LAHORE

GLIMPSES

OF A GLORIOUS HERITAGE

NAZIR AHMAD CHAUDHRY
Lahore 1998

SANG–E –MEEL PUBLICATIONS

25-SHAHRAH-E-PAKISTAN (LOWER MALL) LAHORE (PAKISTAN)

954.9143 Nazir Ahmad Chaudhry
       Lahore : Glimpses of a Glorious
      Heritage /Nazir Ahmad Chaudhry.-
      Lahore: Sang-e-Meel Publications,
      1998.
         566p. : Photoes
         1. Pakistan - Cultural History.
      I. Title

Published
By
Niaz Ahmad
Sang-e-Meel Publications
Chowk Urdu Bazar Lahore
Showroom 25-Shahrah-e-Pakistan (Lower Mall) Lahore
Ph.No.7220100,7228143. Fax No.7245101
Email Ihr01660 @ paknet1.ptc.pk
http://www.sang-e-meel. com
Lahore 1998

Printed
By
Printing Professionals
Lahore. Pakistan

I.S.B.N.-969-35-0944-7
Copies,1000
Rs.1200/-

Title Painting: "Time to rejoice" by Ustad Allah Bakhsh courtesy Shehla Saigol.
Back page painting 'amusements' by Ustad Miran Bakhsh
Photography Tanveer and Zulfiqar Ali

LAHORE

GLIMPSES

OF A GLORIOUS HERITAGE

"Heer – Ranjah" By Ustad Allah Bakhsh Courtesy Shehla Saigol

By
the same author
War of Independence
and repression of Muslim
Urdu as official language in Punjab
Preservation of Archives
Calendar of Persian Documents

Minar-e-Pakistan

ACKNOWLEDGEMENTS

First of all I place on record the debt of gratitude I owe to my benefactors Mr. M. Anwar Zahid and Mr. Muhammad Saeed Mehdi. It was due to their blessings that I got an opportunity to study these aspects of the history of Lahore and hence this book. In connection with material for this compilation I express my thanks to the Punjab Archives staff particularly Mr. Muhammad Ramzan, Librarians, University Library, Public Library, Quaid-e-Azam Library and Mr. Muhammad Iqbal of Alhamra Library who were of great assistance. Ch. Abdur Rashid got me unpublished theses and dissertations from Social work Department on women and some localities of the walled city, for which, I am greatly indebted to him. I am grateful to Mr. Saeed Malik who allowed me to use his work both published and otherwise. My Thanks are also due to Mr. Saifullah Khalid who so graciously lent me books from his rich collection.

I would like to thank Mr. Zulfiqar Ali Zulfi, an artist and a colleague who helped designing, layout and visuals for the book. Mr. Zulfi also saw it through the press and worked hard. The work put in by Mr. Noor Ahmad for typing out the script and its transfer to the computer was a labour of love. He worked untiringly late after office hours for months. Ch. Ghulam Hussain and Siddiq Bhatti also helped in typing out some chapters. My thanks are also due to Mian Khuda Bakhsh and Nasir Malik who helped correcting the proofs, a laborious job indeed. My friends Iqbal Bosan, Dr. Athar, Dr. Khalid Saifullah, Dr. Bhatti and Azhar Majid were all along a source of inspiration. Mr. Habib-ur-Rehman, my assistant, helped me a lot in this project and without any grumbling. I am really grateful to him. I am also indebted to Mr. Najeeb Akram who did most of the work on the computer i.e. spacing, justification and alignment etc. He continued to work for me inspite of illness of his mother. My special thanks are due to Mr. Yousaf Kamal, formerly Commissioner Lahore, who would always make very sincere suggestions. Infact I started finalising the script, when he asked for some information about the origin of Mayo School of Arts, for his son, at Princeton.

As I conclude writing this book I remember most my (Late) father, who first brought me to this city at a young age in connection with my studies. Last but by no means the least I am grateful to the members of my family and my children who so unwillingly allowed me to stay out long hours in connection with this publication. They were always disappointed, as I broke the promises so often.

Lahore 28.9.1998   NAZIR AHMAD CHAUDHRY

"Time to rejoice" Painting by Ustad Allah Bakhsh.

To Ali, Farid, Varda
their Mama Ji & Baji

Shish Mahal – Lahore Fort

Chauburji

City, a view from Fort

Contents

Badshahi Masjid

Ranjit Singh Samadhi

ILLUSTRATIONS

INTRODUCTION

Lahore is not only a historic metropolis but a city of destiny, I would assert. For ages it has been a brilliant symbol of a gracious way of life. It was the abode of great people, both in the spiritual and worldly realms. It has the imposing reflections of its Muslim builder's towering ambitions and cosmopolitan tastes. The complex variety of Lahore which has grown up from the wilderness, when Changez Khan's hordes destroyed its suburbs, to the 20th century developments, is distinct character of the city in various phases and provides a testimony to its cultural legacy. There is a fascinating and colourful panorama of extraordinary personalities with varying social changes in different periods with Mosques, Mausoleums, Fort, Gardens and their grand remains that embodied the aspirations of its mighty rulers.It is not easy to describe Lahore's heritage. The history of the city is an integral part of the story of human efforts of the rulers and the ruled as a whole and ideally this has to be unveiled within the context of cross cultural pollination. The city is an embodiment of a community and the community expresses its corporate consciousness in public monuments which are visible tokens of common heritage. The grand cities of the past possessing the same and their citizens, being custodians of the heritage care most for the same. We also need this more than any one else. Alas! no care has been taken and the explosive urbanization and callous neglect and misuse has surged up the slopes of Mosques, minarets and palaces alike. What we need to convey to our successors is that we should take definite and concrete measures to safeguard this glorious heritage.

But the evidence is otherwise. It reveals that if anything has survived in the grand cities of destiny these are the Holy Cities after their material power and glory had come and gone. Makkah and Madina would not have survived their glory but for the Holy Prophet and Kaaba. If any Jerusalem survives, it will be Jerusalem of the Wailing Wall and the Dome of Rock and not because of Jewish Plazas. If any Rome succeeds in retaining its identity and its appeal, it will be the Rome of Peter and Paul and not of Augustus and Romoulus. If something of Lahore survives it is because of the sanctity of the city (Data Ki Nagri) which is due to Hazrat Data Ganj Bakhsh and saints like Hazrat Mian Mir.

Lahore is city of traditions. It is known as the cultural hub and heart of Pakistan. It is as old as the recorded history of this region. Due to its survival through hazards of history, its typical location on a Highway towards India, it has emerged as a Cultural Centre of its own type.

The origin of Lahore is lost in hazy maze. It was born and founded somewhere between Ist and 7th century A.D. It is, however, inferred by historians that its mythical founder was LOH s/o Rama, a character of Ramayana. It was a Hindu Rajput principality having close links with States in Rajputana. It is with the arrival of the Muslims and conquest of the area from Hindu Raja Jaypal that some recorded evidence becomes available especially when Mahmood Ghazanvi after its occupation appointed Malik Ayyaz its Governor, who originally built the city wall. The city was a witness to the onslaught by Alexander the Great from Macedonia when he crossed the Ravi to punish the Katheas. It withstood the loot by hordes of Changez Khan who devastated the country upto Multan. How amazing it would have been to be a Lahori when Hazrat Data Ganj Bakhsh himself would be preaching and inviting the public to the opening of the first mosque built by him known as 'Khishti Masjid' and leading the prayer. From slave dynasty to the conquest of Lahore by the Mughals led by Babar, the city passed through many upheavals, devastations, developments, peace, war and economic growth. Throughout it was a seat of the North Indian sub-continent. With the arrival of the Mughals there ushered in an era of prosperity, stability and general welfare of the people and city. The Mughals brought with themselves a rich culture with strong traditions of arts and architecture, living standard and administration of the country. They glorified the city by building palaces, fort, mosques, mausoleums, citadels, courts, canals and similar other institutions. How amazing it would have been to see Emperor Akbar the Great holding his Court in the Lahore Fort and the nobility and the gentry moving in the morning towards the palace. It was certainly exciting to find Jahangir, the future Emperor of India, spending his youth in Lahore Fort and Dara Shikoh attending on Hazrat Mian Mir. One would be absolutely stunned to find Shah Jahan on completion of Shalamar camping in the garden and enjoying the playing of over 200 fountains for which the water was brought through a canal from about 100 miles. It is a magnificent history and Lahore is the custodian. In the living history, Lahore emerged as a brilliant symbol of gracious way of life with majestic reminiscences of its creators. In this period it grew from wilderness to the principal seat of the Empire of India and Akbar used it as his capital and seat of Government for over 15 years.

Since the foundation of the Muslim rule in Punjab with Lahore as its headquarters the cultural interaction started taking its course. It reached its zenith during the Mughal period. The city enjoyed envious position during the reign of Akbar.

Dr. P. Hardy observes that in Mughal times, Akbar and his successors presided over, where they did not personally foster, an imperial court culture, shared and contributed to by the Muslims and non-Muslims alike. By the eighteenth century, the Mughal courts had become schools of manners and good taste even for opponents and rebels. As Dr. Percival Spear has well said, 'an observer who visited only the cities of Mughal India might have supposed that India was mainly a Muslim country and that Persian was the current language'. Persian had been the language of the court under the sultans of Delhi and of the Deccan, but under the Mughals it also became the language of the Hindu political elite and higher civil servants.

Both Babar and Akbar revitalised Persian literature in India by attracting Persian poets to India, but Akbar extended its appeal to non-Muslims by having parts of the great Hindu epics, the Mahabharata and the Ramayana, translated into Persian from Sanskrit. By Jahangir's reign, members of Kayastha writer caste had attained proficiency in ornamental Persian epistolography. In the early eighteenth century, a Hindu mystic, Khatri Bhopat Rai, expressed his spiritual experiences in a Persian mathnawi and Lala Anand Rai used Persian to express devotional themes from the Ramayana and Bhagavad Gita. A remarkable form of cultural syncretism expressed through Persian was historical writing by Hindu historians in a Muslim idiom. Ram Lal, in his Tuhfat al-Hind (The India Present), 1735-6, followed Muslim convention so far as to state that the establishment of the Muslim rule in India was divinely ordained and that when Shivaji, Aurangzeb's Marhattas antagonist, died, he departed to hell.

The Mughal architecture, that architecture of drama and pageant, set the fashions of public building for the Rajput prince and for the British civil servant. Its unique combination of the Muslim tradition, outside India, of light and air, expressed by the vaulted arch, the dome, expansive courtyards and audience chambers, with Hindu traditions of massive solidity and ornate decoration, found expression in the triumphant structures of Akbar.

In painting, the Mughal and Hindu princes and courtiers were to patronise a remarkable synthesis of Persian techniques and Indian preoccupations. The Mughals introduced to India the miniature style of Behzad, a painter at the court of Sultan Husain Baiqara of Herat (1470-1506) with its personal portraiture in three-quarter profile, its combination of garden landscapes and walled setting and its rich colour patterns. By the middle of Akbar's reign, Indian influences were becoming noticeable in greater attention to human and animal detail, in the introduction of Indian flora and fauna and in a largeness of construction reminiscent of Hindu mural decoration. Akbar had his own palace studio with over one hundred painters, of whom all but a handful were Hindu.

Despite some disapproval among the Muslim theologians and lawyers, music flourished early in the thirteenth century among the Indian Muslims under the auspices of the Chishti mystic order. All the Mughal rulers except Aurangzeb were patrons of music. In 1666, a Muslim, Faqir Allah, compiled his Rag Darpan; partly a translation into Persian of a Sanskrit work, the Rag Darpan describes the principle of musical composition and the rags or melodies appropriate to different times of day and to different seasons. Probably it was in the sphere of music that Hindu and Muslim cultural traditions came nearest to a synthesis.

It was in the syncretic but none the less living language of Urdu that the court culture presided over by the Mughals bequeathed its most lasting legacy, one into which society outside the audience chamber and the courtyard also entered. The most acceptable theory today is that Urdu originated in the Ghaznavid province of the Punjab in the eleventh and twelfth centuries as an impregnation of old Punjabi with Persian vocabulary and idiom, after which the new dialect was, so to speak, transported to Delhi

A gradual rejection or submergence of the Mughal culture has been a feature of the modern history of India; it is well, therefore, to stress its hold over the imaginations and sensibilities not only of the Muslim and Hindu ruling elite but also, and particularly in northern India, over the general urban population. While the Muslim and Hindu elite showed a common fondness for the chase and for ostentatious living, the common people of the towns joined together in celebration of the Muslim festivals of Nauruz and Shab-i-Barat and the Hindu festivals of Dasehra, Holi and Diwali. All classes attended celebrations at the tombs and shrines of saints and enjoyed the showy displays of the great office holders with illuminations, jugglers, rope dancers, magicians, cock-fights and bear-fights.

It is in the light of the above background that the cultural heritage of Lahore needs to be seen. The inculcation of various characteristics and traits in the lives of Lahoris and their living underwent a change. This also gave birth to a distinct and diverse society which continues till date in Lahore. The currents and cross currents of their socio political interaction caused changes and refinements of standards in daily life living, eating, dressing, education, marriages, pardah, hospitality, manners, dealings, behaviour and the other disciplines governing day to day activities.

The disintegration of the Muslim Empire, ensuing anarchy, Sikh rule and British occupation till the independence are again historical events and Lahore has boldly lived through these periods. It is a pride possessing this rich cultural heritage which has emerged during the last over 1000 years. A couple of books have been written about the history and architectural remains of Lahore and inspite of the competence of authors some aspects have been left untouched. The urbanization and technological advancement is over looking this historical heritage be it economic reasons or industrialization. The cultural institutions, traditions upheld so far are on the decline and a time will come when these may not be available for those who may like to learn about this precious and proud heritage. It is not possible in any way to re-create and depict character of the city life in totality in this small compilation but an effort has been made to collect and narrate what is available and accessible from the contemporary and old available sources.

Lahore having been the seat of many imperial dynasties possesses interesting historical reminiscences. It happened to be in an area which is known as camping ground of earlier Aryans and their civilization. It was Punjab which was home of Buddhism and classical ground of Aexandar's conquests which influenced Brahmanism. It had all along the crowning position in the sub-continent. Being the chief city of the Punjab, Lahore has been a land of great traditions and of interest to the students of history and general reader. Dating back to the time of Subuktgin and Mahmood it was here that the Muslim rule took its roots in India. Qutab-ud-Din Aibak took over as Sultan of India in Lahore. It was Lahore where Ranjit Singh deprived Shah Shuja-ul Mulk, his guest from Kabul, of the famous Koh-i-Noor (diamond)

The heritage of Lahore cannot be and should not be judged from the architectural remains in existence at the moment. The Sikhs and Afghans laboured diligently to deprive it of its architectural embellishments. The Partition of the sub-continent, the great migration and pressure of urbanization has accellerated the pace of rendering the monuments useless objects but we are still lucky to have a few, despite the cruel fate to which these were subjected by despots.

The study of past is a source of curiosity and pleasure but it is only for the reflecting mind that it leaves deeper impression who will see the past with care and draw comparison of great value and worth. The British annexation brought peace and prosperity to the area and there ushered in a new era of thriving cultural, industrial commercial activity and economic well being for the common man. Improvements were effected in the city in all the fields whether these were roads, public health, sanitation, sewerage, schools or hospitals, etc. Consequently the dreary expense of crumbling ruins, old mounds and the desolate and barren tracts charmed into a scene of life again. Above all the British rule brought in the valued price of personal liberty to its subjects irrespective of caste and creed and ensured that decency and order which prevailed in the city.

A city is not just its bazars and buildings or monuments. It is its atmosphere and ambience, its moods of joy and sorrow, fairs and fun, pains & pleasures and above all the colourful life of its people who constitute its spirit and soul. While historical accounts might be available in various publications nowhere coverage of the life of the city has been depicted elaborately. In the volume in hand an effort has been made to recapture some aspects of life of the city. The Hub of Lahore is the walled city which grew up during the Mughal times. It influenced and shaped the style and life of its residents without any distinction of caste, colour and creed, not much has changed in the city over the centuries and it was only after 1947 that the scene took a different turn and that too was on political and economic side leaving the culture intact.   The bazars, most of the lanes and streets remain unchanged. But the change, yes, it is there, no Hindus, and no Holi and Dasehra, no Gurdawaras and Temples with their rich and colourful "Pujaris". The composite culture evolved over a period of one thousand years in the city is continuing in respect of food, dress, customs, manners, living and language. The people enjoy the life and privileges of an Independent country of their own which is under no body's domination. The social life by and large appears to be harmonious and tension free. If economic scene of Lahore was dominated by Hindu Banias before Partition it has now been replaced by the Muslim Seths who own chains of departmental stores, factories, industries and foreign investment divesting the scarce resources of this poor country.

There might have been great deficiencies infact finding, description and presentation in this compilation but I have set the ball rolling and do hope that more intelligent and competent people would improve upon and cover the left over. There is no dearth of brilliant, able and professional writers and critics, who belong to this city and who can certainly attempt better accounts of Lahori life including its bygone dates and sharply emerging metropolitan characteristics brought by hazards of urbanization. It is high time, those in power could also take measures to save this vanishing glory, and separately plan for the influx of immigration to the city. How desolate and disappointed the Lahori will be when he does not encounter with the usual characters which formed an integral part of the city life. How about the city without its winding and circuitous streets without its normal characters. He will simply be disappointed when left without the scenes of the cameos, gay and grim, comic and tragic amusing and annoying pathetic & pleasurable which in reality portray the real life. We need to look-after and preserve this as an institution of our proud heritage.

In describing each subject an effort has been made to make the presentation as comprehensive as possible. Each chapter is a self contained study precisely tracing the history, evolution and present status of the subject. In adopting this method the idea was that the reader should be able to have a complete view of a given subject in a chapter with its background and the latest. Although the subject encompasses many aspects and is very vast, the compilation has been divided into 20 chapters starting with brief political history and then moving on to other features.

The First Chapter is a simple and very brief description of the historical facts starting with the founding of the city. A Hindu principality under the Rajputs, its occupation by Muslim (Ghazanvides, Ghauris, Tughlaqs and Pathans) dynasties. This followed the Mughal conquest and their rule over three centuries. The disintegration of the Mughal Empire led to the local disruptions, Afghan onslaughts, and subsequent Sikh rule. They also met the same fate after death of the Ranjit Singh whereafter the British finally annexed the territory. The Independence movement and emergence of Pakistan led to their departure. This period has been mentioned only factually. Infact it is a resume of the events. A few paragraphs have also been added for the period from 1947 to 1997 mentioning very briefly the Governments in succession. Although Lahore continues to enjoy the privilege of being a Provincial seat throughout history, yet it remained capital of the Indian empire during the reign of emperor Akbar.

The Second Chapter is about the touring of the city to explore the history of the walled city, the city without wall. This in brief takes one to re-live in the narrow and winding streets and bazars where once the princes and nobility moved. This is from Lohari Gate to Lohari Mandi, Haveli Nau Nihal Singh, from Bhati Gate to Tibbi, Hira Mandi, Gumti Bazar and then a walk from Mochi Gate upto Lal Khoo, Rang Mahal, Haveli Mian Khan and Shah Alami, witnessing the most beautiful monument of Muslim period, the Mosque of Wazir Khan and the known Mohallas of old Lahore is in final route. From Chowk Wazir Khan to Old Kotwali, Bazar Rada Tailian, extending up to Azam Cloth Market, Kucha Villayat Shah, Chowk Chuna Mandi and straight on to Haveli Dhian Singh and the side road leading to Yakki Gate, Sheranwala and Masti Gate completes the tour. Lot of changes are taking place, the old houses being dismantled and converted into markets and shops, small bricks being replaced by large sized bricks and re-inforced concrete which is changing the living, use and pattern of social set up also.

The next chapter is about known Saints of the city. They include Hazrat Data Ganj Bakhsh, Hazrat Mian Mir, Miran Hussain Zanjani, and Madho Lal Hussain. The Muslims conquered this part of the sub-continent and established their rule by appointing Malik Ayyaz as Governor of Lahore. But Islam was preached and proclaimed by our Sufi Saints who were also great scholars, men of learning and piety. They convinced the locals and converted them to Islam. Hazrat Data Ganj Bakhsh came from Ghazani and lived for 34 years in the city of Lahore conferring great benefit to the people by his learning, piety and preachings. He was also a great author of his time. He is among the great exponents of sufi thoughts in relation to religious practices and explains Quran as a Code of Life.

Hazrat Mian Mir was also a man of great fame, universally esteemed for his piety and learning. He devoted his whole time to the prayers and meditation and possessed great spiritual power. The same is about others. Brief descriptions of their lives, their association with the city and their tombs has been

21

discussed. They were infact the prime force in effecting change in this Hindu city converting them into Muslims and are the source of spiritual light and guidance till date. Since their presence in the city changed the pattern of social and religious life from pagans to preachers, laying foundation of Islam in this part of India is their big contribution towards the city's history.

The next chapter is about Lahore's architectural heritage and some of the public buildings. If we examine the Muslim Architecture as a building produced we find a remarkable diversity where materials vary from stone through baked and unbaked brick to wood and construction techniques from solid veneered masonry over concrete like cores and from burnt to unburnt brick. Similarly the designs have many forms as there were people who embraced Islam all over. An analysis to these seemingly diverse factors reveals that there are certain unifying principles. Historians report two major regions from which forms were adopted into Islamic architecture, one is Anatolia (Syria) and the second is Mesopotamia (land of Tigris and Euphrates). From here the influence reached the adjacent Persia and it further carried its impact into Afghanistan, Pakistan and India. The main striking feature includes the paradise garden, intersecting elevated paths, water tanks, fountains and plantations. The hypostyle congregational mosque has a mixed origin but exclusive Islamic features. The polychrome tile ornament is a major factor in Islamic architecture. Treatment with glazed tiles survived and flourished in areas where too baked bricks were used in building. Specimens can be quoted from India to Atlantic coast with masterpieces of Masjid-e-Shah at Isphahan and Masjid Wazir Khan at Lahore. The period influencing this part of the sub-continent may be called formative period and includes architecture presented by Samanids and Ghazanvids which ended with Seljuks. The Muslims during Ghauri period brought classic Seljuk forms of architecture to India where it altered its form due to special conditions despite dynastic disputes. These ideas flowed from one era to another. Especially the painted tile travelled everywhere. The Mongol devastations were followed by colossal architecture of their Timurid successors with its small scale of exquisite ornament in tile stucco and even in marble. Similar developments appear in the stone architecture in India during Sultanate period. The period thereafter is termed as post-classic period and starts with Mughal's occupying India in early 16th century. The Mughal India appears indeed to have been inspired in its architecture from Safavids of Persia. Of course inheriting Timurids from which they then transformed independently.

The architectural remains of Lahore, sensuous in their exploitation of colours, textures, materials, intellectuals in its vigorous application of intricate formal patterns and spiritual in essence at once seduce the art lover. There is a dazzling variety in the Muslim architecture, which stuns the students of architectural history. The Muslim architecture is woven into a fabric. The heritage's two major cultural stands according to western scholars are termed as Romano-Byzantouro and Mesopotamian. They created buildings unified by certain principles based on ancient traditions yet uniquely indigenous.

Seen in this background the city's architectural heritage is indicative of the Royal patronage when the major constructions were raised either by Emperors or by the nobility. Unfortunately their successors could not contribute except to deprive and deface the monuments of their stones and other precious materials. The British in turn left the city in much better form than their predecessors. Although in the early years they demolished many buildings to use the material, yet they brought in their own style of architecture which may be called Mughal Gothic. They raised brick (burnt and large sized) buildings for public purposes and avoided use of stone, of course from cost point of view. They, however, also took measures to preserve some of the architectural remains. It is unfortunate that the left over "Lot" of our heritage, is not even being maintained properly. In the Chapter on architecture an effort has been made to introduce the subject, give historical description of some of the important monuments and their main architectural features. Some select buildings raised during the British period have also been discussed with details, background and evolution of each institution which may be of interest to the reader. The post partition period hardly provides any material for discussion and is without typical architectural characteristics. Infact all over the city, box type construction is taking place which can be termed "no Architecture". Briefly stating from Baradari of Mirza Kamran to the inauguration of Garhi Shahu Bridge, (The Chief Minister Punjab inaugurated a 980 meter-long, three-lane Garhi Shahu Bridge on June 13, 1998) covering a period of 475 years is a history and we must know our city and its history.

Chapter V covers Art and Artists of this city inretrospect. Tracing in brief the patronage of Muslims during the Mughal period down to the late 18th century, the Sikh period and damage to the culture and art during the anarchy has been mentioned in these pages. The revival of arts during the British period, emerged as a necessity and as a motive for trade to find about Indian products for European markets. The setting up of an Industrial School of Arts for the local craftsmen and its subsequent evolution is a landmark on the art scene of this city. It helped produce and prepare a class of artists, painters and craftsmen who left their mark in various fields. The paintings, architecture, designing and other technologies received special attention. An effort has been made to briefly encompass various schools of paintings during the British and post – Independence period. It is not a comprehensive survey but a brief of the subject, which is indeed very vast, controversial and sensitive. As a corollary to explore raw materials, Indian products and their markets in England and Europe vis-à-vis raw materials and consumption areas in India, the British initiated the institution of Museum, originally in Presidency towns i.e. Bombay and Madras. They extended the same to Punjab after annexation. This led to the establishment of district museums and a central museum at Lahore. Although ravages of time have deprived us of quite precious parts of this collection yet whatever exists as a museum of the city is of great value and an asset. It did not come into existence as a museum in the sense we take it now. It was essentially an industrial exhibition, remains of which provided foundation of the museum. This chapter covers the evolution of this institution.

The conquerors of India mostly coming from North were from cold regions with streams and rivulets. For permanent abodes in the city they laid foundations of palaces and gardens, which are in existence till date. They gave the concept of garden houses, lawns, falls, fountains and out- houses. Lahore was generally known for its green splendour during the Mughal period. Although the Sikhs destroyed the Muslim heritage yet one or two of these were maintained. Shalamar is one of them which was renovated by Ranjit Singh.

During the British period a green belt was provided around the walled city and a small canal from the Ravi brought to irrigate the garden around the city and other green patches. Unfortunately after partition this exists no more. The land grabbers and squatters have eaten up everything and the city faces the worst pollution hazard. A Chapter on the subject reviews the old gardens of the city, the situation obtaining during the British period and the post-partition development.

We next move over to a description of the Arts Council which appeared in the city in December, 1949. With the efforts of art lovers and financial assistance of the Government the organization developed into a full-fledged institution and contributed to the promotion of art and culture. Later the need for latest equipment and facilities in the form of auditoria cropped up and that was also met by the Government. From a private body it was taken over by the Government, in 1983. The Provincial Government invested heavily and provided auditoria and machinery at quite a bit of cost. The artists are benefitting to a great extent from these facilities. The extent of its activities has made it a national level institution which hosts even international programmes. The Chapter briefly covers the history, growth and promotional work of the Arts Council for the last about 50 years which has richly contributed to the cultural scenario of the city.

Lahore has been a great repository of performing arts particularly those of 'classical', 'folk', 'popular' and 'modern traditions'. The sheer enormity and diversity of its cultural expression in music and dance are the envy of many. The traditional history of theatre dates back to 200 – 100 B.C. There is no evidence about the theatre in Harrappan and Indus Valley civilization except some hints about dance. There are diverse arguments about the routine Sanskrit drama, shadow plays and puppet shows etc. There is another argument that theatre was first conceived in humble origins and the plays were first composed in regional languages. Aryans adopted regional language plays and techniques. According to Hindu writers Sanskrit theatre was sophisticated with fine poetry and dramatic literature. Theatre in Hindu culture received a sacred significance with numerous rituals accompanied by the construction of play-houses and stage consecrated before performances. Theatre became a religious function, entertainment and means for education. This being historically so in the sub-continent the western theatre reached through western educational institutions. The Natak and Notanki having its birth in rural masses also travelled to city centres where emerged the modern stage. In Lahore except for Hindu religious functions details of which are not available with us nothing is known upto the British period. During the British period theatrical companies used to visit the city and modern theatre started in colleges and later in private clubs. After partition besides the educational institutions the Arts Council emerged which religiously attended to this performing art and provided a proper stage for the theatre. The pre-partition Parsi theatre based in Bombay and Calcutta had also appeared on the Lahore scene occasionally which was essentially commercial. Whole time writers used to write the script who were employed for the purpose. The regular performances at the Arts Council for this promotional activity have helped explore talent and provides an opportunity to the youngsters. The private theatres have come up and Lahore has a special audience temperament for stage plays. In the Chapter on theatre some information has been compiled with some facts and figures of dramas performed at the stage of Alhamra.

The cultural heritage depicts the personality of any country. It is by culture that the society is recognized and the level of its status within comity of nations is determined. This part of the sub-continent is custodian of rich cultural heritage with lively music and traditions of dance. The music and dance is associated with our social customs, living, happy and gloomy occasions and times of rejoicing. Be it a village or city each has its own criterions of performance. If the farmers celebrate the harvesting, the urban population rejoices in organizing their national festivals where these relate to industrial exhibitions and crafts. Even otherwise the wealthy and well off have their musical evenings. Of late due to fast means of communication the pattern of entertainment has changed. The people of the city have their evenings out while the youngsters enjoy the popular music and the seniors relax with their instrumental and classical recitals. Until partition the music and dance due to inter-action with other religious communities was quite prospering. It, however, met a set back on the partition of the sub-continent. There was a slump for quite some time and although it is not receiving the priority it used to have in public and private sectors, yet the Government is contributing its bit towards its financing and promotion. Folk songs are generally regarded as most valued popular art as these are the outcome of peoples desire to express themselves. Similarly folk dances free from all restraints and rituals are performed by both male and female. These are completely secular in character. Of all the classical dances which were patronized in Lahore, Kathak is still practised and performed. Folk dances, particularly on fairs and festivals are the crowd pullers. The chapter on music and dance takes care of this subject.

Each society within its given limits has its entertainment, amusements and fun which passes down traditionally. It is in accordance with the social and economic conditions of the area, the products, the status of place, climate and general exposure of the public to the outside world. Lahore has a typical background and evolution of its cultural traits and known for its amusements, funs, 'akharas' and traditional 'takyas' which developed with the city. These were a part and parcel of routine life of citizens and the outlets and places meant for the youth and professionals and served as entertainment centres. Most of these were located outside the walled city where people spent the afternoons. Most of these have disappeared and only a few left and function as wrestling clubs. Chapter XI briefly covers the same.

Prior to partition, Lahore had a mixed population. There were Muslims and other religious communities. The city population by way of inter-action evolved a pattern in which all the sections of society participated in each other's functions without any discrimination. Basant was generally assumed to be a function of Hindus but it was more a function of Lahoris. The entire population celebrated the festival which marked the change of the season. Over a period of time the enthusiasm of general public has increased manifold and it is now an established festival of Lahore irrespective of its genesis. The nitty-gritty of Basant, participation of people and spirit of celebration have been discussed in Chapter No. XII.

Cinema in Lahore was not known till the end of the 18th century and only silent movies appeared in Talkies of Lahore. The main points for showing of such silent films were Bhati Gate and Mcleod Road. With the technological advancement and availability of sound it became the most popular. The Talkies turned into cinemas and it turned out to be a major source of entertainment. The development of film making, evolution of studios and the post partition scenario indicates that Lahore became a centre of film production in Punjab. Classic films were produced based on social and moral problems. Cinema is a very powerful medium. Its impact as a medium of instruction, propaganda and entertainment needs no emphasis. The cinema emerged as an industry in 60s and Lahore gave known artists and investors to this industry. A brief coverage of the cinema as a medium of entertainment and its growths as an industry has been detailed.

Eid is an Arabic word meaning thereby to return year after year or recur again and again. Like all religions Islam has also provided festive occasions for Muslim Umma. These are not only celebrations but opportunities to jointly participate in the rejoicings. It serves as a forum of spiritual unity among the faithful. All the nations and religious entities have their own special festive days or some other religious events to celebrate. Many societies and countries enjoy the same declaring these occasions to be national holidays.

Muslims have three Eids i.e. Eid-ul-Fitr, Eid-ul-Azha and Eid Milad-un-Nabi. Eid-ul-Fitr is celebrated on the end of Ramzan Sharif. Eid-ul-Azha after performing Haj. Eid Milad-un-Nabi is the date of birth of the Holy Prophet but is the latest development. Muslims celebrate these occasions by observing the Eids as most befitting days of pleasantries by also looking after their poor and economically weak sections of the society. People throughout the year wait for the day when relations and friends get together at least once a year. Visits are exchanged, children receive gifts and 'Eidee'. Infact the philosophy behind providing such an occasion is to sanctify year long pre-occupations by recreation and relaxation in a jolly good manner. The occasion of Eid is celebrated with zeal in the city of Lahore. Another most colourful event of Lahore is Mela Chiraghan which is held at the Shalamar to celebrate anniversary of Madho Lal Hussain. People from city and suburban towns flock to the place to attend the festivities which are really colourful. They put on new clothes and spend on eating on the function. The place is full of temporary eatries, talkies, circus shows and a number of amusements. Lot of people come singing and dancing to the shrine of Hazrat Shah Hussain. In this chapter nature of both these festive functions and public enthusiasm as celebrations have been covered.

Travel and Tourism is probably the most important aspect of human activity. Travelling has been undertaken for business purposes as well as for pleasure. This needs the basic facilities of stay and food. With the passage of time and better economic condition, travellers and tourists have been wanting to have better facilities and services. During the Mughal period Lahore, being located on highway connecting North-West with Indian sub-continent, had all around seraes where travellers used to put up, take rest and get fresh for the next destination. The British regulated it in the form of providing rest houses. While seraes and rest houses on the highways took care of tourists and those working for the Government, the people coming to the city had, however, problems which were solved by private entrepreneur through organizing hotels and restaurants where visitors could stay and have food of their choice and on payment basis. Quite a few hotels and restaurants flourished during the British period in the city on the Mall and around Railway Station. While the hotels served the purpose of stay and food, the restaurants catered to the needs of local residents who purely come for variety in the meals or used to eat out as a fashion. Chapter XVI relates to the situation of hotels, restaurants and clubs in the city.

Pakistan came into being on 1947 and with the birth of this new State quite a few countries established their cultural centres in the city. These institutions generally provide library and reading room facilities with their literature and publicity material. They conduct and coordinate their cultural delegations and have their programmes in the city which include social and cultural gatherings. The chapter on the subject covers the existing cultural institutions in the city with reference to their activities.

Lahoris are proud of their cuisine. There are certain dishes which have taken their shape through an evolutionary process through ages. The people settling in Lahore throughout the last one thousand years brought with them their own food and cooking techniques. The Lahori dishes are different from those available in other parts of the country. The cookery and cuisine of Lahori homes has a special taste which are prepared with special recipes, spices and ingredients. Special food is cooked, sold and made available on special times. The evening meals would differ from routine lunch food. In compiling information in this chapter a small physical survey was carried out to note down the available points.

Handicrafts are the representative of any city's artistic genius embodying in it the folk art, traditional motives and patterns. These reflect the aesthetic sensibility and artistic creation of a society. Over a long period of time generally punctuated by outsiders and settlers various arts developed with the passage of time in the city. Infact the incoming arts got naturalized and their merger with indigenous technique gave birth to new and better varieties. With the passage of time the crafts of the city have to be known not only as means of utility and aesthetic sensibility but also determined the level of city's status and personality Vis-a-vis civilization. Chapter No.XIX on crafts makes mention of the city's crafts which include pottery, gold and silver work, brass and copper wares, enamelling, wood carving, lacquer work and fabrics etc., etc. An effort has been made to give the reader a picture of the crafts covering the Mughal period to the Sikh Rule, the British period and the post-independence scene. The traditional crafts have undergone many changes. In the pages on the subject, the available information has been consolidated.

The history of women is no different from the other parts of the world. The womenfolk historically were considered to be a private property. With the growth of human civilization they were thought to be treated in a better way i.e. considered community instead of commodity. It is a matter of record that women/girls were sold for Rs.50/- to 60/- up to the Sikh period. The slavery is no different from this and till date in backward areas the women are treated as servants. The male exploit them for all purposes. The dawn of civilization, the education of women and general economic betterment, especially in the 20th century have, however, changed the status of women. Factually the British rule brought a big difference in life and status of women in the city. With the education and their exposure they are now working on equality basis with men. They have their share in almost every walk of life. They are in the services, in the legislature, in the Cabinet and a woman has held the Prime Minister's slot twice. From being treated private property to Premiership this is really a big change. This chapter deals with the routine life and state of women in pre-partition and their role in the freedom movement. Their contributions after partition and role in national re-construction.

Prostitution is the oldest profession. It is not exactly a pleasant reflection that the oldest commercial aim of the humanity has been exploitation partiality to woman. The consequent gossip of venal love and discussions about the same begin with an apology. According to some modern writers the changes in Governments and social organization to the existence of prostitution may be reasonably and frequently admitted to be only and the least harmful influences upon mankind. Some say, are prostitutes more dangerous than a political pressure group? The dim little windows of red light districts might be presumed to have far least effect upon any healthy youngster than the contemplation of all scenes of murder acted on T.V. screen. The parallel to public morals does not by any means arise only from sexuality. The undermining of ideals of conduct is much more harmful. The history of torture is far more drastic than sexual perversion. But inspite of this the talk about the prostitution is always calandestine a hypocrisy, more so in our society. Accounts on the subject reveal that the sale of sexual satisfaction has been an integral part of urban life of mankind throughout. According to L. Basserman "at no time and in no city in the world have prostitutes and their trade been more active than at Athens and Corinth during the golden age of Greek Civilization. In modern Paris, London and Tokyo unpaid and paid sexual pleasures have come to be enjoyed to a certain extent in separate compartments of society. But in ancient Greece every sphere of urban life was dominated by worship of Aphorodite." Infact in Greece there existed State brothels. It is not clear why the Greek so enthusiastically involved themselves in the cult of prostitution. Possibly they hoped by this expedient to escape homosexuality. Solon, a Legislator and the Philosopher first prescribed a brothel for the Athenians in order to preserve them from the homosexuality. He acquired a suitable building and ordered supply of suitable women and girls from slave traders. He also fixed a low entrance fee to his establishment for which he was praised by Athenians. This brothel by Solon was followed by others. The merchandise grew more copious and the atmosphere more agreeable. The inmates achieved popularity. The change occurred in the wage earning groups of young women exposed to aggression. Thus a system of organization started. Some amongst the women (more clever) even purchased girls from the slave market and trained them to become prostitutes. Corinth, a harbour settlement was perhaps the oldest and most frequented city of prostitution in Greece.

The Greek authorities also levied taxation on prostitution in Athens and such other lucrative trade centres. The position in the sub-continent was not different. The economic conditions, slavery, illiteracy, exploitation of poor by the rich , some time religious freedom and rituals helped spread the profession in this part of the world. It received patronage during autocratic rule and kingship when the rulers would enjoy the best of the venal entertainments. In India during the British period according to an account written by Elphiniston, slave trade helped to a great extent in setting up of the brothels mostly in urban centres. Young girls (between age of 5 –10 years) used to be purchased and sold approximately from Rs.50 to 60, trained and educated for this profession only. During the Sikh period, it is said that almost half of the population of the city consisted of prostitutes. The Maharaja and nobility could enjoy the benefits of the trade.

The Hira Mandi as it came to be known is not a place of sin only. If it caters to one time pleasure seekers it also served the educational needs where music and dance were taught. Irrespective of the religious sentiments in respect of prostitution I have no hesitation in remarking that existence of Hira Mandi helped curtail crime to a great extent in the city. A typical class which is served there, otherwise would make the living of gentry miserable. It would be a mistake to take Hira Mandi only a prostitutes street which is certainly not. Even though some of its inmates carry on this profession for a living. The courtesans, home was essentially a place of culture where the nobility and gentry would enjoy the accomplishments of these women in fine arts, music, poetry and dance. The imposition of laws curbing prostitution resulted otherwise. The disease has spread in the city and one need not essentially visit the place. The perpetual mistakes of the civil authorities and the administration in dealing with the phenomena are more dangerous than the prostitution itself. This chapter carries glimpses of the profession, and, the institution in historical perspective.

With the above contents of this compilation if I have been able to convey some thing about the heritage of Lahore to the reader I have reason to rejoice. I am sure more will be written to preserve the traditions of this legendary city by the brilliant and professionals.

1

LAHORE
Through The Ages

The history of Lahore is infact that of Punjab. Prior to the Muslim invasions, we know next to nothing, except legends of it being a Hindu principality and founded by Loh son of Rama, hero of Ramayana. In the following paragraphs, is a very brief outline of its political fortunes under the various dynasties which succeeded on the downfall of the Hindus in the Punjab.

From the numerous ruins, old villages, and deserted wells and other archaeological evidence there can be no doubt that at one time Lahore was a fertile part of the country. It is difficult to say to what period these prosperous signs may have belonged; but, considering the wars and dissensions that took place in and around Lahore, it may be presumed that this was depopulated on the fall of Mughal empire. The invasions of Nadir Shah and of Ahmad Shah Durrani followed by anarchy and the loot and lawlessness during Sikh period brought its prosperity to a halt. The British occupation in 1849 brought back normalcy and ensured law and order and projects for the welfare of area and city were undertaken. The glory of the city of Mughal period was certainly not restored but there was peace, and welfare of common man was ensured. It became a city of educational institutions, and as seat of Government has expanded manifold. Except for a short while, when on partition it suffered a setback but now it is one of the biggest cities of Pakistan and custodian of a proud heritage.

RULERS IN RETROSPECT

For purpose of reference, since its Muslim occupation we may, for the interest of readers give names of rulers of Lahore which are as under in seriatim:-

YEAR	NAME & SOVEREIGN	DYNASTY	PARENTAGE
1001 to 1032	Mahmood	Ghazni	Son of Subuktgin
1032 to 1040	Masud	-do--	Son of Mahmood
1040 to 1049	Maudud	Ghazni	Son of Masud
1049 to 1077	Abdul Rashid	-do-	Son of Maudud
1077 to 1098	Ibrahim	-do-	Son of Masud

1098 to 1114	Masud	-do-	Son of Ibrahim
1114 to 1117	Arslan Shah	-do-	Son of Masud
1117 to 1152	Bahram Shah	-do-	Son of Masud
1152 to 1159	Khusrau Shah	-do-	Son of Bahram Shah
1159 to 1188	Khusrau Malik	-do-	Son of Khusrau Shah
1188 to 1206	Shahabuddin	Ghauri	Usurped the throne
1206 to 1210	Qutab-ud-Din Aibak	Slave of	
1210 to 1210	Aram Shah		Adopted son of Aibak, deposed
1210 to 1236	Shamsuddin	Balban	Altamash, son-in-law of Aibak, succeeded
1236 to 1237	Rukanuddin	-	Feroze Shah, son of Shamsuddin
1237 to 1239	Razia Sultana	-	Daughter of Altamash
1239 to 1241	Bahram Shah	-	Son of Shamsuddin
1241 to 1246	Alauddin Masud	-	Son of Rukanuddin
1246 to 1266	Nasiruddin	-	Son of Shamsuddin
1266 to 1286	Ghiasuddin	Babbu	Adopted son of Shamsuddin
1286 to 1288	Kaikabad	-	Grandson of Ghiasuddin
1288 to 1296	Jalaluddin Feroze	Khilji	Usurped the throne
1296 to 1316	Alauddin	-do-	Nephew of Jalaluddin
1316 to 1317	Shaukatuddin Umar	-do-	Son of Alauddin
1317 to 1321	Mubarak Shah	-do-	Brother of Shahabuddin
1321 to 1325	Ghiazuddin or Ghiasuddin Malik	Tughlak	Conquered the throne
1325 to 1351	Alaf Khan	-do-	Son of Ghazi
1351 to 1389	Feroze Shah	-do-	Nephew of Ghazi
1389 to 1389	Tughlak Shah	-do-	Grandson of Feroze Shah
1389 to 1392	Abubakr	-do-	Son of Feroze Shah
1392 to 1394	Muhammad Shah	-do-	-do-
1394 to 1394	Sikandar Shah		Son of Muhammad Shah
1394 to 1398	Mahmood Shah	-do-	Son of Muhammad Shah
1398 to 1398	Taimur or Tamerlane	Mughal	Invaded India
1398 to 1421	Ghizin Khan	Saiyid	Made Emperor by Taimur
1421 to 1435	Mubarak Shah	-do-	Son of Ghizin Khan
1435 to 1445	Muhammad Shah	-do-	Grandson of Ghizin Khan
1445 to 1450	Alauddin Shah	-do-	Son of Mahmood Shah
1450 to 1488	Bahlol	Lodhi Pathan	Usurped the throne
1488 to 1517	Nizam Khan	-do-	Son of Bahlol
1517 to 1526	Ibrahim Shah	-do-	Son of Nizam Khan
1526 to 1530	Babar Shah	Mughal	Descendant of Taimur Conquered Delhi
1530 to 1540	Humayun	-do-	Son of Babar
1540 to 1545	Sher Shah	Pathan	Usurped the throne

1545 to 1553	Salim Shah	-do-	Son of Sher Shah
1553 to 1553	Muhammad Shah	-do-	Nephew of Sher Shah
1553 to 1556	Humayun	Mughal	Regained his throne
1556 to 1605	Akbar Shah	-do-	Son of Humayun
1605 to 1627	Jahangir Shah	-do-	Son of Akbar
1627 to 1658	Shah Jahan	-do-	Son of Jahangir
1658 to 1707	Aurangzeb	-do-	Son of Shah Jahan
1707 to 1712	Shah Alam	-do-	Son of Aurangzeb
1712 to 1713	Muhaiuddin or Jahandar	-do-	Son of Shah Alam
1713 to 1719	Farrukhser	-do-	Grandson of Azimul Shan
1719 to 1747	Muhammad Shah	-do-	Son of Azimul Shan
1748 to 1761	Ahmad Shah	Durani	Son of Jahandar
1762 to 1797	Sikhs		Under Sikh Misals divided between Gujjar Singh, Lahna Singh and Sobha Singh commonly known as "three hakims"
1797 to 1798	Sikhs		Ranjit Singh s/o Maha Singh, chief of SUKHARCHAKIYA misl. Secured formal grant of Chiefship of Lahore from the Shahzaman (of Kabul) the Durrani prince
1799 to 1839			Maharaja Ranjit Singh
1839 to 1846			Kharrak Singh, Nau Nihal Singh, Hira Singh, Jawahar Singh, Lal Singh. British and Sikhs fought at Mudki, Ferozeshah, Sobraon and occupation of Lahore by British
1846			Lahore became a protectorate of British and Council of Regency
1849			Final British occupation of Lahore

At the time of the first Muslim invasion in the latter part of the seventh century (A.D.) Lahore was in possession of a Chauhan Prince, of the family of Ajmer. In A.D. 682, according to Ferishta, the Afghans of Kerman and Peshawar, who were Muslim wrested certain possessions from the Hindu prince. A war ensued, and in five months seventy battles were fought until the Afghans, having formed an alliance with the Gakkhars of Salt Range of the Punjab compelled the Raja to cede a portion of his territory. The next mention of Lahore is the Rajputana chronicles. Rajputs of Lahore are mentioned to have rallied to the defence of Chittaur, when besieged by Mussalman forces in the beginning of the ninth century. In A.D. 975, Subuktgin, Governor of Khurasan, and father of the celebrated Mahmood, advanced beyond Indus. He was met by Jaipal, Raja of Lahore, whose dominion extended from Sirhand to Lamghan, and from Kashmir to Mooltan. On the advice of a prince of the Bhatti tribe, the Raja formed an alliance with the Afghans, and, with their aid, withstood the first invasion. On his succession to the throne of Ghazni, Subuktgin repeated his invasion and battle was fought in the

Back Side of Badshahi Masjid 1846 Courtesy Punjab Archives

vicinity of Lamghan. The Raja was defeated, and begged for peace. It was agreed on the part of Subuktgin for the recovery of balance of the stipulated ransom. On reaching Lahore, Jaipal cheated and imprisoned those deputed to receive the treasure. On learning intelligence of his perfidy, Subuktgin, in the words of Ferishta, "like a foaming torrent, hastened towards Hindustan".

Another battle ensued, in which Jaipal was again vanquished, and he retreated, leaving the territory to the west of Indus, in the hands of Subuktgin.. Chagrined at his double defeat, he burnt himself to death outside the walls of his capital. The invader did not retain the conquest he had made, for in A.D.1008, a confederation, headed by Anangpal, son of Jaipal, again met the advancing army, now commanded by Mahmood, son and successor of Subuktgin, in the vicinity of Peshawar. In the battle which ensued the naphtha balls of the Afghan army, according to Ferishta, spread dismay among the Hindu soldiery, who fled, suffering a great slaughter. Lahore was allowed to remain intact for thirteen years longer. Anangpal was succeeded by another Jaipal, called by Al-Beruni, Narjanpal, while Mahmood pushed his conquests into Hindustan. But in A.D. 1022, he suddenly marched down from Kashmir, seized Lahore, Jaipal II fled helpless to Ajmer, and the Hindus principality of Lahore was extinguished forever. A final effort was made by the Hindus in the reign of Maudud, A.D. 1045 to recover their lost sovereignty but after a fruitless siege of six months they retired without success; and thus, says Al-Baruni, "the sovereignty of India became extinct, and no descendant remained to light a fire on the hearth". Lahore was left in charge of Malik Ayyaz, a favourite of Mahmood of Ghazni, whose name appears in many anecdotes of the sayings and doings of the Emperor. He is said to have built up the walls and fortress of Lahore and his tomb, by the 'Taksali' or old mint, is still revered by Lahoris as the burial place of the founder of Muslim Lahore.

From the above account it will be observed that the princess and people of Lahore played a prominent part in that long continued struggle between Islam and Hinduism which marks the introduction of the former into India. The strong social action and reaction, which took place between the two religions in this part of India was resolved by toleration of Muslims who did not interfere with religion and rites of Hindu locals. Even now the Muslims of the Punjab are perhaps less bigoted towards other communities.

EARLY MUSLIM PERIOD

During the reigns of the first eight princes of the Ghaznavide dynasty, Lahore was governed by viceroys; but in the reign of Masud II (A.D. 1098 - 1114) the seat of Government was temporarily moved to Lahore, as the Seljuks having deprived the house of Ghazni of most of its territory in Iran and Turan, the royal family were compelled to take refuge in their Indian possessions. Lahore was again made the seat of empire by Khusrau, the twelfth Ghaznavide emperor, and continued so until the fall of the dynasty, in A.D. 1186, and the establishment of the house of Ghor. The Ghaznavides, especially the later ones, seem to have been a tolerant race, and to have adopted a conciliatory policy towards their Hindu subjects; we find them employing troops of Hindu cavalry, and some of them even adopted on their coinage the titles and written character of the conquered race. Their popularity may further be inferred from the continual disturbances which arose at Lahore after their expulsion.

During the Ghorian and Slave dynasties, Lahore was the focus of conspiracies against the Government; indeed, it appears throughout the subsequent history of Muslim rule to have been the rendezvous of the Tartar, as opposed to the Afghans. In A.D. 1241, Lahore was plundered by Changez Khan; and in A.D. 1286, Prince Muhammad, the accomplished son of Sultan Ghiasuddin Balban, perished in an encounter with the Mughals on the banks of the Ravi, the poet Amir Khasrau being taken prisoner by his side.

During the rule of Khilji and Tughlak dynasties, Lahore does not appear to be prominent in the political history. It was once plundered by the Gakkhars, and mention is made of Mughal colonists taking up their abode in the vicinity of the city, the place of their location being still known by the name of Mughalpura.

The year 1397 is memorable as the date of the invasion of Taimur, the "firebrand of the universe". Lahore was taken by a detachment of his forces, but Taimur did not plunder. On his departure, Lahore was left in possession of Syed Khizar Khan, an Afghan noble, native of India, whom he appointed viceroy.

From their period, the city was alternately in the hands of the Gakkhars and the ruling dynasty, until in A.D. 1436, it was seized by Bahlol Khan Lodhi, one of the Afghan chiefs, who rose to power on the overthrow of the Tughlak dynasty, and eventually became Emperor. In the reign of his grandson Sultan Ibrahim, Daulat Khan Lodhi, the Afghan Governor of Lahore, revolted, and, invited to his aid the great Chughtai prince, Babar, who had long meditated an invasion of Hindustan, which he claimed, as the representative of Taimur.

THE MUGHAL PERIOD

Babar came, saw, and conquered. He was met by an Afghan army, composed of the supporters of Sultan Ibrahim, in the vicinity of Lahore; but it was defeated. Babar did not remain long at Lahore, but, after a halt of only four days, marched on towards Delhi. He did not, however, get further than Sirhand on this occasion. Daulat Khan Lodhi, who had invited him to Hindustan, being dissatisfied with his reward of a jagir, had already begun to intrigue against him. He, therefore, returned to Lahore, and having parcelled out the provinces he had conquered among his nobles went back to Kabul. The next year, Lahore was reported to Babar as hotbed of intrigues but attempt was made to oppose him at the Ravi, but the force melted away before it was attacked, and Babar, without entering Lahore, passed on further towards Hindustan. This was his last expedition, and it ended (A.D. 1526), in the decisive victory of Panipat, the capture of Delhi, and the foundation of the Mughal or Muslim Empire in India. This opened the chapter of entire Indian occupation instead of Lahore (Punjab) which had all along been considered a part of Afghan Kingdom.

The reigns of Humayun, Akbar, Jahangir, Shah Jahan and Aurangzeb, the successors of Babar, may be considered as the golden period of the history of Lahore. The city again became a place of royal residence; gardens, tombs, mosques and pavilions sprang up in every direction; the population increased, suburbs arose until the city became, in the language of Abul Fazal, "the grand resort of people of all nations", and celebrated for its fine buildings and luxuriant gardens. To this day almost all that is architecturally beautiful at Lahore is referable to the period of early Mughal Emperors.

On the accession of Humayun, the Punjab, together with Kabul and Kandahar, became the "apanage" of Mirza Kamran, Humayun's younger brother, who seems to have given the first impulse to the architectural adornment of Lahore, by building a palace, with a garden extending from Naulakha to the river Ravi. During the struggle between Humayun and Sher Khan (Sher Shah Suri) the Afghan usurper, Lahore served as the place d'armes of the Mughals, and, on the temporary expulsion of the former from the throne, it narrowly escaped destruction. Sher Khan at one time thought of razing it to the ground, and transferring its inhabitants to Sialkot and, on his death-bed, he lamented his not having done so as one of the biggest errors of his life.

Humayun after his exile of fourteen year returned in triumph to Lahore (A.D. 1554) and was received with every demonstration of joy by the inhabitants. After his death, at Delhi, A.D. 1556, and the accession of Akbar, the peace of Lahore was again disturbed by Hakim, the younger brother of Akbar, who descended from Kabul, of which province he was Governor, and seized Lahore in A.D. 1563. He was soon expelled. In 1581 he made another attempt, but the siege was raised by the advance of Akbar in person. From A.D. 1584 to A.D 1598, Akbar made Lahore his headquarters, and undertook from thence the conquest of Kashmir and the operations against the Afghan tribes of the frontier. It was during his residence at Lahore that Akbar developed the principles of religious toleration liberality for Hindus, for which he is known. His Court was full of the learned (of every creed), and the arena of religious disputations between conflicting sects. It is related that the Emperor erected two buildings, outside the city, for the entertainment of devotees of every kind; one, called Khairpura, for Jews, Gabrs (or fire-worshippers) and Muslims and another called Dharmpura, for Hindus. Weekly meetings were held for discussion, in which Bir Bal, Abul-Faizi, Abul Fazal and other independent thinkers, took part. Alchemy, fascination, and magic were also practised. According to one historian, the Emperor himself is said to have become an adept in the former art. In the same spirit of eclecticism, Akbar revived the old Persian, festival in honour of the sun, and appointed Abul Fazal superintendent of fire-temples. A portion of the building, called Khairpura is said to exist in the vicinity of Daranagar, on the left of the road to Mian Mir, and there is a memento of the imperial partiality to sun-worship in an enamelled figure of the sun visible to this day, on the front wall of the palace. Tod notices a similar decoration at Udepur; "a huge painted sun of gypsum in high relief, with gilded rays, adorns the Hall of Audiences.

The literary circle which followed the Imperial Court appears to have been peculiarly active during its sojourn at Lahore. It was here the voluminous history of Muhammadanism from the earliest period upto the thousandth year of the Hijri era, compiled by order of the Emperor, was finished and revised; and it was here that the translation of the Mahabharata and the Raja Tarangini into Persian was undertaken. The list of poets, writers and historians who wrote and rhymed in Lahore between A.D. 1584 to A.D. 1598 is too long, but there is one among them who deserves special mention in the history of Lahore, namely, the historian Nizam-ud-Din Ahmad, the author of the Tabaqat Akbari the first historical work of which India forms exclusively the subject matter. He died in A.D. 1594, and was buried in his garden at Lahore. The tomb of this celebre, to whom Ferishta owed so much in the compilation of his history, is not traceable even his name and his work are but little known to the modern literati of Lahore. It is also worthy of remark that Akbar's able minister, Todar Mal, the best revenue officer (who pioneered the basis of a proper revenue system) perhaps the Mughal Government ever had, and the ideal or an Oriental financier, expired at Lahore.

It was during this period that some Portuguese missionaries, at the express request of Akbar, proceeded from Goa to the Emperor's Court at Lahore. They arrived with sanguine hopes of Christianizing the country, and in their journal, they describe Lahore as a "delightful city". On their arrival, they were taken to the imperial residence, situated "on an island in the river"; and, being introduced to the Emperor, presented him with a splendid image of the Virgin (Mary), which he received with the greatest admiration. But notwithstanding this good beginning their hopes were not realized, and they eventually returned to Goa. Akbar's successor, Jahangir, however, was more liberal than his father. He allowed some

Portuguese Jesuits to establish a mission and build a church at Lahore, and even assigned stipends to the priests. But this liberality ceased after his death. Shah Jahan, a more strict Mussalman, withdrew the pensions and pulled down the church; but some traces of it still remained when Lahore was visited by the French traveller Thevenot, in A.D. 1665. A crucifix and a picture of the Virgin were even then observable on the gateways of the palace.

It was about this period also (A.D 1584) that Lahore was visited by some British (Messrs. Fitch, Newberry, Leedes and Storey, members of a company). The former left an account of his travels, but gives no detailed description of Lahore. In A.D 1594, the Emperor Akbar quitted forever the city associated with the brightest period of his reign; and until his death was engaged in military operations.

Prince Salim succeeded Akbar in A.D 1606, under the title of Jahangir. His reign commenced, as usual, with a rebellion and Lahore felt the effects of it. Prince Khusrau, the eldest son of the Emperor, seized the suburbs of Lahore and laid siege to the citadel. His army was quickly defeated by the imperial troops, and his followers punished.

Jahangir was fond of Lahore. In A.D 1622, he fixed his court here, and when he died, at Rajauri, in Kashmir A.D 1627, it was his express wish that he should be buried at Lahore. He was interred, accordingly in the garden of Nur Jahan, his devoted wife; and , through her exertions, the mausoleum at Shahdara, one of the chief ornaments of Lahore, was erected to his memory. In the immediate vicinity is the tomb of Nur Jahan herself, a humble imitation of that of Jahangir, as well as that of Asif Jah, her brother, the historian, soldier and wazir, and in the latter capacity in common with his sister, a great opponent of English interests in the Court of Jahangir at the period of Sir Thomas Roe's Embassy.

On the death of Jahangir, Lahore was again (A.D 1628) the scene of a struggle between rival claimants to the throne, which, as usual, terminated in the execution of the vanquished. On the one side was Shahryar, younger son of the late Emperor, supported by Nur Jahan (whose daughter by her former husband he had married) and on the other, Shah Jahan, supported by his father-in-law Asif Khan. Shahryar seized the treasury at Lahore, and proclaimed himself Emperor; but he and his supporters were speedily attacked and defeated by the energetic Asif Khan, and the prince himself, with the two cousins, was taken prisoner. They were put to death at Lahore and Shah Jahan and his sons remained the sole direct representatives of Jahangir. Nur Jahan survived until A.D 1646, but her influence ceased forever with the death of Shahryar. From that date she lived in seclusion, and devoted herself to the memory of her husband. She and a faithful female attendant are buried side by side in the tomb she had constructed during her lifetime.

Between A.D 1628 and 1657, Lahore enjoyed an interval of peace and prosperity under the munificent rule of Ali Mardan Khan, and Hakim Ali-ud-Din, who is more commonly known by his title of Wazir Khan; but during the struggles between the sons of Shah Jahan Lahore warmly espoused the cause of Dara Shikoh, the eldest son and, according to a point of view, the rightful heir to the throne. Dara Shikoh had his residence at Lahore, and was popular due to his engaging manners and generous disposition, and by the interest he took in the welfare of the city. He collected a history of all the holy men and conventual institutions of the place, and had, as his spiritual adviser, the eminent Lahore saint, Mian Mir, a liberal-minded Mussalman. When pursued by his brother, Aurangzeb, in A.D 1658, at a time when his cause was almost hopeless, Lahore supplied him with men and money; and, when his wife died, during his hurried retreat to the western frontier, Lahore received her last remains. His name is still held in affectionate remembrance at Lahore, and the Badshahi Mosque erected at Lahore by Aurangzeb, a few years after this event, was built from the proceeds of the confiscated estates of Dara. During the reign of Aurangzeb, Lahore had but little connection with the political events of the time, as the attention of the Emperor was chiefly directed to quelling the rising power of the Marhattas in the Deccan and the rebellion of the tribes of Rajputana.

From the death of Aurangzeb to the accession of Ranjit Singh, the fate of Lahore was singularly unfortunate. As the capital of an outlying province, it was naturally the first to suffer from the weakness of the decaying Mughal empire. Ruled over by governors inadequately supported, it became the center of Sikh insurrections. The Sikhs, who had been kept under subjugation during the energetic rule of Aurangzeb broke out into revolt under "Banda", and seriously threatened Lahore. The Emperor Bahadur Shah, the son and successor of Aurangzeb (A.D 1712) marched to Lahore, with a view of crushing the rebellion, but died before he could achieve any decisive success. One of the gates of Lahore, the Shah Alami Gate was called after his name, and the fact furnishes some testimony to the popularity of this prince, whose toleration was a great contrast to the bigotry of his predecessor. It has been said, indeed, that "had Bahadur Shah, and not Aurangzeb, succeeded Shah Jahan, the family of Taimur might have occupied the throne of Delhi. His death was followed by the usual contest among the sons; Azimul Shan, a younger son, but more popular than the others, endeavoured to seize the throne and oust his elder brother, Jahandar. A conflict ensued between the brothers and their respective partisans outside the city walls; Azimul Shan was driven away and fled precipitately to the Ravi, which he tried to cross on an elephant. But the river being in flood he was drowned. The struggle between Jahandar and Farrukhser for the throne, and the dissensions and intrigues in the court of the latter, encouraged the

Sikhs to further excesses; they defeated the governor of Lahore in a pitched battle, and it became necessary for Farrukhser to take some measures for their repression. He appointed Abdul Samad Khan, a Turani nobleman, and an officer of known vigour as viceroy of Lahore who achieved a brilliant success over the rebels, and took Banda himself prisoner, whom he despatched to Delhi. Abdul Samad was succeeded in the viceroyship by his son Zikariya Khan, under the title of Khan Bahadur, and for twenty-one years (A.D 1717–1738) Punjab was peaceful. The weakness of the Court of Delhi raised the viceroy into a satrap, who, safe for a time in his palace at Begampura, viewed with complacency the failing powers of the house of Taimur and rise of the Marhattas.

AFGHAN PERIOD

At length, in 1738, the citizens of Lahore heard with dismay of the approach of a new enemy from the west, led by the Turkomani warrior, Nadir Kuli Khan. On the 18th November, 1738, he crossed the Indus, passed rapidly without boat or raft, the Jhelum and Chenab rivers and pushed on to Lahore. A faint show of resistance was made at Wazirabad, and again in the vicinity of Lahore, but to no purpose, and at length the invading army encamped in the Gardens of Shalamar. Zikariya Khan, the viceroy had no particular affection for the Court of Delhi, and was soon convinced that discretion is the better part of valour. He brought twenty lakhs of rupees and a vast array of elephants, and presented them before the throne of the invader; the result was that Zikariya was confined in his Governorship, and Lahore, this time escaped pillage. On the 29th December Nadir Shah left Lahore for Delhi.

In 1746, a marauding band of Sikhs had collected at Eminabad where Yahya Khan sent troops to disperse the Sikhs, who fell upon the detachment with fury and overpowered it. The news of this disaster exasperated the viceroy, who despatched another overwhelming force, under the command of Lajpat Rai who succeeded in defeating the insurgents. Those who were taken prisoner were brought into Lahore, and executed on the north side of the city, then known as the horse-market, but since the period of Sikh rule by the name of Shaheed Ganj, or place of martyrs; and the spot of the execution is indicated by a shrine erected in the memory of Bhai Taru Singh, the chief martyr, who, though offered pardon, if he would consent to part with his long hair, the outward badge of his faith, preferred death to apostasy.

Two years from this event in A.D 1748, a more powerful enemy appeared before the walls of Lahore, in the person of Ahmad Shah the successor of Nadir Shah, who had no sooner established himself on the throne and marched into India. The viceroyship at Lahore was then a bone of contention between the two sons of Zikariya Khan, Yahya and Shah Nawaz Khan; while the Court of Delhi looked on, too weak or too indolent to interfere. To aid his cause Shah Nawaz encouraged the advance of Ahmad Shah recollecting that his father had not fared ill at the hands of the western invader. Ahmad Shah advanced; but his army was small, and Shah Nawaz Khan having prevailed over his brother, thought better of his treachery. He met the invading forces but was disastrously defeated and Ahmad Shah took possession of Lahore. Ahmad Shah having passed Lahore, met with a check in Sirhand and returned the way he came. Mir Mannu, son of the Delhi wazir, who had distinguished himself in the battle, was appointed Governor of Lahore.

At the close of 1748, Ahmad Shah again crossed the Indus, but the invasion was this time warded off by the bold front at the banks of the Chenab and diplomacy by Mir Mannu. The following year it was renewed with better success. The invader marched without opposition to Lahore, and halted at a short distance from the suburb of Shahdara, where Mir Mannu had entrenched himself. He crossed the river and set up his camp in the vicinity of the Shalamar Gardens. For four months Mir Mannu made a good defence. At length, as provisions and forage began to fall short, he imprudently risked a general action. On the morning of the 12th April, 1752, he marched out of his entrenchment, and took up a position near the village of Mahmood Buti. A battle ensued which was sustained for some hours, with doubtful success on both sides, but at length the tide was turned by a charge of the Durrani horse, and Mir Mannu retired into the citadel. The next morning, however, finding further resistance hopeless, he went to the tent of Ahmad Shah to make his submission, where the following dialogue is said to have taken place. "How is it", said Ahmad Shah, "that you have not, long before this, come to do homage to your lord and master?" "Because", replied Mir Mannu, " I had another master to serve." "And why", rejoined the Shah; "did not your master protect you in this hour of need?" "Because," returned the other, "he knew that Mir Mannu would take care of himself" "And supposing", continued the Shah, "You had been victorious?" "I should have put you in an iron cage and sent you prisoner to Delhi, " was the reply. "And now that I am victor, what, "asked the Shah, "do you expect at my hands?" "If you are a tradesman" said Mir Mannu, "sell me; if an executioner, put me to death; but if you are a prince, be generous." The conqueror struck with admiration at the dauntless bearing of his youthful adversary, called him the Rustam of India decorated him with a jewelled sword, and confirmed him in the post of viceroy of the Punjab. But Mir Mannu did not live long to enjoy his newly acquired title; he died soon afterwards, A.D 1752, leaving an infant son and a widow. The latter succeeded as guardian of her son, and for a time vainly endeavoured to keep upon good terms with the Courts of both Kabul and Delhi; at length, however, her duplicity was discovered, and the Delhi wizier summarily put an end to her intrigues by having her seized in her own house and carried off a prisoner. This violent act afforded the Durrani a pretext for a fourth invasion (A.D 1755 – 56). Lahore was occupied without opposition and placed under the conqueror's son Prince Taimur; but an act of intolerance on his part, in defiling the sacred tank at Amritsar, roused the fury of the Sikhs, now a rapidly rising sect. Sikh horsemen swarmed round the city walls, and assumed so threatening an attitude, that Prince Taimur thought it prudent to retire, and Lahore, for the first time A.D 1756–58, fell into the hands of the Sikhs. Their leader, Jassa Singh, a carpenter, at once assumed the prerogatives of sovereignty, and struck a coin, bearing the inscription. "Coined by the grace of the Khalsah." Their occupation this time, however, was short-lived; they were expelled by a new enemy in the Marhattas under a chief named Ragoba, whom Adinah Beg Khan, the deputy of Mir Mannu had invited to his assistance. With their help, he was installed on the viceregal throne (A.D. 1753); but he enjoyed his success only a few months. He died leaving a name still held in some respect as that of the last Mughal Governor of Lahore.

The success of the Marhattas led to a fifth invasion by Ahmad Shah (A.D 1759), which resulted in their disastrous overthrow at Panipat, A.D. 1761. One Buland Khan was made Chief Magistrate at Lahore; but the government machinery was powerless, the Sikhs again assumed a formidable appearance, and they besieged his successor, Obaid Khan, in the fort of Lahore. A sixth descent of the Durrani scattered the Sikh forces, and inflicted on them a terrible slaughter, near Ludhiana. He returned by the way of Lahore, and left one Kabli Mal Governor, the country being ravaged by the Sikh horsemen. The successes of the Sikhs in Sirhand incited Ahmed Shah to undertake his seventh invasion; but he retired, somewhat precipitately, without having effected his object. Kabli Mal was ejected, and the Sikhs again became master of Lahore. In 1767, Ahmad Shah made his eighth and last invasion, but had to retire without success, harassed by the ever-present Sikh cavalry,

During thirty years following the final departure of Ahmad Shah (A.D. 1767-97), the Sikhs were left to themselves, and increased in wealth and numbers. They gradually divided themselves into independent misls, or bands, under the command of hereditary chieftains, having a common place of meeting at Amritsar. Lahore meanwhile, was portioned out amongst a triumvirate of Sikh chieftains named, respectively, Gujjar Singh, Lahna Singh, and Sobha Singh who are spoken of to this day as the "Three Hakims". The first had his stronghold in a brick fort between Shalamar and Lahore, which still bears his name. Lahna Singh in the citadel; and Sobha Singh in the garden of Zebinda Begum, which he turned into a fort, now known by the name of Nawankot.

In the year 1797 (A.D), the spell was again broken. Shah Zaman, the successor of Taimur on the throne of Kabul and the brother of the unfortunate Shah Shuja, made a new attempt to establish a Durrani empire from Kabul to Ganges. His advance created the liveliest sensation. In the beginning of the cold season, Shah Zaman appeared before Lahore. But his expedition was arrested by bad tidings from home, and he retired, after exacting a subsidy of thirty lakhs from the few wealthy merchants. The next year, it was renewed with no better success; but the event is interesting as being the first occasion on which Ranjit Singh, son of Maha Singh chief of the Sukharchakiya misl, came prominently into notice, and made the first step towards obtaining the sovereignty of the Punjab by securing from the retiring Durrani Emperor a formal grant of the chiefship of Lahore. The history of Lahore is henceforth merged in the history of its great ruler Maharaja Ranjit Singh.

THE SIKH PERIOD

In 1799 Ranjit Singh became master of Lahore that was then in possession of Sardar Chet Singh, son of Triumvirate Lahna Singh, after a short contest, in which Ranjit Singh was aided by the treachery of the leading men. In 1801, Ranjit Singh assumed the title of Sarkar, established a mint, and commenced his career as a sovereign. In 1802, he obtained the celebrated gun Zamzamah, a huge piece which Ahmad Shah had used in the battle of Panipat, but had left behind at Lahore, as too unwieldy to take back to Kabul. The gun had hitherto been in possession of the most powerful of the misls, the Bhangis of Amritsar, and came to be regarded as the talisman of Sikh Empire. Hence its capture by Ranjit Singh added greatly to his prestige. From this period, the tide of success flowed on apace; Jhang, Kasur, Pathankot, Sialkot, Gujrat, felt the power of his arms, and the Chiefs of Mooltan, Jullundher, and Kasauli, were glad to ward off an attack by timely submissions, and acknowledgement of Ranjit Singh as lord paramount. In 1812, he became possessed of the person of Shah Shuja, and of the gem Koh-i-Noor; effectually opposed the hitherto irresistible progress of Afghan invaders, and re-occupied the fort of Attock. In 1814, he suffered his first reverse, in an attempt to conquer Kashmir; but he so far succeeded as to obtain from the Governor a formal recognition of the paramount authority of the Lahore Darbar. In 1818, Mooltan was besieged and taken by his forces, and the province annexed to the empire of the Maharaja. In 1819, Kashmir was at length conquered. This was followed by the annexation of the Derajat, or tract of country between the Indus and the Suleman range; and Peshawar was captured in 1823.

"Ranjit Singh died in 1839, lord of the Punjab from the Suleman range to the Sutlej, and from Kashmir to beyond Mooltan, an empire little less in extent than

Chowk Wazir Khan Painting by Zulfiqar Ali Zulfi   ......

that of Jaipal, having a regular army and three hundred pieces of artillery. But the Hindu supremacy, revived by him, was hollow and unsubstantial. It was based, not upon a national movement, but upon the military ardour of a religious sect whose action he united by the force of his personal character. Hence, like other empires which have been similarly constructed, it was destined to perish mole suo its foundation being thus unstable, with no leading principle to give it coherence – for the consolidating system of its founder had destroyed the bond of union which once existed in the yearly Gurumata, or assemblage of Sikh chieftains at the Sacred tank, without even the prestige of antiquity – the moment the directing power was weakened, the fabric of Government fell to pieces, and the very source of its strength, the large well-disciplined, army became the immediate cause of its destruction.

The political drama which followed the death of Ranjit Singh amongst his successors and counters is not very useful to narrate. It may be said that there was nothing like a political faction. There was, to a certain extent, what may be called a Dogra party, composed of the Jammu family who had risen into importance in the later years of the Maharaja, with their adherents; and the Khalsa party, represented by the Sindhanwalias, who were related to the family of Ranjit Singh. But neither of these parties dreamt of such a thing as the public good. Personal or family considerations and "zanana" intrigues were the mainspring of their public acts, and their first object was to carry favour with the army.

Under Ranjit Singh the principle Sikh feudatories in the Lahore district were Mit Singh of Badhana, Jai Singh of Manihal near Patti, and Gyan Singh of Bahrwal.

The successors of Ranjit Singh threw themselves alternately into the hands of the one party or the other, as it suited their interest or caprice, and it hereupon became the object of the party out of favour to get rid of their obnoxious rivals. The first act in the drama was the murder of Chet Singh, a minion of the imbecile Kharak Singh, Ranjit Singh's successor. This was done in pursuance of a concerted design between Nau Nihal Singh, the heir apparent, and the Jammu party; but no sooner had the object been attained than Nau Nihal turned against his friends.

Kharak Singh died in 1840. Nau Nihal Singh, who, there is reason to believe, had hastened his father's death by poison, was the same day killed by the fall of a portion of an archway, as he was proceeding on foot from witnessing the cremation of his father's remains. The ashes of father and son rest side by side beneath two small domes to the left of the mausoleum of Ranjit Singh.

The death of Nau Nihal Singh, was followed by a struggle between the mother of the deceased prince, in concert with the Sindhanwalia party and Sher Singh, a disowned son of Ranjit Singh, aided by Dhian Singh, the Jammu prince and favourite of Ranjit Singh. The soidisant queen-regent was aided, strange to say, by Gulab Singh, the brother of Dhian Singh, held the fort, and it became necessary for Sher Singh to besiege them. The siege lasted for four days, from the 14th to the 18th January, 1841. This resulted in the submission of the queen and her party, and the coronation of Sher Singh.

Sher Singh in his turn fell a victim to a coalition between the Sindhanwalias and the Dogra chiefs. On the 15th September, 1843 he was assassinated by Ajit Singh, the Sindhanwalia Chief, while inspecting levies at a country seat called Shah Balawal. Having succeeded in their attempt, the Sindhanwalias forthwith turned their hands against their late ally, Raja Dhian Singh, who was shot down and cut to pieces within an hour of the death of Sher Singh, at the summit of the accent into the fort from the Hazooi Bagh. This led to a second siege of Lahore by Hira Singh, son of Dhian Singh, aided by the Khalsah army animated by the prospect of high pay and plunder. The wall was breached; Ajit Singh, the assassinate, sprang over the north-east angle of the fort, and was cut to pieces in the place where he fell; Lahna Singh, already wounded, fell into the hands of the soldiery, and was shot and hacked to death.

For a little more than a year Hira Singh was virtual ruler, in the name of Dilip Singh; the son of the Rani Jindan, a queen of Ranjit Singh; he fell owing to a personal quarrel with the Rani, and his unpopularity with the fickle Khalsah army. He fled, with his adviser, Pandit Jallah, pursued by Jawahir Singh, the Rani's brothers, and troops of Khalsah horse. From Shahdara the pursuit was closely kept up for some twelve miles, until the Pandit fell from his horse, from exhaustion and was cut to pieces. Hira Singh continued his flight, and headed his pursuers; but imprudently stopping at a village to get a draught of water, he was surrounded and slain, after a desperate resistance. Jawahir Singh, in his turn, became unpopular with the practorians of Lahore, and was deliberately shot on parade. Lal Singh, the paramour of Rani Chandan, then became nominally wazir; but the Government was really the will of the army at Lahore. Irritation at the defensive preparations made by the English Government, restlessness, and desire for plunder prompted the invasion of British territories on the 11th of December, 1845. The battles of Mudki, Ferozeshah, and Sobraon, and the occupation of Lahore followed; then at length, in the words of a local ballad, "sorrow was silenced, and the Sikh empire became a story of the past".

The signature of the treaty of peace at Lahore on March 9th 1846 was followed by importunate requests on the part of the Darbar that the Governor-General would lend a British force for the protection of the young Maharaja and his capital pending the reconstruction of the Government. The request was granted, but with the distinct assurance that the force would not be allowed to remain beyond the end of the year. When, however, the time came for its departure, at the earnest request of the most influential chiefs, Lord Hardinge gave a reluctant consent to a more permanent occupation. Then followed the celebrated assembly of the Sikh chiefs in the Darbar tent of the Resident and the new convention signed on December 16, 1846. A Council of Regency was appointed and the British Resident became the real depositary of authority throughout the province. The British troops had hitherto been quartered in the fort, but it was now determined to build a permanent cantonment; and before the end of 1847 sufficient barracks and bungalows had been erected for the requirements of the garrison. The cantonment occupied a strip of land to the south of the city. A spacious Residency, now occupied by the Secretariat offices, was constructed and the Anarkali tomb converted into a church. The occupation, however, was not intended even then to be final. The arrangement was to last for eight years only, till Maharaja Dilip Singh should attain his majority. But circumstances occurred to change the whole policy of the Government towards the Punjab. Moolraj rebelled at Mooltan, and before the middle of 1848, the whole province was in flames. Lahore itself remained unmolested, but even here the position at one time was believed to be critical. All doubts were removed by the fall of Mooltan and battle of Gujrat (February 22nd 1849). On March 29th Lahore was once more the scene of a gathering of Sikh nobles. The young Maharaja took his seat for the last time on the throne of Ranjit Singh and in the presence of Sir Henry Lawrence, the Resident, and Mr. Elliot, the Foreign Secretary and the nobles of his court, heard Lord Dalhousie's proclamation read, and affixed his initials, in English characters, to the document which transferred the kingdom of the five rivers to the Company, and secured to him an annuity of 50,000 pounds a year. The British colours were then hoisted on the ramparts, and Lahore became the capital of a British province.

THE BRITSH PERIOD

On 31st March, 1849 the Governor General of India constituted a Board of Administration for the Punjab which consisted of:

John Lawrence
Henry Lawrence
C.G. Mansel

The Board was given a charter in respect of Administration of the newly occupied territories with brief details and guideline regarding the measures to be taken. It also laid procedures for the civil, revenue and criminal justice, settlement of the lands and development of the country.

From 1849 to 1853 Punjab was administered by Board of Administration with a say, and the work conducted and supervised by Members. In 1853 John Lawrence was appointed as Chief Commissioner of Punjab which assignment he held upto February, 1858. On 1st January, 1859 he was appointed the Lieutenant Governor of Punjab. A list of the officers and Governors who held charge of Lahore (Punjab from 1849 to 1947) is given below for purpose of reference and interest of the readers:-

MEMBERS OF THE BOARD OF ADMINISTRATION, LIEUTENANT GOVERNORS AND GOVERNORS

Henry Lawrence		
John Lawrence	**Board of Administration 1849-1853**	
Charles Gronville Mansel		
Lieutenant Governor		
Lawrence John Laird Mair, G.C.B.K. C.C.S.I.Chief Commissioner.	1853	1859
Sir Lawrence John Laird Mair, G.C.B.K. C.C.S.I.Lieutenant Governor	01.01.1859	25.02.1859.
Montgomery Sir Robert G.C.S.I. K.C.B. I.C.S.	25.2.1859	10.1.1865
Mcleod, Sir Donald Friell, K.C.S.I. C.B.	10.01.1865	01.06.1870
Durand, Sir Henry Marion, K.C.S.I. C. B.	1.6.1870	20.1.1871
Davies, Sir Bobert Henry, K.C.S.I	20.1.1871	2.4.1877
Egerton, Sir Robert Eyles, K.C.S.I. J. P.D.L. C.I.E, I.C.S.	2.4.1877	1882
Aitchison, Sir Charles, K.C.S.I. C.I.E. L.L.D.I.C.E.	02.04.1882	02.04.1887
James, Sir Broadwood Lyall	02.04.1887	1892
Fitzpatrick, Sir Demns, K.C.S.I., I.C.S.	1892	1897
Young, Sir William Mackworth, K.C.S.I.	March 1897	06.03.1902
Rivaz, Sir Charles Montgomery, K.C.S.I.	6.3.1902	27.4.1905
(GAP)	27.4.1905	19.10.1905
Rivaz, Sir Charles Montgomery, K.C.S.I.	19.10.1905	06.03.1907
Ibbestson, Sir Denzil Charles Jelf, K.C.S.I.	6.3.1907	22.5.1907
T.G. Walker, Sir (Officiating)	1907	
Ibbestson, Sir Denzil Charles Jelf, K.C.S.I.	12.8.1907	23.1.1908
T.G. Walker, Sir (Officiating)	1908	
Dane, Sir Louis William G.C.I.E., K.C.I.E., C.S.I, I.C.S.	25.5.1908	28.4.1911
Douie, Sir James McCorne, K.C.S.I, I.C.S. (Officiating)	28.4.1911	5.8.1911
Dane, Sir Louis William G.C.I.E., K.C.I.E., C.S.I, I.C.S.	5.8.1911	26.5.1913
O'Dwyer, Sir Michael Francis, K.C.S.I., I.C.S.	1913	Nov.1919
GOVERNORS		
McLagan, Sir Edward Douglas, K.C.S.I., K.C.I.E.,	27.5.1919	3.1.1921

Halley. Sir William Malcolm, G.C.S.I.O., G.C.I.E., K.C., S.I., I.C.S.	1924	1928
De Montmorency, Sir Geoffrey Fitzhervey, G.C.I.E. K.C.S.I., K.C.I.E.K.C.V.O., B.E.	1928	1932
Sir Sikandar Hayat Khan (Acting)	1932	
De Montmorency, Sir Geoffrey Fitzhervey, G.C.I.E. K.C.S.I., K.C.I.E.,K.C.V.O.,C.B.E.	1932	1933
Emerson, Sir Herbert William, G.C.I.E., K.C.S.I., C.B.E. (Acting)	1933	1934
Sir Sikandar Hayat Khan (Acting)	1934	
Emerson, Sir Herbert William, G.C.I.E., K.C.S.I., C.B.E.	1934	1938
Craik, Sir Henry Duffield, K.C.S.I; I.C.S.(Acting)	1938	
Craik, Sir Henry Duffield, K.C.S.I; I.C.S.	1938	1941
Glancy, Sir Berurand James, K.C.S.I, K.C.I.E, I.C.S.	7.4.1941	7.4.1947
Jenkins, Sir Evan Meredith, G.C.I.E., K.C.I.E.	8.4.1947	01.08.1947

The British from 1849 onwards took steps for settlement of territory, restored law and order and took measures for the development of the area under directions from the Governor General / Viceroy of India. A brief mention may be made of the city's position during the War of Independence in 1857 (termed as Mutiny by British) which led to no result except the persecution of Muslims whom the British considered their rivals as they had taken over from them.

WAR OF INDEPENDENCE

The following account of the events of 1857 is taken from the Punjab Government Mutiny records and explains the nature/extent of involvement and how they were controlled.

The important move which gave us a foothold in North India when the empire seemed well high overwhelmed by the flood of mutiny which had burst forth so uncontrollably in the North-Western Provinces, was the disarming of the troops at Mian Mir. The danger on the morning of May 13th was far greater than had been conceived. A plot had been laid for the simultaneous seizure of the fort and the outbreak of the troops in cantonments. To understand the importance of this move it must be borne in mind that the fort commands the city of Lahore; that it contains the treasury and the arsenal; that a Ferozepur, 50 miles distant there is another arsenal, the largest in this part of India; and had these two fallen, the North-Western Provinces and the Punjab must have been, for the time being, irrevocably lost, the lives of all Europeans in these regions sacrificed, Delhi could not have been taken, India must have been ab initio reconquered. The designs of the conspirators were frustrated. By 5.00 a.m. on the 13th, three companies of Her Majesty's 81st Foot marched into the fort and relieved the native infantry guard; while the ringing of the ramords as the remaining companies of that regiment of the parade-ground at Mian Mir obeyed the order to load sounded the knell of sepoy power in the Punjab. The three regiments of native infantry and one of light cavalry were cowed by the stirring sound and by the sight of twelve horse artillery guns charged with destruction to them should they resist. The infantry piled arms and marched off with silent and angry astonishment. The cavalry unbuckled their swords and threw them on the ground, and the capital of the Punjab was saved. The next night, May 14th, at 10.00 p.m. Mr. Roberts, the Commissioner, accompanied by one military and two civil officers, brought Mr. Montgomery a paper, in the Persian character, which had just reached him with an injunction of secrecy from the writer. He writes. "It was a report from a police officer stationed on the Sutlej, giving a confused account of the attack on the Ferozepur entrenchment that afternoon by the 45th Native Infantry. It gave no account of the result of the action. We conjectured that my express of the previous day to Brigadier Innes had failed of its design that the sepoys had gained the arsenal, had crossed the bridge of boats, and were in full march to Lahore. In the earnest deliberation which ensued other circumstances occurred to our minds which seemed to make our position in Lahore critical to the last degree. A Punjabi Police Corps, the only one we had to carry on the civil duties, and which furnished personal guards to all the civil officers at the station, was reported to be disaffected. (Happily this turned out to be quite false). Lieutenant Gulliver, Engineers, volunteered to ride off to cantonments to acquaint the Brigadier with what we had just heard, and beg him to do what he could to defend himself. Messrs Egerton, Deputy Commissioner, and Elliott, Assistant Commissioner, went round the station to take note of what might be going on. They returned reporting all quiet. Shortly afterwards, Lieutenant Gulliver also came back, hearing from Brigadier Corbett the joyful news of the repulse of the outbreak and the comparative safety of Ferozepur, the Brigadier having received a despatch direct from Brigadier Innes. There could be no doubt that there had been a plot arranged between the Lahore and Ferozepur brigades for on the same forenoon (May 14th) I received two hasty notes from Brigadier Corbett saying that all the troops in Mian Mir were preparing to desert bodily. This caused a panic among the residents of Anarkali, and a rendezvous of all male residents took place at the central jail. The guns and Her Majesty's 81st Regiment, however so quickly got ready that the natives retired into their lines. Some who did escape were seized by the villagers of the tract called the Majha, and taken to Mr. Thomas, Assistant Commissioner at Kasur, the chief town of that part of the Majha which lies in the

Lahore district, and on the direct route to Ferozepur. Mr. Thomas sent them into Lahore. The stalwart Sikhs who form the population of the Majha were wholly on our side throughout. Many villages have been almost decimated by the number of recruits who have flocked to form our new regiments in memory of the bygone days when they bravely fought against us under the banners of the Khalsa.

Defensive measures were at once adopted in Anarkali as follows: The fort was provisioned for six months for 4,000 men, and every gate blocked up but one. All the men of the various Punjab regiments who happened to be on leave at their homes in this neighbourhood were called in and collected under the command of Captain Travers. They furnished pickets for guard all round the central jail and at other places where danger seemed to threaten. A company of volunteers from the European residents of Anarkali was raised in 36 hours to the number of 130 men, and for some days Anarkali was guarded only by a half company of Subhan Khan's Police battalion, and a few ordinary police. A rendezvous was appointed, and danger signals arranged. A chain of mounted police was thrown out along the roads leading to cantonments, which for a length of time were patrolled during the night by the junior civil and military officers of the station. The usual precautions in regard to ferries, sepoys' letters, were vigorously observed. On the 26th and 27th the Guide Corps passed through on their famous march to Delhi, and about a week afterwards the movable column under Brigadier Neville Chamberlain arrived. On June 9th two men of the 35th Native Infantry, which was one of the regiments composing the column, were blown from guns on the Anarkali parade-ground, by sentence of a drum-head court-martial, for sedition and intended mutiny.

On the 30th July, the 26th Native Infantry mutinied at Mian Mir, and murdering Major Spencer, their commanding officers, one non-commissioned European and two native officers, fled. They escaped during a heavy dust-storm, which concealed them from observation and kept us in ignorance of their route. They were destroyed by Mr. Cooper, Deputy Commissioner of Amritsar, on the banks of Ravi. This event showed the necessity for some means of tracking and (any) future body of deserters, especially as the loyalty of the remaining regiments was very doubtful. Four strong police posts were established in villages which lie beyond the plains upon which the cantonment is built, and the men were instructed to throw out chains of sentries and to watch narrowly all passers-by. On the 17th September Mr. R.B. Egerton, Officiating Deputy Commissioner, was called suddenly down to the south-west part of his district in order to prevent the taint of Kharral insurrection from reaching the Mussalman population of that part of the country. Mr. Perkins, Assistant Commissioner, was also for a few days stationed at a remote police post into the boundaries of which emissaries from the insurgents were known to have come. The appearance, with Mr. Egerton, of half a regiment of Wales' Horse and other demonstrations, deterred the Kharrals of the district from joining their rebellious kinsmen. Mr. Egerton was out on another occasion for three or four weeks in company with the Commissioner, Mr. Roberts, in the Gugera district on similar duty. The civil charge of this important station was confided on these occasions to Mr. R. Berkeley, Extra Assistant Commissioner.

Lahore is Pakistan's historic and interesting city; the cultural heart of the country. Its faded elegance, busy streets and bazars and wide variety of Muslim and British architecture make it a city full of atmosphere (of) contrasts and surprise. Due to its location on the main road of invaders from the North, those who visited the city gained some understanding of the cultural influences that shaped the city life, its traditions and environment as a whole.

It has been the capital of the Punjab or the areas that form part of Punjab for the last over1000 years. First from 1021 to 1186 under Ghaznavide Muslim dynasty founded by Mahmood of Ghazni, then under Ghauris and later under Sultanate of Delhi. It reached its full glory under Mughal rule from 1524 to 1752 as already mentioned in preceding paragraph. The Mughal Emperor Akbar the Great held his court in Lahore for 14 years from 1584 to 1598 and made marvellous additions to the architectural foundations of the Fort and city. Jahangir and Shah Jahan similarly made their own contributions. Beautiful palaces and tombs were built and gardens laid out. The last and great Mughal Aurangzeb gave Lahore its most famous 'Badshahi' Mosque.

The downfall of Mughals and anarchy in Punjab areas provided a fertile climate for the establishment of a Sikh state which continued until late 1840s. The British who had been contained on that side of the River Sutlej had their eyes on this fertile region and in the garb of tourists and visitors had surveyed in detail the potential of the Punjab plains which was ultimately to form greenery of their empire. The British after defeating the Sikhs in the wars formally took over Lahore in the year 1849. On 31-3-1849 the Governor General of India constituted a Board of Administration for the affairs of only the conquered territory. The headquarters of the Government were established at Lahore. The old Residency still in existence in the Civil Secretariat and forming part of the Chief Secretary's office was made the office of the Board of Administration. Needless to state that prior to occupation in 1849 the British have been continuing their relations with the Sikhs through their Resident stationed at Lahore. The Residency building belonged to one of the French officers who had been engaged by Ranjit Singh to train his armies. General Ventura the owner of the Residency building died leaving behind a daughter and a wife (local Kashmiri) who shifted to Ludhiana. This building previously on rent was purchased by the British for an amount of Rs.400. The Board of Administration for the affairs of Punjab was headed by Sir Henry Lawrence, later

Lord Lawrence with Mr. John Lawrence and Mr. C.G. Mensel as members. Mr. P. Melvel was the Secretary of the Board. The Board under a written code of administration covering revenue, administration, judicial, civil and criminal justice, police administration and policy towards local landed aristocracy and general public started operating at Lahore. Lahore became the divisional headquarters and Mr. D.F. McLeod was the first Commissioner and Major. Macreggor the first Deputy Commissioner of the city. The Anarkali area which was under use as a camping ground for the army during Ranjit Singh period was formally declared as cantonment. Some of the arsenal, armoury and the treasury alongwith offices were located in the Palace (Fort). The cantonment area of the Anarkali existed on alluvial plan which infact had been built on the ruins of the successive city. It was most unhygienic place, water pools would appear here and there and inspite of some trees there was a lack of gardens. The important monuments in the area were Bara Dari of Wazir Khan and Anarkali Tomb. The Bara Dari of Wazir Khan was used as the first museum of Lahore and later on (as) Anarkali Book Club. The Anarkali Tomb which had been previously used as residence by Raja Kharak Singh was converted into a church and hence till date the road leading from the Board of Revenue to Secretariat is known as Church Road. In 1851 there were around 100 deaths of European army officers in the Anarkali cantonment due to cholera. The Sanitary Commissioner opined that this had happened due to unhygienic conditions and the cantonment should be shifted at once. Accordingly a plan was drawn to shift the cantonment to a dreary plain and jungle six miles from Anarkali ahead of Hazrat Mian Mir, towards east. The cantonment was located here and connected with Anarkali with a road approximately built at a cost of about Rs.14,000 generally called the Mall Road. The area around Mall Road extending upto Lawrence Gardens was called as Donald Town. This included the localities towards Mozang and Regal Chowk, flats and modern residences on the Beadon Road behind the Hall Road quarters, Birdwood Road upto village Mozang and then adjoining the Race Course and GOR 1 which were European bungalows, some sort of garden houses built of western style. Towards north-east the areas of Naulakha, the Railway Officers Colony and on its left the locality of Qilla Gujjar Singh, the Railway station across which lies the Railway Hospital and village Garhi Shahu.

As the Board of Administration settled, the territory, Lahore due to expansion and increase in the administrative machinery, became the Chief Commissioner's headquarters for the affairs of Punjab. It may be added that at that time Punjab included the Frontier and Derajaat Divisions. Delhi was later detached from the north-western province and added to Punjab. Lahore remained the Chief Commissioner's H.Q., from 1853 to 1858. From 1859 onwards it became the Lt. Governor's Province. The Secretariat expaned and the Departments due to their increased pace of work had their various new offices set up. The institutions of Revenue and Financial Commissioners loading with work the Department of Education, Health, Irrigation and Public Works came into existence. The emphasis of the Government was on the development projects to enhance production of the Province in agriculture, exploit mineral and industrial potential of the country and attend to the welfare of the common man. In 1857 according to the British there was a Mutiny in the army which was later on termed as War Independence by the natives. It started at Barrackpur, Meerat and Barelli etc. and spread like wild fire throughout the country. The rebel forces and the freedom fighters occupied the city of Delhi which was retaken by the British forces after an effort of four months. The situation of Lahore has already been narrated somewhere else in this chapter.

STRUGGLE FOR INDEPENDENCE

The reasons for the war of independence were manifold. These were political, economic, religious and administrative. The British took the Muslims as their natural rivals as they had captured the country from them. The Hindus considering the Muslims as their rivals as former rulers hated them and connived with the British. The Muslims ignored the western education which had replaced the Mughal system of administration and thus themselves became extinct from the services / administration as they did not qualify for jobs. The jagirs and grants given by Muslim rulers to Muslim nobility were taken away and the Muslims economically became crippled. The Europeans exploited the resources of their Indian empire, used their raw material, finished the same in Europe and resold the same to Indians. The Christian missionaries under full protection of the Government had started conversion of local Indians without any obstruction. These reasons led to a war against the British which, however, did not succeed and instead strengthened the British rule. They adopted repressive measures lest the Muslims recaptured their lost power and also they were the victims of the British. This policy also worked in Lahore. The Hindus were brought forward whereas the Muslims remained behind and only menial jobs fell to their share. Considering this degradation of Muslim community of India, Sir Syed Ahmad Khan launched his movement for western education and loyalty to the British so that by way of education Muslims could get a share in the Government. The founding of Aligarh Institution in 1875 was the first brick towards this building. Lahore also did not remain behind and also fully participated in these efforts by way of supporting Anjaman-e-Islamia, Lahore, the Scientific Society of Lahore, Muslim Educational Conference and Anjaman-e-Hamayat-e-Islam. In the year 1891 the concept of Legislative Council for the Province of Punjab was sanctioned and this too was located at Lahore.

Another most important aspect of the political currents in the late 19th century which took the shape of an organization was the founding of Congress Party by a British officer viz A.O. Hume in Calcutta which started making efforts for safeguarding the interests of the Hindus. For sometime the Muslims also cooperated but later they learnt that it was only fighting for the cause of Hindus. Consequently Nawab Waqar-ul-Mulk and some of the Bengali Muslim Leaders founded the Muslim League in 1906 at Dacca. Its Head office was in Aligarh but its support areas were majority Muslim provinces and Punjab was the leading one. Later on in 1905 when Hindus resented the partition of Bengal, purely an administrative decision, this was annulled by the British due to protests and it cautioned the Muslims for their rights. Consequently all along there was an agitation through available press/papers in Lahore for the cause of Muslims. In 1922 Lahore fully participated in the Khilafat Movement and there was a lot of agitation against the Government in favour of Turkey. Lahore had its share in this movement and quite a few families in protest migrated. The history of freedom movement under Quaid-e-Azam from Khilafat Movement till the implementation of 1935 Act, elections of 1937 and rule of Congress in for out of seven provinces cleared the Muslim leadership the ultimate goal of Hindu leadership. Before backing out of the Congress from the Lucknow Pact and their outright opposition of Muslim rights in Nehru Report, Dr. Sir Muhammad Iqbal from Lahore gave an idea of a separate State for the Muslims. This proposal was made by Dr. Muhammad Iqbal in his presidential address of 1930 session of All India Muslim League at Allahabad. The negative attitude of the Hindu community all along contributed to the unity of the Muslims. It was this attitude of the Hindus that the Muslim leaders thought of saving the Muslim masses from the exploitation of Hindus capitalists. Dr. Muhammad Iqbal initiated the idea of separation. There were people before him who had advocated partition but Iqbal was the first important figure who profounded the idea from the platform of the Muslim League. In the presidential address to the League's session at Allahabad he discussed the problems at length. He clearly explained that the principles of European democracy cannot work in India. The Muslims of India were the only Indian people who could be rightfully described as a Nation. His famous remarks, which earned him the title of Father of Pakistan Idea, were I would like to see Punjab, North-West Frontier Province, Sind and Baluchistan amalgamated into a single State. Their Government within the British Empire or without the British Empire formation of a consolidated North-West Indian Muslim State appears to be the final destiny of the Muslims at least of North-West India".

It would be observed that again it was the Lahore leadership both intellectual and political that gave the idea of a separate State for the Muslims. This idea of Pakistan is a real landmark in the history of the sub-continent. It established the two-nation theory and on this basis justified not only the need for a separate homeland but demarcated areas which were to form this country. The Government of India Act 1935 provided for complete autonomy for the provinces in which the Congress achieved a big success. However, after coming into power the Hindu leadership ordered hoisting of Congress flag and rendering of 'Bandey Matram'. Hindi was also introduced in the schools and colleges and slaughter of cow prohibited and attacks on mosques became frequent as they had forbidden the 'Aazan'. This aroused the feelings of Muslims and Jinnah, till now, a messenger of Hindu-Muslim unity decided and devoted himself for a separate homeland for the Muslims. After the 2nd World War the congress demanded a promise for independence before helping the British authorities. The demand was not accepted and the congress Government ceased to function. In October 1937 the Muslim League was re-organized and branches established at all places and efforts made to have the widest possible support and strength from the masses. When the Congress resigned in November, 1939 the day of deliberations was celebrated by the Muslims throughout India.

PAKISTAN RESOLUTION

On 23-03-1940 Muslim League had to hold its annual session at Lahore under the presidentship of Quaid-e-Azam. Mr. M.A. Jinnah alongwith Maulvi Fazal-ul-Haq reached Lahore on 21-03-1940 to attend the famous historic session. He went straight to Mayo Hospital to enquire about the health of injured 'Khaksar'. On 21-03-1940 a meeting of All India Muslim League was held. New members of the League were elected on the same night at the residence of Nawab Shah Nawaz Mamdot on Empress Road the manuscript of Lahore. Resolution was prepared in English Language in which Sir Sikandar Hayat Khan, Malik Barkat Ali, Nawabzada Liaqat Ali Khan, Ch. Khaliq-uz-Zaman and Maulana Zafar Ali Khan participated. Maulana Zafar Ali Khan translated it into Urdu. On 22-03-1940 a meeting of the Muslim League was convened in which Nawab Shah Nawaz Mamdot presented his welcome address. In an extempore speech of 100 Mounties Mr. M.A. Jinnah said Hindu-Muslim unity is impossible and impracticable. He explained Hindu-Muslim unity is merely a dream for both Hindus and Muslims belong to two different religions, philosophy, social, customs, creeds, conventions and educational and literary inheritance. They neither interline nor intermarry. To yoke together two such nations under a single state, one as a numerical majority and the other a minority, must lead to growing discontent. Mussalmans are a nation, according to any definition of nation and they must have their homeland, their territory and their state. They have different epics, different heroes and different episodes. Their history, historical events and religious heroes are different. Hero of one nation is considered the enemy of the other. Victory of one nation is considered to be the defeat for the other. They are two separate nations, so they must have a separate, independent and sovereign state where they could lead their lives according to the tenets of Islam, in harmony and peace.

Nawab Sir Shahnawaz Mamdot, President of the Punjab Muslim League invited the Central Muslim League to hold its annual session in Lahore. On 22nd March, 1940, at 2.30 p.m. the annual session of the Muslim League started with the recitation from the Holy Quran. Then Anwar Qureshi read Mian Bashir Ahmad's famous poem, "Millat Ka Pasban Hay Muhammad Ali Jinnah".

On the significant day of Friday 23rd of March, 1940 in Minto Park, Lahore, about one hundred thousand Muslims attended the historic meeting. It was Leagues' 27th Annual Session, which was presided over by the Quaid-e-Azam M.A. Jinnah. Maulvi A.K. Fazal-ul-Haq, Sher-e-Bengal, Chief Minister of Bengal moved the famous historic Lahore Resolution. It was passed unanimously on 24-03-1940. It was seconded by Chaudhry Khaliq-uz-Zaman and others like Maulana Zafar Ali Khan, Sardar Aurangzeb Khan, Haji Sir Abdullah Haroon, Nawab Ismail Khan, Qazi Isa Khan, Mrs. Muhammad Ali Jauhar, I.I. Chundrigar and Dr. Muhammad Alam.

TEXT OF THE RESOLUTION

The Lahore Resolution resolved at the Lahore session of the All India Muslim League held on March 23, 1940.

This session of the All India Muslim League emphatically reiterates that the scheme of the federation embodied in the Government of India Act, 1935 is totally unsuited to and unworkable in the peculiar condition of this country and is altogether unacceptable to the Muslims in India.

2. The Muslims in India will not be satisfied unless the whole constitutional plan is reconsidered de novo (anew) and that no revised plan would be acceptable to the Muslims unless it is framed with their approval and consent.

3. Resolved that it is the considered view of this session of the All India Muslim League that no constitutional plan would be workable in this country or acceptable to the Muslims unless it is designed on the following basic principles, namely, that geographically contiguous units are demarcated into regions which should be so constituted, with such territorial readjustment, as may be necessary, that the areas in which the Muslims are numerically in a majority as in the North-Western and Eastern Zones of India should be grouped to constitute "Independent States" in which the constituent unit shall be autonomous and sovereign. That adequate, effective and mandatory safeguards should be specifically provided in the

constitution for minorities in these units and in these regions for the protection of their religious, cultural, economic, political, administrative and other rights and interests in consultation with them, and in other parts of India where the Mussalmans are in minority, adequate effective and mandatory safeguards shall be specially provided in the constitution for them and other minorities for the protection of their religious, cultural, economical, political, administrative and other rights and interest in consultation with them.

This session further authorizes the Working Committee to frame a scheme of constitution in accordance with these basic principles providing for the assumption finally by the respective regions of all powers such as defiance, external affairs, communications, customs and such other matters may be necessary.

The next day on 24th March, the Hindu press captioned boldly, Lahore Resolution as the Pakistan Resolution. After it, M.A. Jinnah accepted it as the Pakistan Resolution. He then announced that no power on earth could hinder the establishment of Pakistan.

The Pakistan Resolution provided that no constitutional plan would be workable or acceptable to the Muslims less than an independent country which mainly on the principle that geographically continuous units were demarcated in the region to constitute a separate Muslim Homeland namely "Pakistan". The British Government offered to set up a Constituent Assembly after the War to determine future constitution of India wherein minorities would be assured of their rights. The Muslim League accepted but the Congress rejected the offer. During the winter, 1941-42 the course of war took an unfavourable turn for the British and political situation in the sub-continent became a cause of concern for them. To placate the Indian opinion a Mission headed by Sir Stafford Cripps was sent which proposed a new Indian dominion after war but these proposals were again turned down. In August 1942 when the Japanese invaded India, the Congress passed a Resolution requiring the British to quit India on which Government declared it an unlawful organization. Mr. M.A. Jinnah observed that movement by the Congress was an invitation to civil war and instead demanded that the British should first partition the sub-continent and then quit. In 1945 Lord Wavell held a Conference at Simla on the subject but it broke down on the question of participation of Muslim members in which the Congress opposed the nominations by Muslim League.

After failure of the Simla conference elections were held in the winter of 1945-46 in which the Muslim League captured all the Muslim Seats. At the end of Election, a Cabinet Mission was sent by the British Government, which started deliberations. The Congress was not prepared to accept partition of sub-continent. In the meantime Mr. Muhammad Ali Jinnah held a Convention of the Muslim League at Delhi in which it was declared that nothing less then self-determination was acceptable to the Muslims otherwise they would resist the decision by force. The Cabinet Mission failed and announced the Union of India at their own.

INTERIM GOVERNMENT

When in the absence of proper safeguards, the Muslim League rejected the Cabinet Mission, the Congress agreed to join the interim Government. The five seats meant for the Muslims were filled with the nationalist Muslim leaders. This led to a wild reaction and the country came to be rocked by Hindu-Muslim riots on an unprecedented scale almost bordering on civil war. In order to ease the situation, the Viceroy appealed to the Muslim League to join the Interim Government in October 1946.

As the year 1947 dawned, the Hindu-Muslim struggle gained in intensity and severity. The country was on the brink of civil war within the interim Government, there was acute bitterness and the Hindus and the Muslims pulled in opposite directions. It was in the context of this grave situation that Lord Attlee, the Prime Minister of Great Britain, made a statement on February 20,1947. The statement declared that power would be transferred to the responsible Indians by a date not later than June, 1948. It was added that if an agreed Constitution was not worked out by a fully representative Assembly by that date, the Government would have to consider to whom the power of the Central Government in the British India should be handed over on the due date whether as a whole to some form of the Central Government or in such other way as might seem most reasonable and in the best interests of the Indian people.

MOUNTBATTEN AND HIS PLAN

In March, 1947 Lord Wavell was replaced by Lord Mountbatten as the Viceroy. On June 3, 1947 Lord Mountbatten announced his plan for the transfer of power. According to this plan, the provincial legislative assemblies of Bengal and the Punjab were asked to meet in two parts, one representing the Muslim majority district and the other the rest of the provinces. The members of the two parts of each legislative assembly sitting separately were to vote whether or not, the province should be partitioned. If a simple majority of either part decided in favour of partition, division would take place. This was a preliminary step of temporary nature as for final partition detailed investigation of boundary questions will be needed for which a Boundary Commission will be set up.

Both the Congress and the Muslim League accepted the Mountbatten plan. The provinces of the Punjab and Bengal each were divided into two provinces. On a referendum a district of Assam Province also joined the East Pakistan. Similarly referendum was also held in the North Western province and the people of the province opted for Pakistan. The Indian Independence Bill was introduced in the British Parliament and on receiving the Royal assent in July, 1947 separate provincial Governments were set up for Pakistan and India on July 29, Quaid-e-Azam was nominated as the Governor-General of Pakistan. On August 14, 1947 Pakistan was established. That was the culmination of a long struggle, which the Muslims of the sub-continent had waged for a separate homeland in the name of Islam and Lahore was an important and focal center of this struggle.

On 30th of June, 1947 the Punjab Boundary Commission was established which heard the viewpoints of all the political factions and considered various proposals for dividing the territories of both the dominions i.e. Pakistan and India. This Boundary Commission was headed by Sir Cyril Radcliff and had 11 hearings in the city of Lahore. Finally Sir Cyril Radcliff gave his award on 12th August, 1947 which divided Punjab into East and West Punjab. The West belonging to Pakistan.

The Constituent Assembly of Pakistan met at Karachi on 14-08-1947 and Viceroy Lord Mountbatten addressed the members. Quaid-e-Azam Muhammad Ali Jinnah was of course the first Governor-General. Pakistan came into being in the name of Islam. Quaid-e-Azam was very clear on this issue. He expressed his views in this respect on various occasions.

It is, however, unfortunate that Quaid-e-Azam soon parted us on 11th September, 1948 and could not see establishing the Islamic State as dreamed by him. The leaders of the Muslim League tried to continue his mission and in the year 1949 passed the famous objective resolution which provided guidelines to enforce Islamic System in the country. The text of objective resolution lays down the broad principles of our Islamic Government.

Lahore as will be seen from the above has all along remained a very important center of political, cultural and social activities. As in the past its Constituent Assembly met in the Assembly Chambers. The first Governor of Punjab was Sir Robert Francis Mudie. Immediately on partition, Lahore was caught in the frenzy of problems of the migration the biggest immigration of history and thousands of Muslims evicted from East Punjab were coming to Pakistan – their new homeland. Their properties and assets had been looted, their women raped and tortured, the youngsters brutally murdered and those left over pushed into Pakistan. These innocent hordes were coming on foot, railway and carts and whatever means they could find. Thousands were murdered on their way to Pakistan. Thousands crippled and many handicapped before their arrival. They were to be provided shelter, food, medicines and help/assistance to settle in their new homeland. This was an uphill task. First of all they were placed in camps as their temporary abode. The Mohajir Camps were set up around Walton, Lahore Fort and in many open spaces around Railway Station. The administration of the newly set up State was without any resources. They had no money, no transport, and no means to immediately extend required assistance. However by help of the local people it arranged for food and assistance to their brethren. The unhygienic condition in camps created many health hazards but somehow after a respite the Mohajirs were dispatched to other parts of the country where till recently there had been many problems of settlement and rehabilitation. A separate Ministry of Rehabilitation was established but it required decades before Mohajirs could find homes and means to earn livelihood. With the influx of Mohajirs there was also shortage of food supplies. This situation continued until late 50s. Lahore faced all problems and its citizens worked day and night for the settlement of refugees.

In 1955 the Government of Pakistan decided to set up One Unit of the 4 provinces located in the Western Wing. With this came into being the Government of West Pakistan and Lahore became the Headquarters of the West Pakistan with one Constituent Assembly, one Secretariat and Ministers for various Departments. The effort was well intent in the best interest of the National integration and development strategies. In the year 1958 Martial Law was imposed and Lahore was the H.Qs., of Martial Law zone 'A'. Field Martial Muhammad Ayub Khan, Commander of Armed Forces replaced Mr. Sikandar Mirza as Martial Law Administrator and abrogated the Constitution of 1956. He replaced the same in 1962 in which he brought the idea of Basic Democracies. West Pakistan was governed by Nawab Amir Muhammad Khan of Kala Bagh who had been appointed Governor of Punjab in June, 1960. Malik Amir Muhammad Khan, a Nawab, a graduate from the Oxford and honest/strong administrator from Mianwali was a very competent administrator and agriculturist who managed the province of West Pakistan in absolutely up-right manner. It was during this period when Indo-Pak War of 1965 broke out. India had launched air attacks on Lahore. Then followed the Tashkent Declaration wherefore Zulfiqar Ali Bhutto, the then Foreign Minister rebelled against Field Martial Ayub Khan's regime. There was agitation and Lahore became a center of protests in support of Bhutto who led his newly formed Peoples Party. On the resignation of Field Martial Muhammad Ayub Khan, General Yahya Khan became Chief Martial Law Administrator.

In the year 1970 the political conditions obtaining throughout the country were so depressing and disgusting that the Government thought of dismemberment of one unit. This had been set up in the best interest of the Western Wing but it was argued that the people from far-flung areas faced lot of problems due to centralization of powers. Apparently the political groups wanted more and more power in the shape of Ministries and jobs by way of establishment of Secretariats at all the four provincial Headquarters. This movement succeeded and in July, 1970 West Pakistan was again divided into four independent Secretariats, Governors and

Chief Ministers with full-fledged Ministers running the affairs of their respective provinces. Lahore remained back as Headquarters of Punjab. In 1971 the disaster of East Pakistan took place and Dacca fell to the Indian forces. The Bengali Nationalists with the help of Indian forces established independent country known as Bangladesh. Zulfiqar Ali Bhutto who had raised slogan of separate East and West Wings became the civilian Chief Martial Law Administrator and Lahore was the Martial Law Headquarters of Punjab. Lahore remained under Martial Law from 1970 to 1973 wherefore Zulfiqar Ali Bhutto was thrown out by General Zia-ul-Haq, who placed the country under Martial Law in 1977 which position continued till his death.

Throughout this period of about 40 years, Lahore remained Headquarters and seat of Government but has not been able to make any planned and substantial development and growth. Inspite of huge expenditure in the name of development there are hardly any industries contributing to national economy except that it had haphazard expansion and population measured to about 80 millions. The general sanitary and public health conditions are very poor. Incidentally Lahore was lucky to have two Chief Ministers who were residents of Lahore. Let us see what they contribute and leave for the city's economic and cultural heritage. For purpose of reference a list of the Chief Ministers and Governors who had Lahore as Headquarters of the Province, of Punjab, is given for the reader's interest.

S. NO.	Name of the Chief Ministers	From	To
1.	Nawab Iftikhar Hussain Mamdot	15-08-1947	31-12-1948
2.	Mian Mumtaz Muhammad Khan Daultana	07-05-1951	30-07-1953
3.	Malik Feroz Khan Noon	31-07-1953	20-01-1956
4.	Sardar Abdul Hamid Khan Dasti	21-01-1956	30-04-1956
5.	Dr. Khan Sahib	01-05-1956	16-07-1957
6.	Sardar Abdur Rashid Khan	16-07-1957	27-03-1958
7.	Nawab Muzaffar Ali Khan Qazalbash (Leader of the House)	28-03-1958	15-10-1958
8.	Shaikh Masood Sadiq	09-06-1962	03-07-1964
9.	Khan Habibullah Khan	12-06-1965	30-06-1966
10	Malik Khuda Bakhsh Bucha	01-07-1966	04-11-1967
11	Malik Qadir Bakhsh Jhakkar	10-11-1967	05-01-1969
12	Malik Meraj Khalid	07-05-1972	06-11-1973
13	Malik Ghulam Mustafa Khar	12-11-1973	15-03-1974
14	Mr. Muhammad Hanif Ramay	15-03-1974	14-07-1975
15	Nawab Sadiq Hussain Qureshi	15-07-1975	04-07-1977
16	Mr. Muhammad Nawaz Sharif	09-04-1985	30-05-1988
17	Mr. Muhammad Nawaz Sharif (Care Taker)	31-05-1988	02-12-1988
18	Mr. Muhammad Nawaz Sharif	02-12-1988	07-08-1990

19	Mr. Ghulam Haider Wyne (Care Taker)	07-08-1990	08-11-1990
20	Mr. Ghulam Haider Wyne	08-11-1990	24-04-1993
21	Mian Manzoor Ahmad Wattoo	25-04-1993	18-07-1993
22	Sh. Manzoor Elahi (Care Taker)	19-07-1993	20-10-1993
23	Mian Manzoor Ahmad Wattoo	20-10-1993	12-09-1995
24	Sardar Muhammad Arif Nakai	13-09-1995	03-11-1996
25	Afzal Hayat Khan (Care Taker)	17-11-1996	20-02-1997
26	Mian Shahbaz Sharif	20-02-1997	

List of Governors for the period 1947- 1998

1.	Mudie, Sir Robert Francis, K.C.S.I, O.B.E.	15.08.1947	02.08.1949
2.	Sardar Abdur Rab Nishtar	02.08.1949	26.11.1951
3.	Mr. Ismail Ibrahim Chundrigar	26.11.1951	01.05.1953
4.	Mian Amin-ud-Din	02.05.1953	23.06.1954
5.	Rahimtoola Mr. Habib Ibrahim	June. 1954	Nov., 1954
6.	Gurmani, Nawab Mushtaq Ahmad	27.11.1954	31.08.1957
7.	Mr. Akhtar Hussain, H.PK.	02.09.1957	31.05.1960
8.	Malik Amir Muhammad Khan	01.06.1960	18.09.1966
9.	General Muhammad Musa, H.PK. H.Q.A. M.B.E.	18.09.1966	19.03.1969
10.	Mr. Yusaf Abdullah Haroon	20.03.1969	25.03.1969
11.	(GAP)	25.03.1969	31.08.1969
12.	Air Marshal Nur Khan, H.J; H.Q.A.; S.PK.	01.09.1969	31.01.1970
13.	Lieutenant General M. Attiq-ur-Rahman H.Q.A.,S.PK;M.C.	01.02.1970	July 1970
14.	Mr. Ghulam Mustafa Khar	23.01.1971	12.11.1973
15.	Nawab Sadiq Hussain Qureshi	12.11.1973	14.03.1975
16.	Mr. Ghulam Mustafa Khar	14.03.1975	31.07.1975
17.	Alhaj Brig. Muhammad Abbas Khan Abbasi	31.07.1975	06.07.1977
18.	Mr. Justice Aslam Riaz Hussain	06.07.1977	18.09.1978
19.	Lt. Gen. Sawar Khan H.I.(M). S.BT.	18.09.1978	01.05.1980
20.	Lt. Gen. Ghulam Jillani Khan	01.05.1980	31.12.1985
21.	Makhdoom Muhammad Sajjad Hussain Qureshi	31.12.1985	08.12.1988
22.	Gen. (Retd.) Tikka Khan	09.12.1988	06.08.1990
23.	Mian Muhammad Azhar	06.08.1990	24.04.1993
24.	Ch. Muhammad Altaf Hussain	25.04.1993	19.07.1993
25.	Lt. Gen. (Retd) Muhamad Iqbal Khan	19.07.1993	06.03.1994
26.	Ch. Muhammad Altaf Hussain	26.03.1994	21.05.1995
27.	Mr. Justice Muhammad Ilyas (Acting)	22.05.1995	16.06.1995
28.	Lt. Gen. (Retd) Raja Saroop Khan	19.06.1995	06.11.1996
29.	Mr. Justice Khalil-ur-Rahman (Acting)	06.11.1996	11.11.1996
30.	Kh. Ahmad Tariq Rahim	11.11.1996	11.03.1997
31.	Mr. Shahid Hamid	11.03.1997	Till date

2

EXPLORING HISTORY
Tour Of The Walled City

Lahore has a friendly, relaxed atmosphere. It is a fine place to watch the world rush by. The improbable mix of painted trucks, cars, bullock carts, buses, handcarts, scooters with whole families aboard – mum riding side saddle at the back, holding a baby, a toddler standing in front of dad, holding on to the steering, and possibly more children too, lodged precariously, hanging on for dear life. Motor bikes carry at least three youths, sharp dressers – skinny knees sticking out in a row.

There are tongas, scooter rickshaws with engines pop-popping madly as they weave perilously through the other traffic. There are women in purdah and women not in purdah carrying enormous bundles on their heads. The bullock carts are often loaded, overloaded with metal. Heavy industry seems to use primitive transport.

Lahore is undoubtedly ancient. It waxed and waned in importance during the Sultanate, as at times Dipalpur and Multan were more important. But the Muslim rule began here when Qutub ud din Aibak was crowned in Lahore in 1206 and thus became the first Muslim Sultan of the sub-continent.

But the real flowering of Lahore was during the Mughal period. It was Akbar's capital from 1584 to 1598. Jahangir loved the town and he and his wife Nur Jahan are buried at Shahdara. Shah Jahan was born in Lahore and added buildings and even Aurangzeb, not noted for fine buildings, gave the town the Badshahi Masjid and the Alamgiri gateway to the fort.

During the eighteenth century, as Mughal power dwindled, there were constant invasions. Lahore was a suba – a province of the Empire. There were subedars, provincial rulers with their own court. These Governors managed as best as they could, though for much of the time it must have been a rather thankless task to even attempt. The 1740s were years of chaos and between 1745 and 1756 there were nine changes of Governor. Invasions and chaos in local government allowed bands of warring Sikhs to gain control in some areas. Lahore ended up being ruled by a triumvirate of Sikhs of loose character and the population of the city invited

Bhati Gate

Ranjit Singh to invade. He took the city in 1799. Holding the capital gave him some legitimacy; he became Emperor.

The Sikh period was bad news for the protection of ancient buildings. Some survived, misused and knocked about a bit, and a few new ones were added. Nevertheless, descriptions of Lahore during the early 19th century refer to it as a "melancholy picture of fallen splendour". Henry Fane mentions marching ten miles "chiefly through the ruins of the ancient capital". The Sikhs carted off large amounts of material from Mughal building to use in decorating Amritsar. The British added a great many buildings, plenty of "Mughal Gothic", as well as some shady bungalows and gardens. Earlier on, the British tended to build workaday structures in sites like the Fort, though later they did start to make an effort to preserve some ancient buildings.

The bazars in the old city are the ones people dream about – tiny alleys, some of which will admit a rickshaw, a string of donkeys or carts – and pedestrians have to leap into doorways to give room. Some alleys are only possible single file.

The Shahi Mohallah, behind the Fort is the Tart's Quarter and contains the places where gentlemen can see dancing girls. In this area are some splendid embroiderers. The alleys give access to tiny booths that have a counter and a bench for potential customers to perch on. If one shows interest, the proprietor sends for tea immediately. Over tea, he displays his wares, producing suit after suit, piece after piece, lengths of rich cloth, satins and silks, velvets and chiffons – embroidered in various styles and colours. Enough to bring out the sybarite in a puritan!

Fashions are discussed: Perhaps madam would like silver thread on black velvet; Flowers; Or geometrical designs; What kind of neckline? And on the sleeves? These purchases take all day, the shopkeeper noting the details in his book. And the cost, for what is no mere dress, but rather, a work of art, is moderate. It is possible to buy ready-made too. Infact, orders may take too long to be feasible for passing travellers. Similarly, one can spend an age at the goldsmith.

What more could any one want? Spices, vegetables, books, gold and silver, brass, jewellery, junk jewellery, antiques, carpets, kitchenware, brooms and buckets, feather dusters, shoes, pots and pans, garlands of money (for weddings or as presents to whores), garlands of flowers for shrines, blacksmiths and locksmiths, carpenters and furniture vendors, tea shops, snacks and food vendors, milk shops with huge vats of milk, South Asian fast-food, and piled displays of those highly coloured, rather substantial sweets. There are assorted quacks – hakims and vaids, and specialists of all kinds, to give one a beautiful complexion or sort out sexual disfunction or minor aches and pains. There are tooth pullers and streetside dentists, false teeth makers with alarming advertising material. There are cages of smelly chickens. Sellers of make up, kajaal (eyeblack) and Swiss Miss lipsticks and nail polishes. Pictures of Imran Khan and other idols. Oranges, juice sellers, chunks of sugar cane piled in fancy shapes, cane juice, parched grain, sheep's head, and meat buzzing with flies whilst a man hacks with a large cleaver. A man produces a basket of scorpions or a snake; their venom is used for making "Sunday oil", an aphrodisiac.

Washing lines dangle, odd spaces are occupied by a cud chewing buffalo or a few goats. There are sellers of tobacco, stalls where parts of the hubble bubble hukkas dangle. There are so many cloth sellers, selling cloth for shalwar kameez, for what you will. The vendor will pull down and throw open so many bales with a careless gesture. It is hard not to make a purchase when the many has displayed half the goods in the shop – pressure salesmanship! There are sellers of suitcases and bags, for travel agents. Cats and dogs dine under stall fronts under stollen discarded offal. Kite-flying kids stand on top of the houses and every year on kite stand on top of the houses and every year on kite flying day they put powdered glass on their kite strings to cut those of their rivals. The streets below are thronging with people, many of whom are kind and friendly and enjoy stopping to chat with a stranger from another land. This being the general prevailing city condition the ideal course would be to take along the reader and roam in the streets entering through various historic gates of the walled city.

LOHARI GATE

In the brief history of the city a mention has been made of the gates in the citadel of Lahore. Emperor, Akbar the great, built the original city wall with 12 – 13 gateways. The ravages of time played havoc with this wall which is almost extinct now. The city, itself, considered to be one of the most beautiful in the Indian sub-continent, also did not escape the pillage and plunder. During Shah Jahan's reign according to an account by a Spanish Monk, the city was large and capacious. It was expanding and people had sort of garden houses outside. The city streets and bazars were well ordered, decorated pavilions of various colours and large gateways. The streets were over-crowded and it was difficult to cross on a horse or camel and only in wider streets camels and elephants were seen moving the small carts. Mughals lost to the Afghans who subsequently handed over to Sikhs, and unfit as they were to rule the country, the city was spoiled and ruined. During Sikh period economic conditions worsened. The population deserted and this place of culture reached its lowest ebb.

As already mentioned, the wall has disappeared but some gateways are in existence and if one discusses Lahore and its culture it means the downtown and the old walled city. It will, therefore, be only appropriate to walk through this

City Street 1854 Courtesy Punjab Archives

historical city giving brief glimpses of the city streets, houses, bazars, and monuments as they appear today.

The main gates still in existence are Bhati Gate, Lohari Gate, Delhi Gate, Sheranwala Gate and Kashmiri Gate. Entering the city through the Lohari Gate one has either to come through the over-crowded Anarkali Bazar or approach via Circular Road from Lower Mall and Bhati side sniffing a lot of cow dung and road dust and that too if you have the good luck to escape the pushes and beats of the tongas, carts, rickshaws, taxis, hand carts and other two wheelers. Right in front of Lohari Gate where used to be a garden around, laid by the British, one finds concrete and cement plastered buildings, shops, khokhas and stalls. On the right garlands and flower sellers. On the left is the optician market and fruit sellers sitting just under the doorway/gate. The gate is over 20 feet in width, about 20 feet in height and on upstairs some occupants permanently residing. This gate was re-built for the third time in 1864 by Sir Robert Montgomery, the then Governor of Punjab. Moving into the bazar on the right side one finds grocery shops and stores of dry eatable stuffs. On the left there are quite a few shops which sell kababs, Cutlets and cooked food. The bazar has some really good eating points with Shaikh Chatkhara House outstanding, where almost all the items, which are cooked and sold in Lahori style. Nearby there are sweetmeat shops with oven hot bread and Nan Kulchas. The Lohari bazar after reaching the Bokhari chowk crossing turns left, to 'Lohari Mandi' which on its right side has the famous 'Haji Nehari House' and on the left meat and a few grocery shops. The bazar and city streets present a really deplorable scene. These are stinking and smelling. It is really very difficult for an outsider (especially visiting the city for the first time) to breathe properly. On both sides of the bazar open sewerage drains carry filth and refuse which includes everything.

Across the Lohari Mandi one turns left to Chowk Jhanda but just before that on the right side is 'Kucha Kharasin'. 'Kharas' is a word, which is used for a 'Grinding Mill'. In the olden days grain was ground in this area by using the bullocks which pulled the grinding mill but these days these are operated with electric motors. There you get the fresh and pure wheat floor or 'basin' of grams or whatever you like. Turning left from Chowk Jhanda is an area of about one kanal which although filled with lot of paraphernalia provides a space to the residents for their marriages, and other occasions and a space to get together. From here the street leads us towards the west and we reach the famous Victoria Girls High School which was Haveli of Nau Nihal Singh. This lofty Haveli was one of the most magnificent buildings of Lahore City. It was built by Nau Nihal Singh s/o Maharaja Kharak Singh, as his private residence. It has numerous spacious chambers, halls and balconies. The roofs are decorated with mirrors. The walls are richly and tastefully ornamented with glasses and artificial flowers. After occupation of the British and even till date it is used as Girls School. The façade of Haveli has been recently spoiled where cheap painters tried to renovate the stucco tracery work. In front of the Haveli there is another open space which is called "Maidan Bhaian Wala" from where following Kucha Shah Inayat one enters Bhati Gate Bazar. On the left of Bhati Gate, which takes the visitor to the Police Station and outside, rightwards is the Shrine of Data Sahib, and, on left Mori Gate.

From Kucha Shah Inayat moving up north the bazar is dirty and full of heaps of rubbish. Quite stingy, filthy and foul smell leads one to the Faqir Khana Museum. This museum belongs to the Faqir Family who worked as 'Wazir' and 'Hakim' of Maharaja Ranjit Singh. This old city museum has quite a few antiques, portraits, furniture pieces and other art works since those times. The building, which was constructed in traditional style with small bricks till about 15 years back, was in its original condition. Unfortunately the custodians have got it repaired in cement plaster, whitewashed and spoiled its original architectural character. The same road goes up to Tibbi Police Station and in the same premises is located old Tehsil of Lahore and you are just in Chowk Chakla now given a different name of Novelty Chowk or Taranam Chowk. Just close to the gate of Police Station is the Tibbi Gali, which used to house quarters of courtesans, where people used to go for a good time. Unfortunately this is now in a very bad state of decay. From Chowk Chakla westwards one finds Bazar Shaikhupurian which is now Shoe Market and some other shops. On the right side moving eastwards one passes through the main bazar i.e. Chakla which leads upto 'Pani Wala Talab'. On both sides of this bazar there are residential quarters and some singers and dancers reside upstairs. The shops are mostly small hotels and music instruments makers such as Dholak, Harmonium and Tabla. Half way through this bazar on your left is the Roshanai Gate, which leads you to the Fort and Badshahi Mosque through Hazoori Bagh. From 'Pani Wala Talab' coming downwards one follows Gumti Bazar. Interestingly on our visit we found artificial jewellery makers who were finishing the Bangles with hand and to most perfect precision. For one hundred bangles he would charge only Rs.100/-. This bazar again leads towards Lohari Mandi and both sides of the bazar are full of cloth merchants and shoemakers, fruit sellers and small hosiery shops. In between Lohari and Gumti there is the small old Masjid, Bohr Wali.

In contrast to the description narrated in the Mughal period the maintenance of the buildings appears to be quite shabby and poor. The people were generally ill dressed with pulled and drawn faces. The feeling was that they are in depression. Most probably the hygienic conditions are effecting general health conditions. However, one of the significant aspects of attitude of residents on questioning was their hospitality. Every person would invariably ask for a cup of tea, drink or any other service. An insider revealed that Lahore has no parallel of its stingy mornings and aromatic evenings.

BHATI GATE

This gateway is traditionally attributed to the settlement of a clan known as 'Bhatti Rajput" who were made to settle inside this gate after Muslim occupation of the city by Mahmood Ghazanvi. They infact came during the period of Governorship of Malik Ayyaz. They had only agreed to reside on the condition that the gateway will be known by name of their tribe and hence it came to be known as 'Bhati Gate'. Like the city walls it was destroyed and damaged and was rebuilt during the British period. Bhati Gate is very busy chowk as out-side, on the Circular Road, the Ravi Road Lower Mall, Mohni Road, and the road coming from Bilal Ganj and Lohari all converge here. It is all along lively and awake till late in the night. There used to be theatres, cinemas and other local street shows and small entertainments. Its close proximity to the shrine of Hazart Data Ganj Bakhsh has created a great hustle and bustle all the day especially of those visiting Data Sahib. The Chowk is full of eatables, hotels, soft drink stands, and shops of Kababs and fish sellers, fruit vendors, and milk and lassi shops. This is the center of transport pliers and one can get buses and wagons in all directions. The garden immediately on the left of Bhati Gate and facing Data Darbar used to be the beautiful place but it has been badly spoiled by Lahore Municipal Corporation by putting up "khokhas" and small shops and rented out for money. Consequently it has badly effected hygiene of the locality. The old ditch around the city wall has taken the shape of open drain. It is the biggest hazard to the city dwellers. Immediately in front of Bhati Gate on road side a Tonga Stand, on the left a tubewell, wrestling club, some fruit vendors and just around the Gate a Police Station on the entry. Entering the Bhati Bazar one finds grocery stores, vegetable shops, Kabab shops and kitchen-wares and plastic stores etc. The bazar is narrow and it is really very difficult in the morning and after-noon to cross without rubbing shoulders. The general cleanliness is in a poor shape, drains are open and smelly. The living conditions of the people continues in a manner as they used to live centuries back. Their typical Punjabi dialect, noise of the vendors and rush of the children and ladies in the bazar takes one to a totally different world, as compared with the life in recently developed colonies in the city suburbs. A few paces in the Bazar, one finds on right Kucha Patrangan. About 80 years from now Maulvi Asghar Ali Roohi, the teacher of Maulvi Muhammad Shafi, used to live in a house in this Kucha. He was a fountainhead of learning and scholarship, and known far and wide for his 'dars' of Holy Quran. He had later started giving 'dars' in Gumti Bazar also. Dr. Maulvi

Inside Bhati Gate

Muhammad Shafi who was later principal of the Oriental College, also used to live near the Kucha during his days as a student.

A little ahead of Kucha Patrangan is "Nayan di Gali" the 'Barber's street. At the end of this gali there used to be a house where Shaikh Gulab Din, an Advocate used to live. Shaikh Gulab Din belonged to Sialkot and had such command of Urdu that he had translated the laws of evidence and common usage.

Next to Nayan di Gali, to the right, is Mohallah Jalotian across which was the house where Dr. Muhammad Iqbal lived for several years. Adjacent to this was the Cho-Mohallah where the Khatib of Unchi Masjid Maulvi Imamuddin lived. From Cho-Mohallah, one could go to Noor Mohallah to the left of the bazar and to Mohallah Shish Mahal on the right.

In Mohallah Shish Mahal lived Dr. Muhammad Hussain who had come to Lahore after the war of 1857. He and Dr. Rahim Khan, whose mansion was situated on Dhani Ram Road, adjacent to Traders Bank near Anarkali, was considered the most competent doctors of the day. Dr. Muhammad Hussain was the Honorary Physician and Dr. Rahim Khan was Honorary Surgeon to the Viceroy.

From Shish Mahal onwards, you can go to Rai Bahadur Mela Ram's Haveli of which nothing now remains. It was one of the splendours inside Bhati Gate. The Rai Bahadur and his son Rai Bahadur Ram Saran Dass, were followers of the "Sanatam Dharm" and were widely respected. The son, was a great patron of poets and writers in 1880, when Lahore was linked with Amritsar by rail, the Lahore Railway Station was built by Mian Sultan of Landa Bazar, Mian Muhammad Bakhsh Dol Gar of Mochi Gate and Rai Bahadur Mela Ram, were noted contractors of those days.

Rai Bahadur Mela Ram and Rai Bahadur Ram Saran Dass used to celebrate every Hindu, Sikh or Muslim festival with great ceremony. Every Sunday there used to be a musical soiree at Rai Bahadur Ram Saran Dass's bungalow outside Bhati Gate, according to one account. Invitees belonged to all creeds; prominent among the participants were Allama Iqbal, Sir Abdul Qadir, Sir Shahabud Din, Mian Sirajud Din, Raja Narindranath, Raja Sir Daya Kishan Kaul, Nawab Liaqat Hayat Khan, Nawab Ahmed Yar Khan Daultana, Sikandar Hayat Khan, Mian Muhammad Nasirud Din, Khan Bahadur Syed Maratab Ali, Sardar Sundar Singh Majitjia and Sardar Joginder Singh. In other Kucha, Moti Tibba, used to live Sir Abdul Qadir.

It is a fact that Lahore's Bazar Hakiman and Amritsar's Kattra Hakiman owned their importance to Hakim Hissamud Din, who used to practise at both places. He was the personal Hakim to the Maharajas of Kashmir and the Phulkian States. His uncanny diagnostic ability had spread his fame far and wide. Apart from this he was an upright man of God and people were as keen to seek his blessings as his medicines.

A little ahead of Hakim Shujaud Din's house was the residence of Faqir Syed Iftikharud Din. Since he was a distinguished member of the Faqir Khana and held an important position in Government, his house usually saw gathering of Government officials. A special feature of these gatherings is reputed to have been complete admixture of Iftikharud Din's Muslim Hindu friends. These include Lala Harkishan Lal, Dyal Singh Majithia, Ch. Ahmad (father of Faiz Ahmad Faiz), Mirza Sultan of Tibbi, Naseerud Din nephew of Nawab Imamud Din. Syed Iqbal Ali Shah and Syed Maratab Ali Shah, lived in this bazar.

Moving further ahead, we would come to the Kucha of Astana Sharif where the Lal Masjid built by Faqir Syed Jamalud Din is located. Next is a small graveyard, which has the mazaar of Faqir Syed Ghulam Mohyud Din. Opposite this kucha is the mosque built by Hakim Abdullah Ansari, who was founder of Bazar-e-Hakiman.

On the left of the bazar is kucha Fakir Khana where Faqir Syed Zafarud Din used to live and there be also the house where Mir Nazir Hussain Nazim lived all his life. A few paces from this is the house of Faqir Syed Hasanud Din and his 'imambara.' Syed Ali Shah lived here: his fame as an artist needs no recounting, and despite the fact that he never adopted painting as his profession, the leading artists would come to learn the art of painting from him from Bhati Gate up to Tehsil.

Then we come to kucha Tehsil where the Tehsildar of Lahore used to hold his court. Maulana Muhammad Hussain Azad also lived in this kucha for a long time. There is a bazar here which used to be called 'Seemyon ka Bazar' but is now known as Judge Bazar, it was here that Sir Shahabud Din's house and press was located and the house of Syed Mohammd Latif, author of the history of Lahore.

Where Tibbi ends, on left is Bazar Shaikhupurian. In a corner of this bazar is a house in which Muharram Ali Chishti used to live, who was the editor of 'Rafiq-i-Hind' and was known as a 'King Maker'. He often used to arrange 'Qawwali' sessions and was known for his hospitality. There was an old haveli close to his house where Mirza Abdur Rahim lived, whose eldest son Mirza Muhammad Said was author of 'Khawab-e-Hasti' and 'Yasmeen'.

In Tehsil Bazar, a little ahead of Daan Gali, there is another kucha called Bhahron ki Tharrian where three brothers Khwaja Nabi Bakhsh, Khwaja Karim Bakhsh and Khwaja Amir Bakhsh lived. The brothers were, the life and soul of the gatherings that were held at the baithak of Hakim Shahbaz Din every evening. Their fearless criticism and their knack for discovering a person of true worth played an active role in shaping the career of many young poets and writers. Iqbal never used to recite his verse in public till he had shown it to the three brothers. 'Nala-e-Yateem,' Hilal-e-Eid', 'Tasver-e-Dard' and 'Sham-o-Sahir' were all poems, which Iqbal had first shown to the three elders before reciting them in the annual sessions of the Anjaman-e-Hamayat-e-Islam. Khwaja Ferozeud Din, Barrister, who was Iqbal's brother in-law, was Kh. Rahim Bakhsh's son, and Kh. Abdul Majid, author of the voluminous Jaameul Laghat, was Kh. Karim Bakhsh's son.

In front of Mashriqi Dawakhana, established by Hakim Faqir Muhammad at Hira Mandi's junction with Barood Khana and Chowk Sarjan Singh, there was a well which was famous throughout the city for its cool water. On the edge used to sit Rai Bahadur Sanjhi Mal, bare-bodied and wearing only a dhoti, dispensing water from the well to every thirsty wayfarer. The Rai Bahadur was among the first group of graduates from the Punjab University and had joined the Provincial Civil Service. After his retirement, he had given up all wordily pleasures and spent the rest of his life in serving the needy tell old Lahoris. Due to hustle bustle in the Bhati Chowk and surrounding areas some writers call it "Chelsea of Lahore".

MOCHI GATE, RANG MAHAL & SHAHALMI

Rai Bahadur Kanahya Lal in his note-worthy account titled 'Tarikh-e-Lahore' refers to 13 disasters which the city of Lahore suffered at the hands of invaders. The first was when Sultan Mahmood Ghazanvi occupied Lahore as Jai Paul had backed out allegeance of the Sultan and helped Raja of Kallinger against Sultan Mahmood. The city remained under siege for some time and after opening of the gates there ensued a fierce battle. It is said that the city was almost de-populated, the residents ran away and during the battle a big portion of houses was burnt. It turned into ruins. Sultan Mahmood before returning to Ghazni appointed Malik Ayyaz as Governor of Lahore who rehabilitated the city. It is remarked that the first 'Mohallah' or quarters, which was inhabited and reconstructed, was Lohari Mandi that is inside Lohari Gate.

The city suffered at the hands of numerous others and built and re-built many times until it found political stability in period of the Mughals and there was peace and prosperity. The nobility and royalty both contributed towards architectural heritage and the city abounded in wealth and population. Emperor Akbar provided 30 feet high brick wall to the city with 13 gates. We just had a tour of the western part through the Lohari Gate towards Lohari Mandi, Haveli Nau Nihal Singh, Tibbi, Hira Mandi and Gumti Bazar. The second round was from Bhati Gate to Tibbi and the third is now from Mochi Gate to Shahalmi.

Mochi is infact a corruption of Moti or Pearl. It was so called after the name of a Hindu employee, Moti Ram, who was an officer of the Emperor Akbar and resided at the gate and was incharge of the Security. The corruption in the name occurred during the Sikh period when it came to be called "Mochi" the gate was in bad shape during the Sikh period and was demolished early during the British period and bricks sold. It does not appear to have been re-built thereafter.

Mochi, Akbari, Shahalmi and Taxali Gates are not present any more. Delhi, Lohari, Bhati and Sheranwala Gates exist, some in the old, some renovated and some under siege by squatters and Qabza groups. Beyond these Gates are labyrinths of streets and mazes of bazars known by their old names, interconnected and interwoven. Taking a tour of these lanes and by-lanes, one can happily get lost in them, perhaps it is like getting lost in history. For a long time in the past, Mochi Gate was entered through the passage or bazar on either side of which two old derelict barracks housing the police force and the station house stood. These have been pulled down giving way to a rectangular box building, a type, that has become commonplace in the post independence era. May be it can be identified as post-independence architecture, or actually a non-architecture building fashion.

The common entrance to Mochi Gate has now become heavily overcrowded and encroached upon by all sorts of permanently and temporary shops, shacks and shanties all doing roaring business, of course. The encroachments have obliterated the entrance so that coming by the Circular Road, in a car or rickshaw, one is likely to miss or not place the Mochi Gate.

The entry point is packed with shops selling nuts, grams, sweets and dry fruit nuts. Immediately adjoining is the police station building, the office on the right side and the residential quarters on the left. The construction is very recent and in brick and box type. This leads us into the lane direct to the mosque of Muhammad Salah. Anyhow before entering the bazar itself, one sees on the right hand side the huge structure of Mughal Haveli which is typical of old big houses with a large wooden gate and entrance rampart. At the entrance of the Mochi Gate Bazar, actually at the confluence of Bazar Lal Khoo and Bazar Sadakaran, is perched a small beautiful mosque atop the shops. This is Masjid Muhammad Saleh. Muhammad Saleh was a diwan in the Punjab province during Shah Jahan's era. This is a three domed mosque built in 1659 A.D. or around 1078 Hijri, Five steps lead from the bazar to the mosque courtyard and two at the back lead down to Kucha "Chauhattian". Since the level of the road that runs through the bazar has been raised, it is now higher than the level of the shops located under the mosque.

All along the bazar, which is nothing but a narrow passage, not allowing more than three or four persons to pass through, are shops on either side selling firecrackers, kites, dry kitchen provisions, toffees, sweets and such stuff. This narrow passage leads one past the Lal Khoo and on the Chowk Nawab Sahib. Astride the Lal Khoo are the old, about 80 to 100 years, Kabab shops and in front

Inside Lohari Gate Painting by Ghulam Mustafa

a very famous sweetmeat shop. These two shops still provide the traditional old menus the old Lahori tastes of these eatables are maintained and prepared with well-guarded recipes.

The "Lal Khoo" is now disused. But out of faith or love for a saint who might have been associated with this place, people light candles and oil lamps at the perch. Right in front of the "Lal Khoo" is the "Qazi Khana" which is partially covered and leads to the main mohallahs of the Mochi Gate. At the turn of century in Qazi Khana used to live Maulana Muhammad Hussain Azad, the author of "Aab-i-Hayat" and a teacher of Oriental Studies at the Government College Lahore. Also he was one of the initiators of free style verse in Urdu. This laureate lies buried in the Karbala Gamay Shah area, at a stone's throw from the Government College.

Walking through the Lal Khoo bazar is like traversing through mediaevalism. Without being covered, it gives the impression of an Arab Souq. Because of the narrowness flanked on either side by tallish over-projecting abodes, the sunlight hardly ever reaches it. The shopkeepers are seen squatting amongst their overflowing shop wares, doing a roaring whole-sale business of their commodities – commodities which end up in remote villages and mufassil towns of the Punjab. The Lal Khoo bazar ends at Chowk Nawab Sahib from which on the right one detours to Akbari Mandi and on the left to the main mohallah and streets of Mochi Gate and straight on towards "Chauhatta" Mufti Baqar. On the left are two historic buildings the "Mubarak" Haveli and the "Nisar" Haveli. Mubarak Haveli is the place where Ranjit Singh is said to have tricked Shah Shuja, the deprived ruler of Kabul into parting with the "Koh-i-Noor" which now forms part of the crown jewels stacked away in the Tower of London.

Mubarak Haveli is a building in the pseudo Mughal style with hefty wooden gates leading into the foreyard which leads to the main courtyard in the centre of which is a huge water tank. All around on the first storey are the living quarters, their arched windows looking over the courtyard. From these two havelis on to the "Chauhatta" is the bazar with many large multi-storeyed brick buildings with baithhaks brimming over to the adjoining platform (Tharras) which provided open-air places for friendly meetings and discourse across the street.

Arched doors and windows with extended porches are the features of these buildings. This locality in the yonder past must have been the abode of many an affluent of the society. Chau (four) Hatta (big shops) Mufti Baqar must have been a four shops possession of a court official at one time. From this place a few arterial bazars with side lanes emanate in the same pattern which we have seen on the way from Mochi Gate. An old pipal tree under which there is a mausoleum which marks the Chau-Hatta. The characteristics of this narrow bazar are a few mausoleums here and there, some revered with daily candle lighting, some with an

Lohari Gate

annual urs and some just left in solitude. The two oldest establishments in Chau-Hatta being run by fourth generation heirs are a bakery and Pakora shop. From the Chau-Hatta onwards, the bazar again narrows down and then widens again past Kattra Wali Shah that is a big enclosed and gated Mohallah of over 1000 residents. Here again is a pipal tree under which there is another mausoleum and still another two, a few yards onwards with beautiful canopies atop and well cared after structures. These graves are attributed to the soldiers of Ghaznavide armies, who fell on the land of the Hanood and were buried there.

Pressing onwards, one comes to Chowk Ghazi Ilum-ud-Din Shaheed leading to Rang Mahal through Bazar Sirianwala and on right-hand side to bazar Tezabian (acid maker). This Chowk once had a very big well called "Boharwala Khoo" which provided cold water to the community. This well is now covered over by shops. In this Chowk also still remains a hundred years old sweetmeat shop of Haji Sahib whose "Qatlama" was a talk of the town once. Bazar Sirianwala must be a seventh and a half wonder of the world shops selling goat trotters, goats head etc. Shopkeepers sit around these commodities and over the shop-floors serving thousands of Lahoris.

Onwards one again passes covered bazar narrowing itself towards "Kasaira Bazar" in which pots, pans and utensils are sold. The display of utensils previously of brass and now of aluminium scrap, plastic and steel, provide a masterly attraction. At one time noises emanating from the craftsmen's hammers and anvils, giving shape to utensils was a part of the scene. Rounding to the left through this bazar, one finds oneself in Chowk Rang Mahal from the narrowness of the streets and bazars that one has covered from Mochi Gate onwards. This is an open place, once a very wide maidan, but now congested and overspilling. On the left is the Rang Mahal Mission High School, now of course, Government Rang Mahal High School where once taught great teachers like K. L. Rulia-Ram, Kahn Singh and Khadim Rizvi. This centurion of a school building is in a state of dilapidation and decay as is generally with our education system. Alas!

The passage from Rang Mahal to Shah Alam Gate (there is no gate here now!) is a journey of a mile through a river of throngs, chaos, disorder, noise and commercialism. Travel through "Shahalmi" by motorised vehicles is treacherous and pedestrian travel is equally dangerous. Shahalmi before the partition of the sub-continent was a hub market providing all sort of whole-sale provisions to the Mandi oriented and muffasil towns of the Punjab and beyond. The trading was in the hands of the Hindu community that did a roaring business. This place lay destroyed during the riots, which pre-dated the partition and was virtually levelled to the ground. But the new entrants, added to, spoiled and spilled over by

Amusements of old Lahore Painting by Ustad Miran Bakhsh 1919

generations of entrepreneurs over the past half century, thereafter rebuilt it. Now, not only it is brimming over the seams but also it has tentacled into side lanes and residential mohallahs. It still exists the central whole sale market which sells and supplies finished goods not only in Punjab but to a big part of the Northern areas.

All sorts of imaginable commodities can be had in this place - there is no end to the list of articles from the needle onwards which are available in Shahalmi. In historical perspective this is a place of vast trading like the Shahalmi of yonder years.

Walking through this golden mile of extreme commercial and trading activities is not without physical danger and the vehicular travel is a challenge even for the daring. However, having dared to walk through Shahalmi, the journey ends at the Circular Road, which in itself is another eighth wonder of traffic engineering. Standing on the junction one is only a few hundred meters from Mochi Gate, where one started this journey through history, mediaevalism and modernity Pakistani style. This Chowk has only recently been got vacated by the Chief Minister Punjab under police action. It has slightly eased the crossing of the traffic from Shahalmi to Bansanwali Gali.

DELHI GATE, CHUNA MANDI & SHERANWALA GATE

After completing our tour of the city through Lohari Gate, Bhati and Mochi Gate up to Rang Mahal and Shahalmi, the final phase may be covered by an entry through Delhi Gate. As already mentioned there were 13 Gates and Delhi Gate is one of them. There is no particular reason for naming the Gate as such except that it was so called due to its opening towards Delhi, on the High Road from Lahore, and in that direction. Marching on the Circular Road from Shahalmi, Mochi Gate, Akbari Gate (no longer in existence except the Akbari Mandi), just opposite Landa Bazar one takes a left-hand turn and travels towards the walled city. The old area outside Delhi Gate under occupation of gardens and ditch can no longer be seen instead, on both sides there are under cloth shops, kitchen wares, plastic wares, house-hold shops, some hand carts and stalls and fruit vendors, ring sellers, opticians, bangle sellers and so on. The original gateway of the Mughal period was destroyed during the Sikh rule. The gate now in existence was re-built by the British. The gate has an entry space of over 20 feet in width and in circular shape from within, with rooms all around. The length and width of the gate and the area on the first space can be judged from the fact that on the left side, on the first floor of the gate, there is a full-fledged High School for Girls functioning. On the right side the area is in occupation of quarters. Adjoining, left-hand stair wall of the gate, are located beautiful Hammams made by Wazir Khan, the Governor of Lahore

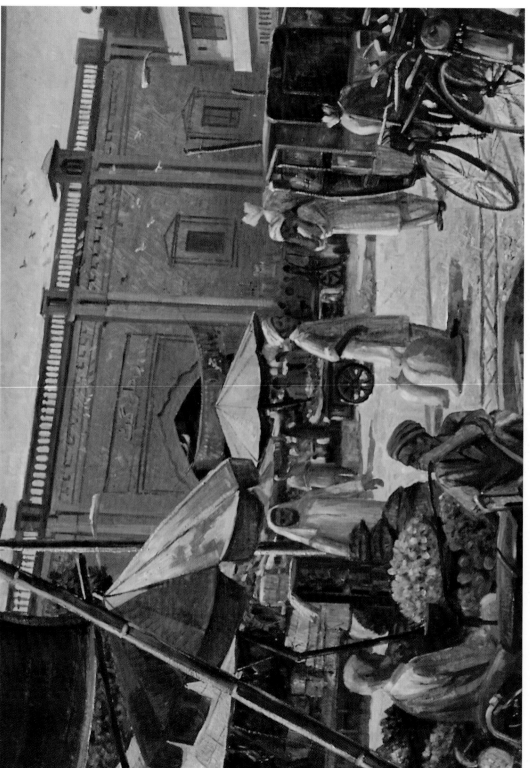

Delhi Gate Painting by Zulfiqar Ali Zulfi

during Shah Jahan's period. These Hammams have a built up area of over 2000 sq.ft., that is preserved now. Whatever the use of Hammams during the Mughal period these are beautiful pieces of architecture, designed for a purpose with arrangement of light and air. Inside the domes are nicely done up in stucco-tracery. The patterns of flowers, paintings of the birds, leaves and flowers are simply superb. These Hammams which had been lying neglected were renovated and re-opened for public in 1991 by the present Chief Minister. There exists a small library and a reading room in a part of the monument. A visit to the building leads one into the city life of 16th century that is no more. Coming out of the Hammams, taking left turn, one moves in the bazar towards Masjid Wazir Khan. In the bazar about 100 meters from the Delhi Gate there comes a Gate which is called 'Sufaid Gate'. Nothing is either written or known about the background except that this is an entry point to Chowk Wazir Khan from where the bazar leads to Chowk Purani Kotwali. The Sufaid Gate is constructed of old small burnt bricks in lime mortar and should be coming down any moment, as it is in a really bad shape. On left side of Chowk Wazir Khan is Masjid Wazir Khan, in front Chowk Purani Kotwali behind which a modern market has been built. We have separately discussed the beauty of Masjid Wazir Khan as an architectural monument that is one of the two best mosques in the world. However, a visit at site sadly reflects about the care and attention the State and public attaches to this heritage. It is utterly neglected, without any maintenance and as if there was none to lookafter. Continuing this way it may lose half of its life. Further Qabza groups are multiplying the encroachments and natural decaying factors are causes of its deterioration. Continuing with the bazar from Chowk Wazir Khan one will find that there is a upward height. This is because Lahore was founded on a mound and subsequently built and re-built on the accumulated debris of many centuries. From Chowk Purani Kotwali the bazar leads towards Chuna Mandi. All the houses both or right and left have been converted into shops. This bazar which is now being renovated and converted into proper shops had its old name as 'Bazar Rada Tailian' replaced by Azam Cloth Market's extension. Infact Azam Cloth Market has its extension known as Kashmir Block in this bazar. The bazar and street at the widest points is not more than 8``-10`` feet and with open drains running on both side of the walls leaving very little space for movement. In parts sewerage system has been laid but does not appear to be working. On reaching upto Chowk Jamia Masjid, Chuna Mandi from where on the right side 'Bangla Ayub Road' leads us out to Sheranwala and Yakki Gates. On the same road Mosque Maulana Ahmad Ali is located. There is a historic Sikh Monument 'Gurdawara Janam Asthan Sri Guru Ram Das Jee'. Guru Ram Das Je was the fourth Guru of Sikhs and was founder of the Sikh sacred city of Amritsar. From Chuna Mandi on the left side the street leads towards Rang Mahal and at about 200 yards, on right, the bazar ends on the Kashmiri Gate. Straight on, the bazar is slightly wider but in a bad state of repairs due to sewerage line and demolitions of 'Tharras' by the civic authorities, it leads one to the Masjid Gate of the Fort that is just opposite Masjid Mariam Zamani. On left is the historic Haveli Raja Dhian Singh. From Haveli Dhian Singh a tortuous and circuitous bazar leads towards Sheranwala Gate where a portion of the city wall still exists and then are found the Circular Road in front dividing the city and the Badami Bagh locality.

The Chuna Mandi has the historical place of Haveli Dhian Singh who was a Commander of Ranjit Singh and his son Hira Singh very near to the Maharaja. This Haveli saw many upheavals on the fall of Sikh rule. The Haveli was converted into a Zilla School that later on became Central Model School and is located on Lower Mall Road now. The Haveli was also used as premises of the first Government College Lahore and now is the Nawaz Sharif Girls College for Lahore.

This completes our tour of the city. Before winding up it may be added that the city is situated about 2 miles from the river Ravi. It is built in the form of a parallelogram. The area within the walls exclusive of the citadel is 461 acres. It stands on an alluvial plain traversed by river. The city is elevated and has a high ridge than its running east and west on its north side. Most feel that the elevated ground has a large component of debris of centuries. The River Ravi is no longer mighty. With its diversion by India it is not a danger for the city that people have constructed upto its banks. Practically it is now reduced to a big drain taking all the sewerage water of the city. When we talk of the city and mention its peculiar features, it means the old walled city located within the city gate. The city is an irregular trapezium. It widens on the north. Only a part of the city wall exists around Sheranwala Gate and the remaining has just disappeared with lofty houses instead. Describing other localities outside the city, which emerged separately during the Mughal, Sikh and British periods or on creation of Pakistan would require another volume. Consequently we are not touching. Of these the older ones are Misri Shah, Shad Bagh, Ghoray Shah, Landa Bazar, Naulakha area, Gowalmandi, Qila Gujjar Singh, Beadon Road, Mozang, localities around Lawrence Road, Raj Garh, Krishan Nagar, Sant Nagar, Karim Park and Sanda etc. This also leaves aside the modern colonies of Gulberg, Model Town, Garden Town, Township, Defence, Johar Town, Tech Society, Canal View etc., etc.

3

SAINTS OF THE CITY

Islam is a force of the volcanic sort, a burning and integration force, which, under favourable conditions, may even make a nation. It melts and fuses together as a whole, series of tribes, and reduces their internal structure to one uniform pattern, in which no survivals of pre-existing usages can be detected. The separate strata disappear; their characteristic fossils are crushed out of recognition; and a solid mass of law and tradition occupies their place. Hinduism, transfused as it is by mysticism and ecstatic devotion, and resting ultimately on the esoteric teachings of transcendental philosophy, knows nothing of open proselytism or forcible conversion, and attains its end in a different and more subtle fashion, for which no precise analogue can be found in the physical world. It is in the context of this basic philosophy, that we have to see the role of saints in preaching Islam, in general, in Lahore and help the rulers in establishing Muslim rule in areas under the principality of Lahore.

Lahore was historically a Hindu state until its occupation by the Muslims by Ghazanvids. It was during this era that Muslim missionaries and saints came over, preached Islam and convinced people to embrace Islam. The arrival of Muslim rulers effectively changed the local cultural patterns through interdiction. The discipline in life, the living, eating, housing, clothing and the intermixture of people (locals and the conquerors) caused adoption of each other's language, customs, manners and a variety of things. The most important impact and change was in the social fabric which under-went transformation due to conversions. Islam preaches and practices equality of all whereas Hinduism was an embodiment of caste ridden wretched rituals and untouchability. This change had far reaching effect on matrimonial relations and brought order in society and respect of a person as a human being with his rights and obligations. Due to the teaching of the Muslim Saints, large-scale conversions also took place and people became aware of the ills of social inequity in Hinduism and the kind of justice which Islamic system provided to all without discrimination. This change totally revised the existing cultural patterns, which were typical to a Hindu society. The Islamic education, jurisprudence, and laws totally differed from Hindu Vedic codes and had great appeal and attraction for a simple straightforward living, without exploitation of the poor. It set the start of new social order more participative for the common man. The habits, the dresses, the living, the food, system of justice, appreciation of each other's problems laid foundation of a new social order which gradually evolved its pattern without involvement of the state. People found the change positive, easy and less problematic. Who introduced this and who nourished it is none else but these great saints. Quite a few of them hailed from Afghanistan, Persia, some from central Asian States and Iraq etc. The reason was that Islam came to those areas much before. It is therefore only fair and historically correct that Saints who either accompanied or followed the Muslim forces spread Islam in the sub-continent. The beginning was made at Lahore when the Ghazanvis occupied the city. Those scholar saints who accomplished this mission were many but the information, which has trickled down, is sketchy as documentation and historiography starts in the later phase of Muslim rule in Punjab. The early period is not very rich source-wise. One can mention a few names like that of Shah Ismail, Syed Yakub Zanjani and Hazrat Data Ganj Bakhsh, but the number is much more the mission was continued and accomplished by their disciples. Detailed narration of the saints who lived and worked in Lahore is not in the scope of this article and, therefore, I am briefly discussing a few who are well known and because of whom the city is known in the world of spiritualism.

SHAIKH ISMAIL MUHADDITH

The first great Muslim scholar-saint, who came to Lahore and who moved about among the people of this city and helped them to the path of righteousness, was Shaikh Ismail. The historians in their chronicles usually assign him the title of "Muhaddith", the traditionalist. He hailed from Bukhara and came to Lahore during the early Ghazanvid period. Kanyha Lal in his history of Lahore gives 412 A. H. as the year of his arrival in Lahore. The writer of "Khazinaul Asfia" mentions 395 A.H., which is the reign of Sultan Mahmood of Ghazani. It is just possible that he might have accompanied the armed forces of Mahmood Ghazanvi. It is further narrated that he was the first Muslim Missionary in Lahore who recited Holy Quran. He spent his life in teaching and preaching Islam. It is said that hundreds of people of Lahore were converted to Islam due to his humanistic approach and his charismatic personality. He would address his audience for hours in a way that went to their hearts and moved them deeply. He lies buried on a raised platform on the left side of the present Hall Road. It is one of the earliest tombs that stands without a dome. It had once a huge garden around it, which was sold by greedy trustees. Its poor neglected structure is a standing testimony to our indifference to a great man who once adorned this city and worked devotedly amidst unfavourable circumstances for the spiritual regeneration of its people. He infact laid the foundation of Islam in Lahore.

MIRAN HUSSAIN ZANJANI

Miran Hussain Zanjani and his brother Yaqub Zanjani who were born in Zanjan in Khurasan, came to Lahore around 557 A. H. The consideration of "Tabligh" and Islamization of the people of newly acquired territory in Indian sub-continent apart from the main attraction was that the city abounded in people of high spiritual attainments and deep erudition. According to a narration Hussain Zanjani and Ali Hujweri were disciples of the same teacher. The day Ali Hujweri entered Lahore the funeral of Hussain Zanjani was being taken to graveyard and Hazrat Data Sahib led the funeral prayer. This tradition is based on the story related by Nizamud Din Auliya in "Fuwaid-al-Fuwad". But it has now been proved to be historically untrue, because Hussain Zanjani lived in Lahore during the early part of the seventh century (A.H.) when he met Muinudin Chishti who came to visit Ali Hujweri's tomb, and according to tradition spent forty nights there for spiritual illumination. According to Dara Shikoh, Muinudin and Hussain Zanjani met and enjoyed each other's company. Hussain Zanjani died in 604 A.H. and was buried in the locality, which is now known as Chah-i-Miran. It was once situated in a beautiful garden known after his name but the garden has disappeared due to the ravages of time. His tomb stands on a raised platform and has no dome.

Syed Hussain Zanjani lived in Lahore for over 36-37 years and during this period thousands embraced Islam due to his preaching.

SYED YAQUB ZANJANI

The shrine of Syed Yaqub Zanjani lies adjacent to the Lady Aitchison Female Hospital, situated between the Shahalmi Gate and Lohari Gate, now on Hospital Road. It occupies a place, which was once the rendezvous of great scholars and poets who came from far and near and gathered here to exchange notes and enjoy discussions on subjects of common interest. It was known as "Tila-e-Bokhari" (Mound of Bukhara). It had a large tract of land and a mosque, attached to it but neither of them is there today. A poet, Abdul Aziz Zanjani during the reign of Muhammad Shah, the Mughal King, wrote a long poem in praise of Lahore. In it, he mentions the tombs of these Zanjani Brothers as centers of great spiritual benefit. According to Hadiqa-tul-Aulia, Syed Yaqub Zanjani was a saint of very high order who had great knowledge both worldly and spiritually. He came to Lahore purely as a tourist and settled here. The name of his father was Syed Ali Hussani. He died on 16th of Rajab A.H. 604.

SHAH ABUL MAALI QADRI

Shah Abul Maali is said to be attached to the Qadriya mystic order. According to Maathar-i-Lahore his name was Shah Khair-ud-Din Muhammad but was called Shah Abul Maali. He was author of many books on Mysticism. He also wrote "Munqabat" for Hazrat Ghaus-e-Azam and "Tuhfa-ey-Qadriya" in connection with the miraculous manifestations of Ghaus-e-Azam, "Gul Dasta-e-Bagh-e-Moonas-e-Jan" and "Zafaran-e-Zar" were also amongst his works. Shah Abul Maali was a Kirmani Syed. His father Syed Rehmatullah bin Mir Syed Fateh ullah Kirmani were three brothers. Syed Rehmatullah, Shaikh Daud Bandgi whose mausoleum is in Sher Garh and the third one is Syed Jalal Din who lies buried in Kotan Syed Jalal in Sind. He was the spirtiual successor of his uncle. Shaikh Daud of Sher Garh, about whom Badayuni speaks eloquently in his 'Tarikh'. He was one of the very few contemporary sufi saints about whom Badayuni talks so lovingly. He states that hundreds of people daily visited him and accepted Islam at his hands. Abul Maali is said to have been born in Lahore in AD 1552 (960 A.H.) but went to Sher Garh to be initiated into the path of sufism. Under the supervision of his mentor he spent most of his youth engaged in strenuous spiritual exercises. When he was 51, he returned to Lahore in A.D. 1602 (101 A.H.) and after the death of his uncle spent the rest of his life in the city for the service of the people.

He is said to have been a saint of great piety and accomplishments. It is said Mullah Nimat ullah once came to see Hazrat Shah Abul Maali. At that time another person came with a beautiful 'Tasbih' and presented to Shah Abul Maali. Mullah Nimat Ullah thought in his heart that the Tasbih was very good and that if the saint had the spiritual power, he would know his secret wish and may pass it on to him. After sometime when Mullah Nimat Ullah begged leave, Hazrat Shah Abul Maali gifted him the 'Tasbih' with the remarks that read 'Darood' on this and you will be greatly blessed by the God Almighty.

Another incident is about Mullah Shah's great love and reverence for Hazrat Ghaus-ul-Azam. When he felt that if the great saint was also aware of his devotion. He had a dream in which he was standing without a turban or 'Amama' and Hazrat Ghaus-ul-Azam came and presented him a 'Dastar' and told him that he was not unaware of him (Mullah Shah) and knew about him being here and that is why he gave gift of 'Dastar'.

Next morning an attendant of Shah Abul Maali came and conveyed that Shah Maali had called him. When he met Shah Abul Maali he gave him (Mullah Shah) the 'Dastar' and remarked that it was the same, which Hazrat Ghaus-ul-Azam, had granted him last night. He was a great scholar and entertained great love and reverence for the founder of the Qadriya order Shaikh Abdul Qadir Jillani about whom he wrote several booklets. He shared this love with his dear friend and confident, Abdul Haq 'Muhaddith' who began his 'Tadhkira' of sufi saints of the sub-continent with a detailed notice of Shaikh Jillani, as a token of his deepest regard for this outstanding genius of the Muslim world. They often met and talked and discussed moral and spiritual problems and a collection of their correspondence is available which throws light on their attitudes. Abul Maali was a poet of great calibre. His Persian ghazals are on the style of Hafiz of Shiraz. Besides the 'Divan', seven of his treatises on different subjects are known to exist. His books reveal him to be a scholar of eminence who was inspired by his love for Shaikh-e-Jilans and was sustained in spiritual equipoise by his intimate friendship and personal devotion to Shaikh Abdul Haq. His sayings and activities are recorded in a book compiled by his son Muhammad Baqir.

He died in 1615 AD (1024 A.H.) at the age of 64 and lies buried in a tomb situated on the road parting off from Mcleod between Lahore Hotel and Orient Hotel. It is called Shah Abul Maali Road. It is a point of great festivities on two Eids occasions.

HAZRAT DATA GANJ BAKHSH

Hazrat Data Ganj Bakhsh is the most luminous figure of our history. While Muslim warriors conquered these parts of the sub-continent by force, the Muslim Saints identified themselves with the people, and interpreted Islam to them as a rational approach to better life in this world and hereafter. The people were not converted to Islam under any pressure of the armed forces; they accepted Islam voluntarily because of the appeal of the message of Islam as conveyed and preached by Muslim missionaries.

By common consent Hazrat Data Ganj Bakhsh is a great Saint of the sub-continent. Hazrat Data Ganj Bakhsh was born in Ghazni, a small place in Afghanistan. Located at a higher altitude it is a cool place in summer. The winter is windy and cold. When Ghazanvids were in power, this town was known for its grandeur as it happened to be the capital of their empire. It is said, it is contemporary to Harrappan and Indus valley civilization. It was the centre of trade with Khurasan and Sindh. It was a medieval walled city with expansions of areas called "Mohallahs" developed outside the walled city. Two of these Mohallahs were known as "Hujwer' and 'Jalab'. Hazrat Data Ganj Bakhsh's, family lived in the locality of Hujwer. In his book Kashful Mahjub he categorically prayed for Ghazni "becoming the abode of Saints and venerable men." Many books mention 400 A.H. or 1000 AD as date of birth but some writers by analysing the contemporary historical events argue it to be 1002 AD. Hazrat Data Ganj Bakhsh was a Hasani Syed i.e. a descendent of Hazrat Ali. Generally recorded is Ali

Mausoleum of Hazarat Data Ganj Bakhsh &
Old Mosque 1920 Painting by Ustad Miran Bakhsh

Hujweri s/o Muhammad Usman s/o Abul Hasan Ali, who was son of Abdur Rehman s/o Shah Shuja s/o Abul Hassan Ali s/o Asghar s/o Daud s/o Imam Hasan who was son of Hazrat Ali. Those of 'Alids' who survived at Karbala sought refuge in distant lands. (There is a narration that some survivors of the tragedy came to Lahore and among them Bibi Rukayya, the chaste lady, whose tomb is revered as Bibi Pak Daman) Some question this, but dispersal after tragedy of Karbala is confirmed. Among them were the forefathers of Hazrat Data Ganj Bakhsh, apparently an affluent family, with a religious devotion, piety and learning. Being in Iran, the family of Data Ganj Bakhsh was largely Iranised. They had married Iranian Women. In the deviation of writing the book Kashful Mahjub in Persian, instead of Arabic, is evidence that the spoken language of the family was Persian. May be his mother was also an Iranian.

The original name of Hazrat Data Ganj Bakhsh was Abul Hasan Ali when he came to be known as Saint, he was surnamed 'Data Ganj Bakhsh' because of his generosity. In Kashful Mahjub, Hazrat Data Ganj Bakhsh has referred to himself as Ali Bin Usman-bin-Ali-al-Jallaby-al-Ghazanvi-al-Hujweri. He was named after his grandfather.

Hazrat Khawaja Gharib Nawaz, Muinudin Chishti, the celebrated Saint of Ajmer, meditated at the tomb of Hazrat Data Ganj Bakhsh. After a period of forty days, he was, it is said, greatly affected by the graces showered upon him at this holy place and it was here that he got the spiritual illumination. At that moment standing at the foot of the tomb, out of respect for the great saint said:
"Ganj Bakhsh-e-faiz-e-alam mazhar-e-noor-e-Khuda Naqisan ra pir-e- kamil, kamilan ra rahnuma"

It is generally thought that from that date the Saint came to be called Ganj Bakhsh. The couplet is inscribed over the marble arch on the entry gate of the tomb. Some, however, feel that the Saint was so known even during his lifetime. Hazrat Data Ganj Bakhsh had great and brilliant knowledge of Quran, tradition, history, jurisprudence and logic etc. that is testified by the treasure trove in the classic 'Kashful Mahjub'.

The supreme mission of the Saint was to make the people understand true Islam. He had great skill in discourses, debates and profoundness of thought. Hazrat Data Ganj Bakhsh, as referred to in Kashful Mahjub has written seven other books. These are

    i)   Minhajuddin containing account of various Sufis
    ii)   Asrarul Khiraj Wal-maurat means of livelihood
    iii)   Kitabi Fana-o-Baqa
    iv)   Al-Hallaj
    v)   Kitab-al-byan li-ahl-al-Iman

vi)   Al-Riayat li Haquq Allah

vii)   A book on the subject of Faith

Hazrat Data Ganj Bakhsh was himself a poet. He has quoted numerous verses in Kashful Mahjub and this shows his developed taste for poetry. The Saint, it appears from his writings, travelled extensively. The places visited include Amul in Tabaristan, Farghana, Azarbayjan, Tabrez, Baghdad, Balkh, Merv, Baward in Turkman, Damascus, Samarkand, Egypt, Herat, Nishapur, Hijaz, Isphahan, Khurasan and Kirman etc., etc.

Hazrat Data Ganj Bakhsh was a scholar Saint. His classic work Kashful Mahjub is scholarly exposition of various subjects. A deep and thorough study leads one to discover the genius of spiritualism in the form of sayings of Hazrat Data Ganj Bakhsh. Prof. Masud in his book on Data Ganj Bakhsh has copied and calculated 536 such 'Aqwaal', to quote one:

"You must know enough to know that you do not know"

According to 'Fuwaid-ul-Fuwad' by Hazrat Nizamuddin Aulia of Delhi when Hazrat Al-Khattali asked Hazrat Data Ganj Bakhsh to proceed to Lahore, he expressed surprise at the order, for, Shaikh Zanjani was already there. But he was asked to follow the orders without questioning. When Hazrat Data Ganj Bakhsh reached Lahore, the first thing he noticed was that funeral of Hazrat Shaikh Zanjani was being taken out and Hazrat Data led the funeral prayer. It thus dawned on him why his Shaikh had asked him to proceed to Lahore.

Shaikh Al-Khattali who was the Qutab of the age was a man of great spiritual vision. He must have visualised that the Seljuks were likely to rise. Islam had recently entered Punjab and there was great scope of work. There is controversy among the writers about the date of arrival but it is around 1034 or 1035 AD. Two Sufi Scholars preceded Data Sahib in case of Lahore. These are Shah Hussain Zanjani and Shah Ismail. Shah Hussain Zanjani died in 1034 and his tomb is in Chah Miran. Shah Ismail died around 1048 and his tomb is on the Hall Road.

According to Sayed Muhammad Latif and Tahqiqat-e-Chishti one of the first persons to become Muslim at the hands of Hazrat Data Ganj Bakhsh was Rai Raju, who was the Naib Hakim of Lahore. On conversion to Islam, he was named Shaikh Hindi by Hazrat Data Ganj Bakhsh. There is likelihood that under the influence of Rai Raju many others converted to Islam.

There were large conversions in the area of Bhati Gate which had been named as Hujweri Gate. On complaint, the ruler, Sultan Masud referred the leader Jai Singh and other Hindus to Data Sahib where they all embraced Islam on forceful eloquent and convincing arguments of Data Sahib. Data Sahib also

Mausoleum of Hazarat Data Ganj Bakhsh & new Mosque, 1998

decided that the name of the Gate might neither be Hujweri Gate nor Jai Singh and instead be called Bhati Gate as before.

Hazrat Data Ganj Bakhsh acquired great fame and came to be recognised as the Qutab-ul-Aqtab. He had during this period many disciples who came to him for religious instructions. He had 'Khanqah' and a Mosque in his lifetime. This Mosque was re-built in 1279. It was damaged later, around late 1960s during an earthquake. It is said that when originally being built some of the locals pointed out that the 'Qibla' of the Mosque was not exactly in the western direction and appeared towards north. On learning the objection the Holy Saint himself one day led the prayers and after that asked the people who had objected to see if the '"Qibla"' was wrongly placed. When they saw they found it directly in line with the Holy Kaaba. It was the Ist 'karamat" of the saint.

As already mentioned the most important book of Hazrat Data Ganj Bakhsh was Kashful Mahjub. The book took quite sometime to finish and he summed up his spiritual experiences in the same. This was also the first work on Sufism written in Persian. Hazrat Data Ganj Bakhsh was also a scholar of Arabic but to communicate easily with his readers, he wrote it in Persian. This book was translated into English by Prof. R. A. Nicholson. He was Professor of Arabic and sometimes lecturer in Persian at the University of Cambridge. The Ist English edition appeared in 1911, second in the year 1936 and yet another in 1959. In the introduction Hazrat Data Ganj Bakhsh noted that the book was written in answer to some issues raised by Hazrat Abu Saeed Hujweri in regard to Sufism. The book seeks to explain divine mysteries, way of truth and stages of Sufism which one covers in his communication and effort to reach the Creator.

THE KHANQAH/SHRINE OF HAZRAT DATA GANJ BAKHSH

The Khanqah came into existence, when infact Hazrat Data Sahib came to stay in Lahore. It was on a mound west of Bhati Gate. A mosque had also been raised by the Saint alongwith Khanqah known as "Khishti Masjid". The Mausoleum of the Holy Saint, according to Tehqiqat-e-Chishti was constructed by Sultan Ibrahim a successor of Masud Ghazanvi, the son of Mahmood Ghazanvi, in whose time the Holy Saint came to Lahore. According to Syed Muhammad Latif's History of Lahore "Having lived for thirty four years in Lahore, during which time he conferred great benefits on the people by his learning and piety, he died in 465 A.H. (1072 AD) and was buried close to a mosque which he had himself built. The Mausoleum was constructed by Sultan Ibrahim. Maulana Jami, in his book 'Nafaht-ul-Ans' and Dara Shikoh his 'Safina-tul-Aulia', speak in high terms of accomplishments of Data Ganj Bakhsh as a religious preceptor and from the times of Ghazanvids being upto the present day his memory has been held in the greatest veneration by all classes of people. He was a great author of his time. A fair is held at the tomb each Friday, which is largely attended by Muslims and Hindus.

These days while generally there is always an atmosphere of fair on all the week days, on Thursday there is much more number of the faithfuls. This scribe saw people from all communities at the tomb including Sikhs, Christians and Parsis. While the donations and nazranas normally come to lacs even in the surrounding bazars there is always a hawker like loud invitation "Is there anyone in need of food"? One of the Mausoleum arches contains the word 465 A.H.

The mausoleum of the saint is in a square shape encircled by seven arches on each side with an outer Verandah and an inner circle of same number of arches i.e. 28 x 7 on each side. The grave in the tomb itself is on a raised platform. One has to climb 3 steps to enter. The tomb has a gate and three openable windows. All the arches, pillars, window frames are in carved marble. The entire floor is also in marble. The entrances on the eastern side were re-built by Auqaf Department with two big entrance doors, one for ladies and the other for gents.

On the south there are again two main doors where people leave the footwear. The Shah of Iran donated one of these doors which has Iranian "gold in-lay". The original mosque which was built by Hazrat Data Sahib was re-built by Sultan Ibrahim, repaired and was finally demolished in nineteen hundred sixties.

According to Syed Latif, the floor of the entrance to the Mausoleum and the door frames as well as platforms on the right and left was built by the Mughal Emperors. Ranjit Singh himself later came to hold the shrine in great reverence and made many offerings. He contributed Rs.1000 on the occasion of each Urs of the Holy Saint. Maharani Chand Kaur wife of Maharaja Kharak Singh built a Vaulted chamber in the Mausoleum where Holy Quran is recited day and night. Other constructions on the perphery of the shrine appear to have been raised by devotees of the Saint. There other royal gifts given to the Shrine from time to time were wells and villages in the vicinity of the Khanqah which were made. It also appears from Tahqiqat-e-Chishtai that a well called Muhammad Khan Tangsalwala, which was then near the Medical College was given as Nazr to the Khanqah by Ranjit Singh, who had also given as 'Nazr' two or four other wells. These were, during the construction of the cantonment of Anarkali taken over by the British, but in lieu thereof the British gave five times the area of land taken over on the other side of the River Ravi. Originally this land was also Muafi but later on the British withdrew the exemption due to the non-cooperation of the Zamindars.

The proper mausoleum is a fine specimen of marble workmanship. As already mentioned, the 'Khishti' Mosque or the Mosque in brick came down during late sixties due to an earthquake. The Mosque has now been shifted from its original place towards further west. A magnificent arched, concrete structure in

Moti Masjid – Lahore Fort

Turkish architectural style has been raised in blue tiles with two high cone style minarets which are gold plated. The mosque has a vast area underground where "Langar cooking" goes on. The offices of the management of the Auqaf and some parking areas are also there.

A couple of years back under directions of the Government to extend the premises and provide more space to the faithfuls and visitors, the Government has acquired the entire area east of Darbar. Which included private quarters and the area under occupation of Islamia High School, Bhati Gate. Now the main entrances to the Darbar will infact start from the Circular Road. A vast underground area has been provided. The construction work remained suspended till recently and under directions of the Prime Minister Nawaz Sharif now the work has again been resumed. All the arches on the Ist floor in the eastern block with under ground construction complete, which extends over a vast area, are exactly of the same style as those of marble on the mausoleum. With the accomplishment of this project a lot of space would become available for visitors. The mosque also having taken a bit of the shrine sufficient space for prayers and those in waiting has become available. The earlier construction of boundary, big gates of Langar Khana, and ablution place have been demolished.

The Saint is highly popular with people and whenever one visits, one finds a large number of people praying, reciting Quran and invoking blessings of the great Saint. According to Syed Latif, Dara Shikoh has written in his book that any person who visits the Mausoleum every Thursday, for forty days consecutively, his wishes are fulfilled. The death anniversary of Hazrat Data Ganj Bakhsh is celebrated on 18th of Safar each year. On Muharram the Mausoleum is given "ghusal". The Mausoleum, to conclude is the spiritual centre of Lahore and it is difficult to visualise Lahore without Data Sahib. So Lahore is also called 'Data Ki Nagri'.

In the absence of much material on biography of Hazrat Data Ganj Bakhsh, his classic Kashful Mahjub projects a living message of the Saint as a man of highly eminent stature in the domain of spiritualism. He was a Sufi, a Saint, a Scholar, a Poet, a Philosopher, a Teacher, a Muslim Missionary and an embodiment of the best in Islam.

According to a narration he had a luminous personality, tall in stature, neither thin nor fat, with white and ruddy complexion. He had dense beard, penetrating eyes a harmonious and magnetic personality, verily a prince among men.

Hazrat Data Ganj Bakhsh held that culture really meant the collection of virtuous qualities. He defined culture as "Dwelling with praiseworthy qualities".

A man was cultured if he acted with propriety towards God in public and private. Hazrat Data Ganj Bakhsh held that culture was not the prerogative of any particular race, and if a person acted with propriety he was cultured even though a non-Arab, and conversely an Arab if he acted improperly was uncultured. In the matter of culture, mere intelligence did not go very far, it had to be backed up with knowledge. He held that those who have knowledge are in every case more honoured than those who have intelligence. For him piety in word and deed was the Sine-qua, non-of culture.

The expansion of Data Darbar Complex undertaken by the Nawaz Sharif Government, on completion the project would have a three storey complex consisting of a basement for parking vehicles, a sama hall, Musafir Khana toilets and ablution site, a roof garden fountain water ripples and fibre glass domes surrounded by arcade approaching the mausoleum. In addition to the Administrative Block, Langar Khana, Quran Mahal and stores have been rebuilt adjacent to the complex.

The Complex will povide entry and exit facilities to thousands of devotees from the four gates approaching from Darbar Road, and Zaildar Road in addition to the golden gate and ladies gate in the proximity of the shrine. Devotees and Philanthrophists plan to erect a golden gate at the main entrance of the complex facing Circular Road which has opened up to the East. Thousands of devotees attend the Qawwali during the Urs and for the last many years it was held at the nearby ground of the school.

The addition at the Data Darbar Complex was planned and executed in 1992 at a cost of Rs. Six crores on the directives of Prime Minister Nawaz Sharif. After excavation of grounds and construction of parts of basement, unfortunately the scheme was abandoned by the Peoples Party Government in 1994. The Peoples Party authorities wanted to include a shopping plaza in the complex in place of a Sama Hall. The idea was, however, resisted by the Data Darbar Committee. After a period of two years, the work was resumed to the original design in 1997 under orders of Prime Minister Nawaz Shrif who gave the target period of one year. The total cost, however, will come to Rs.25 crores since the preliminary construction in 1992. The project is being executed by Lahore Development Authority. Mr. Ishaq Dar, a Federal Minister has been appointed Chairman of Darbar Committee, and is looking after the construction work under strict orders of the Prime Minister. The Prime Minister is being kept informed about the progress. During the last 50 years, this expansion will be the major addition which will cater to the requirements of devotees for another 50 years or so.

HAZRAT MIAN MIR

According to Dara Shikoh the name of the Saint was Mir Muhammad alias Mian Mir and he was addressed as 'Mian Jio' out of reverence and respect. He was born in Sistan in 938 A.H. a city lying between Bhakkar and Thatta (Sindh). The language of this area was Sindhi. His father's name was Qazi Sain Ditta bin Qazi Qalander Farooqi, who descended from Hazrat Umar Farooq. Hazrat Mian Mir, first went to Shaikh Khizar for spiritual guidance in the mountains of Sistan. At 25, with the permission of Shaikh Khizar, Hazrat Mian Mir left for Lahore, for worldly education and knowledge. Here, during the reign of Akbar, the Madrasah of Maulana Saadullah was the most established seat of learning with great men of letters to teach and guide. For some time he received instructions from Akhund Nimat Ullah, who was a disciple of Maulana Saadullah. Hazrat Mian Mir used to visit the Mausoleums and gardens during daytime or sit at isolated places under trees, in jungles or sometimes around the river. The saint avoided meeting people and did not sleep for many years.

Prince Dara Shikoh was the disciple of Shah Muhammad alias Mullah Shah, from Badakshan; in turn a disciple of Mian Mir. Mullah Shah was a man of much piety and was a great orator of his time, and a poet. Both Mian Mir and Mullah Shah pre-deceased Dara Shikoh who constructed a spacious mausoleum of Mullah Shah and had also commenced building a more superb shrine over the remains of Mian Mir, when he was murdered at Delhi by his brother Aurangzeb. The costly stones on the tomb of Mullah Shah were removed later by Ranjit Singh for their temple at Amritsar.

Hazrat Mian Mir was a born Saint and in the realm of spiritualism happened to be "Avaisi" and was from the direct 'Taabeen' of the Holy Prophet. According to Dara Shikoh, Mullah Niamat Ullah narrated that Mian Mir learnt everything but never revealed anything about himself. Mian Murad Naqi tells that Hazrat Mian Mir used to suspend his breath and spend the whole night meditating and praying. For some time Mian Jio went to Sirhand where he developed pain in his ankle, and during this period Haji Niamat Ullah looked after him.

Hazrat Mian Mir did not like to have many disciples and would only accept who appeared generally in search of spiritual light. He had no known source of food and for days he would remain without food. One day his brother came to see him but as he had no food for him he got worried. He asked his brother to stay and himself went out into the garden and started praying until his brother came to call him that a young man had brought the food and was waiting for him. On reaching home, and on inquiring, the reply of young man was that God had sent him food. The young man, however, did not join as he was fasting.

Dara Shikoh in his work has dealt with at length the accomplishments of Hazrat Mian Mir. Dara Shikoh writes that "although my grandfather had little faith in Fakirs, he, however, entertained the greatest esteem for Mian Mir (Bala Pir)". He once invited the Shaikh. He accepted the invitation and went to King's palace. The Emperor received him with great respect. There was a lengthy discussion. The Shaikh chiefly concentrated on the instability of the world. The oration of the saint had such an effect on the Emperor's mind that he expressed a desire to become Shaikh's disciple and abandon the world. The Shaikh, however, admonished him to continue in his worldly pursuits observing that kings had been made for the protection of God's people and that in attending to this he too was discharging an important duty, entrusted to him by the Creator and he may continue to perform that duty. The Emperor was much pleased to hear this from the Shaikh and said to him 'Tell me, Oh' Shaikh, if you want anything " Will you promise to give it to me," said the Bala Pir. "Most certainly, I will grant it, "rejoined the Emperor. On this the Holy Shaikh said my only want is that your Majesty would not give me the trouble of "coming to you again". With this assurance from the Emperor, that he would not be troubled to visit him again, the Shaikh withdrew. Since the Emperor benefitted from the company of the Faqir, inspite of his promise, wrote two letters to Hazrat Mian Mir asking for prayers and spiritual favours especially in connection with attack on Kandhar by the Iranian Ruler.

After the death of Emperor Jahangir, Shah Jahan visited Hazrat Mian Mir twice. On both the occasions Dara Shikoh was there. He writes in his book that there were light and lengthy discussions and the King was so impressed that he always used to say he has not seen any pious 'Darvesh' like Hazrat Bala Pir. The first time, the Emperor entered the closet of Pir Bala; he was accompanied by four persons. The first thing the Shaikh remarked was that the King should be just and caring for his "ra'ayyat" and should divert all his energies for the betterment of the empire. For, if the public at large is well off, the Government will be rich and thus a strong and stable Kingdom. Dara Shikoh was suffering from disease which had been declared incurable by 'Hakims' and a period of over four months had elapsed. At that time Dara Shikoh did not know Hazrat Bala Pir. The Emperor took him to the Bala Pir and with reverence and respect requested that all the Hakims have shown their helplessness and only his kind prayers could help. The Shaikh picked up the bowl he used to take water, filled with water, read something and gave Dara Shikoh to drink. After drinking that water, the disease disappeared within a week. During the week Dara Shikoh again sent someone for prayer and Hazrat Mian Mir said that in four days, at such and such time, you will be fully fit and exactly at that time and day "I was all O.K.," writes Dara Shikoh.

The second time Shah Jahan visited the Shaikh he was accompanied by the same people. He had fine and detailed talk and requested for blessings on which Hazrat Mian Mir advised him that whenever he did some act of benevolence and a Mussalman was happy, at that moment pray for himself and not ask anything except for 'Rehm' of the Almighty.

The Emperor remained with the Shaikh for some three hours and then left. According to Sh. Muhammad Lahori after departure of the King, someone asked Hazrat Mian Mir about the meeting. The Faqir observed kings are perfect and embodiment of widsom and his arrival, sitting and discourse had little to do with him. The Emperor had brought a 'Shawl' (as turban) for the Faqir and a rosary chaplet (string of beads) of dates. The rosary or 'Tasbih' was retained but the shawl returned.

Dara Shikoh in his work writes that once Hazrat Akhund Mirak Shah went to see Hazrat Mian Mir and I (Dara Shikoh) sent a letter for the Bala Pir. The Akhund was received with great kindness. The letter had been tied by the Akhund in his turban end but he forgot to deliver. In his heart the Akhund started thinking that he had not seen any 'karamat' of Hazrat Mian Mir. Hazrat Bala Pir took out the letter from his 'Dastar' with his own hand and read out in detail.

Hazrat Mian Mir used to say that after his death he may be buried in saline land so that the bones also dissolve after sometime. He also addressed his friends and asked them that his shrine should not be made a commercial point.

Shaikh Abdul Wahid Banbani, who served Hazrat Mian Mir for two years, narrated that once Hazrat Bala Pir was lying in the garden of Mirza Kamran Baradari and he was massaging his aching foot and "I suddenly noticed, a python coming towards them. When it reached nearer, I told the Shaikh a python was coming. He said let him. When it reached near, the Pir got up but kept sitting. The python also sat just in front of Hazrat Mian Mir. The python spoke something. The Shaikh replied 'all right it will be like that'. The python got up, took three rounds of the Pir and went away. When the python disappeared, Abdul Wahid asked about the exchanges, the Shaikh replied that the snake conveyed that he had decided that when he will see him (The Pir) he will take rounds around him and would only then leave. Hazrat Bala Pir agreed and he went away after taking rounds.

Mullah Muhammad Sialkoti, who had been in attendance of Bala Pir for twenty years narrated (according to Dara Shikoh) that one day the Shaikh was sitting outside his 'Hujra' with some disciples. Suddenly a windstorm developed and it started raining. Hazrat Mian Mir said that now was the time to move in. On this, Mian Natha, a very dear disciple and close friend said, if permitted he could see that the clouds disappear and they would keep sitting. Hazrat Mian Mir was seriously annoyed and snubbed him that you want to show your own super-natural powers and miracles. Beware not to repeat such words interfering in nature's system. It was not desirable. Instead one should go by the things as ordained by the Almighty.

Hazrat Mian Mir died in Lahore in 1045 A.H. (1635 AD) at the advanced age of 88 years, having lived in Lahore for a period of about sixty years. He breathed his last in the room in which he resided in Mohallah Khafipura.

His longevity is said to have been due to his practice of suspending the breath to which he was accustomed to, and it is said he used to respire only once or twice in the course of a night. When he began to feel the weight of years, he breathed four times in the night. In piety, virtue, beneficence and learning he had no equal in the country in the age in which he lived. He had great respect for the saint of Gilan, the Pir Dastgir, and never mentioned his name without ablution.

The dome over the tomb of Hazrat Mian Mir is supported by a quadrangular tower rising from a large platform of marble, reached by a flight of steps of the same material. The courtyard is spacious and paved with red sand-stone. To the west of the dome, in the same courtyard, is a beautiful mosque, and to the south and east are chambers for the accommodation of the Darveshes and travellers.

The lower portion of the tomb of Mian Mir and of the mosque attached to it, covered with marble, is the work of Dara Shikoh. The upper portion, built of masonry, is the work of Aurangzeb, who, with the materials collected by Dara for the tomb of Mian Mir and the construction of a road from Chowk Dara to Mian Mir, built the Badshahi mosque at Lahore, bearing his name. According to Dara Shikoh, the saint was buried in the suburbs of 'Alam Ganj and Darapur, described as half a kos distant from the town, but no vestige of this has been left by the urban habitation now. Mullah Abdul Hamid Lahori writes in his Badshahnama: -

"His reverend tomb is in the village Ghiaspur in the vicinity of 'Alam Ganj' in the capital of Lahore". Besides the fair on the anniversary, other fairs are held at this mausoleum during the two months of the rainy season, on each Wednesday. They are called the Budh fairs". The author of the Badshahnama says: "His Majesty (Shah Jahan) used to say that, in his whole life, he had come across two fakirs having the knowledge of God; one Mian Mir and the other Shaikh Muhammad Fazlulla of Burhanpur. His Majesty felt the greatest reverence for both these saints." We have stated in the historical chapter of this work that Shah Jahan, while Emperor of Hindustan, twice paid a visit to Mian Mir, on his march to Kashmir and back.

Presently the shrine of Hazrat Mian Mir, has its original boundary on one side intact. On western and southeastern sides the "Qabza" Groups and land grabbers have totally occupied, the area. There a mushroom growth gives the look of a third rate locality on the northern side. A small piece of land, about 20 kanals, is lying vacant but the gradual process of occupation through, 'Katcha' houses, is in progress. The Baradari on the eastern side, which was built by Dara Shikoh, is in a very bad shape and badly in need of repairs. The courtyard of the shrine has now lengthy patches of cement & mosaic looking as walk ways, with old red stone patches. The raised plinth around the Mausoleum was most probably damaged and had been removed and now repairs are under way. On the eastern side of shrine practically a small graveyard has developed over a period of time where the "Sajjada Nashins" and local influentials had their graves. A mosque on the western side of mausoleum, recently painted and renovated, exists. There is no indication of grave of Mian Natha, which according to Dara Shikoh was near the place of Mausoleum of Hazrat Mian Mir. There does exist a grave in the Baradari, with a sarcophagus (one-piece marble) on which it is written in Persian "Nadira Begum wife of Dara Shikoh". She died somewhere in the North, but her body was brought and buried in the graveyard of Hazrat Mian Mir as wished by her.

Maharaja Ranjit Singh removed most of the marble on monuments in and around Lahore. He used to see monuments himself and then order removal of marble & other precious stones, for the Sikh temple at Amirtsar. He ordered the same in case of Hazrat Mian Mir mausoleum, and while on his horse the labour and masons were ordered to remove the stone suddenly his horse became frightened and he fell down. Ranjit Singh got up, stopped the masons from demolition of work and committed an amount of Rs.6000 for the annual "Urs" of saint which continued until the British period. Now the shrine is under control and management of Auqaf Department of Punjab Government. The encroachments on the vacant land around the "Mazar" and onslaught of land grabbers who are raising construction in the name of offices of Political parties is going on – which is unfortunate.

HAZRAT MADHO LAL HUSSAIN

Hazrat Madho Lal Hussain was born in A.H. 945 (A.D. 1539) in Lahore. His ancestors, says the author of Tazkira, were originally Kayashtha Hindus who embraced Islam in the time of Feroz Shah. But Baba Buddh Singh is of the opinion that his great-grandfather or grandfather, who became a Mussalman, belonged to the dhata clan of the Rajputs. At the birth of Hussain, the family was sunk deep in poverty. His father, who was called nau Shaikh " Usman" was a weaver. Hussain never learned this trade.

Shah Hussain was put under the charge of Abu-Bakr at a very tender age and became a "Hafiz" when he was ten-year-old. Then Shaikh Bahlol of Chiniot (Chiniot, Jhang district), who learnt the doctrine of "fana" from a Sufi of Koh-panj-shir came to Lahore and made Hussain his own disciple. After a few years Shaikh

Bahlol returned from Lahore and left Hussain to continue his study of the Sufi Practices at the shrine of Data Ganj Bakhsh in Lahore. For twelve years he served the ashes of the Pir and followed the strict Quranic discipline. He is said to have spent many a night in a standing posture in the River Ravi, repeating the Quran. At twenty-six he left that Pir and became a student of Maulana Sa'dullah, with whom he read many a book on Sufism. Some time after this, as he was coming out of the house of his teacher with the fellow students, he thought he had found the secret of God. Happy at his success he threw in the well the Quran, which he had in his hand, but his companions were enraged at this act. He thereupon asked the book to come out. It came, and to the surprise of his companions it was dry as before. Hereafter Shah Hussain discarding all rules and regulations began to dance, sing, and drink. He became mystic. The excesses of Shah Hussain became scandalous and reached the ears of Shaikh Bahlol at Chiniot. The Shaikh was so much upset that he journeyed to Lahore to see things for himself. His talks with his disciple convinced him of his saintliness and he went back satisfied to his native town. Shah Hussain wore a red dress and came to be known as Lal Hussain or Hussain the Red. Shah Hussain was very fond of dancing and singing and mixed freely in the company of dancers and musicians. The Qadris, to whose sect Shah Hussain belonged, generally loved music and dancing which, they thought helped them in their divine contemplations, but they never went to the extreme which Hussain reached. Hussain clean shaved his moustaches and beard and refused, according to the author of Hasnat-ul-afifin, to accept those persons as disciples who were unwilling to shave their faces. This idea of Shah Hussain and his neglect of the religious duties of a Mussalman aroused suspicion, and some officials thought of punishing him; but by pointing out to them their own neglect of religious duties, Shah Hussain escaped punishment. He is essentially taken by the writers as a sufi saint with typical traits. Shah Hussain's sufism was of a peculiar type and presented a curious medley of Persian and Indian characteristics. In his mystic ideas and beliefs he was more Indian than anything else but in his daily life he followed the style of the Persian sufis. Lal Hussain was fortunate to have been born, to live, and to die during the reign of Emperor Akbar whose fondness for religious men and especially the Sufis was proverbial. Akbar, it appears from the writings of Dara Shikoh, knew Shah Hussain. Prince Dara Shikoh writes: "Prince Salim and the ladies of Emperor Akbar's harem believed in his supernatural powers and entertained respect for him". The Tahqiqat-i-Chishti states that Prince (late Emperor) Salim was greatly attached to the saint and appointed Bahar Khan, an officer, to record his daily doings. These records, which were regularly submitted for the perusal of the Prince, were later on compiled together with the sayings of the saint and were named "Baharia". The Baharia is said to be replete with incidents

Mausoleum of Hazarat Madho Lal Hussain

relating to the supernatural power of the saint. Having become a Sufi, Shah Hussain began preaching in public. A Brahman boy of Shahdara frequented these religious scenes and showed keen interest in his teaching. This attracted the attention of the saint, who soon became attached to the handsome youth. This attachment developed so much and so rapidly that if on any day Madho failed to come, Shah Hussain would walk down to his house. This sort of friendship was not liked by the parents, who tried to dissuade their son from meeting Hussain, but to no effect. Desirous of separating their child from the Sufi, they proposed to take him to the Ganges on a certain festival day. When Madho informed the saint of his impending departure, he was much distressed and begged the boy not to go with his parents. However, he promised Madho a bath in the company of his parents on the appointed day. Madho thereupon refused to accompany his parents, who proceeded alone to Hardvar. After a few days the saint asked the boy to close his eyes, and when he did so, Madho found himself on the banks of the Ganges along with his parents who had reached there by that time. After the bath he discovered that he was back in his house at Shahdara. On their return the parents confirmed their son's statement that he bathed with them on the appointed day. This miracle, says tradition, so much impressed Madho that he confessed the Muslim faith and became a Mussalman. Another story about Madho's conversion is that the attachment of Shah Hussain for Madho was disagreeable to the parents and created suspicion in the people's mind. But Shah Hussain unmindful of all would go to the boy's house when he was prevented from visiting him. Very often the parents would tell him that Madho was absent and Hussain would return disappointed. One day when he had been refused permission to see the boy, he walked down to his house for the second time. On reaching the place he saw people weeping and wailing. On inquiry, he was told that Madho was dead. The Faqir laughed aloud and walking to the dead body exclaimed: "Get up, Madho, why do you sleep at this hour? Get up and see I am waiting for you.' Upon this, continues the story, Madho jumped on his feet and followed Hussain out of his parental house, never to return there again, and became a Mussalman.

The love of Shah Hussain for Madho was unique, and he did Madho Lal's on was known all that lay in his power to please the boy. Once, seeing his co-religionists celebrating "Holi" and being desirous of doing the same, he bought some gulal (pinkish-red powder) and threw it on Hussain. Shah Hussain at once joined him in the fun. Basant or the spring festival, like Holi, was also celebrated each year by Lal Hussain to please Madho.

Madho Lal Hussain was held in great respect by the people, and the Hindus, though they seem to have turned Madho out of their fold, could not master their credulous beliefs in the supernatural miracle-performing power of the saint and esteemed him just as much as their Muslim brethren. Madho Lal Hussain died at the age of 53, a comparatively early age for a saint. His death occurred in A.H. 1008 (AD 1593) at Shahdara, where he was duly buried. A few years later as predicted by the saint, the grave was swept away by an overflow of the Ravi. Thereupon Madho exhumed the corpse and carried it to Baghbanpura, where it was buried with pompous formalities. After his death Madho was buried by his side. Latif describes the tomb as follows: -

"The tomb is situated north of the village of Baghbanpura. There are signs of two tombs on a high platform, one of Madho and the other of Shah Hussain, the actual tombs being in an underground chamber. A wall surrounds the platform with a gateway to the south. Between the platform and the surrounding wall is a space left for the devotees to go round, - the platform being lined on all sides with lattice-work of red stone. North of the enclosure is a tower in which is reverentially kept the impression of the Prophet's feet (Qadam-i-Rasul) and to the west is a mosque. This mosque was constructed by Moran, a wife of Ranjit Singh. Lal Hussain appears to have had friendship among the holy men of his time. He was an intimate friend of Chajju Bhagat who, the tradition says, called him Shah Hussain for the first time. He used to meet Guru Arjun whenever he came to Lahore.

Hazrat Lal Hussain's Sufism was of a peculiar type and presented a curious medely of Persian and Indian Sufism. In his mystic ideas and beliefs he was more Indian but in his daily life he followed the style of the Persian Sufis.

Shah Hussain has left no poetic works. His only work is a number of Kafis of a highly mystic type. His verse is written in simple Punjabi, slightly overlaid with Persian and Arabic words. It excels in expression of thought and has a clear flow. In its simplicity and effectiveness it is superior to Ibrahim Farid's Punjabi. It lacks the brilliance of Urdu poetry but is remarkable for its just proportion of words and powerful sense of rhyme. His versification is smoother, his similes more relevant, and his words simpler but more effective than those of Ibrahim. His poetry is of a less orthodox type but is not as saturated with Indian thought as would be the poetry of Bullhe Shah. Like his character, his poetry is a curious mixture of Sufi, Indian, and foreign thought. The essential feature of his poetry, which strikes the reader is that it is highly pathetic and, piercing the heart, creates a mystic feeling.

SHAH ABU ISHAQ QADRI (MEHZANG)

Another disciple of Shaikh Daud Kirmani and dear friend of Abul Maali, was a scholar saint, Abu Ishaq Mehzang who came from Bukhara and on the order of his preceptor, after successfully completing his tenure of spiritual training, settled in Lahore in the locality now known after his name as Mozang, where he established a 'Khanqah' and a religious seminary. Shah Balawal, a contemporary of Mian Mir and a disciple of Shaikh Shams ud Din Qadri who was himself the disciple of Abu Ishaq, passed several months of his spiritual training in his 'khanqah' and recited the Quran daily for several years. Abu Ishaq was a scholar of great standing and his 'madrassah' was a centre of great learning where hundreds of people came from far and near to get education in 'Fiqah', 'Tafseer' and Tradition. His tomb is situated in Mozang. He died in A. D. 1577 (985 A.H.)

There is a story about the tomb of the saint. It is said that a trader namely Abdullah bin Abdul Qadir used to go to Arabia. Once his ship was trapped by a whirlpool in the gulf and when he lost all hopes, he remembered the saint and prayed for help. He suddenly saw that Hazrat Abu Ishaq came, lifted the ship on his shoulders took it out and left it in the calm waters. When the trader returned home (Lucknow) with lot of profit, he wanted to see the saint but was informed that he had expired. The businessman built the tomb of Hazrat Ishaq in Mozang. The shrine is near Mozang Dispensary, opposite Abu Ishaq Street.

MIAN WADDA
(SHAIKH MUHAMMAD ISMAIL LAHORI)

Another personage of very high calibre Shaikh Muhammad Ismail is commonly known as 'Mian Wadda'. His involvement with matters of spiritualism did not lead him to adopt a negative attitude towards matter mundane.He was a great scholar of Quran and Tradition and belonged to the Suharwardy order. He devoted his life to teaching the Quran and Traditions. His seminary had been the centre of religious learning, serving the people of the city for centuries. He was Hafiz-e-Quran and belonged to village Tarkranm in Potohar. His father's name was Fateh Ullah whose ancestors were agriculturists but he was a man of piety and spiritual and worldly knowledge. He lies buried in village "Jabba" on the river Chenab.

Mian Wadda's parents shifted to "Lange" where he became a student of Makhdum Abdul Karim, who was a saint and great scholar. Mian Wadda acquired worldly knowledge and served the teacher with great zeal and devotion. The teacher entrusted him the assignment of grinding flour manually. One day the flour did not reach in time and when a student was sent to find out the reason of delay, the student found that Sh. Ismail was reciting Holy Quran and the grinding wheels were moving automatically. The student reported back the position to the teacher who saw this himself and decided that he (Mian Wadda) will not do this duty and instead he was deputed to carry milk from the cattle farm. But one day the teacher found, while sitting on a rooftop, that the 'milk cans' were lifted above the head of Mian Wadda who was carrying the same to house. It was at this time that

Makhdum Abdul Karim, informed him that he had attained the objective of spiritualism and that he should leave. Thereafter the Shaikh left the place and started Quranic education first at a place called "Langay". Later on he shifted to Lahore. Here in Lahore he came to the locality called "Tailpura" in a mosque comparatively less attended but remained restless. On a pious person's, advice, he spent 40 days 'Chilla' on the mausoleum of Hazrat Data Ganj Bakhsh. Thereafter the mosque he settled in was full of students and due to problems of space shifted to another mosque (now towards the west of the "Daras"). By chance there was a Hindu "Jogi" living there, who did not want to leave the mosque. Mian Wadda told him that he had to go. When he heard this, he said, the mosque will also go with him. Mian Wadda remarked, Well if it wants to go –let it. The "Jogi" took his bag and baggage and asked the mosque to accompany him. The mosque started moving. Hazrat Wadda got annoyed and hit the mosque with his stick and said " Oh Mosque don't move, people will pray here till the last day." The mosque stopped moving. During Emperor Alamgir's period, the Khanqah was given a grant. There is a story that an illiterate person came to Mian Wadda and stated that his wife was 'Hafiz-i-Quran' and did not allow him the fulfilment of conjugal rights until he learnt the Quran. He therefore requested the Mian that he may be taught Quran in a day. Mian Sahib replied it was not possible but the person was greatly dejected and appealed for help and reconsideration of his request. Mian Sahib asked him to stay for the night and offer the prayer with him standing on his right next day. When next day 'Namaz' was over and Mian Wadda said 'salam' and looked right side all those in that row became Huffaz 'Hafiz-e-Quran' and those on the left could read i.e. 'Nazira' Quran. Lot of people became his followers and it is said that he had remarked that his blessings would continue from his shrine. People say that whosoever is dull minded, eats grass from the shrine even now learns the Quran quickly. His mausoleum is located on Shalamar Link Road. He died in 1085.

SAIYID MUHAMMAD SHAH MAUJ DARYA

Hazrat Muhammad Shah bin Syed Safiuddin Kalan commonly called Mauj Darya Bokhari was descendent of Mir Syed Jalal ud Din, usually called "Mir Surkh" of Uch Sharif. He was known for his piety and was 'Sajjada Nashin' at the shrine of Uch in Bahawalpur region. How he came to Lahore has a story behind. Emperor Akbar was facing great difficulty in conquering the fort of Chittor inspite of his having mobilised all resources. At last the king himself reached but nothing appeared hopeful. He consulted the astrologers who advised him to implore the spiritual help of Mian Muhammad Shah Mauj Darya.

The Emperor went barefooted to the 'Fakir', whose prayers in behalf of his Majesty were believed to have had an effect of reducing the hitherto impregnable fortress. The 'Fakir', at the King's earnest solicitations, made Lahore his residence and Akbar himself made it his headquarters. Akbar granted him a jagir of one lakh rupees in Batala, and also houses, on a large scale. The Saiyid died in 1013 A.H. (1604 AD) and was buried in the present mausoleum. His shrine is held in great reverence. His descendants too hold this day in much respect. Maharaja Ranjit Singh entertained a great respect for this shrine and paid an allowance of forty rupees a month for its maintenance besides making other presents. The tomb was built in 1000 A. H. (1591 AD) by Emperor Akbar, during the lifetime of the saint.

4

ARCHITECTURE

S ince it is just a narration of the cultural aspects of Lahore, it is necessary to
introduce the reader to architectural heritage of the place. How contributions
were made towards these landmarks by various dynasties and rulers during
different periods and how the architectural features of this historical city have been
defaced and disfigured is a monumental account. And we can only describe a few
glimpses and no more.

Architecture generally speaking is a practice of building, design and its
resulting products. Its customary usage refers only to those designs and structures
that are culturally significant. In terms of importance, the architecture is to building
as literature is to the printed word. There are three conditions of a good building of
construction. Number one is 'Commodity'. Number two is 'Firmness' and
Number three 'Delight'. But to put it more plainly one can say that the architecture
must satisfy its intended uses. It must be technically sound and must convey the
aesthetic meanings. Generally the best buildings are often so well constructed that
they out-last their original uses. These, thereafter survive only as beautiful objects
and can become documents of cultural history. Such achievements and architecture
that testify to the nature of society become the landmark in history. In all
probability these achievements are never wholly the work of individuals.
Architecture is a social Art. Architecture is inevitably influenced by technologies
applied but building technology is conservative and knowledge about it is
accumulative. This can be explained, for example, by stating that pre-cast concrete,
for instance, has not rendered the bricks obsolete. Whatever the latest
developments or post-industrial traditions, the technical demands on the building
remain the same i.e. to exclude the enemies, to circumvent gravity, to avoid
discomfort caused by heat or cold, rain, wind or vermin. These cannot be ignored
even with the use of best modern technology. The availability of alternate
suitable material fostered the crafts to exploit them and influence the shape of
buildings has not reduced in any way the importance of timber as a building
although relatively becoming scarce. Similarly the stone and marble are chosen as
important material because these are incombustible and can be expected to

endeavour. It is sculptural material. However, its use is because of other declined substitutes. Building with stones and bricks is called masonry. These elements cohere by use of mortar, lime and sand etc. In the 19th century the steel appeared on the scene which was certainly stronger than wooden frames and then in the 20th century the steel with new forms facilitated the inforced concrete construction and the present era has found profusion of aluminum with anodized coatings provided cladding which is light weight and maintenance free, glass and important inputs, Infact the processing of glass in various forms has revolutionised the exploitation of natural light and transparency.

The above main characteristics of architecture have to be seen as to how they appeared in the city of Lahore during Hindu period, the Mughal period, the British occupation and Post-independence period. For this purpose historical survey of Lahore is pre-requisite in retrospect to give a clear idea of the heritage of the city.

Lahore is a metropolis, which may claim the attention not only of the historians but also of the general readers. It is situated in a classical ground and has been a centre of earliest struggles between Hinduism and Islam. It served sometimes as seat of Government and some times H.Q.s of northern Province of Indian empire but whatever its capacity it was a place of importance. Abul Fazal describes it as a grand resort of people of all nations. By Hindu historians its origin is traced to 'Rama' whose sons Loh and Kash founded the twin cities of Lahore and Kasur respectively. The Muslims claim that the present city and Fort were founded by Malik Ayyaz the Governor of Lahore on behalf of Mahmood Ghazanvi. His tomb is inside the city and is greatly revered by the Muslims. There are also traditions of its Rajput origin and it was one of the earliest Rajput State in West India. To some extent this version is also supported as Lahore was a Hindu principality at the time of the Muslim invasion. The name 'Lahore' is not peculiar to the capital of Punjab. There is a Lahore in Afghanistan. Another as a seat of old Rajput State; one in the Peshawar area, another in India and a Lahore in Mewat State in Rajputana. The exact date of foundation of Lahore is apparently impossible to discover but can be approximately guessed from the fact that the city existed and the place was important in the 7th century. However, its recorded history starts from the period of its occupation by the Muslims. At the time of arrival of the Muslims first, a Chohan Prince of the family of Ajmer was ruling the city. There are reasons to believe that due to its exposed position of a grand road from north to India, Lahore was a deserted place before its occupation by Mahmood Ghazanvi. According to reliable references the seat of Government had been transferred from Lahore to Sialkot. It is also mentioned that Lahore was generally asserted as a region rather than a city. It is also stated that Mahmood Ghazanvi and his General Malik Ayyaz, on occupation of the city established a garrison in a fort (a sort of "Purana Qillah") on the ruins of old Rajput strong-hold. The Lahore (modern) falls far short of glowing description given by earlier historians, in size and population which is one of the biggest cities of Pakistan. But the circuit of its wall originally did not exceed 3 to 4 miles and its population at the close of the 19th century was not more than 97,000. The streets of the walled city were/are narrow, worm-like and general aspect of the city with the exception of northern side is neither imposing nor picturesque. However, a closer survey of the city and its environment will considerably modify the first impression that Lahore formally covered a larger area than it had in the 19th century (the walled city and fort) and again at present its extent can be gauged from the ruins which covered the surrounding country. However, more specifically speaking, from Shahdara to Shalamar and Ravi to Raiwind with a radius of 15 to 30 miles the area has a bursting population and haphazard grown localities, which have multiplied civic problems in the absence of proper planning. Infact there are no dimensions to measure the expansion/extension speed. No yardstick and laws are followed with respect to building and architectural features, which have just defused the monuments of the Muslim period. The domes are cramming, the monuments withering and gardens disappearing without any let or hindrance or control by the State. Few cities of the world have suffered more from invading forces and from anarchy than Lahore during the last over 200 years. The Afghans, the Marhattas, the Sikhs had their work of destruction in addition to the British who also added some frigid colonial buildings to the city as a requirement of their administration. As far as true architectural contribution was concerned it ended with Mughal rule. But it is certain from the recorded history that until Mughal rule the city had architectural pretensions worth the name. On the other hand in the number and importance of monuments the profuse use of glazed tiles and enamelled frescoes as an architectural decoration, the domes and semi-domes gateway we have all the characteristics of the Mughals or what may be termed the style of Indo-Muslim architecture. The Muslim period monuments of Lahore are a complete history as far as the subject of architecture is concerned. A special mention may be made of Kamran's Baradari, Lahore Fort, Shalamar Gardens, Wazir Khan Mosque, Jahangir's Tomb, Badshahi Masjid and countless number of tombs in the city which continue to suffer fate of decay. A brief description of each monument would be necessary to highlight the architectural features of these monuments but before that one may explain the main characteristics of the Mughal architecture.

The Islamic concept of Mosque as a place of prayer differs from the Christian church. The desert climate in which Islam became established required protection from heat, wind and sand storms. The initial proto type was a simple wall in rectangle containing an ablution place with portico a "Qibla" wall towards Makkah, had in its centre a Mehrab with a nearby pulpit or 'Mimber'. The structural elements were the arch and the dome. Roofs were flat unless forced upward by vaults with no windows. The mosque had at least one dome or minaret from which call to prayer was issued five times daily. This basic plan is followed to this day and has been source of main architectural development throughout. There have been contributions by the structural forms as Islam expanded in Iraq. Islam architecturally borrowed extensively from the Turks from constantniple. Iran is renowned for brick masonry vaulting and for glazed ceramic veneers. The finest examples of Islamic Architecture in Iran are found in Isphahan.

As far as Indo-Pak sub-continent is concerned the Mughal architecture was essentially based on Persian traditions and developed further in North-Western India in ways peculiar to that region. It is impossible to separate the Mughal religious architecture that erected to glorify the Mughal Empire. The great three emperors of the 16th and 17th centuries. Their most impressive monuments are imperial tombs, palaces, superb gardens and mosques in the city of Lahore. With this background one can visualize the thematic approach of the builders and architects in raising monuments. Just in passing, a reference before describing the Mughal monuments may be made to exceptions which are tombs of Shah Musa around Railway Station which is from the Pathan period and mosque of Maryam Zamani near eastern gateway of fort. Three localities at Lahore are traditionally connected with Ghazanvi period and cared as places of great sanctity. These are the tombs of Malik Ayyaz in Taxali Gate who built the walls and fortress of Lahore. The tomb of Syed Ishaq in quadrangle of Masjid Wazir Khan and tomb of Data Ganj Bakhsh who entered Lahore around the period of Mahmood Ghazanvi.

To the Mughals we owe introduction of what now forms three striking characteristics of the old city of Lahore. In the first place there grew up new style of architecture that was very splendid and elaborate. The next was their love for picturesque nature, a pleasing feature in their character, which is seen in the planned gardens with walls and fountains. There is appreciation of natural scenery combined with solitude for the preservation of the dead which leads to the erection of numerous enclosed tombs. Lahore with its gardens, tombs and ornamental gateways must have been in the days of its splendour a fine specimen of an Indo-Mughal City. Its splendour did not escape devastation at the hands of time on the disintegration of the Muslim rule. Infact little is left from the architectural heritage of the city and one has to assess their significance which survived the ruthless Afghans and violent/wild Sikhs who laboured diligently to deprive the city of its architectural embellishment. Many monuments were destroyed and many deprived of their ornamental details and only skeletons left. Despite all this some have survived which can be genuinely termed as specimens of architecture, and pride of the city. As already mentioned the first Muslim who contributed to the city of Lahore was Malik Ayyaz a General of Mahmood Ghazanvi who built the city wall, the mint and monument in the fort (non-existent now).

The other important monuments which might be termed as the earliest from Mughal period is Kamran's Baradari. One time on the right bank of River Ravi, this magnificent and very substantial old edifice, standing now in the middle of the River Ravi. For centuries Ravi has struggled to annihilate its walls and was partly successful, and in the late 1950 the garden was washed to a great extent and the monument damaged but the main edifice stood unaffected. It was built by Mirza Kamran s/o the Emperor Babar and brother of Humayun. The garden around Baradari was beautifully laid with walkways and fountains. The massive arches of the monuments are painted in diversified colours. The water tank with fountain and a few old trees standing, the monument reminds one of the glorious past of the Mughals. During the British period it was used as Telegraph post and later on as a Rest House. This imposing structure is made of solid masonry in brick with stairs and a dome in the centre. The Chief Minister, Punjab, Mian Muhammad Nawaz Sharif took special interest in the restoration of this monument and managed raising a protective "bund" of stones around the monument. A portion of garden was also restored. The Tourism Department has set up a motor boat point for picnic by the people of the city who cross over to Baradari for an outing or picnic. Till the close of the 19th century when the river had changed its course, this building was also used as a Toll House on the boat bridge on the river, during the British period.

At Shahdara, on the opposite bank of Ravi, the Hydraotes of the Greeks, three miles Northwest of the town, on the grand imperial road to Peshawar, is the mausoleum of Jahangir, the son and the successor of Emperor Akbar. A monument of surpassing beauty, the finest ornament of Lahore, and the most magnificent edifice in India after the Taj. The entrance to this superb building is through two massive gateways of stone and masonry opposite each other to the North and South. These lead to a square enclosure, or caravan 'serae', five hundred paces in length with an interior court of four hundred paces, lined with cells, which were intended for the accommodation of travellers and mendicants who resorted to the monument. From this enclosure is reached another, on a larger scale, giving a full view of the garden in front, about six hundred yards square, which is traversed by four-bricked canals proceeding from the centre, and in which innumerable fountains were introduced, but these are now in ruins. By a straight and broad path through the garden, we come to a square platform of a reddish free stone. The entrance to this spacious quadrangle is gained by a handsome gateway of marble and enamel, the whole structure being surrounded with a piazza, or corridor, with

Jahangir Tomb

cells for the accommodation of the visitors. The corridor is adorned with a profusion of marble ornaments, arranged in a most elegant mosaic, representing flowers and texts from the Quran. The resettes and arabesques over the arches, which are executed with extraordinary skill and taste, and are in a perfect state of preservation, are particularly striking. The walls are decorated with paintings and inscriptions in mosaic of most chaste workmanship. A covered staircase of twenty-five steps on each side of the quadrangle leads to an imposing and splendid platform of tessellated pavement, at each corner of which is a minaret four storeys high, inlaid with zigzag band of variegated marbles and magnificent blocks of yellow stone, and capped with a cupola of white marble rising to the height of ninety-five feet, and a winding staircase with sixty steps. From the summit of these beautiful towers, the most prominent feature of the structure, a full view of the surrounding country is obtained. The parapets of marble round the roof, and the elegant marble fret-work surrounding the galleries of the minarets, which imparted a lightness to the structure, were removed by Ranjit Singh, who replaced them with masonry work. The marble fretwork of the uppermost storey had been restored by the British Government.

In the interior of the mausoleum is an elevated sarcophagus of white marble, enshrining the remains of the Emperor, the sides of which are wrought with flowers of mosaic in the same style of elegance as the tombs in the Taj at Agra. On two sides are most beautifully carved the ninety-nine attributes of God, on the top is an extract from the Holy Quran.

In the sides of the body of the structure are four large arches, three of them closed in with perforated marble screens, the fourth being kept open for ingress. The pedestal on which the tomb stone stands, is covered with beautiful stones let into the sides. Even the shading of some of the roses and other flowers is preserved by the different colours of the stone. The floor and walls of the chamber are of the purest marble.

Jahangir, on his death at Rajaouri, in Kahmir, in 1627, A.D., expressed a wish to be buried in the garden of his lovely and accomplished wife, Nur Jahan, at Lahore, called Dil-kusha, thus paying her the last tribute of affection. He was accordingly buried here, and this superb edifice was raised to his memory by his son and successor, Shah Jahan.

Muhammad Saleh, in his Shah Jahan Nama, furnishes the following particulars relating to the construction of the mausoleum of Jahangir:-

"His Majesty was, at his own desire, buried in one of the gardens across the Ravi. Following the tenets of the Sunni faith, and the example laid down by his illustrious ancestor Babar, His Majesty further willed that his tomb should be erected in the open air, so that the rain and dew of heaven might fall on it. In pursuance of this will, the Emperor Shah Jahan, his son and successor, built a lofty mausoleum of red sand-stone, measuring one hundred yards in length, round the tomb of his father, the tomb itself having been built on a raised and open platform of white marble inlaid with precious stones and wrought with works of peculiar beauty. Notwithstanding the nature of the edifice, the mausoleum took ten years to build, and cost ten lakhs of rupees."

A portion of the garden wall that surrounds the structure has been washed away by the Ravi. The building suffered much at the cruel hands of Lahna Singh, one of the three Sardars who governed Lahore before the establishment of the Sikh monarchy, and by the ruthless vandalism of Maharaja Ranjit Singh, who stripped off most of its choicest ornaments to decorate the Sikh temple at Amritsar. The Maharaja gave it as a residence to a French Officer M. Amise, who caused it to be cleared out and put in order, but this officer died soon afterwards. The apartments were subsequently given to Sultan Muhammad Khan, brother of Dost Muhammad Khan, whose barbarous Afghan host did much to injure the monument by kindling fire in the halls, and stealing its valuable stones. The edifice had however been kept in proper repair by the British authorities.

THE SERAE OF JAHANGIR

The spacious serae of Jahangir is to the west of the mausoleum of that Emperor. It has two stately gateways, one to the north and the other to the south, both richly decorated with marble and red sandstone. To the west of the serae is a large mosque, with three splendid domes, supported by arches, the middle arch being lofty and decorated with flowers of marble stone beautifully set in red sand-stone. The gate to the east leads to the mausoleum of Jahangir.

The serae was used as the manufacturing depot of the NorthWestern Railway. It is unquestionably a beautiful and spacious building, but badly neglected and misused by the local visitors.

Opposite the tomb of Jahangir, to the west, on a detached piece of ground, enclosed by high walls of solid masonry, is the tomb of Mirza Abul Hasan Asif Jah, the brother of Nur Jahan, and 'Wazir' of the Emperor. It is built in brick, in the form of an octagon, and supports a built dome of the same material. Asif Jah died on the 17th Shaban, 1051 A. H. (1634 A.D.), or four years before his sister. According to Mulla Abdul Hamid, Lahori, author of the Badshah Nama, who saw the commencement and the completion of his edifice, it was built by Shah Jahan in four years, at a cost of three lakhs of rupees. It was well-known for the beautiful glazed tiles which decorated its arched entrances; but of these decorations little is now left. The whole of the interior, with the floor, was covered with white marble, inlaid with costly stones, and the walls outside were embellished with a variety of stones, which were all removed by Ranjit Singh to decorate the temple at Amritsar, and used partly in building the marble summer-house in the Hazoori Bagh of Lahore. The edifice stands on a platform, the side walls of which were covered with the red limestone. At each of the four corners of this square was a reservoir of water, now, however, in ruins. The whole of this beautiful structure was in the midst of a spacious garden with fountains of water and beautiful walks, traces of which are still to be seen. Like the serae of Jahangir's mausoleum, the high and majestic gate of the tomb is towards the south. The mosque attached to it had been converted into a European residence by the British.

The sarcophagus of the tomb is of pure marble, and the Arabic inscriptions on it are in the same style as those on the tomb of the Emperor. Near the mausoleum of Jahangir is the tomb of Nur Jahan (i.e. light of the world), the consort of Jahangir, whose life is equally romantic and eventful. She died on the 29th Shawal. 1055 A. H. (1638 A.D.), at the age of seventy-two, and was buried in the structure which she had herself caused to be erected. The marble sarcophagus was of most chaste workmanship, being of the same size and quality as those of Jahangir and Asif Jah at the same locality, with the names of God in their various significations engraved on it. It has, however, been removed. The vaulted rooms were all covered with marble and wrought with flowers of mosaic, but these were removed by Ranjit Singh. It is now a plain building of one storey, with four main arches, and eight oblong openings in the centre, with three rows of arches beyond, the whole diameter being 135 feet.A recent visit to the tomb revealed that the land grabbers were just in the vicinity of the place and likely to spoil the surroundings which needs to be checked with an iron hand. Yet another horrific news was in the press about a road being planned through the premises which will be really a matter of shame if allowed to materialise.

WAZIR KHAN MOSQUE

The Mosque of Wazir Khan was built on the site of the tomb of an old Ghaznivid saint in A.D. 1634 by Hakim llm ud Din, a Pathan of Chiniot, who rose to the position of 'Wazir' in the reign of Shah Jahan. It is remarkable for the profusion and excellence of the inlaid pottery decorations in the panelling of the walls. Local legend say that artists were sent for expressly from China to execute the work; but there is no authority for this association, nor is there any trace of Chinese style in either the design or the execution. Its origin is manifestly Persian, and the descendants of the craftsmen employed to this day pride themselves in their Persian origin. It will be observed that in these arabesques each leaf and each detached portion of the white ground is a separate piece of pot or tile, and that the work is strictly inlay and not painted decoration, although it appears so. The panels of pottery are set in hard mortar.

In the mosque itself are some very good specimens of Perso-Indian arabesque painting on the smooth chunam walls. This work, which is very freely painted and good in style, is true fresco painting, the buono fresco of the Italians, and, like the inlaid ceramic work, is no longer practised, modern native decoration being usually fresco or mere distemper painting. The reason of this is that there has been no demand for this kind of work for many years. Though the builder was a native of the Punjab, the style is more Perso-Mughal and less Indian than that of any other building in the city. Two chronograms inscribed on the walls gives the date of the foundation of the mosque. One Sijda-gah-i-Ahl-Fazl. "The Worshipping Place of the sons of Grace". Another "Bani" Masjid Wazir Khan. "The founder of the mosque is Wazir Khan." From the minars of this mosque the best view of the proper city is obtained.

Proceeding to the left of the building along a street which is remarkable from the overhanging balconies,(mostly pulled down,except one which is likely to disappear any moment) carved with a profusion of geometrical tracery and ornament, the visitor will observe the gilt melon-like domes of the Sunehri Mosque, or Golden Mosque, which was built in A.D. 1753 by Bikhari Khan, a favourite in the court of the widow of Mir Mannu, a lady who governed Lahore for some time after the death of her husband, the gallant opponent of Ahmad Shah. It is said that having incurred the displeasure of his mistress, he was beaten to death with shoes by her women. The domes are pretty, and the situation, at the junction of two roads, is picturesque; but there is nothing of architectural interest in the mosque itself.

Since Masjid Wazir Khan is the master piece of Architecture in the city of Lahore it is necessary that its plan, the interior and general features are discussed slightly in detail.

The plan of the mosque is a perfect rectangle with its sides 280 by 160 feet. The Qibla wall contains a niche in its centre which is projected outside the back wall.

The façade of the main entrance on the eastern side of the mosque, is covered with multi-coloured glazed tiles (Kashi Kari) and inscriptions headed by "Kalima" on its lintel alongwith the date (1045/1635) of its final completion. There are other inscription on its right and left wings. The main entrances's interior is beautifully arranged on the right and left, with turrets and balconies which have made this whole construction imposing indeed.

Through the entrance within the centre of the corridor's western side, we enter the courtyard of the mosque itself which is a huge rectangle and consists of an

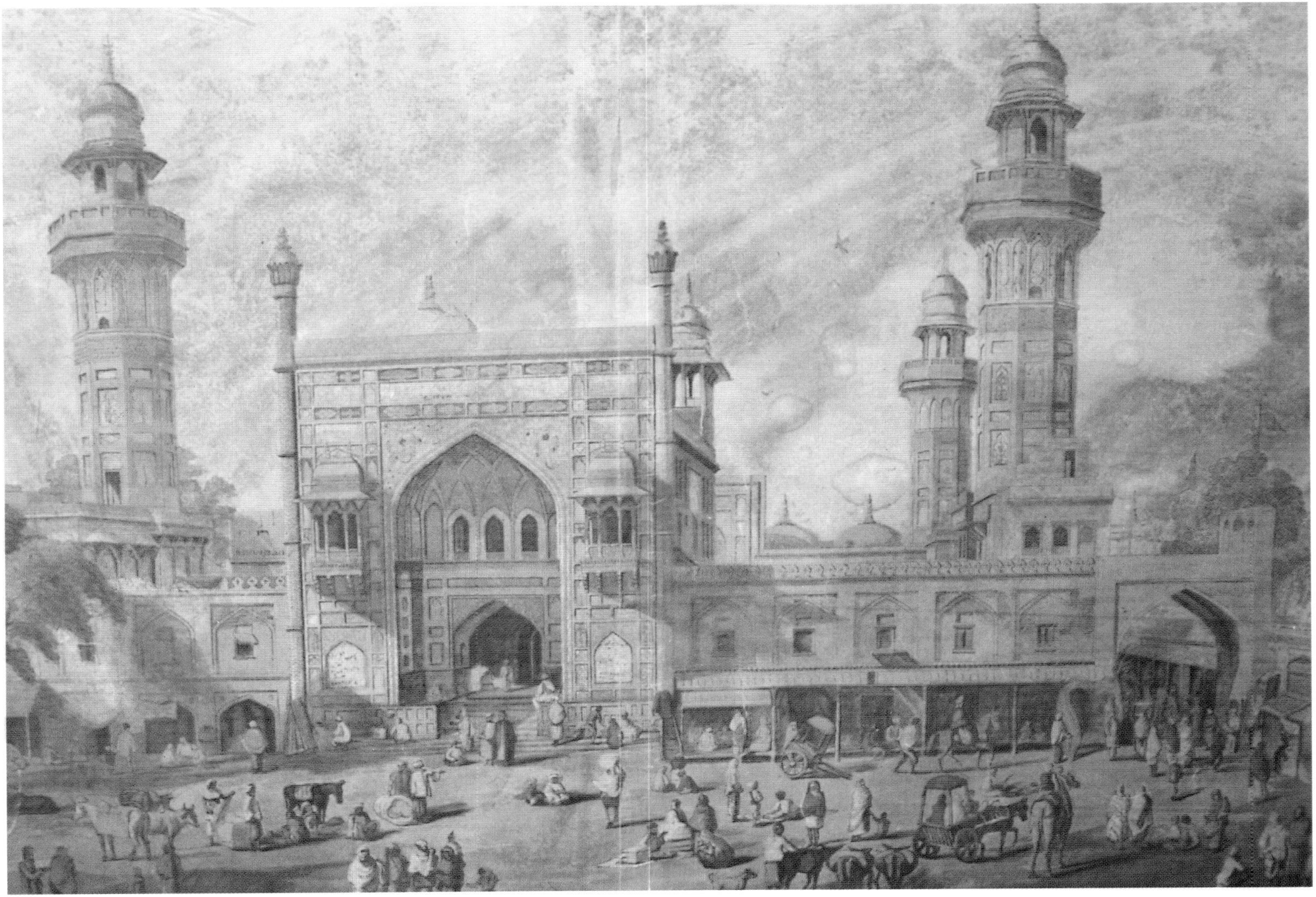

Wazir Khan Mosque Courtesy Punjab Archives

upper and a lower part which is almost square in shape, contains a water basin for ablution, as well as the tomb of Shaikh Ishaq Gazruni towards the south-west. But the visitor immediately looks at the façade of the prayer chamber of the mosque towards the west which may be called the main part of the mosque.

It consists of five porticoes, the central one of which is larger and higher than the others on its right and left and is architecturally called the fronton of the mosque.

The prayer chamber consists of five porticoes on its façade and each portico carries a dome over it, which is cusped in shape and double in construction. The half-domed front of the central portico and the Mehrab in the centre of the back wall are connected with the central dome. The central-niche of the mosque is also projected outside the back wall, which is quite evident in the plan of the mosque. Particularly the prayer chamber of the mosque's plan will show that on its northern and southern ends separate apartments have been made which are quite independent so that the prayers within the mosque may not be disturbed by street noise.

A prominent feature of the mosque is its four minarets which stand on the four corners of the court-yard. The stair-cases built within them carry one to their tops. They are erected on square bases and about the middle of their height they assume in octagonal shape which continues up to the canopies resting on projecting balconies and having domes over them. They are also artistically decorated with "Kashi Kari" harmonising with the embellishment of the rest of mosque.

The floor of this mosque from its entrance to its back wall is very artistically paved throughout, the bricks being set in very beautiful geometrical patterns, with their thin edges being visible. The design which is a geometrical layout harmonises with the entire decorative scheme of the mosque. These geometrical patterns require a careful study which will also manifest other points of the mosque's set-up. In short, the floor gives an additional charm and beauty to the entire building of the mosque.

The architect of the mosque must have been an extremely competent person who has very carefully designed the whole structure. He has protected the court-yard and the central part of the prayer chamber from any sort of outside noise or disturbance by erecting rooms around the court-yard and sitting apartment on its north and south sides. But at the same time to create architectural beauty, he has also added pavilions in the middle of the northern and southern wings.

The material used in the construction of the Mosque is a small tile-like brick universally used by the Mughals when stone was, not obtainable or, too costly. The only stone in the building is used for brackets and some of the fretwork "pinjra". The walls were coated with plaster 'chunam' and faced with a finely-sifted quality of the same material tooled to a marble-like surface and coloured. All the external plaster work was coloured, a rich Indian red, in true fresco, and the surface afterwards picked out with white lines in the similitude of the small bricks beneath. The extreme severity of the lines of the building is relieved by the division of the surfaces into slightly sunk rectangular panels, alternately vertical and horizontal, the vertical panels having usually an inner panel with arched head, or the more florid cusped 'mehrab'. These panels, where they are exposed to the weather, are generally inlaid with 'Kashi', the effect of which must have been very fine when the setting of deep red plaster of the walls was intact. The origin of this variety of 'kashi' in the Punjab seems obscure and the method of manufacture uncertain.

The façade of the sanctuary is practically covered with 'Kashi' and is divided into the usual oblong panels. A beautiful border is carried rectangularity round the centre archway, and inscriptions in Persian characters occur in an outer border, in a long panel over the archway, and in horizontal panels along the upper portions of the lower walls to right and left. The spandrels are filled in with extremely fine designs. A 'mudakhal' pattern runs along the parapet of this façade, up the sides of the heightened central portion and round the lower gallery of the 'Minars'. The two panels on right and left of the central archway bear inscriptions, as do also the two panels on each side between the smaller arches.

The decorative work covering the western elevation of the vestibule building is a beautiful treatment of the small domes over the kiosks.

"The design of the 'minars' is particularly good. The division of the height into its several parts is most admirable. From above the parapet of the square, strong base rises on the octagonal shaft-the change from square to octagon giving a degree of lightness, while the division of the surface into rectangular panels suggest rigidity. Again the shaft rises from above a dividing band to geometrical pattern and, still preserving its octagonal section, is cleverly divided into sixteen narrow pointed panels, from the heads of which spring a most graceful tracery of ''alub kari''or pendentive work drooping gently outwards to carry the gallery with richly coloured borders and pinjra parapet. From the gallery rises an elegant kiosk with sloping caves supporting first an octagonal drum, and above this a circular one which curves slightly outwards to support the pointed and ribbed dome with its lotus final.

The internal decoration is extremely rich and elaborate and is executed in fresco on an exquisitely fine 'chunam' surface. The painting demanding first attention is the covering of the internal walls and cupolas of the sanctuary. Round the lower part of all these walls runs a dado four feet in height, of arabesque design, usually surrounded at each change of surface-level by a gracefully flowing floral border and narrow bands of plain colour. Monotony is avoided by frequent variation in the arabesque patterns, and while all are characterised by grace and admirable discretion, one pattern is particularly fine. The field is deep ochre ("old gold') with a bold strapping superposed in rich red, relieved at each edge by a white line, which is again divided from the field by a fine black line. At certain points where the strapping interlaces, it passes through cartouches of pale natural blue relieved by white and black lines in the same manner as is the strapping. Simple leaves and flowers trail graceful along the straps; and garlands on the blue cartouches encircle the intersections, passing over the under. The deep yellow field, appearing as beautifully shaped panels beneath the plane of the strap work, bears pink naturalistic iris plants, and conventional rose-like flowers with leaves. The floral border is in naturalistic colours on a deep purple-brown ground, and is divided from the filling by narrow bands of pink and green, with white lines between. Many of the white lines in borders and strapping are drawn in agraffito, and so are saved from any possibility of crudeness.

Above the dado, the walls are divided into rectangular panels, alternately horizontal and vertical, the vertical ones having the cusped Persian mehrab shape painted within them, and those which are horizontal having both ends similarly shaped. The spandrils so formed are usually in deep colouring dark red or blue or other rich ground, with conventional flowing patterns of flowers and leaves in naturalistic tints. The field of the upright panels usually bears a finely drawn, gracefully growing flower, or group of flowers, issuing from conventionally indicated grassy ground or from a very chinese 'martoban' or vase. Wherever the 'martoban' is used, it is used, and treated as though copied from blue and white pottery, and is generally standing in a kind of 'chilamchi' or bowl, with a thin stem. The leaves and flowers are tinted in quasi-natural colours, with a certain amount of shading and variety of tone, and are always freely outlined and "fibred" with black. On the background frequently float Persian clouds.

The variety of flowers introduced to these designs, and the appreciation and 'verve' with which they are drawn is remarkable, and shows what lovers of flowers the Mughals were. One sees this, too, constantly expressed in their illuminated books, in their landscape and garden subjects occurring in domestic mural paintings, and more particularly in the elaborately constructed flower-beds in their 'baghs' and around their tombs.

The cupolas are divided into gracefully designed panels, in which the balance of rich and delicate colouring is most admirably preserved, and the applicability or fitness of the enrichment never ignored. The beauty of the panelling is well shown in the right half of panels and the balance of colour, approximately, in the opposite half. The effect of the decoration of these cupolas and walls in the soft warm glow of the light reflected from the sun-lit pavement without is very beautiful, strongly suggesting tapestry. The pavement within the sanctuary was probably covered with an extremely hard, deep, maroon-coloured cement, and in the early part of the day, when the sun strikes under the arches, this would have lent an added richness to the colour within; but, as the heat of the day increases, the reflection draws gradually away, permitting cooler tones to sooth the heated bodies of those who seek shade and peace within the sacred precincts. To an artistic temperament there is a wonderful fascination in watching the great shadows, towards evening, quenching the glowing sunlight as they glide over the quadrangle. The cool band projected by the tall south-east minar, stretches out over the pavement and meeting the circumscribing wall, bends up and presently over it, to be broken into fantastic shapes as it makes its way across the endless expanse of terraced house-tops of the city. When the broad shadow of the sanctuary facade steadily pursuing but ever losing ground, steeps the base of the opposite minar in purple grey, the 'kashi' jewels high above glint in the ruddy light of the sinking sun like the scintillations of a glorious opal. Then as the mournful cry to prayers swells out throbbing over the seething bazars, and good Muslims begin to enter barefooted at the low archway, one feels that it is only where the sun is most fearsome that its potency can provide such a background, and that the most picturesque human conceptions can find such fitting concrete expression.

This practice of embellishing mosques with the sacred texts was in practice from the very beginning. However, the display of verses on the walls of the Wazir Khan Mosque stretches from its main entrance to the hindmost wall of the praying chamber. This whole display is a fine specimen of Islamic calligraphy harmonizing with the general scheme of decoration.

The façade of the main eastern gateways; central part's upper lintel over the central arch bears the 'kalima' in 'nasta'liq' style of writing along with the date A.H. 1045/1635 A.D. when the mosque was finally completed. Similarly on its right and left, the rectangular panels bear the name of Emperor Shah Jahan, during whose reign this mosque was built and the year of its foundation is noted in chronological Persian writings.

SHALAMAR GARDENS

This impressive Mughal monument is on the Grand Trunk Road, five kilometers (three miles) towards the east from the centre of Lahore. One should make an effort to be at Shalamar Gardens when the fountains are playing, which is daily at 10-11 a.m. and 4-5 p.m. in summer and 11. a.m 12 noon and 3-4 p.m. in winter. The flowers are at their best in February and March.

Shah Jahan built the Shalamar Gardens in 1642 for the pleasure of the royal household, which often stayed here for days or weeks at a time. In design, it conforms to the classic Mughal conception of the perfect garden and consists of three terraces of straight, shaded walks set around a perfectly symmetrical arrangement of ponds, fountains and marble pavilions, all surrounded by flower beds and fruit trees and enclosed within a wall. Incredibly, the whole garden took less than 18 months to build. Carrying water from the Hassle canal, a canal into raised tanks outside the garden solved the problem of creating sufficient water pressure to feed the hundreds of fountains.

The garden was designed to be entered from the lower terrace, which was opened to distinguished members of the public. Honoured guests then moved against the flow of the cool waters to discover new and greater delights at the middle terrace, which was used for entertaining. Only intimates of the royal family were permitted to experience the supreme serenity of the upper terrace, the royal inner sanctum.

These days, visitors troop straight on to the upper terrace from the Grand Trunk Road. The terrace is divided into quarters by ponds splashed with fountains and has nine buildings, including the octagonal towers at each corner of the building's three rooms, the walls and ceilings of which were once covered with frescos, opening on to a wide verandah overlooking the garden through five gracefully cusped arches.

The emperor's sleeping quarters are in the centre of the eastern wall, across from the Hall of Public Audience, which gets through the wall and out of the garden. The emperor walked through this hall daily to show himself to the public gathered in a separate walled garden outside. The arcaded pavilion on the northern side of the terrace is the Grand Hall, which was once covered with frescos and used for ceremonial functions. The little house in the northeast quarter, built by the Sikhs earlier in the 19th century, was used as a guest house. William Moorcroft, the prodigious English explorer, stayed here in 1820.

The middle terrace is four meters (13 feet) down and reached by two flights of steps on either side of the Grand Hall. Between them, a cascade carries water down from the upper ponds to the great central pond, a broad square of water upon which plays 150 fountains. Between the cascade and the pond, and surrounded by a marble railing, is the emperor's marble throne, where he sat in the moonlight listening to his musicians play and watching the girls dance.

The Turkish bath house is set in the wall in the southeast corner of the terrace. Its changing room and cold and hot baths were once decorated with pietra dura inlay.

Two pavilions on either side of a waterfall guard the steps between the middle and lower terraces. In rows along the marble wall behind the waterfall are hundreds of little cusped niches. Flowers in golden vases occupied them by day, and lamps by night, so that, when viewed from the lower terrace through a double row of five cusped arches, the waterfall was a shimmering sheet of light.

The lower terrace, the least exciting, has two gates decorated with glazed-tile mosaics, two corner towers and a Hall of Private Audience once decorated with white marble and frescoes.

Shalamar a most striking and remarkable feature of Mughal architectural planning is a system for water to flow. Whether it is a sleeping chamber, a hall of private or public audience, a pleasure garden – or even a memorial for a dead monarch, the focal object is almost invariably flowing water. The Mughal's love for flowing water was immense.

Art historians eulogize masonry art of Mughal architecture but have said little about their skill and love for fountains and falls.

Shah Jahan was known for his skill in architecture and horticulture even before he ascended the throne in 1627 A.D. The first masterpiece of the Shalamar series of gardens was laid by him under the command of his father, Jahangir in 1618-19 A.D. at Srinagar, Kashmir. The natural terraced terrain of the place was indeed a boon for a refined aesthete like Shah Jahan. In about 1643 he planned a garden in Lahore. Inspite of difficulties to create a real terraced garden, which became popular by name of Shalamar. He called the upper terrace as "Farah Bakhsh" (delightful) and the middle and lower terraces as "Faiz Bakhsh" (bountiful).

In the absence of any earlier instance, the concept of a terraced garden with enclosure walls, pavilions, and canals running through the centre, is considered an innovation by the Mughals. The fountains running throughout the length of the central and intersecting canals, and symmetrically arranged in the tanks add beauty to the structural patterns of the garden.

The length of the central and the intersecting canals running over the Ist terrace i.e. Farah Bakhsh is 1480 feet and 1500 feet in the third terrace. A large tank measuring 220 x 190 occupies the central place in the second terrace while two others of lesser dimensions have been placed, one each in the Ist and the 3rd terraces. One hundred and five fountains are placed in the first terrace; 153 in the second and 156 in the third terrace thus bringing the total count to four hundred and fourteen. In addition there are three cascades and the famous "Sawan Bhadon" and of course, provision to irrigate the greenery of the Shalamar.

The hydraulic system followed for the Shalamar gardens is complicated as well as very interesting. As the natural physiography of the plains, lacks springs and the natural gredient, did not provide an adequate quantity of water with desired hydraulic pressure the foremost priority was that of devising means to overcome

Main Entrance of Wazir Khan Mosque Courtesy Punjab Archives

this difficulty. First of all a spot with just enough height was selected on the left bank of River Ravi before it reached Lahore.

The first step undertaken was to branch off a canal from the Ravi at Madhopur about a hundred miles upstream where the river emerges from the mountains to the plains. The canal, which came to be known as Shah Nahr or the Royal canal, was designed by Ali Mardan Khan in such a way as to arrange the flow of water upto the southern portion of the Shalamar, considerably higher than the river flowing on its north. Mullah Alaul Mulk Tuni also helped later to achieve the desired results and "Nahr" was flowing full with water from Madhopur to Lahore. The canal later on came to be known as 'Hassle' canal and finally Shalamar distributory till its closure in 1958 as a result of non-availability of water in pursuance of the Indus water Treaty with India.

The water of Shah Nahr was used for two purposes: (i) Irrigation of the complex of gardens including Shalamar, and (ii) filling of the canals of the upper terrace and the main tank in the middle terrace. The same water, now in the upper-terrace canal, was also used to run the 'abshar' – the Central Marble Cascade and separate the fountains of the middle terrace.

The water was also used to irrigate gardens and for filling the first terrace canal to supplement canal water flow. A well, with persian wheel, ensured the constant supply of clear water. An overhead reservoir was constructed which stood at a height of about 25 feet from the bed level of the Ist terrace. The reservoir consisted of two inter-connected tanks. The water lifted from the well was discharged into the main tank meauring 61'-6" x 17' 6". Three holes, each with 4" diameter, transferred the water to the next tank of 17'-6" x 12' 6" dimensions. The latter served as the filtration tank where sand particles with water would settle down. The water then travelled to two chambers, 11'-3" x 7'-2" and 4'-3" x 7'-2" size, through four holes positioned vertically. The depth of all the tanks including the chambers was kept uniform at 4'-6". The reservoirs were built in solid brick masonry and outlets, where provided, have been chiselled out in one-piece of red sand stone Block.

From the western side of the large chamber a 6" dia outlet provided water to the pipe which was downed and kept underground while another such outlet was also placed in the eastern chamber of lesser dimensions."

To feed these fountains two more connections, one on each end of the east west canal, were given. The western connection took its supply, through an aqueduct along the western perimeter wall, from the overhead reservoir situated on west of the uppermost terrace, from where the water supply to the Ist terrace was also augmented as mentioned earlier. A well, located near the north-eastern Burj of the Ist terrace, supplied water to the eastern end via an overhead reservoir and aqueducts running on the perimeter wall.

Coming back to the upper terrace we find that the water supplied from the Shah Nahr multiplied by that discharged into the canal by playing of 105 fountains would not hold itself within desired limits unless channelized properly with precise calculations. The hydraulic engineering achieved another feat by utilizing this surplus water for the running of the main marble cascade and 153 fountains of the middle terrace.

At the end of the Central canal, just near the pavilion, eight feeding points in the form of outlet pipes, four from each side of the channel, were provided for the fountains of the main tank of the middle terrace, "Sawan Bhadon" and eventually for the running of the fountains of the 3rd terrace. The extraordinary thickness of the solid brick masonry has always proved a barrier against ascertaining the exact layout of these pipelines. Their positioning, however, suggests that they pass under or close to the central baradari.

Similar difficulties are faced with the central tank of the middle terrace where 152 fountains are arranged in 4 rectangles in an impressive symmetry. The floor of the tank has been laid in a six foot thick solid brick masonry in lime mortar. It, once again, rendered it impossible to know the exact routes of the pipelines laid under the thick and heavy floor. Faced with this difficulty especially during a leakage, archaeologists and conservationists had to seek the help of nuclear scientists to locate these pipelines. The "sealed radiation source" method cleared the picture to some extent. We now surely know that all the fountains of the central tank were interconnected. It was, indeed, also necessary to produce harmony in their playing.

CASCADES

This tank served as the main reservoir to supply water to "Sawan Bhadon" and to the fountains of the lower most terrace. After filling the tank, the water split into two small cascades, on eastern and western sides, and flowing over the "Sawan Bhadon" discharged into the canals of the lower terrace. A part of the water in the central tank was channeled through pipelines to feed the fountains of the 3rd terrace. Eleven pipes served as feeding points for the purpose. The arrangement of these lines was made on a sophisticated and precise plan to make maximum use of the water in the tank. Three pipelines were used to feed 3 parallel rows of fountains in the central canal of the 3rd terrace: four pipes fed the five fountains located in the inner basin of "Sawan Bhadon" while the remaining four pipelines supplied water to two cascades of the "Chini Khana."

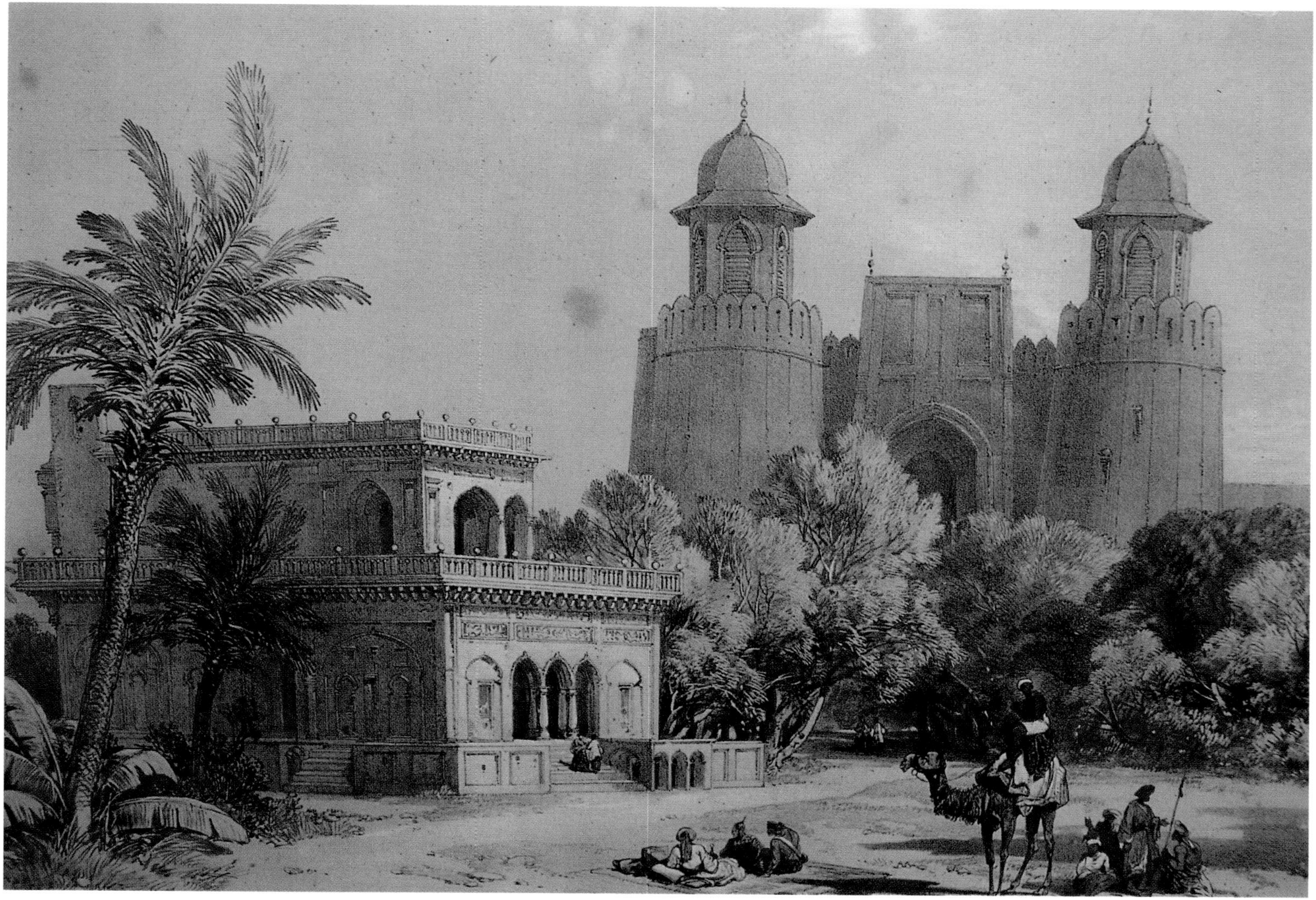

Alamgiri Gate Lahore Fort Courtesy Punjab Archives

The water from the cascades and fountains filled the canals of the 3rd terrace. Its disposal was finally arranged through drains under the Baradari at the northern most end of the central canal. Outside the perimeter wall of the garden, this water was used to irrigate Mahtabi Bagh, a fruit garden, and a large tank situated in it. The surplus water was drained out.

LAHORE FORT

With a galaxy of Muslim monuments Lahore richly deserve to be the custodian of proud Architectural heritage. The main buildings of this period are found within the Fort. The Fort is the only place in Pakistan, which represents the different phases in the development of Mughal architecture. It infact possesses the work of four Mughal Emperors. The place gained prominence during the reign of Emperor Akbar, who demolished the old mud fort and constructed a new one of brick masonry. Later on, his successors Jahangir, Shah Jahan and Aurangzeb made numerous additions in the main building areas. The buildings of the time of Akbar and Jahangir are mainly of red sandstone with a preference given to the use of Hindu beams and brackets and decorative figures of animal like lion, elephant and peacock as well as sculptured gargoyle. The buildings of their successors, Shah Jahan and Aurangzeb – the Moti Masjid, the Naulakha pavilion and the Shah Buri Shish Mahal are in a striking contrast with the former, with the use of white marble in place of sandstone and exuberance of the Persian motifs in the form of pietra dura work and mosaic of coloured stones.

"The only important extinct monument of the time of Akbar is the Masjidi (Masti) Gate. Built in 1566 A.D. as one of the entrances into the fort, its archway opens between two massively projecting bastions. In contrast can be seen a very well-laid area of the residential places, called Jahangir's Quadrangle, which was founded by Jahangir in 1617. The latter's fondness for nature is evident from the provision of a wide-open lawn with water fountains playing in the middle. The living rooms have a pillared frontage, each pillar, being facetted, shows a deeply carved chevron motif and supports a typical bracket of Akbari style – the bracket, which is directly derived from the older Hindu tradition, has a marvellous serpentine design with elephants riding on the top. Here one gets a glimpse of that style of architecture which Akbar followed. But it is in the reign of Shah Jahan that architecture achieved excellence. Shah Jahan's fondness for natives led him to go in for soft construction in white marble and create those architectural forms, which appealed to feminine beauty and grace. His khwabgah (sleeping room), built in 1633, still preserve the marble doorframe and exceptionally beautiful marble screens. The Diwan-i-Khas is an open arcaded pavilion wrought in the choicest marble. Its beauty is further doubled by the nicely cut marble screens on the west,

Diwan-e-Aam

Diwane-e-Khas

the decorated parapet, and the ornamental floor well-laid with geometrical patterns together with a cup-shaped beautiful cistern inlaid with pietra dura work. Of this latter art the most beautiful example is the Naulakha. It was built in 1633 A.D. With its curvilinear roof this dainty little marble summer-house, renowned for its extremely minute and delicate pietra dura work wrought in precious stones, can easily boast of having the finest piece of inlay work in Asia.

Another richly decorated building is the Shah Burj or the Shish Mahal Palace of Mirrors which was constructed in 1631 A. D. It was called Shish Mahal because of the elaborate mosaic of convex mirrors set in stucco tracery and gilt work with which the entire interior of the building was once decorated. This building formed the harem portion of the fort. In front of the Shish Mahal is an open marble court, a fountain playing in the middle. In the centre of the tank of fountain there is a platform made of marble where now a days on State visits instrumental music players sit and perform. A channel to an 'Abshar' (cascade) on the southern side connects this fountain. The cascade shows chevron design wrought in variegated marble of different colours so arranged that illusive ripples are caused when water flows over them.

Quite distinct from these pleasure resorts is the serene beauty of the Pearl Mosque built in 1645 A.D. The effect is produced not only by the use of chaste marble but also by the noble proportion of the parts, superb curvature of its cusped arches and spherical shape of the domes.

Of the last phase of the Mughal period in the Fort, the Alamgiri Gate built by Emperor Aurangzeb in about 1673 A.D. speaks of the great change that had come over the Mughal Empire in this sub-continent. It makes a great contrast with the Masjidi Gate of the time of Akbar. In its fluted towers rising above a lotus bud and having a kiosk as the crowing element, the Gate speaks of the softness and noble demeanor that came in with passage of time. The other most majestic monument is the Badshahi Mosque built opposite this gate in 1674 by Aurangazeb's foster brother and Master of Ordinance Fidai Khan Kuka. Conceived in a grand scale and constructed in chaste material the mosque calls to prayer by its tall minarets placed by an imposing gateway. (Architecture and details discussed elsewhere).

No description of the Fort will be complete without describing the framed wall outside the Shah Burj Gate – the only specimen of figure representation that survives from the Mughal period in Lahore. The decoration which was started during Jahangir's period in 1624 A.D. was completed in the reign of Shah Jahan in 1631. The pictures are decorated in mosaic and stand out boldly in gorgeous colours. They exhibit scenes of sports and daily life which enraptured the Mughal emperors. Here we can see elephant-fight, bullfight, camel-rise, chaugan (Polo

Play) and others in various moods and poses - a glimpse into the court life that the Mughals were keenly fond of, is found with ample depiction of the cultural life of the city. It is however unfortunate that this precious heritage is not being maintained and instead being misused. The fort is regularly used for dinners etc by the Government. Above all, the rulers try to please the visitors by arranging fireworks which are shortening the life of this precious heritage.

Outside the Fort there are a number of monuments of the Mughal period, the most significant being tomb of Emperor Jahangir at Shahdara, built by his son and successor, Shah Jahan in 1637, and the famous Shalamar Gardens, built under the command of Emperor Shah Jahan in 1642. These monuments evince much of the strength and solidity noted into Muslim architecture of the period, with exquisite decorative work at places like the sarcophagus of emperor Jahangir. In all these buildings there is in their spaciousness and setting something of the character of the nature-loving monarchs so fond of running water and lush green meadows. Thus, the masterly hand of these versatile builders can be seen at the tomb of Jahangir or the Shalamar Gardens where nature and man appear to have linked themselves so beautifully together.

THE BADSHAHI MASJID

The next and most important monument probably the last of Mughal period is Badshahi Masjid due to which the city is known all over. It is one of the biggest mosques of the world with distinct and proud architectural features. The Masjid was built under orders of Emperor Aurangzeb Alamgir and the project executed by Fidai Khan Kuka in 1674 A.D.

The general plan of the mosque shows that, originally, only one main gateway on the east was constructed. The present exit on the south through the 'dalans' appears to have been used as an emergency way out. This main eastern gate is a most imposing structure having a half-domed double portal. It stands on a high terrace with its own height of seventy-seven feet, which is approached by a twenty-foot high flight of twenty-one steps. This entire composition appears majestic in front of the Fort. It really looks extremely imposing when one observes it has twofold functions: dignity as the approach to a Royal mosque, and its use as residential quarters for the 'imam' and scholars etc. Its front and rear elevations are almost identical. The crowning central part of the eastern facade is a handsome perforated parapet, which is studded with a regular line of small cupolas. Just below this line there are two rows, one above the other, of pigeon-holes in regular order according to the number of the cupolas. This is a scheme of architectural embellishment, and at the same time the whole composition to the right and left of this most imposing facade, holds two pinnacles with cupolas over them which lend

Badshahi Masjid,

added aesthetic appeal. Then, between two rows of small panels, there is a long horizontal rectangle that contains the historical inscription of the mosque, bearing the name of Emperor Aurangzeb as the builder of the mosque, the date 1048/1674 and the name of Fidai Khan Kuka, who supervised its construction. This whole rectangle is very artistically designed on a white-marble slab in 'pietra-dura' technique. The spendrils of the multifold pointed central arch bear marble Shamsahs (sunflowers) which are fixed there in an embossed form. The concave surface of the arch carries mural decoration in various colours. On the top of the four corners of this gateway small turrets with suitable cupolas acting like sentinel guards break the skyline. There are porticoes beside the central scheme which serve as windows to admit light and air to the rooms of both the ground and upper floors of the gateway. There are also double storeyed verandahs attached to these rooms, facing the main passage through the gateway on both its wings. The upper-floor plan reveals the arrangement of the staircase, and here can be seen the great skill of the architect who designed this gateway as an independent building with so many functions in view.

The present floor of red-stone, quasi-square slabs is the latest work of the Renovating committee. The old system of flooring was more scientific and stable than the present one, because if any defect developed in the present floor, the whole slab will have to be either replaced or reshuffled.

The architect of this mosque has arranged, with great far-sightedness, the surface of the courtyard on the west with one step six inches higher than the eastern part. It extends over a breadth of about 238 ft. to the southern and northern walls of the 'Dalans'. The central part of this raised portion rises another step of equal height, which runs along the prayer chamber and is 275 ft. long. This gradual rise in the courtyard towards the west, like a terrace, lends additional grandeur to the facade of the 'Ivan' (prayer chamber).

The water tank in the centre of the courtyard is for ablution. It is 50ft. square, 1½ ft. high from the floor, and about 3ft. deep. It is fed by the old well (present tubewell) and from the Lahore Municipal Corporation's main water supply.

The floor of the prayer chamber, on a solid plinth about 5 ft. high, has also been renovated by large marble slabs with borders of hard black stone, which has undoubtedly added great charm and life to the mosque. These marble slabs are carefully cut to the size of a prayer carpet, properly fixed and artistically polished.

The whole vast courtyard of the mosque, with the exception of the space of the back wall of the prayer chamber and some exits, is enclosed by a uniform corridor known locally as the 'dalans'. It is about 21ft. high with a plinth 3ft. from the floor. Its parapet is studded with a uniform pattern of crockets.

The whole mosque is ornamented with a uniform parapet all round the building which has a regular range of crockets ('kungras'), having an elegant 'Mudakhal' design. The crockets of the parapet of the prayer chamber in particular are faced with red stone slabs, which are also ornamented with white marble inlaid in parallel outline and fret cutting designs in relief, and the crockets of the 'dalans' are covered with a thick layer of lime plaster.

The whole structure of the mosque is built on ordinary masonry with lime and bricks, and based on an accurate system, a feature of Muslim architecture. Throughout there is a uniform system of multifoil pointed arches geometrically based on four points. These multifoil arches are called 'Margholas' by the local masons. This system of arches from the gateway to the last 'mehrab' gives a completely harmonious effect, and this is an important basic characteristic of Muslim architecture.

On the western side towards the Qibla- stands the prayer chamber which may aptly be called the main body of the mosque. It consists of the 'mehrab', within the centre of the back wall. This prayer chamber, consists of two oblong, arcaded chambers. The three crowning domes stand above the larger western chamber, having vaulted bays between them and the smaller chamber facing the courtyard has a flat vaulted roofing arrangement, being divided into a scheme of bays and ante-chambers similar to the larger chamber. The floor of this prayer chamber has a plinth about 5ft. high which is approached by flights of steps in the porticos. The facade of the prayer chamber towards the east, having the central front on, holds five porticos having multifoil pointed arches of equal size on the right and left. The middle ones on each side afford entrance to its interior by a flight of steps.

The Badshahi Masjid's, mehrab is in the centre of its back wall. The central square portion of the Ivan of the mosque is covered with decorative marble slabs and the central bulbous double dome stands on the portion which is based on squinch system of arches.

The present mimber or pulpit of white marble is a renovated one, the original 'mimber' was either removed or destroyed by the Sikhs when they occupied the mosque for their military operations.

The most conspicuous features of the mosque are its three crowning bulbous domes on the top of the rear chamber of the prayer hall. The central dome is larger and higher than the other two to the right and left. They are covered with regular layers of marble slabs and are most artistically erected on a squinch system. The vaulted bays between these domes rest on pendentives. The adjoining smaller chamber of the hall, having a flat, vaulted roofing arrangement, also falls within the whole arcuated set-up of these domes.

In reality, the domes are composed of inner and outer shells of masonry with distinct spaces or voids, between the domes. They are known as double domes. By building two domes in one, in the form of an inner and outer shell separated by a void, the proportions of both the exterior, and particularly the interior, were much improved. This innovation of the double dome has also helped acoustics by controlling and transmitting the sound of the sermon rising from the mehrab beneath the central dome in such a way as to avoid an echo. It also helps keeping the temperature of the mosque under control.

The minarets of the Badshahi Masjid have three storeys, which stand on a solid plinth of about 20ft. high, which some people would also include as an independent storey. They are octagonal and plain. The height of each minaret is 143 1/2ft. excluding the top pavilions with their cupolas as well as their plinths. The original pavilions were lost in the earthquake of 1840 and they were restored. Access to the summit is gained by a flight of narrow steps of red stone in the interior. Although simple in their design and plain in their tall, and tapering appearance, the minarets are conspicuous for their size and entirely proportionate to the size of the mosque and placed at the Four Corners of the quadrangle after careful consideration by the architect.

The various decorative devices and ornamental embellishments relieve the monotony of the flat red stone on the exterior and the white surface in the interior. The walls of the mosque, both internally and externally, have the following varieties of decorations:

The central square chamber of the Ivan, including the mehrab of the mosque up to the height of the cornice serving as the base of the central dome's squinch system, is supported by a square of multifoil pointed arches. It is built entirely of the best quality of white marble. The concave of the midway cornice of this square just below the squinches has an ornamental frieze, which is full of carved acanthus leaf motifs employed in a regular alternating order of a smaller and larger leaves and matches the arrangement of the acanthus. This unusual and most charming feature of the frieze design in marble carving has a decidedly local influence. The upward points of the leaves and downward hanging ends of the rosettes are most effective.

The walls of the mosque are internally covered with red-stone slabs which have been very carefully panelled in low-relief carving of decorative rectangular motifs in regular composition and rhythm in some cases, these decorative panels are artistically arranged with flat inlaid margins in strips of white marble, which undoubtedly enhance the general beauty of this relief ornamentation on the surface of the red stone.

The third variety of decorative motifs, which are generally defined as 'arabesques', are cut out of white marble and inlaid on the red-stone surface in low relief, i.e. embossed. They are found on the mosque's prayer chamber and on the soffit of the arch of the fronton which just on its inside edge, forms a continuous scroll of ornaments.

Sikhs hardly contributed anything to Lahore and instead deprived the monuments of stone. They disfigured the buildings and the gardens and palaces. The death of Ranjit Singh brought the downfall of the Sikhs and anarchy followed.

LAHORE 1849-1947

On disintegration of Sikh state the British, who had already established the political and military network, finally, took over the country of the Sikhs. The British acquired the absolute right and set up a government of their own under the orders of the Governor General of India. A Board of administration for affairs of the Punjab was set up at Lahore on 31.3.1849 which was headed by Sir H. M. Lawrence as President. Mr. C. G. Mansel and John Lawrence were the members, Mr. P. Melwell was appointed as Secretary of the Board. The Board established its office in the Residency, which was already working in Lahore. The present CS office and Record Room in the S&GAD, (of Civil Secretariat) formed the Residency to which certain rooms were added for setting up office of the Board & Secretariat.

Lahore was made Divisional Headquarters headed by the Commissioner. Mr. D. F. Mcleod was the first Commissioner and Mr. Boring was the first Deputy Commissioner of Lahore. The British army which had conquered the entire Province was also in occupation of Lahore. They established a cantonment in the Anarkali, area of the city. Infact this was already having some residential quarters of the French and other offices of Sikh Army who used to command and train forces during Ranjit Singh's period. There was a garden in the area in which important monuments were Wazir Khan's Baradari, which was also known as Nakhla Wazir Khan and Anarkali Tomb, The British Residency and Chauburji Gateway.

The river Ravi, as mentioned elsewhere, used to flow until late 18th century near the Fort and city but changed its course and deserted its old channel and turned towards north leaving only an arm wandering through its old course around the city coming westwards of the district courts, Secretariat and Chauburji garden. A very small stream flowed under the fort walls. Shortly after occupation of the city, change started taking place, the waste and desolated areas started being occupied for residential purposes. The uneven grounds interspersed with crumbling mosques, domes and gateways, huge shapeless mounds of rubbish and very old brick kilns started disappearing. The European population gradually increased and the city started spreading eastwards. The debris was used for road making or construction of offices. Anarkali became civil station as also the Cantonment. The eastward expansion of the city comprised of Donald Town, Lawrence Garden and Government House. The Anarkali was abandoned as a Cantonment in the year 1851–52 due to mortality in troops on account of cholera. The deaths according to the Sanitary Commissioner of the Province were due to the bad arrangements, unhygienic and unhealthy conditions in the area which was also without sewerage. The new site for cantonment was selected about 2 miles further east of the Tomb of Hazrat Mian Mir. It was a dreary arid plain separate from the city by broken ground and abounded by Jungle.

Generally speaking the vicinity of the city although well-wooded yet the trees were deficient in size and variety. The only tree found generally was 'Kikar' and there were some trees of mangoes, Piple and date-palm in some of the ancient gardens which belonged to old Muslim nobility and had been badly spoiled during the Sikh period. The general aspect of the city was not very imposing and it could not claim to be of picturesque beauty. Hindu buildings were practically non-existent and Lahore could only show architectural worth of imperial city belonging long ago to the Muslims, within the city the streets were narrow, winding, some of the balconies (over hanging) of wood were carved and coloured. People were fond of putting bright colour clothes. With the establishment of the British, control works of public welfare started. The public welfare works undertaken and metalled roads introduced. The initial work on establishment of educational institutions started and railway lines laid. The biggest railway workshop was established in Mughalpura area. The city was provided with water supply system and a proper drainage/sewerage etc. The telegraph and post offices were set up. Above all Lahore being provincial headquarters controlled the entire Province in respect of Revenue, judicial and financial matters. The Financial and Judicial Commissioner offices came into being which later took the shape of Chief Court in respect of judicial matters and Board of Revenue in matters of financial arrangements. The irrigation system was planned and an irrigation Secretariat established. A canal crossed Lahore between Mian Mir Cantonment and the city. Infact this was a branch of Bari Doab Canal, which derives its water from the river Ravi near Madhopur. Records indicate the British faced lot of difficulties while providing water and sewerage to the city due to tortuous and narrow streets. A better drainage and storm water channel could have been possible but due to resistance of public ignored.

The soil around the city was alluvial debris of ages which had raised the site of city to a considerable height above the river. The city is built on several mounds rising to a height of 50 feet and with depression at many a places. The city walls which were of 30 feet height were reduced to about 15 feet. Outside the city wall there existed a deep moat since Mughal period. This moat had outlived its military purpose with commanding of the territory by the British up to the Durand line and it was merely an offensive ditch. The British got it filled with water from the canal and laid garden around the entire walled city. The city wall had originally been built by Emperor Akbar and repaired during the Sikh period. There were 13 gates in the city walls namely.

Bhati Gate.   Masti Gate.
Taxali Gate.   Khizri Gate.
Roshnai Gate   Yaki Gate.
Kashmiri Gate.   Delhi Gate
Akbari Gate.   Shahalmi Gate.
Lohari Gate   Mori Gate
Mochi Gate.

Some of them were repaired and renovated by the British.

The Lahore in 1860s put up quite a different scene than it was 30 years ago. Soon after annexation the vast expanse of uneven ground, runs of successive cities thrived with luxuriant vegetation picturesque, public and private edifices had risen and gardens and plains, intersected by metalled roads were very often visible. People enjoyed peace and prosperity because of a settled Government. The administration was headed by the Chief Commissioner of Punjab in the year 1853, instead of Board of Administration and to further streamline the same the Province was declared as Lieutenant-Governor's Province, in 1858. It continued as such till it became a Governor's Province.

With the British in power no major and monumental work of architecture appeared in public sector on the royal style. However, public buildings, institutions/offices were constructed by the Government according to need and within available resources. With the construction of the first metalled road i.e. Mall connecting Anarkali and Mian Mir Cantt., European shops and stores appeared on the Mall. The areas around Lawrence Garden, Regal Chowk, Hall Road, Government House, Opposite High Court and the localities around Mall were called Donald Town. On the north eastern side lay the Railway Station and Railway Employees Colony generally known as Naulakha. Bungalows and residences around the locality of Mozang on Temple Road, Queens Road and Bird-Wood Road also appeared generally occupied by Europeans. The Residency had taken the shape of full-fledged Secretariat. A book club was set up in the Baradari of Wazir Khan which place was later occupied by Lahore Museum temporarily. The Anarkali Tomb was converted into a Church. This is why the road from the

Board of Revenue side leading towards Anarkali Tomb is still known as Church Road. The population of the city also started increasing.

The following may be mentioned as the principal buildings and institutions raised by the British between 1849–1947.

The Lahore Central Museum (detailed elsewhere) developed from the Exhibition of products of Punjab held in 1864. The building of the Museum is essentially of indigenous character and made in parts. It is of red brick structure and most imposing and stands opposite the University Hall. Its foundation was laid by Prince Victor on February 3, 1890 and the Museum shifted from it was temporary accomodated in Tollinton Market in 1894. The museum was also provided with a Technical Institute, a lecture hall and a classroom where later Lantern lectures continued for a very long time. Major area of the building was roofed in an iron column and special care had been taken to secure abundance of light leaving space for advantageous arrangement of the collection.

When the proposals for museum were considered a thinking started developing with the administration that indigenous industrial arts should also be promoted, preserved and training/educational facilities provided to the locals. By chance on the death of Lord Mayo Viceroy and Governor-General a fund was raised in the memory of late Viceroy. This fund was collected and administered by a Committee. The Committee recommended that a part of this collection be spent on the construction of Industrial School for the indigenous arts for the Punjab. Mr. Lockwood Kippling's services were requisitioned from the Government of Bombay who was given the assignment. He held the charge of both the Mayo Industrial School of Art and Museum for quite some time. It will be seen that the building of Mayo School of Art is contiguous with the museum. This was the thinking of the then officers that educational institutions should be put up in line in a close proximately so that they could benefit from each other and there should be more co-ordination. This is why the University building was located opposite the Museum and Mayo School of Art. The Government College premises are inter-connected with the University campus. The Oriental College and Law College were also later located close to the Senate Hall, on the north of the campus.

The British style of buildings was totally different from the Mughals. These were erected splendidly pompous Victorian public buildings in the style that has come to be called Moghul Gothic. Some also term it classical but some say it was frigid classical. But it is certainly different than that of the Mughals. No monumental works were undertaken others than public buildings. The list of such buildings is also not very large and include among others the Lahore Punjab University, District. Courts, Government College, High Court, Punjab Assembly Building, Lawrence Montgomery Hall, and Atichision College etc., etc. Since the style and features are the same, I only intend to briefly describe them as some of them have already been mentioned in one context or the other elsewhere.

THE GOVERNMENT HOUSE, LAHORE

Government House has been built around the tomb of Muhammad Qasim Khan, (a cousin on the mother's side of Emperor Akbar) who died at Lahore during the reign of Shah Jahan, and was buried here. Qasim Khan was great patron of wrestlers, and to the west of the present tomb he inhabited a Mohallah, or city quarters, and built an extensive mosque. Of the buildings of this Mohallah only the mosque had survived the wreck of the time during the reign of Ranjit Singh, who converted it into a magazine for manufacturing powder and his soldiers quarters. During the British period the Masjid became Nazul property, but it was subsequently released on the application of Sardar Khan, Lambardar of Mozang, who dismantled it and sold the bricks at a great profit. The large well attached to the mosque, which was filled with powder, exploded by accident, killing two zamindars and several bullocks on the spot. Upto the time of Maharaja Ranjit Singh, the ground close to the tomb, was used for wrestling purposes, and the tomb was called the Gumbad Kushti Wala, or the wrestlers dome.

Towards the close of the Maharaja's reign Jamadar Khushal Singh uncle of Raja Teja Singh built around it a nice house, of octangular form which was used by himself and the officers of his contingent. The house was surrounded by a garden, close to which were the barracks of troops under the command of Khushal Singh. The building was utilized as Government House, when Henry Lawrence made it Residency and Sir Robert Montgomery used it as Government House. No part of Jamadar Khushal Singh's house is in existence but the old tomb can still be seen in a portion of the lower storey of the house. The interior of the dome was used as the dining room, and a very admirable dining room it was made. The arches around it serve as recesses for sideboards, the room being lighted through slit in the dome. The walls are decorated with enamelled pottery-work, and the alcoves of the central hall are embellished with fresco designs. Some very fine trees are grown in the grounds and there was a nice swimming pool.

The Tomb around which Khushal Singh built his house had crypt/Burial chamber underneath. In the square portion of the tomb there are three alcoves. Above the well-decorated cornice there is an alcove in the centre of each side. The super-structure of the tomb used as dining room has stucco tracery in low relief. According to some writers it was done in 1853. M. B. Jones, in his work titled Palaces of the Raj, lived as a guest in the Governor's House sometime between

Government House Lahore 1859

Government House Lahore 1863

1849-1853 when Henry Lawrence lived in the same with his wife, according to Jones.

It was infact the upper storey of the tomb of Muhammad Qasim Khan, a cousin of Akbar the Great, and dated from about 1635. The room below the tomb was properly served for a number of years as the kitchen when the cooks would use the sarcophagus as a table. In spite of being built round a tomb, the House had a happy and friendly atmosphere. There were no unpleasant ghosts, apart from an elemental, which used to haunt the grounds near the main gate earlier in this century. Thus it would seem that the spirit of Muhammad Qasim did not object to later generations feasting in his tomb if indeed the sarcophagus contained his bones, for according to some accounts, he was buried elsewhere. He probably feasted here himself having built the tomb in his own lifetime, as was customary, and used it as a House of pleasure until he died. As he was a great patron of wrestlers, the ground nearby was the scene of many wrestling matches, which continued to be held here long after his death; so that the tomb came to be known as Kushti Wala Gumbad, or the "Wrestlers' Dome."

During the Sikh period the tomb and garden around remained a place for manufacturing of gunpowder and as soldier station. The grounds nearby were used for wrestling purpose and tomb was, therefore, called Kushti Wala Gumbad. This means that tomb was visible during the Sikh period and later on concealed by construction raised around both by Sikh and the British.

After annexation of Punjab in March 1849 Mr. Boring, the then Deputy commissioner of Lahore, first occupied this house. Thereafter Major Macreggor became Deputy Commissioner and lived in this house. Later on Colonel Sir Henry Lawrence President of the Board of Administration brought the offices of Residency from the old building (for Civil Secretariat) (CS Block close to Anarkali Tomb) to this place. This house was acquired at the suggestion of Mr. Robert Montgomery the Commissioner of Lahore by giving in exchange to Raja Teja Singh a house and land in Sialkot at his own request. The property at Sialkot was confiscated and belonged to Dewan Hakim Rai.

Col. Napier, Civil Engineer Punjab got executed the conversion of house into Residency through Public Works Department. The changes in the building starting in March 1851 were completed in 1853. The Residency building was named as Governor House in 1859 (during the period of Sir Lawrence and Robert Montgomery when they were Governors in 1859). Additions and alterations throughout have been made in this building surrounding the tomb, which too housed a kitchen and a dining room. The construction around the house is in the British style, which may be termed as Indo-British.

Government House Lahore 1998

Government House Lahore 1998

The Governor's House is a vast amorphous Complex. It totally lacks any planned development and extensions are haphazard lacking style and design.

The Governor's House is spread over on a total area of 67.81 acres out of which 25 acres approximately are under Lawns, 20 acres under fruit and vegetable garden the other areas are under Fish lake, high mound, roads etc., etc. There are some 38 rooms excluding verandahs on the ground floor of the House, of which nine are bathrooms and 35 rooms excluding verandahs on the first floor, of which ten are bathrooms. The Prime Minister's Wing including ten rooms and two bathrooms lies on the first floor, while the President's Wing comprising ten rooms with two baths lies on the ground floor. The Governor's suite has seven rooms in all, out of which two are bathrooms, two dressing rooms and the rest are bedrooms. Family and Guest Wing has nine rooms in all, out of which three are bathrooms, three dressing rooms and three bedrooms. In all, there are at present 73 rooms in the Governor's House including 19 bathrooms. This in short shows the development, which has taken place in the House during the past 150 years.

The House contains a good selection of old paintings and various Wings have been decorated appropriately for the President & Prime Minister's staff along with other state guests. The Darbar Hall is for the visitors and small gatherings.

The Routine office work is done on the ground floor. The Governor's House due to its historical background and role of the Governor, which is Constitutional only, can be termed as an institution and this historical building should be preserved. These days there is a lot of talk about its disposal by public and press to collect money but one wonders as to how much it could fetch and what purpose it would serve compared with, its historical significance which is invaluable.

ANARKALI TOMB, THE FIRST "CHURCH"
CIVIL SECRETARIAT (Gen. Ventura's Residence)

Anarkali's tomb is well-known as the first parish church of the Protestant community of Lahore, but the records of the period have brought to light the existence of an even older "church" hitherto unknown. Like many other old buildings in Lahore, Dhian Singh's Haveli or place has served many purposes since it was built during the Sikh times by Mian Dhian Singh, the young Rajput who was chamberlain to Maharaja Ranjit Singh and subsequently Prime Minister to Maharaja Sher Singh, whose murder was arranged with his connivance. He himself was murdered by his accomplices immediately after. It appears from old official records that this haveli, which is situated in the Hira Mandi, inside the old Taxali Gate of the city, was fitted up as a place of public worship for the Christian garrison

of the neighbouring fort and it is, therefore, presumably the first building ever used for this purpose in Lahore. In response to an enquiry made by the Honourable court of Directors of the East India Company, it was explained that the Garrison Engineer had spent Rs.341-7-6 "for fitting up Raja Dhian Singh's house at Lahore as a temporary place of worship." The Government of India referred to it as "the church in Dhian Singh's house." The fittings constituted of 40 benches, three punkhas, a book-stand and bamboo chicks.

In later years the building was known as the Government District School and as such is remembered by the older generation. It was also the first home of the Government College when opened on January 1, 1864.

FIRST CHURCH

Many of the old tombs and mosques of the Mughal period, which are still to be found dotted about in Lahore, were, at one time or another, utilised as residences or offices. For example, there is the mosque of Dai Anga near the railway station which was the residence, in the early 1850's, of Mr. Cope, editor of the Lahore Chronicle, and was afterwards used for many years by the Railway as the Traffic Manager's office. Government House is built round the tomb of Muhammad Qasim Khan, a relative of the Emperor Akbar; the masjid of Shah Chiragh housed the Accountant-General's office for many years and also occupied by the Session Court; but none of these buildings has served so many or such varied purpose as Anarkali's tomb. The romantic tragedy connected with the construction of this tomb is so well-known that it will be sufficient for the purposes of this to write up and recall the reported fact that Anarkali was a slave-girl who was buried alive in 1599 by order of the Emperor Akbar, who suspected her of having a criminal intrigue with his son, Prince Salim. Afterwards the Emperor Jahangir on his accession to the throne, had the tomb built over the grave of the unfortunate girl. It was completed in 1615.Some writers do not agree with this version and assert that it is fiction and the tomb is that of some one else. During the time of the Sikhs, this tomb was occupied by Sardar Kharak Singh, Maharaha Ranjit Singh's heir-apparent, but was subsequently given to General Ventura, who converted it into a private residence (Syed Muhammad Latif's "Lahore"). When Punjab was annexed by the British Government, the tomb was used partly as a residence for some of the clerical staff and partly as an office, temporary rooms were also added around it for use by the officials. On the 15th March, 1851, the Secretary to the Board of Administration, Punjab, reported to the Government of India that "the Board's offices having been removed from the old Residency, the tomb which they formerly occupied has become available, and has lately been used, by permission of the Board, for Divine Service on Sundays"" Sanction was at the time obtained for

Anarkali Tomb

the expenditure of Rs.1,000 on fitting up the tomb so as to serve as a place of worship for the Protestant congregation, civil and military, of the station known as Anarkali. Apparently the temporary structure round the base was then demolished. Four years later, in 1855, the Revd. Dr. Carshore, Chaplain, applied for sanction to increase the seating accommodation by giving access to the recesses or arches round the upper storey, and the necessay structural alterations were carried out by the Public Works Department, including the construction of an outer staircase, as the existing "steep and narrow staircases could not in any way be remodelled without incurring the expense of pulling down and rebuilding the turrets in which they are built. In their present state, they are certainly very inconvenient and not at all adapted to the purpose of giving free access to the proposed sitting on the upper storey of the church". It may be noted, however, that after years one of these spiral staircases remained in use to supplement the new outer staircase. This spiral staircase is till date in use. The outer staircase being exposed and opened to the officials working in the archives section prefer the stair in the turret.The tomb is now used as Punjab Archives office.

Early in 1857, the Chief Commissioner of the Punjab consented to the consecration of this place of Christian worship, and over fifty members of the congregation submitted a petition to the Bishop of Madras (Dr. Dealtry), then on visit to the Punjab as representative of the Metropolitan, asking him to consecrate it. Among the signatories were two future Lieutenant-Governors of the Punjab (Sir Robert Montgomery, then Judicial Commissioner, and Sir Robert Egerton, then Settlement Officer); Lieutenant-Colonel H. Fraser, officiating Chief Engineer; Charles T. Elliot, Assistant Commissioner; Charles Hathaway, Inspector of Prisons; Dr. C. Manners-Smith, Civil Surgeon: Lieut. J. J. McLeod Innes, Engineer; and the Revd. Joseph James Carshore, D. D., Chaplain. The ceremony of consecration was performed by the Bishop on the 24th January, 1857, the church being named St. James and it is on record that Dr. Dealtry was "glad to find that the tomb at Anarkali, in which he preached in 1847 as Archdeacon of Calcutta, had been neatly fitted up for Divine Service". From this it may be gathered that the tomb had been occasionally used as a place of worship three or four years before formal permission was given by the Board of Administration for its regular use on Sundays.

In the early seventies, when the Revd. J. R. Baldwin was chaplain, it was found necessary to make a further increase in the sittings, and this was effected by throwing out a wooden gallery, supported on substantial wooden pillars, round the inner side of five of the upper arches. At the same time, the vault of the dome was colour-washed blue and was decorated with tinsel stars to represent the firmament. This crude specimen of "Art" disfigured the interior of the building. St. James'

General Ventura's Residence Now Chief Secretary's Office

church was known in later years as the Pro-Cathedral, when the Lahore diocese was created and Dr. French was appointed its first Bishop; and it continued in use as "the Mother church" of the diocese until the present Cathedral was completed. Anarkali's tomb lay vacant for some years after it was given up by the ecclesiastical authorities, but in 1891 it was again converted into an office for the storage of Secretariat records, and is still used for that purpose. The sarcophagus, which had been put away in one of the turrets when the building was first converted into a church, was placed on the spot from which the altar had been removed. It remains to be seen what further changes time has in store for the old tomb after the removal of its present contents to the new Secretariat Buildings promised shortly to be constructed for the last about sixty years by the Authorities.The writer has been sitting in the tomb while working in the Archives for about 15 years.

Members of the Cathedral choir may be interested to learn that it was in the old parish church of St. James that a full-sized organ was substituted for the harmonium which had been in use for many years, and that this organ was transferred to the new Cathedral, where it was succeeded in course of time by the present organ. Mr H.R.Goulding choir of St. James, when the "old" organ was used for the first time, and many years later he sang in the cathedral choir when the new organ was first used. It may also be interesting to mention that the "mixed choir" of St. James' included at one time Lady Davies, wife of the Lieutenant-Governor; Miss Lindsay (choir leader), a daughter of Mr. Justice Lindsay of the chief court; and the two daughters of Bishop French. Among the men were Mr. (afterwards Sir Robert) Egerton, Mr. Thornton, Secretary to Government; Mr. (afterwards Sir) Mackworth Young.

Mr. B.H. Baden-Powell, Mr. J. A. E. Miller, Secretary to the Financial Commissioner, and Colonel A. H. Bamfield, Inspector-General of Police, who was for some time choir-master.

The Headquarters of the Government of Punjab (i.e. Civil Secretariat) popularly known as "Daftar Lotsahib" is located on the right side of the Lower Mall while coming from P.M.G.'s office towards M.A.O. College. It is bounded by Commissioner's Office on Devsmaj Road on the north and Chishtia High School and the locality of Santnagar on the west. On the south it is encircled by Law College ground, Government Press and People's House on Vedak Road. How the Provincial Head Office found its location on this place is really an interesting story and infact is connected with the history of annexation of the Punjab by the British.

The British officers (e.g. Sir Henry Lawrence) moved like waves, in the Sikh Darbar, occupied Punjab under a well conceived plan and established the seat of Government (for the newly acquired territories of the Punjab including North Western Frontier Province) at Lahore bringing it at par with other settled areas of the rest of India. Students of history would remember that the anarchy that followed Maharaja Ranjit Singh's death in Punjab allowed and encouraged the British to interfere in and influence the affairs of Lahore Darbar. The British, under the terms of treaty of 1846, were entitled to maintain peace and law and order in the Sikh territories till Maharaja Daleep Singh could attain majority. This control of the British became so deeprooted that even 'Maharani Jindan' would always consult, in private, and act upon the advice of the British Resident.

For all this business with the Sikhs and correspondence with Governor-General at Calcutta, the British Resident had to set up an office at an appropriate place which would consist of English and Persian Offices and was to be manned by British and native staff members. To accommodate the offices they selected the building then, commonly known as "Anarkali House". This building, according to the then available evidence, happened to be in the area called "Anarkali Garden" on the left bank of the River Ravi towards east of the tomb known as "Anarkali's Tomb". The Engineer of the British force stationed at Lahore requested Sir Henry Lawrence, the Resident, on August 4, 1847, for the expenses on the conversion of "Anarkali House" and buildings attached thereto, into a Residency for the Resident and the assistants of the office. The Engineer wrote the following.

"Rough Estimates of the probable expenditure of converting General Ventura's House at Anarkali into a Residency Lahore August 4."

"The building consists of a range of low and ill ventilated rooms, 7 on the ground floor and 5 in the upper storey. These have been thoroughly cleaned, plastered, white-washed and furnished with glass doors. The two end apartments with the addition of a bed-room on the south, have been prepared for the use of Principal and Senior Assistants. An Apartment on the upper storey has been roofed in, with the addition of a sky-light chupper for the Resident. A new upper verandah on pillars has been added along the entire front".

"The Anarkali's Tomb adjoining the House, has been cleaned, whitewashed, and fitted for office purposes and residence for clerks".

"It is now proposed to build 4 rooms at the back of and attached to the main buildings. The centre room to be 55 feet long by 40 feet wide and 30 feet high. The side rooms to be 26` X 22` feet with a Verandah 12 feet wide, partly enclosed for dressing and one bath room. These walls on account of the looseness of the soil require a foundation of 10 feet deep brick masonry".

"The whole building when complete is designed for the accommodation of the Resident and assistants a sufficient range of out-office and stabling is to be provided and the existing Ground House and Sheds enlarged to afford cover for a company and half of the Infantry and 80 Sawars. A mud wall 6-1/2 feet high with

Chauburji, Secretariat, Anarkali Tomb & the River Ravi

an interior banquet to enclose the premises in the rear and with side unoccupied by buildings".

"The expenses for these alterations and additions, according to rough calculations made by the Engineer came to Rs.24,900".

In this manner the British Residency was set up in the present building occupied by the Chief Secretary's Office. This "Anarkali House" or General Ventura's residence is said to have been built by General Jean Baptiste Ventura, a French General who had been employed by Maharaja Ranjit Singh to train his army. According to representations made by his widow later, this General, like some other civil and military officers of the Sikh Government had rendered services and "took deep interest and pains to promote the British cause in the Sikh court secretly and openly both which the reports of Capt. Wade and Alexander Burns forwarded to Government during the life of Ranjit Singh will show". It was General Ventura, who, in opposition to several members of Ranjit Singh's court exerted himeslf to remove evil impression from the hearts of Sikhs and facilitated the way for the progress of the force headed by Capt. Wade and Mackeson who were escorting Prince Taimur for placing the late Shah Shuja on the throne of Kabul. This indicates that when, after annexation, the "Khalsa Sarkar" property stood confiscated to Government, the persons who had been in league with the British (for annexation of Punjab) were exempted. The records further prove that in addition to this house, which was converted into Residency, the other property of General (Jagirs and shares in the factories) in Ludhiana District were also allowed to continue with him and his successor. When Punjab was finally annexed, General Ventura was duly compensated for his house and furniture in Lahore. The documents (Proceedings 13th July Nos.21-2 General department 1850) establish that in 1850, General Ventura put in a claim of indemnity for his house and furniture at Lahore and in reply to a letter from the Punjab Government, the Governor-General observed that while he was "willing to agree that the General should receive that compensation of Rs.2000/-," he could not assent to the suggestion that the General should receive the compensation of Rs.10,000/- for the house. It was further pointed out that as the Punjab Government was satisfied General Ventura had no claim as a matter of right to the house in question, yet the Government had already dealt with him liberally but was not inclined to be so liberal as to the grant of compensation for the property to which, it is clear, the General had no claim. Consequently the Punjab Government addressed the General as under:

"I have the honour to inform you that the Government of India referred to the Board of Administration the claim advanced by you for compensation on account of the house at Lahore now occupied by the President of the Board and its establishment which was formerly the Residency and also on account of furniture. The Board in consequence made a report to the Government on the subject and the result is that the Government has fixed the sum of rupees 2000 as compensation to you on account of furniture left in the house but has declined to recognise any claim in your faith to compensate for the house itself.

The Board requests the favour of your referring them in what way you would wish rupees 2000 to be remitted to you."

This indicates how General Ventura's House, in the first instance, was converted into Residency and later on, in April 1849, when the Board of Administration for the alairs of Punjab, was constituted, became its Secretariat. The Board of Administration consisted of two Members with a President and had one Secretary and one Deputy Secretary. The Board and its Secretariat continued to occupy this building as their Secretariat for Punjab until it was replaced by the Chief Commissioner and subsequently by the Lt. Governor. When the Chief Commissioner / Lt. Governor moved to the Governor House, the building became Chief Secretary's Office and since then it has continued as such.

With the expansion of Governmental activity, new offices/ departments were created and to house them, new blocks were raised from time to time around the Chief Secretary's office. In 1917, on a move by Sir Edward Maclagan, it was proposed to erect a tablet in the Secretariat to commemorate the fact that the building (Chief Secretary's office) was occupied by Sir Henry Lawrence and Sir John Lawrence as Residents at the court of Lahore. The Government Consulting Architect was requested to design the tablet which was executed in white marble with lettering incised and filled with lead. Its cost was installed complete, for Rs.240/- at that time. The tablet is still there on the left-hand side on the entrance to the Chief Secretary's room. The writing on the tablet is as under:

"Jean Baptists Ventura, General in the service of the Maharaja Ranjit Singh erected this building in its original form, and lived in it for many years. It became the British Residency in 1847 and was occupied by Henry Lawrence and John Lawrence as Residents at the Court of Lahore, and, after the annexation of the Punjab, as Member of the Board of Administration."

Till the Partition, the Secretariat compound consisted of mainly Chief Secretary's block and around it the Police Block, Ministerial Block (now C.M.'s office and Ministers' rooms) and Finance Commissioner's Block, Law Department and Health and Local Government Department. The only office located outside the Secretariat was of the Chief Engineer Irrigation and Chief Engineer Buildings (later on Irrigation and Communications and Works Department). It was housed in a building opposite to the Punjab Public Library building and Young-Husband Hostel. After Independence, the manifold increase in Governmental activities necessitated more accommodation for offices and the new blocks now housing the Planning and Development Department, Agriculture, Industries, Forest and Wildlife and Food Departments, were constructed at the end of corner of Bank Road and Church Road. In the main Secretariat compound the block presently occupied by Home Department, Health Department and Estate Office etc., were also raised after Independence.

The Secretariat mosque designed on the lines of "Masjid-e-Nabwi" was also constructed after partition. It will be interesting to note that as back as 1890, there existed a shed which was used as a prayer platform by the Muslim employees of the Secretariat. It is said that this shed was prepared through the efforts of Kh. Tassadiq Hussain, the then Mir Munshi of the Punjab Secretariat. In 1891 it came to the notice of the authorities that the Muslims were converting the platform into a permanent structure which had originally been authorised as temporary shed. The platform was located on the right side of the Anarkali Tomb and some Muslim employees had made a 'Pacca' wall around it. The Municipality and Secretariat authorities objected to it. The matter was brought to the notice of the Chief Secretary who ordered that a thatched or timber roof may be allowed to be put on iron or timber posts. It continued as such till Independence. After the creation of Pakistan, the present mosque was completed at a cost of about Rs.2 lakh, mainly contributed by the Secretariat employees. The Government only donated a sum of Rs.25,000/- and the land.

It would also be interesting to note that from 1849 to 1900 these Secretariat buildings housed the Departments which were administering the affairs of Punjab and NWFP Province. In 1901 the NWFP was made a separate province and till 1947 the Secretariat was only for the Province of Punjab. From 1947 to 1955, it housed the departments which were responsible for the administration of West Punjab. From 1955 to 1970 it accommodated the Secretariat of the defunct West Pakistan Government and from Ist July, 1970 onwards it again became the seat of the Punjab Government.

It may be added that the expansion of the Departments/Offices and shortage of accommodation as also construction of a proper and suitable building for the Secretariat has been engaging the attention of the Government since long. A proposal was made as early as 1909 in which it was thought to enter into a bargain with the trustees of the Dyal Singh College for sale of site and building of the Secretariat to raise new one from the proceeds. This could not materialise due to the valuation of the site and building of Secretariat (estimated by the Government as Rs. 51/2 Lakh for starting negotiations and the offer of Rs.2-1/2 lakh from the Trustees).

Again in 1918 there was a proposal for shifting of the Secretariat to Charing Cross area but its fate is not known as no records are available. After the emergence of Pakistan, there was a proposal for the construction of new Secretariat during West Pakistan Government time (in sixtees), but the schemes could not materialise due to the Indo Pakistan War of 1965, probably, and also because of the ensuing financial stringency. There were Press reports in mid seventies about the construction of a New Secretariat in the old Race Course area but the Government, it is felt, is still looking for a suitable site. Any way it is expected that whenever a modern Secretariat building is raised with a befitting design, the old building, now known as Chief Secretary's block, will be protected as a historical monument.

GOVERNMENT COLLEGE

The Government College Lahore was opened on January 1st, 1864 by an order of the Lt. Governor Punjab. Its establishment was subsequently confirmed by the Government of India in April, 1864. In the same year i.e. 1864 the Institution was affiliated to the Calcutta University for examination in Arts. Dr. G. W. Leitner of the Freiburg University then a Professor of Arabic and Muhammadan Law at King's College London was appointed as Principal. As Dr. Leitner could not assume immediately, Mr. C. W. Alexander of Trinity College Cambridge was appointed as stop gap arrangement. The college was temporarily located in the first instance alongwith Zilla School in a portion of Raja Dhian Singh's Haveli. A couple of rooms on the first floor consisted of a Boarding House. The benefit of locating the college in this city building was the meagre staff of the college, which was occasionally, helped by school teachers especially Mr. Beddy, the Headmaster. The first college class consisted of 9 students who matriculated from Calcutta University and almost all the students of the college were given scholarships. The value of the stipend ranged from Rs.10/- to 15/-. The first examination of the students sent up was that of F.A. of the Calcutta University in 1865.

In the year 1871 the college commenced the series of migrations which ended in its arrival on the present site. The old building in the city had long been found unsatisfactory and in April, 1871 the college was removed to a large bungalow in Anarkali, part of which later survived as an Ice Factory. One of the old students of the college remarked in his memoirs that it was later in the year 1873 that Dr. Rahim's Kothi near the Veterinary College was hired. The Boarders first lived in out-houses and subsequently in 'Bans Mandi' known as "Chotay Lal ki Kothi". The Hostel kept on shifting. Sometimes in big house which was rented in the area of Mozang and sometimes in Anarkali and Court Street.

This picturesque building with a large centre clock tower, is situated on an eminence to the east of District Kutcheri and north of the public Gardens known

Government College

differently at different times, Anarkali Gardens, Company Bagh, Gol Bagh and now Nasir Bagh. The structure of the building is in Gothic style, and contains accommodation for a college, a large Examination and Lecture Hall, used also for Convocation purpose, and two large rooms, one for a Library, and the other for Models etc.

The College till about 1890 consisted of twelve large class rooms, and four small ones, or sixteen in all, of which eight were in the lower and eight in the upper storey.

By the side of the above there are again four large class rooms and four small ones, or eight in all, of which four are in the lower and four in the upper storey. The two rooms beyond, connected by a wide arch, are used as a Library and Model rooms while the rooms above these are used as Principal's and Assistant Principal's rooms. The Examination and Lecture Hall is 55' x 35' with a gallery of 10 feet wide all round, access to which, as well as to the upper rooms and the Library is gained by a masonry staircase. Access to the upper rooms of the College, is gained by a wide staircase, in an octagonal tower, at the north –west corner of the building. The connecting passages and the verandahs are 10 feet wide.

The outer walls, outer face of inner verandah walls and all the exposed parts of the superstructure are of large, well shaped bricks, carefully dressed and laid in Flemish bond, with straight and fine joints. The outside brick-work is finely dressed, and the moldings and ornamental portions are neatly executed.

The roof of the class rooms is made of large slates, laid with an overlap of eight inches, over Deodar Planking, of inch thick resting on Deodar battens, one foot apart from centre to centre. The roof of the Verandahs, gallery and passages is flat, and rests on Deodar beams. The building was designed by W. Purdon, Esq., Superintending Engineer, and constructed by Rai Bahadur Kanhia Lal, at a cost of Rs.3, 20,537. It was commenced in 1872, and was completed in five years. More than double of the accommodation has been added to the above construction after 1900 especially after 1947. The Bokhari Block, Staff Block, a block adjoining old Law College Block, Cafeteria and still a block coming up on the North close to Saleem Model High School.The Principal's office and staff now sits immediately near the oval theatre or at the start of the building. If one enters the College from Kutcheri street and moves up on the mound the first room with a porch is that of the Principal.

The College has a big Library, containing thousands of books. There is also a well-stocked Museum of apparatus and a good collection of Minerals, rocks and folios, presented by the Geological Department of the Government. (some material was also transferred from the Lahore Museum in the very early years.)

Two Boarding Houses before partition was one for Hindus and the other for Muslims. The old Presbyterian Church near the College had been acquired and converted into a gymnasium for the College. The old Dawk Bangalow adjoining the College, was reconstructed as a residence for the Principal or Vice-Principal and new out-houses for the College were also built. The unsightly waste land behind the College compound was levelled as a cricket-ground.

The College Union Club held weekly meetings for debates at each of which one of the Professors, or Assistant Professors presided. Subjects of literary and practical interest were discussed at these meetings. The members also had a Club and a a Reading-room on the tables of which the leading English and Indian Journals were always to be found. The Union Club was maintained by private subscriptions, and, with the amounts collected, the club was able to hold its various athletic sports and play frequent matches. After 1947 lot of accommodation has been added. This includes new blocks on the northeastern side of the old building and a large double storey building towards Oriental and Law College. With its becoming autonomous it is learnt that plans are afoot to declare it a Degree awarding institution.

It may be added that in the year 1994 this College was made autonomous with a Board of Governors. The College now formulates its own policies in respect of academics and other activities including financial matters.

THE DISTRICT COURTS

This building is situated on the Lower Mall, on the high ground opposite the Government College Lahore. The masonry throughout is of the best description, faced with dressed bricks; the moldings over pillars, arches, doors and windows being in cut bricks.

The principal facade is 233 feet in length, the breadth being 61½ feet. This part is double-storeyed, the lower 18½ feet, and the upper 17 feet in height. The wings, which have a single storey only, are each 166 x 51 feet by 18½ feet in height.

In the middle of the southern line is the Deputy Commissioner's Court-room; and on either side of it are the English and Persian Offices. To the left are the Assistant and Extra Assistant Commissioner's Court and to the right the Treasury Office and the Pension Pay Office. Towards the west of the courtyard is the District Treasury, and to the east the District and the Police Mal Khana, Police Office, Nazir's Office, the Office of the District Superintendent of Police and the Courts of Extra Assistant Commissioners.

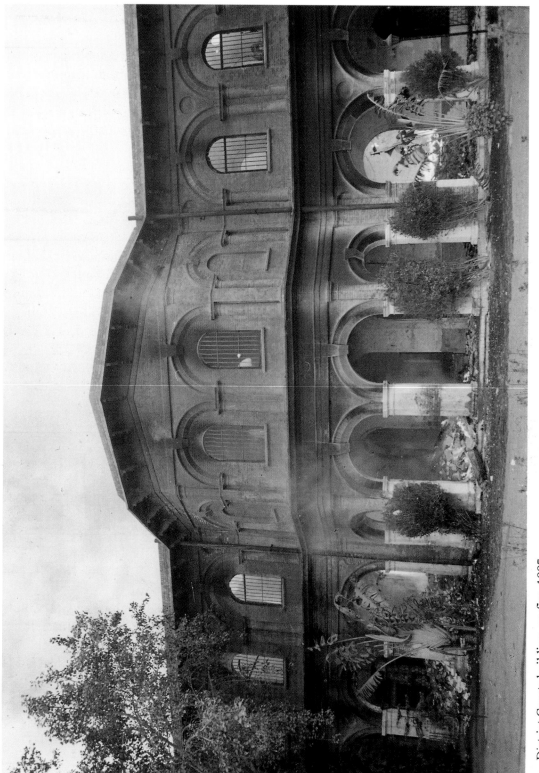

District Courts building, on fire, 1997

The floors of the upper rooms were used as Record rooms, the record-keeper's room being above the Deputy Commissioner's Court Room.

A masonry staircase obtains access to the upper floor in one of the rooms at the back of the Deputy Commissioner's court room. The main outer cornice is of red-sand stone properly cut and supported on corbels of the same description.

The area covered by the building is 32,564.5 superficial feet and the cost was Rs.95,420-8-5.

A block on the eastern side of the existing old block was constructed by Government in the year 1993. The pleaders were allowed separate space for their offices. The new block follows the same kind of structure but not really exact. The details and main contours of building are generally the same but quality wise it hardly matches the old construction.

The District Courts, since the inception of British rule in Lahore in 1849, had held a sanctity and were the symbol of maintenance of Law and Order. An unfortunate incident, which took place in early 1998, was the burning of the District Court complex. There was a sectarian trouble in a local graveyard allegedly by Sipa Sahaba who killed over a dozen people. The Shia community took out a protest march, which started from Mochi Gate. They damaged public property on the roadside and violent mob also set on fire the District Court's old building. The Deputy Commissioner's Office and the entire old block was seen ablaze. The 150 years historical record, was all burnt. This buried history and made the authority and sanctity of Law a laughing stock of the street urchins.

THE LAHORE HIGH COURT

Before discussing about the building of the High Court, it is necessary to very briefly detail the background of the coming into being of a Chief Court in Lahore. The Board of Administration was invested with plenary authority and control in all Departments. As agents and representatives of the Governor General in matters of Civil Judicature and police they had the powers conferred upon them of Dewanee and Nizamat Adwalet.

The annexation of Punjab was followed by the creation of a Board of Administration on 31st March, 1849 having joint responsibility in all important matters, but otherwise each having separate charge of the Political, Revenue and Judicial administration respectively in the territory. The Board had powers of a Saddar Court of Judicature and a Saddar Board of Revenue. The country was divided into Divisions, the Divisions into Districts, and the Districts into Tehsils. The Divisions were under the charge of Commissioner, who also acted as Superintendents of Police and Revenue and exercise appellate powers in civil and criminal cases. The Districts were controlled by Deputy Commissioners who also

District Courts building, after restoration 1998

acted as Magistrates and Collectors. They were provided with Assistant and Extra Assistant Commissioners. The Extra Assistant Commissioners also acted as Assistant Magistrates and Deputy Collectors. The Tehsils were supervised by Assistant and Extra Assistant Commissioners, but were otherwise governed in some small measure by the Karders (subsequently termed Tehsildars) who constituted the Courts of the lowest tier regarding petty, civil and criminal cases.

In the files of Criminal Law a Penal Code known as The Punjab Crimes Act was the first instrument to be applied in the Province. Petty Courts in the Tehsils to deal with petty cases were created. For intricate matters the Courts of the Magistrates and Sessions were set up, with the Court of the Commissioner at the apex as the highest Appellate Court. In the Civil Jurisdiction, Revenue Officers were given the authority to hear cases pertaining to land property.

In 1853 the Board of Administration was abolished and the Chief Commissionership was established with John (later Lord) Lawrence as Chief Commissioner, and two Principal Commissioners separately appointed for Judicial and Administrative work. The Judicial Commissioner was the Chief Judge of appeal and his Court was the final appellate court; and he also held some other portfolios. On 1st January, 1859, the whole administration of the Province was entrusted to the Lieutenant-Governor. In the realm of Criminal Law, a new Penal Code and Criminal Procedure Code were applied in 1862 followed inter alia by the transfer of heinous cases for trial to the Court of Sessions in 1865. In the Civil Jurisdiction, a code called the Punjab Civil Code was applied to the Province in 1853-54 ; this consisted of a complete set of rules and orders issued in the past covering among others substantive civil law, principles of procedure, matters regarding local customs and personal law, with comments thereon. It was strictly a Departmental Manual for the guidance of officers and was drawn up by the Judicial Commissioner.

This state of affairs would have continued for sometime, but for an objection raised by Sir Barnes Peacock in 1861 that the Government could not make laws for the Non-Regulation provinces by mere circulars and executive orders. He opined that the first of such orders made by Lord Dalhousie as related to the period of emergency in 1849 had the force of law, on the doctrine that they were Acts of State, but that subsequent orders issued after the country had settled down to an era of peace could not be covered by that doctrine and had to be passed through the medium of a Legislative Council. The opinion aroused a general doubt as to whether or not any law at all could be said to have existed in the Punjab and whether the whole series of departmental instructions issued by the Government under the Board of Administration were not one continuous series of illegal acts. To cover up the infirmity, a provision was made in the Indian Councils Act in 1861 clothing with legal sanction all laws, orders and regulations hitherto made for the Non-Regulation provinces by the Governor-General or by a Lieutenant-Governor. This was a temporary solution and did close the issue for a short time, but as we shall see later, doubts arose again and invited legal attention in 1867-70.

In 1865 an important Act was framed, namely. The Punjab Courts Act, XIX of 186. By the provisions of this Act, inter alia seven classes of Courts were brought into being in the Civil Jurisdiction, starting from the Court of the Tehsildar at the bottom to the Court of the Judicial Commissioner at the top. Suits relating to land revenue, rents and produce from the land were transferred to the Civil Courts from the Revenue Courts. Thus, leaving aside the Judicial Commissioner all the subordinate officers who were not only judicial officers but administrative and revenue officers as well.

By 1864, the necessity of expanding the judicial machinery became necessary. In December, 1864, Mr. Cust introduced into the Governor-General's Council a Bill for the formation of the Chief Court of the Punjab. The Bill having officially come to the attention of the Judicial Commissioner, Mr. A. A. Roberts, the Judicial Commissioner immediately recorded his views and opinion on the said Bill and forwarded it along with his letter dated 20th January, 1865, to the Secretary to the Government of the Punjab. Mr. A. A. Roberts took exception to that portion of the Bill which provided a reference of cases to the High Court of Judicature at Calcutta where there was disagreement between the two Judges of the Chief Court (under certain stated conditions). By a subsequent letter dated 29th March, 1865, the Judicial Commissioner pointed out to the Secretary that as the Report of the Select Committee on the Bill had not yet come under the consideration of the Governor-General's Legislative Council, a copy of his correspondence should be sent to the Government of India for their attention. Accordingly, on 30th March, 1865, the Judicial Commissioner's views were transmitted to the Home Department of the Government of India by the Punjab Government. Unfortunately, it seems the views did not reach the Government of India in time to give the Council or the Select Committee sufficient time in hand to cogitate or reflect on them with care and satisfaction. Thus, when the Chief Court Act, XXIII of 1865, received the assent of the Governor General on 17th April 1865 it did not provide for the changes that the Judicial Commissioner so staunchly advocated. But then, as fate would have it, the Chief Court Act, though enacted, had a short life. Shortly after the Governor-General granted his assent to the passing of the Act, the Law Officers of the Crown intimated that as the Act had been passed, before the Secretary of State's sanction, conveyed in his dispatch of the 17th March, 1865, was received by the Government of India, the Act had no force of law. It was therefore deemed expedient to re-enact the law. The Government of India, intimated that necessary steps for the re-enactment of the Bill had been taken and that the new Act would be passed into law on the 16th February 1866 and would come into operation on the following day.

The Chief Court Act, IV of 1866, received the assent of the Governor-General on 16th February, 1866, and came into operation on 17th February, 1866 in Punjab. It was of further interest that under Section 2 of Act IV of 1866 Mr. A. A. Roberts, Judicial Commissioner, automatically became a Judge of the Chief Court and that Mr. Charles Boulnois, Barrister-at-Law, had been appointed as the second Judge.

The Lieutenant-Governor of the Punjab Commissioned Mr. A. A. Roberts to receive the statutory declaration oath from Mr. Charles Boulnois, and commissioned the latter to receive the declaration from the former. Mr. A. A. Roberts, reported to the Government on 19th, February 1866, that he had received the declaration of Mr. Charles Boulnois under Act IV of 1866 and that both the Judges had entered on the execution of their duties under the said Act. By further letter of even date, Mr. A. A. Roberts, wrote to the secretary of the Government of the Punjab, that the Judges proposed, subject of the sanction of the Lieutenant-Governor, the appointment of Mr. J. W. Smyth to be the Registrar of the Chief Court. The next day, i.e. on 20th February, 1866, Mr. Charles Boulnois wrote to the Secretary to the Government of the Punjab, to confirm that he had received that declaration of Mr. A. A. Roberts under Act, IV of 1866, which he was submitting. By virtue of seniority, Mr. Justice A. A. Roberts took rank and precedence over Mr. C. Boulnois in the Court as Senior Judge. Mr. C. Boulnois may therefore be treated as the first permanent puisne Judge. Mr. C. Boulnois was, previous to his appointment as a Judge of the Chief Court, a Judge of the Small Causes Court, Calcutta.

The Chief Court Act, IV of 1866, constituted the Chief Court of the Punjab as the ultimate Court of Appeal from the Civil and Criminal Courts in the province. The Chief Court was also vested with Extraordinary Original Civil Jurisdiction, Supervisory Jurisdiction over Subordinate Courts, and the power to try European British Subjects committed to it for trial in lieu of the High Court at Fort William in Bengal. This is how the structure of the judiciary developed in Lahore for the province which ultimately needed a proper premises and court to function.

The previous arrangement merged into the newly created set up and the Chief Court started evolving itself into a proper High Court. This evolution of judicial set up was necessary to completely take along the reader with the history of High Court.

THE HIGH COURT BUILDING

The Gazetteer of the Lahore states that the Civil Secretariat was erected in 1845, the Chief Court building in 1865 and the Financial Commissioner's Office in 1867. Actually there was no Chief Court designed building in 1865 but there is a rectangular commodious building in what is now A. C. S. Block, present Civil Secretariat, which, prior to the creation of the Chief Court in 1866, housed the Court and Offices of the Judicial and Financial Commissioners. Mr. A. A. Roberts was then the Judicial Commissioner of the Punjab and he had his Court and office there.

In August, 1865, correspondence was exchanged between Mr. A. A. Roberts, Judicial commissioner, Punjab and Mr. T. H. Thornton, Secretary to the Government of the Punjab, about the accommodation that would be required by the former with the establishment of the Chief Court. In that correspondence. Mr. A. A. Roberts stated that in addition to the accommodation occupied by him and his office, one Chamber for a second Judge, one large Court room and one room for the Deputy or Assistant Registrar would be required. Such accommodation, Mr. A. A. Roberts pointed out, existed in the rooms then occupied by the Financial Commissioner in the same building. On 13th February, 1866, Mr. T. H. Thornton, intimated to Mr. A. A. Roberts, that the Lieutenant-Governor had, with a view to affording the Chief Court the requisite accommodation, decided to temporarily vacate his office in the Secretariat buildings for the benefit of the Financial Commissioner, so that the Financial Commissioner could vacate his accommodation in favour of the Chief Court. By this date it was apparent, from advices from Calcutta, that the Chief Court would be established as from the 17th February, 1866, and that Mr. A. A. Roberts and Mr. Charles Boulnois would be the Senior Judge and Puisne Judge respectively of the new Court. Accordingly the Chief Court took over the accommodation in the whole building previously with the Judicial and the Financial Commissioners. The very fact that the road coming from North of secretariat, parallel to Lower Mall (between L.DA and Evaucee Trust office) is still named as Court Street, testifies that the Chief Court was in Scretariat and the road led into that was closed later. This was probably in 1958.

Today, the old Chief Court building houses the offices of the Finance Secretary and deputy Secretaries and subordinate staff of the Services & General Administration Department. There are two old blocks, both facing inwards, occupied by the Services & General Administration Department in the Civil Secretariat today. One is a large rectangular block and the other a thin long one running east to west; the thin long one is in the north and the other large one is in

Lahore High Court

the south. Both these blocks are located in the north-western portion of the Civil Secretariat. Of these two blocks, the older one is in the south and the thin long one, where presumably the Financial commissioner used to sit, in the north block. The older block is the one which was previously the Chief Court of the Punjab: its eastern portion comprises one large hall, which was the main court room, but which now has been partitioned into smaller rooms.

The plans for the erection of the new Punjab Chief Court building started in 1877. By 1879 correspondence was well under way between the Public Works Secretariat and the High Court with regard to the lay-out of the premises. In January, 1880 the question as regards the selection of the site of the new Chief Court buildings was taken up formally. The Secretary Punjab, P.W.D. suggested to the Registrar of Chief Court that the new building should be constructed on the open piece of ground between the Agra Bank and the old Bank Club buildings.

The old Agra Bank building is now the Central Police Office II on Bank Road. This proposed site of the new Chief Court would therefore be the open ground now lying between Bank Road, Lower Mall and Church Road, that is to say, the open ground opposite the Civil Secretariat, now belonging to the Government College Lahore.

The whole area south of the Mall from the Town Hall to the present Tollinton Market, and bounded by Library Road, part of Church Road, Bank Road and the Lower Mall was (in 1880) an open area. This was a part of the Anarkali Division and this is the southern portion of the Anarkali Gardens referred to by the Registrar of the Chief Court. The place a little to the south of the Museum. Assuming Court House Hotel was somewhere where the P.W.D. Secretariat now is, the place a little to the south where the Museum now stands would fit in correctly with the description.

The same month, it appears, the matter regarding the site was referred to the Lieutenant Governor who opined that the original site proposed opposite Mr. Smyth's house between the Multan Road and the Mall should be considered. An old map from the "Plan of the city and Environs of Lahore" (1867) shows this proposed site: it is the triangular plot between Multan Road, Cust Road and Lake Road, namely, where the University ground now is. This is the site suggested by the Governor.

However, this is not the place where the new Chief Court was built. Unfortunately, the correspondence between the P.W.D. and the Chief Court relating to the final site is not available, but, the Chief Court was finally constructed on the Upper Mall near the General Post Office.

The Gazetteer of the Lahore District for the year 1883-84 states that the foundations of the new Chief Court were sunk in 1882-83 and brought to plinth level and that the collection of materials for the superstructure was taken in hand, but that the work was then at a standstill for want of funds.

It was not until September, 1887, that the Chief Court building, though not totally complete, was ready for occupation and steps were initiated by the High Court for the Lieutenant Governor of the Punjab to formally declare the premises open in November that year, but in the absence of any further reference, it is not possible to state whether any ceremony was held or not. However, it is, clear that by September, 1887, the Punjab Chief Court shifted from Civil Secretariat to its new premises on the Mall, where it stands today. The old building was handed over to the Financial Commissioner.

K. B. Syed Muhammad Latif in his monumental work "LAHORE- Its History, Architecture, Remains and Antiquities" (1892 Edition) states inter alia the following about the new Punjab Chief Court Building:-

"The details of the superstructure were designed by Mr. Brossington, a skilful architect, and the work was executed under the supervision of Mr. J. E. Hilton, Ex-Engineer, who completed it in March, 1889 the total cost being Rs.3,21,837".

The whole structure, which is in the form of a quadrangle is built of solid bricks, in lime mortar, with all moldings, cornices and projections of specially molded bricks and the arch-fillings of terra cotta trelliswork. One great peculiarity of the work was that no chipping of bricks was allowed.

The front arches of the Judges verandah and the porch outside, and portions of the main towers, are built of Nowshera marble, with marble trelliswork. The roof of the main court room is of double Allahabad tiling, and that of the rest, flat filed and terraced. The floor of the central hall is of marble, and that of the rest of hexagonal tiles. The roof are of Deodar wood and the doors of teakwood, with carved devices on the stiles as well as on the frames. The Waiting Hall, Court Rooms and the Judges' Chambers are furnished with a dado of encaustic tiles of various patterns laid in Portland cement.

The front row of rooms, to the north, consists of a central hall, 55' x 35', approached through a large porch by a broad flight of marble steps. To the right and left of this hall are spacious Bench rooms, each 55' x 40' and in the wings beyond, four smaller chambers for four judges, with retiring-rooms and bath-rooms, a private passage leading direct to the Bench rooms from the chambers.

On the west, facing the Accountant-General's Office, rooms are provided for the Jury, the Bar, Bar Library, Deputy Registrar, the Translating Department Readers' Room, and the Superintendent of the Vernacular Office.

In the block opposite, on the eastern side, there are the Registrar's Room, Committee Room, the Court Library, the English Office, and rooms for the Head Assistant and subordinate clerks.

On the south, large rooms, 35' x 25', for the English and Persian Records, form the two wings, with rooms for the Record-keepers and the Treasurer, leaving a gateway in the centre, forming the carriage entrance to the quadrangle.

On all four sides, both inside the quadrangle and round the outside of the entire building, are spacious verandahs, bringing the whole of the courts and offices into direct communication with one another.

The two towers, which form the central feature, are carried up square for one-half the height, above which, they are fluted and have bold cones thrown out, somewhat after the model of those of the Kutab Minar at Delhi. The total height of the central towers to the vane is 95 feet and that of the two at the end 72 feet. The end towers contain circular staircases leading to the top.

The verandahs are, in all cases, carried up to the full height of the inner walls, the arches being nearly two thirds filled in with trellis, or tracery work in terra cotta, to keep out the glare.

All the verandahs of the principal front are surrounded by a massive cornice of the old Arabic honeycomb pattern.

A marble fountain in the midst of the court-yard laid out with green shrubs, contributes materially to the picturesqueness of the whole structure.

According to an old Register of Buildings maintained by the Public Works Department for the year 1915, the Chief Court in 1889 comprised of the main building, Senior Reader's room, Translators' barracks, out-houses for menial staff, Police Lines, Cook House and Latrines. Other structures are also shown but against later years.

The new Chief Court was originally designed to provide accommodation for three Judges, but during the progress of the work certain additions were made to provide for a Court of four Judges. Before the Court came to be occupied, the number of Judges had been raised to four and within two years after the Court moved into the new premises, there were six Judges. An expanding array of work and an increase in the number of Judges, raised problems of accommodation. There was no space for the Translation Department and the Printed Record Branch, which had grown alarmingly within a matter of just a few years.

From 1890, correspondence was well under way with regard to major additions and alterations to the Chief Court building. It was proposed that year to add an upper storey over the two wings of the main building, but the proposal was dropped for next year in favour of another suggested by the Public Works Department, which was to add a new block to the rear or southern part of the main building. The estimated cost of Rs.83,398/- for the latter proposal , approved by the Judges, was submitted to the Government for administrative sanction, but was refused; the Lieutenant-Governor remarking that not more than Rs.30,000/- or at the most Rs.35,000/- could be earmarked for a plain block to be erected at the back of the Chief Court building. In subsequent correspondence exchanged between the representatives of a sanguine Bench and a parsimonious Lieutenant Governor, the matter was aborted and nothing further happened.

By 1893, seven sets of quarters in Mr. Gouldsbury's Chambers adjacent to the Court (presumably on Fane or Turner Road, but unidentifiable now), had come to be rented by the Chief Court for accommodating the office staff. Two rooms on the western side of the Chief Court were also constructed that year to serve as Suitor's Sheds, for the suitors waiting for the Deputy Registrar or their cases before the two Judges whose chambers were located in the west wing of the Chief Court building. Simultaneously, in the month of August, the Suitor's Sheds in the south, which had originally been built when the Chief Court had been constructed, but not being properly shaded, had been used by the office, was converted to provide rooms for accommodation to the Chief Court Bar Association, to relieve the congestion in the main building. The three rooms (inclusive of the Jury Room) in the western wing of the main building vacated by the Bar Association were made available for the Court's Offices. The Suitor's Sheds referred to here are today the rooms occupied by the High Court Bar Clerks' Association; the newly constructed Associations Rooms referred to above are today the premises now occupied by the Advocate General, the Superintendents, Establishment and Administration, the Treasurer, etc., and the three rooms given up by the Bar in the main building, as stated above, are the Court Rooms.

In 1895, a Carriage Shed was built in the open space of ground lying vacant on the western corner of the Chief Court compound, to provide temporary shelter to carriages coming into the premises.

In 1902, the pressure for additional accommodation was again felt. The Lieutenant-Governor was invited that year, who came to see the Chief Court premises to see what arrangements could be made for granting additional accommodation. Subsequent to the Governor's departure, it was decided to lodge a formal request with the Government to carry out certain minor works in the main building and to provide for one additional Court room and four Judges Chambers and for the addition of three rooms to the barracks at the back, two on the side behind the Police Guard at the south-east corner of the barracks and one on the south-west corner. By December that year it was also decided in a Judges Meeting that the Government be requested to construct two blocks on either side of the southern entrance to the quadrangle to provide four rooms and two toilets in all (two rooms and a toilet on either side) with verandah, so that three of them could be given over to the Bar. It was further decided that the two outer rooms of the Bar Association Building (Old outer block) be extended and a verandah be placed on both sides and in front of the same.

The extensions to the southern entrance to the quadrangle were completed in 1905. The Chief Court Bar Association shifted from the old outer block and entered their new premises in the southern entrance to the quadrangle. The cost of construction of the new Bar Rooms was Rs.16,887/- The minor works in the main building and the addition of three rooms to the barracks was also completed in 1905, but it seems that the extra rooms were all added to the western portion of the barrack. It may be mentioned here that in December 1903, two additional Refreshment Rooms with verandah for use by the native officials of the Chief Court were also completed. They were constructed at the back of the then Resfreshment Rooms which were situated behind the Servants Quarters in the Chief Court compound.

In 1909 steps were taken to provide for additional Record Room accommodation. In that year, the arrangement that existed consisted of storing records in different places in the main building away from the godown intended for that purpose. It was therefore decided to add one room to the rooms occupied by the clerks to the west of the Bar Association building (old outer block) and to convert the Clerks' Rooms into Record Rooms. The proposed new Record Room was added and alteration to the Clerks' Rooms was completed within a few months. The year had not run out when the Section Branch of the Chief Court, which was located in the old Accountant General's Office, was requested to shift from those premises in order to make accommodation for the Divisional Judge of Gujranwala and his establishment. It was therefore decided to construct on the premises a new block of four rooms in such a way that further rooms could be added later, but in order to secure Government's administrative sanction, the Judges decided to content themselves by requesting for a cheaper alternative, namely, by requesting for sanction for the construction of two rooms only for the Section Translators. The said rooms were constructed in 1911-12. The old Register of Buildings also speaks of a "Section Translators Room" having been built in 1911-12.

Under the Government of India Act 1915, the question as of the conversion of the Chief Court into a High Court assumed manifestations of reality. The proposal was accepted by the Secretary of State in 1916. The Great War delayed it but by 1918 the matter became certain. In view of this pending move, the remodelling and extension of the Chief Court building to provide for the extra accommodation was required and which was long overdue became a necessity.

Plans were discussed that October and approved by the High Court in February 1919.

It was proposed to have two new blocks to constitute two symmetrical wings on the northeast and northwest corners of the main building, forming, with the main building, three sides of a quadrangle open towards the Mall. Each block was to contain two Bench Rooms and three Chambers with retiring rooms and lavatories. There was also to be a room over each porch, to be used as a Meeting Room or Waiting Room. Administrative sanction for the incurring of the estimated expenditure of Rs.4,97,300/- was also demanded. Though the Government granted its approval in December, 1919, funds were made available in piecemeal. Rs.1,00,000/- was granted in the budget for 1919-20 but was subsequently withdrawn. The said figure was again re-allowed and budgeted for 1920-21. Subsequent grants permitted the balance expenditure to be incurred and by the end of 1923 the two blocks were ready. The Opening Ceremony of the two new blocks was held on the 23rd October, 1923, when His Excellency Lord Reading, Viceroy of India formally declared the wings open.

In 1929, the question of more accommodation again cropped up. The High Court requested the Public Works Department to provide plans for elaborate alternations to the main building, addition of certain wings and a separate block for the Court's Offices, etc. The same were prepared and delivered to the High Court, the estimated expenditure being shown as Rs.10,00,000/-. Considering that so large a sum would be involved on patch work extensions, etc., the judges requested the Consulting Architect to submit an estimate for the dismantling of the whole of the quadrangle and the building of a suitable three storied block to accommodate the whole of the High Court's office and Court requirements. The Consulting Architect submitted the revised plan for the three storied structure, with the estimate of expenditure running into Rs.18,00,000/- Both the proposals were submitted to the Government, but the Government indicated its inclination in favour of the first scheme which provided for additions and alterations

The same year Government gave administrative approval to the estimated expenditure of Rs.9.32.030/- for the execution of the 'Patch Work' Scheme. The full amount was never budgeted. In 1933, only Rs.78,017/- was provided to meet the expenditure for the construction of the new Bar Association Rooms and extension of Chambers "L" and "M" then occupied by Curie and Abdul Rashid JJ. This amount was duly applied. The Bar shifted to its new building in 1935. The remaining works to be executed remained in abeyance and by May 1936 the same were given up by the High Court on the ground that there had been a reduction in the number of Judges. In order to utilize this saving, the High Court side by side requested for administrative approval for installation of a cooling system.

In August 1936, the Sessions Court shifted from its old premises adjacent to the High Court to the Lower Mall. Four out-houses previously attached with the Sessions Court thus were transferred to the High Court. In October that year, the Legal Remembrancer's Office also shifted from its old premises adjacent to the High Court and six menial quarters previously attached with that office, were also transferred to the High Court.

An immediate need for further accommodation became felt when 4 to 5 additional Judges were expected to be appointed for Lahore in 1964. To provide for their immediate accommodation, three rooms had to be converted into four Chambers and one Chamber was constructed in the Court Room of Mr. Justice Sajjad Ahmad Jan. Side by side, plans were discussed with the P.W.D authorities and the Consulting Architect for the construction of another wing in the main building, contiguous to the present General Branch, corresponding to the two blocks already existing in the north-east and north-west of the main building (which were built in 1923). In April, 1966, the High Court submitted the necessary schedule of new Expenditure amounting to Rs.7,72,000/- for the major extensions, for provision of funds in the Budget for 1966-67, but the Government only provided Rs.5,00,000/- in the said Budget. Consequently the High Court was constrained to renew its request for the balance of Rupees Two Lacs odd for provision in the Budget for 1967-68. The plans prepared for the proposed new extension show that the layout of the new block was similar to the two blocks already existing, except that the first storey will contain equivalent accommodation to that existing on the ground floor.

The present Supreme Court is located in one of the borrowed wing of the High Court. In 1959, the Supreme Court did make some attempt to acquire independent premises for itself and the name of the "Patiala House Estate" (opposite the Governor's residence on the Upper Mall) was even suggested in that connection, but the exorbitant costs incidental to its acquisition compelled the Central Government to drop the matter in its exploratory stage. The price of the land comprising the "Patiala House Estate" was then stated as Rs.20,000/- per kanal, a sum which was considered too high. Little was it realized that by 1966 the value would jump over by a hundred per cent. The "Patiala House Estate" is now the site of three Ministers' Bungalows and Hotel Pearl Continental. However, the Federal Court and Supreme Court, having their seat at Lahore, have never had any independent accommodation; they have all along been accommodated in borrowed portions of the High Court Building.

The above is a brief account of the various substantive and major additions and alterations made in the High Court building from time to time, not to speak of the innumerable different minor alterations and adjustments made which have not been taken into account in this brief article.

These days the repairs and restoration work on the High Court building is on. There was a comment in the Press that the repair work, of Lahore High Court by ordinary contractors not trying, to preserve the original architecture may spoil the beauty of one of the historic buildings of Lahore.

Architecturally a combination of Indian and Arabic style, the LHC building was constructed in 1889, designed by architect Brossington. The building has been completely in coherence with the ambience and culture of the city. There are two minarets and two bastions on the front corners, 95 and 72 feet high.

These days work is being done on the domes of the minarets. New marble tiles are replacing the old marble, however the repairs have destroyed the original globular shape of the domes. Also the original marble was mellow, which is being replaced with brand new white marble.

It is learnt that an estimated Rs.150,000 to Rs.200,000 will be spent on the new tiles of Naushera marble quality. "It is not an easy task to fit marble tiles of one square foot in the roundness of a dome, and only an expert can do it properly," said a mason working there. "It looks as if rice-paper is being pasted there," remarked an expert of Conservation Society, commenting on the replacement of the marble tiles. He thought there was no need to replace the marble tiles. "A hundred year old building should look a hundred years old. There was no need for such cosmetic repair". He called the project work by contractors without consultation of specialists. "Not much money is required on the restoration of old buildings." The Lahore High Court and some other buildings on The Mall are listed under the Punjab Special Premises Act 1986, which is meant for the conservation and protection of these buildings. The present repair work is totally against the law."There is no awakening of the law," said an architect. The prevailing conditions within the LHC premises are also pathetic, the green lot has become a dumping ground where a heap of waste has been placed. "Probably they want to use it as fertilizers," noted a lawyer. The road on the premises has become a thoroughfare being used by all and sundry as a short cut to Turner Road. The premises has become a parking lot where lawyers and other people park their vehicles on either side of the road. "It does not give a pleasant view of the building from The Mall," commented another concerned citizen. Some people have installed photo-stat machines there, making it a congested place.

In addition to repairs and restoration a new/additional accommodation is under construction. The entire architecture of the Lahore High Court building will wear a new look after the completion of a new building for judges' chambers, being constructed on the Turner Road side of the Lahore High Court.

Keeping in view the shortage of court rooms and increase in judges in the Lahore High Court this project was recommended in 1992 by the Chief Justice. However, the project started in 1993 at an estimated Rs.75 million.

The addition to the Lahore High Court building will be completed by the end of this year, claimed an officer of the buildings department. The new building will have 12 court rooms and judges' chambers. The judges' chamber building will have five floors including a basement, lower ground floor, ground floor, first and second floors. This building will house a library, dispensary and a cafeteria for judges, lawyers and litigants.

To maintain the historical building of the Lahore High Court it was also decided in 1992 to fix marble plates on all domes of the building that these had fallen off. The stone plates of two of four domes in the front of the Lahore High Court building were damaged but had been replaced from time to time temporarily. The Lahore High Court suggested replacement of damaged and odd-looking tiles from the domes to maintain the historical beauty and grandeur of the building.

A fountain is also being made and it will have 46 nozzles and one carambola, near the Attorney General's office besides new parking lot reserved for vehicles of lawyers entering from the GPO gate of the Lahore High Court building. The fountain will cost from Rs.150,000, to Rs.200,000, said an officer of Punjab Buildings Department dealing with the construction work of the Lahore High Court building.

PUNJAB UNIVERSITY

The beginning of the modern education system started almost immediately after annexation. With the efforts of Mr. D. F. Mcleod, Lt. Governor of Punjab and with the establishment of Punjab University College in 1869 things moved quickly indeed. The establishment of a full-fledged Education Department in 1854 made a history of education in India on the issuance of famous dispatch by Sir Charles Wood. In the Punjab, Department of Public Instructions was established in 1856. In 1858 it was proposed that a Central College be founded at Lahore. In April, 1861 Lord Halifax (Sir Charles Wood) approved the formation of a school of a superior order at Lahore which would serve as the nucleus of the College sanctioned in 1856. In 1853 an Anatomical School was established at Mian Mir which was proposed to be converted into a Medical School by Mr. C. M. Smith, Civil Surgeon, Lahore. The Medical College was, infact, opened at Lahore in October 1860. In 1863 Government College, Lahore was established with Dr. Leitner as its Principal. The Forman Christian College was established in 1866. The colleges established in Lahore were attached with the University of Calcutta.

Punjab University Hall

There was a strong dissatisfaction expressed on this account mainly on the basis of distance from the Centre which was like London to Rome. Further the curriculum and method of examination of University of Calcutta were unsuitable. Dr. Leitner, the Principal of the College alongwith other Scholars felt about the narrowness and the superficiality of curricula of that University and founded Anjaman-e-Punjab, a vernacular literary society on 1.1.1865 for revival of ancient oriental learning, advancement of popular knowledge, literary and scientific discussions and association of local learned classes with Government officers. The Society established free public Library and Reading Room. The Society proposed to establish an Oriental University in Lahore. They also approached the Governor in this behalf. The Governor sent up a proposal for the Oriental University in 1866. Later a strong committee for establishment of Lahore University moved a more practicable proposal in May 1867. The Government of India, however, expressed its sympathy but advised for improving the Government College, Lahore with enhanced grant. In 1868, the Governor again took up the matter with the Government of India. After lengthy correspondence and insistence of the Governor, Punjab University College was established on 8-12-1869 which was to promote the diffusion of European sciences as far as possible through medium of vernacular language.

Lt. Governor Sir Donald Mcleod as its Chairman held the first meeting of the Senate of the Punjab University College on 11-1-1870. The Oriental School was also attached with Punjab University College in December 1870 (also founded in 1870). The Punjab University College and Oriental College were a pair of precocious but delicate infants, with precarious means of life and uncertain habitation. The University College was a teaching and examining body as well as a learned society. It had a Senate and a consulting body in all matters of public instructions. In October, 1871 the first examination was held for award of certificates of matriculation. Very rich donations were made by the local Chiefs including Maharajas of Kashmir, Patiala and Kapurthala. In 1876 Government College Delhi was closed and transferred to Government College, Lahore. In Lahore an Educational Conference was held in 1871 in which the question propounded was 'is Punjab ready for a University of its own'?. The Conference answered strongly in affirmative requesting local and Supreme Governments conferring Punjab College the powers to grant degrees. Lot of efforts were made by Anjaman-e-Punjab, and the gentry, headed by Dr. Lietner for establishment of University at Lahore. The Governor General considered this request and forwarded it to the Secretary of State for recommending the case. Lord Lytton had received this request at a very favourable time. The success of Afghan policy in which Punjab-Frontier forces took a prominent part convinced the Viceroy to support the

Punjab Exhibition building 1863

Finishing Touches being given to Punjab Exhibition Hall (later Tollinton Market), a photograph probably taken in Dec. 1863

Lahore Central Museum 1868

proposal of influential persons of the Punjab. Viscount Cranbrook in the Foreign Office (Secretary of State) considered the Viceroy's dispatch and sanctioned the introduction of a Bill in the Legislative council to transform the Punjab University College into a University to confer degrees in Arts. In February, 1880 the Government of India asked the Punjab Government for supporting material to put forward the Bill.

The Punjab University Act No. XIX of 1882 was published in the Gazette of India dated 7-10-1882 and the Punjab University was formally called into existence on 14-10-1882 by a Notification issued by Sir Charles Aitchison, Lt. Governor of Punjab in pursuance of provisions of the act. The first meeting of the Senate of the Punjab University was held at Barnes Court, Simla, on 14-10-1882. The Punjab University held inaugural convocation on 18-11-1882. Since the inauguration of the University College Dr. Lietner was Registrar and he continued in that capacity in the University until November, 1885. From the beginning the University College attempted direct teaching in two spheres. Firstly of learning in classical and vernacular languages and secondly professional training in Law. The Oriental College continued two sections i.e. Oriental Languages and Literature and of general knowledge conveyed through media of Urdu and Hindi. Classes in vernacular civil engineering were held at College of Lala Ganga Ram. These classes of civil engineering were transferred in June, 1888 to the Mayo School of Arts where they continued for a very long period.

In 1886 Faculty of Medicine prepared regulations for the degrees of Bachelor and Doctor of Medicines. The control and administration of Medical College, however, continued to vest in the Government. Under Act of 1904 affiliating system was adopted and various colleges were attached to the University. The Punjab University Hall on the Mall was founded on January 4, 1905, The Lt. Governor, Sir Charles Riwaz, laid the foundation stone. In 1910 the Syndicate acquired a site in proximity to the Senate Hall for erection of a Library designed by Ram Singh. The foundation stone of the library was laid on 27-1-1911. By 1910 at least ten institutions had been affiliated to the Punjab University. The University also established certain Departments for direct higher teaching in early 20s. Various Departments gradually emerged and Chemistry was one of them. In 1919 the University proposed to have a Chemical Laboratory which was constructed and completed in 1922-23 by plans and designs given by a Government architect – Mr. B. M. Sullivan. In 1920 the University decided to erect a suitable building for Oriental and Law College. It was in place of Convent building which had been acquired by the University in 1913. Law College building was erected in 1922 at a cost of Rs.1.00 lac towards which Rs.30,000/- were contributed by Maharaja of Kashmir. The Oriental College got a permanent Board in 1925 immediately behind

Law College. A hall was also constructed in between both of these institutions in 1926. Due to shortage of accommodation and rapid growth of University in 1926 a new and handsome Senate Hall was created, finished in roman style and named as Hailey Hall in honour of the distinguished governor and scholar Malcolm Hailey. The Hailey College of Commerce was established in 1927. The Montmorency Hall (in Law College was founded in 1930). The hostel behind Law College premises, one used by students of Law College, known as Woolner Hostel was built in the year 1930. Similarly Oriental College Hall now known as Shirani Hall was founded on October 1930.

The Punjab University continued to function at its premises on the Mall and Kutchery Road till late in 50s. It was, however, felt that the campus had fallen short of accommodation as due to direct teaching through various Departments it had expanded manifold. It was, therefore, decided to have new campus for the institution as the number of affiliated colleges had also arisen to 124. An area of about 10 Sq. Miles was given by the then Governor, West Pakistan – Malik Amir Muhammad Khan for the campus in the south of the city on the canal. The first building to be raised was an Auditorium. By now almost all the Departments including Law College and Commerce College have shifted to this new campus. A number of hostels have been provided and the University is almost residential. The entire structure is in western style and box type blocks have come up with no care and consideration for the local architectural traditions. Consequently the rooms and apartments are hot in the summer and cold in the winter. The University can hardly take a pride in owning any type of architecture. It is just accommodation and nothing else except for the beautiful location, which is on both sides of the canal and makes a picturesque view, with poplar trees planted on both sides of the canal. By now almost 95% of the offices and academic activities have shifted to the new campus and only one or two Departments i.e. Fine Arts Department and Chemical Technology are in occupation of the old campus, which can certainly boast of its classical style of architecture.

THE TOWN HALL

The Town Hall of Lahore City now known as Metropolitan Corporation Hall was known as the Victoria Jubilee Town Hall, which was declared open by His Royal Highness Prince Albert Victor, with a great ceremony on 3rd February 1890. It is a lofty building from the roof of which an extensive, but not very diversified, view is obtained of the surrounding parts of the city, the ascent being by a spiral staircase. The chief feature of the Hall is its lofty room on the second floor. The Hall, which has been built on the Oriental Principle is 80 feet in length, and 40

Town Hall, Lahore

feet in breadth. The general colouring is in shades of green and sage. The centres of the arches are beautifully decorated with stucco work in white plaster on a yellow ground. The doral paintings are in Venetian red. The Floor is laid with teak planks, nicely planned and polished in the usual way. The Hall is a place where the "wise and quiet debate", spoke His Royal Highness at the opening ceremony. The excellent floor also admits of its being used for dancing.

Outside the building, the fountain presented by Raja Harbans Singh constitutes a great attraction. The fountain is painted green, in imitation of bronze, and the four cupids on the pedestal are white. It is beautifully situated and the enclosure in front of the building, is surrounded by plants, and is intended to throw out jets in several designs.

This handsome building was begun in the year 1887, the foundation stone being laid by Sir Charles Aitchison, late Lieutenant-Governor of the Punjab. The building is dedicated to the joyful memory of the fiftieth year of the reign of Her Most Gracious Majesty the Queen Empress, and is used as a Town Hall and Local Fund Office. It had been built by the Municipal Engineer, Mr. Bull, after elegant designs were furnished by Mr. Pogson, a Madras Architect, and had cost Rs.60,000 in construction. Mr. Pogson was awarded a prize of Rs.500 for the best design out of many submitted.

THE AITCHISON COLLEGE

The Punjab Chiefs College, named after Sir Charles Aitchison, late Lieutenant-Governor of the Punjab, is the outcome of a movement which, originated in the suggestions made in 1869, by Captain Walter, Political Agent at Bhurtpur, took shape in the formation of the Mayo College at Ajmere, and the Rajkumar College at Kathiawar .

The germ of the Aitchison College was a school at Umballa where the wards of Court of the Umballa District were educated. This institution was founded in 1864, and was virtually a day-school; the boys living in detached houses of their own, and only attending the Superintendent's residence for the purpose of instruction. The enforcement of a common rule of life was under such difficult conditions, if not impossible; and the boys were so few in number –in 1886 the number was only 12 - that games could not be organized, and little benefit could be gained from social intercourse. The teaching establishment was limited to the Superintendent and two native assistants, who must have had considerable difficulty in dealing with boys of ages varying from about ten to twenty. As a result, the educational attainments of the Umballa wards seem to have compared unfavourably with those boys getting education at the ordinary Punjab Schools. In 1874 a proposal was made to widen the scope of the Umballa School, so as to make

Aitchison College

it available for boys living in other parts of the Punjab; but funds were not forthcoming, and it was not until 1882, when the Lieutenant-Governor, Sir Charles Aitchison, interested himself in the matter, that a systematic effort was made to develop the Wards School into a Chiefs College.

Sir Charles Aitchison, though keenly desirous of founding an institution for the sons of the Punjab aristocracy similar to the Colleges already existing at Ajmere and Rajkote for the Chiefs of Rajputana and Kathiawar, wisely refrained from imposing any ready-made scheme of his own. He contented himself at first with eliciting opinions, and trying to awaken the interest of the Chiefs and gentry of the Province. Correspondence on the subject began in 1882, and the plan hung fire until in 1884, when, at the request of the Local Government, Mr. Coldstream, the Commissioner of Umballa, submitted a set of "rules for the constitution and management of the Punjab Chiefs' School, Umballa." These rules may be regarded as the frame-work on which the Present constitution of the College is based. Control was to be vested in the "Principal and Headmaster," with a Committee of Management. The course of studies was to be submitted to the Director of Education for approval, and annual examinations were to be held by the Inspector of Schools. In addition to the teaching staff, Musahibs were to superintend the boys after school-hours. Those eligible for admission were defined as (1) wards of Court (2) relatives of Ruling Chiefs (3) youths of respectable families; a classification which has been retained, and which is noticeable as giving the Punjab Chiefs' College a less exclusive character than the name might imply. Fees were fixed at 12 per cent, on the income of wards of Court (the rate adopted in the Umballa School), and for other boys at Rs.50 monthly for each set of rooms.

The framing and circulating of the rules for the new institution was followed in 1885 by a Resolution in which the Lieutenant-Governor reviewed the progress of the scheme and sketched a programme for the future. "The school," he said, "which it is now proposed to be founded, should be a place where the young nobility of the Punjab will find in generous emulation full opportunity for the exercise of energies which are not too often allowed to lie dormant, and where they will undergo the discipline and receive the education necessary, in these days, to fit them for the positions of public usefulness to which from their social standing they are naturally called." After describing the scope and constitution of the proposed College, he appealed to the Chiefs and aristocracy of the Province for donations, promising that the Punjab Government would contribute a sum equal to that raised by subscriptions, in addition to a yearly grant-in-aid. The Maharaja of Patiala had already offered Rs.50,000. This munificent gift led to others: Rs.20,000 from the Raja of Kapurthala, Rs.10,000 from the Maharaja of Kashmir, and Rs.5,000 from the Raja of Faridkot : Rs.85,000 thus being subscribed to the College by the end of

1885. In 1886 the Nawab donated Rs.12,000, and many lesser sums were subscribed, the total amounting to over two lakhs of rupees in 1888, when a second appeal on behalf of the Building Fund of the College was issued. The Maharaja of Kashmir then supplemented his previous gift by Rs.25,000, Mian Ghulam Rasul of Peshawar gave Rs.10,000, and the Raja of Poonch, Rs.5,000 sums which rendered it possible to complete the main building and add a third block to the Boarding-houses. The total sum raised by private subscriptions amounted in the end to Rs.2,56,000, the bulk of which was contributed by Ruling Chiefs. Interest, and the contributions of the Government of India and the Punjab Government, brought the total available for the College Building Fund to Rs.4,82,100 ; all of which, except Rs.1,400, was expended by 1891. The College also received a free site of 150 acres from the Local Government.

Thus Sir Charles Aitchison's appeal for funds met with a liberal response. Opinions may differ as to the wisdom of spending all the money collected upon bricks and mortar. Rs.4,82,100 as an endowment for an Indian Eton,was not a huge amount and part at any rate might have been set aside as a provision for the future. A school without an endowment reserve fund is always tempted to economize on its teaching staff when the fee-income falls off – a policy which lowers its reputation and brings about a sense of insecurity. Expensive buildings, it may be added, entail corresponding expenditure in establishment and upkeep. That the Aitchison College has been able to pave its way is mainly due to two causes: first, the decision of the Punjab Government to give it an annual grant-in-aid and secondly, the foundation of thirty scholarships, a plan initiated by Sir Charles Aitchison in 1886. The interest accruing to the College from scholarship endowments and other savings was Rs.8,200, making, along with the grant-in-aid, an assured income of Rs.17,000 annually, enough to guarantee the services of a qualified teaching staff even if the income from fees diminished.

The history of the college as an organization may be said to date from the first meeting of the Committee of Management and the "Visitors" (now known as the Council), in January 1886. The main resolutions then adopted were that the new institution should be located at Lahore upon a site previously selected, adjoining the Mian Mir Road, and that steps should be taken to acquire the site, and to invite the submission of plans for the College Building.

The decision to substitute Lahore for Umballa was a foregone conclusion. The central position of the capital, along with its educational and social advantages, made it the natural home of an institution intended for the whole Province. The particular sites available at Lahore were reported on by a special committee at the end of 1885. Shahdara, on the banks of the Ravi, two miles from the city, had been at first proposed, and was recommended by the Sanitary Commissioner on account of the free drainage into the river-bed; but the land to the north of the Mian Mir Road was eventually preferred. The advantages of this site were reported in detail. It lay above the level of the irrigating channel, so that excessive flooding would be impossible, water having to be raised for cultivation - a recommendation by the way, which would not now hold good, canal-water having been brought on to the grounds from a higher level - and the irrigation channel referred to have a sufficient fall for the purpose of drainage. There was a practically impermeable stratum of clay below the surface soil, protecting the well water (reached at 24 feet) from surface pollution. The well-water was certified to be fit for drinking, and Municipal water was within easy reach, and could be laid on if desired. These points are worth enumerating as evidence that the College occupies as healthy a site as is obtainable in the Lahore Civil Station. The general health of the students fully bears out the judgment of the committee, serious illness being virtually unknown. A few cases of fever occur from time to time, but the boys appear on the whole to enjoy better health at school than at their homes, where they probably live in far less sanitary surroundings. From other points of view there is everything to be said for the present location of the College. Situated on the outskirts of the Civil Station, it adjoins Government House grounds, and is within easy reach of the Lawrence Gardens and the business parts of Lahore, while in the opposite direction there is open country and ample room for expansion. The neighbour of Mian Mir, which is only at a distance of two miles, makes it easy to arrange matches with the garrison, and to witness Assaults-at-arms and other military functions. The Government College (classes in which are attended by the senior students) and the other Colleges and schools of Lahore are all readily accessible. Invitations to garden parties at Government House and social gatherings else-where, which give the boys an opportunity of making the acquaintance of their elders, can be availed of without inconvenience. The Aitchison College, in short, has advantages of position which fall to the lot of few schools in India.

The next question which occupied the attention of the Managing Committee was the choice of a design for the College Building. Two of the designs sent in-those of Mr. Kipling and Bhai Ram Singh, of the Lahore School of Arts, and of Colonel Jacob, were partially approved of, and it was decided to combine them if possible. The School of Arts were offered an honorarium for the use of their design, and Colonel Jacob was asked to adapt it to his ground plan. Thus the elevation and the arrangement of rooms are by different hands. The joint design was finally accepted by the Committee at a meeting held in September of the same year (1886). Its picturesqueness is beyond dispute: the building is probably the most handsome of its kind in the Sub-Continent. The façade of the verandah with its interlaced Moorish arches, and the fine proportions and graceful outlines of the large hall command general admiration. On the other hand, the dome is dwarfed by the massiveness of the rest of the building, and the colouring detracts from the architectural ornament, red marble side by side with Lahore brick being an ineffective combination. Some writers comment that apart from aesthetic considerations, there are structural defects involving wastage of space and materials, the result of altering a ground plan so as to make it fit an ornamental design. The eastern portico, for instance, is an objectless appendage, the rooms required for the Principal and staff are cramped and difficult to access, and the class-rooms beneath the dome have been cut down to inconveniently large, as compared with the class-room accommodation. The plan, in short, bears evidence of practical utility having been sacrificed to artistic effect, and the parts on which most money has been spent such as the roof "kiosks" have least to do with school purposes. These were the observations made by some in early years.

The building contains a large hall (utilized for roll-call and on public occasions), nine class-rooms, a science laboratory, a library, and a few smaller rooms. A school museum is housed in the upper gallery.

The consideration of the plan of the Boarding-houses and minor buildings was postponed until representative opinions from Chiefs and others had been obtained. Eventually it was decided that each boy should have the following accommodation: - a sleeping room, 18 ft X 16ft., with two bathrooms attached; a kitchen; quarters for two servants and a "syce" ; and stabling for a horse. In connection with the scale of fees charged by the College, it is worth remarking that the boys have as comfortable quarters as they would get in a European club or hotel. Two blocks of such rooms were taken in hand by the Public Works Department, each accommodating about sixteen boys. In 1888 a third block was added, intended for scholarship-holders and boys paying reduced fees. The outer dimensions and appearance are the same, but it is divided into cubicles, 16 ft.X 9 ft., separated by wooden partitions, and is thereby able to accommodate over forty boys. The Boarding houses have no architectural embellishments, but are excellently adapted for their purpose. Each block takes up three sides of a quadrangle, the space in the middle being laid out in grass and flower-beds. At the extremity of the wings are suites of rooms intended for Musahibs, or boys for whom special accommodation is desired, and in the centre are large halls, used as mess and recreation rooms.

In May 1886, the Committee decided to transfer the boys of the Umballa Wards' School to Lahore without waiting for the new buildings to be completed, and three bungalows were accordingly hired for their temporary accommodation. These were occupied, not without inconvenience as the number increased, from November 1886 to April 1889. At the next meeting, in October, a scheme of studies was sanctioned, and the educational staff appointed, the latter consisting of the Principal, three Assistant Masters, and two Oriental Teachers. Two Musahibs were added to assist in superintendence after school-hours. In this meeting Sir Charles Aitchison made the important announcement that the school would henceforward be placed under the control of a Governor, and that "it was advisable that this appointment should be held by a military officer of some standing, in order to ensure that a proper tone might be given to the training of the students, and the discipline of the institution duly maintained." General Black, C. S .I., who was named for the post, had been Secretary to the Punjab Government for many years, and was intimately acquainted with the aristocracy of the Province. In the early years of the College, when the first and most difficult task was to gain public confidence, his influence and local knowledge were of great value.

Progress had been rapid during 1886, for Sir Charles Aitchison's term of office was drawing to a close, and he was anxious to see the College start before his departure. All the preliminaries were now in readiness; it remained only to inaugurate the undertaking with a ceremony which should mark its importance. On the 3rd November the foundation-stone of the main building was laid by the Viceroy, Lord Dufferin, in the presence of a distinguished company, including H. R. H. the Duke of Connaught and the Rulers of Kashmir, Bahawalpur, Jind, Nabha, Kapurthala and other States. The feature of the occasion was the address delivered by the Lieutenant-Governor, in which he traced the development of the scheme from its inception, and explained the nature and object of the future college. "Hitherto," he said, "the native aristocracy has participated but little in the benefits of our system of education. From the middle and lower ranks native society is rising up year by year by an ever increasing number of candidates for honours in our academical institutions and for positions of responsibility under the Government; while those who are the hereditary leaders of the people are being elbowed out of the positions which they are naturally expected by their fellow-country-men to occupy, but for which under the altered circumstances of the times they have in most cases as yet failed to qualify for themselves. As stone is placed upon stone in the visible structure of this edifice, and tier upon tier rises from the level plain, let it be our earnest hope that there may rise a still fairer edifice in which the aristocracy of the Punjab shall be the polished corner stones, bright example to their fellow-countrymen of true manliness, of the highest culture and the gentlest manners that the times can boast of." Lord Dufferin followed with a few eloquent periods, concluding with a proposal that the new institution should henceforth bear the name of its founder, and be known as the Aitchison College. The appropriateness of the change of title cannot fail to have struck his audience. It was only fitting that Sir Charles Aitchison's name should be associated with the project of which he was the originator, and in which he had evinced, from first to last, such an active and personal interest. The bust of the founder which had been placed in the central hall serves as a visible reminder of the debt which the College owes to his single-hearted zeal.

With the laying of the foundation-stone, and the arrival of the boys of the Umballa School at Lahore, the preliminary period of the history of the College came to a close. Its constitution, finance, and future home were assured. The promoters had made their share, and its fate now rested with the management and staff. In the end of year 1888 Sir Charles Aitchison paid a farewell visit to the college and gave the students a few forcible works of advice declaring them to be blue blood of the Province, who should make use of opportunities to qualify for the position of honour devolving upon them by banditry right. The school building was completed in 1890 and during ensueing years few additions were made.

After Independence, the college grew into a public school and it made a rich contribution to the educational life of the country. A junior section was added to the college to provide education for boys under ten years and to act as "feeder" for the Preparatory School. However, the class character of the institution remained its dominant feature, and its overwhelming clientele continued to be derived of from the landed aristocracy of the country.

The Peoples Party Government completely stripped this college of its aristocratic character, and decided that thenceforth only talented boys will be admitted to it, regardless of their class background. Aitchison College, therefore, ceased to be a Chiefs College. As a result of this change of policy, an overwhelming majority of the boys now admitted to this college comprises the sons and wards of persons having professional backgrounds (medical men, engineers, businessmen etc.). Aitchison, lays great stress on its boys taking part in a wide variety of activities, besides classroom work.

Education at Aitchison is divided into three stages; yet the curriculum has been designed as a well-integrated unit. These stages are:

(a) The Junior School;
(b) The Preparatory School ; and,
(c) The Senior School.

Besides instruction in all modern academic fields of arts, sciences, and languages, Islamic Studies are included in the curriculum as a regular subject of study. Of late there has been a criticism against the English medium institutions but the fact of the matter is that this college has doubtlessly produced quite a few great men who made their mark in services and other fields.

MASONIC LODGE

The 90-Shahrah-e-Quaid-e-Azam, is the only recently fixed brass plate outside this classic structure in the Charing Cross Square on the Mall. Until early 70s this building was commonly called as "Jadoo Ghar". Nobody had ever seen the entry or exit of any person or activity in routine at the premises. The Masonic lodge doors had always been haunted and full of awe and suspicion. It is a mystery replete in an enigma.

This building belongs to Free Mason Organization. Masonry is a Movement established throughout the world and generally known as a secret organization with its secretive activities. It is believed that it started in the late 17th century in Europe and anti-Christians inspired by heretical writings. Some believe that the Ultimate goal of the movement was to up-root the entire religious and political order of the world and so some regarded it as Jewish conspiracy. What is right and wrong is not ascertainable. However, this much is said that it was a secret brotherhood, which according to them used to help its members and others in need. What was their attitude towards Muslims may be seen from introductory paragraph in the book titled "The Knights Templars" by C.G. Addison (published in London in 1853), which records. "To be propagated by the sword was a vital principle of Muhammadanism. War against infidels for the establishment and extension of the faith was commanded by the Prophet, and the solemn injunction became hallowed and perpetuated by success".

"A century after the death of Muhammad (PBUH) the Moslems had extended their religion and their arms from India to the Atlantic Ocean; they had subdued and converted, by the power of the sword, Persia and Egypt, and all the north of Africa, from the mouth of the Nile to the extreme western boundary of that vast continent; they overran Spain, invaded France, and turning their footsteps towards Italy they entered the kingdoms of Naples and Genoa, threatened Rome, and subjected the island of Sicily to the laws and the religion of their Prophet. But at the very period when they were about to plant the Quran in the very heart of Europe, and were advancing with rapid strides to universal dominion, intestine dissensions broke out amongst them which undermined their power, and Europe was released from the dread and danger of Saracen dominion.

In the tenth century of the Christian era, however, the ferocious and barbarous Turkomans appeared as the patrons of Muhammadanism, and the propagators of the Quran. These were wild pastoral tribes of shepherds and hunters, who descended from the frozen plains to the north of the Caspian, conquered Persia, embraced the religion and the law of Muhammad, and became united under the standard of the Prophet into one great and powerful nation. They

Masonic Lodge 1859 Now lady Maclagan School Office

overran the greater part of the Asiatic continent, destroyed the churches of the Christians and the temples of the Pagans, and appeared (A.D. 1084) in warlike array on the Asiatic shore of the Hellespont in front of Constantinople. The terrified emperor Alexius sent urgent letters to the Pope and the Christian princes of Europe, exhorting them to assist him and their common Christianity in the perilous crisis. The preachings of Peter the hermit, and the exhortations of the Pope, forthwith aroused Christendom; Europe was armed and precipitated upon Asia; the Turkish power was broken; the Christian provinces of the Greek empire of Constantinople were recovered from the grasp of the infidels; and the Latin kingdom of Jerusalem was reared upon the ruins of the Turkish empire of Sultan Soliman. The monastic and military order of the Temple was then called into existence for the purpose of checking the power of the infidels, and fighting the battles of Christendom in the plains of Asia. "Suggested by fanaticism," as Gibbon observes, but guided by an intelligent and far reaching policy, it became the firmest bulwark of Christianity in the East, and mainly contributed to preserve Europe from Turkish desolation, and probably from Turkish conquest.

Many grave and improbable charges have been brought against the Templars by monks and priests who wrote in Europe concerning events in the Holy Land, and who regarded the vast privileges of the order with indignation and aversion. This clarifies to some extent the spirit and philosophy of the organization.

It is also asserted by some that it crept into State organization for various Governments and were most influential and effective in higher orchelons of bureaucracy. The members were reportedly perfect in recognising each other without creating suspicion in and around. People say that since it originated in U. K. the colonies of Great Britain had their share too, from this organization. The masonaries started their activities in Punjab and established their ranks and files in the city of Lahore in early 19th century. It is said that Generals Ventura and Avitable were the first Free Masoners to the city of Lahore. Infact both of them were French army men who had escaped from the Napoleon War and had been engaged by Maharaja Ranjit Singh to train his army. They were given handsome emoluments and other fringe benefits in lieu of their services. When the British moved into Punjab, their Army units were held in the organizational set up and they had their meetings in the city. It is told that the masonic organization used to hold their meeting inside Sheranwala Gate and Naulakha localities. They continued with their meetings at their appointed places secretively until they thought of building their own Grand Lodge/Free Mason Lodge in Lahore.

The building of the District Grand Lodge of Pakistan or Freemasons Hall Lahore looks somewhat old fashioned but still an imposing structure that forms one sector of a circle of building surrounding Charing Cross, on the Shahrah-e-Quaid-e-Azam in the centre of modern Lahore. Although itself only about eighty five years old, its history and that of its predecessor dates back to the period before the formation of the District Grand Lodge of the Punjab.

In 1859 Lodge "Hope and Perseverance" No. 782 was formed and the following year a building was constructed in the Old Anarkali section of Lahore on what to this day is known as Lodge Road. Mr.Justice R.S. Sidhwa in his book on the District Grand Lodge has given an account of the laying of the foundation stone. From this book we learn that the Brethren of the Lodge together with many residents and one hundred and fifty native Chiefs assembled for the ceremony on 6th September 1859, at which Wor. Bro. H. D. Sandeman officiated. The building was completed by February 1860, to become the first permanent Masonic establishment in Lahore. It was in this building at an Emergent Meeting of Lodge "Hope and Perseverance" No.782 on 12th March 1869 that the District Grand Lodge of the Punjab was established. In late 1872 Lodge "Hope and Perseverance" No. 782 by a unanimous vote, transferred the title of the building and property to the district to be used as its headquarters.

The original building served the needs of the District until 1889 by which time the facilities had become inadequate. Early that year an office room was added on the southern side and a library, reading room and lavatory on the northern side. Before the end of the year the District sanctioned the construction of an enclosed verandah and a reception room. These additional rooms not only completed the required facilities but added to the aesthetic value of the building. In the year 1900 the Banquet Hall was enlarged and in 1902 a large Hall 45'x3' was added to the south end of the District Building at an estimated cost of Rs.7,000. No other major additions or alterations were found necessary until the structure was extensively damaged by a severe earthquake on 4th April 1905. An examination of the damage revealed that it was due, in part to the piece-meal construction of the additions. To guard against the possibility of a similar occurrence in the future, the Board of General Purposes decided to completely demolish the damaged sections and to reconstruct those portions as a unit. Consequently the members of the Board framed an estimate of the work which amounted to Rs.13,500. During April and May, 1905, attempts were made to obtain a grant of Rs.15,000 from the Grand Lodge of England to cover the intended rebuilding including furniture and fittings, but the Board of General Purposes was informed by Grand Lodge that any such grant was improbable. However, in June, the estimate for demolition and rebuilding was approved by the Board and the work was started. In the same month an appeal to the Grand Lodge for a loan of Rs.15,000 was also turned down. In March 1906, the revised estimates of the cost were found to have soared to approximately Rs.21,500. This increased estimate was approved at the district Grand Lodge Meeting held at Lahore on 7th April, 1906, with the condition that the District should mortgage its property in favour of the Governing Body of the Punjab Masonic Institution to secure the said loan. It was not until 10th September, 1906, that a resolution was formally passed at the Autumnal Meeting of the District held at Simla, allowing the property at Lahore to be mortgaged without possession in favour of the Trustees of the Punjab Masonic Institution as security for a loan of Rs.20,000.

"The extensive repairs and additions to the Temple at Lahore (Lodge Building) were finally completed by the early part of 1906 and the District Grand Lodge met for the first time in the reconstructed Temple on 7th April, 1906."

For three years the building offered good service to the District without inviting any criticism. But, at a Meeting of the District Board of General Purposes held at Lahore in March 1910, Wor. Bro. Major G. K. Walker moved a proposal – the first of its kind – that a new District Grand Lodge building should be built, in view of the accommodation in the Masonic Temple being inadequate Wor. Bro. Walker suggested that money should be raised by the sale of the existing property and the issue of debentures to Masonic Bodies and Masons in the Punjab. After discussion, a Committee was appointed, consisting of Wor. Bros. Sir D. P. Masson, Lt. Col. Arthur Grey, Major G. K. Walker, C.A. Owen and the District Grand Secretary to find a suitable site and ascertain the value of the existing property. In August 1910, the District Board of General Purposes considered certain proposals with regard to this subject.

In March, 1911, certain concrete steps were taken to collect funds to finance the building costs of the new Temple. Bro. Dudley, the Municipal Engineer of Lahore, prepared plans and estimates for the new Temple. The cost of construction of the new building and out-houses with the site, and new furniture and electric installation all worked out to Rs.1,50,000. It was estimated that a sum of Rs.70,000 would probably become available by sale of the existing Temple (on Lodge Road), leaving a sum of Rs.80,000 to be raised by loan. Considering that the rate of interest at which the District Grand Lodge would be able to secure a loan was 5% the annual estimate required to meet the interest on the loan was worked out at Rs.4,000. The Board of General Purposes found that the average annual receipt of the District Grand Lodge General Fund was roughly Rs.10,000 against which the expenditure was Rs.6,000 thus leaving a credit of Rs.4,000; just enough to meet the annual interest on loan of Rs.80,000. In order to work out a plan to enable the District to pay off annually some part of the principal also and not merely the interest, the Board decided to create a Building Fund and to call upon all Lodges in the District to contribute at the rate of 8 annas per member per quarter or Rs.2 per annum. This was intended to yield approximately Rs.3,400 per annum on an estimated membership of 1704, this being the number of members on the Roll of the District on 31st December, 1910. The Board also estimated a further yield of Rs.1,000 form enhanced rental from Craft Lodges using the Temple. Accordingly, a list of all the Craft Lodges showing the number of members on their Rolls on 31st December, 1910, and the amounts payable by them towards the Building Fund was prepared and circulated on March, 1911. A covering letter from the District Grand Secretary, Punjab addressed to Wor. Maters of all Lodges in the Punjab, requested that the Circular be placed before their Lodges at their next meeting and an intimate to the District whether the Lodges would agree to the contribution proposed of 8 annas per member per quarter for the creation of the Building Fund.

At the District Grand Lodge Meeting held at the Freemasons Hall Lahore, on 15th April 1911, a new Committee consisting of Wor. Bros. The Hon'able H. P. Burt, Major R. Head and Major Bailey, was appointed with full powers, subject to approval by the D.G.M. to negotiate and complete the sale of the existing Temple and premises on Lodge Road and the acquisition of a new site and construction thereon of the proposed new Temple. This was found necessary as many of the members of the old Committee had left or were no longer in the station. At that Meeting, the D.D.G.M. in the Chair referred to the contribution which it was proposed to levy on all Lodges in the District to pay off the fund to be raised for the construction of the new building and felt that there was not a Lodge in the District on which the levy would press heavily. He hoped the scheme would very soon be regarded as complete and settled and that before very long the construction of the new building could be commenced.

Before the Autumnal Meeting of the District in September, 1911, a good many replies were received from the various Lodges in the District offering their full support to the quarterly levy on each member for the purpose of creating the Building Fund. The Committee which had been formed, to arrange for the sale of the old Temple, select the new site and arrange for plans and estimates for the new Temple, had by that time made considerable progress. That Committee selected an excellent site, the property of Government, in the very heart of the station and made an application on behalf of the District for the purchase of the same. At the District Grand Lodge Meeting held at Simla under the Banner of Lodge "Himalayan Brotherhood" No.459 on 11th September, 1911, the D.G.M. referred to the progress made by the Committee in warm terms and hoped that the District would be in a position to proceed with the project at an early date.

In 1913, strenuous efforts were made by the Committee to expedite matters. His Honourable the Lieut. Governor was approached again, which led to enquiries being initiated by the Governor as to the requirements of the District with regard to the site. Thus, by the Autumnal Meeting of the District held at the Freemasons Hall, Simla, under the Banner of Lodge "Himalayan Brotherhood" No.459 on 8th September, 1913, the D.G.M. was able to report that much headway had been made in the matter and that the Punjab Government had intimated their intention of purchasing the existing Freemasons Hall at Lahore and its compound for conversion into a Public library, and of selling to the Fraternity the site at Charing Cross opposite the Queen's statue, for the new Temple, if suitable terms could be arranged for these two transactions. The D.G.M pointed out that negotiations in the matter were not proceeding with the Deputy Commissioner of Lahore and since the site at Charing Cross was very valuable that the sanction of the Government of India would probably be necessary to its sale, but which, he had every reason to believe, would be granted.

At the Meeting of the District held on 13th April, 1914, the new D. G. M. Rt. Wor. Bro. The Hon'able H. P. Burt, intimated to the Brethren the further progress made by the District with regard to the sale of the existing Temple and the acquisition of the new site for the construction of the proposed new Temple. The D.G.M. stated that the Committee appointed by them for the purpose had been successful in negotiating the sale of the existing Temple to the Government for Rs.1,07,590 and the purchases from the Government of a plot of land measuring 13 Kanals and 126 sq. ft. at Charing Cross, the corner of the Lahore Zoo known as the Deer Park at the junction of The Mall (now Shahrah-e-Quaid-e-Azam) and Queens Road, for Rs.32,590. The D.G.M. stated that one of the conditions insisted on by the Punjab Government regarding the sale of the new site at Charing Cross was that the building to be constructed by the Fraternity should be an ornament to the locality, with the result that the District had decided to engage the services of Mr. Sullivan, the Consulting Architect to the Punjab Government, for the preparation of the necessary drawings and plans and to submit such plans for the approval of the Government.

Before the next Meeting of the District held at the Freemason's Hall, Simla, under the Banner of Lodge "Kitchner" No. 2998 on 7th September, 1914, the D.G. .M was able to report that the sale of the old Temple to the Punjab Government was completed, that the District was in possession of the new site at Charing Cross, and that the plans for the new edifice were complete and ready in all respects for execution and that he hoped that construction of the new Temple would begin soon. (Bro. Mohan Lal was appointed the Contractor to construct the building).

At the above Meeting, the names of Wor. Bros. L.H. Leslie Jones, H.L.O. Garrett, Dr. C.C. Caleb and J. A. Swainson were added to the Committee previously appointed to arrange for the construction of the new Temple, to make up for a number of members of that Committee who had left Lahore.

The foundation stone laying ceremony of the new building took place on 1st April, 1916. This ceremony and the District Grand Lodge Meeting, held on that day, were both tied together and were therefore attended by far the largest gathering ever assembled at a District Meeting held at Lahore in the past. Apart from the members of the District, there were no less than 86 visiting Brethren. Another reason why so large an assembly of Masons was present was because the Installation Ceremony of Rt. Wor. Bro. Col. H. T. Pease, the new District Grand Master of the Punjab, was also fixed for that day. This investiture ceremony constituted an integral part of the District Grand Lodge Meeting. Thus, after the new D.G.M. was installed and the D.D.G.M. and other District Grand Lodge Officers appointed. The District Grand Lodge was then adjourned temporarily and the Brethren proceeded to the site at Charing Cross. There they assembled in Max Minck's Building (now the building where Goldsmith's jeweller has his shop) where they clothed themselves in Masonic Regalia and proceeded across the road to the shamiana erected at the site of the new Temple. Here the District Grand Lodge sitting was formally resumed for the purpose of laying the foundation-stone of the new Masonic Temple. The foundation stone that was laid was not a new one, but the original corner Stone which Wor. Bro. H. D. Sandeman had laid on 6th September, 1859, in the old Temple on Lodge Road. This original Corner Stone was brought from the old building and relaid at the new site according to established Masonic custom. After the ceremony, the D.G.M. whilst addressing the Brethren, thanked those Brethren who, from time to time, had served on the Building Committees and by whose efforts the plans for the erection of the new Temple had borne fruit. After the ceremony was concluded, the Brethren formed a procession and returned to Max Minck's building to unclothe. The District Grand Lodge Meeting was then resumed at the old Temple for the completion of the remaining Masonic business, which having been accomplished, the Lodge was closed in due form.

In the last quarter of 1917, the new Temple at Charing Cross was complete. When the D.G.M. had presided at the District Grand Lodge Meeting held at Freemason Hall, Lahore, on 1st April, 1916, the day that the Corner Stone was laid at the new site, he had hoped that this would be the last of the District Meetings in the old Temple, but work on the new Temple had not progressed expeditiously and the same was not ready for occupation even by the 7th April, 1917, when the next Regular Annual Meeting of the District was held at Lahore. Every effort was therefore made to expedite the completion of the new structure.

When the new Temple was ready for occupation a Special Meeting of the District Grand Lodge was convened for the 29th November 1917, for the dedication of the new Temple. The Special Meeting was well attended and at an impressive ceremony, the new Temple was dedicated to Masonic purposes according to an ancient custom. The records are not clear regarding the use to which the old building was immediately put. However, it is still standing and it is now occupied by the Lady Maclagan School for Girls.

Towards the end of 1918, steps were taken to find ways and means to pay off the debt secured to finance the building of the new Temple. The District Board of General Purposes at its Meeting held on 17th December 1918, decided to create a Building Fund to assist in paying off this debt and to provide means for the proper upkeep of the new building. The Board made two recommendations: firstly, to increase the rents charged from the several Masonic Bodies using the Temple, and secondly, to levy a contribution of eight annas per member per quarter for the Building Fund. The Board's recommendations were duly accepted and approved by the District Grand Lodge at its Regular Meeting held at Freemasons' Hall, Lahore, on 29th March 1919.

In February, 1931, the question of repairs to the Masonic building at Lahore was set up. A brief flash back with regard to the subject would not be out of place. The condition of the external facings of the District Grand Lodge building was first brought to the notice of the District Board at its Meeting held in July 1930. Mr. Brentford, A.R.I.B.A., was asked to go over the building and he submitted an estimate for the entire stripping and replastering of the external walls, amounting to Rs.36,000. It was also found that the basement of the building remained damp and unhealthy which slowly affected the plaster facing. At the same time the heavy cornice around the whole of the top of the building showed signs of disintegration and imminent collapse. A special Premises Committee was formed to look into the matter which finally decided to re-face the building and to apply for a loan from the Punjab Masonic Institutions. Some time later, at a Meeting of the District Board of General Purposes, the Board recommended the District to take a loan of Rs.50,000 from the P.M.I. to meet the cost of those repairs, etc. The Board also appointed a special Sub-Committee comprising of Wor. Bros. Owen Roberts, Col. G. I. Davys, Lt. Col. H.L.O. Garrett, Lt. Col. C.A. Gill, Dewan Amar Nath Nanda, C. A. Durham and G. Reeves-Brown, to examine the estimates submitted by the architect, obtain all details and report to the District Grand Lodge on the subject. At the meeting of the Premises Sub-Committee held in January, 1931, the Committee recommended that a loan of Rs.50,000 be asked for from the Punjab Masonic Institutions to cover the expenses of re-plastering the entire external facings to the building, to instal sanitary flush system and electric heating in the Temple. These recommendations were accepted at the Annual Meeting of the District Grand Lodge of the Punjab held at Freemasons' Hall, Lahore, on 28th March 1931. The major repairs were thus started.

At the Annual Meeting of the District held at Lahore on 26th March, 1932, referring to the District Grand Lodge building, on which a great deal of work had been done and money had been spent, the D.D.G.M. expressed the hope that the improvements would benefit the District for many years. The D.D.G.M. could not avoid mentioning that the District had gone back to where it stood ten years ago as the new debt incurred, placed the District in almost the same position as it was when it originally borrowed money to construct its Temple.

After the major repairs in 1931, the District building did not require any special attention for a number of years, till, in August, 1955, the Premises Committee of the Board of General Purposes, sanctioned the sum of Rs.900 for repairs to the District Grand Lodge building at Lahore.

Seven years later, i.e. in June, 1962, the Premises Committee was again called upon to inspect and prepare estimates for repairs to the roof, coping and interior of the District Grand Lodge building. The Premises Committee, however, only recommended repairs to the roof and coping and directed that they be given top priority before the monsoon and that all other work be carried out at a later date, which was accordingly done.

The question of repairs, maintenance and improvement to the building again cropped up in May 1963, when a joint meeting of the Finance and Premises Committees was held to discuss this matter. The building was in a deteriorated condition and major repairs were required as they were considerably overdue. After much deliberation, the joint Committee discussed and fixed certain priorities and the District Grand Secretary was requested to go ahead with the repairs. Brethren and Lodges were also requested to specially contribute to the Building Fund of the District. (Rs.1,710 was received as voluntary donation up to the Autumnal Meeting of the District in October, 1963).

In July, 1964, the matter with regard to extensive repairs to the District Grand Lodge building was taken up again. The Finance Committee duly approved a sum of Rs.5,140, against Rs.17,240 recommended by the Premises Committee, for repairs to the roof, removal of corbelling, repairs and colour-washing and white-ant treatment. The Finance Committee did not consider it desirable to sanction a large outlay on extensive repairs as it was thought that a stage had been reached when the building required pulling down for a new one to be built instead, for which investigation was initiated.

The problem of the District Grand Lodge building at Lahore engaged the attention of the District once again. At a Meeting of the District Grand Lodge at Rawalpindi in January, 1965, the D.G.M. intimated to the Brethren that the District had initiated a move with the Government of permission to dismantle the existing building and to construct a 6-7 storied commercial building instead, the major

Masonic Lodge 90-Shahrah-e-Quaid-e-Azam 1917

portion of which could be utilized by commercial houses and the income of which could be utilized towards Masonic and Non-Masonic charities but, unfortunately, in view of protracted delay, it was necessary to give up the idea and to go in for large and important repairs and alterations which were imminently required to make the structure safe and secure. The D.G. M. stated that he felt that roughly Rupees Two Lacs would be required and as the district had no funds available it was necessary to approach the Brethren for donations. Accordingly, the D.G.M. requested Wor. Bros. Lahore, D.D.G.M., Wor. Bros. Lt. Colonel J.J.V.C. Cunningham, Asst. D.G.M., to form Committees and collect opinions and advices from the Brethren all over and bring a detailed proposal before the District Grand Lodge at the next meeting. The Committee so set up went into the matter and the final consensus of opinion was that the Brethren should advance interest free loans to the District, repayable to them after a stated period. Accordingly, at the Annual Meeting of the District in March, 1965, the D.G.M. issued an appeal for funds, and assured the Brethren that the loans would be redeemed no sooner the Government granted sanction for the construction of the commercial enterprise and the rents started coming in. Pursuant to this request, roughly Rs.10,250 was collected by the District, but as the Government sanction was not received, the money was returned after some time to the Brethren.

Inspite of the fact that repairs to the present building have continually been required it remains in service and, although dwarfed by an adjacent and magnificent structure, the WAPDA building designed by Edward Stone, is still a pleasing piece of architecture which with its sweeping driveway and high porte-cochere, retains a stately and serene air of grandeur. On the ground floor, heavy teak doors open into a waiting hall floored with marble tiles and panelled in teak. This panelling was constructed in memory of the late Rt. Wor. Bros. Edwin Woodall Parker, P.D.G.M. To the left of the waiting hall on the ground floor is the clock room, the library containing more than 2000 volumes and the District Grand Master and Secretary's offices. To the right is the main dining room where, over the fire-place is displayed a bust of Lord Kitchener, and one or two side rooms. From the waiting hall, a broad marble staircase leads upto an inter storey rotunda, noted for its tall stained glass windows depicting the three ancient Grand Masters of Craft Masonry. From the rotunda, winding staircases on either side ascend to the upper storey where are located the Temple and other rooms on either side. The winding staircase opens out into an open verandah in front of which is the balcony. On the left is the dressing room and the Temple connected by a small passage. This Temple, which is used by the District Grand Lodge and the Craft, Mark and R.A.M. Lodges and chapters, has a squared pavement of black and white marble, teak panel wainscotting and an ornate domed plaster ceiling. On the right hand side are the various rooms used by the Christian degrees. On the ground floor, just beneath the rotunda, is the Bar-cum-Club room. Below the ground floor is the basement, where the District Office, kitchen and some residential rooms are situated. These lower rooms in the basement open on to a pleasant lawn and garden.

Plans were not been shelved for the construction of a new District Grand Lodge building at the same site. If the plans materialise, a 6-7 storied structure will be constructed, part to be used for Masonic purposes and the balance to be let out to bring in income for the District Charities as well as for maintenance and support of other Masonic buildings in the District. If ever such a building comes into being, the original Corner Stone, the stained glass windows and many other furnishings of the present building will be utilized in the new one, to perpetuate the link with the beginning of Masonry in the Punjab.

In the year 1974 the Pakistan Peoples Party Government was in power and under the orders of the Prime Minister, Mr. Zulfiqar Ali Bhutto, this building was taken over and the organization apparently banned. Pakistan Peoples Party made its Headquarters here in this building and continued to occupy until it was ousted by the Martial Law regime. Some of the Martial Law offices were also set up for a short period here but due to very poor maintenance and neglect the building was in very dilapidated condition. The roofs were leaking, the rain water used to flood the under ground portion and quite a few rooms of first floor were rendered useless and had given way. A part of the building on ground floor was handed over to the Punjab Council of the Arts a newly established organization in the city in the year 1975. They continued their offices here in the building and their dancing troupe rehearsing in its hall immediately on right-hand, on the entrance, which is beautifully panelled and floored with teakwood. The basement was occupied by the Artists Association for its office and the "Artists Equity". The Punjab Council of the Arts was dislodged from the place in 1980 and the building was taken over by the Tourism Directorate, which later on became the Tourism Development Corporation. During this period too the building continued to be in a very bad shape and the Tourism Directorate also was shifted to Shadman Colony. The Masonic Lodge was taken over by the Chief Minister Punjab for his Secretariat. A Banquet Hall was set up. The Chief Minister used to give audience to the people here and dinners to the guests and VVIPs. It so continued until there was a political change. On the fall of the Government, the interim period Chief Minister Mian Afzal Hayat declared that this building would be used for a Museum for the Pakistan Movement Archives. Infact with round the clock efforts documents, photographs and craft items were collected and a proper museum organized. On 27th January 1997, the President of Pakistan Mr. Farooq Ahmad Khan Leghari inaugurated this Museum and glowing tributes were paid to the Chief Minister for establishing the Museum which was the dire need for the education of younger generation. Some nucleus staff was appointed to make the Museum functional. This arrangement continued until Feb. 1998 when under the orders of the Government the Museum was shifted and the place apparently declared to be used by the Chief Minister secretariat.

During the pace of transitional period beginning late 80s when it has been taken over for Chief Minister's Secretariat, reportedly over three crorers of rupees have been spent on the renovation of this building. The building has been partly restored but the restoration work leaves much to be desired. The original plot of land of the Lodge has been added up with another piece of land towards the Zoo side, which belonged to Blood Bank of the Health Department. Another gate has been opened towards the Zoo for an entry exit to the Mall. It is understood that when this building was taken over by the Government, the Masonic Organization, which still survives in the city of Lahore, filed a writ petition in the Lahore High Court where the occupation of this building was declared illegal as it was a private property. The Government probably have filed an appeal in the Supreme Court of Pakistan where the same is under-adjudication.

The reader might be feeling bored with this lengthy account which may not be very interesting. For example the details of committees and members, but I feel it is necessary to give the reader an idea as to which people held membership, what was their status and how they penetrated into the Government for interests of the Masonic Oraganisation. With such an effective set up the Society members were in a position to manoeuvre anything for the Brethern.It was that this effectiveness which enabled them to get this valuable piece of land and subsequent loans and other assistance

PUNJAB ASSEMBLY BUILDING

The first Punjab Legislative Assembly met, on April, 5th 1937 in the Council Hall, situated in the Punjab Civil Secretariat, Lahore. The Council Hall is now under occupation of the Education Department and Chief Minister's Secretariat where some Section Officers with their staff sit. The monogram of the Punjab which was most probably designed on the formation of the Council and is in vogue in modified form till date is in the Punjab Archives in the historic Anarkali Tomb.

The foundation stone of the present Punjab Assembly building at Lahore was laid on November 17, 1935 by Sir Jogendir Singh, the then Minister for Agriculture Punjab. It was designed by Mr. Bazel M. Sullivan, the Superintending architect, Punjab. It took 3 years to build. The first session of the Assembly, in the

Punjab Assembly & Summit Minar

building, was held on 10th November, 1938. Since independence, the present Assembly Building at Lahore has been the permanent seat of the Punjab Assembly and the West Pakistan Assembly. The building is a classical piece of architecture raised in pompous Victorian style during the British period. It has a most imposing gate-way facing the Mall. The entrance has typical round supporting pillars with Spanish style roof. The steps and floors are in red-stone. Immediately on entrance comes the lounge and stair ways leading up to the Assembly Hall where there are entrances on right and left through lobby. Just opposite to Speaker walk way to his Chamber, is the room of leader of the House and on right side of the Hall is the Governor's Gallery. As already pointed out the building is in semi-circle and both on right and left spacious corridor divides the blocks of room which are occupied by the Ministers and their staff. Downstairs there are offices dealing with the matters pertaining to MPA, establishment of the Assembly, Question and Answer Sections, Library and Security staff. The rooms are centrally air-conditioned and panelled. The Assembly Complex extends over an area of 112 Kanals out of which 148 Kanals are under lawns and open spaces. On the north east of the building (big site) there is hotel Falettis. On the east PIA building and WAPDA House. On right side of the Assembly Building there is MPA's Hostel and Al-Falah Building. Just in front of the main gate of the Assembly at a distance of few yards is the Summit Minar which was raised in 1974 in commemoration of meeting of Heads of Islamic States at the Punjab Assembly Building.

The Assembly Chamber is semi-circular in shape. The present seating arrangement, in the Hall, is designed to accommodate 271 members, including Ministers. In addition, there is speaker's throne, Secretary's Table and the Reporter's table. On the left side of the Speaker's throne, is the Governor's Gallery with 12 seats meant for the visitors of the Governor, and on the right side of the throne is the officers Gallery with 12 seats, meant for the Secretaries to the Government.

Adjoining the Chamber, on all its sides, is the Members Lobby which serves as their retiring room, during the meetings of the Assembly. There is a Visitors Gallery and a Press Gallery over the Chamber. The Chamber is fitted with a modern Conference System/Public address stystem.

The Press Gallery is stituated over the Speaker's throne and facing the Members seats. It has 12 seats.

The Visitors Gallery has a seating capacity of 132. It is divided into various enclosures: the VIP Gallery, the Speaker's Gallery, the Ladies Gallery, the Front Press Gallery and the Members Gallery.

The Assembly Library is situated on the Ground Floor in three separate rooms. It is the oldest legislative Library in the Country. It has a collection of

30,000 volumes on Constitutional Law, Parliamentary Practice, Political Science, History, Pakistan Studies, Islam and Social Sciences.

HISTORY OF THE ASSEMBLY

The Provincial Assembly of the Punjab, like other parliamentary institutions in the country emerged through a long process of constitutional development during the pre-independence and post-independence period. The Indian Councils Act, 1861, which provided for the inclusion, through nomination, of certain non-official members, in the council of the Lieutenant Governor when it was to transact legislative business as the legislative council. The provisions of the 1861 Act were modified by the Indian Councils Act, 1892. This latter Act provided (i) for the nomination of non-official members on the suggestion of certain recommending bodies. (ii) for discussion of the budget in the Council and (iii) for addressing questions to the Executive.

The first Legislative Council in the province of the Punjab, under the Indian Councils Act, 1861, was constituted in 1897. It comprised of ten members, both official and non-official. The General Clauses Act, 1898, was the first enactment, in the history of the Punjab, made by the Legislative Council. The meetings of the Council were presided over by the Lieutenant Governor himself.

The element of election in the Legislative Council was, for the first time, introduced by the Indian Councils Act, 1909, through the Minto-Morley Reforms. The legislative Council was given power to pass resolutions, on the budget, as also on matters of public importance, which, however, were of a recommendatory nature.

Punjab Legislative Council under Government of India Act. 1919: - The first World War gave impetus to the growing demand for self-government and the new constitutional reforms, under the Montague-Chelmsford scheme, were introduced by the British Government, through the Government of India Act 1919. The reforms established partially by responsible Governments, in the provinces, under a system known as "dyarchy". The Legislative Council of Punjab, under this Act, comprised 83 members, of whom at least 70% were to be elected. The Council was to elect its own President and Deputy President and until such election, the Lieutenant-Governor was to appoint its President. The term of a council was 3 years.

The first Legislative Council, under the 1919 Act, was constituted in 1921, the second in 1924, the third in 1927 and the fourth, which was constituted in 1930, continued up to 1937.

Mr. M.S.D. Butler, ICS, was nominated as President of the Council from January 3, 1921 to March 21, 1922 Mr. H.A. Casson, ICS, was the nominated

President from May 10, 1922 to January 16, 1925. The Council elected Sh. Abdul Qadir as its President on January 17, 1925. Sir Shahab-ud-Din was elected as the President of the Council on January 4, 1927 and he continued in his office till 1936. He was succeeded by Chaudhry Sir Chhotu Ram whose tenure lasted from 21st October, 1936 to 31st March, 1937.

Dr. Sir Muhammad Iqbal was elected to the Legislative Council of the Punjab constituted in 1927.

Punjab Legislative Assembly under the Government of India Act, 1935: - The demand, for more responsible government grew stronger. The British Government held a series of round table conferences, in London, from 1930-1932, with representatives of various parties, in India, and formulated certain constitutional reforms. These reforms were eventually embodied in the Government of India Act, 1935. This Act introduced Provincial autonomy, which was no doubt, of a controlled type, but still it was an improvement over the previous system of dyarchy. Under this Act, the Punjab Legislative Assembly had 175 seats, divided into various categories: 42 General (Hindu) seats, 84 seats for Muslims, 31 seats for Sikhs, 1 seat for Anglo-Indians, 1 seat for Europeans, 2 seats for Indian Christians, 1 seat for representatives of commerce, Industry, Mining and Planting, 5 seats for land-holders, 1 seat for University, 3 seats for labour representatives, 1 general seat for women, 1 seat for Sikh Women and 2 seats for Muslim women.

The first Legislative Assembly of the Punjab, under the Government of India Act, 1935, was elected in 1936. It held its first Session on April 5, 1937. Sir Shahab-ud-Din was elected as its Speaker on April 6, 1937. The second Legislative Assembly was elected in 1946 and it was convened on March 21, 1946. Diwan Bahadur S.P. Singha was elected as its Speaker on March 21, 1946. Sir Sikandar Hayat Khan was the first Premier, of the Punjab, from 1937 to 1942. The Second Premier was Malik Khizar Hayat Tiwana from 1943 to 1947.Legislative Assembly of Punjab under the Pakistan (Provisional Constitution) Order, 1947: - On August 14, 1947, Pakistan came into being under the Indian Independence Act, 1947. The Government of India Act, 1935, with necessary modifications, was adopted as the provisional constitution vide the Pakistan (Provisional Constitution) Order, 1947.

From August 14, 1947, all sitting Members of the Legislative Assembly of Punjab, elected from constituencies included in the Province of West Punjab, were declared to have been elected to the Legislative Assembly of West Punjab under the Pakistan (Provincial Legislatures) Order, 1947. It had 90 Members. The first session of this assembly was held on January 5, 1948. Khan Bahadur Shaikh Faiz Muhammad was elected as Speaker of the First Legislative Assembly of West Punjab on January 9, 1948. Nawab Iftikhar Hussain Khan Mamdot was the first

Chief Minister of the West Punjab, after Independence, from August 15, 1947 to December 31, 1948. This Assembly was dissolved in 1949. In 1950 the Province of West Punjab was renamed as the Province of the Punjab. The Legislative Assembly of the Punjab was reconstituted in 1951 as a result of Fresh elections. It had 174 Members, its first Session was held on May 7, 1951 and on that day Dr. Khalifa Shuja-ud-Din was elected as its Speaker. This Assembly held its last meeting on 31-3-1955. Mian Mumtaz Muhammad Khan Daultana was the Chief Minister of Punjab from May 7, 1951 to July 30, 1953. He was succeeded by Malik Feroz Khan Noon, from July 3, 1953 to January 20, 1956.

Provincial Assembly of West Pakistan Under Constitution of 1956: - From October 15, the territories of the Provinces of Punjab, the N.W.F.P., Sindh and Baluchistan and the states of Bahawalpur, Khairpur, Amb, Chitral, Dir and Swat and the Tribal Areas of Baluchistan, the Punjab and NWFP, were all incorporated into the province of West Pakistan, under the Establishment of West Pakistan Act, 1955. The Provincial assembly of West Pakistan, under the said Act, had 310 seats divided into various categories: 10 General seats, 290 Muslim seats and 10 seats for Women. The Provincial Assembly of West Pakistan, constituted under this Act, held its first meeting on May 19, 1956. Ch. Fazal Elahi was elected as its Speaker on May 20, 1956.

The Chief Ministers during this period, include Sardar Abdul Hamid Khan Dasti (21-1-1956 to 30-4-1956) Dr. Khan Sahib (1-5-1956 to 8-3-1957) Sardar Abdul Rashid Khan (9-3-1957 to 27-3-1958) and Nawab Muzaffar Ali Khan Qazalbash (28-3-1958 to 15-10-1958).

The Constitution of Islamic Republic of Pakistan was passed by the constituent assembly on February 29, 1956 and was assented to by the Governor General on March 2, 1956. The Provincial Assembly of West Pakistan, under this Constitution, had 300 members, while for a period of ten years 10 additional seats were reserved for women. This Constitution provided that until a Provincial Assembly for the Province of West Pakistan was constituted under the Constitution, the Legislative Assembly constituted under the establishment of West Pakistan Act, 1955, shall exercise the powers and perform the duties of the Provincial Assembly of West Pakistan under the Constitution.

Preparations for the first general elections to the National Assembly and the Provincial Assemblies under the Constitution of 1956 were under way when the President of Pakistan annulled the Constitution, dissolved the National and the Provincial Assemblies and imposed Martial Law in the country, on October 7, 1958. Soon, the President abdicated and the Chief Martial Law Administrator assumed the office of the President.

Provincial Assembly of West Pakistan Under Constitution of 1962:- The President promulgated the 1962 Constitution which came into force on June 8, 1962, when the first meeting of the National Assembly was held and Martial Law was abolished. The basic institution, under the Constitution, was the Electoral College, consisting of 80,000 Electors. Each Province was divided into 40,000 Electoral Units and the residents of each unit elected, for a period of five years, from among themselves, an Elector, on the principle of adult franchise. The Electors so chosen constituted the Electoral College and elected the President, members of the National Assembly and Members of the Provincial Assemblies. The Governor of the Province was appointed by the President and he also had a Council of Ministers composed of persons not members of the Provincial Assembly. The Provincial Assembly consisted of 155 members of whom 150 were elected by the members of the Electoral College of the Province and 5 seats were reserved for women, who were elected by Members of the Provincial Assembly. The term of the Assembly was 5 years but it could be dissolved earlier.

The Provincial Assembly of West Pakistan, under the Constitution of 1962, was constituted in 1962. Mr. Mobin-ul-Haq Siddiqui was elected as its Speaker on June 12, 1962. A no-confidence motion was carried against him and Ch. Muhammad Anwar Bhinder was elected as Speaker of the Assembly from July 16, 1963.The Provincial Assembly of West Pakistan was re-constituted in 1965. Ch. Muhammad Anwar Bhinder was re-elected as its Speaker. The leaders of the House, in West Pakistan Assembly, during this period, were Shaikh Masood Sadiq (9-6-1962 to 3-7-1964), Khan Habib Ullah Khan (12-6-1965 to 30-6-1966), Malik Khuda Bakhsh Bucha (1-7-1966 to 4-11-1967), and Malik Qadir Bakhsh Jahkkar (10-11-1967 to 5-1-1969).

On March 25, 1969, President, Muhammad Ayub Khan, relinquished his office and handed over all powers to General Agha Muhammad Yahya Khan, Commander-in-Chief of the Pakistan Army, who forthwith, assumed the office of the President and abrogated the Constitution, imposed Martial Law and also assumed the office of the Chief Martial Law Administrator and dissolved the National Assembly and the Provincial Assemblies.

Provincial Assembly of Punjab Under Constitution of Pakistan 1973:
First Assembly 1972-1976.Under the Provisional Constitution order, 1969, it was provided that notwithstanding the abrogation of the Constitution, the State would be governed in accordance with the Constitution of 1962 but this would be subject to any contrary provision in the Provisional Constitution Order, or any Regulation or an Order, from time to time, by the President/Chief Martial Law Administrator. The Province of West Pakistan was abolished from July 1, 1970. The Legal Framework Order, 1970, provided for setting up of a National Assembly and

Provincial Assemblies of East Pakistan, and for each of the four provinces of West Pakistan, Elections to be held were Direct and on the basis of adult franchise. The elections were held in December, 1970. After secession of East Pakistan, from Pakistan, on December 16, 1971, President General Muhammad Yahya Khan handed over power to the leader of the majority party in West Pakistan, Mr. Zulfiqar Ali Bhutto, who assumed the office of the President and Chief Martial Law Administrator. The first ever civilian Martial Law Administrator in Pakistan.

The Interim Constitution, promulgated by the President and ratified by the National Assembly, commenced on April 21, 1972. This Constitution was replaced by a permanent Constitution passed by the National Assembly on April 10, 1973 and authenticated by the President on April 11, 1973. This constitution commenced with effect from August 14, 1973.

The Provincial Assembly of Punjab, elected in December, 1970, under Legal Framework Order, 1970, held its first meeting in March, 1972. This Assembly had 196 seats. Mr. Rafiq Ahmad Shaikh was elected as its Speaker on May 2, 1972. The Constitutions of 1973 declared that Assembly as the first Provincial Assembly under the said constitution.

Second Assembly – April 1977 to July 1977:- According to the provisions of the Constitution of Islamic Republic of Pakistan, 1973, the Provincial Assembly of the Punjab had 240 General Seats, 5 seats for minorities and 12 seats for women. Elections to the Provincial Assembly were required to be held by direct and free vote on the basis of adult franchise and on the system of joint electorates for Muslims and Non-Muslims. The first elections, to the Assembly, under the Constitution of 1973, were held in March, 1977.

Thus the second Assembly, under 1973 Constitution, was Constituted in 1977. It held its first meeting on April 9, 1977. Ch. Muhammad Anwar Bhinder was elected as Speaker on April 11, 1977.

The Chief Ministers of Punjab, during the period of the First two Assemblies, included: Malik Miraj Khalid (7-5-1972 to 6-11-1973), Malik Ghulam Mustafa Khar (12-11-1973 to 15-3-1974), Mr. Muhammad Hanif Ramey (15-3-1974 to 14-7-1975) and Nawab Sadiq Hussain Qureshi (15-7-1975 to 4-7-1977).

Third Assembly, 1985 – 1988:- On July 5, 1977, General Muhammad Zia-ul-Haq, Chief of the Army Staff, imposed Martial Law throughout the country and assumed the office of the Chief Martial Law Administrator. He suspended the Constitution, dismissed the Federal and the Provincial cabinets, dissolved the Parliament and the Provincial Assemblies. Later on, when Chaudhry Fazal Elahi, President of Pakistan, resigned, General Muhammad Zia-ul-Haq assumed the office of the President also.

Since the Constitution was held in abeyance, the Martial Law regime laid down the procedure for next elections through the houses of Parliament and Provincial Assemblies (Elections) Order, 1977. The concept of separate electorates for Muslims and non-Muslims was introduced in 1978. According to this system, the voters, enrolled on the electoral rolls of Muslims, were entitled to vote for the Muslim Members, while the non-Muslim voters were eligible to elect their own representatives. The number of seats, reserved for non-Muslims, in Punjab Assembly, was increased from 5 to 8, bringing the total number of seats, in Punjab Assembly, to 260.

The elections to the National Assembly and all the Provincial Assemblies were held, on 25th and 28th February, 1985, respectively, on non-party basis. The members of each Provincial Assembly elected persons to fill the quota of seats reserved for the respective Province in the Senate. The Constitution was revived in March, 1985. The elections held, in February, 1985, under the Houses of Parliament and Provincial Assemblies (Elections) Order, 1977, were declared to have been held under the constitution of 1973. Although the Federal and the Provincial Cabinets were formed, after the elections, under the constitution, inspite of that Martial Law was not lifted until December 30, 1985.

Thus, the Provincial Assembly constituted on the basis of the February 1985 elections were the third Provincial Assembly, under the 1973 constitution, as the first assembly was constituted in 1972 while the second was constituted in 1977. However, the 1985 elections were the second general elections, held under the 1973 Constitution, as the first were held in March, 1977.

This Provincial Assembly consisted of 260 members, of whom 240 had been elected against general seats, 8 against the seats reserved for non-Muslims and 12 against the seats reserved for women. The total number of lady members in this Assembly was 16, as 2 women had also been elected against general seats, in addition to 12 women against the seats reserved for ladies and 2 women against the seats reserved for non-Muslims. The first session of the Assembly was held on March 12, 1985. Mian Manzoor Ahmad Wattoo was elected unopposed as Speaker on April 9, 1985. Mian Manzar Ali Ranjah was elected as Deputy Speaker on the same date. They took oath of their respective offices on April 10, 1985.

Mian Nawaz Sharif entered upon his office as Chief Minister on April 9, 1985 and secured vote of confidence of the Punjab Assembly on April 10, 1985.

The elections to this Assembly were held on non-party basis. However, later on the Punjab Branch of Pakistan Muslim League was re-organized and a dominant majority of MPA's joined Pakistan Muslim League making it a majority party in the Assembly. Only 10 members formed an Opposition Group under the leadership of Makhdoomzada Syed Hasan Mahmood. After the death of

Makhdoomzada Syed Hasan Mahmood, the Opposition Group, in the Assembly elected Mian Muhammad Afzal Hayat as Leader of Opposition, in October, 1986.

On May 29, 1988, President, General Muhammad Zia-ul-Haq, dissolved the Federal Cabinet and the National Assembly, Following suit, the Governors of the Provinces dissolved their respective Provincial Cabinets and the Provincial Assemblies on May 30, 1988.

General Elections, 1988:- After dissolution of the Assemblies, Care-Taker Cabinets were appointed in the Centre and the Provinces. In Punjab,

Mr. Muhammad Nawaz Sharif was appointed as the Care-Taker Chief Minister. The President announced that the next General elections would be held on non-party basis and fixed November 16 & 19, 1988, for elections of the National Assembly and the Provincial Assemblies, respectively. The President, General Muhammad Zia-ul-Haq, died on August 17, 1988. When an Army C-130 plane carrying him along with top Army Officers and the American Ambassador to Pakistan, crashed near Bahawalpur and non-survived.

As scheduled the elections to the National Assembly and the Provincial Assemblies were held on 16th & 19th November, 1988, respectively. These elections were held on party basis in pursuance of the decision of the Supreme Court. The Assembly had been constituted on the basis of the said elections.

The Provincial Legislature consists of the Governor and the House, known as the Provincial Assembly. The Governor is empowered to promulgate an Ordinance, when the Provincial Assembly is not in session. He summons and prorogues the Assembly and has the right to address the Assembly. A Bill, passed by the Assembly, becomes an act of the Provincial Legislature only after it has been assented to by the Governor, who may withhold his assent or return the Bill for reconsideration by the Assembly.

The Governor invites such Members of the Provincial Assembly to be the Chief Minister who commands the confidence of the majority of the Members, of the Provincial Assembly, as ascertained in the session of the Assembly summoned for this purpose and may also remove him if he is satisfied that the Chief Minister has lost the confidence of the majority of members of the Assembly. He also appoints and removes the Minister, on the advice of the Chief Minister. The Governor may dissolve the Assembly on the advice of the Chief Minister, or in his discretion subject to the previous approval of the President if a vote of no-confidence is passed against the Chief Minister and a situation arises where an appeal to the electorate is necessary.

The executive authority of the Province, which extends to the matters with respect to which the Provincial Assembly has power to make laws, vests in the Governor who may exercise it personally or through officers subordinate to him.

All executive actions of the Provincial Government are expressed to be taken in the name of the Governor.

The Chief Minister is the leader of the majority party in the House and is the Leader of the House. The Chief Minister is also the head of the cabinet of Ministers to aid and advise the Governor in exercise of his functions. The cabinet is collectively responsible to the Provincial Assembly.

The Constitution provides that the Governor invites such member of the Provincial Assembly to be the Chief Minister who commands the confidence of the majority of the members of the Provincial Assembly, as ascertained in a session of the Assembly summoned for this purpose. Other Ministers are appointed and removed by the Governor on the advice of the Chief Minister.

The duties of the Chief Minister are laid down, in detail, in the Constitution and the Punjab Government Rules of Business. He communicates to the Governor all decisions of the Cabinet relating to the Province and proposals for Legislation, and also provides such information relating there to as may be called for by the Governor. He also authenticates schedule of authorised expenditure. Mr. Muhammad Nawaz Sharif became Chief Minister through a resolution on April 10, 1985. He was elected as President, Pakistan Muslim League (Punjab Branch) on January 30, 1986. He continued as Chief Minister of Punjab and Leader of the House in Punjab Assembly till its dissolution on May 30, 1988.He was appointed as Chief Minister, Punjab, in the Care-Taker Cabinet constituted until the next elections to the Assembly. During the General elections, 1988, he was elected to two National Assembly seats from Lahore and Sialkot and two Provincial Assembly seats from Lahore. He again retained the Provincial Assembly seat. The Punjab Assembly re-elected him as the Chief Minister on December 2, 1988. Later, he was also elected as President, Islami Jamhoori Itehad.

WAPDA HOUSE

Wapda House was conceived in early sixtees primarily to house offices of rapidly expanding Water and Power Development Authority (WAPDA) with its headquarters at Lahore. The most attractive location in the city, the fourth corner of the spacious Charing Cross in the immediate vicinity of Assembly Chambers on the Mall, was chosen for this magnificent building which was to enjoy the status of the most beautiful building not only in Lahore but also in the entire country for a long time to come. For this purpose existing "Mela" Ram and Jodha Mal buildings across the Mall, opposite Freemason's Hall were purchased and demolished to obtain 33 kanals and 6 marlas of prime land on the Egerton – Mall Road juncture. New York's famous architect, Edward G. Stone undertook designing of the building, and construction work was initiated in October 1963. M/s Gammon Pakistan Ltd. were awarded contract for civil works while M/s Ally Brothers (Pak) Ltd., M/s Jaleel Brothers and M/s Paktrack were assigned the tasks of electrification, air-conditioning and providing light respectively. The building was completed in 1967.According to WAPDA it produced a unique blend of old and new architectural rendering. It has been so designed as to meet not only the physical needs of Wapda but also to symbolise the nation's high aesthetic standards, as the building is still rated as one of the greatest and most attractive buildings of the recent period.

Consisting of nine storeys, including two below the ground level, the 115 feet high majestic structure has an arcaded two-storey block spanning the centre site, and a seven storey tower rising above this block. The height excludes 12 feet height plexiglass dome at the roof over the central 65 feet diameter rotunda which makes it stand out amongst all the surrounding buildings.

The building has three main wings: the Tower Section facing Al-Falah, the Mall Wing along the Shahrah-e-Quaid-e-Azam and the Egerton Road Wing facing the Assembly Chambers. Parking space for more than 100 cars has been provided in the sub-basement around the grand 400 seat auditorium which is even today considered the finest venue for holding conferences, seminars and similar functions in the town. The auditorium has a tastefully laid stage with a wide screen for projecting films from two 35 MM. projectors installed across the hall. The building has entrances from all the three sides with main entrance facing The Mall.

A unique feature of the building is the sunken garden, about 11 feet below the ground with direct access from the upper basement and the auditorium below. The Mughal style fountains when in operation present a charming view enhancing the beauty of the building. Lush green park bordered by beautiful flower beds constitute the colourful corner of the site.

Amidst the offices on all the nine floors rests beautiful dignified mosque on the first floor in which more than 300 persons can pray. The design of the mosque, though different from the rest of the building, goes well with the main building's architectural theme.

The building is provided with two banks of four lifts each with a service little Centralised toilets on each floor.Although the lower floors of the building were rented out in the beginning to house private offices the entire building is now in Wapda's own use with only outer peripheral show-room type rooms rented to banks, airlines and a few other trading concerns.

About 17,000 tons of cement and 5,650 tons of steel went into construction of Wapda House in addition to large quantities of best quality wood, plate glass and other masonry items. The building with large scale plumbing works of the highest

WAPDA House

quality, lighting and finest air-conditioning plants and ducts have comfortably stood test of 30 years' use for which the credit also partly goes to excellent maintenance of the building which is looked after by a strong contingent of cleaning and repairing staff employed for round-the-clock check on wear and tear of the building. The project incurred a total cost of Rs.40.39 million (1967) which included entire civil, electrical, air-conditioning, carpentry and other works.

The above was a resume of the architectural remains of the Mughal period, the British times and the post independence era. The subject is very wide and with many dimensions. Encompassing in this compilation is neither possible nor technically and professionally my subject. It would however give an idea of the assets we own in terms of city's heritage. The brief historical facts were mentioned to put the reader in picture to better appreciate the value of the monuments. The most important thing is as to how we are looking after this heritage. Are we saving or expediting their decay. A reflection reveals that we are certainly not doing justice. Like Sikhs and the British we have divested the monuments of their valuables. We are misusing them like aliens and taking no measures for their preservation.

The British style of building was totally different from the Mughals. They created splendidly Victorian public buildings in the style that has come to be called Mughal Gothic. Some also term it frigid classical. Whatever name may be given the fact remains that it was certainly different than the one already invogue, in the city. No monumental works other than the public buildings appeared in the city. All such buildings are not large and massive. These are mostly functional in charter and public oriented in nature.

After 1947, as already mentioned in the preceding paragraphs nothing much of architectural significance happened in late 60s. Infact the long tradition of Muslim architecture was broken by the British Rule, which resulted in colonial style of architectural pattern in some buildings. On partition Pakistan had no more than a few architects in the country. The early years of the history of Pakistan might be taken as a period of transition. There were reasons of resource constraint, problem of refugee settlement, and deficient technical know how. However there appeared to be a traditional desire of Muslim architecture, at least an anxiety to have that type of architecture using the latest building techniques. The population grew at phenomenal rate and the buildings came up with vulgar designs and built by non-descript overseers and inept architects. The only buildings which appear to have been designed were of some residential houses in some big cities. Some time later the change that appeared in the architecture was expression of fair-faced fronts, with re-inforced concrete framed structures. Some modern treatment of interior by younger group of architects also came in. The removal of the dividing line between the exterior and interior of the building and consequent closer integration of the lawn, the houses were the special feature adopted in the cities. There was however a change in 1961 when the Government of Pakistan took a decision to build capital city at Islamabad. There was a competition between International architects but the press opined a clamour for the adaptation of Muslim style for the public buildings. Committees were formed and seminars held to interpret Muslim architecture. The net result was that while the people sympathized with the nation's desire to reflect about the same means were non existent. For example, while one school of thought looked for the obvious imitation of superficial forms and symbola of Muslim architecture, which could only be anachronistic and uneconomic in conjunction with modern materials and methods of construction others advocated a more rational approach to the best traditions in Muslim architecture, which included the sensitive integration of the garden and landscaping with the principal building as in the Shalamar Gardens the variety of textural decoration as in Jahangir's Tomb, and the expert use of scale as exemplified in Badshahi Mosque. Most critical students of Muslim architecture are aware that Muslim settlers are reputed to have adopted the use of indigenous materials and local buildings within the sub-continent as elsewhere.

With such strong and clear traditions, nostalgia for the external forms of Muslim architecture without close attention to modern methods of construction and advance in technology was pointless. The controversy on the subject continued to rage within the country, with a resulting conflict and confusion in the minds of architects. By this time young architects having foreign training had started coming back to the country. In the field of public buildings some efforts were made in capturing the spirit of Muslim architecture especially the offices. The use of traditional building material, construction methods duly scaped in Muslim tradition, gave special distinction to such identities and as an example the Secretariat Building (P&D Branch) can be quoted. The building is reportedly purely functional short in traditionalism, simplicity of design and economy of structure coupled with interesting visual effects created by pillars and classical structure specifically in locating blocks. During the sixties the new buildings in private sector that appeared in Lahore city can be termed as Industrial architecture is that of Wyeth Laboratories. In its functional simplicity and freshness of approach it really remains a landmark amongst industrial buildings. The 70s sought a new direction in the contemporary architecture in the city qualified architects grew in number, many of them were trained from abroad and exposed to new idea and uninhibited by the constrains of traditionalism. However, their design appeared to have merged in public building are not worth mentioning except pigeonhole houses and multistoried flats at scattered spots. The reason for encouragement of this sort of architecture appears to be urbanization, escalating prices, pressure on land, resource constraints, growing population and absence of State policy towards architecture. This is why the majority of these modern edifices are devoid of aesthetic appeal as well as functionally poor with climatic and environmental problems. Some architects had however, managed to strike a balance between economics and harmony and have been able to produce response to harsh environmental condition. The structures by British with a uniform design have disappeared but at the same time Muslim features of geometric curvilinear motifs have also disappeared.

Architecturally, the Mughal period is characterized by the integration of landscape and buildings. Landscape designing was itself a highly developed discipline which aimed at using both running and still water, formal gardens and tiered terraces to achieve a fusion of textures and colours. Shalamar Gardens in Lahore are fine example of this unique attention to open spaces. Mughal buildings are specially striking because of the deep understanding of mass and scale inherent in them.

As evidenced in Mughal buildings perhaps the finest contribution to the Pakistani architectural heritage was in the vast field of surface treatment and decoration. Surface decoration emphasized and heightened the sculptural qualities of the form of the building. Excellent enamelled tile work, exquisite geometric marble lattice work and arabesques from decorative motifs on many buildings, combining with existing modes, such as calligraphic inscriptions and geometric relief panel treatments were noteworthy features. Finding a rich store of coloured marble and onyx, the Mughal craftsmen of central Asia were inspired to embellish monuments with magnificent inlaid stone panels. Many remarkable buildings like Jahangir's tomb in Lahore have inlaid stone panels.

It may be remarked in passing that the material used in the roof of Naulakha Pavilion was evolved from the use of bamboo in the form of curved cornice to drain excessive rainfall. Similarly there was pre-dominant use of local materials in other parts of the Punjab. From ancient times the indigenous architecture in this part of the Sub-Continent especially in Punjab and Lahore was dictated by the climate. The fierce sun and devastating night cold in the hot Punjab plains swept by swollen floods and rocky mountainous environment always played an important role in planning and building for the communities. In this part of Punjab particularly mud plaster houses were a natural response to environment. The mud/clay is in plenty and a house can be constructed with little cost and re-built when required. Mud is cool in summer as it is natural insulating material. In case of damage to house it can be easily built and raised afresh. Indoor smooth mud-plaster forms the walls and niches. The wooden shelves are used for supporting the house-hold effects. It can also be kept clean easily. Maintenance wise mud plaster costs very little. This was so generally in Punjab and quite a few mud brick buildings, reinforced with wooden beams, rising over winding and narrow streets existed in the city. However one major change in the post partition construction became the use of burnt brick although its use had been in abundance during the British regime. It has become a requirement of the city dwellers now a days. Most of the houses in the extended parts of the city are raised with pucca bricks. The muddy houses are only found in the Katchi Abadies which are also being gradually upgraded with subsidy from the Government.

The abundant availability of modern building materials is cement, enough supply from brick kilns, availability of steel and wood and its substitutes steel doors, windows of different materials, glass, and miscellaneous other items have also changed the pattern of architecture after the late 70s. While the middle class generally comes in for construction of houses with pucca bricks only the well off go in for RCC construction i.e. steel and concrete is used in columns and re-movable walls provided in bricks. The houses are now designed not keeping in view the climate instead air-conditioning and heating have taken care of this aspect. The mobility inside house of the residing members and lawns is mostly incorporated in the plan of the houses. In late 70s there was a trend to have hedges but after 80s security becoming a problem the people now prefer to have security walls. The only post-partition structures of public buildings which have emerged in the city are some hospitals, some colleges and school buildings. On the Mall the State Bank Building, WAPDA House and Arts Council (generally called ALHAMRA) have been constructed. We have already mentioned elsewhere about Gymkhana, Hotel Pearl Continental, Avari and Holiday Inn. These buildings hardly give any Muslim or Classical architectural look, instead they have been made to the requirement of the client. These buildings have been constructed in RCC and are controlled by Air-conditioning for purposes of hot and cold weathers. The recently constructed children's Hospital on Ferozepur Road can be termed frigid classical as at least it looks a sort of classical structure although columns structure with filled walls, it has had fair face treatment in red bricks. The other addition in the architecture of the city can be mentioned as over-head bridges, under-passes, bridges on the River Ravi a monument known as Yadgar-e-Pakistan near Lahore Fort, Summit Minar, Fortress Stadium, Cricket and Hockey Stadiums and an Open Air Theatre on the Ferozepur Road. The Yadgar-e-Pakistan or Minar-e-Pakistan is an RCC 'minar' raised to commemorate the memory of passing Pakistan Resolution at that place. It is on a raised plinth and about 100 feet on each side in square. The height of the Minar is 110 feet. Whatever the genesis of construction, it hardly represents our heritage, history or any mode of architecture except that it is a minar with a poor look in the vicinity of Majestic Minars of Badshahi Mosque.

With the over-whelming increase in transport and vehicular traffic from other cities towards Lahore two Bridges on the River Ravi have been built. Both the bridges are wide enough to take one way traffic with the facility for pedestrians, Motorcyclists and others. Both the bridges have been constructed on RCC Columns with lengthy lintel beam slabs and treatment on the surface. Of course users have to pay the toll-tax. While one bridge near the old railway bridge is most probably in place of the old boat bridge around Baradari the other bridge was only recently inaugurated (in the year 1997) three miles downstream, from Kamran's Baradari, connecting the city with Lahore –Islamabad Motorway. The building on the Mall especially those of State Bank of Pakistan is a poor piece of modern construction with hardly any features or characteristics to be commented about. The WAPDA House building located in the Charing Cross on the Mall, now known as Faisal Square/Chowk is again a modern RCC building, Air-conditioned and designed by Mr. Edward Stone. This building, however, due to its large size has marred the classical structures which exist in the shape of Masonic lodge (Chief Minister Secretariat) and Shahdin Building on the west. The other buildings which gives very gaudy and pigeonhole impression is the Alfalah Building in this area which inspite of its height hardly impresses. This building has been raised from contributions of civil servants. It is mostly rented out and poorly maintained. On the southern side there stands the most imposing Punjab Assembly (built in 1935-37) which has been described separately in this book. In between there is Summit Minar which was raised to commemorate the holding of an Islamic Summit in the Assembly Hall, in February, 1975. The Summit Minar is surrounded in triangular style tent like blocks in an area of about 3 kanals. Some time a sort of Museum was maintained under this but usually remains closed. In the adjoining ground close to the minar is located the beautiful canopy which was constructed in the late 19th Century to mark the Jubilee Year of Queen Victoria. With our little taste and respect for the monuments and sculpture, the statue of Queen Victoria had been removed and only Canopy stands in the ground. A couple of years back THE HOLY QURAN was placed under the Canopy which hardly appeals as a replacement instead anyway this is how it is. The building of Hotel Avari, Pearl Continental, Holiday Inn are essentially modern structures raised with modern materials on prime locations in the city and essentially meant to make money. These building being commercial ventures are well maintained but hardly representatives of any school of architecture.

The city of Lahore has expanded manifold. If it consisted of 90,000 soles in the year 1890 it was over 60 lacs in the year 1990. The walled city is just an Island in an Ocean, haphazard & erratically grown localities in all directions surrounding the city starting from Ravi northwards the city is touching Kamoke with residential colonies on both sides of the highway. After Kamoke practically there appears any vacant land. The localities and colonies on this road are Shahadra, Ferozewala, Imamia Colony, Ruchna Town, Kala Shah Kaku, Jia Musa, From Ravi towards Shah Pur, Begum Kot, Kot Abdul Malik etc. etc.

Coming downwards from Ravi, the city includes, Qasim Pura, Qila Lachman Singh, Timber Market, the Ravi Road, Karim Park, Sanda, Bilal Ganj, Mohni Road, Sant Nagar, Krishan Nagar, Raj Garh, Sanda Khurd, Sanda Kalan, Out fall , Riffle Range, Riwaz Garden, Sham Nagar, Gulshan Ravi, Jaffriea Colony, Chauburji, Islamia Park, Rustam Park, Nawankot, Shera Kot, Said Pur, Shahnoor, Mustafa Town, Kharak, Allama Iqbal Town, Hassan Town, Awan Town, Canal View, Ittefaq Town, Society, Shahpur, Niaz Beg, Choong, Mohlanwal. Mohafiz Town, Judicial Colony I, II, III. Westwood Colony, Jauhar Town, University Town, Wahdat Colony, Muslim Town, Income Tax Colony, Alhamd Colony, Urdu Bazar, New Anarkali, Old Anarkali, Mozang, New Mozang, Bahawalpur House, Samanabad, Pakki Thatti, Shah Kamal, Rahman Pura, Icchra, Shah Jamal, Shadman, Gulberg-I, II, III, Waltan, Choungi Amar Sidhu, Nishtar Park, and so on.

These localities go right up to Bhai Pheru 30 miles on the Multan Road. On the Ferozepur Road starting from the District Courts would come the Old Anarkali, Mozang, Nia Mozang, Shadman Colony, Ichhra, Old Muslim Town, Shah Jamal, Garden Town, Model Town, Model Town Extension, Township, Revenue Society, Green Town, Valanshia Town, PCSIR Society, Postal Colony, General Hospital Colony, Choungi Amar Sidhu, Walton, and so on. Until 15 miles towards Kasur this area again is filled with factories and newly raised colonies. These localities have emerged without any respect to roads, sewerage and water supply, health and education facilities. Starting eastwards from the District Courts would come the localities of Qila Gujar Singh, Garhi Shahu, Aitchison College Colony, Zaman Park, Dharam Pura, Mian Mir, Cantt., Mughalpura, Shalamar Colony, Ghazi Road, Railway Colony, Upper Mall Scheme Saddar and Baidian etc. Leading towards south would come the areas of Missri Shah, Shadbagh, Singh Pura, Mehmood Booti, Kot Khawaja Saeed, Gujjar Pura, Begum Pura, Ghoray Shah, Pak Mint and so on. These would give the idea of haphazard growth of the city which inspite of the Government's best efforts have hardly any standard facilities. During rains, quite a few areas become ponds and casualties take place due to rainwater, over-flowing gutters, leakage of electric power supply, crumbling Katcha and Pacca Houses as also epidemics, which spread out due to unhygienic and filthy conditions.

For the last over 10 –15 years the Government have been consistently spending millions to drain out water but since expansion is without any planning it has hardly proved successful. The walled city, which was provided drinking water facilities in the year 1863, can now hardly cope with the requirements. The same is the condition of educational facilities. The people wander about finding political recommendations for admission of their children in the educational institutions

Above all the population growth, is over 4 per cent and catastrophic and telling heavily on the resources of the city. This has hampered any systematic development and thus no architectural growth. A gap has occurred after the departure of the British which hardly appears to be bridged in the coming years inspite of educational and technological advancement.

We have gone through the architectural heritage of the Muslim period, the Sikhs. (who only dis-figured and defaced the city) and the British period which brought in the Victorian style structures and then the post partition period. Of the last there is nothing worth-mentioning which may be counted as a landmark in the field of architecture. There are only a very few buildings (already mentioned elsewhere) which include the extension of Academic Blocks of Government College, Lahore, the State Bank Building near the Regal Chowk and the WAPDA House in the Charing Cross. The other buildings, which have come up after partition, are Academic Blocks of Engineering University, Mian Nawaz Sharif Hospital, Sheranwala Gate, Minar-e-Pakistan, Extension of Distt. Courts, Planning & Development Department Block, Civil Secretariat. Some constructions in Mayo Hospital, Alfalah Building, Alhamra Arts Centre, Fortress Stadium, Social Security Hospital, Multan Road, Gaddafi Stadium, Cultural Complex, Permanent Art Gallery, MPAs Hostel near Assembly Chambers, Children's Hospital, Ferozepur Road and New University Campus.

The Academic Block in the Government College is a modified version of the Gothic style construction already in existence at the premises.

The addition to the Mayo Hospital came up in the shape of Emergency Block, Eye Hospital, Paediatrics Wing and Orthopedic Block. All the construction is without any regard to the contumely of architectural features or keeping any relation with the existing structure raised even in the British period.

Nawaz Sharif Hospital in the old city, Social Security Hospital, on Multan Road, and Punjab Institute of Cardiology are just modern constructions without any outstanding features worth mentioning. These are air-conditioned without any regard to the climate, light or ventilation etc. The Children's Hospital on Ferozepur Road, has a brick façade which is quite impressing. The Summit Minar, Minar-e-Pakistan and a Sculpture-like construction near Garden Town hardly gives an idea of as to which school of thought they belong to. The Fortress Stadium close to the Cantt and Gaddafi Stadium on Ferozepur Road have a reasonable seating capacity but without any proper arrangements for the audience from the heat and rain. The temporary shelter type coverage in the Gaddafi Stadium gives a very ugly look.

The addition of shops and a commercial plaza around the Stadium has made mockery of the stadium place as a playground. The Hockey Stadium adjacent to the Gaddafi Stadium raised on lofty columns with lintel construction is quite spacious and takes in thousands of spectators. It is a good functional playground.

The other main building on The Mall is that of Alhamra. A heavy brick structure quite imposing in between Hotel Avari and Government House. It is learnt that the architect designed the slanting walls impressed by Mausoleum of Shah Ruken-e-Alam at Multan. Functionally, only the management and users know but looks to be with architectural features blending with local provisions. The elevation of the building is quite attractive and well conceived. It initiated a new chapter of brick construction after a long break in the city.

"I fall up on the thorns of life – bleed" Shelly Painting by Ustad Allah Bakhsh

5

THE ART
And Paintings' Scene

The origin of painting is traced centuries back in the regions now forming Pakistan, when traders and travellers indulged in rock carving and drawings on the silk route specially depicting human and animal figures. Archaeologists track their origin to 3000 BC. Then come the pottery paintings in plains leading to pre-Harrappa civilization. The excavation at Harrappa led one to conclude the town planning, emergence of urbanization along order and symmetry. The advancement of technology and trade gave impetus to artistic expression, which appear in Terracotta figurines stone statutes fairly done with strong expressive power. Skillful design of jewellery beads, etchings with variety of shapes and sizes is indicative of the evolutionary stages of Arts and crafts. A careful study reveals that figurines are modelled playfully and finished with flair raising them to the level of artwork. The skill of necklaces, bracelets, rings, ear-rings, casting bronzes and statutes was the end product of long practised Arts. This was followed by sculpture where the realistic figure apparently referred to Greek influence. The master pieces in sculpture and pictographic seals indicate the level reached. About paintings, the evidence of decoration of pots, although a facet of paintings, cannot be treated on the same level as that of statutes. The amazing artistic scene flourished for centuries but disappeared around 1900 BC and was succeeded by agriculturists' settlement during which period growth of art appear to have met a setback. In Punjab 'finds' at Harrappa bear evidence of cultural landmarks. In the northern areas the Gandhara culture reveals much about the stage of cultural awareness. Archaeologists assert that Aryans influence over-whelmed the Indus Valley civilization, which was followed by Persian influence. It was too diverse and noteworthy in architecture and is evident in the Mughal period. The evidence of the repetitive "Persian Columns" in carved panels and motifs of cypress tree, lotus flower is still in use in contemporary architecture. The Greeks succeeded Persians who lost to Mauryans and their inscriptions are evidence of the Buddhist school of Gandhara sculpture. The city of Sirkap (Taxila) has temples, statutes and wall paintings which is proof of the growth of Arts. There appears to be a gap after the Kanishka period of over one thousand-years. The missing link is between

"In the stilly night"Painting by Ustad Allah Bakhsh

Buddhist murals till the Mughal School of painting, except that of some claims of fresco painting in the intervening period but nothing about the pictorial Art as such.

During the Sultanate period nothing substantial has been found except deduced references by scholarly illustrations on manuscripts. In the later period the work of known artist Behzad finds, mention in various annals with composition, decoration, layout and architectural background. The mural painting, however, is reported to have received the patronage of Khilji and Tughlaq rulers in India. The decoration of buildings with floral and geometrical patterns has been instrumental in the education and learning of the Arts.

The Mughal period saw remarkable change where the Arts found fertile climate. They were highly cultured and patronized music, poetry, history, Arts and architecture. Of course this build up found its basis in the proceeding progress and tradition of Indian art. The enormous out-put during the Mughal period has survived to a reasonable extent in the sub-continent and is also found all over the world. The personal interest of the Mughal Emperors gave birth to a school of miniature painting, and great calligraphists and 'Naqqash' not only contributed to the creative work but also trained and educated natives. As a consequence the art historians discovered an emergence of Rajistan and Pahari School of paintings. The interaction of foreign and local artists gave birth to fresh and hybrid style in treating the Indian subject of painting. The treatment of Rajput style and Mughal School differs in women-wear, loose trousers and pyjama etc. This phenomenon appears to have given way to various schools of art in the beginning of the 19th century. The indigenous institutions declined with the arrival of western thought and education and governing system. However, as far as Punjab is concerned first came the Persian & Central Asian influence and then during the 19th century there emerged the Sikh school of paintings. Portraits of people sitting in chairs were specially done up during this period.

Punjab was the latest child of the British Empire in India. It put an end to the Sikh Rule in March 1849. With the change of system of administration and introduction of western style of Government the British brought in western educational system and accordingly the founding of schools and colleges and art institutions on European lines was introduced. Some art critics feel that the Westerners who entered as traders and tourists taught the locals to paint scenes and sites confirming to "Englishman's romantic notion of the west".

One Mr. B. H. Baden Powell on the instance of Educational Committee in Punjab supported by Col. Maclagan and Dr. Hunter of Madras proposed that a school of art and industry be established. It was proposed that a school of design to teach drawing and designing should be a Branch, first to be established. The proposal fell through due to difficulty of funds and was again taken up in 1868 in which it was suggested that a school such as it is desirable to be established to embrace instructions in ornamental art and as applicable to manufacturers. The proposal was again dropped due to difficulty of funds and taken up in February 1868 in which it was suggested that a school was desirable to impart instructions in Ornamental Art as applicable to manufacture and decoration of buildings and actual execution of work. A beginning was to be made with the first branch which would consist of teaching free-hand and geometrical drawing, so as to enable students to appreciate the forms as applicable to manufacture and soon after that, as might be (when a little experience had been gained) for actual work in those branches which suited most. It was, therefore, proposed to have a suitable room properly lighted and furnished, a drawing Master, a small stock of Art examples, models, designs. To begin with a room attached with the central museum was to be done up for the purpose and services of a drawing master was proposed to be obtained from Madras School of Art with small stock of elementary examples, models proposed to be obtained from Educational Division of South Kensington Museum. The school was to have two branches one for the drawing and design and the other for the course of mechanics with a workshop (for the proposed school of art) which was to be raised from the memorial fund.

The Punjab Government requested, the Government of India, in the home Department on 18.7.1973 that Mr. J. L. Kipling, Professor in the School of Art Bombay, a gentleman believed to be well-known to the Government of India, had been recommended to the Lt. Governor of Punjab as a person eminently suited by attainment and experience, to start the proposed Industrial School of Art. The Government of India was requested to sanction the proposed arrangement and nominate Mr. J. L. Kipling as Principal of the School of Art as soon as the Government of Bombay spares his services. His salary was fixed at Rs.800/- P.M. to be defrayed from the Provincial Government revenues. Acceding to the request of the Punjab Government, the Government of India and Government of Bombay allowed Mr. Kipling to report to the Punjab Government who arrived in Lahore on the morning of 24th April 1875. The Provincial Government asked Prof. Kipling to submit definite and detailed proposal for the establishment of new school in accordance with general principle laid down by the Secretary of State and in the light of special work and preliminary thinking and work already done at Lahore. On 27th of May 1875 Professor Kipling, the Principal of Lahore School of Art, reported to the Government that as a temporary measure he had started his office and classroom in the house (lately) occupied by Mr. Harrison. The school of carpentry was making drawing boards, desks, easels table etc. And he had ordered books, casts, and examples etc. from England for the school. It was suggested that for permanent arrangements, he advised, locating the Art School near the Museum.

¨Rind Kharabat-i-Diwana-i-Ma¨ Omer Khyyam
Painting by Ustad Miran Bakhsh

He suggested the place occupied by G. P. O. and one near hospital close to the Badshahi Mosque but as an interim measure he suggested to hire some house, as building a school was to take place in about two years. He also submitted plans for the organization suited to the local requirements and capable of expansion as occasion may direct.

Mr. J. L. Kipling suggested the out-line of the courses of instructions which pertained to elementary outline, geometry, outline from objects, plant drawing, modelling architectural drawing and drawing from living models including painting from the living models. With this course of instructions, procedures were laid for admission to the school and thus started working the New School of Industrial Art as an institution in Lahore that is till date a place of Art Education. The school progressed and was joined by students from all communities i.e. Hindus, Christians and Muslims. The School got separate premises in 1878 prior to which it was part of the Museum with proper workshop equipped with tools and machines and photo lithographic studio functioning. The work done at school was recognized all over India and Britain. The school attended to Lot of wood carving, plastic work and interior in various Government buildings.

Such was the artistic scene obtaining at Lahore by the close of 19th century when late Professor J. L. Kipling founded the school in Lahore, stretching up to Peshawar and the entire area got the much needed profile. His personal efforts & interest re-invigorated the art activity, which had vanished with the glory of Mughals in this historic city.

Lahore was actually the only city of art activity, which essentially emerged as a requirement of the promotion of industrial Arts and Crafts much concerned with manufacturing of local products. The institution and education at this place promoted indigenous crafts of India and very little was produced in oil and water painting by the students and teachers of the Art School. Sher Muhammad of Lahore who was a student of the Lahore Art School designed the title page of the exhibition catalogue held at Delhi in 1902-3. About the paintings Mr. Percy Brown in his introduction to the catalogue remarked " of the school of art style of paintings, two portraits of Punjabis by Sher Muhammad of the Lahore School of Art deserve special mention. They show knowledge of technique and a familiarity with the intricate modelling of the human face, that places them considerable above the ordinary work of this kind." In the 1920s and 30s one finds some artists active in Lahore. Chughtai's work was first printed in the Modern Review of Calcutta and then published by the Editor as "Chatterji's Picture Albums". "In Album No.6 we find call of the Cuckoo" and "the Lamp Fails" by S.N. Gupta, who joined the Mayo School of Art as teacher in 1913 and later on became the Principal and also Curator of the Lahore Museum. Gupta was a pupil of Abindranath Tagore and brought the new Bengal School of painting to Lahore. E. B. Havell, who was earlier Principal of the Art School of Calcutta, wrote: -"In the Punjab section, there is far more evidence of an Indian artistic renaissance, but the painters of the Lahore School, as far as the Wembley Exhibition goes, seem to be still struggling towards self-expression without being quite sure which way they are aiming at."Lionel Heath, Principal of the Mayo School of Art (1914-29) wrote in his article "Modern Indian Art at Wembley" in the British Empire Review that: -

"The Punjab artists may be congratulated on having set a high standard of merit and also upon having formed a very definite style of their own. The Punjab artists are now in the forefront of this movement."

Among the Lahore artists who came in for special mention were S. N. Gupta and Roop Krishna, both pupils of Abindranath Tagore. About Abdur Rahman Chughtai, Heath observed: -

"The new school of thought may be represented by the work of A. R. Chughtai, who shows a beauty of line and composition in his drawings that is admirable. In his paintings, his colour is simple and decorative, while the form is well expressed, as is evident from his "Devdasi", a temple-dancing girl. Mr. Inayatullah, Mr. Muhammad Hussain Qadri, Mr. A. R. Asghar, are all represented by only eight paintings but it is safe to say that these exhibits leave an impression of personality and force." This was the art scene obtaining in Lahore in 1920s and till 40s forming the Arts continued flourishing, in Lahore. Most important centre of artistic activity was Mayo School of Industrial Art, and most of the artists who gained prominence were old students of this School or teachers. Most of them used to paint in Bengali style. The work of alumni of Mayo School, displayed in exhibitions all over India was also published in Urdu Magazines. The work of A. R. Chughtai, Inayatullah, M. H. Qadri and A. R. Ejaz was also published in the Calcutta Art Journal "Rupam" and the famous general magazine "Modern Review" in the 20s, 30s and 40s. The "Chatterjee's Picture Albums" brought out by the editor of "Modern Review", contained paintings by M. H. Qadri and A.R. Ejaz together with work by the famous Bengali artists. S. N. Gupta was the moving spirit behind this movement. When he retired from the Principalship of the Mayo School in 1942, Mian Muhammad Hussain became the Principal. He signed his paintings as M. H. Qadri. Outside the School, Roop Krishna was another practitioner of the Bengal Style.

Two European women painters threw a challenge to this whole group. Amrita Sher Gil in the 30s and Anna Molka Ahmad in the 40s. Amrita Sher Gil was the daughter of a Sikh aristocrat and a Hungarian mother. She was born in Budapest in 1913. At the age of eight her parents brought her to India where she stayed, with one brief interruption, until she was 16. From 1920-34 she studied art in Paris, and in 1934 returned to India. In 1941 she died. Hers was a short life; but in her last seven years she painted a number of canvases which are, in the opinion of our few honest critics, some of the most important pictures painted by an Indian painter since the great Rajput schools of the eighteenth century. Many influences are traceable in her work. The treatment of Ganesh Puja, a scene showing the worship of the elephant-headed god as practised in the villages of Northern India, and of Camels, an experiment in composition, derives partly from Basholi, Kangra and Mughal painting. The almost sculpturesque technique of The Procession and of Hill Women blends the draughtsmanship she learnt in Paris with a compassionate vision of the unhappy Indian people.

She seems to be thrilled with the discovery that India is shrieking aloud for artistic interpretation by someone who could eschew false romanticism with a resilient technique and a genuine tenderness. Few artists in contemporary India have handled colour with quite the passionate joy which Amrita Sher Gil brought to it and yet all these gay and bright colours communicate the essential melancholy of this land and her inhabitants.

This struggle to realize herself through paint dominated her and she remained an experimentalist throughout her young life. Waging an uncompromising war against complacence, and straining to achieve greater control over her medium. She returned to India in July 1939, but painted very little in the atmosphere of uncertainty, which prevailed, with the outbreak of war. But when Amrita settled down in the village of Saraya, where her husband was appointed Medical Officer at her uncle's sugar factory, she was conscious of a new phase in her work.'I can't waste time,' she had cried incessantly during this period, as though she had a premonition of her impending death. And she had relentlessly pursued her painting, exploring all kinds of ideal forms, colours and constructions, with a view to the new synthesis she had been intent on achieving between the canvas and India. In 1940 she moved to Lahore, where she died of a sudden illness. She died in December, a few days before her exhibition, which was likely to open in Lahore.

In late thirties another European woman artist came to Lahore in 1940. She was Anna Molka Ahmad, wife of Shaikh Ahmed, the artist. She set up the Fine Arts Department of the Punjab University from where a stream of graduates came out who spread all over the Punjab as art teachers in schools and colleges (after Fine Art was introduced as a subject in colleges due to Mrs. Ahmed's efforts). She practised the orange-mauve formula (not Impressionistically but Expressionistically that is with bold brush strokes and deep rich colours) but she looked down upon the Bengali Oriental style, writing in her magazine "Vista"(1959):

About "these well-known artists, i.e. Mr. Abdur Rahman Chughtai and Mr. Muhammad Hussain, Tagore observed, neither did he see sunshine nor did Chughtai or Muhammad Hussain. Soft harmonies of colour, dreamy eyes and languid limbs and the billowing garments of olden days seem to hypnotize us as we gaze at their work". But the impact of the virile painting of the younger generation awakes us. There is a tremendous change.

Mrs. Ahmed encouraged her students to paint village scenes and village people in a realistic way and their work bears the stamp of her training. She said "I teach my students tonal painting, that is varying of tone of colour from dark to light, but I practise colouristic painting, using colours of different light values for each shade of light and dark."

Shaikh Ahmed, Anna Molka's husband, was a highly talented artist who taught for some time in Mayo School but left in 1950 because he could not work with the Principal, Ghulam Nabi Malik, who had taken over in 1947. Shaikh Ahmad was a prominent figure in the art circles of Lahore in the 40s because he had a very social nature. His style was meticulous to a degree, the opposite of that of his wife, but he had a restless temperament and his studio was full of unfinished portraits. Another important artist of Lahore was Ustad Allah Bakhsh. He came to Lahore in 1939 after a long stay in Bombay, of the same age as Chughtai and equally dedicated, he too lived almost like a recluse but unlike Chughtai, he had a few pupils always working with him. His adopted son Abdul Aziz learnt to paint exactly like him while the grandson, Abdul Majid painted historical scenes based on published drawings, which he suitably modified. To briefly state preceding Independence leading painters of Lahore were A. R. Chughtai and Ustad Allah Bakhsh. It will therefore, be only befitting and appropriate to narrate briefly about the life and work of these artists who are known as "Masters".

ABDUR RAHMAN CHUGHTAI

Born in Lahore on 21st September 1897, after passing middle school, he joined as a Drawing Master in the Mayo School of Art. He worked for some time as Drawing Master in Mission School, Gujranwala and later, in 1916 became teacher of PhotoLithography in Mayo School at Lahore. His painting work was published in Modern Review of Calcutta. The early work of Chughtai available to view in "The Indian Academy of Art Journal" shows from the beginning his literary preoccupation and eagerness to paint ideas beautifully. He was, it is stated, a famous name in the first quarter of this century as Modern Review was the most authentic magazine of India in those days. When the Magazine, started publishing "Chatterji's Picture Albums" in 1918 a painting by Chughtai was included in each of the six volumes that were brought from January 1920. The India Academy of

published paintings of Chughtai in each of the first four issues. Chughtai also took part in exhibitions all over India and won many prizes. The climax was his participation in the great British Empire Exhibition held at Wembley in 1924. For this eleven of his paintings were selected which were more than that of any other Indian artist. In 1928 an illustrated edition of the Diwan-e-Ghalib titled "Murraqa-e-Chughtai" was published.

It was in those days when this most beautiful book of art and literature was published in India and became a best seller, with the result that Chughtai became a household word. All the paintings of the artist were commented as meticulous and delicate."Murraqa-e-Chughtai" and "Naqash-e-Chughtai" built the image of the artist. The illustration in Murraqa and verses of Ghalib made a combination with certain similar features of the work of the artist and poet. Both are sweetly sad and wistful. Poetry of Ghalib is full of meaning and Chughtai too is one of those rare artists who like to convey an idea through pictures and to give it a literary content: "The flights of fancy of the poet and his utter disregard of the realities of the surrounding world, in his ghazals, is matched by the imaginary archaic dresses and the fanciful flowers and trees and old architecture which forms the setting of most of the pictures. The musical cadences of the poetry are paralleled by the rhythmic cursive lines of the figure drawing and the drapery and the arabesque decorations in the background. The dreamy drunken eyes of all the people in the pictures match the rapt emotional mood of the poems. Finally, the atmosphere of unreality, of twilight times, of "a light that never was on sea or land is well translated by the subdued colours and deep shadows that overcast most of the pictures."

The line work of Chughtai in his art works is very prominent. The faces and figures are rendered in meticulous uniform, fine line with flowering dresses, rich gathers and scarves and the ample dimension. These provide an occasion for the display of virtuoso line work in depicting the folds of the dress and its border decorations. The buildings too are rendered in decorative design and in the same way the flowers. The quality of line is indeed very fine free flowing, unfaltering and rhythmically cursive. The colour is softened and subdued and deeply suffused by the technique of colour application on the pattern of Bengal School.

The early work of Chughtai, such as that printed in the "Indian Academy of Art Journal", is indistinguishable from the work of the Bengal School in technique and style but the "Muraqqa" paintings are differentiated by the use of Muslim dress for men and women and by the use of Muslim architecture and Muslim arabesque decoration on dresses and buildings and in the back ground. Another important feature of the style that Chughtai developed in his "Muraqqa", as distinguished from the Bengal School, was the profusion of linework and drawing in such features as the flowing dresses and their folds and decoration, the architectural

background and its ornamentation, the imaginary flowers and shrubs and trees and the sheer beautification through floral and arabesque designs in the background. In the Bengal School, there were very few features in the picture that had been linearly depicted and mostly it was made up of colourful washes and misty effects of dusk or dawn.

Another important work is his Hindu publication, titled "Chughtai's Indian Paintings" which was published from Delhi in 1951. It contained his paintings on Hindu and some Buddhist subjects. Chughtai did this work prior to 1947. This book includes only 21 of the 200 paintings that Chughtai claims to have done on Hindu and Buddhist subjects, Painting light and fanciful drawing, heavy surrounding brown green shadows and luminous centre and those wholly arbitrary shading and lighting were derived from Bengal. Dr. Tara Chand in his foreword to this book observed that "Chughtai's fame as an artist of great sensitiveness refinement and skill is well established. Many years ago he stormed his way into the heart of art lovers by his portrayal of medieval themes in beautiful lines and soft melodious colours which had an individuality of their own. In the exhibition his paintings attracted notice and held visitors spell bound by their languorous sweetness, and by the magic of their composition.

These qualities were strikingly displayed in his publications like the Muraqqa-e-Chughtai and Naqash-e-Chughtai's paintings, which all received tributes from art critics of India and abroad. His new paintings concern themselves with subjects drawn from the rich lore of Hindu tradition and mythology, scenes from the life of Krishna and Radha, the dance of Sive and as the lord of the mountains, Buddha's asceticism, love lorn heroines playing on the Veena and attracting gazelles by their music. Rajput knights holding vigil accoutered with arms, or rushing forth to battle, and motherly love and affection and passionate longing and waiting for the beloved.

The romance of India which the painters of the courts of Mughal, Rajput and Pahari Princess depicted so brilliantly has come to life again in the paintings of the Chughtai. And also their style of portraiture, which is exemplified in the portraits of Manlala, A Barmaki, Zubaida Khatun, and Saint's Daughter etc.

Chughtai's art has been ripening with time and as Iqbal pointed out it is moving towards its own perfection. He has consistently endeavored to realize one aim-portrayal of the joy and beauty of India's wonderfully rich, composite and variegated life as seen through the eyes of a poet-artist who has identified himself with all the aspects of this life and who has sought to rise above all differences of race and creed.

Chughtai like A. N. Tagore and Nandalal Bose has made valiant efforts to keep the traditions of Indian Art alive, and his contribution to the understanding of

Indian art and culture and to the advancement of India's recognition in the realms of art achievement has been of a high order.

His art has been commented on three important aspects. In the first place in all his works dominant is its architectonic quality, besides figure works. His landscapes are so characteristically Indian and convey a deep sense of space and proportion in composition. His trees, stalks and flowers are animated with an almost human intention. The figures, men, women and children give the impression of life, and carry their heads with determination and purpose. Whenever Chughtai directs his talents he leaves an ineffaceable mark in each painting. His amazing mastery of line and composition entitle him to a position of honour with the great artists of West and with old oriental masters. Professor Kashmira remarks that: -

"Some time Chughtai plays with light and shade after the manner of Rambrandt and sometime he draws the human form and feature in the spirit of Holbein. In some of his pictures he is an abstract as Van Gogh, Paul Gauguin or Manet. As a draughtsman he is as consistent as Igres and old Chinese Masters, but first and last he is himself, he is Chughtai the artist of India and none else. There is no doubt that he is one of the most important figures of our times. He has played a leading role in Modern Indian Art for the last twenty-five years. His position in Indian art is comparable to European Masters of the Nineteenth century."

The other major publication of Chughati title "Amal-e-Chughtai" came out in 1968. It illustrated the verses of Iqbal. The painting in the book show a change of palette that occurred after his publication 'Murraqa'. Many pictures have bright, yellow and green landscape in the background. Some pictures have contrasting colours as scarlet and green inprofusion as "The Virtuous" the young Farmer. There are other paintings with bright colour schemes in which standing figure of a maiden is shown robed in yellow with long pink scarf with green foreground green and orange background. Chughtai's style is different from that of Mughal miniature painters because the Mughals never show the picture so close to viewers as Chughtai does. Nor did they paint bust or half or three quarters of figures when they made portrait. This is apparently the influence of photography to cut short the figure at the bottom border. The most remarkable view of Chughtai painting is his composition. He places the figure on the paper in such a way, arranging their postures and gestures so effectively with a setting of trees or buildings or designs so impressively that the elements of the whole picture falls into a well-knit, well-balanced totality and artistic unity. Another noteworthy feature of his work is the use of architecture to provide framework for the compositions. They also provide Chughtai an occasion to indulge in favourite floral and decoration additions. This influence in his work is precisely due to his earliest art education in copying the designs on the walls of Wazir Khan's Mosque where his uncle Miran Bakhsh worked as "Naqqash".

"Sometimes, Chughtai draws and paints these designs behind and beside the figure in panels or squares or rectangles, without the excuse of a building on which to make them. This is in the tradition of Persian miniature paintings in which areas of beautiful designs are made part of the picture quite arbitrarily and we see what look like carpets floating frontally over the scene. Some of the finest and most prominent can be seen in "Sharfan-Nisa" where a vertical panel or screen seems to stand behind her, and also in 'Zubaida Khatun' behind whom a white wall is covered with arabesque."

Illustration of the poetry of Iqbal had to be quite different. To create the effect of massiveness and monumentality, Chughtai often uses in "Amal-e-Chughati" the stylistic device of inflating and enlarging the figures, ignoring consideration of realism. Such is the picture of the bearded old man entitled "Wisdom" and the picture of the Kashmiri woman with her child titled "Under the Apple Tree". The same "exaggeration is found to be of some extent in other paintings."

The impression of glory and grandeur is also created by Chughtai by bringing the image close to the viewers on the picture plane, as in "Retrospect", showing a very grim looking women holding an upraised sword. Inspite of bringing the image close and magnifying it, the painting remains a miniature because only the outline of the face and the features are rendered in line while the undulations of the face and the bony and muscular structure is not at all touched. Linear decoration is provided depicting prominently the dress, always ample and expensive, on which the folds are laboriously drawn. The careful, continuous, uniform, unfaltering and wiry line is used very realistically. The curves are smoothed and the lines drawn rhythmically.

USTAD ALLAH BAKHSH

Ustad Allah Bakhsh (1895-1978) was a most prolific and a very versatile artist who literally produced thousands of paintings during a period of about half a century. Born in Wazirabad, he was initiated into the craft of painting in his hometown at the age of five. He became an apprentice of the local signboard painter, Master Muhammad Abdullah after many years of grounding in the art of lettering, he got a job in the railway workshop to paint words and designs on railway carriages. He also worked in an English Automobile Firm. A very significant change in his life, as an artist came when he went to Calcutta and joined the theatrical company as Scenes Painter. That experience exercised a strong influence on him as can be seen in the numerous theatrical paintings that he

"In the moonlit night" Painting by Ustad Allah Bakhsh Courtesy Shehla Saigol

produced. From Calcutta he came back to Lahore and tried to eke out a living as a painter but without success. So, in 1914 he left for Bombay and there he was able to get a chance to work with an artist Muhammad Rafi, who was running an art studio with some apprentices in the employment of Hindu businessman, Lala Ram Lal. They were engaged in painting Hindu religious and mythological pictures mostly of krishna. He also worked there as photographer, retoucher, portrait and landscape painter. There he had his introduction with Hindu Mythology, which played an important role in his future career. This experience had a long-lasting influence on his work and he came to be known as Allah Bakhsh Krishen because of a number of paintings of lord krishna that he made.

He lived for five years in Bombay returned to Lahore in 1919 and started work as commercial artist in 'Paisa Akhbar.' He worked day and night at his paintings and finally began contributing his paintings to Bombay and Calcutta for exhibitions. In 1923 he won first prize in Bombay. His reputation spread far and wide. In 1937 he went to Patiala where the Maharaja had invited him to his Durbar. After the death of old Maharaja, he returned to Lahore permanently in 1938. For some years he worked in Kapur Printing Works as an artist. After Independence he retired to his own studio in Muslim Town, Lahore. The Hindus were his major clients and painting of Hindu subjects, especially Krishna, was his favourite activity. All that changed, when Pakistan came into being, in 1947, and there was no demand for paintings of Hindu subject. Allah Bakhsh had, of course, been painting other subjects too and now he turned all his attention towards painting the Punjab rural scene. Therefore one important aspect of his multi-dimensional work is a celebration of Punjab village life.

Critics find it difficult to survey comprehensively the work of Ustad Allah Bakhsh because there is such infinite variety in it and generalizations are difficult to make. Even classification of the work into categories is not easy because there are so many. However, for the sake of discussion, we can roughly divide his work into eight categories i.e. theatrical figures in flat colours/ coloured lines, theatrical figures in three dimensions, Punjab Village life scenes, farming scenes, figures in architectural setting, trees & bushes, cloudy and misty scenes and large compositions of fanciful figures.

A tableau in coloured line and flat washes is one style of the Ustad in which he painted subjects that had a narrative basis. For example, a woman could be shown in a dancing pose with other women at the back playing on musical instruments. The dresses in these paintings are highly decorative and jewellery is given much prominence. The poses are conventional and theatrical and the faces are almost all similar and very doll like, which is illustrative, and anecdotal picture making.

Allah Bakhsh in three dimensions paints the same kind of theatrical scenes. Again there is much emphasis on costumes and the rendering of silk and velvet material and jewellery, but in this group of paintings, the work is minutely and smoothly finished. For example, in one picture a man stands at the back holding out jewellery in each of his outstretched hands while in the foreground a woman is half kneeling and reaching out towards one of the jewels. The poses of the figures are very artificial and the treatment of the drapery is very conventional and the faces are stereotyped.

In Punjabi Village Life Scenes, Allah Bakhsh has painted many canvases showing a long line of people either going to a wedding or to a festival or some occasion that calls for social celebration. In these he depicts realistically the common people, their facial types, their dresses and their customs such as musicians playing on long iron tongs and people taking all kinds of banners in the processions as they go to the sites of the festivals or women carrying baskets of clothes and gifts on their heads as they wind their way to a wedding. He shows young and old, men and women, babies and children in their typical dresses. It is all very realistic but somewhat stiff and conventional. Every part is depicted in detail. In Farming and Ploughing scenes, the mass and volume of the animals and the men is much more powerfully depicted. The bullocks especially are painted with much empathy and show very close observation and masterly rendering. One such painting is hanging in the Gallery of the Lahore Museum and another in the Civil Secretariat, Lahore. The light in these pictures is very soft and diffused and so there are no strong shadows on the figures of the animals and the men and their details are equally clearly spread out from one end to the other.

Figures in architectural setting. Allah Bakhsh often paints a beautiful female figure or two in an architectural setting, that is, against the background of an arch or a jali (latticework in stone) or a parapet. In the foreground and center, there may be a carpet with its own elaborate design. In the foreground, there is this figure, elegantly composed, often in some dance pose. One picture for example, shows a woman sitting with her hands raised in prayer while in front of her lies the Holy Quran on a bookrest called 'Rehel' behind her is a stone lattice window, and below that the dado at the base of the wall with a row of octagons, she is sitting on a richly designed carpet. This picture reminds one strongly of Chughtai but the difference is that the figure has very realistic proportions and the drapery has very realistic wrinkles and the light effect is very prominently shown on the figure.

Trees and Bushes, a large category of the late Ustad's paintings shows trees or rather tree trunks, quite often lopped off at the top and cut short at the upper edge of the painting. Mostly they are bare trunks arranged in a variety of very natural compositions, leaning sideways or across each other and so on. Each picture is painted in a different colour scheme and with new light effects so that no two are alike. They are almost like abstract paintings in which the tree trunks have been used as the basic imagery and the whole composition has been built up with that. It seems obvious that these remarkable paintings have not been done to please his clients but for his own pleasure.

There is another important sub-group of these tree paintings in which instead of the tree trunks the artist has shown thick clusters of vegetation deep down in the forest. Sometimes in the middle there is the figure of a man, perhaps a hermit or a poet, with some light playing on him. There is an air of mystery in these pictures and one is left guessing the meaning of it. The artist adopts a new and interesting style of brushwork to render this thick foliage. He makes short sharp scribbling movements with the brush and creates little curls and zigzags that depict leaves in a mattered form. Trunks are hardly visible in these woodland scenes but sometimes-twisted branches are shown. The varying shades of green and brown and many related colours are also depicted with great mastery. These and the tree trunk paintings discussed above are wholly original in style and owe nothing to tradition. They form a delightful and a very remarkable contribution of Allah Bakhsh to Pakistani Art.

Misty and Cloudy Scenes. Just as Allah Bakhsh could create a great painting with no features in it except waves of water, so he could use a dust storm as a subject. A masterly painting entitled "Dust Storm" is hanging in the Modern Gallery of the Lahore Museum. There is nothing but a play of colour in this very large painting. On the low horizon there is bright yellow and orange and above that the dark purple threatening dust storm and some cloud formations. Two small leafless trees are bending under the force of the wind at the bottom left.

He has painted a number of pictures in which the whole scene is covered with clouds or smoke in yellow and orange and blue and purple colours. In these clouds of smoke or vapors are dimly shown faces and figures sometimes of a few and sometimes of a crowd, like superhuman creatures of another world. These mystical visions have rendered dreamily dim contours but in rich and vivid colours, as in a stormy sky or as in a huge conflagration. They are masterpieces of colour control and brushwork.

There are other paintings in which clouds or mist does not render the atmosphere vague or smoke but crowds and masses of faces and figures are depicted quite clearly in all kinds of fanciful and strange forms. They are masterpieces of inventiveness and skill in composition. Such is the huge painting entitled "Tilism-e-Hosh Ruba" in the Lahore Museum. It shows an old magician standing below and creating all kinds of super natural creatures such as 'jinns' and fairies and also princess and princesses, warriors and wrestlers and so on. The sheer ingenuity and fertility of the artist's imagination is as remarkable as the skill with which he has been able to arrange them on the canvas. Then the distribution of light and shade and the arrangement of the colour scheme further add to the beauty of the painting and makes it an outstanding work of art. There is one such painting in the Permanent Art Gallery of Alhamra.

There must be many creations of Allah Bakhsh that are not covered in the above categories that have been discussed but enough has been said to show that there is immense variety in his work and also many levels. Some of those showing Punjabi rural life are very conventional illustrations in which there is no characterization and no force of line in the drawing or any striking effects of light or colour. But on the other hand there are the wonderful woodland scenes in which the tree-trunks make strange patterns and the dense foliage creates a mysterious atmoshere.

Nature is a marvel to the Artist and he sees in it a Beauty which common folk are unable to appreciate. The whole phenomenon of creation, whether in the seas, mountains or land, in the sunset, or in sunrise is a source of ecstasy and delight to him. He signs and worships identifying his whole self with the soul of the Universe, and translates the works of his brush and pencil accordingly.

Allah Bakhsh has produced some masterpieces which depict Nature in all its glory and grandeur to the minutest detail. They are a source of inspiration and a surprise to the lovers of Art as they represent Nature in variegated colours and its ever-changing forms as ought to be seen by the Artist.

"Husn-i-Kohsar", "Chandni", the Spring" and " the Poet" are some of the pictures, which are diffused with utmost brilliance and splendour, introducing the Artist as a man of originality and skilful genius. Then again his paintings, "the Sunset", "Moonlight" and "the Light of Life" are exquisitely charming and full of softness, which directly interpret Nature in all resplendent details. Allah Bakhsh's idealism and mysticism finds itself in his pictures. He unfolds himself with directness, which is his own. He does not linger but reaches the destination directly and with intense realism. His conception of life is not indebted to artificial and outward influences but is real with a tinge of idealism. His "grouping" is unique and village life study is full of real touches. He does not believe in any "ism" and he represents every class of mankind, fantasy, a land of fairies, where landscapes are invested with a dream world atmosphere, like a child's storybook. Indeed, he has brought to these creations the fresh untutored mind of a child coupled with the craftsmanship of an accomplished painter. In one sense he is almost a metaphysical artist, with animism strangely primitive in its interpretation of life, not confined in its animate form, but embodied in rocks, in trees, rivers and mountains." In his infinite variety of delineation of tree forms, Allah Bakhsh has captured something of the robust delicacy. His art is thus derivative only from his own fertile mind, and an inborn sense of form and design. Its poetic quality, and poetry is inseparable from his paintings, seems to flow from some inner emotional source, and his personal purity of vision.

Some of his works showing Punjabi rural life are very conventional illustrations in which there is no characterization and no force of line in the drawing or any striking effects of light or colour. But on the other hand there are the wonderful woodland scenes in which the tree-trunks make strange patterns and the dense foliage creates a mysterious atmosphere. Most remarkable are the cloudy misty scenes, shot with colour, in which visionary faces and figures appear, half-visible. All these show masterly control of the medium and are really fantasies in colour. With command of so many styles and with output so enormous, one cannot but recognize Ustad Allah Bakhsh as one of the greatest of Pakistani art.

Allah Bakhsh is particularly remarkable for the personal mysticism and symbolism of his imaginative paintings, for his unbelievably prolific output – his meticulous craftsmanship, and his highly developed sense of rhythm, colour and design. The variety and piquancy of his media are infinite; watercolour diluted with milk; watercolour thickly laid on and scraped with a palette knife, oil and watercolour mixed poster, tempera and oils pure and simple. His subjects range from faithful, carefully thought out scenes from every day life through the intricate composition of his enchanted woods, the colour jewelled in their intensity, the pattern alive and flowing, to the subdued rock and earth formations, of a world of almost Blake-ish anguish an underworld of deeply rooted beliefs and moral precepts. It is difficult to reconcile Allah Bakhsh, the conscientiously truthful, kind portrayer of Punjabi rural life, with Allah Bakhsh, dreamer, the creator.

HAJI MUHAMMAD SHARIF

Among the painters who migrated to Pakistan from Indian states, on emergence of Pakistan, one was Haji Muhammad Sharif whose forefathers worked as court artists with the Maharaja of Patiala. He was born in 1905 at Patiala. His Grandfather and father were court painters. He got his early education from Lala Sahoo Ram, who was one of the pupils of Basharat ullah, the father of Sharif. He however later on also received training from Ustad M. Hussain Khan of Delhi, whose great care polished the artist in Haji Sharif.

In 1924, his work was exhibited in London and he won much admiration. He was decorated as a Member of the British Empire. In 1945, he retired from service, in Patiala and (at the age of 60) he came to Lahore. Here he was employed to teach at the Mayo School of Arts, where he continued to do so till 1968, when he again retired. In 1960, President Ayub Khan got arranged an exhibition of his work and gave him a small stipend for life. Later Prime Ministers and Chief Ministers of Punjab also rewarded him. Haji Sharif's presence in Lahore helped to renew an interest in the traditional miniature painting at the Punjab University and the Mayo School of Arts.

His work is scattered all over India and also in other countries but in Pakistan the largest collection of some twenty-four paintings was acquired by the Idara Saqafat-e-Pakistan, Islamabad, for their National Art Gallery. A few paintings are with the Mayo School of Arts.

Like all miniature artists, he made copies of the artwork of the old masters but besides that he made his own innumerable original compositions. These mostly feature one or the other of Mughal Emperors whose features were adopted by the miniature painters as part of their training. These show the bust with arm within an oval outline. The throne and the bolster cushion are elaborately decorated with arabesque design and so is the hem of the dress and collar and cuff. Always they are shown wearing many pearl necklaces and jewels and plumes on their turbans. He is very fond of stippling the surface of the dress. The face is sometimes in profile and sometimes three-quarter. Each has certain traditional features like the shaven face and big pointed moustache of Akbar. However, one does not expect much characterization in these decorative little miniatures.

Most impressive are the equestrian portraits of the same kings and unknown princesses that Haji Sharif was fond of making. For example, there is an equestrian portrait of Shah Alam. The king is sitting erect in the saddle holding the reins with the left hand and a long spear with the right. The face is in profile and enclosed in a nimbus. The horse is gently trotting, with one front leg raised. The more lively is the portrait of Emperor Jahangir and Queen Nur Jahan riding two splendid horses, side by side. The horses are shown running in very natural poses. Jahangir appears in contemporary portraits and the queen could be any beautiful lady. She is wearing a jewelled crown even though she is out on a hunt and has a hawk on the right hand. The background of forest and mountains is very feeble but a small locality with a mosque and houses in the distance is in correct perspective.

Haji Sharif also painted some elaborate kingly processions in which the king is riding on an elephant. A very impressive procession shows Emperor Akbar riding an elephant while attendants walk along, in the foreground, and two horsemen in the front and four behind. The crowd is not formally arranged though the four horsemen behind are moving in pairs. The faces of these four look almost alike and those of the crowd too are not much differentiated except for the fact that some faces are bearded and others not. The lower figure of the elephant is hidden by the crowd but the head is well drawn. As usual, the horses are excellently done. It is the overall composition that makes the picture so impressive, with the elephant in the centre and in the foreground the crowd of walking attendants and two horsemen in front and four at the back. These latter are carrying two pennants in front and four at the back. Rising over it all is the "howdah" of the elephant on which Emperor Akbar is sitting, with the 'mahawat', the elephant (driver), in the front and the umbrella bearer behind. Highest of all rise the colourful umbrella, the symbol of royalty.

In these days when the art of miniature painting is almost forgotten, his work is a matter of satisfaction. Certainly, the procession scenes are the most noteworthy contribution of the late Ustad and they show all the best characteristics of his work, his elaborate composition, his minute arabesque decoration and his superb drawing and balanced figure work, has set the standards for the youngsters to follow.

The post partition period was much different. The Fine Arts Department became active in the Punjab University. Similarly the colleges in Lahore also introduced this subject and there was an atmosphere of flourishing artistic activity in the city. There arose a group of talented young artists who began with realistic work but soon started modern paintings under the influence of Shakir Ali who joined the Mayo School of Arts in 1952 and later became its Principal. Shakir Ali (1916-75) had received arts education in Bombay, the Slade School of arts London, in Paris and in Prague. He had his style of paintings in which he made human figure, horses by reducing them to their basic structure. He had masterly economy in his style and tremendous force in his line.

The young artists who became active in early 50s included Ahmad Pervez, Shaikh Safdar, Shamza, Qutab Shaikh, Ali Imam and Moeen Najmi. The first three who were very creative are all dead. Qutab Shaikh left for Germany, Ali Imam has not been very active and is managing an art gallery at Karachi and Moeen Najmi (late) was also not very productive. Shakir Ali was much older than this lot but he mixed freely with them and became a part of their social and artistic life. He convinced the young artist towards modern abstract paintings as against the realistic group led by Anna Molka Ahmad, whose stronghold was the Fine Arts Department of the Punjab University.

AHMAD PERVEZ (1926-79)

Was a most remarkable and prolific painter. From 1955 to 1964 he lived in London and there developed a purely abstract style in which short swift strokes, arcs and ellipses, whorls and circles, were used to build up a design that seemed to explode and erupt and fly apart but was firmly held together in a coherent pattern. The design of thick lines was filled with intense bright colours which many critics and reviewers called gems and jewels. His work is the most vibrant and animated and intense and colourful that has been produced in Pakistan.

S. SAFDAR (1924-84)

He was born in Gujrat (Pakistan) but lived in Bombay from 1941-1948 where he learned art the hard way before working in the commercial art market. He was much influenced by the Ajanta and Ellora style drawings and paintings that he saw people doing in Bombay and his earliest work shown in Pakistan was of this type. Later, he enmeshed the same figures in a network of Cubist patterns and space divisions, which made a strange but attractive combination. More convincing were these abstract space divisions when he used leaf motifs and the patterns of fields as seen from the air. His drawing was strong and firm and he had an unerring sense of colour always.

SHAMZA (1928-85)

Began by painting village women (like his "Jatti") whose forms were made up of triangles and other geometrical shapes and whose faces were distorted in the Cubist manner in an effort to combine the profile and the front view. The colouring was mostly flat. He also left for London in 1956 and there developed a delicate abstract linear style in which he made either a connected network or separate small forms with single or double semicircle, C or B forms, things that looked like chessmen. Towards the end of his life he was painting another series called "Roots" in which a tree or plant was drawn in a quite fanciful manner whose roots were convoluted to look like Urdu for Arabic alphabet.

MOEEN NAJMI (1926-97)

Was another of the early group of Lahore painters. He has been more prominent as a promoter of art and used to teach at Aitchison College in Lahore. On the rare occasions, he painted, his work is semi-abstract in which architectural features are used to create Cubist effects. Just as the buildings are depicted in the form of stay glimpses, so the colour is laid on roughly, shading off at place into blank canvas. However, the total composition is delicately balanced.

AHMAD KHAN

Is a versatile artist. In the 70s, he was painting purely abstract pictures, using large squares and circles that filled the canvas and were painted in flat colours. Since then he has been doing very little painting but has been expressing himself in a variety of other ways, such as treating a silver foil chemically to create coloured effects on it and adding calligraphy here and there.

COLIN DAVID

Paints full figure paintings that are not portraits as much as compositions. The figure is always at some distance and the face is not given much importance so that it is either in profile or averted. There is no idealization and the colours are neutral, almost flat. It is in the arrangement of the elements of the figure on the canvas and the total colour pattern, in which lies the appeal of the picture. He was once fond of enlivening the canvas with a small area of bright colours. The main figure is usually in one corner of the large canvas. His nudes are another class.

KHALID IQBAL

Emerged in the early 60s as a prominent painter of portraits and landscapes but later on, he concentrated on landscape alone. He studied at the Slade School of Arts, London, and taught at the Fine Arts Department of the Punjab University, (1956-65). He also taught at the Mayo School from 1966-81. He also headed Alhamra Arts Academy for many years. His early pictures were usually distant views, with a broad sky and a broad foreground and in the middle a narrow strip of trees and mud houses join the horizon. Later, he started painting clumps of tall thin trees fairly close up. Brighter colours are found very rarerly in his work, sometimes, as in trees with red flowers. His work is very subtle and sensitive and executed with consummate skill. The exact place and time is very well captured. A very well respected senior artist of Lahore.He is mostly neutral in the artist factions and is widely respected as a person and an artist and painter.

The list of Lahore group during 70s would include the names of Ghulam Rasul, Ijaz Anwar, Askri Mian Irani, Zubaida Javed and Ijazul Hassan. Ghulam Rasul is a landscape painter and a student of Anna Molka Ahmad. He has distinct style of his own in which he paints indigenous features. He is presently serving in the National Council of the Arts. Ijaz Anwar is a watercolour painter and has beautiful paintings of the old city of Lahore. He revels in depicting the carved wooden balconies and the ornate plaster mouldings with details of streets and bazars. He maintains total harmony despite so much variety of details.

Askri Mian Irani now teaching at the Art College is basically a designer and earlier he created paintings which were more like textile designs. Later he changed and paints calligraphic style using lot of gold. He has created a balance between painting and design elements. The features of Arabic words of a religious touch through design are found in the works. Alhamra has recently published a book of his works. It so appears that he has somehow been acknowledged as a painter instead of merely a designer at least by Alhamra. Ijazul Hassan may be considered as one of the artists to arise in Lahore in the 70s because he had already held four solo exhibitions by 1980 but actually he came into prominence only in the 80s when he changed his subject. At first he was painting people because he was much moved by the social and political movements of the early 70s and wanted to express the aspirations of the people" as he himself has written. However, he came to notice only when he gave up his social approach for an aesthetic one and began to paint trees and plants in close up views, leaf by leaf and flower by flower. Though his work is quite literal, it is enlivened by light effects, which are appropriately varied, and by apt indications of receding plains and distances. The lay out is neatly balanced, and the picture is often divided into panels. Of late he is busy in politics and doing little work. His wife Dr. Mussarat Hassan, again a landscape painter is doing quite a bit in landscapes. Mian Ijaz has written a good book on paintings and might have contributed a lot in the field of Arts but somehow he, probably finds little time. The later period includes the names of Zubaida Javed, Ghulam Mustafa, Shahid Jalal, Khalid Mahmood, Iqbal Hussain, Dur-e-Wasim and Zulfiqar Ali Zulfi.

ZULFIQAR ALI ZULFI

Of the latest lot Zulfi is the most versatile artist. His specialization is land scape in oil but he is equally good at pastels and water colours. Presently he is serving as Assistant Director at Permanent Art Gallery Alhamra.

6

FOUNDING THE MUSEUM

The really imposing red-brick building, standing on the Mall, opposite Punjab University Hall, houses Lahore Central Museum which is supposed to store relics of our history and cultural heritage. Some term the existence of such building as colonial legacy but one should not really forget the contributions which were made by the British Rulers in establishing institutions and taking up monumental development projects for the welfare of the common man and prosperity of their dependencies. Discussing something about cultural heritage would remain incomplete if the history of museum was not traced. It is generally believed that the museum came into existence out of industrial and agricultural produce exhibition of 1864, which was arranged at Lahore, but the factual position slightly differs.

THE INDUSTRIAL EXHIBITION

An exhibition was organized for a greater show at London to introduce the agricultural, mineral and industrial products of Punjab in Europe. While this was to serve for introducing Indian products and crafts in Europe, it was also to create awareness in the Europeans as to which resources of the Empire could be exploited and to what extent. It meant to create awareness about the potential market of products and industries in the newly acquired territories. The establishment of museum took place much earlier rather as early as 1856. Infact the movement for Museums started in Madras where earlier a few museums were established in some cities in the beginning of the 19th century. The Punjab being the latest addition to the British Empire, was occupied in 1849, but the British administrative system, educational pattern and various other measures were adopted quickly to bring it at par with the management of the other Indian territories. What happened was that one Muhammad Azim produced a pamphlet, at the Chronicle Press, Lahore, in 1855 containing abstracts of some papers published by the Bombay Times of 13th December 1854. This leaflet carried extracts from the documents laid before the Madras Government in 1843 by the Resident at Travancore on the subject of establishing District Museums. This paper stressed the importance of establishing the Museums, which were beginning to be recognized in India as important educational institutions after they had been, in this light, regarded, for half a century throughout the rest of the world. It was pointed out that the Government should not lose sight of merits of those who first pressed them for consideration of Government as popular institutions. The museums and observatories might be scattered in hundreds all over India to the infinite advantage of everyone without imposing any outlay on the public exchequer. This indicates that before accession of Punjab many museums were in existence in Bombay, Madras and Bengal. The Resident of Travandrum, Major General Cullen, made a definite proposal regarding information and material i.e. mineral, industrial and others noticed by the engineers and officers posted in the districts. He felt that it was not advisable to transfer the same (products) to Headquarters. i.e. Madras and instead it would be preferable to form and set up local museums. He thought of a small museum for every Collectorate for which a room might probably be set apart in each 'Kutchery' or Court House. This Museum would be under the charge of the Collector assisted by the Engineer and the Medical Officer. This, according to him would afford a better person to look after the contents. The advantage of having such a museum in a public building, under the charge of the Collector was further evident as no person was likely to be more interested than the Collector himself in possessing such a museum for his own information and reference and he would, doubtlessly, himself as well as his Assistants, promote the objects of it to the utmost of his power. In a public building it may be rendered at all times available for the inspection of every person interested in the subject and to the scientific travellers who would not only derive much interesting information themselves but would probably occasionally contribute to the value of the collection by their own remarks, resources and suggestions. The objectives in setting up these Museums were that: -

"From these Local or District Museums, contributions might, from time to time, be made to some general Depot at the Presidency, to be also placed under an officer of the same Corps, perhaps most appropriately under the Secretary to the Department of Public Works, under the Board of Revenue, for, it ought, in all respects, to be a Government measure without which it cannot be expected to succeed; and surely it will be well worth the care of Government to promote an undertaking that is likely to be attended with little or no expense to it, and yet offers so apparently certain and expeditious a mode of drawing up a memoir on the resources of this Presidency. The Museums in the provinces being under the Collectors and Civil Engineers, it is but following up the plan to place the General Museum at Madras under the Board of Revenue, and Head of the Civil Engineer Department, as the body most interested in giving effect to the views of

Government, and thus completing the chain of communication. Any other plan would work with equal certainty. It would be an object also, of course, to furnish specimens to the scientific bodies.

The formation of these Local Museums under the countenance of the Government, would probably also induce Members of the service at out-stations, to meet together occasionally, to examine and discuss the subjects of interest presented for their consideration; nor would their researches, be limited to the mere collection of minerals, but that they would naturally, and in due time, be extended to every other branch of information comprised under the head of Statistics. No work has yet, appeared that has offered more minute and valuable statistical information for the time it was written, than that of Francis Auehman, on Mysore, Malabar, and Canara. It might indeed, in many respects, still be considered valuable to such enquiries. The more influential natives of the several Districts would also probably take considerable interest in such an undertaking, more especially when they perceived that it was likely to lead to the encouragement of agriculture or trade, by suggestions for the primary tracts of Malabar, are most singular and extensive, and yet unexplained, carbonaceous deposits.

The Museum is intended to offer a repository for every variety of Raw Material, animal, vegetable, and mineral, which the East supplies, used as food, medicine, or clothing, or convertible, by the application of human industry, into any thing that becomes subject of merchandize: of all tools, instruments, machines, and implements, made use of in the process of transformation, and of the manufactures themselves which are the result.
The articles will be arranged under a double system of classification, the first referring to the locality from which they are obtained and the second referring to their characters.

By this means strangers in Bombay will discover, at a glance, the whole contents of our bazars, find directions where and how to procure them and be able, in a few hours, to acquire all the information regarding them that can be obtained. They will see what are the products of other countries, and may, if proceeding thither, be made aware at a glance of all that is known regarding them at Bombay, and for this determine the facts on which we are ignorant, in reference to which enquiries will be most important."

DISTRICT MUSEUMS

On receipt of this leaflet and considering its contents it was important to introduce the agricultural, industrial and mineral wealth to British Traders through these Museum establishments, the Financial Commissioner of Punjab Mr. Mcleod

Lahore Central Museum

issued instructions to all the Deputy Commissioners and field officers for setting up the District Museums. After issuing orders, he submitted the matter to the Chief Commissioner for his approval forwarding, for the information of the Chief Commissioner, a copy of the Circular (No.15 of 1855) to the address of Commissioners of Division relating to the establishment of Museums, together with a copy of the private pamphlet referred to therein. He thought the measure proposed by him will meet with the approval for the resources of the country and give direction to the efforts of those who may be desirous of effecting improvements in Agriculture, machinery and the Arts. The instructions circulated contained the objectives and modes through which the collections had to be built. These instructions provided a Charter for the Museums and basic guidelines for the field officers to establish and build up the Museums in Punjab. The instructions read "As it appears to me very desirable that some systematic efforts should be made, towards collecting specimens of the natural products of the Punjab and having these reserved permanently accessible to all, who may be desirous of informing themselves upon the subject. He forwarded some copies of document, formerly submitted to the Government of Madras in connection with a proposition for the formation of District Museums; subordinate to a central Museum at the Headquarters of the Local Government."

These papers according to him contained, suggestions of a useful and practical character. While adopted for general application – and in his opinion suitable, in the main, for adoption in the Punjab; with such modifications, as circumstances may point out to be necessary or desirable. It was hoped, that in such districts there will usually be found some individuals at least, connected with the civil administration, or the Engineering Departments of the Medical Service, who take interest in such enquiries; and would willingly take charge of a Museum, such as was contemplated and the mode in which it suggested itself that the object might here be best carried out, was, that in such locality so many specimens of such natural products for useful or interesting character that may be discovered as there were Districts in the Punjab to each of which, one such specimen should be distributed with a note of its destination, locality in which found, and uses (if any) to which applied.

The museum of each district would be composed after collective specimens obtained from other Districts, added to those procurable within itself and these museums might be extended, besides natural products, specimens likewise of the more durable and uncommon manufactures peculiar to each locality the more interesting objects of natural History and such like.

The Commissioners were directed to take this subject into consideration and after communicating with the District Officers and through them, with such others as may be likely to aid or take an interest in the undertaking, and that there were to get back on subject, in detail, as it might appear to them necessary. No details were asked and only names of interested and entrusted, the assignment were to be communicated to purpose of nomenclature and identification, of specimens; their proper uses, proper classifications etc., etc. In the event of the proposed arrangement being carried out, wholly or in part; the Central Museum might perhaps, with advantage, be made to contain; besides the products of the Punjab specimens likewise from other parts and in many ways it might be expected to possess resources not possessed by those of the Districts. It might be found possible to secure for its scientific supervision such as would enable it to afford material aid and advice to the subordinate ones.

It was this detailed proposal which had been initiated by Mr. D.F. Mcleod in 1855 and his order to the Commissioners that the Chief Commissioner of Punjab accorded his approval to the establishment of District Museums in Punjab and a Central Museum at Lahore. The exact wording of the Government approval communicated reads that "In reply to inform you that the Chief Commissioner's approval of the instructions issued by you relating to the establishment of District or Provincial Museums in the Punjab and of a Central Museum at Lahore. You are at liberty to arrange the details of the scheme as sketched in the papers under acknowledgement." Mr. Temple Secretary to the Chief Commissioner conveyed these orders of Chief Commissioner. These orders formed the basis of the setting up of a Central Museum at Lahore. The Museums at the Districts including Lahore were to be funded and financed by the Local Government funds. As revealed in later correspondence the Lahore Central Museum got an amount of Rs.1000/- to 2000/- annually. The Museum at Multan was given grant of Rs.1000/- and the one at Delhi Rs.600/-. Museums were also established at Sialkot and Amritsar.

CENTRAL MUSEUM AT LAHORE

Where and at what premises the Museum was set up for the Ist time. It is learnt that it was somewhere in the Baradari of Wazir Khan, where afterwards the Anarkali Book Club was located. The working of the Lahore Central Museum is also confirmed from the Notification issued on October 2,1858 regarding a meeting at the Museum Premises. The notification reads: "With reference to the Notification which appeared in the Punjab Gazette, Vol.II, No.31, dated 19th June, 1958, it is hereby announced that a Committee, composed of as per Mr. W. D. Arnold, President Museum, will meet at the Rev. C. Stoggett, Lahore Museum at 10 A.M.Capt. Hucainson on the 22nd November next. Capt. Ralph Young for the examination of such candidates (being other than natives of India, for whom separate provision will be made) for Extra Assistant Commissionships, as may appear before it." W. D. ARNOLD Lahore October 2nd, 1858 Director of Public Instruction for the Punjab. This notification confirms that the Central Museum was working in 1858, which was spacious and commoditious enough to cater to the requirements of other departments. This arrangement appears to have continued for quite sometime. In Sept. 1860 Mr. R. H. Davies, Secretary to Government of Punjab was informed by Mr. T. H. Thoronton, Curator to the Lahore Museum that "I have put myself in communication with the Superintendent of Geological Department in the Lahore Museum as desired by His Honourable the Lt. Governor, and that the ethnographical casts, whose arrival I had the honour to report in my last docket have been now arranged in right cases occupying the two octagon rooms on either side of the entrance to the Museum."

"In the left hand rooms are arranged for the caste belonging to Hindu and all original tribes. In right hand rooms for those of Pathans, Turks, Tibetans and other foreign tribes."The arrangement order was also got approved from the Governor. The ethnographical casts were extremely interesting. The general resemblance of the aboriginal tribes whether from the eastern or the western tracts, was shown in a very striking manner and an admixture of aboriginal blood can also be traced in the features of some of the low caste Sardars, which on this account, have been placed in juxtaposition with them.

LONDON EXHIBITION 1864

"In the year 1861, the Punjab Government set up District Committees headed by the Deputy Commissioners which were given the task of collecting products of Punjab which were to be sent to London for an exhibition being arranged there. Mr. T. H. Thoronton in his instructions to the Deputy Commissioners specified their duties to take immediate measures for making known the objects of the exhibition, its conditions, making rough selections, transmission of articles. The collection of articles was to be contributory and inducing the public. Guidelines were also furnished about the nature of articles; "Raw Product" was to be preferred, with reference to items of commercial value excluding common bids of raw produce. With regard to Art and Manufactures which promoted material for the future Museum, items were to be of quality which could compete with those of other parts of India "Good specimens of Shawl weaving "Koft Gari" of Gujrati work, gold and silver brocade, Lacquered pottery, wood emamelling; Papier Macheivory work, silk, velvet and fine cotton fabrics were considered acceptable. Through poster (advertisement – locally printed) the objectives were explained and it was also circulated. It further elucidated the objective as –

Punjab Exhibitions 1864

Tilinton Market 1998

a) The exhibition will be held in May 1864 in London on the pattern of 1851 exhibition.
b) The Lt. Governor set up a Committee consisting of financial Commissioner Mr. D. F. Mcleod and Curator Central Museum, Lahore. Mr. Thoronton Secretary to Government, Commissioner, Lahore and D. C. Lahore
c) Setting up of District Committees and criteria for selection of articles.
d) To create awareness in Europe about progress in India.
e) Medals for participants etc.
f) Perishable articles not to be included.

The letter of Mr. T. H. Thoronton to Mr. R. H. Davies confirms the position of the museum, its existence in Lahore, contents of some rooms and opening of ethnographical sections with detailed comments which of course, was done under orders of the Governor of Punjab. The Punjab Government issued instructions as well as the circular to establish a Central Museum at Lahore in 1861 and that Mr. T. H. Thoronton, Secretary Punjab Government was also its curator in 1861.

The correspondence preserved in the Punjab Archives indicate that the Museums were established and maintained at Delhi, Lahore, Multan, Amritsar and Sialkot. All these Museums were founded by the Local Government Department. This leads to the conclusion that the Central Museum with its Curator was there since 1858 as independent institution and entity.

The exhibition place was developed as a separate project for an event exclusively although motive at initial stages was knowledge and exploitation of resources. The Curator of the Museum was only a member of the Committee to co-ordinate and supervise work of exhibition (at London) on the pattern of 1851 exhibition held at the same city.

This Museum was arranged at a temporary shed type accommodation on the Mall opposite Director Public Instruction's office later known as Tollinton Market. This building is still there awaiting its fate at the will of the political bosses and land grabbers as it has emerged as a prize point. The efforts of some sane elements for its allocation for extension of Museum appear to have borne no fruit. The day is not far when the Tollinton Market structure will be pulled down.

When the exhibition closed in April, 1864, the whole building was of course occupied for a considerable time by the debris of the collection; and after it was all cleared, the building remained empty partly for sometime. In October, 1854 on the occasion of the great Durbar, it was used as the place of distribution for all "Khilluts" Subsequently the building was (one half) re-roofed and re-floored with pucca flooring and then divided into two parts by a beautiful double screen of glass and carved wood which being double, formed passage across the centre from door to door; access being gained to either part of building by doors on the screen itself. The screen with its carved work, was executed in the Railway Workshop at Mughalpura.

When these arrangements were complete, the remains of old Museum collection were removed into the end of the building farther from the bazar side, while the other end was left vacant, and several public entertainments were held in it. Subsequently the other half was also re-roofed and with a view to protect from dust, the screens already alluded to, were raised to the roof, by a construction of Gothic frame-work and glass to match the original screen below. This, done, it was found that the requirements of the Museum were greater than the one-half of the building could provide, for, and consequently the other half was taken up also. The original division was maintained to contain the raw produce and Natural History together within an annexe containing antiquities. The newly acquired half was devoted to manufactured products, fine Arts, ethnographic specimens and the collection of coins.

Once fixed in the building and distributed as just detailed, the collection began rapidly to increase. Besides the remains of the old Museum that existed since 1858 in the building occupied by the Anarkali Book Club, a considerable addition resulted from the Exhibition of 1864. Nearly all the raw produce that survived the exhibition during several months, a number of models, and a number of manufactured specimens, were taken over for the museum, and these of themselves, when set out for inspection, formed the nucleus of a very interesting collection. The contribution of the Government of Bombay in this behalf was commendable. A large collection of carved furniture of inlaid ware, of Cambary Agats, of 'kim-cobs', and other fabrics was set up; and of the remaining that were unsold, the Government presented to the museum, such specimens, as might be selected. The articles retained for the Museum were a series of Cambary Agats, and a number of specimens of silk and cotton fabrics and "Kim-Cob's".

The subsequent growth of the collection had been the result of some purchases, but principally of the contribution of various districts pursuant to a circular issued by the Government.Quarterly lists of the contributions were notified in the Gazette but the more important acquisitions in various departments and noteworthy were the antiquities, natural history and ethnography.

Antiquities: Foremost among these deserve to be mentioned is a beautiful collection of the carved friezes and fragmentary sculptures from the Yusafzai area, a complete series.

Another interesting addition was relic of Greek art i.e. the base of the Greek columns of the Ionic order which was discovered by General. A. Cunningham near

Mayo School of Arts

Sehah-ki-dera in the Rawalpindi district. This place is supposed to be the site of the ancient Taxila. Major Hall contributed to the Museum a large stone figure of Buddha and also a beautifully sculptured figure from the ancient Taxila.In the Ethnographic Department the museum was helped by Dr. Cayler and Dr. Leitner.Dr. Cayler contributed a number of specimens illustrating the products of Ladakh, and later complete collection of dresses, manufactures and agricultural products of these countries. Dr Leitner donated collection of dresses and other curiosities that he brought from Little Tibet and the Daro country. These included some interesting Tibetan manuscripts, and a number of other specimens. A place had been proposed for a complete ethnographic gallery of dresses, exhibition of the costumes of the various tribes in the hills and plains of the Punjab.

The building had been also beautified by presentation of two marble statues and some other specimens of marble vases. The total number of contributions to the collection upto 31st March 1868 was over hundred specimens. The Museum was very favourably situated and place of attraction for local visitors, and the numbers that visited the building commencing December 1867 was:

| December 1867 | 255 | February 1868 | 12,256 |
| January, 1868 | 735 | March 1868 | 8,539 |

Prior to 1868 the Museum was supported entirely by local funds. But thereafter a budget grant, generally of 1,000 rupees a year was voted and out of this sum the Secretary would pay according to the requisition of the Curator. A special grant of Rs.500/- was made in March 1866, His Honourable the Lieutenant Governor recorded a minute in which he expressed the desire of the Government to maintain and improve the institution and a sum of Rs.200/- per museum was thenceforward devoted to the Museum, of which Rs.100/- was to go to the Curator. The whole building had been ornamented in colour by stencil-plate round the arches. Sixty-five glass cases had been made up. Four hundred and thirty-eight feet of table or case stands fitted into the building. Besides this, a cabinet for the collection of silver and gold coins was completed. A considerable part of the collection had been named and ticketed in English and the vernacular. By a letter from the Secretary to Government dated 23rd July 1866, Mr. Roberts, headed a Committee, consisting of Financial Commissioner, the Commissioner of the Lahore Division and Deputy Commissioner of Lahore were appointed as the Central Committee, with the curator as their Secretary ex-officio. The establishment of Museum at that time consisted of a 'Moonshi' one 'Darogha' in charge, (who was also the incharge of the Magazine in the Fort). He was paid for by Local Fund an allowance of Rs.100 per month, an English writer was entertained on Rs.25/- per month, who was expected (besides copying letters) to assist in preserving specimens labelling boxes and cases, and be able to mount pictures, varnish, paint, and make himself generally useful. Since the number of visitors so largely increased, another Farash was entertained as two men were required at least to dust and keep clean the building all the day.

On 15th April 1867 the Punjab Government vide its circular No.15 issued the following instructions to all Commissioners in the Province regarding Museums:

"The arrangements for re-opening the Lahore Central Museum in the building erected for the exhibition (of 1864) being now nearly complete, I am desired by the Honourable Lieutenant Governor to invite your assistance and that of the officers subordinate to you in completing and extending the collection.

While the various Local Museums in the Punjab are designed primarily to illustrate the products, trade, industry and Arts of the Districts in which they are situated, the Central Museum at Lahore is designed to represent the products and manufactures of the whole Province, and with this object it is divided into four departments:

A.	Raw products	C.	Antiquities, coins, &
B.	Manufactured articles	D.	Natural History

I am to suggest that there be formed, in each district of your Division, a Committee of cooperation, to correspond with the Central Committee at Lahore; that Tehsildars and the Saddar Station have any objects of interest or curiousity in the way; and that the people be encouraged by rewards to bring such objects to notice. The small expenditure required for this purpose can be met from local fund; and for expenses of carriage to Lahore, or for the purchase of manufactured articles or other valuables which it may be desirable to obtain, the Curator of the Central museum will be able to supply funds. Since the exhibition place was a temporary structure, it was again specially done up and preparations made for housing and now locating the Lahore Central Museum in that place for which the instructions in question were issued by Government. As per reports of Government the additions and acquisitions were notified in the Gazette. These collections were received from all over the Province for the Lahore Central Museum.

In his report on the Central Museum Lahore, submitted in May 1869, Mr. B. Powell, the then Curator briefly described the new additions to the Museum, important out of which were sculptured figures of Buddha (Greco-buddhist), coins and dresses in the ethnographic section. The building was reportedly not in a satisfactory condition and it was proposed to have a suitable building for the rapid increase in the interesting collection. He stressed the justification to have a good Museum for the Province. The Museum was also visited by His Highness the Amir of Kabul.

The Museum remained in the exhibition building for a long period. In March 1872 a Committee, was set up known as Mayo Memorial Committee to establish a suitable Memorial in honour of the Late Viceroy. The Committee accomplished its objective by raising contributions and free will offerings and collected Rs.66,053/-. Regarding the use of the funds; further a special Committee was set up which recommended that half the amount be used for a School of Arts and half to replace the condemned building of Museum of which Rai Kanyha Lal even submitted a design. This was conveyed by Mr. Brandrath, the Commissioner of Lahore, to the Provincial Government. The Committee also recommended that the Government might join the Museum to the School of Arts. The newly appointed Principal, Lahore School of Arts in his letter dated 27 May 1875 advised that from the Arts Teacher's point of view the connection of the School of Arts with the Museum is most desirable as the present building was not weather proof and unsuitable for Museum in the summer months, the valuable collection was likely to suffer both from heat and wet and new museum building was an emergent necessity. It was also felt that Museum should follow the commencement of the Arts School. The names of Mr. Purdon and Major Mant were suggested for design. Lengthy correspondence and discussions continued about location, funding, design and other connected matters and finally after 30 years temporary abode in "Ajaib Ghar" the Present building was decided to be constructed in 1887 as a result of public subscriptions to commemorate the Jubilee of Her Majesty Queen Victoria. The foundation stone was laid in 1890 by His Royal Highness Prince Victor, the Prince of Wales. Mr. Lockwood Kipling was then Curator of Central Museum Lahore. The design of the building was prepared by Sardar Sahib Ram Singh. The building was completed in 1893, and all the collections were immediately transferred to it.

Because of Kipling's association with Art, and Art school as also syallabus the Museum was mainly taken advantage of by the students of the Mayo School of Arts, who used the exhibits in the museum under the supervision of their teachers for the purpose of getting ideas for new designs. Some other colleges also used to send their students under charge of their teachers to study the collections chiefly in the Geology, Natural History and Sculptures Section. Lectures and Study shows were also held. Additions and acquisitions was a continued process. The Treasure Trove Act helped a lot in adding to the collection of coins. Purchases were also effected in respect of Art and manufactured items included Paintings and drawings. Punjab hill painting series were acquisitions of the late twenties. All the galleries were open to public except the new gallery which was mostly used by the Principal, Mayo School of Arts for his exhibitions of craft work.

During this period most purchases were source of new acquisitions especially in painting section. These paintings were arranged choronologically from the Persian, Mughal, Rajput, Kangra and Sikh Schools, with revival of painting through the Calcutta School were more noticeable parts of the collection. Mr. S. N. Gupta catalogued and illustrated the same. Museum was always a place of exhibitions by the Fine Arts Society and in the like manner there were other exhibitions.

The Lahore Museum continued to grow and gained much from the archaeological excavations and remains in the country but these were mostly industrial products, artifects, statutes and archaeological fragments without any systematic arrangement. Inspite of this it was the most precious and valuable asset for cultural history of the area. In 1947 the collection was divided between India and Pakistan, which gaps will take long to complete. The condition of Museum in respect of its maintenance and gradually after partition until the Punjab Government came to its rescue in late 1950s. The building at that time was in a bad shape with broken floors leaking roofs and no electricity. The institution was without any laboratory, workshop and other public utilities etc.

The Museum was closed for quite sometime to re-organize and re-habilitate the same. Extensive repairs were carried out both to the building and the wood-works. Additional construction took place. A Carpentry, a laboratory and studio emerged along with canteen, parking and a shop. Separate sections were organized for study of manuscripts, paintings and cataloguing work accelerated. The compound of the Museum was done up in consultation with horticulturists and a properly landscaped lawn developed. Of course, additions continued to be made, staffing position multiplied against the pre-partition nucleus arrangement. During this re-organization and re-doing the industrial exhibits/ material were transferred to the Industries Department leaving the Museum only with cultural and historical assets. The pattern of acquisitions of antiquities has too undergone a change. While in the pre-partition days the field officers used to help collect antiquities for the institution now acquisitions through purchases is the only mode for which, of course, the funds are limited and Government's priorities otherwise. Inspite of these constraints the institution has reasonably added to its collection of antiquities, manuscripts, documents and books both through public, generous donations and purchases. The Museum authorities are short of display space and they need additional accommodation where they will be able to put up more galleries and sections of unique collection of great educational value. Presently as the Museum exists it can be divided into 7 Sections: i.e.Historical collection, 2. Ancient Hindu Section, 3. Buddhists sculpture, 4. Islamic, 5, Muslim relax, 6. Paintings, coins and 7. Pakistan struggle Section.In 1965 some steps were taken towards the renovation of Lahore Museum by Mr. B. A. Kureshi, the then Chief Secretary and later Chairman of Museum's Board of Governors. The Museum was re-organized and new additions made. For example, the historical Jain Temple and ethnological I and II Galleries were added in late 1960s. In 1973 the new Gallery of Pakistan Movement was created. The Pakistan Postage Stamps Gallery was set up. Other additions are galleries containing manuscripts, calligraphic illustrations, specimens of Arts and crafts, and coins and medals section.

The Museum has a reference library. Donations by men of letters added to the collection of library. The library has lot of materials on Pakistan Movement, including files of the Daily 'Zamindar' and 'Inqalab'. The extracts from vernacular newspapers are also available here. Microfilm and Photostat facilities are available. The Museum has now a conservation restoration laboratory. Services like cafeteria, curio shop, carpentry, auditorium and committee room are also there. The museum has kept up its tradition and runs educational programmes and lectures. A bi-annual bulletin is also brought out regularly.

The Museum has invaluable historical collection on cultural history of Pakistan from the earliest to the present times. Some objects have come from other parts of the world. The objects from the sites of Harrappa and Mohenjodaro, displayed in the gallery, unfold the world's earliest town planning and sewerage system. The undeciphered script of seals stands to be a mystery for archaeological scholars. As a whole all these finds represent Paleolithic, microlithic and Neolithic periods of Pakistan's history.

The Hindu collection depicts their beliefs, mode of life of the community. Their collections consist of carved stone, fireplace from Jaipur that is important for its artistic craftsmanship. It shows Krishna, Radha and Rukmani, flanked by two large shells showing Durga Maheshamardni with female attendants. The architectural fragments include columns in red sandstone from Jain Temple and Murta from Salt Range of the Punjab (seventh century), discovered by Sir Stein. Another significant item is the ninth century statute of Divine Couple, Shiva and Oarvati, in the form of Hara Gauri or Uma Maheshvera. They're rare epigraphic specimens in the Hindu, Buddha and Jain Gallery. The museum has also valuable Tibetan, Burmese and Nepalese collections.

Buddhist Sculpture collection in the Museum is unique. It is evidence of a wonderful civilisation which once flourished in Gandhara region. The sculpture of fasting Sidhartha of second century is notable for its artistic accomplishment. It manifests the Greek and Roman influence in the region. The sculpture depicting the miracle of Sarawati is a master piece, as it has been carved out from sixty-eight figures in motion into one stone mass. It belongs to the second century. The sculptures displayed in the gallery present complete sequence of the story of

Buddha from his birth to death. The Buddhist specimens also include pieces of Kushan at Mathura. Statutes, reliefs and architectural fragments represent Jainism.

The Islamic collection of the Museum manifest cultural history of Muslims in the fields of Miniature paintings, manuscripts, calligraphy, architecture and various kinds of crafts including wood work, papiermache, arms, carpets, shawls, textiles, ceramics, jewellery and remarkable and rate items as the large sized carpet of the Mughal period, a Safvid Sword, the famous astrolabes produced at Lahore. Humayun's wood-carved Quranic verses of Ayatual Kursi, and Wooden door of Akbar's time.

The recently established manuscript section contains about a large number of manuscripts of the Holy Quran in Arabic, Persian, Urdu, Punjabi, Pashtu, Turki, Sindhi, and Hindi languages, transcribed in various styles of writing on palm leaves, hide, and paper, made of rug, cotton and other materials. The Kufic Quran is a unique specimen of the Seljuqi period. There are many other pride items in the collection, some of which are Herati Quranic manuscript of Shahrukh's time; the Quran transcribed for Egypt's Mamluk Ruler Abu Saeed Jaqamaq; Khannsh-e-Niazmi from the library of Jalal-ud-Din Khan of Azerbaijan; illustrated Shah Nama of the time of Shah Suleman (1667-94), oldest manuscripts of Devan-e-Talib-Aml, Royal manuscript of Sahih Bukhari from the Library of Shah Jahan and Aurangzeb Alamgir, Devan-e-Hafiz inscribed by Abdul Rashid Delmi, text of Tafsir by Abul Faizi.

The Museum has a treasure of miniature paintings. The earliest examples are from the manuscripts of Kalpasutras, the Jain religious text from Gupt (India) of the fifteenth century. The folios from the medieval remance of Lurck Chanda, painted by Malva in the beginning of the sixteenth century, are also valuable. The Mughal paintings display Persian influence and subsequent developments under the Mughals themselves. The productions of their own type in the world. Modern painting collections include specimens of almost all modern painters of Pakistan like Abdur Rahman Chughtai, Ustad Allah Bakhsh, Zain-ul-Abidin, and Anna Molka owes its existence to the donations made by Faqir Jalal-ud-Din Trust, Maulana Hifzur Rahman, Khawaja Abdur Rahsid Kamil and many others. This collection retains the original glass model of the famous Koh-i-Noor. The painting section also includes the pride works of the earliest masters of Bengal School, like Rabindra Nath Tagore, A. K. Haldar, S. N. Gupta and K. Mazumdar.

The Museum includes the earliest issues of coins, known as Punch Marked, produced in the fourth century B. C. and subsequent periods. It also contains the first Muslim coins issued by Mahmood of Ghazni in Lahore, bearing the inscription of Mahmoodpur, the then name of Lahore. The collections are housed in lockers and scholars can see on request. However, for instructional purpose, the Gallery of

Coins and Medals has been recently organized with a display of replicas of the originals. Sadequain's donation to Lahore Museum is also highly valuable. This is his largest collection of personal belongings consisting of paintings, calligraphy and family manuscripts. His mural painted ceiling in the Miniature Paintings Gallery and panels of calligraphy in the Islamic Gallery represent his monumental work.

The Museum in its present condition, according to the management presents panorama of our history and culture from the earliest of modern times. The most significant latest addition to the Museum is the establishment of freedom gallery, which contains pictorial scenes of the struggle of Muslims in the Sub-continent. This is significant but slightly different aspect of the museum in cultural and historical assets especially due to negligible original material. People are really shy to donate.

A Board of Governors presently manages the Lahore Central Museum with its own rules and regulations under the administrative control of the Information and Culture Department. Unfortunately the bureaucratic controls have all along played a negative role and hampered academic growth of the institution. An institution, where the management consists of technical and learned people has been reduced to clerical establishment that shuttles between Secretariat Sections and various Departments. The museum is a repository of our history, Cultural heritage and has lot to offer to the students of art and scholars and there is a need to give it real autonomy and managerial control which hitherto rests in the bureaucracy. A visit to place always enriches one's knowledge.

7

THE GREEN SPLENDOUR
Which Is No More

The travellers who visited Lahore in the olden days have described the city in their writings as a "Grand resort," a city of old and modern fame, the seat of the mightiest empire and "the city of enchantment". We do not know what that enchantment was which attracted Lalla Rookh (Lalla Rookh by Moore) to Lahore or lured the Mughal Kings, queens and princesses to make their abodes here and build mosques, forts, mausoleums and lay gardens, to enhance it. But we do know that during the Mughal period Lahore was a city of gardens known far and wide for its green grandeur.

Today, from Shahdara to Shalamar, and over the whole of the area around the old walled city, the eye of the wanderer catches the sombre sight of hoary domes, tombs, turrets, mosques and minarets which once adorned the imperial capital. They are poor reminders of the pageantry of the past which is no more there.

Going down the Grand Trunk Road, we come across groups of coal-coated craftsmen, labourers and workers hurrying down to the Railway Workshops and other factories instead of princess who once strolled under enchanting shades of evergreen cypress groves of the Shalamar Gardens. Wandering along the Multan Road, the curious visitor sees neither the lovely Zeb-un-Nisa nor her lively gardens but only a "gateway", in the pattern of the garden of Paradise" (Quranic inscription on the Chauburji Gateway) defying decay even in its deplorable dilapidation; and one feels like writing an eulogy on the departed glory of Lahore.

Historians are not certain about the history of Lahore until the period it was occupied by Muslims. The pre-Muslim history of this splendid city can be simply termed as legendary, which is confined to casual notes in the annals of the neighbouring states with inferences from the accounts of earlier Muslim writers and numismatic evidence, However, Archaeologists conclude that Lahore must have been founded between Ist and 7th centuries of the Christian era. Since recorded evidence, if any, about the grandeur of this city, its buildings, domes and gardens date back to the Muslim period, one can only say something with certainty from thence onwards. The establishment of Muslim Empire in India gave birth to a number of institutions which were peculiar to the Muslim culture. The arts and architecture of Muslims is in itself a separate subject of study and has no parallel whatsoever in the history. It would be only fair to observe that the story of art in India is only as societal as with the name of Muslims and Lahore. It has invariably been seat of the Government, throughout the Muslim rule, the importance it might have received need not be over-emphasized. The Lahore Fort built by Emperor Akbar, the Badshahi Masjid raised by Emperor Aurangzeb, Jahangir Tomb built by Nur Jahan and Shah Jahan and a number of other buildings and tombs, are symbols of the glory the city enjoyed in the past. The Muslims were not only fond of erecting buildings but also laid out gardens throughout the length and breadth of their Empires. Lahore got its share which is manifest from Shalamar and many other gardens non-existent now.

The gardens of Lahore can be divided and described in four periods, Viz. The Muslim period (1526-1800) the Sikh period (1800-1846), the British Period (1849-1947) and post independence period 1947-1997. According to available accounts, the Mughal Period would include: -

Shalamar Gardens.	Dilkusha Gardens
Gulabi Bagh.	Mirza Kamran's Garden and Baradari
Inayat Bagh.	Gardens in the Lahore Fort.
Angoori Bagh	Garden of Zeb-un-Nisa.
Mehtabi Bagh.	Naulakha Gardens.
Garden of Mohabat Khan.	Bagh-e-Dara.

It would seem that the Sikhs were not fond of nation-building works as during their short-lived rule they only exploited or developed remains of the past. It would thus be appropriate to say that the old gardens of Mughals in the suburbs of Lahore were divided amongst Sikh Sardars and simply renamed. As such, the names narrated in different books and accounts are as under: -

Hazoori Bagh.	Teja Singh Bagh.
Badami Bagh.	Rattan Chand Bagh.
Khushhal Singh's Garden.	

The British were not fond of laying out magnificent gardens comparable to those laid in the Muslim period but they believed in developing well planned cities with greenery all around. They gave Lahore: -

Lawrence Gardens (now known as Jinnah Garden.)	Public Gardens on Lower Mall.
Soldiers Garden.	Green Belt around the walled city.

The post independence period, like the British, did not contribute much to the city. The early years were full of settlement hazards which were deeply routed in economic depravation and political instability. It was in the late sixtees that the industry and agriculture took off. Then followed the catastrophe of the fall of East Pakistan and it took quite sometime before the development started. The late seventies and early eighteees found some additions but the migration played havoc with the architectural beauty of the city. The population influx due to migration from India, movement of population from rural to urban areas brought great strain on the resources. The open spaces, the gardens, grounds and green belts were greatly occupied, forcefully or otherwise. The weak administration, the corrupt bureaucracy, poor management caused haphazard growth without any care for city planning. There was no attention to leave open spaces and developing parks and gardens to the point of even minimum required limits. The reader would note from the account in the following paragraphs that most of the gardens which even survived the Sikh and British rule have totally disappeared.

Badami Bagh has disappeared and instead a very dirty locality has come up. It is also used as a Bus and Truck Stand for the traffic coming to Lahore with quite a few markets of spare parts of vehicles. During rains, the area being low lying is always under water, with the sewerage gushing out garbage.

Raja Teja Singh Bagh or Raja Dina Nath's Bagh, there is no evidence and only ill-planned houses and 'Mohallahs' have sprung up. The same is true of Rattan Chand Bagh. The population of city which was less than a million in 1947 has crossed the figure of 6 millions. Unfortunately matching and requisite facilities which are essential from public health point of view have been completely ignored. However, following Parks and Gardens have been added by the post partition administration of Lahore.

The Yadgar-e-Pakistan Park.

Iqbal Park.

Forest Park.

Pain Bagh on back of both sides of G.T.Road

University Park, New Campus, Punjab University.

Guslhan-e-Iqbal Park, Allama Iqbal Town

Lahore Park on Raiwind Road.

Jallo Park, near Village Jallo.

Race Course Park.

Liberty Park, Gulberg, Lahore.

SHALAMAR GARDENS

The word "Shalamar" is a combination of Turkish and Sanskrit languages. 'Shala means house as in "Dharamsala", "Patshala", and "Mar" in Turkish indicates joy. Thus Shalamar would mean the "house of joy". It is not certain as to when these gardens came to be known as "Shalamar Gardens" but it can be authoritatively said that these were known as "Farrah Bakhsh" till Shah Alam's period (the successor of Aurangzeb). Syed Latif, the author of "history of Lahore" narrates that Ranjit Singh named the Gardens as "Shahla Bagh". Shahla in Persian means "sweet heart" and 'Bagh' means 'Garden'. Thus "Shahla Bagh" means the garden of "Sweet heart". The Maharaja is reported to have styled it as such in all his official correspondence and the "Lahoris" even now, call Shalamar Bagh as "Shahla Bagh".

About 4 miles Northeast of the old city, the gardens are located on the left side of Grand Trunk Road (Lahore -Wagha Road). The land was, probably, selected for its fertility and height level as it happened to be the old bed of the Ravi commonly called "Majha". The garden is in the form of an oblong parallelogram surrounded by a high wall of bricks with three successive terraces each raised 12-15 feet above the level of the other. The total area covered by the gardens come to about 80 acres in the 19th century.

It is said that before laying out these gardens, the first major task to be undertaken was the construction of a canal to bring water at a level from which there should be a reasonable fall for running the fountains. This assignment was entrusted to Ali Mardan Khan, the great canal engineer who also built the Delhi canal. The canal, which took off from the River Ravi, 100 miles upstream, was completed by 1633 and was known by the name of "hasli" canal. This used to intersect the gardens and discharge itself in the middle terrace into a large marble basin where from 450 fountains used to sprout water.

Ali Mardan Khan and Mulla Ala-ul-Mulk, on the instruction of Emperor Shah Jahan jointly laid out the garden. The work was completed in 1642. In the same year the Emperor visited the gardens. The cost of garden and building is reported to have been to the extent of Rs.6 lacs and the whole work was completed in one year, five months and four days. According to a legend, Emperor Shah Jahan once spending a night at Shahdara (gardens) then just completed by Empress Nur Jahan, dreamt of a garden like the Paradise, bright with fruits of gold, marble fountains, cool pavilions and every variety of foliage. On waking up he sent for Ali Mardan Khan and Nawab Fazl Khan, and ordered them to re-create for him his "fleeting vision". They accordingly laid out the garden in seven divisions, representing the seven stages of the Paradise. Of these only three are included in the present area. The remaining were, either, not constructed or destroyed. But it

Shalimar Gardens

would be logical to assume that the garden is complete in itself as it is of considerable size with proper walls. The original entrance was to the lowest terrace and on the west as has been customary in the Mughal Gardens. The upper terrace was known as "Farrah Bakhsh", the remaining two were called "Faiz Bakhsh". The central level is the most spectacular. The reservoir, once, had 152 fountains of which only 100 exist now. The central platform is reached by a narrow pavement. The water flows down through the southern pavilion by way of a broad curved marble 'Chute' at the bottom. Over hanging the water, is the marble throne of the Emperor. The footpaths and pavings are of bricks. It is said that the Emperor had given specific instructions about fruit trees and they were brought from Kashmir and Afghanistan. Under the trees were to be grass platforms as they exist at present. The original plantings included mango, cherry, apricot, peaches plum, apple, almond, orange and cypress etc.

The buildings in the Gardens were also of peculiar designs with beautiful workmanship. The number of buildings in the Garden is evidence that most probably this garden was primarily used as a camping ground on Emperors' visit to Lahore. The marble of garden pavilions was stripped off by the Sikhs and was used in decorating the Ram Bagh and Golden Temple at Amritsar. The other important features of this magnificent remnant of Mughal grandeur are firstly, the exact and correct maintenance of water level from the entry to the fountains, irrespective of the height of different levels. Secondly seen from outside, the garden appears to have one single surface of ground with walled enclosure although there are terraces at different levels. The summer houses located towards the northern side of the first terrace were originally a structure of marble which like many other buildings of Lahore could not escape the ruthless hands of Ranjit Singh and was taken away to Amritsar for the Golden Temple. Similarly, the summerhouses of the east and west were also deprived of their marble covers and sold. The niches in the building known as "Sawan Bhadon" in the garden in the 3rd terrace were all of marble and were carried away by Sikh Sardars during anarchy preceding Ranjit Singh Rule. Not only that, the copper used in the fountains was also taken out and sold. The original gates of the Gardens were to the west and east on the 3rd terrace but of these only western was in use in the 19th century while one in the east was bricked up. The doorway towards South of the first terrace on the Grand Trunk Road was only opened by the British. It was originally sleeping apartment for ladies of "harem". South of the Khwabgah across the G.T. Road were the splendid palaces of Royal ladies and the area was known as "Khawaspura".

On the decline of the Mughal Empire, the Gardens were taken as private property of Maharaja Ranjit Singh and by the time the British occupied the Punjab, these were reported to have deteriorated into a dense jungle. Steps were taken by the British authorities to restore the masonry work and put in order the gardens by cutting the jungle. An English gardener from Saharanpur was called who arranged large-scale cutting of trees and their removal for disposal. When the settlement of Lahore was in hand, the question of the maintenance of the Gardens rose and it came to light that when Emperor Shah Jahan acquired the land presently occupied by Shalamar Gardens the original occupants of this tract were given rent free grant in 'Mauza Baghbanpura'. This grant alongwith other 59 plus 22 'Ghumaon' of land was given to one Mehr Munga. The family had since then maintained the Gardens from the proceed revenues of the grant and it is said that they were continuing as such given during the Sikh period. The British after thorough examination of the case on documentary evidence decided that it was advisable to maintain these gardens and buildings in a state of decent repair as a memorial to the fallen greatness of the Mughals. The gardens afforded a pleasant place of rest and relaxation to all classes of the inhabitants of Lahore and the best manner of securing this objective was to allow these gardens to be kept up properly and the grant was kept off the Government rent roll. Nabi Bakhsh the lineal descendant of Mehr Munga of Baghbanpura, was accordingly allowed to maintain the gardens with proceeds from the grant of Baghbanpura as usual.

Presently the garden remains in an utter state of neglect. The old structure and buildings of small brick around garden have disappeared and one with a mission of research can only find small brick mounds at some points. It is a matter of few years that a part of eastern living quarters across the road, which extended over a sizeable area are non-existent. Instead of a Police Station and market with houses have come up. The most ugly mushroom growth of housing colonies by Qabza Groups have totally spoiled the very locale of the garden. The most distressing part of the story is that the Archaeological Department, which maintains the garden, does not even spend what it gets on account of entry fee recovered from the tourists. It is a pity we condemn Sikhs and British for neglect but we have not lagged behind in accelerating the pace of dilapidation of such a beautiful spot. The trees are disappearing, lawns in bad shape, the walls crumbling, fountains not working and rubbish all around presents a very sad scene.

GULABI BAGH

Gulabi or the 'Garden of Rosewater' although not in existence now was located about two miles on the road to Shalamar Gardens. It was laid out by Mirza Sultan Baig who was 'Amir-ul-Bahr' during Shah Jahan's period according to the inscription on the gate which existed in early 20th century the founder of the garden had constructed it as beautifully as any other. It is said this garden had very beautiful flowers. The Shalamar Gardens were encircled by a number of smaller

Shalamar Gardens

Shalimar Gardens

Bagh Mirza Kamaran

gardens to make it more picturesque, like Gulabi Bagh, on the south was the Inayat Bagh and further south the Angoori Bagh on the north was the Mehtabi Bagh, which was beautifully decorated with Baradari and fountains. It is strange that expansion of city has been so aggressive that even remains have disappeared. Of course these parks were public property in the Government ownership and Departments must have taken precautions to save this precious heritage.

GARDEN OF MOHABAT KHAN.

Mohabat Khan's garden, though small in area, was to the south of the then village Baghbanpura and to the west of the Shalamar Gardens. It was surrounded by high brick walls. The garden had many chambers mostly built of bricks. Mohabat Khan who was Commander-in-Chief of the Mughal Army and Viceroy of Deccan, had built this garden. During the Sikh period it was bestowed upon Faqir Aziz-ud-Din on whose death his son Faqir Chiragh-ud-Din sold it to Jahangir & Co., the Parsi merchants in the 19th century, who made alterations and constructed a new gate to the north of this garden.

BAGH-E-DARA

There was another Garden around Shalamar which was built during the Mughal period and was known as Bagh-e-Dara. It was towards east of Shalamar Gardens. During the Sikh period it was given to Dyal Singh, a Sikh Sardar, by Raja Kharak Singh. The Sikhs demolished the buildings and sold the bricks and other materials. Later on, the land was also sold, in pieces to various people.

DILKUSHA GARDENS

The garden laid out by Empress Nur Jahan in Shahdara across the River Ravi were known as Dilkusha Gardens. It is said that these were the same gardens where the Jahangir's tomb was later built. These gardens were damaged a lot when Amir Dost Muhammad Khan's (of Kabul) brother stayed here in Sikh period. In spite of the ravages of time they reflect the taste of the builder and designer.

BARADARI OF MIRZA KAMRAN

The first and the oldest emblem of Mughal architecture in Lahore was the Baradari of Kamran which was built by Mirza Kamran son of Babur and brother of Humayun. It was constructed in the midst of a beautiful garden, the first of its type ever laid out in the city. The River Ravi then used to flow at quite some distance from the garden, but now the Baradari, badly damaged, with only a few plants, stands in the middle of the river. The river has over the centuries been fighting to

Race Course Park

Race Course Park

wipe it out of its way but it has stood the pillage of time. Even now it is a picnic spot for the people who go on boats from the western side and by a causeway from North when the river becomes dry during winter. The gardens were washed away following the change in the course of the river. However, during the tenure of Mr. Nawaz Sharif as Chief Minister, he specially ordered providing a stone protection embankment to the Baradari. Some pavements of the garden were restored. The Baradari was also repaired. A restaurant has also been set up. People hire boats to reach the Baradari and garden for picnic.

LAHORE FORT

The Fort, which was also used as palace by the Emperors, had small garden with fountains and flowers. The flowers would be usually seasonal and according to the taste and preference of each king and usually there were no fruit trees as these would block the open view. These gardens had seats and private rooms on the side-ways and fishponds were also common. The Lahore Fort which was improved by successors of Akbar had two gardens. These were in Jahangir's Quadrangle and the "Pain Bagh" the former is a large open space with a reservoir in the centre with fountains and a marble platform with an approach from causeway. Its grassy lawns were watered by the fountains. No trace of the original plantations are available. The other garden i.e. "Pain Bagh" has pavements made of small red bricks and was a place for relaxation for the ladies of the harem. There exists a water tank and platform in the centre and the side plots have grassy beds and dark green hedges. It is said that originally these plots were enclosed by red stone railings Both these gardens are very well looked after and maintained by the Archaeological Department and are visited by a large number of people on Sundays and holidays.

GARDEN OF ZEB-UN-NISA

About a mile from the District Courts on the right side of the Multan Road, is the building known as Chauburji. It was the gateway of the garden of Princess Zeb-un-Nisa or Zebinda Begum, the daughter of Emperor Aurangzeb. The Princess used the 'nom deplume' "Makhfi" in her poetry. Historians like Syed Nur Ahmad. Syed Latif and Kanyha Lal agree that it was a garden but Dr. Abdullah Chughtai, in his booklet "Lahore during Sikh Period", differs. He is of the view that it was Jahan Ara Begum and not Zeb-un-Nisa, who laid out the garden. Anyway, whosoever was the builder, it is confirmed that it was a garden which extended from the western side of the walled city to Nawankot. It is said that a female attendant of the Princess who was her favourite, had supervised the construction of the garden. On the completion of the garden, when the Princess was going to open the garden, she heard a crowd saying that the Princess was going to open Mian

Bai's gardens. On hearing that the garden was already known by the name of Mian Bai, she bestowed the garden upon her. Later on she laid out another garden in Nawankot with many other beautiful buildings and summer houses in the midst of which she built her Mausoleum which was divested of valuable stones, as in other cases by Ranjit Singh. Only the skeleton of the tomb is left. The gardens and the other buildings which were non-existent during the British period are now a story of the past and the area has become an over populated extension of the city where the houses have come up in a haphazard manner without any plan or scheme. The Chauburji also lost one minaret which was restored only a few years back. A small round about had been developed by Ch. Hafizullah Ishaque, Director-General, Lahore Development Authority after a great fight who also got removed encroachments. The Chauburji (Gate of the garden) was restored due to his personal interest.

NAULAKHA GARDENS

A mention may also be made of Naulakha Gardens. The gardens were laid out by the great Canal Engineer Ali Mardan Khan. It is called Naulakha. It is said, because it was prepared at a cost of Rs. 9 lakh but according to another version it was so called because it gave an annual income of Rs.9.00 lakh. It was plundered during the Sikh period, the bricks sold and stones removed to Amritsar. The lands were brought under cultivation and a separate 'Mahal' of Naulakha came up in the British Period. A portion of the left over ruined building was converted into residence by Sardar Dyal Singh Majitha. These were known as a Ahluwalia gardens during the Sikh Period. Except trees on roads in the area and grooves in the Naulakha Church there is no sign of garden in the area but the greenery speaks of its past eloquently.

HAZOORI BAGH

The space between the Badshahi Mosque and Alamgiri Gate of the Lahore Fort was used by the soldiers. During the Sikh Period, Maharaja Ranjit Singh turned the space into a garden with a Baradari in it and named it as 'Hazoori Bagh'. The building is two storeyed with underground chambers. The ceilings are beautifully decorated with small mirrors. It was built by the Maharaja in 1818 and the marble used in the building was taken from different Mughal buildings like Tomb of Zeb-un-Nisa in Nawankot and that of Shah Sharf outside Taxali Gate. According to one account, the entire Baradari was shifted from the Tomb of Jahangir. The garden with grassy plots is in existence. On Sundays and holidays people from the walled city have there gatherings in the 'Bagh', Punjabi Mushaira

Minar-e-Pakistan

and story tellers "Qissa go" have their sittings in groups a lively tradition, reportedly, continuing over for the last one century or so.

BADAMI BAGH

This garden between the Masti Gate and Sheranwala Gate was also founded by Maharaja Ranjit Singh. The garden was named after some Muslim Princess 'Gul Badam' whose tomb happened to be in the locality. The garden being very close to the walled city was a public garden. The English families used to visit the garden for relaxation and recreation. It was under the management of Mr. Henry Cope, Editor of the 'Lahore Chronicle' in early British period, when the British planned to build a new garden on the Mall, it was sold to the Punjab Horticultural Society for Rs.2500. With the passage of time and floods it lost it glamour as lot of plants, flowers and fruit trees were destroyed. The extension of Badami Bagh Railway Station also affected the garden. On the construction and completion of a garden on the Mall it became less attractive and was completely abandoned. Now a days there is no garden and instead of the area has been converted into the General Bus Stand but the locality is known as Badami Bagh. A mushroom housing growth has totally spoiled the surroundings of the fort replacing the garden.

KHUSHHAL SINGH'S BAGH

The garden of Jamadar Khushhal Singh was reported to be in a good condition during the late 19th century and was in the custody of Ram Singh the son of Khushhal Singh. The garden was taken over by the British Government for construction of some Government buildings and the owner was compensated by grant of land in Sialkot. This is the garden and Haveli where Lahore Government House is located. The garden is intact but not open to public. Of course being Governor's house lot many developments have taken place. It abounds in fruit & other trees.

TEJA SINGH'S BAGH

Towards the north of the city is the locality now known as 'Khooi-Miran'. There used to be a splendid garden with fruit trees, fountains and summerhouses which belonged to Raja Teja Singh and subsequently his successor Raja Harbans Singh. This was covered and the area is now known as Harbanspura.

DINA NATH'S BAGH

A beautiful garden was built by Raja Dina Nath close to the tomb of 'Ghoray Shah' which was known for its beauty and elegance. The remains of the garden and buildings were around the locality of 'Ghoray Shah' across the Railway

Station. It was a noted place for garden parties by the public of Lahore even after the British occupation. But now after partition there is hardly any sign of Bagh there.

BAGH RATTAN CHAND

Another garden known as Garden of Rattan Chand was located outside Shahalmi Gate and as it happened to be close to the walled city it was place of great interest. This garden had numerous fruit trees and a 'Serae'. A part of the garden is still known as 'Serae Rattan Chand'. The place of this garden may be identified where presently the Children Ward and Orthopaedic ward is located. Next to this was the Serae.

LAWRENCE OR JINNAH GARDENS

Covering an area of about 112 acres, these gardens are located on the Mall opposite the Government House. Prior to 1860, this land was lying in desolate wilderness but in that year a small garden was laid out here. In 1868 a portion of the land on the south-eastern side was purchased and the gardens extended. The amount spent is said to have been partly met from the proceeds of the sale of Badami Bagh, Soldier's gardens at Anarkali and partly from Government grant. A part of this garden was under the Horticultural Society of the Punjab along with the botanical garden and was managed by a gardener from Kew Gardens (London). Another part of the garden on the Northwest was given to 'menagerie' or Zoo which was largely built up by contributions and donations received mainly from the Chiefs of Punjab. In 1860 the garden was transferred to the Lahore Municipal Committee and was used as a public resort for recreation. Grounds for tennis and cricket (which even now exist) were also earmarked. On Saturday evenings, the police band used to play in front of Montgomery Hall. The Garden is irrigated from Lahore Branch canal. It contained more than 80,000 plants and shrubs of 6000 different species. The cost of the maintenance was partly met by the Municipality and partly from subscriptions and grant-in-aid from the Provincial revenues. The botanical gardens, it is said, were laid on the recommendation of Agri-Horticultural Society mainly for the purpose of studies by the students of the Medical School on the pattern of Calcutta and Madras Medical Colleges. The old menagerie had developed into a full-fledged zoo with a fine selection of animal species. Additions and alternations have also been made in the original layout plans of roads. The Fatima Jinnah sunken garden is a post-independence addition beautifully laid out with grassy platforms and arched hedges. In the afternoon

Gulabi Bagh

Hazoori Bagh

people walk here to breathe in the cool and airy place. On the Lawrence Road side is the Open Air Theatre on a mound. The addition of the Mughal Garden, on Shalamar pattern on to the southern side is very recent and infact completed only a few years back. This portion has beautiful fountains and pacca pavements. A mosque facing the canteen has been erected in the garden and a Library by name of Dar-us-Salam has also been established which runs classes in Library Science. The other important building in the gardens are the buildings of Cosmopolitan Club, the Commercial Club (since demolished) the Ladies Club, The Open Air Theatre and the Lawrence and Montgomery Halls. Towards the eastern corner of the garden, a children's park has also been developed. One may not forget to mention the cricket ground where even test matches in the Lawrence Garden were also played.

The Lawrence and Montgomery Halls are located on the left side of the Mall Road entrance to the Gardens, the former facing the Mall and latter facing the central avenue of the garden. They are joined by a covered corridor. The Lawrence Hall was built as a memorial to Sir John Lawrence mainly through contributions of the British Officers, in 1861-62. The Montgomery Hall, in 1866 was erected through contributions from the Punjab Chiefs and Nawabs whose names are inscribed on a marble tablet in the building. This was constructed in memory of Sir Robert Montgomery, the Governor of Punjab. The Lawrence Hall was frequently used as an assembly room for public meetings and theatrical entertainments. Both the buildings were under the care of the Municipality, which held them in trust for the Government. The buildings contained some portraits which it is reported were till recently there, alongwith a good Library. This building was later on used as Gymkhana Club. When the Club moved to its new building on the Upper Mall the buildings were used as Academy for Administrative Training by the Government of Pakistan. The Academy moved to Walton and the building, according to Press reports was to be used as a Cultural House. Infact it was allotted to the Punjab Arts Council but later the decision was changed by the President of Pakistan and Quaid-e-Azam Library was established here.

SOLDIERS GARDEN

Towards Northwest of old Anarkali Bazar, there is said to have been a garden with a Baradari known as 'Wazir Khan's Baradari". Immediately on annexation some Regiments of the British Forces were stationed in the barracks built in garden. These gardens were known as Soldiers Garden. To place it appropriately, these were around the present building of Public Library. When the army Regiments moved to newly constructed Cantonment at Mian Mir in 1851-52, these gardens were sold to the Agri-Horticultural Society of Punjab at a cost of Rs.2,000/-. The Government of Punjab, in conformity with orders of the

Government of India decided to lay out regimental gardens in their cantonments throughout the Punjab and NWFP. These gardens coupled with the plantation on Lower Mall now known as 'Gol Bagh' and Riwaz Gardens (There was a garden Opposite University ground which was later on used for residential quarters for Secretariat Officers) came to be known as Public Gardens on the Lower Mall.

GARDEN ROUND THE WALLED CITY

The British, after annexation of the Punjab, took a number of steps for overall development, generally in the whole of the territory and especially, in the capital city of Lahore. In 1863-64 when the Municipal Committee was set up, they initiated a number of schemes for improvement of the city and welfare of the people. An out-let of water was brought from the Lahore Branch of Bari Doab Canal to meet the shortage of water caused on account of the diversion of a stream on the western side of the Fort. The area around the city which was dirty and filthy was cleaned. The ditch around the walled city was filled up and a garden was laid where people would relax in the afternoons. The 'Mochi Gate Bagh' bears testimony to all this as it has been the venue of public meetings and political gatherings during the Pakistan Movement. While most of these gardens have been authorisedly or unauthorisedly occupied by the people by way of shops and houses etc. still some patches of the green belt can be seen. Alas, the city fathers could not ensure their existence, and instead shops & petty markets are being raised and the remaining green parts being occupied by squatters. Only a few trees are left on the southern side of old city facing the Ravi Road. Even those are under threat of occupation in the names of mosques and fake 'mazars' by the land grabbers.

Sikh rule in Punjab (1799-1839) was really a painful period of history especially for Lahore. It emerged after decay of Muslim set up which had been built over a period of centuries. The cultural fabric of the Muslims in Punjab suffered badly. The historic Monuments, buildings, mausoleums and gardens etc., were denuded of the valuable stone which were used at Amritsar. The Sikhs also laid one or two gardens but these were a far cry from magnificence of the Mughal gardens and one may remark that these were poor copies of Muslim rulers. British equally harmed the monuments of Lahore. They levelled many monuments for the sake of bricks required for their offices, and cantonments. They discarded the Mughal style of gardens and themselves set up green belts as prevalent in Europe. The Western style gardens may be termed as parks or green spots. The green belt around the city won the appreciation of every body. The Lawrence Garden, Lahore City's, present day Bagh-e-Jinnah started in 1861-62 and the vast Minto Park – now divided into Minar-e-Pakistan and Iqbal Park, etc. were all antithesis of Mughal gardens. However, there was one exception. It was the Ram Bagh on the

West of Nawankot. This garden started in 1890 and spread over 500 Kanals was built by Rai Pandat Khabardhan. Contrary to the British period gardens, the Ram Bagh, was imitation of Mughal gardens, water reservoirs, fountains, water-falls and houses with hanging walls for working fountains and above all enclosed by four walls. This garden was also called New Shahla Bagh. This garden, last of the Mughal traditions, was destroyed after 1947 by the residents of Lahore, both old and new mainly due to influx of settlers and land grabbers.

POST INDEPENDENCE PARKS OF LAHORE

RACE COURSE PARK

This park was built during Governor Ghulam Jillani Khan's time. The race course was shifted out of the city. As its name suggests it is located on old race course premises, close to official residences i.e. G.O.R-I, opposite the Government Services Hospital. Located near the Bagh-e-Jinnah Lahore, the park consists of over 88 acres of land, around which runs a jogging track. Several walkways criss-cross their way through the park. Among its special features are a Japanese garden, a botanical garden and a row of fountains which come alive when they are lit up at night. There is a lake towards the north of the garden. The lawns are beautifully laid and well marked. During National Horse and Cattle Show and on other festive occasions, the Chief Minister and Government of Punjab host their lunches and dinners on the lakeside.

YADGAR-E-PAKISTAN PARK

The 196 feet high Minar-e-Pakistan built as a monument to commemorate the passage of Pakistan Resolution is situated in the middle of the Iqbal Park (old Minto Park) near the Lahore Fort and the Badshahi Mosque. A fast moving elevator takes the visitors up to the top of the Minar for a bird's eye view of Lahore. There are vast grassy plots around the "YADGAR" which are visited by a large number of people daily. A sizeable number of inhabitants of walled city daily come out and spend their evening time in the park. Of late this park is also used for large size public meetings of Politicians and religious groups.

LINEAR PARK

The park is another garden which was added by the Prime Minister of Pakistan, Mian Muhammad Nawaz Sharif which runs along Model Town on Ferozepur Road for over 7000 feet. It features pedestrian park paths, jogging tracks and two lakes on either end in addition to three high rise and beautifully laid fountains. The area under the park was occupied by some people as a 'Katchi Abadi' on the site of China Camp which was set up here during the 2nd World War. The park lying between Ferozepur Road and Model Town has totally changed the look of the area. It has fountains, fish tanks, beautifully laid rose beds, water channels and walkways. Its proper maintenance attracts lot of visitors in the early morning and in the evenings for jogging and walking and on holidays for picnics.

MODEL TOWN PARK

Also situated in Model Town is the Model Town Central Park around which the residential area is designed. A jogging track runs around the landscaped park, which also houses a small aviary. This was a big pre-partition park and a very wide road encircled it. In the recent years many encroachments have taken place. Two schools, two big markets, petrol pumps and lot more has appeared around the park, changing and affecting its very character. It is rather being ravaged.

JALLO PARK

Just off the Lahore Canal seventeen miles upstream outside Lahore on its left side is situated the Jallo Park. It was again built by Governor Jillani. A really spacious area with lakes, large grassy plots, facilities, drive in spots. It is gradually becoming a weekend resort for the visitors. There was a scheme under consideration of the Government for developing a Joyland with some funding and outside assistance but it is yet to materialise. It was planned and well-conceived park which could be of great use to the over-populated city of Lahore which has outgrown all proportions during the last three decades, but unfortunately it is now desolated. A recent visitor observed that the place is turning into a jungle in absence of proper care and maintenance. Planned in 1977 as an amusement park and picnic spot, this garden covers 450 acres. The main attraction of Jallo Park was the Children's Zoo located there. Animals in the Zoo included varieties of Deer and Antelope, a Zebra, Ostriches, Pelicans and Storks, as well as a Himalayan Black Bear. These animals moved almost in open grassy areas. Several varieties of pheasant, peacock and other birds were found in aviaries, the Zoo also housed several monkey varieties and various reptiles and snakes. Strangely all this is disappearing. Interestingtly while this Government built park is vanishing a private park just near the place is developing like any commercial venture in private sector.

IQBAL PARK

Infact it is adjoining Minto Park (Yadgar-e-Pakistan) with a lake, a stadium and areas for hockey and wrestling. It is mostly used by professionals for matches.

There is great rush on holidays for boating in the lake. Of late it is a neglected state without any attendants.

LAHORE PARK

Another contribution to Lahore by Governor Jillani was establishing a Park on the Lahore Raiwind Road in early 80s. This park extends over hundreds of acres of land. Immediately crossing the Defence & Raiwind Road off the Raiwind Road a small metalled road leads into the Park. It has also a garden with drive in facilities leading to the picnic and amusement points. At the moment it is very secluded with no service facilities like that of restaurant, parking and even there is no entry fee. But one should hope that in a couple of years with the growth and development of city on that side, it will become a very interesting picnic point.

LIBERTY PARK

Another garden very well laid after independence is a park known as the Liberty Market – lying in the posh locality of Gulberg, the garden is very important place for those jogging and coming for morning and evening walk. The City Development Authority is maintaining the park reasonably well with gardens and other horticultural staff. The garden is divided into various levels with amusement facilities for children. The central portion of the park is very shady and the growers of evergreen trees provide relief to those coming in the months of May – August. The walkways and jogging tracks are all in brick. The park is beautifully lit. However of late the L.D.A. has started leasing it out for marriage parties which damages the grassy lawns and flowerbeds.

GULSHAN-E-IQBAL PARK.

Another Park which has been developed by the city's development authority is the Gulshan-e-Iqbal Park. The park has been laid in one of the recently developed locality known as Allama Iqbal Town. It extends over an area of about 100 acres. It was inaugurated by the President of Pakistan, the late Gen. M. Zia–ul-Haq. It has two lakes with boating facilities and many amusement points for children such as train travelling, fishing, dodgem cars, a small aviary and 'Jhoolay'. It is the most popular point of outing for middle class families on holidays especially on Eids and "Taroo" etc. etc. Not many trees stand in the Park except a few on the northern and southern side. There is a beautiful fall on the central mound with lighting arrangements.

8

LAHORE ARTS COUNCIL

T he arts symbolise a society's way of life, both material and ideological. The Body of the arts is, therefore, the visible representation of a nation's identity or image by which it is known and recognised. The level and quality of these arts is taken to be the level of its civilization. "Art, unlike culture, is not the raw material of social life which exists independently of individuals, but a deliberate and superior manufacture created by a body of specialists. It predicates, on the part of the artist, an awareness of things superior to the common run and a level of sensibility higher than of those who are not similarly endowed. Art, therefore, unlike culture, is not merely a passive reflection of way of life but an active agency which can also, to some measure, change and modify it. It prescribes the good and bad in taste, the 'cultured' and 'uncultured' in personality and behaviour, the beautiful and ugly in material surroundings. It thus profoundly influences both value judgements and social behaviour within the community.

Art, therefore, is an important moral social force. The arts provide a sublimated vehicle for the expression of urges, impulses, instincts, dreams, illusions, conflicts, happiness and unhappiness, fulfilments and frustrations of a human group. These means of self-expression are as natural and as necessary to community as laughter or tears, or cries of pain and pleasure, to an individual. The blocking or suppression of these means can have the same pernicious psychopathic repercussions for a people as the forcible suppression of natural instincts for an individual.

Artistic expression, is an important factor in peoples' mental health. Art is an acknowledged source of human pleasure. So much so that this is sometimes mistaken as its sole end. This pleasureableness together with other moral, intellectual, and emotional components, makes good and serious art into the most instructive, beneficial and purposeful means for the utilization of a peoples' leisure. Art thus is an important agent of human happiness.

Culture has defied a precise definition and is often subjected to a medley of meanings - different in varying contexts. Its definition is still a subject of debate, not only in Pakistan, but also in many advanced countries of the world. Undoubtedly, the vitality, vigour and personality of a nation, or a group of people, are reflected in its culture which, infact, means the historical traditions of a people's arts, literature, music and also their love of beauty.

Healthy traditions and enduring cultural landmarks are not created overnight. It takes a country or a city several centuries, if not a millennium, to evolve customs, conventions, social practices and cultural sensibilities which are furbished and enriched by succeeding generations of citizens.

The origin of Lahore is lost in the hazy maze of antiquity. It has been mentioned in the ancient treatises and travelogues. This city of sprightly people has braved the vicissitudes of history, absorbing in their wake the influences of several civilizations which swept it through the ages. Its rich musical heritage, among other cultural hallmarks, is the product of trans-cultural pollination and cross-cultural fertilization of minds spawned by several centuries. This city historically known the world over for its ebullient cultural traditions earned the approbation of being the hub of creative activities before the emergence of Pakistan. The mass exodus of Hindus, Sikhs and others to India in August, 1947, created a sudden void in August, 1947 in the cultural life of the city.

The second largest city of Pakistan, and the bustling provincial metropolis of the Punjab, Lahore has variously been called the city of gardens, 'baithaks' and 'akharas'; the centre of education, art and culture. Over the decades, it has produced a large number of renowned artists, or has welcomed within its folds many celebrities who achieved distinctions in the field of visual and performing arts, scholarship and education, sports and politics.

THE ARTS COUNCIL

Until only a few decades ago, Lahore was reputed for its chain of baithaks located within the walled city where its vivacious citizens used to confabulate in politics, social and community affairs, poetry and music. Large halls and spacious auditoria had not yet emerged on the city landscape; the only exceptions being the two small but useful multipurpose halls which were frequently used by different communities. These were: the YMCA Hall on the Mall, and (the now extinct) SPSK Hall outside Mori Gate. But the baithaks admirably served the cultural needs of the people wherein they primarily dabbled in music.

With the rapid increase, in urbanisation, necessitated by the increasing demographic pressure and due to the culturally corrosive effect of the horizontal expansion of city landscape, the age-old tradition of baithaks faded into oblivion.

Several attempts have been made in the past to fill this void. A number of cultural organizations sprang up in the city with the professed object of promoting drama, painting, sculpture and music. A large number of concerts were held at

Lahore Arts Council (Alhamra) in 1955 Painting by Sufi Waqar

different places in the past several decades, but the absence of a multi-purpose auditorium always remained a bane of these organizations.

The establishment of Arts Council in Lahore in 1949, helped to some extent in fostering musical and other cultural activities in the city, but the scope of these was limited in the absence of proper music and theatre halls and other technical facilities and large auditoria. The situation took a turn for the better with the emergence of a Cultural Complex on the Mall, and the provision of the Open Air Theatre on Ferozepur Road.

To understand the gradual evolution of the Lahore Arts Council's Cultural Complex, one has to go back into the year 1949 when an association of like-minded and culturally conscious citizens formed a society. Named as 'Pakistan Arts Council', its founders included among others, such luminaries as artist M. Abdur Rahman Chughtai, playwright Imtiaz Ali Taj, Agha Bashir, S.S. Jafari, Zafarul Hassan, Justice S.A. Rahman, Mian Mumtaz Muhammad Daultana and not to forget Malika-e-Mauseeqi Roshan Ara Begum and Malika-e-Tarannum Noor Jahan. This association provided the nucleus of an institution that aimed at the revival and further promotion of creative activities in Lahore. The association in the name of Pakistan Arts Council started working in December 1949. It was a body formed under the Societies Registration Act. The objective was promotion of Pakistani culture, fostering creative activities of Lahore.

The Arts Council was inaugurated on December 10, 1949 by His Excellency AlHaj Khawaja Nazimuddin, Governor General of Pakistan. Welcoming the Governor General the members of the Council briefly stated about the objectives which were as under:

- Strengthening bonds and revival of Islamic culture in the context of Muslim Civilization
- Creating awareness about the arts and literature
- Promotion to help development of arts
- Revival of Islamic cultural values
  Creating awareness and educating the new generation about Islamic culture
- Promotion of healthy cultural activities
- Propagation of Pakistani cultural heritage

The establishment of the Arts Council was very well thought as Lahore could generally take pride as custodian of Muslim heritage in India and had been the place where Pakistan Resolution was passed. In the welcome address the significance of fine arts was also stressed. On the occasion of inauguration of Arts Council an exhibition of the art works of Mr. Abdur Rahman Chughtai was also arranged. The exhibition contained 200 paintings of Chughtai.

This was the first exhibition of its own style in Lahore. The art of Chughtai needed nobody's comments as he was acclaimed one of the greatest artists of the world. With this remarkable beginning the organization took upon itself the promotion and enrichment of Pakistani art and culture. The Society, right from the beginning, was dependent on the Government grants. It is learnt, that the Council continued and carried on its cultural activities covering all phases of art and literature and matters improving and the circle of those interested in arts widened by 1952.

FINE ARTS

The exhibition of Chughtai's paintings was followed by an All Pakistan Exhibition in which works of artists of both wings of Pakistan were represented. According to a report about Alhamra in 1952 it was stated that an Exhibition of Australian Art, Iranian Cultural Exhibition, exhibition of books and three photographic exhibitions, several symposiums and discussions on literary topics were held and meetings were arranged to introduce living celebrities like Hafeez Jullundari and Jigar Muradabadi and to commemorate great literary figures like Iqbal. Some film shows were also arranged.

In December 1952 Alhamra's major event was putting up the exhibition of Ustad Allah Bakhsh. In all 244 art works were exhibited which covered a wide variety of themes and mediums. The exhibition was commented upon as remarkable.

Allah Bakhsh's exhibition was followed by the exhibition of Safdar Ali, who hailed from Gujrat. A shy, clean, well-groomed and only 29 years old youngman. Safdar's exhibition consisted of 56 art works. Safdar's work was considered to be of remarkable spatial depth. In still life Safdar accentuated the depth of his composition by placing a starting foreground against a background that is vigorously dynamic. Safdar at that time undoubtedly occupied a permanent place among the younger artists of Pakistan.

The next important exhibition of Arts was by Anwar Jalal Shamza who was considered to be a significant writer and painter. Majid Al-makky writing about his art works observed "He loves to paint all that he feels and finds about him in flowery words and charming colours - oil, pastel or water, not just in the way that pleases his fancy alone, but the subject, its intrinsic beauty and objective charm. He tries to dramatise his paintings with greater emphasis on 'created' beauty and to that end he works with meticulous care and precise decision."

In his work Shamza persistently tried to impress the importance of abstraction in the art of painting and writing - yet his drawings, the arrangement of different forms and figures with their spontaneous curves and contours, skillful manipulation of bold colouring, with the frequent use of traditional decorative motifs, only established his relations with the school he disowns.The abstraction of familiar objects and traditional subjects does not disturb our imagination in most of his paintings because the sure test of an abstract painting, any painting for that matter, is not the reaction to it of first contact, but the effect created by sustained association, Shamza's paintings pulsate with dramatic balancing of parallel verticals relieved by semi-circular flat surfaces here and there, and with most of them one could live in comparative peace.

The set of about thirty sketches that Shamza exhibited, was completed in about 1950. This was, therefore, not the accomplishment of a great master, but the efforts of a budding artist - a young devotee, who had as yet to discover himself. It is a fitting tribute from a young painter to the memory of a great leader, who carved out for his people a mighty state from almost nothing." It needed sustained efforts, great care and devotion to create a gallery of portraits in different mediums and out of a multitude of painters Shamza alone did itand had done it well.

A first look at some works of Shamza might give a rude shock to those who look for photographic likeness in a sketch though camera too has been lying ever since its inception. Shamza had tried to perpetuate a few of the fleeting expressions, "characteristic of the great leader, Quaid at play, the leader addressing a spellbound mass of people, the gentle brother, idol of the millions, a heavy smoker and to achieve all this Shamza has worked faithfully.

The tall, frail figure of the man with an iron-will, captivating powers, disarming arguments starts radiating with greater refulgence. The purpose of the portrait painter has been accomplished".

In January 1955 S. Safdar organised another exhibition at Alhamra, with 49 paintings on display. Commenting on his work Agha Akhtar Ali remarked "Safdar is a modern artist. If you ask him, he will tell you that he is still a student of Modern Art. It is difficult to label him and thus, attach him to any particular school. He is young, intelligent and full of enthusiasm for his work. He is experimenting with various modes and mediums of expression. This in itself shows his keenness of intellect and breadth of vision.While very young, he went away to Bombay, where for sometime, he studied art at the J.J. School of Arts. During this period, he mingled with a variety of people and allowed himself to mature with age and experience. The influence of his stay in Bombay, is visible in his work. Safdar had a good sense of composition and his use of colours was brilliant. Sometimes, his colours, clash and sparkle and set one's mind racing, while at times, they mingled with each other peacefully and harmoniously. Safdar's paintings are not static. They are full of movement and bold designs and patterns. An interesting and critical appreciation of the work of Safdar was given by Hamid Jalal in the following words:

"Abstract painting makes most people feel uneasy and I am no exception. I have always been afraid of embarrassing others by expressing my disapproval of a picture which may really be a Picasso! But with Safdar I am on sure ground. Most of his pictures have a touch of the Orient and that instantly makes me feel at home."

This was the most distinctive feature of the new pictures Safdar was now exhibiting. It was generally missing from the pictures he included in his one-man show at the Alhamra in April last time. Those pictures were experimental, covering a wide range of subjects and showing his fluency in various mediums. Their character, however, was cosmopolitan; Safdar seemed to have taken hardly any notice of his surroundings. The majority of his pictures were ablaze with local colour. Some of his subjects were taken directly from our rural life while others are just as familiar. "Doll" reminds of the days the home made rag-doll was a favourite, until it was deposed by 'walkie talkie' dolls and Walt Disney toys. What makes these subjects all the more attractive was Safdar's approach, which has the directness of a folk-poet and his execution which is as clear as the movements of a folk-dancer. But his pictures were neither gaudy nor crude; they wear the gloss of sophistication, the mark of a refined and sensitive artist, who was also an idealist.

This sophistication and refinement was even more pronounced in the several still-life studies that are on display. They showed his fine sense of composition growing maturity and the courage to experiment with wide sweeps of basic colours. Among his other pictures, his pair of third dimensional panels "Perspectives" had an attraction all their own. Looking at either panel was like scanning the horizon through a pair of binoculars, one eye focussed on a trail of symbols leading in from the past and other on the signposts to the future.

In 1955 - Lahore Art Circle, group members consisting of Razia Feroze, Mariam Shah, Ali Imam, A.J. Shamza, S. Safdar and Moeen Najmi put up a joint exhibition of 30 paintings. This collective canvas of the Lahore Art Circle was wide as the style of its members. I am reproducing a paragraph below which not only indicates about the work of each artist but will enable the reader to assess the stage of work of artists from Lahore in the 50s and 60s as we are essentially portraying the cultural scene and it should give the historian a correct view of the stage and level of development of Art of painting and how it was emerging after the independence.

"The collective canvas of the Lahore Art Circle is as wide as the style of its members is different. Four of them are still bound to oriental traditions and this aspect of their work manifests itself in some form or the other. Razia Feroze transplants on to the canvas, in vivid colours, scenes of rural life; Shamza acknowledges by some sign or the other, his debt of his own social and cultural heritage: Ali Imam focuses attention on our decorative and utilitarian architecture while Moeen Najmi turns a page from popular history into an exquisite picture. Safdar has passed through his phase of environmental consciousness and is becoming more and more cosmopolitan and abstract. Mariam Shah is not weighed down by any prejudices and she paints whatever takes her fancy. Firmly anchored in the realm of realistic painting there is no refracting between her eye and the brush, nor any indication yet of a drift towards abstractionism.

For Imam, Najmi, Safdar and Shamza this exhibition will serve to chart their positions, showing the present stage of their journeys to or within the realm of abstractionism. Ali Imam, a former post-impressionist, is now devoting greater attention to form and design, which is a stride towards abstraction. That Najmi's course is also set for the same destination is obvious from the transformation discernible in his pictures. Safdar has already crossed the barrier and is experimenting with new compositions, designs and colours. His bold black demarcating lines are still there, but seen through his latest pictures he is almost a new personality. Shamza's growing majority has brought with it greater self-confidence. There is nothing timorous in the manner in which he conceives his experimental pictures using basic tints and hues to achieve a colour harmony.

Movement continues to be the keynote of Razia Feroze's pastoral studies, the only significant change in her method is that she has now started painting in poster colours. Her development has been from the realistic to the decorative, with an occasional touch of abstractionism. Freshness, directness and simplicity mark Mariam Shah's paintings. A new feature of her work is the painting of portraits and nudes.

In addition to these major events, other artists works were also shown occasionally in group or solo shows. A total of 24 exhibitions were held at Alhamra by 1959.

The programmes of theatre and music were not more than two dozen. But the management of the Arts Council did find it possible to organise the Council's work on any planned, systematic or clearly purposive basis. The main hurdles were reportedly the paucity of funds and a proper building with facilities which would multiply and accelerate the pace of work and thus obvious a more voluminous and purposeful output. Justice S.A. Rahman remarked "Though we are by no means complacent about the past, we can reasonably be optimistic about the future."

MUSIC

The Arts Council conducted and integrated efforts for the promotion and projection of various arts which were essential components of our cultural heritage.

Right from its inception it made efforts to preserve, propagate, whatever was valuable in our traditions, to discover and establish as our cultural identity. It aimed at popularising the existing arts and bringing them nearer to people and revitalising the dying and decaying indigenous arts and exerted in restoring their rightful place in the cultural set up of the country. It required a bold imaginative and persistent effort with freedom in working both political and bureaucratic system. It did receive government support in unequivocal terms i.e. financial with no interference but as is the phenomenon of all developing countries, the resources, reportedly never matched the demand. However, within the given means the Council tried to enrich new forms of beauty with the help of literature to raise the standards of common morality and behaviour. It increased cultural activity in the city and new artistic groups came up and the seniors worked more hard. The thinly spread lot of performing artists swelled, thus exposure to more knowledge, learning, experience and education which finally helped build our own cultural individuality - a much needed asset for the newly born nation. Fine Arts was followed by Music. A music academy was established in 1957 although programmes and concerts of individual artists and group performers, right from 1949 onwards, were held yet there was no regular teaching faculty. The academy was headed by the late Mr. Feroze Nizami who was a reputed music director and exponent of classical music. Its objectives were two-fold: (i) to create a genuine group of musicians by imparting training in vocal and instrumental music; and (ii) to promote the cause of music in accordance with our national aspirations. Lectures on music appreciation were also introduced, as a supplement to the training in music, which became popular and the class was extended to interested, non-students. It started sitar, violin and vocal classes which were regularly held and Mr. Feroze Nizami was assisted by Mr. Siraj Ahmad Qureshi and Mr. Sardar Hussain. The academy produced every year quite a few students who had learnt all that is best in music in its pure and authentic form. They were taught 'raags'. Later exam system was also introduced, and a proper syllabus on the pattern of the Punjab University was also adopted. Two courses were offered, one for three years and the other for two years. Students were also encouraged to perform for radio and television etc. These classes were disturbed for some time when the old building crumbled down but were restarted in the newly constructed portion attached to Hall I (green rooms, rehearsal room and the rooms now used as store and library). These rooms were constructed before the hall.

Since then the music classes are going on regularly four days a week. The addition has been that of tabla class, harmonium and organ classes. The Arts Council holds its regular programmes of students and amateurs under the title of 'Musicians of Tomorrow' in which students perform and get prizes. In the absence of a proper performing arts academy, the Lahore Arts Council has played the pivotal role of a training centre and a feeding ground for the radio and television stations. Occasionally some foreign students also attend the classes. Countless concerts were held in which musicians like Ustad Umeed Ali Khan, Shaukat Hussain, Sharif Khan Poonchwale, Faqir Hussain, Ustad Ata Muhammad, Hira Lal, Ustad Bismillah Khan, Nusrat Fateh Ali Khan, Salamat Ali Khan, Nazakat Ali Khan, Mehdi Hassan, Ustad Chote Ghulam Ali, Fateh Ali Khan, Amanat Ali Khan, Munni Begum, Roshan Ara Begum, Iqbal Bano, Fareeda Khanum, Ustad Hamid Ali Khan, Rais Khan, etc., etc. performed a number of times. In addition many pop singers and jazz groups from many western countries including Pakistani groups performed here. Infact performance by artists at Alhamra is now taken as token of excellence and standard for any artists successful public appearance.

FINE ARTS ACADEMY

As we know the beginning of the Arts Council was made with an exhibition of the artworks of artist Abdur Rahman Chughtai. One of the main objects of the Council was promotion of arts. Right from commencement the exhibition by individual artists were organized and group shows also encouraged. Quite a few artists not only used to paint and work here but also kept alive the activity. These included Murtaza Bashir, Zain-ul-Abidin, Mariam Shah, R. Akbar, S. Safdar and Ali Imam etc. and artists both from West and East Pakistan worked a lot. There was a demand from amateurs for some training faculty in painting. However, no planned and concerted efforts were made to provide instructional facilities till 1959.

The establishment of music academy was followed, by the creation of an art academy shortly thereafter. It was headed by Mrs. Anna Molka Ahmad. The academy started with evening classes which were open to all, irrespective of profession, age and sex. Here one could study drawing, modelling, landscape, portrait, painting and sculpture. This had all along been a source of interest and many benefitted from what the academy offered by way of practical guidance and instructions. The classes were held in the evenings. In opening of these classes, it was felt that while the Punjab University and National College of Arts catered for education of professional painters and designers, and followed regular courses of study, no such arrangement existed for those in other walks of life, who wished to learn art appreciation, in a practical way in their leisure hours. Due to association of well known artists like Colin David, Aslam Minhas, Miss Nasim Qazi and Mr. Khalid Iqbal, the academy started picking up. For sometime Mr. Murtaza and Sufi Waqar were also on the staff. The academy was housed in the studio huts. Most of the students had jobs in the daytime and used to attend the evening classes as hobby for the leisure hours. In addition many art students studying regular courses came for extra evening classes for practice of life modelling, still life, landscape and portrait painting etc. The commercial artists and art teachers also attended classes to use life models and keep up practice of drawing.

While the academy has had evening art classes for adults since 1961, it also thought of the idea of starting art classes for children sooner or later. In 1962 along came a Sunday children art class, exclusively for children. The children did all sorts of things along with modelling, papier mache painting, mask making, practice drawing and making all kinds of patterns with marble and glazed paper. These students (even now) hold their annual exhibition.

THE ARTS GALLERY

The academy is fully functional till date. The number of which was from 10 to 20 till 1965. For sometime when the old building crumbled this work remained suspended but the Academy's activities again came in full swing with the inauguration of Hall I wherein the foyer area had enough wall space for exhibitions and classes were located in the basement. It was in the year 1984 that the existing modern gallery, with four parts was inaugurated. This provision of gallery infact revolutionised the scope of artworks and exhibitions, which is allowed free of cost to all artists for their exhibitions. The gallery has an area of over 15,000 sq. ft. It has a framed structure with red brick finish consisting of five halls, in drum shape. In addition to group and solo shows by the local artists National Exhibition of various disciplines of arts and the exhibitions received from other countries, under bilateral agreements, are also held here. The Gallery has an accommodation of displaying over 400 paintings at a time. The average number of exhibitions now held annually in Alhamra Art Gallery is 50-55. Amongst VVIPs who visited the Alhamra Art Gallery include General Ghulam Jillani Khan, President Ziaul Haq, Mr. Jiang Ze Min, President of China and Mian Nawaz Sharif, Prime Minister of Pakistan.

DANCE CLASSES

Dance as we all know has been denied the official patronage although classical and kathak dance is part of our heritage. Until 1975 the Arts Council was maintaining its own orchestra and dancing troupe, but with the formation of Punjab Arts Council the troupe was transferred to PUCAR, where it continued to exist till 1982. This troupe visited a number of countries under bilateral cultural agreements and was only disbanded in 1982 when the local press launched a campaign against it in the name of religion. During this period the class of dance, which had started in late 70s, was also closed for about two years. It was only in late 80s that the dance class, as a part of teaching and instructions was restarted. Maharaj Ghulam

Hussain Kathak, a known dance teacher, hailing from Bengal (originally) took the class twice a week. The number of students is not much but the teaching goes on. Ghulam Hussain Kathak only used to teach kathak and as such the teaching, I feel, remained not very intensive. It is understood that Arts Council has now selected a teacher, who should know about all branches of this field. There was also a feeling that the teacher should also be well read to explain the theory along with practicals. Occasionally foreign students also attend the class.

THEATRE

In founding this forum, the Council placed a distinct emphasis on the development of theatre. These efforts ultimately led to the drama which was and is played on stage and television till date although the script and direction standards have deteriorated. But at whatever stage enthusiasts find, it is actually the continuity of the same because Lahore Arts Council's efforts have received and developed theatre to a point where it has now entered a popular stage and it can well be termed as an industry. The medium of drama has always been considered to be a very effective source of communication. The Council's efforts for production of theatre started in late fifties and were at peak in the sixties except for a short break when the old building had given way, the theatre was shifted to a self styled Open Air Theatre at the site of Block III. The theatre is thronging till day, and has been a major area of attention and resource generation for the Council.

The old drama hall which was fabricated out of the evacuee bungalow had a capacity of 159 seats with a small stage, larger in length and shorter in width. The lights had also been devised by way of fixing bulbs in tin cans and fitted in the proscenium arch. There was no light in the hall which could lit the stage. On the back of the hall, there was a two seater cabin for control of lights and sound effects. On the right side of stage there was a make-up room and a very small workshop or carpentry. There were two rooms upstairs, one for the painting class and the other for music classes.

The programmes in the Council generally covered theatre, music, painting, shows by foreign troupes and lectures and seminars but the theatre was the local focus point of attention in every day business. There was a play going on daily right in 1959. There was always a long list of pending applications awaiting turn. On the whole 10 to 15 plays were staged in a year. The applications for play production were entertained keeping in view the theme of the script, plot, characters and dialogues etc. These plays were scheduled for 15 days and sometimes for a month. The productions were well rehearsed beginning with readings, blocking of moves, movements, artists entries gestures and especially face and footwork were attended to including the profile position. Full dress rehearsals were taken by the director who would take it to mark the show. On the Ist day of the performance, brochure was distributed which contained comments and ads to meet expenses of the play. In addition to ads in the brochure the other source of financing the play was sale of tickets which was Rs.10/- per person and reached Rs.30/- in 1974. But for the chief guest everybody had to pay for entry. Another tradition was the dinner by the producer on the closing night after the play. From the start of the theatre at Alhamra in 1959 to early 70s comedy, tragedy, brisk, slow and experimental plays were performed. These were mostly adapted. For original scripts, writers mainly on theatre included Bano Qudsia, Ashfaq Ahmad Khan, Syed Najam Hassan, Khawaja Moinud Din, Sufi Nisar, Athar Shah, Khan Aziz Asree, Salma Jabeen etc.

The period when theatre was developing at Alhamra, stage plays were also performed at the Government College, Kinnaird College, Islamia College and Dyal Singh College. Some private groups also used to have theatre productions. Known amongst these were Ravi Art Circle, Ishrat Rahmani group and Aki-Mi Art Circle which held their performances at Open Air Theatre Bagh-e-Jinnah, Young Men Christian Association and Educational auditorium near Museum. In 1971 the dismemberment of Pakistan was followed by various changes. Politics replaced academic activity at Alhamra and various groups emerged under different people. This led to deterioration in the standards of the stage and mainly due to immature and untrained directors, with no control over the cast and performances. Consequently comedy changed into farce and farce into vulgarity and indecency. This caused emergence of two sections of audience one who wants to see serious plays, mostly adaptations or translations and western plays, but do not pay or spend for such productions. The productions, they always propose to be at the government expense and for the invited audience. Obviously this is a non-viable proposition, in these days of financial stringency government cannot afford this luxury of spending on such productions for all times. The other category of audience which is drawn mostly from the middle class, working and business people, pay and like the comedy obviously for they want entertainment in the city. This has brought in poor scripts with little thought content, adlibbing, indecency and sometime vulgarity. Economics played a vital role in this evolution and devolution of theatre. While serious theatre disappeared, drama emerged as popular entertainment for the masses not only for the pleasure seeking source of the western educated elite class, but for the commonman who earns and spends for relaxation and entertainment. People from the workshops, factories, business houses in and around Lahore who could spend, throng the theatres in Lahore. WAPDA Auditorium remained a centre of these plays but when a bomb exploded this theatre stage shifted to hotels like Salatin, Falettis and Rahat Hall etc., etc. In 1980, the Punjab Arts Council opened two venues i.e. one at Open Air Theatre and the other at 90 Shahrah-e-Quaid-e-Azam. This continued until the opening of Alhamra Hall I. The beginning in Alhamra was made with repeat plays of sixties but financially these could not breakeven. Consequently a new class of financiers emerged who would under-hand purchase the slots of the hall allotted to different people (both artists and others), advance exorbitant fees to comedians and make money. Naturally the Government-financed productions had not been viable and the theatre especially comedy, became so popular that now at least there are three private theatrical halls in addition to two halls of Alhamra where performances daily take place. The ticket rates range from Rs.35/- to Rs.200/- and people pay for it with 20% entertainment duty. Now no one can stop this entertainment which the common man pays for. On the other hand a negligible minority wants western style theatre at no expense. This is obviously not feasible. Here it will not be out of place to make a mention of a controversy between a typical group of fading artists, who invariably find a supporting column in the media and bureaucracy. They start campaigns on regular intervals mostly in the English press. That the standard of drama has gone down and Government must spend regularly to create an audience for such theatre. They insist for this inspite of the fact that they have only brought forth a few adaptations and translations or copies of Indian and German scripts with very liberal thought contents unacceptable in a Muslim society. They are mostly the decaying lot who have lost their saleability and have their network in the English dailies, on television and radio. The other school of thought which is usually condemned by the foregoing as "jestors" label them as 'Mafia' who thrive on state funding. They have no market value and are not booked by producers as they have little public demand. On the other hand the comedians cater to the tastes of common man who work and have made the theatre financially viable proposition. This has actually upset the so-called standards which according to other school of thought is a slapstick comedy, but if the public wants it so, none can stop it. The artists have played havoc but now all types of foreign and Indian programmes on dish have crippled all; what we may not like or term as a non-family entertainment is a routine show on the small screen. Some say its script, some say it is organization but control on one point (Arts Council) is not of much help as private theatre is free from all checks and controls. This academic discussion apart we must keep on fighting to encourage decent family entertainment which confirm to our moral, social and religious values especially keeping in view the ideological foundations of Pakistan. A separate chapter on theatre is being inducted in this book for those who are interested in more details of theatre in Lahore.

As far as the Lahore Arts Council is now concerned it organizes countrywide festivals and workshops in which artists and individuals participate from all over the country. For a check on the quality of the script the procedure followed is that the Arts Council announces certain dates on which scripts are deposited by interested persons. These include actors, producers and members of the public if they so like. These applications are deposited and arranged in a serial or in accordance with receipt attached by the applicants for scrutiny fee. These scripts are then sent to the Scrutiny Committee members. If Scrutiny Committee clear these scripts they remain in the merit list of the script awaiting allotment of dates. Each year to avoid interference and pressure, applications for enlistment of plays are invited. These scripts which have been rejected are so conveyed to the applicants. It is generally rumoured out that slots for theatrical production are not given on merit and that artists are not accommodated for their dramatical activities. The fact of the matter is allotment of dates of drama / theatrical schedule are prepared on merit i.e. criteria of first come first served as approved by the Government. For other cultural activities the Arts Council charges the organizers only nominal rates so as to recover utility charges in respect of electricity, air-conditioning, staff salaries and wear-tear etc. As regards commercial venture there are quite a few people which play in the garb of artists and exploit the organization to make money. They are not willing to pay even the utilities. No organization can subsist without recovery of utility bills as Government grants are being squeezed and reduced. Even for promotional programming there is a limit of the council participation and it cannot be made a regular phenomenon. As far as quality of theatre is concerned, the public demands, viability of production, and financial position of the institution are the main considerations, especially in view of the uniform level and rate of excise duty recoverable from Alhamra as well as from other private enterprises. Even otherwise this poor country can ill afford the luxury of showing stage shows free of cost.

PUPPET THEATRE

While the Council took care of other art forms, it nearly ignored for sometime the children programmes. It started the puppet theatre for recreation of the children in 1959. The puppet theatre gave its first performance on the 22nd of June 1959 thereafter the puppet theatre group held regular and varied performances for the children throughout. This theatre was arranged at a time when the art of professional puppeteers was on the decline. Puppetry as a form of fine art has been neglected. Alhamra started with glove puppetry. It used equipment such as tape recorders and amplifiers and lights etc. Specially devised and movable shows were designed. With the disuse of old building puppet shows at Alhamra got a setback. After deterioration of old building and even after the inauguration of new building it started afresh very late. The puppet theatre was only revived under orders of

General Ghulam Jillani Khan on an initiative taken by Mrs. Naveed Shahzad who directed puppet productions at Alhamra from 1986 to 1993. The puppet theatre is now located in the basement of Council. It has a capacity of about 100 seats and weekly puppet shows are mounted. At times the Council arranges puppet workshops. Quite a few shows are also taken out on request. This effort of the Arts Council is to entertain children, who have very few programmes. It also helps preserving the art and craft of puppetry and provide training facility to the youngsters for future.

BUILDINGS

Since its inception the Arts Council found refuge in an evacuee bungalow on the Mall. According to one account this evacuee property belonged to the Kashmiri Leader Sh. Abdullah. This was a residential building with sufficient open space and poorly maintained lawns and garden. As already mentioned the Arts Council depended on Government grants. In the year 1956 this grant increased and some funds were allowed for refurbishing the old Bungalow meeting requirements of programming, provision of a stage and fabrication of a hall with lights and sound equipment etc. On this stage since the existing building was in a precarious condition nearly collapsing, the Arts Council managers thought of a new building which would approximately cost Rs.13 lacs. Commenting upon the condition of the building and achievements of the Arts Council Justice S.A. Rahman, the then President of the Governing Body, observed that though by no means they were complacent about the past yet he was reasonably optimistic about the future of the institution, provided certain impediments in the way of their further progress were removed. The provision of a proper habitat for the premier cultural organization in West Pakistan was the prime need of the hour. Unfortunately final allotment and demarcation of the building site had been delayed by the departmental process of the Settlement Department on which the Council had no control. He felt that it was imperative that the existing rickety old structure which secures ill with historic name of Alhamra should be demolished and replaced by an edifice befitting national dignity and the historic importance of Lahore. The scope of the activities of Arts Council was conditioned by the accommodation at the disposal of the Council and delay was not desirable in any way. It was thought that they will come over the technical difficulties and both the Provincial and Federal Government will come to the rescue of the organization. The financial assistance of both the Governments was also sought for with a proposal that culture should be given more donations.

The Council was housed, as already mentioned, in an old building surrounded by a wild and unkempt garden with long dusty and completely unlit

Alhamra 1998

drive. The ten years of Arts Council's life until 1959 helped to add to the age and dilapidation of the building as adequate funds according to the Council had not been provided by the Government. In November 1959 with a grant of Rs.4 lacs special repairs were taken in hand. The lawns and garden attended, cleared and partly replanted. Two bathrooms, a green room were prepared, furnished and the entire building was refloored. The main gate and drive were electrified and some decoration of other rooms provided. A canteen in a temporary hut for art classes was completed. Inspite of all this, accommodation fell short of essential requirements. With a persistent demand of funds for the new building the Council fathers also started searching for an architect who could give them a proper design befitting the institution. Contacts were established with Mr. Douglas Harold, Mr. Edward Heran and Mr. Taj-ud-Din Bawani. At a stage it was felt that there was little use of planning until the question of transfer of land was finally settled for, which concerted efforts were required for the ownership of the land in the first instance. It was also felt that there should be a clear line of thinking as to what last was included in an Arts Complex. This needed a big exercise of taking exact measurement and calculation of areas for various proposed sections of the organization. Further it had to be kept in view whether the proposition of engaging a foreign consultant was financially effective, especially when no experienced person was available in the local market with specialised knowledge of Arts Complex.

It was thought that the proposed building project would be taken up in phases. The first multi-purpose hall with a capacity of 1000 seats and the other with 300 seats will be taken up in first and second phase respectively. The auditoriums were to be circular in shape and on raised podium of 5 feet above the ground level to provide under-ground car parking. The building was to be of RCC frame structure and walls were to be of brick masonry and external finish of either concrete structure or cement plaster. This exercise continued throughout. The Council members finalised the rough brief of the facilities to be provided in the proposed building with cost estimates. According to the report finalised by the Council in December, 1967 the total expenditure was calculated as Rs.42,40,000/- on the first phase and Rs.37,20,000/- on the second phase. No evidence is available as to what was the fate of this proposal except that the Council prepared the rough estimates. It so appears that from 1968 onwards the Council was not very serious in programming the cultural activities and rather the pace of work got slow and hampered by some non-cultural activities. In the given atmosphere, the management and climate not being conducive to those at the helm of the affairs were too busy to spare time for pursue the developments proposals. These matters appear to have made a mess and come to an impasse when the Government had to intervene and take over the organization in the public interest in 1973. The Government appointed an officer as an Administrator who was to look after the affairs of the institution. The Department of Culture and the Council itself, however, re-invigorated the efforts for a Government grant to set up a new Cultural Complex as envisaged by the organization earlier. Finally in 1974 the Government allocated funds for the proposed buildings of the Arts Council.

On 7th of December, 1974 the Arts Council entered into an agreement with M/s Republic Engineering Corporation in association with Mr. Nayyer Ali Dada, the Architect, for execution of the project which was mainly the Hall I or Phase I of the proposed Cultural Complex. The then President of the Arts Council Sufi Ghulam Mustafa Tabassum presided over a meeting of the Building Committee on 30-6-1975 and finalised the procedure for execution of building works. The main decisions were that the Director of the Arts Council would be its Project Director who will supervise the work. The LDA was to appoint an Engineer who will verify the bills and also supervise the work of the contractor which will be finally sent by the Council to the Director Finance, LDA for purpose of making payments. This procedure was submitted to the Chief Minister, Punjab in black and white. Mr. Muhammad Hanif Ramay, the then Chief Minister approved the same on 1-7-1975 and laid the foundation stone of the building on the last day of his Chief Ministership of Punjab. After some spadework the construction commenced and continued till it reached the roofing stage. The then Martial Law Administrator Lt. Gen. Sawar Khan thought of utilising this allocation for some better public welfare projects instead of building a centre for the leisured of the few in Lahore. The work came to a stand still. The funds were almost exhausted and it remained so until Lt. Gen. Ghulam Jillani Khan took over as Governor of Punjab. Enlightened as he was, being a man of culture, he foresaw the need of the city for having a cultural centre with a multipurpose auditorium which would ultimately, meet various requirements. He allowed the Administration to go ahead with the project. Mr. Javed Ahmad Qureshi was Secretary Information & Culture, Mr. Omar Khan Afridi was Commissioner Lahore Division and Chairman Lahore Arts Council. Mr. Ghulam Rasool Azhar the Resident Director, Mr. Nazir Ahmad Chaudhry Executive Director Punjab Council of the Arts were involved in expediting the work and accomplishing the project under direct supervision of Secretary Information & Culture. The allocation of Rs.99 lacs had already exhausted. The additional funds were arranged through revision of ADP Scheme and Secretary Information & Culture would take a meeting daily and monitor the progress of the building work. With large number of persons on the Building Committee, acute shortage of funds, demands of contractor and consultant, problems by PWD and LDA it was really a big job to steer through the project. Finally they were able to complete Hall I as it is today in July, 1981. The target date for opening of the hall was fixed as 14-8-1981 on which the Council invited General Jillani Khan to inaugurate. After the inaugural speech the plaque was unveiled and that augured the Arts Council Centre for cultural business. It, however, appeared, most non-cost effective to run the place with huge electricity, air-conditioning and maintenance expenses. But the Council started spending its own money on repeat productions, of course from a grant given by the Government.

The inauguration of hall of Alhamra ushered in a new era of performing arts in the history of Lahore as Alhamra had got a stage which was fitted with the latest facilities. The stage is 80 feet wide with a depth of over 50 feet. There is an orchestra pit covered with removable wooden planks. The orchestra pit is used in musical shows only and for other functions it remains covered when dramatic or other programmes are performed. The stage has a large front curtain of tapestry, a frill hanging with the proscenium arch. There are three flies (backstage) behind the curtain. The curtain and flies are all motorised. There is sufficient space at the backstage for the waiting participants. The stage is connected on south with the greenroom, makeup rooms and rehearsal areas etc. The hall is carpeted and has 758 seats with cushioned steel chairs. The stage lights are fitted in the frontal portion of ceiling. The auditorium is air-conditioned. Entry to the hall is from the Mall Road side with a big foyer or waiting area. The height of the hall is about 50 feet. On the northern side of the hall there is a waiting room and entrance which is generally used for the entry of chief guests to the programmes. In the underground portion of hall, air-conditioning plants are located with a workshop and carpentry on the ground floor and fine art classes on the first floor.

On the front facing the Mall a sizeable place is given as a podium which gives a nice view from the Mall but there appears to have been utter disregard in the design and space callously misused without any planning for the future. There has absolutely been no facilities provided for parking except the driveway which cannot take more than 15-20 vehicles. This being a public place and visited by hundreds of people daily needed a parking area which would not only accommodate the vehicles of those coming for the programmes at Alhamra but the parking could also become a permanent source of revenue for the Council. Had this been properly planned, the Alhamra which has an area of over three acres, an underground parking could take a big chunk of the Mall Road parking rush and thus the organization would never need Government's financial assistance. There also does not appear to have been any consideration to the road level while taking in hand the construction of the building. It is noteworthy that during rainy season sewerage and rainwater enters the premises. The level of the halls is about minus 3 feet from frontal entry gates level and consequently the rain and sewerage water enters the halls and damages the carpet and air-conditioning plants.

Above all the height of the roof of foyer and stage are ill designed for the proper maintenance of the building. Interestingly there is no staircase for going up the roof. Further the roof being of steel trusses the G.I sheets in the absence of proper treatment have started leaking and need repair every now and then. The leaking roof is a headache and a source of trouble for the management. The toilets have not been properly designed and consequently these stink, inspite of best efforts to keep them clean. The negative spaces which have appeared as a result of the sloping, slanting and reclining walls which are hollow are a big problem for maintenance purpose as these are a permanent abode of rodents and similar other species. Further the construction work has been done in lime mortar with little or negligible ratio of cement which has started giving way to the bricks coming out with decay and poor quality mortar mixture.

For about a year after inauguration of the hall the Government allowed funds for the Art Gallery and the Administrative Block. As a continuation of the architectural work the same appears to have been entrusted to the same architect, consultant and the same contractor. The gallery was located on the eastern side of the hall in an elongated shape. On the ground floor is located, one hall for the Administration section and one for Director's office with a small Committee room. On the first floor the Arts Gallery that has been provided is infact divided into four parts; exhibitions with small number of artworks are put up in one or two parts and large collections displayed in the entire gallery. It appears that little attention was paid to the creation of more display space and instead emphasis was laid on blending the brick structure although vertical, and in drum type halls. The lighting system in the gallery is always criticised by the artists and public. The poor construction material invites dampness and spoils the painting works regularly during rainy season. It is very useful part of the Complex where regularly exhibitions are held and accommodation provided to the artists free of cost alongwith other facilities such as printing of brochures, leaflets and cards in connection with exhibitions. The Art Gallery is really a remarkable facility for the artist community and has gone a long way in the promotion of fine arts. Quite a few artists from all over the country have exhibited their work. It encourages the younger generation in art education and attracts public appreciation. Consequently, there develops a market for the artworks and people interested in arts under international standards exchange programmes, with Federal Government, many exhibitions of arts, sculpture, architecture and handicrafts are held which provide ample opportunities to the local artists to see standard of work in the world. In addition to national exhibitions of paintings and groups including solo shows help a

lot in projecting and promoting the discipline. Alhamra Art Gallery, located at a central place in the city and being offered without charges is a big credit to the Punjab Government who finances the Arts Council for all purposes. The gallery, however, needs to be done up afresh in respect of storage, leakages, insufficient lights etc., etc.

IInd PHASE

In the year 1983-84 the Government provided funds for the Second Phase which was meant for Hall II. The construction was again entrusted by the Governing Body of the Arts Council to the same architect and the same contractor as a continuity in the architectural features. This hall was completed in 1985 and was inaugurated by General Ghulam Jillani Khan, the then Governor of Punjab on 22-8-1985. This hall has a capacity of 438 seats with carpetting and furnishing of the same standard as that of Hall I. It is also used for theatrical, artistic and public programmes. The backstage of the hall is linked with the stage of Hall II and the artists and props can easily move from one stage to the other. A waiting room, an office for manager and rehearsal and makeup rooms are attached with this Hall. Again the hall has the same problem of leaking roof and inflow of sewerage and of rain water. Its location on the back of Hall I has made it most unattractive to those who use the place commercially. The ideal course would have been to locate its front on the side of the link road connecting the Mall and Egerton Road,

IIIrd PHASE

As mentioned earlier one of the most avowed object of setting up the Arts Council was preservation of the country's cultural heritage and music was one of its most important component. When the complex covered the theatrical, arts and administration side the Council started making efforts for provision of a music place. For this purpose again an ADP proposal was prepared stressing importance of music the only left over discipline to be covered in the newly established complex, which would remain incomplete otherwise. In September 1985 the proposals were moved for an ADP Project which was approved under special directions of Governor of Punjab, General Ghulam Jillani Khan and the work was awarded in December, 1985 to M/s AFCO Builders. This block was completed and inaugurated by the Chief Minister, Punjab, on 23rd March, 1988. The accommodation in the Music Block consists of a small auditorium with a capacity of 225 seats and a foyer area. It has a conference room facility for about 40 people and some of the accommodation on the ground floor for the administration section. In the basement a Recording Studio has been provided with 12 channels recording equipment and recording booths. The studio is fitted with sound proof material and accoustically most suitable for recording programmes. In the basement there are classrooms for music students also.

In the year 1989 a small canteen was provided near the waterworks. It has a capacity of 15 tables with a kitchenette etc. This was the last and latest addition to the building on the Mall in the Alhamra.

Another remarkable work was also done in the year 1988. This was with the specific interest and effort of Mr. Hafeezullah Ishaq, the then Chairman of the Arts Council. It was a mural. The mural is located on the eastern corner of the building between the Gallery and the Music Block. It is 45 feet in length and 32 feet in height and built in cement concrete. The mural depicts cultural life of Punjab a complete rural scene. It was designed by Mian Ejazul Hassan a famous landscape artist and is depicted on tile, burnt at a Small Industries factory at Multan. This mural is of its own type in the country. The mural was also inaugurated by the Chief Minster, Punjab and is a real work of art located in an art institution which speaks of the cultural pattern in rural Punjab. Inspite of the fact that it is in tiles the colour scheme is perfect and linework realistically drawn. Thematically it depicts of economy, timing and life.

OPEN AIR THEATRE
Cultural Complex Ferozepur Road

The Open Air Theatre is an extension of the Alhamra, the premier performing arts centre of Pakistan. The Ferozepur Road location was selected to take the pressure away from an overly congested Shahrah-e-Quaid-e-Azam and to create a performing arts facility for the newly developed areas of Lahore i.e. Model Town, Faisal Town, Garden Town, Jauhar Town, Township, Gulberg and Defence, etc.

The theatre sits in the midst of large green areas, at a stone's throw from Lahore's famous willow lined canal. Its imposing brick façade set with local regional features such as handmade Multani tiles is an interesting blend of the contemporary and the traditional classicism of the Roman colosseum. The multi-purpose theatre is designed to cater for drama, music, cultural melas and sports activities such as boxing etc.

The hallmark of the concept is the creation of an intimate relationship between performers and audience. Despite its vast arena-like atmosphere everyone feels close to the stage. This is by no mean an architectural feat considering the seating capacity is well over four thousand. Meticulous detailing as far as sound and light systems, i.e. world famous 'STRAND' brand promises to make any performance, an exhilarating experience. Enormous backstage space has been provided for workshops, greenrooms and storage.

Cultural Complex Ferozepur Road

Apart from the open air facilities, maximum and effective utilization of space has resulted in the provision of an elegant auditorium with a seating capacity of 350. A handsome wood panelled small hall and a spacious workshop has also been provided in addition to rehearsal and storage space while the larger hall is generally being used for plays by students and amateur groups, the small hall is put to use for lectures, seminars and discussions. The space beneath the open air also houses temporarily a Craft Complex office of the Punjab Arts Council. Again the most problematic thing is the drainage of rain and sewerage water which enters the auditorium located at a minus level of about 15 feet. Probably it was never foreseen which the management has now to face.

PERMANENT ART GALLERY

The most recent and latest addition to this Cultural complex on the Ferozepur Road is establishment of a Permanent Art Gallery. This art gallery was planned by the Council and the proposal materialised with the blessings of Mr. Anwar Zahid the then Chief Secretary, Punjab. Mr.Anwar Zahid was very kind and considerate to the art institutions. It was his personal interest that he directed the development department to speacially spare funds for this Gallery. It met an outstanding demand of the artists community. Its completion and functioning became possible only in 1996. It has an area of over 12,000 sq.ft., with sufficient wall space for displaying artworks upto 200 at a time both on the ground and first floor. Again the design was given by Mr. Nayyer Ali Dada and it was executed by M/s A.B.S. Contractors. Strangely, architecturally it does not go with surrounding buildings of Open Air Theatre and stadium which are in circular shape whereas the Gallery building is squarish and with glass domes. The experience of the use of the last couple of years is not very satisfactory. It is not very functional. There is the problem of leakage again. The maintenance problems are multiplied as there does not exist the approach to the roof with lot of spouts in the parapet portion of the building. Still the provision of the gallery has fulfilled a long outstanding and important demand of the artists. The city has got a permanent place where a permanent exhibition of the Old Masters is always on. The foreigners, tourists and outsiders, can always see the works of Old Masters and senior contemporary artists. The credit again goes to the Provincial Government which inspite of financial constraints and other prevailing factors has been paying due attention to the development of Art Institutions.

9

THEATRE

When one thinks of theatre, his thoughts take him to ancient Greece, where it used to be a great festival occasion. The statue of Dionysius, the god of wine, used to be carried through the streets, leading a procession to the outdoor hillside theatre, where plays were presented. Several plays, all religious in nature and nationalistic in character, were performed in one day. The spectators were enchanted and thrilled by the dramatic stories of gods and heroes, and had the added excitement of witnessing a contest for the best playwright, who was honoured with a prize.

Discussing theatre would remain incomplete if it were not explained in historical retrospect in the context of its evolution in the sub-continent as a whole. It is because the region is one of the greatest repositories of performing Arts particularly those of classical, folk, popular, devotional and modern traditions. The sheer enormity and diversity of its cultural expressions in music, dance, drama and theatre are the envy of many nations around the world. The need to give this background is that Lahore was the seat of a Hindu principality originally before its occupation by Mahmood Ghazanvi. Further exploring theatre would require a survey of many fascinating inferences that have shaped the cultural life, the classical forms, rituals, practices and ancient plays with deep roots in the folk culture, welded to the village settings. And finally the modern urban environment which has shaped the continual scene of global currency and removed us from all our past. Theatre has multitude of patterns, probes a host of issues, and at times hates some, pleases the few and serves the rich and the poor alike. The literature of Indian performers genres draws heavily at this epic and Puranic literature and the aesthetics of theatre are closely linked to Hindu religious philosophic basis. The vast spectrum of performance genres in India is a reflection of its linguistic, cultural and religious diversity. This sphere of influences which are all along lacking in nature may be categorised as classic, the ritual, the devotional, the folk - popular and the modern. None of the sphere is autonomous and all of them are inter-connected. The classical sphere of performing is characterized by high degree of refinement in performance techniques. The folk and popular traditions are regional in nature and pertain to a specific language area with mass appeal. The ritual performance serves a specific religious group. A ritual end where the fulfillment of a vow, the grading of a boom, the transformation of an individual family or village etc., etc. Highly complex colourful performance form part of a ritual presentation. The devotional performance and those of ritual spheres are independent to achieve the desired goal or end.

Looking back historically it is not possible to fix an exact date for the creation of theatre in India. Yet there are reasons to believe that it came into being sometimes in 200-100 B.C. There was a lively tradition of dance, music and song, which were the accepted branches of performing Arts with a rich heritage of myths and legends. It is learnt that the oldest fragment of Sanskrit plays which dated from first century A.D. reveals a dramatic structure. The Indus and Harrappan civilizations developed a city culture in north-west India now forming Pakistan. Both the Harrappan and Mohenjodaro excavations hint upon the existence of dance, but without any evidence for the theatre. But if the figures indicate dance, music and songs may also have been part of the rituals and festivals of the people of this civilization. The successive waves of in-coming people from central Asia, even if inferior became dominant over the locals. During Vedic age ritual practices arose which were highly dramatic in character. The Hymns were sung and ceremonies were complex and inclusive of elaborate rites with symbolic gestures and physical actions and music. The search for existence of drama and theatre at some specific dates in ancient history is inevitable and leads to the vast body of literature generated after composition of the two great epics. The Mahabarata which makes reference to performers (Nats) amongst whom the actors have been classed. In later history the word 'Nats' was used to describe dancers and pantomimes as well as actors. The Ramayna is the other major epic which also makes reference to Nata and in addition its book of 'nataka'. This term is used for a specific type of drama. There is, however, nothing in Ramayna, which shows the existence of Sanskrit Drama. The Greece inference find a mention as the Greece troupes might have engaged themselves in theatrical performances during rest/leisurely time while marching to this land. The word 'Curtain' in Sanskrit as 'Yavana' is attributed to the Greek influence, which was used at the back of Greek stage, and it arrived in India, with invaders. Another theory is that the Indian drama has arisen from the ritual competition. The personification of these points are illustrated by Patan Jali in his work titled 'Mahabasha'. There have been diverse arguments on the origin of Sanskrit Drama. Sir William Ridchwav argues that drama is the outcome of plays in which reference is brought to the spirit of the dead personified by actors. Some other scholars contend that there were shows in ancient India and these were dictated forms of drama. Some suggested that ancient pantomime coupled with epic recitation had a great deal to do with the formation of drama. One proposal claims that recitation of epic stanzas and competition led to the development of drama. The theatre had its origin and first composition in regional languages. But suffice to say that the earliest plays, which have been discovered, indicate that Sanskrit theatre was fully formed and highly sophisticated. Some of the finest poetry is found in the Sanskrit drama. The survey of the plays and dramatized contests leads us to believe that there was a complex cut of gesture, movements, and pattern and figure expression. Sansakrit Theatre was also multi dimensional and dance and music contributed to its development, although the existence of their inter-action with dialogues and verse is not certain. This was a theatre of imagination, costume and make-up was only symbolic. Later on special plays appear to have been constructed for performances. From all evidence the theatre served religious functions as well as entertainment and education. Sanskrit was not the only language of the plays. Various forms are also found in surviving works but Sanskrit was the language of major male character and although the theatre of this period was multi-lingual. Sanskrit drama was dominant throughout India. As court and temple started the theatre it was exclusive rather than popular in its appeal.

Most of the text of Dramaturgy that ancient India produced is 'Nata Shastra' which literally is Drama Science. But it is said to be more than science of drama. It is a veritable encyclopaedia of knowledge concerning Sanskirt drama and theatre. The Nat Shastra contains numerous chapters which begin with the origin of theatre, its scope, theatre architecture, acting, costuming, make-up, props, dance, music, poetic composition, grammar composition, theatre companies, audience, dramatic competitions, the actors community and ritual observances etc., etc.

A reference may be made as to how music and dance were integrated into performance. From Sanskrit plays one gets the impression that drama was dialogue, drama without the benefit of music and dance except that rare action in certain texts in which the character is said to sing or dance or do both. On the other hand Nata Shastra lays down that dance and song are very much part of the total performance experience. It is also learnt that music was essential to the progress of preliminary ritual and to the consecration of the theatre building. It so seems that the main function was to serve as a part of the preliminary rituals and heighten the dramatic impact of a particular scene. Sudhrata and Bhasha, Kali Das and Bhava Bali are some of the historic names of Indian playwrights whose contribution towards theatre is un-paralleled.

It tells us a great deal about human behaviour and social inter-action, the values and moves of the culture are encapsulated in the play, as they teach us about the life and the continuity between old and the new.

The history of drama in India especially in Sanskrit literature finds exhaustive development in Temple Theatre where audience used to be Brahamans and those of royal blood. The commoners had similar performances in the open. Out of Temples. With the Temple declining the patronage of this art also diminished. The performers were forced to seek alternate means of livelihood and perform outside the sanctified quarter of Temple Theatres cutting and adopting their works to meet the current taste for short and concise performances. This was the situation, which prevailed in India before it was captured by the Muslim invaders from Northwest. All types of performances in India were mostly of religious significance and punctuated by ritual practices. The Sanskrit theatre or the classical theatre of India therefore can only be discussed with careful consideration of its religious and ritual significance. It is learnt that eastern and southern regions of India played a central role in the development of some forms of scripted theatrical genres through ritual performances. The traditional Indian ritual theatre took the shape of performances and then devotional dance also took the shape of a drama Ram Leila, Ras Leila and Dasehra devotional dance dramas. These were the performances of sacred and devotional nature. The rituals and religious performances presented to the drama apart, the commoners had their own popular theatre as well. The "Naqara" (drums) summoned the spectators to performances of a Notanki. In Villages clatters of the drums is all that is necessary to announce a performance. Notanki or Svang has been for decades a popular formation of theatre in the northern region of India. It is characterized by lusty singing and spiritual dancing. In big cities the audience is usually male, who feel attracted due to the presence of women dance and popular songs. The performers also mimic a romantic erotic dance of the film stars. Notanki plays have strong story lines. Details are taken from the great epics, popular legends, historic events and contemporary society and are played before the audience and diverse religious background. The spirit is entertainment, narrative instructions and secular in spirit. It is performed by men and women who are semi-professional. This sort of theatre was popular in rural areas till early 40s but is dying down.

Another type of theatre is called 'Tamasha' which emerged on Deccan side of India. They have two varieties Song type and Folk Drama type. They offer substantial dramatic presentation and song and dance. Tamasha theatre is characterized by loosely arranged mixture of elements. The performances might include traditional songs and dances, skits and devotional songs alongwith lengthy dramatic folk plays. It carries entertainment, traditionally expressed through love songs and drama evoking very often tormantic and comic scenes.

Yet another type of drama perhaps the best known in India, is classically called 'Kathakali'. Kathakali is reported to have born in Kerala in the 17th century from a confluence of historic and cultural circumstances. It is always been a popular form of theatre. Traditionally Kathakali performances are such outdoors in a family compound or near a Temple but in the recent western style performances of stages are also arranged. This dance drama has maintained continuity and integrated in its aesthetic and performance style over the years.

MODERN THEATRE

Modern theatre in India owes its origin, growth and development at urban centres such as Calcutta, Bombay and Madras. The introduction of British higher education system after establishing their supremacy, their next step was to found Universities, which appeared at Calcutta, Bombay and Madras. The spread of English education led to the spread of British Ideas, their values and morals among Indian intelligentsia. This also brought knowledge of British drama and theatre. In early days dramas were performed in English by Englishmen in proscenium arch playhouses as in London. The drama written in Indian language and performed on the stage by Indian actors was not to emerge until the last quarter of the 19th century when private theatres were constructed for the amusement and edification of rich particularly those who lived in Calcutta. Eventually these early attempts led to the construction of public theatres with an appealing to a wide variety of castes and classes of people presented in the language of the region. Shortly the theatre became quickly a powerful weapon to promote social and political reforms. By the late 19th century there was some sort of social unrest on account of theatrical performances. The example was a production titled "The Blue Mirror" presented in Lucknow in 1875 in which a white tea planter was depicted raping an Indian peasant woman and this enraged the Europeans, who stormed the stage and stopped the show. This event and other political developments in the country led to a strict enforcement of censorship rules on all theatres through Dramatic Performances Act 1876.

This survey of the growth and development of Indian Theatre leads us to the conclusion that until 1875 there was no theatre in Lahore except touring theatrical companies visiting the city. The University of Punjab was established in the year 1885 and the Government College established in the year 1863. Prior to this, the British established Lahore as their Provincial seat of Government with all head offices of Railway, Education, Health and Miscellaneous other Departments. Mr.

H. R. Goulding referring to this in old Lahore and talking of the public amusements makes mention of the performances that used to take place in Lahore.

Touring Theatrical Companies such as Christy Minstrels group were brought by Dav. Carson every winter in late sixties. It used to draw crowded audiences to the entertainment and the performances were arranged in Lawrence Hall. Circuses in which equestrian feats formed important feature of the programme, were regular visitors in winter. The Great Australian circus was reportedly to be the best, which also used to visit regularly. In early seventies the Touring Company known as Star Company visited Lahore. They performed in the Lawrence Hall and their programme included instrumental music scene in character and dances etc. The other Companies who brought such entertainments to Lahore were the party of dwarfs, General and Mrs. Tom Thumb, Miss Minnie Warren and commodore Nutt also a strong Japanese Company. In later years, Dav. Carson was succeeded by the well-known Hulssons Surprise Party that combined Christy Minstrel items with balled singing and musical hall turns. By the time the Railway Theatre close to the station yard had been built, not only Hudson's but also theatrical companies such as the Crofton Ferrel and others not so well known, were glad to visit Lahore from time to time. Except for a small semi-private club which gave an occasional performance in the Roberts Institute, there was nothing resembling an amateur dramatic club, but spasmodic efforts were made at long intervals to afford local talent an opportunity of showing itself.

"One such occasion was the Viceregal sojourn in March 1879 when a Lahore audience was introduced for the first time to the beauties of Gilbert and Sullivan' s operas, the piece chosen being "H. M. S. Pinafore". The amateurs responsible for the production did not aspire stage for the whole opera, but limited themselves to selections, which included some of the most popular choruses and solos. An old programme brings back to memory some of the most talented singers and actors of those days gone by, among them being Mrs. Bouquet, wife of the Agent of the Railway who sang "Little Buttercup," and Colonel Medley, a future Agent, who represented the "Admiral". The late Mr. G.E Coats sang the "Boatswain's" song. The selections were followed by two original pieces written for the occasion, one being described as a comedy entitled "our Indian Uncle", by Mr. W. Piercy, Assistant Accountant-General who played the main part: and the other a comic sketch by Mr. Jabez Lightfoot called "Old Brown's Daughter, or which shall I Choose?" In this too, the author played a leading part, In later years, Mr. Lightfoot's talent as a comedian won much appreciation in Simla, Madras, and other stations. Another well-known amateur who took part in Mr. Piercy's comedy was Mr. Phillip Morton. His Excellency Lord Lytton and the Viceregal Staff, His Honourable the Lieutenant Governor, the Raja of Faridkot and other distinguished personages were present at this performance, the proceeds of which were devoted to decorating the new Railway Theatre in the Station yard, near the old level crossing."

"Mr. Piercy was also the organizer of a "Literary and Musical Christian Association" which however, did not long survive his transfer from Lahore. Another noteworthy entertainment was the rendering in the Lawrence Hall of selections from the "Messiah" by a choir of amateur, organized and trained by Mr. Melville, the then Financial Commissioner. One of the solos was sung by our future Lieutenant Governor, Sir, (then Mr.) Mackworth Young."

As already mentioned in preceding paragraphs the English Education at University of Calcutta, Madras and Bombay had caused a deep appreciation of English literature which in turn brought in dramatic performances of Shakespeare and others, in these areas. So far as Lahore was concerned the Government College, Lahore was opened on January 18, 1864 although budgeted in the year 1863. Its establishment was formed by Government on 15.4.1864 and in the same year (1864) the College was affiliated with the Calcutta University for examination in Arts. Dr. G. W. Leitner Principal and Col.H.L. O. Garrett, who was professor of history, in his 'History of Government College' has produced a memoir of L. Kunver Sein M. A., Principal of the Law College who entered Government College as a student in 1891, and who remained on the staff till 1897 (Government College Lahore). It is narrated in the book that "there used to be dramatic performances in our days invariably representations of scenes from some one or the other of Shakespeare's plays. But the staging was seldom of an elaborate nature. One-third year class attempted "A Midsummer Night's Dream" in which he took the part of Thesues. The 4th year class gave a performance of "Julius Caesar," in which Anthony's part was well done. In "The Merchant of Venice", performed by the 2nd year class, Shylock's part was remarkably well done by Mr. Madan Gopal, Aggrwal. Taken all in all, however, our performances bear the same relation to those given today by the College students as Shakespearean stage and acting does to those of the present day. But after all, as Shakespeare himself has it. The best of this kind are but shadows. And the worst are no worse if God amends them.

In the same History of Government College by Professor Garrett, the following paragraph appears:"Sanskrit Plays. In 1902 there took place the representation of portions of one of the plays of Kalidas in the original Sanskrit. This was said to be the first occasion in modern times on which a Sanskrit play was performed in the Punjab. This experiment was repeated in 1903, and was intended to be an annual event but in some years the difficulties proved inoperable".

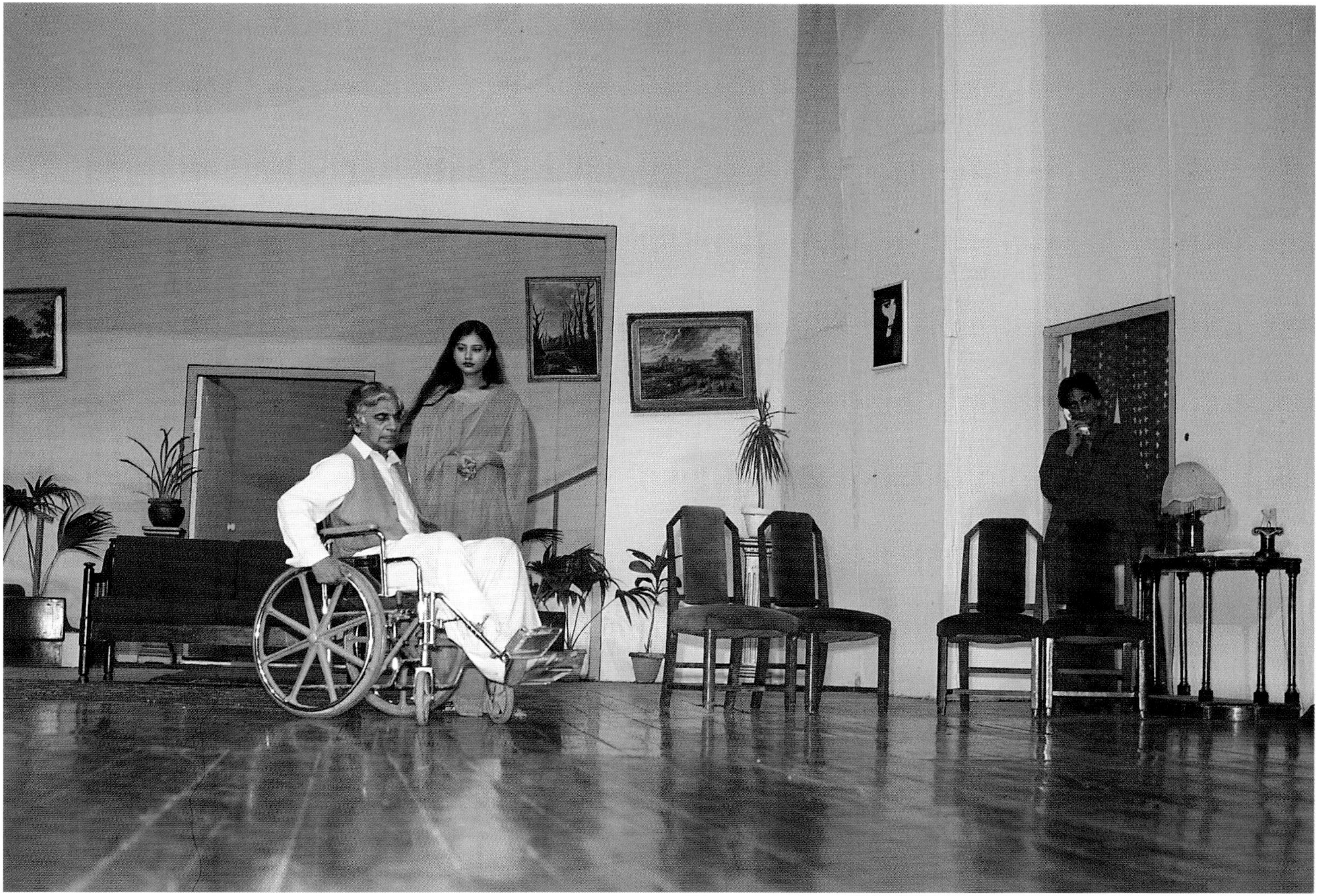

Stage Drama at Alhamra

"The Dramatic Society has continued to flourish, and has staged successfully many dramas of all kinds, ranging from Shakespearean tragedy to broad Urdu and Punjabi farce. In some cases students who distinguished themselves as tragedians, have continued to do yeoman service to the Society after being promoted to be members of the Staff".

The above indicates that Drama both in English, Urdu and Sanskrit had reached Lahore before the close of the 19th century. The Government College also produced Sanskrit Drama, in addition to English and Urdu Plays. The private institutions and clubs were separately producing and showing their own plays from 1875 onwards. In the first decade of the 20th century the theatre became lucrative business as the cinema was still an inception. The Parsis at their theatrical Units in Bombay and Calcutta set up their own Theatrical Companies. It is in these days that Agha Hashar Kashmiri visited Lahore in 1913 and read his poetry in the meeting of Anjaman-e-Hamayat-e-Islam, 'Shookriya Europe' and 'Mauj-e-Zam Zam' which introduced him to Lahoris. This also led him to be introduced as a Dramatist through the Press. According to Maulana Abdul Majid Salak, that as he had cordial relations with Agha Hashar (1916) he advised him for printing and publication of his plays to save them for future. It was agreed that an institution under the title of 'Maktaba-e-Nigaristan' might be established where the scripts of plays would be given duly correction for publication. In the meanwhile Agha Hashar Kashmiri got an employment with Maiden Theatre of Calcutta and the project did not materialize. The status of Agha Hashar Kashmiri in prose and poetry is very well established. He had an extraordinary command on prose poetry and play writing and none could dare to speak for his expertise and fluency of dialogue writing mixed with Persian, Hindi and beautiful metaphors, based on local legends, stories and social problems. Most scripts of his dramas (as originally written by him) are non-existent and only the few, which were printed by Mr. Ishrat Rahmani, are available. The total number of plays written by Agha Hashar is reported to be more than 40.

We have seen the development of theatre right from its beginning in India and Lahore and how it prospered because of ritual and devotional requirements in the first instance and then through the educational institutions due to speed of English education. But this theatre was either in Sanskrit or in Prakrit. The Urdu theatre (actually) is reportedly stated to have emerged in the beginning of the early 19th century. It was at the kingdom of Oudh under the patronage of Muslim Ruler Wajid Ali Shah.

Infact the activities known as theatre were a dance and song drama which during the performance evolved into theatre when repeated later. Some call it opera type drama with its special type of dialogue delivery and presentation. It was one of the important entertainments of the urban population in those days. This drama had no realistic approach towards human behaviour for its popularity on extravagant and visionary faculties. The scripts were based some times on local and sometimes on western stories. It was the nature of this type of play requirement which brought in writers like Agha Hashar Kashmiri whose translations and adoptions were always awaited for and were box office hits until mid thirties of the 20th century. The sudden slump in the theatre was brought by cinema. The actors, the performers and play-writers left the stage and joined film studios thus performing on slightly better terms. The success of the studio of the "talkies" and film producers was sudden. This left only a history and tradition of the popular or commercial theatre remnants of which can still be seen in far flung places (rural) where old plays are still performed on special occasions, under the Shamianas.

RURAL THEATRE

Anthropologists and social historians claim that rural milieu in the Punjab is steeped deep in the long and enduring traditions of theatre which date back to many centuries. In what is now called the Lok Theatre, it was used to project the yearnings, hopes and fears of the people through dialogue that were suffused with rural images and claim that theatre was present in our cultural milieu since the beginning of history.

In the contemporary context, to many people, especially the city dwellers, theatre means entertainment which has become associated with neon signs and phony glitter, with the opulence and gaudiness that mask shallowness. But before their presentations started degenerating, theatrical companies provided a better alternative, especially for the village folk, who were entertained by the millions every year. Although a majority of those theatre companies originated from Lahore, it was not so much of a matter of location as it was a state of mind. If city theatre evoked images of shallowness and superficial slickness, the touring rural theatre brought to the mind images of dedicated artists who spent their lives in a gypsy-like life-style, always on the move, visiting places located through the length and breadth of Punjab's hinterland.

Like in other countries, Lok Theatre in the Punjab also had its osmosis in song and dance. Sung to the accompaniment of simple, indigenously-manufactured musical instruments like flute, Chimta, lyre and dhole, these songs were rendered to eulogise heroes. The dancer depicted various activities and vocations of the people like sowing and harvesting, and the moods of the people in different seasons such as monsoon and spring; and a few religious rites which were performed by followers of different faiths living in a multi-religious and multi-ethnic society.

Those theatres, notankis or svangs, were not housed in large buildings like they are now in urban centres, but were performed under large shamianas (tents) perched outside a village where people thronged to get themselves entertained by theatre-wallahs, whose repertoires had much to attract the attention of village folk. In the villages and in small towns, fairs would be (and still are) the main attraction for the poor. Touring theatre, a majority of which originated from Lahore, did a lot for the villagers by providing them inexpensive entertainment with a variety of items that tickled their sensibilities. Epics and ballads such as Heer Ranjha, Mirza Sahibaan, Sohni Mayyhanwal and Sassi Punnu were used as main attractions to draw large crowds. The form, style and presentation of rural theatre were dictated by an understanding of the image which permeates the hinterland, its culture and customs, and the comprehension level of the people. A theory of performance value was evolved which combined the aesthetic appreciation of the villagers and their understanding of the crafts of the playwrights, and the art of play-acting. Thus, the theatrical language of gestures, customs and costumes, movements and melodic interludes (providing breathing spells to the actors and change of dresses between two acts) were understood by the spectators.

Before the advent of cinema and radio (in the 30s), all large theatre groups were based in Lahore, a place which had not yet attained the status of a large city. In those days in Lahore, theatre was the only source of collective entertainment of the people. Located at different places in the Circular Garden (which once ringed the Walled City), especially outside Bhati Gate, these theatrical companies later fanned out into the countryside, visiting small towns and villages where their presentations were lustily cheered and enthusiastically applauded by entertainment-hungry village folk. Money collected at the 'gates' was enough to convert the cultural ventures into economically viable propositions, besides providing opportunities to the philandering owners (of theatres) to exploit the (mostly financial) limitations of their female employees.

During the second quarter of the 20th century, the best known theatres of Lahore, which regularly toured small towns, qasbas and villlages, were Phajji Shah Theatre; Babu Kaley Khan Theatre; Shah Jahan Theatre; Maula Bakhsh Theatre; and Shama Theatre; which was set up by the legendary actress Baali Jatti, who deserves a special mention. Despite the harsh vicissitudes of life, she tried to hold on to the old tradition of folk theatre. Using all the resources and her ebullient creative talent, Baali attempted to inject vitality and vigour into the fast-decaying rural theatre in the Punjab, but failed to achieve her cherished objective. She was the first woman to own a theatre in the Punjab, perhaps in Pakistan. In the process, she suffered abject poverty and privation, which ultimately took her life. Her 30-

year experience of theatre could not help revive and rescue folk theatre from fading into oblivion.

In the beginning, actresses were not easy to find, and male actors would enact female roles. But the hawkish owners succeeded in luring women (mostly from Hira Mandi) with tempting monetary offers. As all performers in those days were required to croon songs assigned to them in a given play, nautch girls from Hira Mandi (who were trained in the art of singing and dancing) formed the only source for the theatre-owners to tap. They put attractive, good-looking singing girls from that area on their pay rolls, and assigned them the roles of heroines in the plays staged under the banners of their theatrical groups. No wonder, a number of popular heroines of the theatre era ended up enacting the role of wives of the owners in real life, who had earned notoriety for their sly lasciviousness.

Not much authentic information is available about actors and actresses who performed in rural theatre in the Punjab before the advent of cinema, radio and microphone. But we do know of a number of artistes who were associated with this art since the late 30s. Included among them were Khadim Hussain, Master Channi (the brother of famous composer Master Ghulam Haider), Almas, Fazal Shah, Ashiq Hussain (dancer), Manzur Jhalla (Poet and actor), Nazar (film actor), Surriya, Ruqqya Jabeen (katar), Naznin (Maano), Alam Lohar, Khurshid Kuku and Hoor Bano, not to forget Inayat Hussain Bhatti and Baali Jatti, who carried forward the traditions of rural theatre in the Punjab until late 60s, when it started cloying under the unbearable weight of television.

Except for Lucky Irani Circus, whose owner was once the proprietor of a theatre prior to converting his company into a circus, one can now hardly find a theatre group of the size and resources of the companies mentioned earlier.

During its heydays, rural theatre in the Punjab was a much sought-after entertainment of the village folk. Associated with it were a number of truly talented artistes who enacted the roles assigned to them with much gusto, fervour and creative zeal. Those crowd-pulling artistes were paid and looked after well, especially when they were on tour, and a congenial environment was created to get the creative best out of them. However, the inroads made by cinema and the resulting drain on acting talent, took a heavy toll of rural theatre by severely depleting its manpower, resources and repertoires.

The advent of television in November 1964 created further difficulties for the rural theatre which tried to put up a brave resistance, but failed to hold its own in the wake of a massive onslaught by the electronic visual medium.A few theatre groups still float around in the vastness of Punjabi hinterland, and the people associated with these derive some creative and artistic satisfaction, but not much income.

Using several devices to enliven their presentations, they have tried to survive in an environment of stiff competition from this new medium but the odds were against them. Even a Lok Mela held at Islamabad in 1991, which was yet another attempt at reviving rural theatre in the Punjab, proved too feeble an effort to produce satisfactory results.

We have just gone through the brief background of the growth and development of theatre from the ancient times to the 20th century. We have also seen how the folk legends turned into entertainment and how the rituals took the shape of performances thereby causing a self-evolution of a discipline now called 'Theatre'. With the passage of time technological advancement, economic betterment, more literacy and change of social conditions the theatre has also undergone a change. The taste of those in the urban centres is different from the requirements of the folks in the rural side. Over a period of time a class emerged from amongst the performers and those interested in drama who started exploiting the State in respect of inputs for such ventures. While in earlier times writers were dependent on local legend folk stories and ritualistic appearances, this class depended on adaptations, translations from European literature and tried to arrange production at the cost of public expenses. They have all along been successful. They find their islands within the bureaucratic ocean which unfortunately continues to have its grip in the way the aliens managed this land. These connoisseurs inspite of their efforts for a long period have not contributed and created any original material on the subject.

Again there have emerged two classes one which manoeuvres to have theatre of their choice at State expense and the other which works and produces the Drama at their own. Since the Press and Media is also controlled by these connoisseurs they are termed as commercial and slap stick. It is really strange that this popular or commercial theatre subsists at its own but the one liked and supported by the western educated is elite always at the expense of the public, which luxury we can hardly afford. Another interesting phenomenon is that while the popular theatre gets the script the so called elitist dramas are always looking for translations.

During the hey day of the commercial theatre, the need for writing serious and realistic drama was felt by the new urban middle class intelligentsia. A large number of plays in various languages were written on legendary; historical and even political themes. Mirza Qalich Beg in Sindhi and Abdul Halim Sharar in Urdu are notable examples. The Urdu poet and journalist, Maulana Zafar Ali Khan, wrote a play on the Russo-Japanese war of 1905. Many modern and classical plays from European languages were also translated into Urdu and other languages. All this writing activity proved theatrically barren, as the plays were not performed, except occasionally by students in college dramatic societies.

The intelligentsia got a real opening into the world of drama, through paradoxically, the non-theatrical medium of sound broadcasting. In the late Thirties and early Forties, radio provided, for the playwright and the sophisticated play audience alike, the major vehicle to satisfy the demand for dramatic entertainment. The other, and more legitimately theatrical, medium was the amateur dramatic societies especially in the rapidly expanding educational institutions. The radio as well as the amateur dramatic societies depended largely on adaptation of European plays. The most prominent of the radio playwrights was Imtiaz Ali Taj. Among others who wrote radio plays in Urdu was Saadat Hasan Manto, whose main work was put on the air from Delhi and Bombay where he also wrote screen plays before he came to Lahore after independence and also wrote for the stage.

With independence some of the drama lovers in the City generally felt the need of a proper theatre in Lahore. The regular stage productions were going on at the College Dramatic Societies, the Railway auditorium, the Lawrence Hall and private Talkies outside Bhati Gate and one or two on Mcleod Road. Some senior performers & writers patronized by bureaucrats founded the Arts Council where the work started with the exhibition of Paintings and was followed by stage productions. By the end of 50s small theatrical groups emerged and there were societies assisted by the Government which revived and reactivated the stage Dramas in the city. Most of the plays written in those days were translations and adaptations from western Dramas with the only exception of original plays written by Khawaja Moin-ud-Din and Mehr Nigar. In the 50s efforts were also made to produce Agha Hashar's play 'Rustam Sohrab' that may be mentioned as one instance. Since so much is talked about Agha Hashar by a class it will be appropriate to make a mention of his work in the field of theatre. According to Syed Imtiaz Ali Taj the work of Agha Hashar as a playwright either is not appreciated or he is epitomised as Shakespeare of India. Those who are students of western theatre consider him not only as an ordinary scriptwriter but also as one he who was responsible for the down fall of Urdu stage. Those comparing him with Shakespeare, probably do not have enough knowledge of literary value of Shakespeare's writings. The students of English drama always find faults irrelevant of tragedies, empty slogans and cheap stuff which turned him as an ordinary script writer specially the inferior plots of the play which according to them are responsible for the decay of the theatre. Both sides apparently have failed to strike a balance. Those who condemn have not seen the performances of the scripts written by Agha Hashar and also failed to draw a comparison of the theatrical characteristics.   One requires knowing that the stage plays were written in a particular age and in a typical environment.   How did the performers become available and above all, the types of audience they catered for, are the essential points to fairly comment on the merits of the plays written by Agha Hashar and dramas from the western literature.   It is also observed that the language of the play is certainly not written from the point of view of creating literature. Agha Hahsar's period of play writing is somewhere between 1901–1930. The public for which the plays were written liked the crispy language and not the literature although they appreciated the use of quality language with metaphors and similes. (Infact these are comments of the press.) As he grew in age and gained experience the language of his drama also changed with the change of social conditions. The temperament and reception of such production by the general public also changed. Above all Agha Hashar did not know English and without the knowledge of Western plays he created a sizeable part of dramatic literature partly based on his own observation. Another peculiar feature of Agha Hashar's writing was that he had full confidence to lead the actors according to the script.   The element of adlibbing was non-existent. Most of the actors being not well read were bound to go by the lines during performance. The dialogues were of oratory nature and throw of voice was considered a qualification of the artists success. The themes of the scripts were local legends or social satire based on the Indian society.   When the audience became serious in the later years Agha Hashar's plays became dull as they lacked real relationship with the life and accordingly. Syed Imtiaz Ali Taj concludes that "it is not correct that Agha Hashar damaged the theatre rather Agha Hashar could not help to save the dying theatre" Needless to add that until 1913 when he visited Lahore he was not known as a Dramatist. He was introduced as a Poet and read his poetry under the title of "Shookriya Europe" and "Mauj-e-Zam Zam" in the sessions of Anjaman-e-Hamayat-e-Islam. He was advised by Abdul Majid Salak who had felt disappearing scripts of Agha Hashar, for their proper publication and Agha Hashar had agreed to their publication under the title of 'Nigaristan Publication'.   But when he got a job in Maiden Theatre, Calcutta, he shifted straightaway. Infact at that time the Parsi Businessmen were investing in theatrical companies as stage was the lucrative business and the centre of stage productions were Bombay and Calcutta. These Parsi Theatrical Companies employed script writers as their regular employees and Agha Hashar was one such playwright.

The actual fact is that prior to partition there was hardly any theatrical company from Bombay and Calcutta, which had not visited Lahore. This included mainly the "Parsi" Theatrical Groups. The centre of theatrical activities were Bradlay Hall on Rattigan Road and Cinema/Talkies located outside Bhati Gate and some Cinemas on the Mcleod Road, in addition to temporary stages called

"Mandwas". Some other companies from Lahore were Albert Theatrical Company, Pareem Parcharni, Natak Mandli and Punjab Reform Theatrical Company. Rehmat Ali who was a very genuine artist and a person of fine taste owned the last one. The Playwrights included Master Rehmat, Master Qamar, Mir Ghulam Abbas, Syed Dilawar Shah, Muhammad Ismail, Muhammad Shah, Hakim Ahmad Shuja. Agha Hashar also spent some time in Lahore. He also used to come with "Parsi" Theatrical Groups from Bombay who visited and performed in Lahore. The name of his own Company was Shakespeare Theatrical Company. The stage dramas of Master Rehmat Ali became very popular. These included 'Dard-e-Jiggar', 'Baa Wafa Qatil', 'Tasveer-e-Rehmat' and 'Bap Ka Gunnah'. After 1935 the stage deteriorated and drama lost its popularity. There was a sort of political turmoil. The film/cinema replaced the theatre in the early thirties in Lahore. Quite a few popular artists of the films in Bombay were from Lahore. In those days those who remained attached to theatre in colleges included Professor G. D. Sohndhi, Hakim Ahmad Shuja, Professor Ahmad Shah Bokhari and Imtiaz Ali Taj and Prof. Ghulam Mustafa Tabassam. After Independence, Alhamra Arts Council came into being in Lahore. Its founders were literary figures like Agha Bashir, Abdur Rahman Chughtai, Dr. Tasaddaq Hussain Khalid, Justice S. A. Rahman, Imtiaz Ali Taj, Mumtaz Daultana and Madam Noor Jahan. Mr. Khalil Sahafi was the secretary of the Arts Council. All the pre-partition theatre halls had since been converted into cinema houses. Immediately after Partition, no stage as such was available but some of the adaptations were staged in the Government College amongst which one was "Mid Summer Night's Dream". The artists of this period included Safdar Mir, Sikandar Shaheen, Sufi Waqar, Khalid Saeed Butt, Fazal Kamal, Yasmin and Naeem Tahir etc. Until 1954 various theatrical groups were formed and every group including Railway Staff and Government Press officials had the theatrical productions staged in the city. In those days in Alhamra, Imtiaz Ali Taj, under the direction of Safdar Mir produced the translation "Who Killed Me" and " Box and Cocks". Izhar Kazmi produced "Mujrim Kon". Alhamra Group of artists included Safdar Mir, Yasmin, Sikandar Shaheen, Sufi Waqar, Izhar Kazmi, Khalid Saeed Butt and Naeem Tahir etc., etc. In 1955 Ishrat Rahmani started his company titled "Star Theatre Academy" which produced 'Rustam Sohrab" by Agha Hashar Kashmiri in Y.M.C.A. Hall. The Akimi Theatre and Ravi Art also produced some dramas at Alhamra stage. The Star Theatre Company also produced "Khud Kushi" by Saadat Hasan Manto at Alhamra. A detailed study of the dramatic activities of the period by Ishrat Rahmani reveals that during this period Lahore was only a centre of adaptation based plays. There was no original script written. Later on there followed the re-organization of the Alhamra where Kamal Ahmad Rizvi and Safdar Mir produced "Gurya Ka Khel". Naeem Tahir and

Yasmin produced their play titled "Adab Arz" translation of "She stoops to conquer". In those very days Hamid Shaikh produced quite a few dramas at Bagh-e- Jinnah Open Air Theatre.

From 1959 to 1970 all types of plays were produced at Alhamra. These included comedies, tragedies, farce, brisk, slow and experimental plays. Most of them were adaptations and translations. A few original written by Ashfaq Ahmad Khan, Bano Qudsia, Najam Hassan Syed, Atique Ullah Shaikh, Sufi Nisar, Athar Shah Khan, Salma Jabeen and Ijaz Malik etc., etc. The stage dramas were also produced in various colleges in that period including Kinnaird College, Islamia College, Dyal Singh College and F.C. College. The other stages included Y.M.C.A., Open Air Theatre and auditorium on the Mall. After 1971 there were changes at Alhamra due to grouping of artists and different groups started performing at different places outside except Dr. Anwar Sajjad who occupied Alhamra. This dispersal of artists led to further deterioration of quality of stage plays. The dramas were also staged in WAPDA Auditorium, Falettis Hotel, Salatin Hotel, Hotel 786 and Rahat Hall. This situation continued until the Government completed Alhamra Hall-I and a project of plays was taken up officially with the Government funding. It will be appropriate to list the plays for the period from 1959 to 1972, which were performed at Alhamra for purpose of record. These are as under:

PLAYS STAGED AT ALHAMRA
FROM 1959 TO 1972

Qisa Sotey Jagtey Ka	1959 Kh. Moeen ud Din	Kh. Moeen ud Din
Adab Araz	1959 Naeem Tahir/Yasmin Tahir	Naeem Tahir
Saai	1959	Dr. Anwar Sajjad
Bulaqi Badzat	1961 Kamal Ahmad Rizvi	Kamal Ahmad Rizvi
Kanjoos	1961 Raaz Yousafi	C.M. Munir
Aap Ki Tarif	1961 Naeem Tahir/Yasmin Tahir	Naeem Tahir
Nach Na Janey	1962 Saleem Chishti	C.M. Munir
Zena Kadal	1963	Munawar Taufiq
Nagry	1963 Abu Saeed Qureshi	Prof. Kaleem ud Din
Sajjawal (Punjabi)	1964 Akram Butt	Akram Butt
Dawat	1964 Bakhtiar Ahmad/Farooq Zamir	Bakhtiar Ahmad
Jaag Utha Watan	1964 Aziz Asri	Aziz Asri
Khahmkah	1965 Rashid Umer Thanvi	Rashid Umer Thanvi
Lahu Kay Chiragh	1966 Saleem Chishti	Saleem Chishti
Wadi-e-Kashmir	1966 Kh. Moeen ud-Din	Kh. Moeen ud Din
Mirza Ghalib Bandar Road Per	1967 Kh. Moeen ud-Din	Kh. Moeen ud Din

Ik Tery Anay Say	1968 Bano Qudsia	Kamal Ahmad Rizvi
Manzil Manzil	1969 Bano Qudsia	Kamal Ahmad Rizvi
Hunsi Hunsi Main	1969 Ishrat Rahman	Asif ur Rahman
Larrki Ik Sharmili See	1969 Atique Ullah Shaikh	Yasmin Tahir
Darad Ki Dawa Kiya Hai	1969 Intizar Hussain	Nazir Zaigham
Aai Bhi Woh	1969 Salma Jabeen	Jamil Bismil
Chirrya Ghar	1969 Athar Shah Khan	Athar Shah Khan
Main Patloon Aur Naukari	1970 Nusrat Thakar	Nazir Zaigham
Anjaney Loag	1970 Raz Yousafi	Akhtar Tanha
Barra Sahib	1970 Agha Babar	C.M. Munir
Muhabat Aur Bel Bottom	1970 Khalid Abbas Dar	Nazir Zaigham
Paisa Bolta Hai	1970 M. Siddique	Nazir Zaigham
Phir Dekh Tamasha	1970 Sajjad Haider	Sajjad Haider
Who Jo Zinda Rahey	1970 Shaukat Zain	Shaukat Zain
Aj Akhan Waris Shah Noon	1970 Sufi Nisar Ahmad	Saleem Chishti
Ishq Ik Dewaney Ka	1970 Ijaz Malik	Ali Ejaz
Adhi Baat	1971 Bano Qudsia	Kamal Ahmad Rizvi
Cousin Aur Guest House	1971 M. Siddique/M. Sharif	Nazir Zaigham
Nahley Te Dehla	1972 Saeed Anjum	C.M. Munir
Mian Bivi Razi	1972 Shaukat Zain	C.M. Munir

While we have listed the plays it might be of interest to give names of the known artists for this period.

PROMINENT ARTISTS
FROM 1959 TO 1972

Abid Ali	Hamid Rana	Nazir Zaigham
Abid Butt	Jamil Bismil	Nighat Butt
Afzal Ahmad	Jamil Fakhri	Perveen Roz
Albila (Akhtar Hussain)	Kamal Ahmad Rizvi	Qamar Chaudhry
Ali Ejaz	Kh. Abu Tahir	Qavi Khan
Anwar Ali	Khalid Abbas Dar	Rashid Umer Thanvi
Athar Shah Khan	Khalid Saeed Butt	Rehan Azhar
Attiya Sharaf	Khalid Saleem Mota	Rehana Siddiqui
Aurangzaib	Khurshid Shahid	Romana Shafaq
Aurangzaib Leghari	Khurshid Shaukat	Sajjad Haider
Ayoub Khan	M. A. Nadeem	Saleem Nasir
Badih-uz-Zaman	Masood Akhtar	Samia Naz
Bakhtiar Ahmad	Mohsin Rizvi	Saqib Shaikh
Begum Perveen	Mumtaz Chaudhry	Sarwat Attique

C. Semuail	Munawar Saeed	Shakeel Ahmad
C.M. Munir	Naeem Tahir	Shujaat Hashmi
Dr. Anwar Sajjad	Naheed Siddiqui	Sikandar Shaheen
Durdana Butt	Naja (Raj Rani)	Siraj Munir
Fakhri Ahmad	Najma Mehboob	Yasmin Tahir
Farooq Zamir Ghauri	Nana (Rafi Khawar)	Zil-e-Subhan
Ghayyur Akhtar	Nazir Husaini	Zubair Khan

Pending these activities at Alhamra, in early 70s the theatre in the College Dramatic Clubs continued unaffected. Alhamra stage got a slight set back due to group politics in the artist community which finally led to the taking over of the management by the Government wherefore Provincial authorities launched a massive development project. The Art Council got two new theatres, art gallery, accommodation for the classes, conferences and seminars etc. Again a group of the artists started staging the adaptations. The productions were all at the expense of the Government in the name of serious theatre which after sometime were discontinued due to shortage of funds.

In late 80s the Council authorities felt that productions on public expense were not viable due to resource constraint. The facilities were therefore, leased out to private producers wherein they had their own scripts and productions. This led to the emergence of popular theatre, which is generally termed as commercial theatre by those supporting the western style plays. This popular theatre is surviving at its own without any Government support. Generally the saleable cast is booked on high fees and the producers usually make money out of these ventures. There has been criticism by a particular group about quality of popular theatre which is termed as slap stick comedy and the scripts being without any substance. But it continues to thrive at its own to the extent that quite a few private theatrical companies and auditoriums have come up in the market. Inspite of this, this theatre has grown and expanded. Now in Lahore there are three auditoriums viz. the Rabia Theatre, Tamaseel and the Lahore Theatre, which are operating in addition to Alhamra Halls. Most of these halls show comedies with saleable cast. The other theatre conversed by some is so-called elitists' theatre and can only work on Government grants. They believe that the Government should pay for changing the taste and aptitude of people and make them opt for such productions. This school of thought comprises western educated class including fading artists who all along wait for the Government assistance to mount these productions in which artists and stage crews are from amongst them. Till recently the Government due to pressure from these groups, irrespective of the market and resource constraints did provide financial assistance, for these dramas, but for the last year or so this has been stopped and the theatre has been left to its own under the normal laws and regulations on the subject applicable to all. The producers pay 20% Entertainment Duty both at Government run Arts Councils and private forums. The plays are generally staged for 15 days and each new script is scrutinized and censored. The Arts Council subsidizes the performances by the University and College dramatic groups. The known names in the field of drama commercially being staged are Muhammad Qavi Khan, Masood Akhtar, Sohail Ahmad, Khalid Abbas Dar, Aman Ullah, Baboo Baral, Ashraf Rahi, Shauki Khan, Sahiba, Sheeba, etc., etc.

The list of plays staged during 1973-98 along with names of main artists is given below for reference.

PLAYS STAGED AT ALHAMRA FROM 1973 TO 1998

Sotila Shauhar	1973	Sher Ali Zaidi	Nazir Zaigham
Barish Main Larrki	1973	Atique Ullah Shaikh	Atique Ullah Shaikh
Barey Wo Hain	-do-	Younis Adeeb	Masood Akhtar
Sitamgar Tery Liya	-do-	Bano Qudsia	Kalim ud Din
Love Spot	-do-	Zil-e-Subhan	Zil-e-Subhan
Yeh Begmat	-do-	Mushtaq Saifi	Nazir Zaigham
Jeway Pakistan	-do-	Nasir Khan	Nasir Khan
Larrki Ik Sharmili See	-do-	Atique Ullah Shaikh	Irfan Khoosat
Ghar Aya Mehman	-do-	Amjad Islam Amjad	Jamil Malik
Professional Leader	1974	Asif ur Rahman	Asif ur Rahman
House Full	-do-	Jamil Bismil	Jamil Bismil
Ishq Ik Dewaney Ka	-do-	Ijaz Malik	Ali Ejaz
Adhi Teri Adhi Meri	-do-	Iftikhar Haider	Iftikhar Haider
Hum Sub Chor Hain	-do-	Kamal Ahmad Rizvi	Kamal Ahmad Rizvi
Kabarr Khana	-do-	M. Sharif	Ali Ejaz
Tawajo Farmain	-do-	Asif ur Rahman	Asif ur Rahman
Zuban Darz	-do-	Iftikhar Haider	Iftikhar Haider
Tuch Me Not	-do-	Afzal Rahman	Irfan Khoosat
Best of Luck	-do-	Mirza Rashid Akhtar	
Chalo Chuti Hooi	-do-	Prof. Siddique Ahmad	Nazir Zaigham
Ladan Pitti	-do-	Sufi Nisar Ahmad	Saleem Chishti
Yeh Bichary Loag	-do-	Mirza Rashid Akhtar	Mirza Rashid Akhtar
Aik Say Barr Kar Aik	-do-	Siddique Ahmad	Naheed Khanum
Caleen Bold	-do-	Asif ur Rahman	Asif ur Rahman
Nahley Per Dehla	-do-	Saeed Anjum	Ali Ejaz
Jehl Family Main Ath Pass	-do-	Sarwat Attique	Sarwat Attique

Mazaq	-do-	Sajjad Haidar	Sajjad Haider
Mamoon Aur Mamoon Jan	-do-	Mirza Adeeb	Masood Akhtar
Meherban Qaisay Qaisay	-do-	Shoaib Hashmi	Shoaib Hashmi
Dewana Bakar Khawaish Sohiar		Rafi Peer	Salman Peerzada
Kanjoos	-do-	Riaz Yousafi	Nazir Zaigham
Chor Machai Shore	1978	Kamal Ahmad Rizvi	Saleema Hashmi
Paisa Bolta Hai	-do-	Siddique Ahmad	Nazir Zaigham
Andar Aana Mana Hai	-do-	Athar Shah Khan	Qavi Khan
Kanwarey Musibat Kay Mary	-do-	Prof. Ahmad Saeed	Prof. Ahmad Saeed
Aik Chehray Par Kai Chehry	-do-	A. R. Siddiqui	Mian Ashfaq Ali
Hai Koi Aisa	-do-	Sajjad Haidar	Sajjad Haider
Ik Tera Annay Say	-do-	Bano Qudsia	Jamil Bismil
No Lift	-do-	Mushtaq Saifi	Nazir Zaigham
Ishq Kay Musafar	-do-	A. Hameed	Iqbal Afandi
Khatra	-do-	Athar Shah Khan	Naveed Alam
Nach Na Janey	-do-	Saleem Chishti	Jamil Bismil
Ghar Aya Mehman	-do-	Amjad Islam Amjad	Saleem Chishti
Haran De Kar Pass Karin	-do-	Athar Shah Khan	Naveed Alam
Wrong Number	1979	Athar Shah Khan	Masood Akhtar
Ehsas Jay Rishtay	-do-	Mirza Rashid Akhtar	Masood Akhtar
Aik Thi Maina	-do-	M. Sharif	Badi uz Zaman
Damad	-do-	Rashid Umer Thanvi	Rashid Umer Thanvi
Sitamgar Tery Liya	-do-	Bano Qudsia	Saleem Chishti
Shehr Diyan Kurrian Pind Wich	-do-	Jamil Bismil	Pern Cooper
Shetan	-do-	Sufi Nisar Ahmad	Jamil Bismil
Cousin Aur Guest House	-do-	Siddique Ahmad	Nazir Zaigham
Chirriya Ghar	-do-	Athar Shah Khan	Asif ur Rahman
Bura-i- Farokht	-do-	Iftikhar Haider	Iftikhar Haider
Twist	-do-	Sajjad Haidar	Irfan Khoosat
Ulti Seedhi	-do-	Sufi Nisar Ahmad	Iqbal Afandi
Allah De Qasmy	-do-	Sajjad Haidar	Hamid Rana
Seedha Morr	-do-	M. Sharif	Irfan Khoosat
Lahore By Night	-do-	Sufi Nisar Ahmad	Khayam Sarhadi
Kis Ki Bivi Kis Ka Shoher	1981	Kamal Ahmad Rizvi	Jamil Bismil
Rakhwala	-do-	Atique Ullah Shaikh	Ali Ejaz
Laly Di Jan	-do-	Saleem Chishti	Jamil Bismil
Ashraf ul Makhloqat	-do-	Sarmad Sehbai	Sarmad Sehbai
Waiting Room	-do-	M. Sharif	Irfan Khoosat
Thori See Shararat	-do-	Afzal Rahman	Jamil Malik
Hi Hi Ha Ha Ha	-do-	Mian Farooq	Khayam Sarhadi
Baki Bacha Aik	-do-	Shoaib Hashmi	Muhammad Nazir
Adhi Larrki	1982	Shehbaz Sarhadi	Shehbaz Sarhadi

344

Lal Lagam	-do-	Siddique Ahmad	Nazir Zaigham
Madam Dulari	-do-	Siddique Ahmad	Masood Akhtar
Yeh Dil Ka Moamla Hai	-do-	Aziz Asri	Irfan Khoosat
Naam Ka Nawab	-do-	Iftikhar Haider	Iftikhar Haider
Jams Band Ki Wapsi	-do-	Sarwat Attique	Sarwat Attique
Ishaq Per Zor Nahin	-do-	Ashfaq Ahmad Khan	Khayam Sarhadi
Get Out	-do-	Sajjad Haidar	Sajjad Haider
Aap Ki Tareef	-do-	Naeem Tahir	Naeem Tahir
Enquiry Officer	-do-	Babar	Rashid Umer Thanvi
Khamkhah	-do-	Rashid Umer Thanvi	Rashid Umer Thanvi
Mirza Ghalib Bandar Road Per	-do-	Kh. Moeen ud Din	Mehmood Ali
Dard Ki Dawa Kya Hai	-do-	Intizar Hussain	Nazir Zaigham
Lehri In Trouble	-do-	Usman Meman	Usman Meman
Palat Tera DhianKidhar Hai	-do-	Shaukat Zain	Shaukat Zain
House Full	1983	Jamil Bismil	Jamil Bismil
Chor Chor Chor	-do-	Husina Moyeen	Humair Hashmi
Uff	-do-	Athar Shah Khan	Masood Akhtar
Jagty Raho	-do-	Aziz Asri	Aziz Asri
No Problem	1983	M. Sharif	Irfan Khoosat
Begham Mujey Talaq Do	-do-	Jamil Bismil	Jamil Bismil
Jesay Ko Tesa	-do-	Ayoub Khawar	Sarwat Attique
High Jump	-do-	M. Sharif	Dr. Enver Sajjad
By Road	1984	Sajad Hameed	Rashid Umer Thanvi
Chand Ki Siteh Par	-do-	Sufi Nisar Ahmad	Jamil Bismil
Shadi Bohat Zruri Hai	-do-	Nawaz	Irfan Khoosat
Baat Samaj Main A Gai	-do-	Nasir Baluch	Saleem Chishti
Budha Trunk Aur Boski	-do-	Khalid Abbas Dar	Khalid Abbas Dar
Khatra	-do-	Athar Shah Khan	Nazir Zaigham
Phir Daikh Tamashi	-do-	Sajjad Haidar	Jamil Bismil
Who Baat Aur Thi	-do-	M. Sharif	Dr. Enver Sajjad
Aur Ankh Khul Gai	1985	Aslam Bolhsari	Saleem Chishti
Khali Jageh Pur Karain	-do-	Iftikhar Haider	Iftikhar Haider
Zarurat Hai	-do-	Nasir Naqvi	Irfan Khoosat
Adhi Raat	-do-	Saleem Chishti	Saleem Chishti
Waiting Room	-do-	M. Sharif	Irfan Khoosat
Two in One	-do-	Muzafar Nazash	Nazir Zaigham
Anokha Ladla	-do-	Sarwat Attique	Sarwat Attique
Khul Ja Sam Sam	-do-	Mehmood Ali	Qazi Wajid
Zara Suniya Tau	-do-	Ayoub Khawar	Rashid Umer Thanvi
Kis Ko Keh Rahay Hoo	-do-	Amjad Islam Amjad	Jamil Bismil
Meri Jaan	-do-	Aysha Tasleem	Aysha Tasleem
Ik Sitam Aur Meri Jaan	-do-	Nuzhat Ijaz	Naheed Khanum
Damad	1986	Rashid Umer Thanvi	Rashid Umer Thanvi

Hazar Junab	-do-	Hamida Jabeen	Jamil Malik
Safaid Jhoot	-do-	Shaukat Zaidi	Saleem Chishti
Seedhy Hath	-do-	Iqbal Haider	Nazir Zaigham
Neelam Ghar	-do-	Athar Shah Khan	Munawar Saeed
Aap Ki Qasam	-do-	Tahir Malik	Nazir Zaigham
Chirriya Ghar	-do-	Jamil Bismil	Jamil Bismil
Urran Tashtary	-do-	Munir Raj	Khalid Abbas Dar
Muhabat Ka Maray	-do-	Husina Moyeen	Jamil Bismil
Bura-i-Farokht	-do-	Iftikhar Haider	Iftikhar Haider
Tuti Kahan Kamand	-do-	Munir Raj	Jamil Bismil
Tamasha	-do-	Husina Moyeen	Mehmood Ali
Khatra	-do-	Athar Shah Khan	Khalid Abbas Dar
Aap Ki Tareef	-do-	Yasmin Tahir	Naeem Tahir
Naya Makan	-do-	Rahman Zulfi	Nazir Zaigham
Jokar Pokar	-do-	Iftikhar Haider	Iftikhar Haider
Yeh Shadi Nehe Ho Sakti	-do-	Nawaz	Nazir Zaigham
Mazaq	-do-	Sajjad Haidar	Iftikhar Haider
Anar Kali	-do-	Syed Imtiaz Ali Taj	Naeem Tahir
Anokha Doulah	-do-	Shaukat Zaidi	Qavi Khan
Chalti Ka Naam Garri	1986	Munir Raj	Khalid Abbas Dar
Insan Bano	1987	Iftikhar Haider	Iftikhar Haider
Hansna Mana Hai	-do-	Mirza Rashid Akhtar	Jamil Bismil
Achha Too Yeh Baat Hai	-do-	Nasir Baluch	Saleem Chishti
Twist	-do-	Sajjad Haidar	Fakhri Ahmad
Laoot Ka Budhu Ghar Ko Aai	-do-	Munir Raj	Jamil Bismil
Paisa Bolta Hai	-do-	Siddique Ahmad	Nazir Zaigham
Company Bagh	-do-	M. Sharif	Khalid Abbas Dar
Yeh Shadi Nehe Ho Sakti	-do-	Nawaz	Khalid Abbas Dar
Uff Allah	-do-	Athar Shah Khan	Khalid Abbas Dar
Yes Papa	-do-	Amjad Islam Amjad	Khalid Abbas Dar
Sitamgar Tery Liya	-do-	Bano Qudsia	Rashid Umer Thanvi
Miss Bavri	-do-	Romana Begum	Naheed Khanum
Zauja Mohtarma	1990	Nawaz	Ilyas Najam
Nizam Saka	-do-	Munir Raj	C.M. Munir
Shoher Bechara	-do-	Ghayyur Akhtar	Ghayyur Akhtar
Aab Janey Do	-do-	Umer Sharif	Jamil Bismil
Hum To Chaly Susral	-do-	Afzal Rahman	Irfan Khoosat
Urgent Service	-do-	Munawar Shehzad	C.M. Munir
Aao Such Bolain	-do-	Umer Sharif	Naheed Khanum
Lo Who A Gaya	-do-	Shaukat Zain	C.M. Munir
Tamasha To Ab Ho Ga	-do-	Mirza Rashid Akhtar	Khalid Abbas Dar
Allah De Qasmy	-do-	Sajjad Haidar	Jamil Bismil
Bakra Qistoon Par	-do-	Umer Sharif	C.M. Munir

To Bhi To Harjai Hai	-do-	Ayoub Khawar	Khalid Abbas Dar
Dola Dohky Baz	-do-	Munawar Shehzad	Khalid Abbas Dar
Teen Dewaney	-do-	Ayoub Khawar	Khalid Abbas Dar
Ratain Theen Chandni	-do-	Iftikhar Haider	Anjuman
Haran De Kar Pass Karin	-do-	Athar Shah Khan	Nazir Zaigham
Mera Lal Dopata	-do-	Naheed Khanum	Naheed Khanum
High Jump	-do-	M. Sharif	Irfan Khoosat
Paisa Bolta Hai	-do-	Siddique Ahmad	Ilyas Najam
Aap Kaon Hain	-do-	Iqbal Haider	Masood Akhtar
Papu Yar Tang Na Kar	-do-	Tahir Gilani	Irfan Khoosat
Dewany Do	-do-	Ali Azar	Mian Shabeer
Mujeh Shadi Say Bachao	-do-	Shehzad Raza	Masood Akhtar
Hai Koi Hum Sa	1991	Munir Raj	Mian Shabeer
Mazaq Shuru Hai	-do-	Umer Sharif	C.M. Munir
Qasam Tarey Piyar Ki	-do-	Iftikhar Haider	Mian Shabeer
Baja Hai Barat Nahin	-do-	Mirza Rashid Akhtar	Mian Shabeer
Sanam Teri Qasam	-do-	Khalid Mujahid	C.M. Munir
Aadhy Ghar Wala	-do-	Ali Ashraf	C.M. Munir
Ladan Pitti	-do-	Sufi Nisar Ahmad	Masood Akhtar
Load Shedding	1991	Jamil Bismil	Nazir Zaigham
Anokhay Mehman	-do-	Mirza Rashid Akhtar	Khalid Abbas Dar
Jaal	-do-	Shaukat Zain	C.M. Munir
Hello Uncle	-do-	M. Sharif	Ghayyur Akhtar
Nawan Pawara	-do-	Sajjad Hamid	Mian Shabeer
In Say Milya	-do-	Tufail Akhtar	C.M. Munir
Kanch Ka Borreh	-do-	Shaukat Zaidi	Muhammad Zubair
Muhabat Ka Khridar	-do-	Shahid Abbas	Anjuman
Court Marriage	-do-	Noor Sultan	Anjuman
Zara Dekhia To	-do-	Ayoub Khawar	Masood Akhtar
Main Aya Wo Gaya	-do-	Umer Sharif	C.M. Munir
Dulhan Mery Naam Ki	-do-	Umer Sharif	C.M. Munir
Ehsas Kay Rishtay	-do-	Mirza Rashid Akhtar	Jamil Bismil
Teri Jaan Di Qasmain	1992	Munir Raj	C.M. Munir
Sassi Sohni Meyyhanwal	-do-	Jamil Bismil	Jamil Bismil
Yeh Dil Ka Moamla Hai	-do-	Aziz Asri	Irfan Khoosat
Do Doni Chhe	-do-	Aslam Mughal	Nazir Zaigham
Bolana Mana Hai	-do-	Qavi Khan	Haroon Pasha
Pind Tay Paris	-do-	Mirza Rashid Akhtar	Muhammad Zubair
Guzra Howa Zamana	-do-	Iqbal Haider	Irfan Khoosat
Lakhoon Main Aik	-do-	Naheed Khanum	Naheed Khanum
Tauba Tauba	-do-	Ali Sufian Afaki	Masood Akhtar
Qisa Aik Mohabat Ka	-do-	Atique Ullah Shaikh	Irfan Khoosat
Pagal Hi Pagal	-do-	Mirza Rashid Akhtar	Iftikhar Haider
Dekh Magar Piyar Say	-do-	Naheed Khanum	Naheed Khanum

Yas Papa	-do-	Amjad Islam Amjad	M. J. Rana
Barwan Khilari	-do-	Shaukat Zaidi	Muhammad Zubair
Aisa Bhi Hota Hai	-do-	Nasir Naqvi	Masood Akhtar
Lahore By Night	-do-	Sufi Nisar Ahmad	Bindya Begum
Bakalam Khud	-do-	Siddique Ahmad	Nazir Zaigham
Andaz Mohabat Ka	-do-	A. Hameed	Naheed Khanum
Wapas Jana Mushkal Hai	-do-	Munir Raj	Nazir Zaigham
Lakir Dy Faqir	-do-	Sufi Nisar Ahmad	Muhammad Zubair
Ik Sitam Aur Meri Jaan	-do-	Nuzhat Ijaz	Naheed Khanum
Aik Jhoot Aur Sahi	1993	Khalil Ahmad	Usman Peerzada
Dil Tham Ka Betho	-do-	Jamil Qureshi	Jamil Qureshi
Muaff Karna Dosto	-do-	Iftikhar Haider	Masood Akhtar
Paindo Aur Muhabat	-do-	Munir Raj	Naheed Khanum
Yehi Moqa Hai	-do-	Shaukat Zaidi	Nazir Zaigham
One Way	-do-	Asad Nazir	C.M. Munir
Kambal Nain Chaad Da	-do-	Munir Raj	C.M. Munir
First Cousin	-do-	Ayoub Khawar	C.M. Munir
Jehan Demagh Bikty Hain	-do-	A. Hameed	Naheed Khanum
Jhoot Maat Bolo	-do-	Noor Sultan	Naheed Khanum
Kanjoos	1993	Riaz Yousafi	Khalid Abbas Dar
Jookar Pookar	-do-	Iftikhar Haider	Masood Akhtar
Sub Achha Hai	-do-	Iftikhar Haider	Naheed Khanum
Main Pya Teri	-do-	M. Sharif	Naheed Khanum
Aaj Ka Majnoon	-do-	Shaikh Zahid Rafi	Naheed Khanum
Chalti Ka Naam Garri	-do-	Munir Raj	C.M. Munir
Kab Jaigi Susral	-do-	Zahid Akasi	Irfan Khoosat
Barkry Ku Maan	-do-	Khalid Butt	Qavi Khan
Shohar Ho To Aisa	-do-	Shahid Abbas	Khalid Abbas Dar
Oh My God	1994	Iftikhar Haider	Iftikhar Haider
Jhoot Ka Paoon	-do-	Shaukat Zaidi	C.M. Munir
Akhar Ghar Basana Hai	-do-	Iqbal Haider	Naheed Khanum
Modern Thugh	-do-	Sajjad Hameed	Naheed Khanum
Khatay Mithay	-do-	Younis Butt	Irfan Khoosat
Sapney Saajan Kay	-do-	Iqbal Haider	Masood Akhtar
Anndaz Apna Apna	-do-	Mirza Rashid Akhtar	Naheed Khanum
Mauqa Achha Hai	-do-	Iqbal Haider	Masood Akhtar
Seedhay Haath	-do-	Iqbal Haider	Naheed Khanum
Baain Haath Ka Khail	-do-	Nawaz	Ilyas Najam
Aao Gee Piya Gee	-do-	Khalid Abbas Dar	Khalid Abbas Dar
Main Raja Toon Rani	-do-	Mirza Rashid Akhtar	Naheed Khanum
Ishq Ho To Aisa	-do-	Munir Raj	C.M. Munir
Shadi Garr Barr Hai	-do-	Iftikhar Haider	Iftikhar Haider
Bholay Badshah	-do-	Meena Naz	M. J. Rana
No Lift	-do-	Mushtaq Saifi	C.M. Munir

Qaid Main Hai Bulbul	-do-	Naheed Khanum	Naheed Khanum
Dukh Sukh	-do-	Rahman Zulfi	Ilyas Najam
Soney Ki Chirrya	-do-	Iqbal Haider	M. J. Rana
Shadi Na Karna Yaro	1995	Ashfaq Ali	M. J. Rana
Kis Ko Keh Rahey Ho	-do-	Amjad Islam Amjad	Ilyas Najam
Dolha Ho To Aisa	-do-	Zulqernain Haider	Majeed Zaigham
Uff Yeh Shadi	-do-	Munir Raj	Ilyas Najam
Ishq Karana Manah Hai	-do-	Naheed Khanum	Naheed Khanum
Baraat A Gai	-do-	Iqbal Haider	Naheed Khanum
Yeh Larrka Dewana	-do-	Iqbal Haider	Naheed Khanum
Aap Say Kiya Parda	-do-	Iqbal Haider	Naheed Khanum
Jano Sun Zara	-do-	Qasir Iqbal	Ilyas Najam
Bevi Ho To Aissi	-do-	Iqbal Haider	Ilyas Najam
Aashiq Mazaj	-do-	Riaz Akhtar	Naheed Khanum
Nazar Kay Samnay	-do-	Iqbal Haider	Masood Akhtar
Kanglay Sahib	-do-	Nasir Naqvi	Naheed Khanum
Tamasha House	-do-	Munir Raj	Naheed Khanum
Doli Saja Kay Rakhna	-do-	Zahoor Shamsi	Naheed Khanum
Nakhra Gori Da	-do-	Shaukat Zaidi	Naheed Khanum
Yeh Kali Kali Ankhain	1995		
Mazaq	-do-	Sajjad Haider	Irfan Khoosat
To Bhi Kaya Cheez Hai	-do-	Zulqernain Haider	Zulqernain Haider
Hu Ja Pichhy	-do-	Pervaiz Raza	Muhammad Zubair
Papu Sahib	1996	Shahid Abbas	Naheed Khanum
Majnoon 96	-do-	Naheed Khanum	Jamil Bismil
Bhabian Toba Toba	-do-	Munir Raj	Munir Raj
One Way Ticket	-do-	Riaz Akhtar	Qaisar Javaid
Shohar Harjai	-do-	Naheed Khanum	Naheed Khanum
Sharmili Ankhoon Wali	-do-	Naheed Khanum	Naheed Khanum
Sajy Khaby	-do-	Baboo Baral	M. Zubair
Garmagaram Hai	-do-	Noor Sultan	Naheed Khanum
Fuqray Krorr Patti	-do-	Naheed Khanum	Naheed Khanum
Teri Ankhain Jhuki Jhuki See	-do-	Mirza Rashid Akhtar	Naheed Khanum
Baat Ban Gai Gi	-do-	Naheed Khanum	Naheed Khanum
Dekha Jo Chera Tera	-do-	Rai Amin	Jamil Bismil
Nakli Bao	-do-	Naheed Khanum	Naheed Khanum
Dil Ashiq Tera	-do-	Khalid Mujahid	Masood Akhtar
Thank You Madam	-do-	Shauki Khan	Naheed Khanum
Mujey Neend Na Aay	-do-	Naheed Khanum	Naheed Khanum
Munday Shararti	-do-	Munir Raj	Naheed Khanum
Choor Sanam	-do-	Naheed Khanum	Naheed Khanum
Roop Tera Mastana	-do-	Nayyer Ahmad Mian	Irfan Khan
Baly Bhi Baly	-do-	Iftikhar Haider	Iftikhar Haider
Ashiq 420	-do-	Naheed Khanum	Naheed Khanum

Payar Howa Iqrar Howa	-do-	Naheed Khanum	Naheed Khanum
Thagon Ki Barat	-do-	Iqbal Haider	Naheed Khanum
Teray Nakhray Hazar	-do-	Imdad Siddiqui	Munir Raj
Sub Achha Hai	-do-	Iftikhar Haider	Iftikhar Haider
Bakra Saja Ke Rakhna	-do-	Mirza Rashid Akhtar	Munir Raj
Iqrar Karna Mushkil Hai	-do-	Pervaiz Raza	Pervaiz Raza
Larrki Mery Shehr Ki	1997	Iqbal Haider	Iqbal Haider
Raja Ab To Aaja	-do-	Munir Raj	Khalid Abbas Dar
Katoray Pay Katora	-do-	Naheed Khanum	Naheed Khanum
Teray Ishq Nasaya	-do-	Naheed Khanum	Naheed Khanum
Sianey Bewaqoof	-do-	Naheed Khanum	Naheed Khanum
Ho Nahin Sakta	-do-	Mirza Rashid Akhtar	Naheed Khanum
Nat Khat Sayan	-do-	Naheed Khanum	Naheed Khanum
Veri Good Dunya	-do-	Naheed Khanum	Naheed Khanum
Dosari Bevi Taoba Taoba	-do-	Aysha Tasleem	Aysha Tasleem
Kusa Na Kaho	-do-	Baboo Baral	Baboo Baral
Janay Na Pai	-do-	C.M. Munir	C.M. Munir
Ho Jaigi Balay Balay	-do-	Naheed Khanum	Naheed Khanum
Hero No. One	-do-	Dr. Tariq Aziz	Masood Akhtar
Shadi Kra Lao	1997	Shahid Abbas	Muhammad Zubair
Chacha Choor Bhatija Ashiq	-do-	Khalid Butt	Khalid Butt
Rang Baz Sajnan	-do-	Sajjad Hameed	Mirza Rashid Akhtar
Dil Jalay	-do-	Abid Kashmiri	Abid Kashmiri
Bhool Na Jana Phir Papa	-do-	Iqbal Haider	Iqbal Haider
Nakhatoo Kahen Kay	-do-	Irshad Hussain	Irfan Khan
Ik Tera Mukhrra Pyara	-do-	Munir Raj	Irfan Khan
Dil Tera Dewana	-do-	Mirza Rashid Akhtar	Jamil Bismil
Shadi Ik Pawarra	-do-	Munir Raj	Qaisar Javaid
Sahib Bivi Aur Taraqi	-do-	Abid Kashmiri	Abid Kashmiri
Sun Sajnan	-do-	Riaz Akhtar	Masood Akhtar
Ab Kaya Ho Ga	1998	Munir Raj	Masood Akhtar
Ik Pal Chan Na Ay	-do-	Masood Akhtar	Masood Akhtar
Teri Meri Chhoo	-do-	Iftikhar Haider	Iftikhar Haider
Munda Ho Giya Dewana	-do-	Naheed Khanum	Naheed Khanum
Meela	-do-	Baboo Baral	Jamil Bismil
Janam Samja Karo	-do-	Munir Raj	Qasir Javaid
Jawab Drust Hai	-do-	Iqbal Haider	Naheed Khanum
Aai Din Bahar Kay	-do-	Zulqernain Haider	Qasir Javaid
Awara Dewany	-do-	Mirza Rashid Akhtar	Iftikhar Haider
Larrki Number One	-do-	Iqbal Haider	Naheed Khanum

While we are putting up information about the dramas it might also be of interest to mention the prominent names in this field. It may be of some use to those writing on the subject in future.

DRAMA ARTISTS
FROM 1973 to 1998

Abdul Rashid	Humair Hashmi	Munaza Hashmi	Sehar Abbas
Abid Kashmiri	Hussanain Haider	Murtaza Hassan	Seemi Zaidi
Abid Khan	Iftikhar Haider	Nabzar Ameen	Shabana Bhatti
Abida Baig	Ijaz Parwala	Nadeem Zafar	Shabana Jubeen
Afroze Khan	Ilyas Najam	Naeem Kashmiri	Shabana Shaikh
Afshan Qureshi	Imran Shah	Naeem Tahir	Shahid Iqbal
Aftab Haider Shaikh	Inaam Khan	Naheed Khanum	Shakeel Khan
Afzal Ahmad	Iram Tahir	Najam Zaidi	Shamila Shah
Ajab Gull	Irfan Hashmi	Nargas	Shaukat Zaidi
Akmal Rahi	Irfan Khoosat	Nargis	Shazab Mirza
Albaila (Akhtar Hussain)	Irrma	Naseem Vikky	Sheeba Butt
Ali Ejaz	Ismail Tara	Nasheela (Shaukat Ali)	Sheeba Hassan
Amanat Chan	Ismat Tahira	Nasir Butt	Shakeela Qureshi
Ambar Shah	Jaffar Hussain	Nasir Naqvi	Shoaib Hashmi
Amir Butt	Jameel Bismil	Nayyar Ijaz	Shoaib Niazi
Aneeta Amber	Jameel Fakhri	Nazir Hussaini	Shauki Khan
Aneeta Amber	Javaid Hassan	Neelofar	Sidra Khan
Anjuman	Javaid Kaudoo	Nenan Naz	Sobia Shah
Anwar Ali	Javaid Rizvi	Niaz Ahmed	Sohail Ahmad
Arif Gill	Jawad Butt	Nusrat Ara	Sohail Asghar
Arifa Siddiqui	Jawad Waseem	Papu Alaichi	Sonam
Arshad Malik	Kainnat	Pervaiz Khan	Sonya Durani
Ashar Raheem	Kanwal	Pervaz Raza	Syed Kamal Ahmad Rizvi
Ashraf Khan	Karishma Moghal	Qayyum Shehzad	Syed Najam ul Hassan Shah
Asif Iqbal	Kh.Muhammad Saleem	Raffat Gajalee	Tariq Aziz
Asim Bokhari	Khalid Abbas Dar	Raiz Malik	Tariq Javaid
Aslam Rao	Khalid Butt	Rangeela	Tariq Taidi
Aslam Sarhadi	Khalid Moeen Butt	Rashid Ali	Tasneem Kausar
Asma Akhtar	Khayum Sarhadi	Rashid Mehmood	Tauqeer Nasir
Aurangzaib Leghari	Komal Naz	Rashid Umer Thanvi	Teena (Samina)
Aysha Tasleem	Majeed Ahmad	Rehana Malik	Umer Shareef
Ayub Akhtar (Baboo Baral)	Majeed Zareef	Rehana Siddiqui	Usman Peerzada
Benish	Mehmood Aslam	Roohi Khan	Wahed Butt
Bushra Khanum	Mehwish Chaudhry	Rubi Anum	Waheed A. Rashid
C.M. Munir	Mian Shabeer	Rukhsana Lodhi	Waseem Abbas
Chaand Puri	Mirza Rashid Akhtar	Rukhsana Manzoor	Zafar Irshad
Dr. Enver Sajjad	Moeen Akhtar	Rukhsar	Zahid Ali

Fakhra Tanveer
Farkhanda
Farukh Shah
Firdaus Jamal
Ghazala Fareed
Ghayyur Akhtar
Hamid Rana
Haseeb Pasha
Hassan Murad

Mohni
Mohsin Ghilani
Muhammad Nadeem
Muhammad Qavi Khan
Muhammad Zubair
Mujahid Abbas
Mumtaz Zareef
Muna Khan
Munawar Saeed

Sabah Pervaiz
Sahiba Nishoo
Saif Khan
Saleem Chishti
Samina Ahmed
Samina Mir
Samina Qureshi
Sana Butt
Saqib Chugtai

Zahid Butt
Zahid Saleem
Zaiba Shahnaz
Zameer Mirza
Zamurad Khan
Zara Akbar
Zubair Khan
Zulqernain Haider

10

MUSIC AND DANCE

The Music of Lahore, truly speaking, cannot be very different from the rest of basics of music of the sub-continent. It infact revolves around that heritage as its important component. Historically the, impact of outsiders must have created difference of pattern as a result of interaction between the rulers and the ruled. Before, however, getting into the nitty gritty of the subject it is desirable to give some basic information as to what is music.

The music is an organized movement of sounds through a continuum of time. It plays a role in all societies and it exists in large number of styles in a given number of geographic regions or historic era. While there is music in all the societies the specific language is adopted by a few. In western cultures it is defined as an art that is concerned with combined sound, particular pitches to produce an artifact that has beauty or attraction. It expresses something that follows some kinds of internal logic and is exponent of intelligible structure that requires special skill on the part of its character. While its concept is recognizable its clear definition is not easy. There exist undefined border areas between music and other sound phenomenon such as speeches and cultures of the world differ in their opinion of the musicality of various sounds. A simple tribal chant, a broken style of singing or a composition on computer may or may not be accepted as music by members of a given society. For example Muslims do not consider recitation of Quran to be a kind of music although the structural performance is similar to that of secular singing. The social context of sound may determine whether or not they are recorded as music. Industrial noise for that matter cannot be accepted as music. On the other hand experimental music in an auditorium with a proper composition may be included in the list. Somewhat analogous to having a language each society may be said to have a music, which can be called, self-contained system within which musical communication takes place and that like a language must be learnt and understood. Within each music system there may exist different categories usually by degrees of learning i.e. professional versus untrained musicians. The educational level of the members of the society, the choice of the elite versus

Dance Painting by author

masses, patronage by the State, religious authorities or commercial establishments, the manner of dissemination etc., etc. In addition the folk music shared by the population at large, particularly its rural component and transmitted orally, and third category would include popular music, performed by professionals disseminated through media i.e. film, TV, Radio print etc. and generally consumed by the urban masses.

In any system the creation of music is by individual using a traditional vocabulary of music elements. For composition the principal creative force in music is produced by combining music element that a given society recognizes as a system. Innovation as criteria of good composing is considered important and normally carried out with the help of notation in western music but in case of folk and tribal culture composition is done in the mind of the composer who may sing or use an instruction as an aid. Creative Arts in music also include improvisation or the creation of new music during performance but it is always on the basis of some previously determined parameters. The normal method of retaining music and transmitting is oral. Most of the world music is learnt by hearing.

In any music system the creation of melody involves selection of tones from a prescribed set called the scale which is actually a group of pitches supported by specific intervals. The handling of time in music is expressed through concepts such as lengths of notes and inter-relationship among them, relative degree of emphasis on different tones and in a particular meter. The organization of music normally involves the presentation of basic materials that may then be repeated precisely with variations. The composers often unconsciously strike a plan between unity and variety and all pieces of music contain certain amount of repetition in all individual tones, their group of tones or longer units such as melodies is called chord sequences often termed as themes. Again all societies have vocal music and with few exceptions all have instrumental. The simplest instruments are sticks that are stuck together and used to produce sound with the use of body parts as in slapping the thighs and clapping. Such simple instruments are found in many tribal cultures. Certain highly complex instruments exhibit flexibility not only in pitch but also in timbre. On sitar for example one plucked string is used for melody and other plucked strings serve as drones while still others produce fainter sounds through sympathetic vibration. The modern technology has given birth to various types of instruments. The most widely used system distinguishes audio-phones in which the main vibrating units are the resonant bodies of the instructions themselves. For example membrano phones, chordo-phones, earphones and Electro-phones etc., etc.

Music everywhere is used to accompany other activities. For example, it is universally associated with dance. The association of music and poetry is so close that language and music are widely believed to have a common origin in the human history. In some societies it is a combination of religious services, secular, rituals theatrical productions and entertainment of all sorts. In some societies it is an activity carried on for its own sake. A couple of centuries ago it was an entertainment of the royals. Another less obvious information of music is social integration. It serves as a powerful symbol for some social groups. It also symbolises military, patriotic and funerary moods and events. In more general sense music may express the central social value of a society. In most of the world societies musicianship requires talent, special knowledge, training and efforts. There is no evidence that superior music may not rise in one society or community as opposed to another. It would rather be fair to state that various achievements are the results of difference in technology, in degree of specializations achieved and in the value placed at music in a given atmosphere. Individual talent is always recognized amongst most of the people & music specialists exist everywhere as informal leaders and singers in folk culture and in tribal societies. Somehow the musicians have rarely enjoyed great prestige even if music is regarded as indispensable everywhere. In early periods the musicians were regarded as undesirable social deviants. It still remains the case in some parts of the world and sub-continent especially in Pakistan.

With the above background and broad outline of musical domain, music of Lahore may be termed as music of different genres and levels of sophistication. At one point classical music is performed in concert halls for purely artistic reasons and at the other many kinds of functional rural music accompany the life cycle in city streets and agricultural rites in surrounding rural areas of city. In between are many other music genres of different kinds reflecting diversity of its people, their life style, their language, education and impact of the media which has brought into focus the disco music groups and POP singers with individual compositions just out of the fixed parameters by the connoisseurs of music dictionary.

CLASSICAL MUSIC

The origin of classical music may be traced to a Sanskrit treatise, which encompasses music as well. This is Ramayna. It is learnt that the ancient Hindu custom of singing the great epics is still maintained. Both in Mahabarat and Ramayna frequent reference is made to music and it is inferred that the art must have reached the advance stage of development during the centuries when these works were created. The Hindus are almost unanimous in their praise of music whereas Muslims disagree as to its merits. Some Muslims consider the art to be an incentive to evil doing but many Muslim rulers encouraged the performance of fine music. Emperor Akbar maintained large staff of musicians at his court and according to 'Aeen-e-Akbari' His Majesty paid much attention to music and was the patron of all who practised this enchanting art. There were numerous musicians at the court Hindus, Irani, Turani, Kashmiri, both men and women. The court musicians were arranged in seven divisions. One for each day in the week. Then followed a list of 36 principal musicians including singers and performers on the "Been" or "Vina". The 'Tamboora" another popular string instrument, 'Kanun' and the flute etc. This reference is being made specifically as Emperor Akbar made Lahore his capital from 1584 to 1598, and the 'Aeen-e-Akbari' was very much written in Lahore. In classical music there are seven pure tones and 12 impure tones. With surtis or quarter tones three forms were of gramas. The Shadja Grama, Ghandhara Grama and the Madhya Grama. The Ghandhara Grama is lost but the distribution of intervals in other gramas is as follows:-

Shadja Grama

Sa	Ri		Ga	Ma	Pa	Dha	Ni
1 2 3 4	1 2 3		1 2	1 2 3 4	1 2 3 4	1 2 3	1 2
Major tone	Minor tone		Semi tone	Major tone	Major tone	Minor	
Semi tone							

Madhyama Grama

Sa	Ri		Ga	Ma	Pa	Dha	Ni
1 2 3 4	1 2 3		1 2	1 2 3 4	1 2 3	1 2 3 4	1 2
Major tone	Minor tone		Semi tone	Major tone	Minor tone	Major	
Semi tone							

The term grama gradually fell into disuse, and was replaced by Raga, implying an arrangement of sounds. Ragas may be termed as 'Melody modes'. Although all scales now commence from a common tone; traces of the ancient gramas are still to be found in many ragas forms. Ragas are chiefly derived from tribal songs, poetic works, devotional songs and the innovative talent. The less respecting system on which certain ragas may be performed are still closely observed and it is considered offensive for a musician to perform an evening rag in the morning or vice versa. Certain ragas are associated with natural phenomenon. The Raga 'Megh Malhar' for instance is supposed to produce rain. Similarly Raga 'Deepik' has a relation with heat and flames etc.

A Raga can be performed both in free time and in measured time. In free time called 'Allap'. The melodic features of Ragas are exploded gradually in their natural rhythm or flow. In measured time it usually follows the Allap. One of several possible measures is called 'Taals'. The Taal consists of repeating number of time units (Maatra or Counts). That forms cyclical pattern. Then cycle specific points receive different degrees of stress. Taal thus involves both a qualitative element and a quantitative element (accent or stress). For example Jhap Taal has

10-time units divided into 2+3+2+3. There exist many cycle taals but its ranging from 6 to 16 units are most common. Usually going after an improvisation in Allap. A Taal is introduced by a set of composition, which followed by variations and improvisations is based melodically on the Raga but constrained rhythmically by the Taal. The emphasis of Allap depends upon the performer. In 'Khyal' the composition is generally considered subordinate to the improvisations. The Khyal appears to have replaced the 'Dhurpad' because it accommodates a greater display of virtuosity and imagination.

MUSIC INSTRUMENTS

The classical music instruments fall in two categories i.e. those that carry the main melody and those that accompany, in melodic instruments. The voice is considered pre-eminent. Of the many other melodic instruments the most prominent are the plucked lutes, sitar, sarod, vina, flute (bansari), shehnai, etc. The accompanying instruments have three functions. They provide a drone, the secondary melody and rhythmic support to keep time. The common instruments are 'Tamboora', Violin, Sarangi, Harmonium, double ended drum, Kanjri, Ghara, Tabla and Pakhavaja.

FOLK AND POPULAR MUSIC

Most of our population still in rural Lahore being a focal cultural-point, with all facilities for the performers and performances in cities the artists all along try establishing an independent repertoire for music concerts at city forums. The women songs often unaccompanied are sung at weddings generally, on births "Mehndi", and other festivals and other ladies functions. Male songs often accompanied are connected with devotional performances, particular festivals and occasions. Of late, "entertainment" through music purposes is being commercially exploited in the city and the performers and the public enjoy it on the basis of payment. The role of village entertainer has been eroded substantially and the economic constraints in rural area pushed the artists to the city. Consequently POP music groups have appeared who make presentations in the form of a dance, drama, with poor or no composition, playing to the sentimental tunes of the popular music, even if it is vulgar, sometimes. These songs which have no roots in the musical culture are short lived and disappear in no time. However these musical groups are indeed liked by teenage boys and girls. The latest trend is that POP groups perform folk songs in western lyrical style and use the modern orchestra with the help of large number of microphones and other sound gadgets.

Of the religious or devotional music 'Naat Goee' in the last decade or so has got a recognition in the state functions of the city which begin with recitation from the Holy Book, followed by Naat and then the routine proceedings. Of late the abandoned tradition of formal singing, dance performances on wedding ceremonies, occasional private performances, in-house functions and parties have also reportedly revived to some extent. But it is certainly in the higher rungs of the society and not a common feature.

After the Mughal period in Punjab and particularly in Lahore the music did not receive the court patronage. The Sikh Maharaja had a personal liking for the music and dance and he did have intimate individual connection with the singers and dancers and courtseans but no institutional arrangements appear to have existed for the teaching, training and practise of music. It was only on the individual level that people practised music for their living or requirement of some individuals out of the nobility. During the British period music emerged as a discipline and subject of Arts. In the late 19th century and the early 20th century it occupied a place in the curriculum and syllabus of the University of Lahore. The students were taught music and there was a sort of revival at least for those who liked it as an art if not commercial venture. The formation of Church choirs, military musical bands, formation of police bands, occasional concerts at auditoriums i.e. Lawrence Montgomery Hall, Railway auditorium, the auditoriums and forums of the Mission College (F.C. College) and Government College, lent support to this as a discipline. In addition to this State patronage was there which was, essentially, educational in character. The music also developed at the Hira Mandi where singers would engage teachers at individual level and also arranged imparting instructions to young girls. This tradition of engaging Ustads for teaching music in Hira Mandi leads to formation of an informal instructional institution from where great Ustads and exponents of classical music made their mark. These include singers like Barkat Ali Khan and Ustad Chhote Ghulam Ali Khan etc. The post partition period remained slack for sometime but the 60s saw it flourishing and quite a few female singers in the folk, classical and light classical, coming out of Hira Mandi captured the scene. Their list appears in some other Chapter of this Book. After enactment of Prohibition of Prostitution the music too got a set back but still it continued to grow as it had to cater to the needs of newly emerging media branches of radio, film and TV. The Lahore of 70s also found quite a few teaching academies for music both in public and private sector. The subject is also taught in schools and colleges. It is in the charter of duties as one of the functions of the Arts Councils. The local talent also learns a lot from visiting musical troupes, which perform in the city.

Lahore inherited musical traditions that go far back into history. Amir Khusrau solidly laid the foundation of classical music in the thirteenth century that introduced the Qawwali tradition. Since then this art has almost exclusively been in the hands of Muslim musicians. In the past three centuries there have been legions of Muslim Masters, and all the prominent Gharanas or schools of classical music were founded by them. The permutations and combinations of the twelve semi-tones, which form the universal basis of music, have been sifted and given individual names.

Broadly, music in Lahore can be classified as traditional or modern. Traditional music includes classical and semi-classical. The modern may include folk, light, Ghazal and Pop music.

The themes of Qawwali are mystical and moral, based on a deep love of the Holy Prophet and the Saints and a desire to be one with the Infinite. The rhythmic pattern of hypnotically persistent beats successfully employed to create a climax of hysterical ecstasy.

The patronage of music suddenly came to an end after the departure of nawabs after Partition. This was catastrophic. Masters like Ustad Ashiq Ali Khan, Ustad Abdul Waheed Khan, and Ustad Tawakkal Hussain Khan, died within a decade and the most famous classical singer, Ustad Badey Ghulam Ali Khan, migrated to India.

In the late Sixties classical music in Pakistan was at the lowest ebb. The accredited representatives of the recognized Gharanas of classical music were Ustad Salamat Ali Khan (Sham Chorasi) Ustad Fateh Ali Khan (Patiala), Ustad Ramzan Khan.

Traditional light classical music includes thumri, dadra, and ghazal. Of these, thumri, and dadra, being products of the times of the nawabs it no longer enjoys the former popularity. Farida Khanum and Iqbal Bano, two notable exponents of this art, are keeping it alive. But the signs are that these two forms of music will finally merge with the modern geet or song, a medium that has become the vehicle of modern Pakistani music. Since Farida Khanum and Iqbal Bano excel also at ghazal singing, this form of musical composition has been brought to perfection. Ghulam Ali and Mehdi Hassan are two other ghazal singers whose styles have captivated listeners the world over.

Sarangi is a string instrument perfectly adaptable to all the nuances of eastern music. The late Ustad Bundu Khan, Ustad Nabi Bakhsh Khan were great exponents of both the theory and practice of sarangi playing. It is acknowledged that a sarangi player of their calibre has not appeared on the musical scene of the sub-continent for centuries. The art of sarangi playing is slowly disappearing, a great loss to the instrumental classical heritage.

In Ustad Sharif Khan of Poonch, Lahore had an outstanding sitar player – he ranked among the finest sitar players of the sub-continent with Ravi Shankar and Vilayat Hussain. Outstanding among the folk instrumentalists of Pakistan include are Munir Sarhadi (Sarinda) Misri Khan Jamili and his disciple Khamisoo Khan

(Alghoza) Sain Allah Ditta Qadri (flute) and the late Sain Marna (Iktara) Arif Lohar on Chimta. They all performed with distinction abroad.

The folk music together with Qawwali and mystic music, represents the real culture of the masses, their love and hate, their joys and sorrows, their colourful ceremonies and festivities, and above all their spiritual entity. It includes all the songs and dances spontaneously originating among the common people. Like folk songs all over the world, these songs too are predominantly strophic in pattern – the same music is repeated for each stanza. This pattern is most suitable for simple lyrical pieces with regular metres and uniform stanzas; mahiya, gidda and Jugni are some of them.

Similarly the epic love poetry of Heer Ranjha and Mirza Sahibaan and mystic poetry of Mian Muhammad & Sultan Bahu are sung in specific mode (sur) and have their own distinct style of presentation. Present folk artists like Arif Lohar, Reshman, Hamid Ali Bela, Shaukat Ali and Ata Ulla Khan Isa Khelvi have performed all over the world. Modern singing is characterized by the use of Western instruments and is wholly confined to light music. There have been no modern trends in classical music. Lately electronic instruments have also come into vogue.

Because of the extemporaneous nature of classical music and the improvisation freely employed in the exposition of classical ragas, the masters never felt the need for a notation system. The teaching of music was oral. Recently however, composers have acutely felt the need for notation. Instead of evolving an indigenous system, however, the Western notational technique was introduced and is being generally used, even though it has proved inadequate for classical music. After the death of Ustad Muhammad Sharif Khan his son Ashraf Sharif has established himself as a really good sitar player. Lahore can genuinely hope of him to replace his father.

Following is the list of Artists(Music) who made a mark in Lahore during the last five decades. Some of them came from Tibbi Area and some otherwise:-

Abdul Latif Khan
Abdul Waheed Khan
Akhtar Ali Khan
Akhtar Hussain Khan
Ali Bakhsh Khan
Amanat Ali Khan
Amanat Ali Khan Fateh Ali Khan
Amjad Ali Khan
Asad Amanat Ali Khan
Ashiq Ali Khan

Imtiaz Ali Khan
Johar Amanat Ali Khan
Kale Khan
Kh. Khurshid Anwar
Machhar Khan
Mian Ilum-ud-Din
Mubarik Ali Khan
Murad Ali Khan
Nazakat Ali Salamat Ali Khan

Badar uz Zaman
Barey Ghulam Ali Khan
Basharat Ali
Bhai Arora
Bhai Lal
Chhote Ashiq Ali Khan
Chhote Ghulam Ali Khan
Feroze Nizami
Ghulam Ali
Ghulam Haider Khan
Ghulam Hassan Shaggan
Ghulam Hussain Khan

Ghulam Rasool Khan
Hameed Ali Khan Fateh Ali Khan
Hamid Ali Khan
Hussain Bakhsh Guloo

Payare Khan
Qadir Ali Shaggan
Rafaqat Ali Khan
Rafique Ghazanvi
Riaz Khan
Rustam Fateh Ali Khan
Safdar Hussain Khan
Salamat Ali Khan
Saleem Hussain Khan
Sardar Khan
Sharafat Ali Khan
Sultan Fateh Ali Khan

Tassaq Ali Khan
Umeed Ali Khan
Zakir Ali Khan, Akhtar Ali Khan

LIGHT MUSIC SINGERS

Abdul Sattar
Abdus-Shakoor Bedil
Abrar ul Haq
Ali Bakhsh Kasuri
Ali Bakhsh Zahoor
Anwar Rafi
Arif Lohar
Barkat Ali Gotewala
Barkat Ali Khan
Bashir Mahi
Bashir Niaz
Fazal Hussain
Fida Hussain
Ghulam Abbas
Habib Ali
Hamid Ali Bela
Imdad Hussain

Inayat Abid

Inayat Hussain Bhatti
Jamil Anjum
Mehdi Hassan
Muhammad Anees
Muneer Hussain
Munir Hussain
Nazir Amritsari
Niaz Hussain
Pervaiz Mehdi
Raja Ali
S.M. Batish
Sain Akhtar
Salim Raza
Salman Hameed
Shahzad Nagi
Tahir Iqbal
Zahoor Hussain

Zareef

FEMALE SINGERS

Afshan
Anwar Bai
Arifa Siddiqui
Asha Posley

Noor Jahan
Noor Jahan Junior
Raeesa Khanum
Rehana Yasmeen

Bahar Bakhsh

Baali Jatti

Balquees Khanum

Eidan Bai Hassain Wali

Eiden Bai Akhian Wali

Fareeda Khanum

Humera Channa

Iffat Sami

Inayat Bai Derwali

Iqbal Bano

Irene Parveen

Kausar Parveen

Khurshid Bai

Mala Begum

Malika Pukhraj

Mukhtar Begum Amristari

Munnawar Sultana

Mussarat Sami

Nasim Begum Amritsari

Nazir Begum

Rifat Aisha

Roshan Ara Begum

Rubina Qureshi

Sardar Bai

Shabnam Majeed

Shahida Aziz

Shahida Perveen

Shamshad Begum

Shamshad Kausar

Suriya Khanum

Tahira Syed

Tassawar Khanum

Ummat-ur-Rashid

Waheeda Khanum

Zahida Parveen

Zarqa

Zeb-un-Nisa

Zeenat Begum

Zil-e-Huma

Zubaida Khanum

SARANGI PLAYERS

Baba Ali Bakhsh

Balley Khan

Barkat Ali

Buddhey Khan Kasuri

Chhote Kaley Khan

Chunnu Khan

Fazal Elahi

Ghulam Muhammad Kasuri

Gul Muhammad Alias Gullu

Haider Bakhsh Faloosa

Hussain Bakhsh

Jhandu Khan

Mehr Din Khurshid

Nabi Dad Khan

Nathu Khan

Phathu Khan

TABLA PLAYERS

Akhtar Ali

Akhtar Hussain Khalifa

Allah Rakha

Altaf Hussain

Buddhey Khan

Faqir Bakhsh Peshawari

Fateh Din Guldam

Fazal Hussain Kasuri

Khadim Hussain

Manzoor Hussain

Miran Bakhsh Gil Walia

Muhammad Iqbal

Nabi Bakhsh Kalrya

Qadir Bakhsh

Sadiq Hussain Dhati Dhara

Safdar Ali

Haji Fida Hussain

Imdad Hussain

Inayat Khan

Irshad Ali

Janul Hassan

Karam Elahi Kasuri

Karim Bakhsh

Shafqat Ali

Shaukat Hussain

Talib Hussain

Tufail Ali

Ustad Niaz Ali

Zaffar Hussain

SITAR PLAYERS

Abdul Latif Khan

Ashraf Sharif Khan

Athar
Hussain

Farukh Bashir

Fateh Ali Khan Patialwi

Ijaz Hussain

Majid Khan

Manzoor Hussain

Muhammad.Alam

Muhammad Saleem

Muzafar Akbar Khan

Sharif Khan Poonch Waley

Siraj Ahmad Qureshi

QAWWALS

Abdul Raheem Fareedi

Ali Bakhsh Khan

Mubarik Ali Khan Fateh Ali Khan

Muhammad Boota Gegum Koti

Santoo Khan

Bashir Ahmad Fareedi

Rashid Ahmad

Muhammad Ali Fareedi

Hafiz Atta Muhammad

Bhai Bora

Nusrat Fateh Ali Khan

Ghulam Farid Maqbool Sabri

Aziz Mian

Badr Miandad

Mehr Ali Sher Ali

Ghulam Hussain/Qurban Hussain

Bakhshi Salamat

MUSIC DIRECTORS

Akhtar Hussain

Akhtar Hussain Akhiyan

Ashiq Hussain

Baba G. A. Chishti

Bashir Wazir

Habib Hussain

Khadim Hussain Faizi

Khalid Ahmad

Khalid Asghar

M. Ashraf

M. Javaid

Musleh-ud-Din

Master Inayat Hussain

Mohsin Raza

Muhammad Ali

Muhammad Asrar Ahmad

Rashid Atray

Rahman Varma

Sabbir Hussain

Safdar Hussain

Safdar Niaz

Salim Iqbal

Shehryar Mian

Shehryar

Master Abdullah
Master Ghulam Ahmad Chishti
Master Ghulam Haider

Taskeen Chishti
Tassadaq Hussain
Tufail Farooqi

CLARINET PLAYERS

Baqar Hussain
Feroze-ud-Din
Master Alamgir
Master Sohni
Muhammad Shafi

Muhammad Sharif
Muhammad Siddiq
Saddiq Ali Mando
Ulfat Hussain

PIANO PLAYERS

Master Allah Divya
Master Inayat Hussain

Master Sadiq Ali

FLUTE PLAYERS

Arif Jafari
Baqar Hussan
Haji Umar Hayat
Inayat Ali

Khadim Hussain Haidri
Sain Allah Ditta
Sain Ditta Qadiri
Sain Sadiq Ali

SAROD PLAYERS

Bhai Mehr

Faiz Fareed

VIOLINIST

Akram Farooqi
Kafait Hussain
Asghar Ali
Javaid Iqbal
Khalid Fareedi

Khalid Pervaiz
Muhammad Sadiq
Sardar Latif
Sardar Hussain Hashmi

FOLK SINGERS

Ashiq Jat
Fazal Jat Abbas Jat
Tariq Lohar
Muhammad Siddique

Muhammad Younis
Manzor Hussain Bhatti
Pathane Khan

DANCE

The dances of Lahore have graduated to the stage from the marble floors of the Mughal courts, on the one hand, and the green and golden fields on the other: the genre of the one is classical, that of the other, folk. Classical dance acquired a wider appeal when the Mughals opened the gates of their palaces to the dancers from Hindu temples. The transition from the skill or appeasing inanimate gods to the art of pleasing a live audience led to modification, adaptation and, eventually, to standardization.

Among the classical dances, Kathak is highly praised. Katha means story, and Kathak has its root in this word, evolved from a simple dance form of telling a story to a complicated series of rhythmic patterns, brilliant variations heightened by flawless timing. With the development of the technique, the pauses of silence began to be used to enhance the exciting movements of lightening pirouettes. The "boles" (rhythmic syllables) which are spoken during the dance have become a highly technical series of word patterns. Intricate hand movements and foot work, facial expression, use of the eyes and the language of gesture took many years of study with learned masters, and thus the technique survives today.

The impact of the Mughals on Kathak was so pervasive that the costumes of the royal courts even provided patterns and styles for its dancers. The dress, worn to this day, consists of brightly-coloured; tight-fitting trousers under a diaphanous costume called 'angrakha'. The soft, flowing bell shaped shirt is full length and like the sleeves, is unlined. Women wear an embroidered waistcoat to emphasize their natural contours.

A singer and one, two or occasionally more instrumentalists provide the musical accompaniment of Kathak. One provides the melody and the other rhythm. The most essential instrument is the tabla (a pair of small upright drums). The 'refrain' is the repetition of a musical phrase within a given time-scale called taal. Folk dances generally follow the cycle of the seasons, portraying the mood and emotions of the people tending the soil, harvesting the yield and winnowing or processing it through machinery. In all its varied forms of exultation, folk dancing reflects the element of organic oneness and ethnic continuity characteristic of the country. Jhoomar and Luddi for instance are popular throughout slight variations in formation providing local colour.

'Jhoomar' (meaning spinning, or going round and round) is danced in a circle accompanied by clapping synchronized with the movement of the feet, the swirl of the body and the beat of the rhythm. As the dance progresses, the participants break into different forms of patterns, until a crescendo is reached and the circle is reformed through a graduated process of reversal. Jhoomar is popular with women, but men dance it with equal facility and greater vigour.

Both men and women dance 'Luddi', but separately. Any kind of celebration, whether it is a wedding or a victory in a wrestling match, it is an occasion enough for luddi. It is danced most frequently when the fields have been prepared for sowing. While the men's version is fast, the women's is slower and more graceful. The women, positioned in a circle, click their fingers and clap their

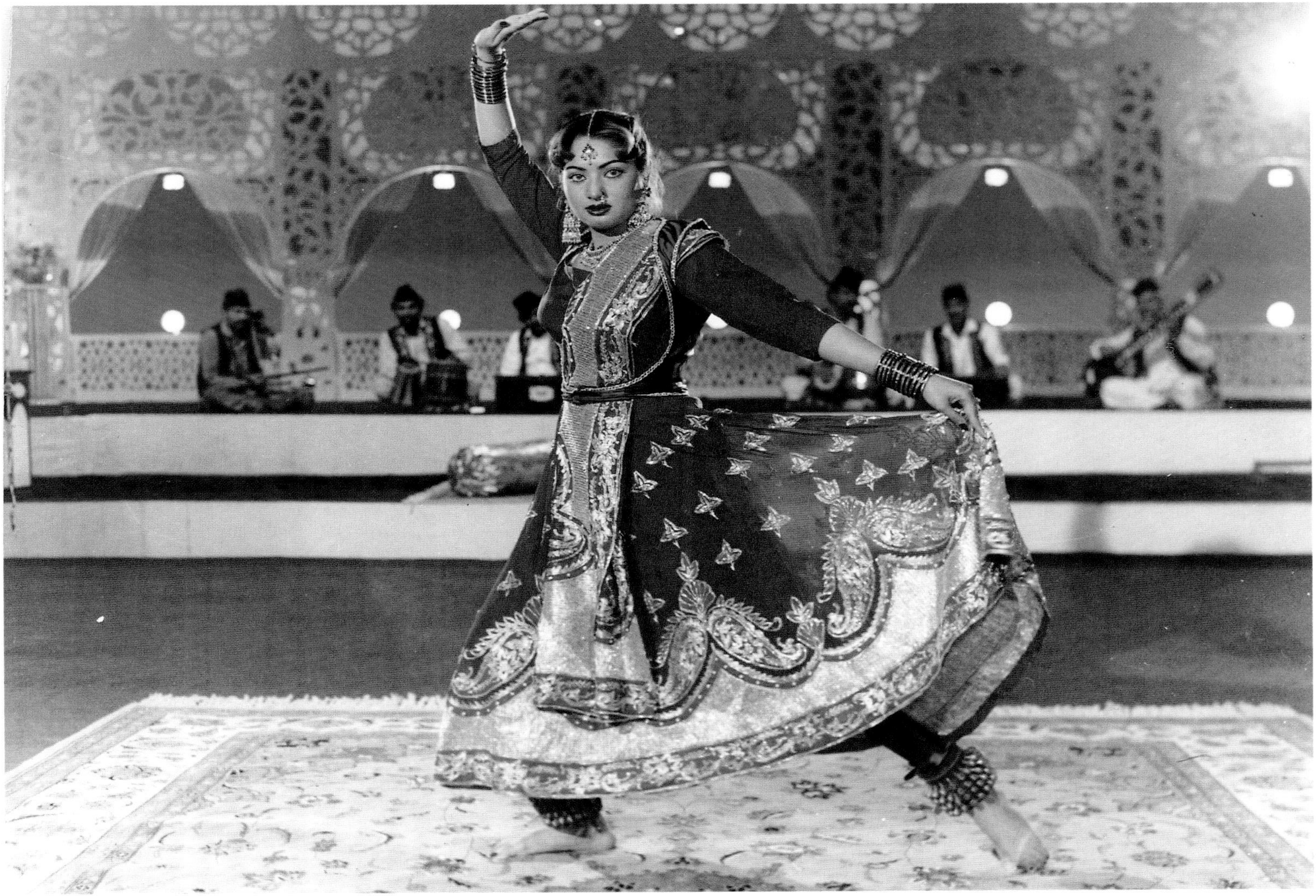

Dance

hands, moving by short jumps and half-turns, accelerating their rhythms according to the beat of the drummer playing on the dholak (oblong drum).

Another popular dance, mostly for women, is 'Sammi'. It has a slow movement accompanied by a sad song associated with the tragic love story of Princess 'Sammi' and Prince 'Dhola'. To the beat of a somewhat subdued drum, the dancer's hand and foot movements follow a well-drilled routine involving periodic clapping and, for variation, at times the clicking of sticks held in each hand.

'Bhangra' is also another remarkable folk-dance. Usually danced at the onset of spring to celebrate the harvesting season, it is a favourite of the Punjabi peasant. It is punctuated by a song and at the end of every line the drum thunders. The last line of the song is taken up by all the dancers and repeated in a chorus. Bhangra varies from one place to another and is more of a spontaneous expression of joy than a dance with formalized steps. Dancers surround the drummer in a circle, each with his own individual steps, shout, wriggle their shoulders, and swirl on one foot, often holding a piece of cloth with both hands over their heads.

In Lahore the Government through the Punjab Arts Council did form a troupe of female and male dancers who worked from 1975 to 1982. But due to a campaign in the press about its being un-Islamic, the female troupe was banned. All these dances are performed in the Lahore city on different occasions. It could be a marriage party, a friends feast, national festival, or performances for the visiting state guests. Dance is the most important element of the cultural life of a place and the international language of any country and we need to partronize the same at a much better level than the hidden corners of Hira Mandi or private parlours.

11

AMUSEMENTS, FUN, AKHARAS AND TAKYAS

Amusement is a requirement of each social set up. Whenever any society evolves through a process of time it develops its amusement to enjoy themselves after the work to earn livelihood. It is, however, generally a feature of spare time. We have seen elsewhere that amusements include games, singing, dancing, reading, writing, gambling, smoking, intoxicating and of course dining. These have continued to exist in all the societies in peace time except war, even those sometime after the wars were decided and some time, on the result of a fight or wrestling between warriors.

We know that during the Sultanate period Polo was played and Sultan Qutab ud Din Aibak died during this game in Lahore. This also continued along with the horse riding and hunting as a past time during the Mughal period. Of course singing and other literary pursuits also received patronage of the court during various periods. The conditions slightly differed as the Sikhs had occupied during anarchy by loot without any organised political background or training. They indulged in low-level practices. The holding of dance parties was most favourite amusement of the Sikhs given to voluptuousness and debauchery. The Sikhs would show their wealth by such festive entertainments to their friends and allies. The poor and those without money would spend their leisurely hours by taking 'Bhung' and its other formats. Opium eating was also one of their favourite enjoyment. Chess and playing cards was also common. The position and atmosphere however changed during the British period. Education was regulated, schools and colleges opened and the living became more civilized due to better economic, and the social intercourse and attitude towards amusement and living of the common man changed.

Cricket started to be played in early sixties of the 19th century after British occupation of Lahore and the first cricket ground in city was the Minto Park, near the fort where Europeans used to play the game. Racing and Polo also continued side by side. There was the Anarkali Cricket Club whose members were mostly drawn from the Clerical Staff of the offices. Billiard was also played and matches were also held in the Lawrence Hall. Tennis courts also came into being but all these games were generally supervised, conducted and participated by Europeans working in the Government. Mr. A. C. Seymour of the Provincial Civil Service has the credit of introducing Football in Lahore. He raised a team from the Punjab Volunteers. The first match was between Lahore and Ferozepur. Soccer was another game, which soon got popular in Lahore and there were teams from Railway Employees and Punjab Volunteers who held matches. Hockey was also introduced in the later period and became popular with Lahoris.

WRESTLING

Wrestling is a favourite amusement with the young Lahoris. Unlike the English game, the attack is not confined to parts of the body above the waist; but the combatants, two at a time, use their strength freely, and one endeavors, by dexterous tricks, to throw the other so that his back may touch the ground flat, and as soon as he succeeds in his attempt, the game is won. The trial of skill is made before a large assembly of people in the open air. The moment the victory is gained, the louder Wah Wah! (Bravo! Bravo!) from the enthusiastic and admiring multitude fills the air. The victor is lifted up by the people of his party, riding on the shoulders of another man, is carried in triumph, and followed by a band of musicians, round the assembled multitude, whom he salutes with both hands, the spectators, on their part, would crown him with wreaths of flowers, in acknowledgement of his prowess, and present to him with a sum of money which is collected for the purpose. The Rajas of various states, in pre-partition times were great patrons of this game and engaged the wrestlers.

In addition to these regular games reading of light literature, exchange of visits between the families and friends was a common feature. Smoking etc. was also a pastime of the middle class, retired and slightly educated people of the city. Taking drugs (Bhang, Charas, Opium) and liquor was confined to illiterate classes. Some people were used to sniffing. Athletics at the Akharas and other out-door games i.e. lifting, throwing heavy weights were also the evening outlet of youngsters. Kabbadi was also occasionally played in the open in the after-noon especially during rainy seasons. Kite flying, skilful turning of wrist and 'tapil' in the moonlit nights were also amongst the amusement of the city. While not falling strictly in the category of amusement, another pastime and prevalent practice in the city was animal fighting. This included calf and ram-fighting etc., around open spaces in the town or its vicinity. Large crowds used to assemble on the occasion and the people took great delight in watching the proceedings with keen interest when actual fight between birds or animals took place. There was lot of excitement, which ensued, when the game was over. They were always betting when professionals were participating in these fighting. Horse races were also held but were poorly organised and also without betting.

Gambling in various forms some time with cards and with dice was popular amongst the people of wealthier classes. Hawking was also regarded a particular field sport by the rich and wealthy. Hounds were also kept to run after deer (now after rabbits) or to bring the wild bore to bay. All the above games still exist in one form or the other except that their modes have changed due to availability of time, resources, space, participants, teams and above all freedom in some cases. The walled city amusements if exclusively described took the following shape.

FUN FAIRS, GAMES,

In old Lahore traditionally before partition, there were plenty of games and pastimes, fairs and festivals, recreations and diversions to keep one amused all the year round. One had to walk into the street to be entertained by one or the other professional jugglers, madaris (magicians), bazigars (acrobats), bhands (jesters), animal and bird tamers, snake charmers, singers. The tensions of life were always diverted by these joyful diversions and people had enough time to stand and stare. Lahore like a magnet had drawn them to its environs and kept them happy by its generous patronage.

In the early 19th century the city dwellers were more simple, straight and innocent. They lived as a well knit community without any consciousness of caste and creed. The children, both boys and girls, played together with earthenware, toys, and wooden "gaind-balla" (ball and bat), shared the "peeng" or jhula jhulna (swing) and competed in 'kirhi-kahra', a game in which the participants jump on one leg, pushing a piece of stone through a rectangular area divided into eight sections drawn on the floor with charcoal or chalk. Another favourite game was 'lukanmichi' or hide and seek, in which the children used to hide themselves as one of them singing 'luk chhup jana, makai da dana, raje di beti aai a', pursues them. Up to the age of eight or ten, boys were allowed to play with girls. Thereafter they played different games. The boys moved on to gulli-danda and kanchas (marbles) and the girls took to playing with dolls, to rope skipping and kiklis. The latter involved jumping round in pairs with clasped hands and joined feet moving in unison. Another girl's game was playing with tiny stonepieces called 'gitas'. The boy's gulli-danda is a sport demanding a high degree of skill, quick reflexes, exceptional hand-to-eye coordination, strong wrists and a powerful grasp. Similarly, playing with kanchas or shooting small marbles involves placing a marble ball against the tip of the left forefinger, which is drawn back and quickly released so as to hit the ball against which the blow is intended. The game demands an ability to judge distances and strike the target with precision. Kite

Warestling

flying, was an extremely popular sport during winter months. (Dealt with in detail in another chapter). Another popular pastime was spinning a "latoo" or top by pulling a cotton string wound at its bottom. Tops were especially finished by expert craftsmen who would rub its edges with such precision as to make them spin fast for 15 to 20 minutes.

Girls amused themselves with dolls which, though without the waxy skin (plastic made) and woolly hair of modern makes, were cared for and loved by their young owners. Perhaps the game young girls found most exciting was the marriage of their dolls-guddis and guddas-with those of their playmates. The celebrations included all the traditional ceremonies of mangni (engagement) and shadi (wedding) they had heard so much about from the women around them. They would collect a dowry for the bride and go through the entire exercise of holding negotiations about the reception of the barat and its departure. The game was played in all seriousness, the older girls acting as mothers and aunts, and preparing imitations of special wedding dishes.

Before partition the festivals and fairs, which provided a delightful diversion for the people, were also events of social significance. Celebrated with pomp and show, Lorhi, Basant, Holi, Baisakhi, Dasehra, Diwali, Eid, Moharram and Gurpurav, were symbols of a composite culture for all communities who participated in them. Religious processions attracted large crowds of people who would line up in bazars and stand on balconies of houses to be able to witness them. The great attraction (by Hindus) was the procession of jhankis or floats elaborately set up on bullock-carts with a miniature stage where amateur artists would enact incidents from the Ramayna. Some of the Jhankis depicted colourful scenes from the epic. Seated on them were also singers who entertained the surging crowds. The onlookers used to occupy vantage points in bazars, hours before the arrival of the processions and kept a night vigil to witness the full show, which usually concluded at dawn. People spent lavishly during the festivals, which promoted social intercourse and communal harmony.

The festivals were also occasions for holding "Dangls" (wrestling matches) which carried attractive prizes. "Kushti" (wrestling) was a popular sport and a number of "Akharas" were run by renowned Pehlwans (wrestlers) in different parts of the city. It required several years of hard training to become a Pehlwan, also a special diet of energy-yielding almonds and milk products. The Pehlwans of Lahore were famous all over the country for their physical strength and ingenious daos (holds) to defeat the adversary. Wrestling matches were held in the open air before a large assembly of people. The moment one of the wrestlers succeeded in knocking his adversary flat on his back he was acclaimed a victor and loud cries of wah, wah (bravo) from the enthusiastic and admiring multitude would fill the air.

The victor was lifted and, riding on the shoulders of one of his supporters was carried in triumph followed by a band of musicians. The spectators on their part would crown him with wreaths of flowers. The city was proud of its Rustam-e-Zaman, the world champion Gama Pehlwan, who defeated Zbysco at Patiala in 1928.

The principal fairs or "Melas" of Lahore were those of Baisakhi, Bhadarkali, Basant, Dasehra, Chiraghan, and Kadmon ka Mela. The Baisakhi "Mela" was held in April on the banks of the Ravi where people in thousands took a bath in the river. The great Hindu fair of Bhadarkali was held in Mauza Niaz Beg at Devi Mandar in the month of June. In January-February was organised the Basant "Mela" in the precincts of the mausoleum of Madho Lal Hussain near the Shalamar Gardens which attracted large crowds belonging to all communities. "Kadmon-ka-Mela" held at the tomb of Sakhi Sarwar in Anarkali in February attracted professional drummers who amused the young and the old with their music and dance. The fair of Dasehra, which lasted for eight days, was held at Minto Park, concluding with the burning of the effigies of Ravan and his clan.

All these fairs which were periodically held at appointed places presented lively scenes. Dressed in colourful costumes, people of all communities assembled there for fun and laughter and enjoyed themselves heartily. They looked forward to these occasions with excitement and saved money to buy playthings and other novelties. The shopkeepers from the city would set up stalls of sweetmeats, toys, utensils, fruits and eatables of various kinds. There were magicians, jugglers, acrobats, mimics, actors, singers and dancers, who entertained the crowds with their performances, receiving rewards for the display of their skills. Full of mirth and merriment, the fairs were attended in large numbers enthusiastically.For fun and amusement, one did not have to wait for fairs and festivals. Near at hand were diverse sources of entertainment. There was the "bunderwala" beating his hand-drum to catch the attention of children. He always had two performing monkeys dressed up as a man and a woman. Not to be left behind was the "reechhwala" with his tamed bear who would dance to the tune of his drum. One could not miss the snake-charmer who was always in demand by spectators keen to see a fight between the mongoose and the snake, or the cobra dancing to the tune of the gourd pipe which could be an awe-inspiring experience. The snake charmer would also offer his services for catching serpents that might be hiding in houses. He claimed to do so by playing the pipe "Been". Sometimes he carried around his neck pythons rolling down onto his arms. This was a frightening sight indeed. It seemed there was some kind of affinity between the snake charmer and his snakes who always answered the call of his pipe. The snake charmer also claimed to possess antidotes to snake bite. He sold stones, which were supposed to suck out poison from the bitten spot.

Street jugglers or madaris were a class of entertainers who had sleight of hand as their forte. A "madari" would always be accompanied by a young lad called "Bacha Jamura" who would keep talking to the spectators while the juggler showed his bag of tricks. To the utter amazement of the bystanders, he would take a pinch of dust in his palm and transform it into a silver rupee/coin in a jiffy by the use of his magic wand. Holding the audience spellbound, he would suddenly begin passing the hat. He rarely failed to collect enough money. Then he would start performing his other tricks; changing pebbles into birds, birds into eggs, eggs into plants. He would cough out several metal balls from his mouth one after another, as also thread beads with his tongue. The most exciting of the tricks was the 'vanishing' act in which Jamura would squeeze himself into a round basket two feet high and three feet in circumference. The basket, when opened, would be found empty. Some jugglers could even emit flames from their mouths and pierce their tongues with iron needles, and roses/flowers and colourful pieces of cloth coming out from the mouth.

Bazigars (acrobats) were another class of entertainers who amused people with their feats of skill and daring. One was wonder-struck to witness the agility and pliability of body of these people. One of them who bore on his shoulders six men standing in twos, one above another. There were others who could walk on a rope suspended over twenty feet above the ground. They even ran upside down on the strength of their palms. A popular entertainment especially for children was the puppet show staged by puppeteers who usually visited Lahore during the summer season from Rajasthan. Expertly manipulated by wires and strings, puppet shows were given at street corners where children would assemble and listen to ballads and songs narrating the tales of the kings and queens of Rajasthan.One also came across Chinese groups performing acrobatic feats. One could see trained lads rotating porcelain plates balanced on bamboo sticks held by the toes or placed on the forehead, and turning and twisting the body backwards to pick up straws with the eyelids.

Bhands (jesters) were yet another group of entertainers who appeared from nowhere whenever there was a festive occasion in a family, such as an engagement, a wedding, or childbirth. There were jesters and mimics who spared neither the young nor the old. They would demand a reward according to the status of the family, employing all kinds of bargaining tactics and usually having their own way. Similarly, eunuchs group was a familiar sight on these occasions. They would sing in praise of every member of the family, praying for the long life and prosperity of the newly born or the wedded couple. No one dared to criticise them, for once enraged; they would shower abuses on one and all. When rewarded to their satisfaction, they would sing and dance mimicking professional dancing girls. Their presence on such festive occasions was considered auspicious, the hosts treating them with kindness and generosity. During winter months, folk dancers form Kangra in their attractive hill costumes would sing and dance, revolve large plates balanced on sticks, throw them up in the air and catch them again with the sticks still revolving in rapid motion.

The Bhand shows are the only amusement which has prospered over a period of time and especially after the partition and most of other games are either on decline or extinct.

Travelling circuses and carnival companies when they visited Lahore provided another kind of entertainment. Circus shows were a novelty and attracted people of all ages. Carnivals offered a veritable feast for gamblers, until these were banned by the Government in the mid-thirties. Carnival companies had an extra attraction of amusement parks with giant wheels, swings, and merry-go-rounds. These amusement parks were later merged with the periodic exhibitions held in Lahore. A great novelty that appeared on the scene in 1935 was the dodgem car. It was a mighty attraction at amusement parks and youngsters would make a beeline to take their turn. Consisting of small electrically powered cars, the patrons would drive and try to bump other cars while avoiding being bumped by others. It was a thrilling experience, which in those days cost four annas for a ten-minute ride. Many a daring feat was shown on these occasions. Another was the driving of a motorcycle on the walls of a specially constructed wooden well, called the (maut ke kunwan) well of death, and the other was a daring jump into a watertank from a height of 65 feet by a stuntman after setting himself aflame.

The amusements, fun and games differ with those prevalent in Lahore during pre-partition days. The pace of life has so changed that there is hardly any time left with the people for these enjoyments. Some traditional games and amusements are still in existence but in most invisible condition. These do not make a regular phenomenon of city streets. Some of the items are almost disappearing. These include the acrobatic groups commonly known as (Bazigar) Chinese performers and mixed children play game Lukanmichi in the evening. The pattern of fairs and games has differed through evolutionary process. The small fairs, which were a routine feature of city on one weekend here and on the other weekend there, are non-existent. Life has become so busy due to over population constraints of money, and acute shortage of time that these fairs have either disappeared totally or emerged in a different shape. The people now go out on picnics in-groups of friends and families for a day out in parks, around historical monuments and others on such quite, shady and exclusive places. One would find daily big crowds in and around Yadgar-e-Pakistan, old Minto Park especially in the evening busy in kite flying, having group gatherings and families for a walk in grounds. The Hazoori Bagh in between Fort and Badhashi Mosque is daily busy. Mushaira programme in the afternoon and 'Dastan Go" functions. The Shalamar, Jallo Park, Lahore Park, Jahangir Tomb, Baradari, Iqbal Town Park, Bagh-e-Jinnah (Lawrence Gardems) Race Course Park, Liberty Park and other spots are full of people having an outing on weekends and on holidays. The education and technological advancement has brought another change in the amusements for the people. TV and Radio Programmes have replaced the routine street singers. Air-conditioned cinema houses have replaced the Talkies with the latest films being shown from around the world. The evening games of the children have been replaced by regular theatrical shows being produced at different auditoriums of the government and private managements. There are a couple of clubs where gentry have their games, and other evening programmes. While wrestling is traditionally practised in some of the "Akharas" around the city and also partly looked after by Government Departments. Cricket has emerged as the most popular game in the city. Youngsters on holidays, weekends even otherwise are busy playing cricket matches. Most of the grounds are booked for matches between different teams and even the streets of the city roads are not spared by young children who play and practise in the hope to join one of the teams, at the city, provincial or National level. The hockey is the second game. Both for hockey and cricket there are proper stadiums, now located at Ferozepur Road where International matches are annually held. Full-fledged Department of Sports looks after some grounds and matches in the city on festive occasions. These include Kabbadi, Volleyball, Football, Badminton, Wrestling etc., etc.

Golf is also played in the city in the Lahore Gymkhana Club and Railway Club but it is a game of the rich. A couple of Squash courts are available, again monoplised by a few and not for the common man. The jesters do perform on marriages but the fun on barats, going on horses is extinct. The venue has shifted from Mohallahs to Marriage Halls and hotels.

Above all the Television has played havoc and interfered in the centuries old amusements. It has squeezed the entire world programming through Dish Antenna. There are many programmes with a lot of variety for each age group and most of the people spend the evenings at homes.

Any account of Lahore will not be complete if a reference is not made to the 'Baithaks' 'Takyas'and 'Akharas' of Lahore. "Takya" literally means abode of Faqir or pillow Bolster used as support. Lahore is known through out history as a city of Grandeur. These gardens entail some interesting aspects and that is the use of certain places outside the city shrouded in trees known as 'Takyas'. These takyas were generally located outside the city gates and some slightly in distant gardens. Generally a Faqir used to live in the Takya permanently and people would go from the surrounding areas for exercise, just relaxation or to vile away time. Some times the old and young would equally visit these places and spend their free times in these 'Takyas'. The essentials of Takyas are a well, bathroom, some durries (mats) and some other games sort of thing such as chess, cards and luddo etc. Due to the place being shady, cool, availability of water and bathroom, these were also used for other game purposes as also for condolence meetings. Reportedly the elders of the Mohallah or locality also used to get together here for receiving and deciding complaints. It is learnt that each Takya had also the facilities of a small special area attached where youngsters in the early mornings or in the afternoon, would take exercises. These Takyas served the purpose of Health clubs as also Civic Centres in the modern terminology. One of the important function entrusted to these Takyas was that when the city doors were closed, in the evenings, those coming from outside could stay for the night on the Takyas of the adjoining locality. He would of course move on the next day but there were instances when a person had no relation or acquaintance he could stay for a longer period at the Takya. The Faqir of the Takya was looked after by contributions by philanthropists of the area.

With the passage of time these institutions of Takyas have almost vanished except for only a few points where green trees with water tap, bath and toilets exist. Most of these places have been grabbed by "Qabza Groups." Those supporting this most economical centre catering to various routine needs of people have withdrawn. The old Takyas of the Lahore were as under:-

TAKYAS

The Takya is now an out-dated word and a few know the real places of Takyas in the history of Lahore. If at all a few exist in the city these are used by the addicts and no gentleman would like to go and sit there. The existing Takyas are as under:-

Takya Sabir Shah	Takya Imli Wala
Takya Bhoorey Sain	Takya Taje Shah
Takya Sher Ali	Takya Meeasian
Takya Balmeekian	Takya Khotian Wala
Takya Peer Makki	Takya Lalu Sain
Takya Zaildaran	Takya Kabootar Shah
Takya Saidey Shah	Takya Gudi Sain
Takya Gandi Peer	Takya Sher Shah Wali
Takya Khirki Peer	Takya Jangi

Takya Qutub Shah	Takya Nathe Shah
Takya Sarwar Shah	Takya Khai Wala
Takya Peeraz Ghalib	Takya Surma Sain
Takiya Ghudu Shah	Takya Chet Ram
Takya Maskeen Sain	Takya Sadhoonan

Of the surviving points these are no Takyas. Infact rather these are hiding places of opium caters, drunkards and heroin sniffers. They are generally found in the graveyard continuing with the activity of smoking, Bhang, Charas and gambling etc., etc. Due to these problems the gentry usually avoid visiting such places. Even otherwise with the growth of western education and development, people found other amusement for their free time.

AKHARAS

Wrestling is a game which has always remained important throughout history; Greece, Rome, Egypt, Persia and India were always the centres of this sport and the best wrestlers were considered to be the best commanders and infact at times the Wars were decided on the basis of fights between two wrestlers. In the Sub-continent the wrestling continued as an art since ancient times. For the purpose of teaching and imparting instructions to the youngsters, places were developed around cities with water facility, better and shady trees where the best of the Instructors would impart instructions in the art of wrestling. These places were known as 'Akharas' Lahore as historic place is known for the names of wrestlers the world over. These wrestlers – won many matches both in and outside the country. There were three groups of Wrestlers and Pehlwans commonly known as Kaluwala, Noorwala and Kotwala in Lahore. Various wrestling matches were organized between the trainees and professional wrestlers and at different Akharas. Well known people from different schools of thought used to come to attend these wrestling matches commonly known as 'Dangls'. While on the one hand a great art was being introduced at Akharas it was a useful and safe outlet channeling the energy of the youth who would spend their spare times in this exercise instead of indulging into evil pursuits. The main Akharas of the old Lahore were as under:

The Akharas are almost non-existent except a few. Details of the Akharas as listed by 'Naqoosh' in its 'Lahore Number' brought out in 1962 is as under:-

Akhara Khalifa Boota	Akhara Gama and Imam Bakhsh Pehlwans
Akhara Takya Tajey Shah	Akhara Bandar Shah
Akhara Chanan Qasai	Akhara Khalifa Hussaina
Akhara Ustad Shish Gar	Akhara Takya Nathey Shah
Akhara Nazd Pul Misri Shah	Akhara Takya Khotian Wala
Akhara Veyam Shala (used by Bholu,	Akhara Chowk Barf Khana

Aslam, Akram, Goga and Azam
Pehlwans)
Akhara Bhoorey Shah
Akhara Takya Sher Ali
Akhara Pir Makki
Akhara Takya Pir Ghaib
Akhara Khalifa Bakhshi
Akhara Jani Pehlwan
Akhara Ghadu Shah (belonged and
Used by Rustam-e-Zaman)

Akhara Ghiba Sain, Ram Gali

Akhara Chanan Kababi, Misri Shah
Akhara Boota Mal
Akhara Lalu Sain
Akhara Khalifa Bakhsi
Akhara Balmeekian, outside Taxali Gate
Akhara Balmeekian, outside Bhati Gate

Presently most of them are non-existent and those remaining are being used under the control of some families of wrestlers.

The situation as it obtains in Lahore is again different from the one 50 years ago. The size of Akharas is reduced due to shortage of space and interference of land grabbers. Further the art of wrestling is also on the decline and for all it is also not well at these points. However the following Akharas still exist in Lahore and are generally called Wrestling Clubs.

AKHARAS IN EXISTENCE

Name of Akhara and its venue	Name of Khalifa
Rustam Wrestling Club, Bhati Chowk	Kala Maruwala
Miran Wrestling Club Scheme No.2, Shadbagh	Haji Siddique Pehlwan
Chandi Wrestling Club, Chowk Saffanwala, Mozang	Chandi Pehlwan.
Haidri Wrestling Club, Chah Miran	Nazir Alias Jiru Billa
Kala Jat Wrestling Club, Kot Khawaja Saeed	Kala Jat Pehlwan
Jahangirabad Wrestling Club Chowk Nakhuda, Jahangirabad, Wasanpura	Akram Pehlwan Jelebianwala
Sadiq Wrestling Club, Faizabad, Lahore	Sadiq Pehlwan Meva Mandi Waley.
Khairat Wrestling Club, Amar Road, Shadbagh	Khairat Pehlwan
Kala Spring Wrestling Club, -do-	Kala Spring
Sajjan Wrestling Club, Chah Miran	Sajjan Pehlwan
Yaqub Wrestling Club, Dars Mian Mir	Yaqub Army Wala Pehlwan
Siddiq Wrestling Club, Baghbanpura	Siddiq Baghbanpuria
Ghorey Shah Wrestling Club, Ghorey Shah	Ayub Pehlwan
Pir Makki Wrestling Club, Pir Makki	Haji Akram Pehlwan
Muslim Wrestling Club, Samanabad	Salahuddin Pehlwan
Champion Wrestling Club, Nawan Bazar	Sheeda Pehlwan
Haji Afzal Wrestling Club, Sanda	Haji Afzal Pehlwan
Haq Char Yar Wrestling Club, Sanda, Bund Road	Ahmad Pehlwan Qasai
Billa Wrestling Club, Shahdara	Billa Changar Pehlwan
Ghani Wrestling Club, Shahdara	Ghani Pehlwan

Pappu Wrestling Club (Khai Wrestling Club)   Pappu Pehlwan Chardha Suraj
Sheesah Wrestling Club, Shahdara   Sheesha Pehlwan
Jia Musa Wrestling Club, Jia Musa, Shahdara   Ch. Rashid Pehlwan
Veryam Shala Wrestling Club, Mohni Road   Sohail Pehlwan
Baau Wrestling Club, Tibbi   Shaikh Shaukat
Bhola Gaadi Wrestling Club, Lari Adda   Bhola Gaddi Pehlwan
Bhatti Wrestling Club, Shah Alam Gate   Bhatti Pehlwan
Haider Sain Wrestling Club, Near Lari Adda   Salahuddin Pehlwan

BAITHAKS

In the old city, in the absence of proper educational institutions the instructions in respect of professional performances were imparted at various "Baithaks". These were the large sized rooms and a particular house with large frontal rooms in a street or locality where the students would get together and take lessons from the teachers or the Ustads. Generally these instructions pertained in the subjects of Music, both vocal and instrumental, Calligraphy, teaching Arabic, painting and Persian. Some other such vocations were also taught. These 'Baithaks' also used to serve the purpose of small performances within the student groups but those interested in the Mohallah used to attend the small scale limited functions, which were held in the Baithaks. In pre-partition Lahore, there used to be many Baithaks but with the partition these institutions have practically finished. Still keeping to the tradition there exist some families who allow the use of their Baithaks for these literary and cultural pursuits that of course have a healthy effect on the youth of the Mohallah and also divert their energy for constructive purposes. One of these Baithaks has been taken over by the National Council of the Arts.

Festivals and fairs which provided delightful diversion for the masses and people were also events of social significance. There were many amusement, fairs that were held in pre-partition at Lahore. Leaving aside the Hindu functions, the Muslim had their fairs "Melas" of known saints, Eids, Moharram, Urs Data Ganj Bakhsh, Urs Hazrat Madho Lal Hussain generally known as "Mela" Chiraghan. The Urs of Data Ganj Bakhsh is held with great zeal and respect by people both from home and abroad every year in the month of Moharram. This fair is more of a religious sanctity and people remain busy in prayers and recitation on the shrine. The surrounding area is full with stalls and other attractions for the visitors. There is also a lot of free food for the visitors, which of course remains available throughout the year. The availability of 'Sabeel' of supplying pure, fresh and natural milk to every body is a very distinctive feature of the Urs of Data Ganj Bakhsh. The "Mela" Chiraghan is totally different in character. It is full of amusements.

Basnat Ghulam Mustafa's Painting by Ghulam Mustafa

12

BASANT
The Family And Friends Festival

L ahoris look forward to Basant, the King of all festivals. Weeks ahead large variety of kites appear in the market with "pinnahs" and "dor" of the latest quality. Shouts of Bo-Kata are heard all around. The fresh air blows and thousands of kites, small and large, are sailing up in the sky. It is Basant, the kite-flying festival. All the rooftops are crowded with young and old busy in watching the sport. Kite flying is an emotion and devotion with Lahoris who wax eloquent of their kites and boast of their accomplishments in this field. It is claimed that there is no other place in the world where kite-flying as a sport has attained such commanding heights as in the city of Lahore.

"Kite flying has a long history. A Japanese legend tells us of a 12th century warrior, Minamoto, who was exiled to the island of Oshima and who had his son escape to the mainland by flying away on a great kite. Another legend recounts that a kite was used to hoist tiles to roof the Zojo-ji temple in 1689. The kite has had an incredible variety to forms and colours in Japan, often carrying symbolic representations of prosperity, long life and fortune. However, its invention, which dates back to about 200 B. C., is attributed to China. Marco Polo speaks of kites during his stay in that country. Even today, on the ninth day of the ninth month, the Day of the Kite is celebrated in China with great gusto". It is possible that the kite travelled to Europe through the sub-continent. It is not known exactly when and how this City (Lahore) emerged as the principal centre of kite-flying in the world. The very mention of kite awakens ones memories of childhood. In old Lahore, Basant marks the end of the season which begins after November with the onset of the cold weather. Mostly made of coloured paper and fine bamboo, the kites are as beautiful as big butterflies and almost light alike. There is a large variety of colours, shapes and designs, each with its own merit. There are master craftsmen in Lahore who specializes in making different varieties of kites.

KITE MAKING

The making of a good kite is a real art. The secret lies in perfect scraping and softening of its fine bamboo rods. One batten is fixed to the centre of the frame and another batten is curved as a bow linking the two corners on the right and the left. In older days a large variety of coloured paper of different thickness and qualities was imported from England. The construction of patang and its male version Kup is a very complicated task. The master kite makers have perfected the art of cutting and scraping of bamboo battens. They would invariably guarantee that their kites would never swing right or left, keeping their upright position in the sky in the face of even strong winds. Now-a-days kite makers are engaged in making kites all the year round and by the time the kite-flying season arrives, their kites are ready for action, the bamboo battens having become free of moisture which made them very light and manoeuvreable. The connoisseurs would buy a stock of kites enough to last at least a week if not the whole season.

DOR AND PINNAH

The art of producing the right kind of dor (string or cord) is also perfected in Lahore. The well-twisted and durable thread is rubbed with a mixture of flour paste and levigated glass until it becomes armoured. This makes the "dor" so sharp that it causes blood dripping from many a finger holding it. To prevent this, it is necessary to wear finger gloves. The armoured "dor" is wound on a pinnah (ball) with great skill so that there is a smooth flow of twine to make the kite rise high or low during a kite-fight. Sometimes boiled egg was also rubbed on the twine to even out its sharpness. The common run of players in Lahore usually purchase their dor from the kite sellers who keep it in ready stock. The experts and connoisseurs buy their raw stock of thread reels, called gotes, and get them armoured in their presence by specialists who run this business outside Bhati, Shahalmi and Mochi Gates as well as in Minto Park. But these days everywhere on roadsides the Dor makers are engaged in preparing the specially armoured Pinnahs which are sold at a special price to particular customers.

During the season, children rush to the rooftops immediately on return from school with their guddis and dor. From the rooftops one can have a glimpse of the whole city.

It is after lot of effort and strenuous practice that one learns the skill of flying the kite and keeping it steady in the air. To hold a kite in this way is to hold something alive, something that played in your hand, that jerked and warbled as the dor vibrated with the wind. The kite goes up and up until it appears to mingle with the clouds; it connects one with another world, larger, far larger than ours, at least for the time the Patang remains in the sky. It also links one with other flyers whose kites share the air space with ours. Indeed one feels that kites are a symbol and sign of life.

Basant

Basant

PECHA AND BO KATA

One cannot recall anything that thrills one more than kite-flying in boyhood days. Whenever, one observed the kite moving up towards the clouds, one experiences a sense of power and mastery over the elements. Perhaps, in a way, one identified oneself with the kite itself flying so free and so high above far from the maddening crowd, enveloping in a spirit of freedom and adventure. The kites also signify a hope, a desire for escape, fancy dreams entrusted to a breath of wind, and connected to a string and the hand that clasped it. Some say kite-fighting instead of kite-flying i.e pecha Larana. 'Pecha larana' or to entrap another kite by pouncing upon it from above or below or sideways, depending on its position, is the most exciting part of the sport. The skill lay in crossing dor with an opponent until the vanquished kite, cut loose, floated helplessly over the rooftops at the mercy of the wind. The victor and his team mates announce the defeat of the rival with loud cries of Bo-Kata and throw a challenge for a return pecha. The defeated rival would accept the challenge and send up a fresh kite into the sky. The rules of the game do not permit entrapping the kite till it is high above in the sky. It requires great manoeuvring to entangle or disentangle one's kite from the clutches of the opponent. Sometimes, one hears a shrill commotion on the rooftops and see boys running with bamboo poles to catch a drifting kite. The falling kite in a street or bazar also creates a stir and passers-by of all ages run to catch the booty as a prized possession. Some boys who cannot afford to buy kites often amuse themselves by watching pechas and catching the fallen kites.

Every mohallah in Lahore has its own acknowledged khilaris (expert kite-flyers). As soon as they launch their kites, it is a signal for the small timers to pull back their kites and leave the field open for them. They dare not venture to disturb the Khilaris each of whom has established his sphere of influence.

There is a style of kite-fighting called Khaincha which entails cutting the twine of the rival kite by dragging and pulling it with a sudden jerk. This is a practice followed by some boys who have very little twine and are looked upon with contempt by the Khilaris who would sometimes even give them a beating for attacking their kites in this fashion.

The celebrations on Basant day commence well before day break. Rooftops and terraces are crowded with men, women and children of all ages. It is also a custom to wear yellow dress on Basant day. The women, young and old, also sport "chunis" (headcover) of yellow colour which lends a charm to the festival atmosphere. By daybreak, the sky is ablaze with thousands of kites of different colours, shapes, sizes and designs. The whole atmosphere of the city also reverberates with the triumphant shouts of Bo-Kata and the blowing of trumpets to proclaim victories in kite-fighting battles. There are famous Khilaris in Said Mitha, Wachhowali, Machhi Hata, Sutar Mandi, Rang Mahal, Ravi Road, Sheranwala, Lohari and other areas of Lahore. They challenge one another for pechas. There are also renowned Khilaris who play for heavy stakes in Minto Park. The winners are admired for their dexterity and skill in gauging the winds as well as for their perfection in the tactics of manoeuvring, surging, shielding and stretching during the kite-flying.

Basant is synonymous with old adage "Aiya Basant palla urant" and is a festival in calendar of Lahoris. It has, however, changed its character with the changing times and advancement of technology. The Basant festivities aside, the event has been a historical feature at the Mazar of Hazrat Madho Lal Hussain where Muslims gathered in pre partition days on the occasion in yellow clothes, Sikhs would put up their own in Gurdawara Mangat while the Hindus celebrated the same at the Samadhi of Haqiqat Rai. Lahoris as a whole anxiously awaited the day. The feature was most typical of residents of the walled city. With the departure of Hindus and Sikhs, the yellow and Basanti Clothes are missing but still some male and females are seen clad in yellow colour reflecting a basanti spirit. So the day is celebrated with customary zeal not forgetting the spirit. The Lahoris, by nature, it is generally felt await the days to rejoice and remember and Basant is one such day when young and old celebrate the luscious sport marking arrival of spring season which unveils flowers of hundreds of colours and shades and to mark the occasion as peoples function through inter-action in the name of kite flying derive pleasure and joy. During Maharaja Ranjit Singh's period according to Alexandar Jones it was celebrated in a most befitting manner. "Basant", heralding in Bahar (spring), was celebrated with pomp and show on February 6th. An elephant ride took the Maharaja and his guests, from the Fort to Shalamar Gardens, with soldiers lined-up through the route, presenting a sort of Guard of Honour. The Maharaja's entourage, dressed in 'yellow' basanti colours travelled through a route that was surrounded by Sarsoon Kay Khaits, supplementing the Royal yellow hue. At Shalamar Gardens, Ranjit Singh's tent, embellished with yellow strings, inter-laced with pearls and jewels, valued at over Rs. one lakh, presented an unbelievable sight. After the initial court courtesies, it was followed up with a dance and song sequence by the patronised dancing girls, and lasted well upto early hours of the morning. It was as if those present were substituting for the spring time of maize. A fine scene, a fine view, that was exquisiting enjoyable and remembered and recalled with pleasure. Royal rituals missing, it is now generally taken as a date turning the weather from the winter to spring and celebrating the same with family and friends in the name of Basant. Infact it should be better to be called a folk festival of Lahore. One is really fascinated and the life on the whole jovial, playful and exulserant, the mustard fields blossom yellow in the country side and the moods of the fields romantic too.

Lahore is the centre of Basant celebrations as people around the country gather here for the festival. Generally Basant falls in the month of January and February and exact dates are decided by the Kite Flying Associations with concensus. Of late, another tradition of the night kite flying has been added which is on the night preceding the Basant day. It has added a new dimension to the Basant scene in the city. The sky is full of white kites in the night and those who afford to hire search lights enjoy the game and the kites appear dancing in the flickering lights in the sky. There is an added character. This is a participation of the young ladies who fly the kites and share the celebrations. Added to this the youngsters also arrange at some scale the display of fire works which add colours and risks. About a couple of years back the ladies would only sit in the houses and cook special meals for the male members flying kites, for the family guests and the friends with special food items. But now-a-days they fully fly kites and those who cannot or do not fly kites, help the flyers.

It has also been seen that in some areas where roof-tops have enough space people hire musical groups and bands. Those who do not afford, they play the recorded cassettes. Inspite of soaring prices of daily commodities the activity of kite flying around and on Basant has multiplied. We can compare it with the Europeans who save around the year and buy holiday/destination once a year. The same way Basant is celebrated by Lahori enthusiasts. Another development in some localities and specially in the walled city during kite flying in the night is the drum beating, shouts and firing with Kalashankovs. The city gets on reverbrating with indiscriminate shots and festive songs. People in general are set to fly millions of rupees in gust to get maximum pleasure out of the festivity.

While some enjoy basant on roof tops, lot of old and the young go out in the grounds and open spaces in and around the city and some even walk across the fields at distant places like Jallo Park, Lahore Park, Raiwind Road, Shahdara Park, Lawrence Gardens, Kamran's Baradari, Shalamar etc., etc. Interesting scenes occur when elderly and white bearded, expertly direct the young boys how to fly a "gudda". The occasional string pulling, flying weave and die until it successfully cuts the rival's kite which finally drifts away across the horizon. The old all along never give up passions of basant even though they had grown up. The young boys who are engaged by old help catching the stray kites and learn tricks of the trade.

Kite is the main story of the entire festival. The kite may be described as an object having a light weight frame covered with paper and designed to be carried by the wind and to be handled with a long string tied with it. In Eastern Asian countries, kites have been flown since before recorded history and have deep rooted cultural background. The simplest shape of kite is that it is formed by two thin sticks of bamboo tied into a cross. Such single-surface kites need a proper tail to act as a stabilizer. Bending and tying the cross stick of the flat kite into curved bow shape needs no tail. The tail is attached for beauty. This shape of kite is called "guddi" in our local terminology.

In other Asian countries of the east kites are flown for recreation and pleasure. In Western countries originally kites were used for recreation but later on they had been employed for military observation, meteorological research and aerial photography. Kite flying has now become almost a professional game. It has always been a part and parcel of our culture. It is popular in China and India also. Many Western countries also enjoy it as a sport. Kite flying festivals are celebrated in the Sub-Continent with great fervour. These are also celebrated in Thailand and Britain. In countries like USA, Malaysia and Thailand people fly kites on sea shores. But now in USA kite flying has also been developed for very useful purposes, like photography, advertisement, travelling and for military observation purposes. For these special purposes huge kites are made in specific shapes and sizes. Photography with the help of kites is becoming very popular in USA because it produces beautiful kite's eye view. The world-wide association of kite aerial photography is a group of more than 400 photographers around the world who use kites to lift cameras and to capture beautiful view. Kites have lately been enjoyed in France. In April 1993 two persons established a world record by flying 208 kites called "Flxifoils" connected with each other simultaneously in France. Travelling in a buggy drawn kite is also becoming popular and thrilling in the West. The buggy attains a very high velocity depending upon the blow of the wind. The speed and the direction of the buggy are controllable. These kites are designed and manufactured by experts. In China, people have always been flying kites for their private pleasure and to kill the spare time, and it is popular mostly in children. They have their own variety of designs and sizes of beautiful kites.

The difference between Indo-Pak and the rest of the world is that the former has taken kite flying as a sport in which there is a competition between two players to decide as to who is able to cut the opponent's kite first. Kite 'looting' is another charming and thrilling phase. "Looter" runs after loose kites, carrying bamboos, in parks, on roads and on house tops. Thorny bushes (dhingri) are fixed on the upper end of the bamboo, so that any loose kite may not escape. "Chomoring' is another interesting way to catch a loose kite floating at a certain height. In this process one can catch a loose kite going over any height, with the help of his flying kite. For this purpose normally his own kite is flown with a thick strong string called 'Tandi'. In Pakistan kite flying is popular in limited areas. The festival celebrated named Basant is actually a traditional style to welcome spring and to bid farewell to winter. Kite flying was initially popular in the Walled city and some other congested areas of the town but with the passage of time it has spread throughout the city. Lahoris celebrate Basant in their own distinct traditional style. The day is chosen by the concerned association which is always a holiday falling either in the last week of January or in the beginning of February. A few years back kite flying was popular in Lahore and Kasur only, but now it has become much popular in other cities also.

COST OF KITE FLYING

The strange thing about this recreation is that it has become extremely costly but people do not mind spending. Celebration of Basant has become a source of public relationing. Influential people are invited to different spots for entertaining and obliging them. Previously it used to be celebrated in old "Havelies", old big houses in the city, but now it is also celebrated on the tops of all big hotels, plazas and at the premises of big industries within Lahore.

Around the sixties kite flying was banned in Pakistan. Arguments for banning were that it caused accidents on roads and house tops and that it had become a nuisance for Electricity Department because it disturbed overhead power lines. The case was heard by (Late) Justice M. R. Kiani and the historic decision was given in favour of kite flyers directing them not to fly or "loot" kites on roads and on the house tops without walls. Kite flying has been revolutionised now. About 13 years back there was no concept of night kite flying. The Basant was celebrated at day time only, but now night kite flying in flash lights has become more popular.

NIGHT KITE FLYING

This started in early eighties from Mochi Gate, Lahore. White shining kites are seen in the sky in flash lights at night. Later it became popular in Akbari Gate and Yakki Gate and then it spread like anything. Lahoris enjoy a lot while flying kites at night. It so happens that two teams arrange a competition between them and start flying kites from their house tops making loud noise, on listening this noise rest of the Kite flyers of that area fail to control their emotions and rush to their house tops either for flying kites or for looting loose kites. People from all walks of life enjoy it thoroughly. The special thing about this game is that children, young and old, the rich and the poor enjoy it at the same time. Some of the traditional aspects have not changed at all, for example the competitions at Minto Park (Iqbal Park) have been held for years in a traditional style. Only highly experienced people participate in these competitions. These tournaments have their own regulations where a fresh and amateur player cannot participate. In these competitions winners are awarded trophies, cash prizes or golden lockets etc.

People who are much enthusiastic in this regard are trying to modernise this field. Many educated amateurs are trying to automate or mechanise the manufacturing of kites and costing of thread, for example an enthusiast has invented a device which holds the thread reel (charkhi) which as per requirement, re-winds quickly or lets the thread through during use. This device has actually replaced a helper, who otherwise is necessary to hold the thread ball, it is being commercialised now. The same person has grown specific type of bamboos in the lawn of his house for catching loose kites. This specific type of bamboo is slim, light weight and upto 30 feet long, and bamboos of this type are ideal for this purpose. Similarly there are many other amateurs who make different types of kites for their own use for the celebrations.

KITE AND THREAD BUSINESS

Millions of people in our country are involved in kite and thread business. There are different business opportunities connected with this field. Kite manufacturing business is in a big scale now. Paper, bamboos, glue and thread are the items which are essential for the industry as raw material.

Kite making is a very technical job. Kites made by experts (Ustads) are in a big demand and are, of course, costly. There are different categories of kites like 'gudda', 'guddi', 'maccher', 'patang', 'koop', 'ghoga', 'sharla', 'doli' etc. Kites generally used in competitions are made on order. Similarly the thread used for this purpose is also of different thickness and strengths. Different types of threads are used for flying different types/sizes of kites. The special type of kite 'doli' is the three dimensional kite which is also known as box kite, with its rectangular, open frame but it is very rarely seen.

The biggest and most busiest market of kites is in the heart of Lahore at Mochi Gate. Outside and inside Mochi Gate, even narrow suffocating streets are crowded with the kite shops which deal in wholesale as well as in retail. In winter the market at almost every time of the day is busy and humming with the sellers and buyers. Kites are also now manufactured in Kasur, Gujranwala and Sialkot.

There is a large number of Pakistanis working in the Middle East, USA, UK or elsewhere in the world, who invariably come back just to celebrate Basant in January/February.

Like every thing else in our country, many evils have found their way in this festival e.g. firing with automatic weapons and fireworks in congested areas which quite often claim lives of many innocent citizens every year. Similarly use of metallic wire in kite flying for 'chomoring' purpose has become a permanent problem of WAPDA as well as for the power consumers. It causes frequent power failures and some times very heavy damages to grid stations by short-circuiting on high tension lines. In 1752, Franklin Benjamin, an American scientist also flew a kite with (an insulated) metallic wire to perform an extremely hazardous experiment in France to prove that lightening was infact a form of electricity or a result of electric discharge. This famous kite experiment was performed during a thunderstorm in which he flew a kite that had a metallic-tip. At the lower end of the wire a metallic key was attached, to which he tied a nonconducting silk string that he held in his hand. The experiment was very dangerous, but the results were unmistakable; when he held his knuckles near the key, he could draw sparks from it. The next two persons who tried this extremely dangerous experiment were killed. Unlike the experiments performed by Lahoris, this experiment was very useful which discovered many new concepts of static electricity and led to the invention of electric capacitor.

Kite flying has a strong opposition from some people based on different grounds. Sometimes it is said that it is totally a wastage of money, in some people's view it is dangerous because it causes deaths and injuries; moreover it is purely a Hindu festival. It is also considered that children waste their time while flying kites and do not pay attention to their studies.

Infact it's not the wastage of money but a circulation of money, the money comes from the pockets of the rich and becomes a way of earning for the poor. People are injured in other games, also. The kite flying knows little and people from all walks of life like doctors, engineers, educationists enjoy flying kites.

THE FESTIVAL OF LAHORE

According to one school of thought it is not a Hindu festival and they term it as cultural and traditional game of Lahore. It was in the press that a recommendation has been made to put this game under the Sports Board where it will be re-named as Spring festival (Jashan-e-Baharan), so that nobody may call it part of Hindu culture. Interestingly it has received indirect patronage of the Government as it is included as an item in various festivals like National Horse and Cattle Show and during tournaments by Sports organizations.

Basant is the one occasion when the Lahoris go mad. It is the festival of kite flying for which he waits and saves the whole year – the day when, just for the fun of it, a young, Skilful Romeo will land with uncanny accuracy, his kite on the roof of his Juliet with a sweet little love message inscribed on it, or a passionate, self-composed couplet glued to its tail, and then lift it, as skilfully, and hopefully, with a possible heart-warming verse in reply, hastily fastened to it with fine red thread. Basant falls sometime in January or February, depending on the Hindu

Calendar. As the day draws near, sporty Lahore is plunged into frenzied activity. For the night kite flying we have already made a mention earlier. For the Day, actually the young gets up early and starts the activity.

By mid-day, on Basant, the Lahore sky is studded with a myriad multi-coloured kites and the space between the ground, roof-tops and the top sphere is one vast invisible net of razor sharp thread a dangerous day for pet pigeons and other birds.

On the joyous Basant day, in Lahore, no birds fly. Only high flying vultures and kites escape the neck-chopping 'manjah'. They generally go hungry on that day, for, they descend or swoop down at their own risk.

Kite-flying season is on from the middle of November to the middle of February i.e. winter months, when the sun is mellow and the breeze is lively enough for the kite to lift it and to keep it airborne but now-a-days whenever it is little breezy the kite flyers start the game. But being an outdoor sport, kite-flying is generally done only during winter months. Summer is too hot to permit the sport in the scorching sun.

The string is specially prepared and there are specialists who keep on making their string throughout the year and market it at appropriate time. Proper making of regular the thread is to be strung between two pegs, or trees or poles, exactly fifty yards apart. Then, a coating of thick starch sizing is applied enough to receive the finely ground glass and thick adhesive. The string is then allowed to dry. One reel of 'manjha', or "Gote", pronounced as "goat" consists of 500 yards. The 'manjha' can be dangerous if it is handled clumsily. It cuts fingers. There is a saying that 'manjha' that does not cut the fingers of the kite-flier will not cut the string of the opponent's kite. Of late another dangerous tactic is being used by some of the kite fliers. This is the metal wire which is used for Bo cutting, the rival's kite but there have been casualties when it touches the electric wires/poles and also causes short circuiting.

Regular matches, subject to rules and in traditional style are also held in open spaces. In Lahore, the favourite ground is the Iqbal Park, adjoining the historic Badshahi Mosque and Minar-e-Pakistan. Two wooden platforms of the size of a dining table, are put up fifty yards apart. There can be several such pairs of platforms on the tournament ground. Contestants, each with dozens of kites of different types and reels of 'manjha', and backed by 'seconds' or supporters, swarm all over the place before taking positions as competitioners early morning. The idea behind the wooden platforms is that the contesting parties remain confined in a small, fixed area, and be distinctly above the ground, to enable the umpires to see whether the players are observing the rules of the game. By mutual agreement, then, two players are paired off and they take their positions on the wooden platforms with their "seconds". The judges stand between the two teams.

The match starts at the blow of the whistle. Almost immediately, the contestants bring the kites together like the foils in fencing. Thereafter, the players are free to manoeuvre their kites whichever way they like so that the strings come together. This is called the "Pecha", from the Persian word "Paicheeden", which means tangling. This is the high point of the match, for, better skill will claim the "kill". Heart-beat gets faster, fingers number and wrists a long more can deft. Tension mounts as the kite is subjected to feverish but artistic flicking and flipping. Dextrous loosening and "tensing" of the manjha produces the sorely-needed fiery action, and the climax is reached when the opponent's kite is gnawed away to float down to eager youngsters, looking for "booty".

The judges watch the match closely. They will blow for 'foul' the moment they see a kite being pulled back. When the kite is pulled up, it should not, of its own accord, deflect towards the opponent. This is not allowed.

As soon as a kite is gnawed off, the supporters of the winner raise the victory cry of 'bo kata' which is a distortion of the Urdu words "Woh kata", meaning, "there goes the cut off kite". "Bo kata", with the passage of time, is, now, just "bo". Now-a-days there is a very favourite song sung by a young female singer which is usually played on these matches loudly.

" **Dil huva bo kata**" is the title of the song. In matches played in sober, traditional fashion, unseemly slogan-raising is not allowed. Frequently, after one or two serious bouts, the hands of the contestants are so badly cut that they are unable to participate in any more matches for a week or so.

After a kite has gone upto 1,500 yards, the skill of the flyer becomes ineffective and the judges, unusually, declare the match drawn. A kite can attain a height of 6000 feet which is just fun and no part of a match.

Matches also take place on house-tops but they are neither scientific nor in the traditional style. It is a general scramble and everybody is on his own, in a kind of free for all, in which no rules are followed. But, it is the house-top matches which put the city of Lahore on the boil. The walled city, from cock-crow to dusk, is a virtually bedlam. While the sky is studded with multi-coloured kites – hundreds of thousands of all types and sizes, - aloft and loose, the air is deafeningly thick with full-throated cries of 'bo kata' or just 'bo', and the beating of tom-toms, drums, or just empty "canisters" of kerosene and the sounding of bugles and trumpets.

Short and long-distance verbal duels also occur, but they do not degenerate into serious brawls, for nobody has the time to go downstairs to fight it out, in the lanes and streets. On the ground, thousands of urchins with thorn-topped bamboos, run crazily across roads and from street to street, "looting" the descending loose kites and the dangling 'manjha'.

KITE-HUNTING

Sometimes kiteflying causes accidents, some of which are serious. Scramble for loose kites also leads to falls from house-tops. Every year, the kite-flying festival takes a toll of about half a dozen fatal falls from roof-tops and about the same number of young kite-chasers are hospitalized as "vehicle-hits".

By tradition and by choice about a decade back women, whether they observed purdah (veil) or not, were confined to the lower or the ground floor, leaving the top terraces free for their menfolk. House-wives enjoyed cooking for the competitioners, who were either relations or family friends.
But for the last, say, about a couple of years the young girls/ladies actually, participate in the fun and festivity of Basant.

However like the classification in many other fields the well off arrange very rich programmes. Even in the walled city Haveli owners arrange breakfast, lunch & dinner and invite important people, both local and foreign friends. A large number of kites is stocked with quite a few of attendants to help provide strings and set the kites fly. Some sort of arrangements are also made for drinks, soft and hard, traditional hot "Puri" "kachuries" and number of local food items with sufficient supplies for whole of the day are pre-requisite.

Local hotels invite their customers for the "Basant" parties, on hotel tops and lawns to enhance their clientele. The silver screen faces and their fans also throng the hotels in really colourful dresses to participate in jolly 'gala'. Women organizations and social clubs and groups have their food festivals specially performed for that day. Some of the Newspapers organize Basant functions. Amongst Hotels Pearl Continental, Avari, & Holiday Inn formally organize the basant parties. Some people have their reservations about the celebration being totally Hindu but it has been so adopted and celebrated during the last over 50 years that it has emerged as a typical Lahore feature which attracts people from other parts of the country and there are hardly any prejudices.

The Governor of Punjab attended a Basant function at Hotel Avari in 1998 while the Prime Minister of Pakistan at Haveli Maratab Ali Shah. People enjoying Basant defy the bans. The city which is suffering environment pollution has the worst kind of noise pollution. The walled city remains the most busty centre of activities and Basant is celebrated with zeal and gala. Loud music, drum beating and roars of kite flying creates a special buzzing scene. The kite flying with metal wire, firing and falling from rooftops are the problems in addition to electric supply tripping.

This, however left apart, Basant is essentially a celebration of spring whose advent sparks festivity and excitement. Over a period of time the fascination of the function has spread but it is now becoming wild and noisy and lost some of its innocent colour and charm. One can safely assume that millions if not billions of rupees are spent on Basant activities and the festival also annually claims a few lives in addition to frequent blackouts. But Lahoris take all this in good stride. They are not prepared to let anything cool their Basant fever. So come on let us line it up and enjoy the way the people of Lahore prefer.

13

THE CINEMA

F ilm history of Lahore is not much different from that of India where it began on 7th July, 1896 with the newly arriving film titled Marvel of the century, The wonder of the World at 'Watsons Hotel', inviting the Bombay residents. The attraction was described as "living photographic pictures in life-size" reproductions by M/s Lumiere Brothers. It was called the cinematography and shown at 6, 7, 9, and 10 p.m., on that day in Bombay. Such shows were extended repeatedly and held in that city. The significant aspect of this event is that a concurrent unveiling of similar cinematographic expedition was held at Saint Peterburg, Moscow where the Tsar of Russia witnessed the same. The miracle living pictures were also introduced in China, Australia and South Africa and elsewhere in addition to European countries. Film history was in short erupting, almost simultaneously on every continent and stirring its strange new fever.

The motion pictures were developed scientifically long before their artistic or commercial possibilities were realized or explored. In USA and Europe, pictures drawn animated as amusement using devices that became popular in the parlours of the middle class. It was specifically found that if 16 pictures are made of a movement that occurs in one second and are shown successively within one-second, persistence of vision puts them together and they are seen as moving. Until 1890 the scientists were entrusted chiefly in the development of photography rather than cinematography. Edison is generally credited with devising the original movie machine, the Kinetoscope. Dickson devised the sprocket system, still in use by which the film is moved through the camera. He even succeeded, as early as 1889, in producing a rudimentary talking picture. Experiments in projecting motion pictures proceeded simultaneously in USA and Europe. In France the Lumiere Brothers introduced their cinematography, a combination of printer, camera and projector in 1895 and produced short films depicting motion for its own sake. More elaborate, the theatrical films were produced in USA where circus entertainers, dancers and dramatic actors performed for the cameras. By this time the equipment had been standardized and such films were immediately marketed on an international scale. Mr. D. W. Griffith developed the aesthetics of motion pictures, refined the element of movie making and the first Director to use the close up as a means of emphasis. Between 1915-1920 grandiose movie palaces proliferated and film industry started moving gradually. Hundreds of films were made to meet the increasing demand from theatres. The vast majority of them were Western slap stick comedies and elegant romantic melodramas. Mack Sonnett was known as King of Comedy. He had a talent for creating an atmosphere in which artistic temperament could flourish. Amongst his stage players were Marie Dressler and Charlie Chaplin whose presence in the film assured success. This movie business slightly suffered during the war due to rising costs and over all economic depression. Again after the first World War it became a major industry. The star system flourished and the studio business multiplied.

In 1926 the Warner Brothers introduced the first practicable sound film using a process known as Vitaphone and recording of musical and spoken passages on large discs that were then synchronized with the actions on the screen. The first film released was 'Jazz singer' in 1927. It was a talking picture. Of course it was an immediate success. This was also the end of the silent film era. By 1931 Vitaphone became obsolete and was replaced by Movie Tone System. This was the standard process invented by L. D. Forest. The transition from the silent to sound film was so rapid that the theatre owners rushed to convert their facilities to accommodate sound. The earliest talkies simply used to exploit raw sound, on stage, for novelty.

Cinema in Lahore has no history prior to 1900 and only theatre and other stage performances took place occasionally. The 19th century saw most of the technological developments such as the Printing Press, the Railways, the Automobiles, Telephone and miscellaneous other inventions. One of the most important invention was the development of Photography, the invention of Camera and development of images in a life cycle keeping in view the theory of body movements of the living things. There is a difference of opinion as to where the movie finally developed i.e. whether it was America, Germany, U. K. or France but it was certainly European invention. First appeared the movie without sound and subsequently the sound revolutionized the entire film scene. People found themselves a part of entertainment while sitting in the Talkies. Some assert that it was an improvement on the stage but whatever the arguments cinema/movie emerged as a most potential factor both in the fields of entertainment and social awareness. India being a British Colony had shared the fruits of the technological developments of Great Britain and Europe and consequently Lahore got its share in turn. In the early 20th century the Talkies were operating in Lahore City and later with the addition of innovation in the sound movie the Talkies were replaced by cinemas and most of the places renovated purely from the business point of view.

The people also welcomed this source of entertainment which was competitive, educational and informative in nature with a lot of fresh and reinvigorated cultural liveliness. Before partition the Talkies which were converted into cinemas were located outside Bhati Gate, Mcleod Road and one or two around the Railway Station.

Till late 20s people used to visit cinema houses to watch silent films e.g., Chandramukhi, starring Miss Gohar. The Paris Cinema, outside Bhati Gate, with a roof of corrugated iron sheets used to show such films. Instead of dialogues, there were written titles flashed on the screen which many in the audience read aloud. A few musicians sat near the screen and played their instruments whenever there was a hilarious, sad, or romantic scene, or a sword fight. Their harmonium, tabla and sarangi provided a kind of background music. The cinemas were usually equipped with a single projector and there had to be a break for a few minutes after a reel was shown.It was generally believed that film watching was injurious to the eyes and collyrium was not only a good antidote but also helped in improving the eyesight so outside Cinemas collyrium was sold.

The advent of talkies in 1931 brought about a revolution in the entertainment world of Lahore. The novelty of sound began attracting larger crowds to the cinema houses which began to install new projection equipment of screen in the talkies. Some old cinema houses were remodelled, renovated and new ones opened their doors. Paris Cinema outside Bhati Gate was demolished and Wellington Talkies constructed in its place. There were now three cinema houses in the Bhati Gate area: Crown, Wellington and Diamond. The fourth cinema house, Paramount, facing Crown was added during the mid-thirties. The other major cinema centre was Mcleod Road, with five cinema houses: Regent (old Capital), Majestic, Palace (Old Elphinston), Ritz (Old Excelsior) and Prabhat. The sixth cinema house, Rattan, was built much later. A little distance away, on Abbot Road, we had Nishat and Capital (old Shanti). All these picture houses were now exhibiting Urdu/Hindi movies. There were a few lesser-known cinema houses in other parts of the city. Plaza and Regal Cinemas on the Mall, however, screened only English movies.

The first talkie to hit the screen was Alam Ara starring Miss Zubaida and Master Vithal. Described as an all-talking, singing, dancing picture, it became an instant hit. Haqim Ram Parshed made a fortune from showing it at his cinema house, Capital, on Mcleod Road. This first ever film song, "Dey dey khuda ke nam pe pyare, himmat hai gar dene ki" became a rage and one could hear people humming it in the streets of Lahore. Soon followed a string of films from Madan Theatres of Calcutta, such as Laila Majnu, Shireen Farhad, Inder Sabha, featuring the great singing stars of those days, Master Nissar and Miss Kajjan. The youngsters enjoyed seeing stunt movies form Bombay like Hunter Wali, Toofan Mail starring Miss Nadia. Strangely, the Censors whose main concern seemed to be to keep out films having political overtones and comments against the Government freely permitted kissing scenes.

By the mid-thirties, New Theatres of Calcutta, Bombay Talkies of Bombay and Prabhat of Poona had set a new trend with their social themes. Minerva Productions of Sohrab Modi added a new dimension with its historical themes.

The College and School boys used to visit the cinemas for their matinee shows. Students got concession and by spending four 'annas' could sit in the eight-anna class. Buying a ticket in those days, however, must have been an adventure. The queue system was unknown and the law of the jungle prevailed. It was not uncommon to find one's pocket picked or shirt torn in the melee. The next exercise was to scramble for seats situated in the centre of the hall and during summer those under the fans, as seat numbering was as yet unknown. Among the hit films during the thirties were Devdas, President, Amar Jyoti, Street Singer, Deccan Queen, Achhut Kanya, Jailor and Pukar. These outstanding films had songs, dances and other popular elements. The celebrated stars who attained countrywide fame were K.L. Saigol, Prithviraj, P.C. Barua, Ashok Kumar, Chandramohan, Motilal, Surendra, Najmul Hussain, Ghulam Muhammad, Mazhar Khan and the Billimoria brothers. Among the leading actresses were Devika Rani, Durga Khote, Sulochana, Madhuri, Gohar, Mehtab, Shanta Apte, Naseem Bano, Kanan Devi, Leela Chitnis, Jamuna, Leela Desai, Sabita Devi, Bibbo and Gulab.

Once a week, on Wednesday, there used to be Zenana shows in the afternoon for women and children. Tongaloads of women would come from all parts of the city to see them. Grown ups used to have a liking of romantic themes and visited the cinema houses on Mcleod Road where tickets for the lowest class used to cost six annas. The middle class gentry patronised these picture houses where the general atmosphere was more congenial. There was an orderly display of still photographs of the running movie as also of forthcoming attractions. The film music had struck roots in the people's mind. Film songs were pressed into discs and the gramophone became a familiar feature of many households. Booklets containing film songs were available for one anna each, while those containing full dialogue were sold for two annas each. The first film song that created a sensation was- "Balam ayo baso mere man me" sung by K.L. Saigol in Devdas. But it was the haunting piece from street singer- "Babul mora"- that made Saigol the king of singing. Among the popular songs of the days were "Chal chal re naujawan" by Khurshid, and "Ai chand chhup na jana" by Kanan. The Lahoris were greatly thrilled when Punjabi film songs appeared on the screen with the first popular melody "Kankan diyan faslan pakiyan ne", "Shala jawanian mane" and "Uchi madhani te dud payi ridhkan" followed by several others which were soon on the lips of every film-goer.

Before the release of a new film, the cinema managements would organize a special show for the press in the mornings. This was an occasion to gather friends and relatives for a free show. The viewers were expected to praise the movie in their own circles and impress upon them not to miss seeing it.

A memorable event around 1941 was the maiden visit of Ashok Kumar and Leela Chitnis to Lahore after the resounding success of Kangan, Bandhan and Jhoola in quick succession. Thousands of young people crowded the railway station to catch a glimpse of the stars as they alighted from the train. Later, they appeared on the Regent stage during the showing of Jhoola. "The first successful Punjabi film, Shila, produced in Calcutta, was released in 1937 but it was only after the resounding triumph of Heer Syal in 1939 that Lahore studios came to life and ventured into the production of Punjabi and Hindi films. During the forties, they produced several memorable hits like Gul Bakauli, Sohni Mayyhanwal, Yamla Jat, Khazanchi, Dassi, Khandan and Mangti. The film industry of Lahore owed its success to the contributions made by pioneers like Imtiaz Ali Taj, a reputed writer. Nanak Chand Naz, Editor of the Milap, R.L. Shorey, J.K. Nanda, K.D. Mehra, and Dalsukh M. Pancholi. Those were the days when Malika-e-Tarannum, Noor Jahan, won countrywide fame and became a leading star. Other popular stars among the actresses were Ragini, Swaranlata, Munawar Sultana and among the male actors, Ismail, Narang, Karan Dewan, Ghulam Muhammad, Om Parkash, Pran and Majnu. Music directors who rose to fame were Ghulam Haider, Ghulam Muhammad, Amar Nath and Gobind Ram.

The educated class also used to go to English movies at the Regal and Plaza. While some wanted to learn more about spoken English, others were keen to view provocative love scenes. Visited by the gentry and the elite, these cinema houses presented a different atmosphere. They had introduced a queue system for buying tickets with numbered seats. In the middle stalls, as they called them, seats were available for one rupee and two 'annas' each, whereas a ticket for the lowest class cost nine 'annas' only.

"The cinema houses had found a new source of revenue by projecting slide advertisements. It was quite amusing to see each slide lasting only a second or so in which one could hardly read the full name of the product advertised. The first ever publicity film to be shown was about Dalda Vanaspati (vegetable oil) with a tuneful melody extolling its wonderful qualities. As for smoking one found the dark cinema hall an ideal place to indulge in it without being noticed."

Among the outstanding English films of those days were: All This and Heaven Too, Lady of the Tropics, How Green was My Valley, Gone with the

Wind, Rebecca, Lady Hamilton, Gaslight, Valley of Decision and Spellbound. It was considered fashionable to talk about English movies and Hollywood actors and actresses, My favourite actors were Errol Flynn, Robert Taylor, Clark Gable, Ronald Coleman, Spencer Tracy, Bob Hope, Humphrey Bogart, Charles Boyer, Ray Milland, Gregory Peck, and Laurence Olivier. Among the leading actresses one could mention Olivia de Havilland, Heddy Lamarr, Greta Garbo, Maureen O' Hara, Marlene Dietrich, Vivien Leigh, Greer Garson, Lauren Bacall, Rita Hayworth and Ginger Rogers.

This continued until the fifties and in those days, cinema going was the chief source of entertainment. Seeing a film in the company of friends was something to be discussed and talked about for weeks. The youngsters with the heroes and their exploits. When one speaks from memory about the films one had seen in one's youthful days, the judgement is apt to be coloured by nostalgia. Seeing old films again when one is in advanced years brings pleasant surprises. One realised that one never noticed or fully understood many of the nuisance, as one was too immature to discern them at the time. In retrospect one reflects that not all-old films were as good as one had thought them to be. Memory lends them values that were seldom there, studios burnt looted, investors migrated, lot of artists had to find a proper locale for production which took quite a bit of time before the films and cinema scenes could become renowned. However as in pre-partition days, Lahore had developed a base for the productions, on birth of Pakistan it re-appeared as a fertile and alternative centre for the cinema Industry.

In Lahore like many other noted cities of India the people used to watch silent films, as was the practice all over. Lahore's first silent film, 'The daughter of Today' was made in 1924 almost 11 years after the release of Phalke's Raja Herish-Chandra. In 1925 appeared 'Prem Sinyas' which was followed by 'Anarkali' based on the play of Syed Imtiaz Ali Taj. Hakim Ahmad Shuja, M. S. Dar, and Imtiaz Ali Taj also acted in Anarkali and Lahore entered the main stream of cinema. In Lahore the Actors/Directors known as Bhati Gate Group consisting of Nazar, Hira Lal, M. Ismail, Lala Yaqub, Rafiq Ghazanvi, Gul Hamid, Master Ghulam Haider, Abdur Rashid Kardar were the activists, Kardar sold his property and launched his own production company titled 'United Player' and made quite a few films based on popular local stage plays mostly from the Parsi Theatre. Kardar's silent films included 'Husan Ka Dakoo', 'Sher Dil' and 'Gadarya Sultan'. Muslim Town's studio by Daulat Ram, Pancholi Studio by Dalsukh and Kamal. Movie Tone by R. L. Shorey were the prime institutions, which led the film world of Lahore. 'Sohaag Din', 'Surag Kee Serhee', 'Majnoon', 'Dulla Bhatti', 'Mangti', 'Gul Bakauli' and 'Khandan' etc. were the hits produced in those days. It was Pancholi Studio, which was managed by Devan Sardari Lal. On partition the owner migrated to India and Sardari Lal produced the first Pakistani film in Lahore in 1948 'Teri Yaad' and later 'Ghalt Fehmi' in 1949. The language of the cinema was mostly Urdu, Hindi and Punjabi as it was spoken and understood by a vast majority of people. On emergence of Pakistan the perception of artist was a jester and brothel keeper. Only writers were partially exempted. Good Directors were mostly in Bombay. Cinema in Lahore was a profit-oriented industry but the investment was meagre.

Immediately after partition un-restricted import of Indian films kept the cinema houses full. The local distributors like Ch. Eid Muhammad, Agha G. A. Gul, J. C. Anand, Nisar Murad, Bari Malik and others made money out of this business. W. Z. Ahmad got allotted the Regal Cinema on the Mall and made two films viz. 'Rohi' and 'Waada'. 'Rohi' was the first movie, which was banned by the Pakistan Film Censor Board. In 1948 Nazar and R.L. Shorey founded Kamala Movie tone in 1924 in Lahore. His son R.K. Shorey expanded the business.

Swaranlata made the first Pakistani venture 'Schhai' with the most out-dated equipment. Their second film was 'Phaire'. Hakim Ahmad Shuja's son Anwar Kamal Pasha launched his 'Do Aansoo' with Shahnawaz, Ajmal, Himaliawala, Shamim, Allauddin, Asif Jah, Santosh Kumar, and Gulshan Ara. Sabiha Khanum was the main-stay of the film that was a new find. But the Pakistani cinemas had none of the established or rising stars and suffered a great set back in selling the products without the established artists. Nazar was Pakistan's' first comedian. He appeared in dozens of films and became very popular and was later cast as hero in 'Juddai'. Agha G. A. Gull was one of the first distributors. He established Evernew pictures in Lahore. After partition he also took the management of Pancholi Studio and produced the film 'Mundri'. Noor Jahan and Syed Shaukat Hussain Rizvi produced their first venture i.e. Punjabi film 'Chan Wey'. It was after 'Chan Wey' that Noor Jahan unleashed her prowess in one film after another. As actress her Pakistani films included 12 movies besides 'Chan Wey'. These were 'Dopatta', 'Gulnar', 'Intezar', 'Anarkali', 'Paatey Khan', 'Lakht-e-Jiggar', 'Nooran', 'Neend' 'Ghalib', and 'Koel'. Noor Jahan belongs to that rare class of artists who make any institution out of an individual. The year 1957 brought in a great variety in the selection of subjects in the field of cinema. It brought into limelight the artists like Aslam Pervaiz, Bahar, Nayyar Sultana, Talash, Kamal, Ejaz Durrani, Akmal, Neelo, Allauddin, Shabab Kairanvi and M. A. Rashid etc. Some of the films that appeared in that period were 'Ishq-e-Laila', 'Laila Majnoon', 'Bada Adami', 'Thandi Sarak', 'Aankh ka Nasha', 'Baap ka Gunnah', etc., etc. Then we enter the 60s in which both Punjabi and Urdu films made at Lahore made a debut in the cinema world. Punjabi film 'Kartar Singh' is an all times classic and still remains the best. It was written, directed and produced by Saif-ud-Din Saif. Allauddin as Kartar Singh gave a laudable performance that became a trendsetter in future films. During the same period Zarif and Munawar Zarif appeared as comedians. S. M. Yusuf, a very successful film maker in India came in mid-60s to Lahore and his first film 'Sehaili' was a tremendous success and won Pakistani medals for appreciation in different categories. Khalil Qaiser and Riaz Shahid also emerged on the horizon of silver screen and became known for their exploration. Riaz Shahid's 'Zarqa' was probably the most important production in which Neelo (wife of Riaz Shahid) famous for her sexy and glamorous image gave an authentic and sensitive performance. In late 60s Muhammad Ali and Zeba appeared and in their heyday commanded the industry. During this period Lehri's name may also be mentioned who was entirely a different entity. His humour was an individual slap stick and instead centered around one liner. One of the known producers of this time was Shabab Kairanvi who is considered equivalent to Alfred Hitchcock and his film 'Insaaniat' was a really commendable production in which Waheed Murad, Zeba, Tariq Aziz and Firdous performed.

With the emergence of Nadim, Lahore film world found a trio of stars along with Muhammad Ali and Waheed Murad. Nadim has remained a lone star from 60s till date and has all along shown brightly in the field. Nadim-Shabnam pair made a best team with seasoned Director – Pervaiz Malik and they created some of the best movies. For example 'Aakhari Station', 'Aas', 'Dosti', 'Doorian', 'Aina' and 'Pakeeza' etc., etc. Another Television prodigy Muhammad Qavi Khan has a very long and even full career as performer, producer and director. He took part in 'Riwaj', 'Bahu Rani' and himself produced 'Mr. Budhoo'. Although he could not make a milestone in the film world yet he continued to make his presence feel as a stage performer in a variety of roles. Qavi also acted and produced a Pushto film 'Maen Bani Dulhni'. He is a holder of Pride of Performance award. The 70s saw the entry of Shahid, a graduate with good family background in the film titled 'Ek Rat'. Soon Shahid found place in the galaxy of top male stars and was cast in quite a few films. The 70s also saw husband/wife-cum-director star team of Hasan Tariq and Rani.

By and large inspite of this apparent prosperous industry, the situation and working conditions especially the financial management of this field left much to be desired. The traffic of foreign films and award ceremonies in the country as also film functions organized at international level created an awareness in the community of film kingdom that all was not well and somewhere Government's help was required to streamline the affairs. In 1973 the Bhutto Government considering the deteriorating condition of the industry arranged a seminar in Lahore in which all connected participated from the field. The problems of film industry were discussed threadbare and it concluded with a policy for the promotion of the industry and recommendation to establish National Film Development Corporation (NAFDEC). For initial finances the American Film Producers allowed the use of their funds to the tune of Rs.40 millions. The NAFDEC had been authorised to import foreign films and start functioning as an Autonomous Body. In the later years it was found that instead of supporting low budget for the films NAFDEC tried to control existing cinema activities i.e. registration of producers, raw film permits and approval of scripts. It began to manoeuvre ways to squeeze money from the sick industry. Somehow the NAFDEC could not accomplish the assignment entrusted to it. Lahore's cinema industry has a big contribution towards Punjabi films alongwith productions in other languages and has produced cinematic legend. Sultan Rahi was one such person coming from an ordinary background. He surpassed many super stars and enjoyed great popularity. He became a real model for the person he played in any film. Muhammad Sultan (Rahi) endeavoured many problems to reach this level and had to wait and suffer for months in visiting and residing the outside studios. It was Ashfaq Malik of A. M. Studio where he was taken as an extra in the film 'Bagghi'. In 1971 Iqbal Kashmiri cast him in his film 'Babal' which was a break through for him and he received Nigar Award. Then in Aslam Dar's 'Bashira' he was introduced as "dacoit" and performed the role of committing criminal acts. The film that ungrained the legend of Sultan Rahi deeply in the psyche of down trodden peasantry was 'Maula Jat'. This was the milestone of his success and then he became the legend who could not be killed by any number of evil forces throughout his countless battles in films because he was victim of insane and greedy elements of the real world. It is, however, unfortunate that he was murdered cruelly by un-known assailants on roadside in Gujranwala, on his way to Lahore.

In 1976 actress Sangita emerged as Director and Syed Noor as a writer with their film "Society Girl'. It was a bold subject entirely different from the routine films. In 1977 two comedies were released one after another i.e. 'Bare Mian Devane' and 'Aj Dian Kurian'. These were reasonably successful ventures. Similar other films like 'Sulakhain' by producer Tariq Qureshi and 'Ishq-e-Laila' again the slap stick comedy. Sangita also produced 'Muthhi Bhar Chawal' and 'Ik Chadar Meli Si'. The Hasan Askari's 'Aag' with cast of Babar, Muhammad Ali and Sultan Rahi was not very popular. Shamim Ara's film "Hong Kong' with Babra, Asif Raza, Nanna and Tariq Aziz was a successful and a commercial proposition. The producers of Maula Jat, Mr. Sarwar Bhatti produced 'Chan Varyam' and another film 'Sala Sahib' with Ali Ejaz and Nanna. This was directed by Altaf Hussain. Lollywood cinema manifests a most unyielding tendency of opting for success-oriented formula. If an artist, director, scriptwriter, composer or singer comes out with a couple of big moneymakers in row then every producer runs after him for his next venture. Sultan Rahi, Mustafa Qureshi, Anjuman, Nasir Adeeb and Noor Jahan teamed together in more than 200 movies. The mechanism of such filmmaking followed a set pattern. The producer would first approach Sultan Rahi and if he consented to play the main role, the rest was smooth sailing with Nasir Adeeb, Mustafa Qureshi and Anjuman for other roles. Such a team ensured ready buyers in the distribution market particularly in the Muffasil Punjab.

The Punjabi cinema got a big boost and accordingly the production cost also increased. Sometimes the producers found it financially more viable to shoot Punjabi films abroad. For example Sultan Rahi and Mustafa Qureshi performed in film 'Jat in London'. At the time when Punjabi Cinema was dominating Hasan Tariq made his 'Sangdil' in Urdu with Nadim and Babra Sharif which was produced by Sajjad Gul. The NAFDEC Festival arranged in 1983 gave 11 awards for excellence in feature films. The winners were given cash prizes also. The National Award became a regular feature and continued till 1991. The period of 80s is considered lean in comparison to previous productions with decline of about 8% in 87 compared to 77. The reason for this lean period was decline in the standard of films, stories and characters being lousy and without un-authenticity, poor scripts and repeated roles by actors and musical directions of 'Start, Cut or O.K.' affecting the industry. In 1987 Sajjad Gul produced his 'Choron Ki Barat' a highly entertaining comedy, thriller directed by Iqbal Kashmiri. The film had two alluring young women in the Cast viz. Shushma and Neeli. This film happened to be a stepping stone for Neeli towards the Stardom. In 1990 Aslam Butt introduced Reema and Shan in film 'Bulandi'. The new comers proved their worth and the film was a success. The pair also performed in 'Hina', 'Anchal', 'Chakori' and 'Chandani' etc. Prior to 'Bulandi', Reema had also been cast in Iqbal Kashmiri's,'Qismat'. Reema has established herself as a sharp stage woman who knows the art of acting. The others of her contemporary are Shahida Muni, Madhia Shah and prior to them Babra Sharif had reigned the supreme almost for a decade after replacing Shabnam, The actresses of new generation are required mainly to show all their figures and their prowess at dancing.

In Lahore, the film industry had a long love and hate relationship with TV. The Television was established in Lahore in 1964. In its initial stage it did not affect the cinema business. The mid-70s however, brought in the casting, which gave a real jolt to the filmmakers. The cinema also lost family and middle aged audience who would now prefer to sit in their cosy homes and watch the movie of their choice on VCR/TV. In the 90s the Dish Antenna brought another revolution. Dozens of new channels and networks are now available offering a wide range of entertainment programmes offering films, music; dance, world news, documentaries on nature and above all these are shown round the clock. For all practical purposes a majority of Lahore audience watches the Star TV, Zee TV, EL TV, Sony channel, BBC, and CNN etc., etc. This has given a big boost to the cinema and Bombay Film Industry. The local TV has failed badly in attracting or inviting the viewers to see PTV programmes, which are conservative, stagnant, and without life. The most wretched of the local programmes is stereo type stage drama, which is produced at quite a high cost by engaging the fading performers. Infact there is monopoly of some group of artists who do not allow entry of youngsters to protect their vested interests. The same is true of the programme producers, management and the writers. There is generally an assumption that people even for news switch over to BBC instead of local bulletins.

An overall survey of the film history reveals that quality-wise the discipline has deteriorated. While the stars are the main obsession on cinema there are others in the pantheon. The music director, the composer, continues to have a status second only to that of the star. The lyricist occupies the slightly lower. Then script writing, direction and dancing may likewise had an idealized cause. In some cases the dance provides a road to stardom. Generally speaking what would film suggest about psyche of the audience. It has been observed that countless plots derive in their impact from sexual concerns relating more often to young men and women, whereas there are many other areas of concern and interest in the social life. The mere production of song and dance films, conflicts over marriage, role of master and servant are out-dated formula films and there is need to re-assess this production psyche. At the same time the other image of modern girl with free thinking, accessibility, sexual allurement, insistence on her own say in matters of romance is also not welcome by general public. A balance has to be stuck somewhere when the freedom and tradition could be fruitful for the society.

14

EID-UL-FITR, EID-UL-AZHA
MELA CHIRAGHAN

Since the dawn of civilisation all the communities and religions had their festive occasions, on which they relaxed, rejoiced and enjoyed breaking the routine. This has been true all along. Islam being the last and latest religion is a complete Code and covers all aspects of our social life including rejoicing and festivities. A study into the pre-Islamic social order would reveal that some of the festive events were allowed to continue in Islam with slight modification. The idea was to give continuity to the tradition and cultural life and not to denude the people from their amusements and occasional entertainment. Infact in all the religious cultures of the world there are certain days which are declared as days of rejoicing and there are places of peace. It is in this context that both the festive occasions of Eid-ul-Fitr and Eid-ul-Azha should be considered as a part of Islamic Provisions for the Muslims, the world over. However, as a background to this special event Eid-ul-Fitr started after the Battle of Badr.

The word Eid is derived from the Arabic and means to return, to come again and again. As Eid occasion recurs year after year so they are known, as 'Eids'. But the word Eid also implies feast. There are two basic 'festivals' in Islam, Eid-ul-Fitr and Eid-ul-Azha (Eid-e-Milad-un-Nabi is a later addition). Eid-ul-Fitr means the feast after breaking the 'fast'. It marks the end of the fasting month of Ramzan, that is why a 'Hadith' requires Muslims to eat something (as a mark of breaking the fast) before going out for Eid prayers. On the other hand Eid-ul-Azha prayers precede eating.

The beginning of 'Eid-ul-Fitr' started with the Battle of Badr, the first war between Muslims of Madina and infidels of Makkah. It was fought in the month of Ramzan A. H. 2. It was summer season. The Muslims fought the battle while fasting. Their force consisted of only 313 men, 70 camels, two horses, and only eight swords and six spears. The enemy force was manifest, well equipped with weapons and had on it expert fighters. This unbalanced confrontation was a battle of survival for the Muslims.

The Holy Prophet (PBUH) had prayed earnestly for the Divine help, because if the Muslims were defeated and killed there will remain none to pray and worship. And then the Divine help did come. The Muslims emerged victorious and the enemy was routed and forced to retreat, of course with a threat to come again next year. As the Muslims returned victorious to Madina they heard rumours that Banu Salim were preparing to attack Madina, the only Muslim stronghold. The Holy Prophet (PBUH) well foresaw the danger and prepared to meet the challenge, ignoring the weariness and fatigue of the Muslims after the Battle of Badr he led them to crush Banu Salim, in their own settlement. Banu Salim were already overawed at the spectacular victory of the Muslims. The Prophet (PBUH) stayed there for three days (as was His routine in campaigns) and then returned to Madina. As they returned the month of Ramzan was nearing its end. When the Shawwal moon was sighted the Holy Prophet (PBUH) distributed the "sadaqatul Fitr" among the poor. The next morning, he led the Muslims to an open place outside Madina and offered the Eid prayers.

This was the first ever Eid-ul-Fitr observed in Islam. It was on Ist of Shawwal. It was observed as a day of thanks giving to Allah for granting the Muslims victory over the enemy and for successful completion of the fasting month of Ramzan. So simple an occasion marked with true faith in 'Allah' and renewed determination to serve the cause of Islam. This is the pristine spirit of celebrating Eid-ul-Fitr. It gave the Muslims three lessons. First, thanks to Allah for completion of fasting during Ramzan. Second, to contribute something towards welfare of the poor so that they may also feel happy on the occasion and should not have a sense of deprivation. Third, all the Muslims should come out best dressed and pray together and show national solidarity.

The Eid-ul-Fitr celebrations were kept up during the times of the Holy Prophet (PBUH) and the Four Caliphs. It was observed in a religious and devotional spirit. The Muslims take bath, clean their teeth, put on new or clean clothes, use perfumes, if available, and offer Eid prayers. Before or after Eid, they would help the poor with their "sadaqatul Fitr". After Eid prayers they embrace and greet each other and pay visits to graveyards to pray for the dead. With the Holy Prophet (PBUH) it was a practice to deliver sermons in piety and Islamic teaching, first to men and then to women, who had gathered for Eid prayers.

Sometimes important announcements were also made on the said gatherings. Appeals for contributions towards Jehad Fund were made on these occasions and the faithful would gladly donate whatever they had. Hazrat Bilal (R.A.) was usually deputed to collect these contributions and donations. Womenfolk offered prayers alongwith men but separated from them or were in the back row. Under the Ummayids and Abbassides and later under this pristine spirit was lost sight of. The religious aspect of the Eid remained but it was fossilized into rituals with no attention to the spirit. The religious aspect was over-shadowed by the festive and merry-making aspect of Eid celebrations.

The rulers presumably indulged in personal luxuries, and the common men followed. The merry-making aspect trickled down to the general public also, with evernew innovations.

Until the Mughal period, Eid was still considered a religious occasion and merry-making was mostly confined to the elite families. During the British Rule however, we find the Muslims arranging celebrations more elaborately. Girls used to dye their hands with "Mehndi" on the night before Eid. On the Eid morning men and women, especially children wear new clothes. Children are given "Eidee" by parents and near relatives. Eid melas are held in open places, where merry go rounds and "Panghooras" and shops providing toys and gifts and eatable were set up to attract children. In streets, jugglers and "Madaris" show feats by monkeys, bears and snake and put up their "Shows". Children really enjoy these shows. Now-a-days, these have been pushed back and children have other types of entertainments i.e. visiting Zoo, Museum, Parks, Fun fairs, joylands, cinemas, theatres, films, TV and Videos.

Before partition probably, the exaggerated merry-making element in Eid celebrations was the result of intermixture of cultures. In Hindu culture, almost all-religious and historical festivals like Dewali, Holi, Dasehra are invariably attended by merry-making. So the Muslims also introduced merry-making in Eid festivities also. Exchange of greeting cards on Eid is a borrowed idea from Christians of sending Christmas cards. The present way of celebrating Eid is typical to the sub-continent Muslims. Eid in some countries is not observed the way we do. Special sweet dishes such, as "Doodh Sawayyan" is the traditional dish of Eid. Now we have also added "Sheer Khurma" and custard and other fattening dishes to the simple menu. Pulao was the usual dish for lunch or dinner. Now, we have all sorts of luxurious dishes to offer to guests. Most people prefer eating out with friends. Again there is over-eating and over-spending.

Regarding dresses, one finds the real extravaganza. Orders for new dresses are placed well before Eid. Readymade garments are available to those who prefer them. Cost is no problem. The rich and poor are there to purchase anything. Dressmakers prepare dresses in exotic designs and squeeze many times from the actual cost from fashion-crazy ladies. Weared, used and washed dresses on Eid occasion is not the fashion now. New dress is a must, even in middle class homes. And with ladies, every dress must have matching shoes and lipsticks and purse, all new, of course. The menfolk have their own ways of spending. The employees offer precious presents to their bosses in order to have a good Annual report. The bigger the boss, the more valuable the present. Sweets and fruit "dalla" is a story of the past.

The financial aspect of all this is an upsurge in prices, despite announcements by the Government about reduced prices at Utility Stores. etc. There is a big rush on Utility Stores and Fair Price shops and few people can afford to stand in long queues for hours. Moreover, it is said that quality of commodities offered at such shops is inferior.

Besides higher prices of commodities and other things, there is a disproportionate rise in rates of services. Higher demands of such people as tailors, barbers and household servants add to the miseries of middle class people. While it is usual to raise the prices of food and other eatables on Eid-ul-Fitr the prices of sacrificial animals get sky high on Eid-ul-Azha.

It is often pleaded that the lavish and wasteful expenses need to be controlled. Then there are certain social groups such as film stars and artists and sport stars who unconsciously influence their fans and their age mates. If they come to observe Eid simply, persons under their influence would also adopt simplicity. They are educated and are broad-minded. They should realize the gravity of the present day tendency of lavish spending on Eid. If they mobilize public opinion against this, much of the Eid extravaganza can be eliminated. This is the need of the day and the religious aspect too which is widely neglected. In Lahore the tradition that the Prime Minister, Governor and Chief Minister usually offer their Eid prayers in the Badshahi Masjid.After the prayers the Prime Minister, Chief Minister and Governor meet the general public in the Governor House.

Eid is a happy occasion. We must rejoice but should not waste. Help the poor and attend the needy, which is the spirit of the Festival. Celebration should be austere and graceful instead of making it an extravaganza, which invites reaction from the deprived. However the position is otherwise there are couple of closed holidays the entire population gets busy into merry-making, the factories are closed and similarly the other production units adversely effects the country. This needs to be taken care at the highest level so that we do not waste in the name of rejoicings.

EID-UL-AZHA

This is the other festive occasion religiously observed by Lahoris. For three days the animals are sacrificed. Meat etc., is distributed to the poor. The youngsters have a lot of 'Halla Gulla' kite flying, theatre and cinema going, inviting relations and friends. But again it is not celebrated according to religious ordains. Sacrificing the animals is a ceremony current in Arabs before Islam but it was allowed to continue. The idea was to share your good food with the poor and deprived.

Eid is not just a festivity but serves a reminder to the Muslims that they should share the joys with the poor and neglected sections of the society.

MELA CHIRAGHAN

Lahore can genuinely boast of its most important, by far of all in point of gaiety, neatness, pleasant scenery and the number and variety of the assembled multitude, its "Mela" Chiragh, or fair of lamps, held in Shalamar Gardens on the last Saturday of March and the following Sunday. The fair was originally held for one day only (Sunday), in the month of April; but the time was considered too short, and the season too far advanced, for a spring gathering like this, and the present arrangements were adopted. On Sunday, after sunset "Dias"(Chiragh), are lighted in the premises of the tomb of Madho Lal Hussain, in Baghbanpura, at a distance of about a quarter of a mile from the Shalamar. It is said the Mela originally consisted of lighting "Chiraghs" at the tomb. People stayed at the saint's 'Khanqah' for the night, and used to walk to the garden (of Shalamar) the next morning for the sake of recreation. With the passage of time, however, the gathering at the Shalamar quite eclipsed that of the mother-place, and, although Chiraghs are lighted at the Khanqah, the "Mela" itself is held in the Shalamar, and, after the original name is known as "Chiraghon-ka-Mela". The scene in the garden on the days of the festival is charming and picturesque. The tanks and reservoirs were filled with water, the fountains played, and, this being the time of spring, the gardens were seen to be at the best. To the loveliness of the scene, the pleasant sight of the water flowing on the marble water-falls, the green foliage of the trees and the richness of the garden, adds the diversified colours of the costumes of the people, the hustle bustle of friendly groups of gay visitors, the knots of companions sitting on the green, some eating, some drinking, some listening to music, or watching various performances. The pleasantly laid Mughal garden looks like fairy land, and were invested with a charm which can be better conceived than described. Large numbers of people attended the fair from the neighbouring districts, and a show of horses takes place, at which prizes were given by the Government for the best brood mare and young stock. The attendance at the fair was estimated at 50,000 persons in the late 19th century.In prepartition days Sikhs, Hindus and Muslims used to attend the "Mela" in-groups with great pomp and show. They would come, always dancing, with lathis in hands, and singing (Bolian). These songs were the most important characteristic of the "Mela". The dress would be red (Basanti) and "pagri"(yellow) were considered as the signs and symbols of those attending "Mela". More than Lahoris (people from the city), the crowds were from the adjoining Districts, who would wait all the year long to join the celebrations.

Lighting the "chiraghs", shopping the village style and eating in the festive manner were the peculiar features of the "Mela". The numbers of those visiting the "Mela" have multiplied to lacs these days. The Auqaf Department manages the opening ceremony of the '"Mela"but somehow the visitors feel that it lacks the flare and enthusiasm and instead the Auqaf has made it a sort of official function.

"Mela" Chiraghan (the festival of lights) and the annual urs of Shah Hussain is the only urs of a Sufi poet that is not held according to the Hijra calendar. Traditionally, it is held in the last week of March – the last Saturday and Sunday of the month (and when Friday used to be the weekly holiday it would fall on the last Thursday and Friday). Faithful and devotees from far-flung areas come to the mazar in-groups with great zeal and zest to pay him homage and to get his 'blessings'.

On the occasion of "Mela" Chiraghan (also known as "Mela" Shala Mar Ka) people come performing 'dhamal' to heavy drumbeats, at his mausoleum, they deposit a substantial amount and their precious belongings as offerings. They tie a thread with the grill and pledge some precious offerings for the acceptance of their (dua) prayers. Those participating also light 'chiraghs (earthen oil lamps) on the mausoleum, which called to be lacs of "Dias"or lamps lit, there is not enough space left for these lamps, therefore, the lamps are thrown at a place called 'aawa' (a huge oven of fire) specially meant for this purpose. Then, there are some other people who only come to the shrine to untie the threads after their prayers are fulfilled.

Seeking blessings on the mazar has become a tradition among the Muslims of the sub-continent. "Mela" Chiraghan is also a part of this cultural tradition. The pilgrim's enthusiasm is worth observation. Offering salam at the mazar, offering big amounts as charity among the deserved on the occasion, dancing to the tunes of dhol/drums, thus giving an outlet to their suppressed passions and enjoy themselves. Initially the "Mela" was held in the premises of Shalamar Gardens but the Government on the insistence of Archaeology Department to save the historic garden put a restriction on the "Mela" in the gardens and it is now organized outside the gardens, on all open spaces including roads and streets.

The locality of the mausoleum being a low laying area always gets inundated with rainwater, if it rains. Although the mausoleum is a great source of earnings to the Auqaf Department, it is generally criticized for poor maintenance of the mausoleum except annual whitewashing. A cultural complex in the area is an earnest demand of the local organizations but no step has been taken in this regard by the Government so far. This needs to be considered as Shah Hussain was a great

Eid Prayers

Sufi Poet of Lahore. At one time there was a thinking by the Alhamra to name its Campus on the Ferozepur Road as Ihata Shah Hussain but this did not appear to have materialised. The three-day Celebrations of "Mela" Chiraghan is one of the largest cultural and religious festival of Lahore. 'Chiragh' and 'Dhamal' on heavy drum beats outside the shrine are the two main features of the "'Mela'" that differentiate it from other fairs in addition to the villagers joining in typical red turban dress singing and dancing.

The tomb of Shah Hussain is situated in Baghbanpura, in northern Lahore near the famous Shalamar Gardens. The green dome of this tomb, once visible from quite a distance, is now hidden because of tall residential buildings around. The grave of Shah Hussain faced a similar whisk-away some 400 years ago, when River Ravi swept the grave. Shah Hussain died and was buried at Shahdara. According to some historians, a few years after, as predicted by the saint, the grave was swept away by the overflow of the Ravi. Madho, the favourite disciple of Shah Hussain, exhumed the corpse, and with due formalities, buried it at the present locality.

During "Mela" thousands of Shah Hussain's devotees tread the narrow streets off the main Shalamar Road to reach Shah Hussian's shrine every year. The green dome of the tomb, visible from a remarkable distance, fills these devotees with a tremendous zeal and already accompanied by Dhol Walas, the crowd's feet will tap to give vent to their passions through traditional Punjabi Folk dance 'Bhangara' at the 'Daga' (beat) of the Dhol (drum). All the localities in the vicinity have a jovial mood and festive look. The area reverberates with the thunderclap of drumbeats and dancing feet. The devotees come in large processions carrying 'chadars' inscribed with Quranic verses to lay them at the grave of their spiritual leader to pay him tribute. This thundering reminds one of the ways the great sufi saint of Punjab challenged the rulers of his time with great courage and with candid rhetoric. This candidness also enriched Punjabi poetry with a new genre Kafi. Special shops of eatables of rural tastes like 'qatlama' and 'andrassa' crockery, toys, handicrafts and merry-go-rounds and wings are most important features of the festival. People also take keen interest in a circus and well of death set up near the mausoleum. Makeshift stalls of sweets, bangles and items of reverence at an urs, a circus, death-well and other recreational spots are also among the peculiarities of the "Mela". These stalls can be seen in abundance right from the main road to the inside streets in the whole locality.

The tomb and particularly the graveyard where the mazar is situated is thronged by the 'Malangs' (die-hard devotees) of Shah Hussain from all over the country. Clad in colourful attire wearing big bangles and rosaries, these malangs take puffs of 'charas', 'bhang' and other local narcotics at their special places inside the graveyard.

Malangs & faithful 'play haal' to the tunes of Kafis of Shah Hussain or thundering beats of the Dhol in groups "Sajan de hath baanh asaadi, kikan akhan chhad ve arrya". The situation mostly turns into a sort of competition among the groups of 'malangs' and other young devotees making the whole scenario worth disserving.

Every devotee, old or young, male of female, and belonging to each section of society from all over the country, goes inside the mazar of the grave to offer fateha and put some cash as 'nazrana' in charity boxes there. In the courtyard of the mazar, there is a big 'Much' (oven) always with a fire "Dhowan dhukhay meray murshid wala, jaan phholaan te laal nee". Devotees throw candles throughout the Urs celebrations as a mark of their love for the saint in this 'Much'. Some of the people also throw candles in the oven as a sign of fulfillment of their 'Manat' (wish).

During the time of Maharaja Ranjit Singh, the place was also the centre of the celebrations of Basant, another festivity of Lahoris. It is narrated that Maharaja Ranjit Singh along with his chiefs and troops all dressed in yellow attire, while paying his respects at the shrine on Basant, made an offer of Rs.1,100 and a pair of shawls of yellow.

But now the 'Basant' has become a distinctly full-fledged festival of Lahore. As most of the glitterati exhaust themselves on 'Basant', always celebrated a few weeks before "Mela" Chiraghan, the colours of the "Mela" are not as bright as they used to be due to Basant but these are very much there. "Mela" Chiraghan has become so popular an event that it is simply inescapable to conceive Lahore without "Mela" Chiraghan.

15

HOTELS, RESTAURANTS
And Clubs

Travelling for trade and merchandise dates back to the ancient times where if the Arabs reached the Maldeep in the East, the Chinese would travel up to Central Europe to sell their silk and stone. In case of travelling by sea the ships carried the ration for travelling time but would replenish stores and stocks on their way at various seaports, if destinations were far away. However, in case of travelling by roads, in the plains, through the mountains, the valleys and across the dry and desolate deserts it necessitated the need for night stay, rest and recoupement of rations. These temporary halts also created intermediary markets for the traders and the caravans who carried their goods from one destination to another.

These being the facts of the past over 2000 years travellers' trade and their halts en route their destinations, are mentioned in the holy books much before the birth of the Christ. These temporary halts needed facilities which any person would require to stay for a night or so. The shelter from storm, rain and other vagaries of weather was necessary. Some of these halts were arranged in mountain caves, some times in Jungles and sometimes in any 'Nakhlistans' in the desert. These were improved upon by the efforts of the traders and the local population who lived near the points of stay of the caravans. It was necessitated for both the parties as traders would get safe stay and those arranging for the halts would get money in return for the services rendered. This was the basis for emergence of "Seraes" which came to be regulated by state immediately during the Mughal Rule in India.

Infact Sher Shah Suri was the pioneer who built Grand Trunk Road from Calcutta to Lahore, Lahore to Multan, Delhi to Lahore and Lahore to Peshawar. On all these roads the Emperor built "Seraes" where the travellers could safely stay and local "Mukhtarkars" and "Thanedars" used to be responsible for the security of the guests or travellers. These "Seraes" were used by officials and employees of the state travelling on duty and those carrying official post (DAK).

The institution was so useful that it was reinforced during the later Mughal period. When British occupied India they found it more advantageous and developed and extended it to even remote areas where only routine roads connections existed. They provided Dak and Stage Bungalows along with better maintenance of Seraes throughout India. In case of Punjab this system was made foolproof and effective in late 1860s. In case of Lahore the principal seraes are (1) Muhammad Sultan's, in the Landa Bazar, near the Railway Station; (2) Muhammad Shafi's in Anarkali; and (3) Rattan Chand Dhariwala's outside the Shahalmi Gate. The first two are much frequented by native horse-dealers.

Near the Railway Station is a fine pakka tank, with a colonnade all round it and quarters on the north side, built by Mela Ram, the great contractor, in 1874. It is supplied with canal water, and is much frequented by travellers. There is another large pakka tank adjoining Rattan Chand's Serae, mentioned above, with a Shivala attached.

Kamran's Baradari was used as Rest house immediately on annexation. Later on as the need for such accommodation increased more and more rest houses came into existence. While the Rajas and Rulers of small States set up and constructed their own Bungalows, as they had to occasionally visit Lahore, the Provincial Headquarters, the official needs for on duty visitors were met by providing circuit houses and rest houses of the touring departments. This took care of one aspect of the travelling but those coming to the city as tourists and visitors neither on duty nor as guest of the state needed accommodation for stay and food. Both these items put together necessitated and caused the emergence of hotels where the ordinary visitor or tourist would get local transport, food and stay, of course on payment of charges to the proprietor. According to one British report about Lahore during 1880s the hired carriages in Lahore are still very bad; but some efforts are being made to improve them. The tariff is as follows:-

Class i. –Rs. 1 for the first hour, and 8 annas for each succeeding hour or portion of an hour, up to a maximum of Rs.4 for the whole day.

Class ii. –Eight annas for the first hour, and 4 annas for each succeeding hour or portion of an hour, up to a maximum of Rs.2-8 for the whole day.

The following is a list of the hotels in Lahore.

(1)	Nedou's Sindh and Punjab Hotel	(2)	Montgomery Hotel
(3)	Nedou's Sindh and Family Hotel	(4)	Avenue Hotel
(5)	Caversham Boarding House.	(6)	Punjab Hotel.
(7)	New Victoria Hotel	(8)	Punjab Railway Hotel
(9)	Clark's Royal Victoria Hotel.		

HOTELS OF OLDEN DAYS

It is mentioned in a booklet on'Old Lahore' that "The hotels in Lahore are poor, though there is little doubt that a really good hotel would pay, owing to the influx of travellers at certain seasons of the year. The Punjab Hotel, Mr. Clark's Hotel, the Victoria and the Montgomery are the most frequently visited by European visitors." But, in the late 'sixties, Milner's and Goose's, situated on Mcleod Road, were the two best known and most prosperous hotels then opened for travellers. The latter occupied the large bungalow in which the executive Engineer office is now accommodated. In later years, Mrs. Hillier opened a hotel of a superior class in Caversham, the house at the junction of Ferozepur and Mozang Road, afterwards occupied for many years by Sir David and Lady Masson. In those days, as suggested in the old guide-book, the hotels in Lahore had to depend on the patronage of 'birds of passage'. It was not until permanent or quasi-permanent residents of the station showed a preference for hotel life and acquired the hotel habit that the demand for such accommodation grew sufficent to ensure the success of an up-to-date hotel on a large scale, such as Mr. Nedou established some years later on the Upper Mall in the bungalows now occupied by Messrs. Walter Locke and Mrs. Stiffle.

Another old hotel which did a fairly good business for some years was owned and managed by Mrs. Cunningham. It was accommodated in the large bungalow on the Lower Mall between the Council Chambers and the Small Cause Court. Regarding serving liquor, it was much controlled and the improvement had been gradual and steady, and perhaps attributed, to the efforts of those who first realised that it was necessary to provide healthy recreation for the men. When well-organised dances, concerts and theatricals drew the men away from their tents, the advocates of this reform reaped their reward in getting better results from the annual concentrations and, incidentally, in promoting the cause of temperance without resort to heroic measures. It may be inferred that similar causes were responsible for the general improvement noticeable in this respect in all sections and classes of the European community in Lahore. As mentioned elsewhere, there were no proper places of public entertainment in "Old Lahore" clubs and institutes were open to only a restricted membership, visits from touring theatrical companies were few and far between-what under, then, that men found time hang heavy on their hands and spent too much of it in convivial gatherings uncontrolled by refining influences but with passage of time things were preceding towards normalcy and institutilisation.

With the British occupation of the country the administration of land and people witnessed a major change. The pattern of living changed with economic changes. Means of communication, the transport, introduction of railway line, provision of metalled roads, bridges, revolutionised the entire social and economic scene. Politically there was a transformation from the monarchy. In the first instance anarchy in Sikh period and then a regulated proper civilized administrative set up controlled by aliens brought a total upheaval in the social scene of the city. The establishment of educational institutions and common man's access thereto further enlivened the city life. The entry of locals in services brought far reaching changes in the old social fabric. Life became more settled, institutionalised and security and safety of life and property was owned by state. The economic prosperity ushered in development and progress in all sectors. Better living facilities became available due to sustained growth which envisaged change in the attitude of commonman, life and pattern of living. The inter-action of foreign rules effected a better set of administration. The visitors from outside needed and expected better care, good food and more comforts for which they were prepared to pay. This caused and demanded more comfortable, well furnished, and service oriented facilities for visitors and tourists. Such was the background which brought into existence the institution of hotels and restaurants in the city which infact was an improvement on the stage bungalows, dak bungalows, rest houses, and 'Seraes' usually meant for official purposes. As already mentioned until early 1940s the hotels as an industry and commercial ventures had reasonably entered the scene and the city had quite a few places where tourists, visitors from other parts of the country as well as from abroad used to come and stay. Immediately before partition the Hotels which were functioning were Nedou, Stiffles, the Lorang, Park Luxury and Falettis Hotel. Park Luxury Hotel was located at the site where later on Hilton Hotel was constructed to which name of successors are M/s Avari Hotels. The Lorang Restaurant was across the round about now called Faisal Square previously named as Charing Cross near the Shah Din Building, on the Mall Road. It was a meeting point for most of the literary figures of the time like Abdul Majid Salak, Mahmood Hassan etc. The Stiffles Restaurant on the same side of the Mall was a few yards ahead around the French Wine Shop. It was more British in character as reported in some narrations. Again a place for Lahore connoisseurs of literary figures it served drinks, beverages and a decent choice of Lahori elite class. These were the known restaurants and in addition to that the small cafes, tea stalls were not uncommon. The most known were the restaurant in the YMCA building, Dyal Singh Mansion, Chinese Lunch Home, Tea House and some really very cheap hotels and restaurants did exist near Railway Station around Data Ganj Bakhsh, outside Lohari Gate and in the Anarkali. The post partition scenerio has however totally changed. At the moment brief situation of the city in respect of hotels etc., is somewhat like this.

HOTEL FALETTIS

Extending over an area of over 68 Kanals of land just on the back of the Punjab Assembly building stands the legendary Hotel Falettis. It is infact on the Egerton Road, opposite Transport House and T&T Tower. Hotel Falettis has reportedly over 120 years of service to the visitors to the city of Lahore. The exact year of its establishment could not be traced as the present management of the hotel showed their ignorance of its record. However, as ascertained from the staff, and old employees who have been working for generations in the hotel, it was informed that this hotel was launched around 1880 by one Mr. Faletti, who is generally known as an Italian citizen. Some English-men are reported to have succeeded to Mr. Falettis and managed the place in later year. Around 1940s it is learnt that Rai Bahadur Mohan Singh Oberoi purchased this hotel. M/s Oberoi now own an international chain of hotels in India and some other South Asian countries. M/s Oberoi also owned hotel Flashman's (Rawalpindi), Cecil (Murree), and Dean's at Peshawar.

Like most of the historic buildings on the Mall and in the vicinity this place has also fallen on poor days. Needless to say that in the recent past the architectural heritage of Lahore has been criminally neglected and is disappearing fast without any regard to our history and cultural heritage. Neither the citizens of Lahore nor the State authorities care for disfigurement of historical landmarks. The conservationists also do not have a string likely and to care for the disappearing monuments. Unfortunately this place is also falling prey to that policy of neglect and disinterest toward the city. The management of the Hotel Falettis continued with M/s Oberoi etc. until 1965. Some time after the war, this hotel was declared enemy property. For sometime it remained with the Pakistan International Airline. M/s Oberoi (after 1946, and) till 1965 continued to manage, the affairs and control of the hotel from his HQs in Delhi. Their representative used to regularly visit the hotel with permission from Pakistan Authorities.It is learnt that the management also had plans for renovation and expansion of the hotel but these could not be implemented after 1965 War.

The enemy property board turned over the control of the hotel to PIA. Later, the national carrier expressed its inability to manage the hotel which was then taken over by Pakistan Services Ltd. (PSL). In 1972, the Pakistan Tourism Development Corporation (PTDC) acquired the hotel. Falettis remained under PTDC for over two decades and was run in a typically non professional manner. It has now been auctioned to the highest bidder in a televised ceremony, as a consequence of privatization policy of the Government.

Spread over 8.35 acres of prime land in the heart of the city, Falettis was a symbol of the good life and pattern, that used to be. Its 50 grand rooms and suites are in sharp contrast to the small and lavishly decorated rooms and suites of modern hotels. The rooms at Falettis have a story to tell and not just about the English ladies gentlemen who must have been the early beneficiaries of service at the hotel. It is sad that no record has been kept about life at Falettis during its formative years. It was the only grand hotel till sixties in Lahore both before and after Partition. Its Bengali chefs were experts and known in Pakistani and continental cuisine. They left for Bangladesh in 1971 and were replaced by local cooks. Unfortunately the bureaucratic management spoiled the very reputation of a decent place it put up.

If the clientele of a hotel is any guide to the quality of service, then no hotel could have matched Falettis during its heyday. In 1955, Gardner stayed here for the filming of John Master's 'Bhowani Junction.' Even today two black and white photographs adorn the walls of the suite which have been named after Gardner. One is a smiling picture of the actress herself while the other shows Gardner and Stewart Granger the hero of the movie. Justice A. R. Cornelius, the former Chief Justice of Pakistan, spent 40 years of his life at Falettis. Room No.1 and 2 bear marks of the residence of Justice Cornelius and his wife. Mr. Cornelius died in his room at Falettis soon after the death of his wife.

Other dignitaries who graced Falettis included Mr. Z. A. Bhutto who stayed frequently in room Nos.63 and 64 following his split with President Ayub Khan. He planned his election campaign for the Punjab from his base at Falettis.

Much more important is room No.18 outside which a memorial plaque reads that the Quaid-e-Azam stayed there on July 14, 1929, when he came to Lahore to plead the case of Ghazi Ilm-ud-Din Shaheed. The Falettis needed to be preserved as monument but now it is not being allowed to continue as such. We don't care for history anyway. The ideal course would have been to set up a hotel and tourism institute where this flourishing industry could have contributed towards our economy.

Prior to partition, more managers of the hotel were foreigners, German, Italian or English. One of the earliest demands of the post-partition employees union was for a Muslim Manager. They finally got one but, critics say, at the expense of quality of service. After the debacle of 1971, the management threw open its doors for office space within the hotel premises. It may have seemed a pragmatic move to attract business but this spoiled the environment of the place. Din Tours had a pre-partition presence but now Barber shops, press and political offices could be seen in place of aristocratic use of the place.

What is so special about Falettis anway ? Isn't it just another hotel in the city? To begin with, it is one of the few historically important places left standing in the vicinity of the Mall. And, moreover, the investors now don't build hotels like the Falettis any more. Where else would you find rooms and suites the size of modern apartment? Some suites occupy five to 10 marlas and are complemented by bedrooms, living rooms, drawing rooms, dressing rooms and bathrooms. The hotel has an added advantage. Guests can park their cars right in front of their suites. A stay at Falettis is like being at home. A drive in hotel really.

In good old days there was a rigid dress code for the clients who were expected to be formally attired for dinner. Before partition the English were regular visitors. Landlords from Multan, Sargodha and other parts of Punjab including States always stayed at Falettis during their visits to Lahore. The Members of Assembly from rural areas in pre-partition days and during West Pakistan days used to stay here. Support staff such as cleaners and launderers were not allowed at the front. Now one sees frequent use of the front entrances and a general sloppiness which creeped in after Government control. Falettis has never been completely renovated since the take over. Partial renovation of some wings has taken place but that is merely patchwork. Infact for the last some years its bar was misused. The small auditorium of the hotel was also used for cheap and vulgar dramas. The fate of Falettis is not known and will depend on the new owners when the official handing over takes place.

Over the decades, the people of Lahore have watched glimpses of the past replaced by symbols of modernization. Falettis is still standing but, one wonders, for how long. It may not be out of place to mention here that in the recent past the heritage of the city especially from architectural point of view, is being disfigured. The landmarks of the city are being ravaged and replaced by tasteless commercial pigeonboxes. The most unfortunate aspect is that inspite of better education neither the citizens nor the State is paying any attention to the architecture and hence the haphazard growth and the city is losing its identity.

PEARL CONTINENTAL HOTEL, LAHORE

The Inter-Continental hotels came to Lahore in 1967. It was the city's first step in the establishment of an international class of hotels. Set in 15 acres of sprawling landscaped gardens, the Pearl-Continental Hotel Lahore, is centrally located on the Shahrah-e-Quaid-e-Azam (The Mall), 15 minutes from the Airport and adjacent to the business centres of the city. With 196 rooms, deluxe Suites, Banquet and Meeting rooms, unique type of restaurants and leisure facilities, the hotel launched into meeting a very vital need of the travellers. Eighteen years later, Pakistan Services Limited assumed control of the property and was given the new name of Pearl-Continental Hotel.

Pearl Continental Hotel

In the years that followed, the hotel continued to expand its facilities and provided more and more services to its growing network of clients both from within the country and from abroad. During this period, between the years 1985-1995 there were major changes and improvements in the hotel, with refurbishing of rooms, increase in capacity of its banquet halls, etc.

Last year the P.C. Lahore completed a major expansion programme. This extension was the addition of 289 spacious 4500 sq. ft. rooms and lavish suites to the present 200 rooms five star property. The hotel has a new and impressive seven storied atrium lobby with scenic lifts serving all the guest room floor. From the Lobby with its attractive water features one has direct access to the new Speciality and Chinese restaurants as well as the Café Restaurant.The new P.C. now boasts of the Marco Polo Café. This 170 seater café is the centre of the city's social activities. It provides service for Buffet, breakfast, lunch and dinner. In addition, a very exclusive Tea Lounge, with 21 seats, is open from early morning to late evenings with light snacks and beverages. The Afghan restaurant called "Dumpukht" will be the new star of the hotel shortly. It will offer Afghani cuisine and other barbecued delights both at lunch and dinner. The trendy Muddy's Café will be open day night and will specialize in hot and spicy Mexican cuisine. This was told by the hotel staff to the writer when this information was being collected.

In the Business Centre there will be an addition in the form of a "Club" with a 36 seater restaurant exclusively catering to the executives. Other plans include a Health Club Bar for diet and health conscious folks and of course there is the 24 hours room service. The Pearl's new 289 room's feature fax machines in all rooms, electronic key system which is tamper-proof. There will be mini-safes, double line telephones, mini bar, a state of the art safety alarm sprinkler system, and along with all these upgraded facilities, there will be stylish new décor that will be a cut above anything that the guests would have experienced in hotels in Pakistan. The hotel is functional with lot of these facilities and some provision in the process. State of the art Business/Convention facilities: The hotel's proposed business in the centre will also feature two boardrooms and three private offices with fully integrated system of computers for conferences including flip charts, Video screens photocopying facilities and a very modern audio visual network. The Business centre will feature in-house dining facilities, and full secretarial services. The convention centre will expand over 24000sq. ft. and will be able to offer banquet and meeting facilities for 2000 people. The convention hall itself is 12000sq. ft. equipped with elaborate audio visual system. The recent addition of the Atrium Wing to the existing hotel makes the Pearl-Continental Hotel Lahore the largest luxury hotel in Pakistan. It boasts 500 elegantly appointed rooms and suites, 5 special restaurants, offering local and continental cuisine, a lavish in-house shopping arcade, a state-of-the-art Business centre and a most modern Convention Centre.

Contemporary décor, designer furniture, exclusive silver and tableware; all set against the backdrop of granite flooring and intricate in-lay work of semi-precious stones, create an aesthetic blend and an avant-garde atmosphere. An air of spaciousness prevails throughout the hotel, particularly in the unique (200 feet high) Atrium Lobby dominated by 4 scenic capsule lifts, with new additional banquet facilities for up to 2000 guests and five restaurants, the extended Pearl-Continental is Pakistani's largest and most luxurious hotel.The most interesting feature which is enigmatic and beyond comprehension is that all and sundry complain high costs and dearness but if one goes for a booking the list of reservations is so long that it is difficult to have the same. This is not in case of P.C but all other standard places.

HOTEL AVARI

We know that the capital is only attracted by fertile climate. The investors also remain in search of such sectors. With the tourism emerging as an industry, trade being internationally conducted and international organizations visiting the country for purposes of investment and other business motives, there cropped a need for hotel and catering facilities of international standard. Mr. D. B. Avari and Dinshaw Avari, a business tycoon from Karachi acquired the Park Luxury Hotel in Lahore. This hotel was located right in front of Lahore Zoo on the Mall adjoining the Charing Cross. The place being central and ideally located in the city acquired for the hotel later was re-built by Avari Hotels to meet their modern requirements. It was leased/contracted out to the Hilton. Most probably it worked under the Hilton Franchise. In 1988 it was taken back from the Hilton International chain. It has now a franchise arrangement with that of Ramada Renaissance chain of hotels. Standing amongst other historic land-marks on the Mall this hotel has emerged as a favourite meeting place of businessmen, intellectuals, landlords and professionals alike. On the demise of B.D. Avari in 1988 Mr. Dinshaw Behramji Avari is conducting the business. The service standards of this hotel are of international level and the standard of catering, hoteliering are carefully capitalised to the financed value of hospitality. Infact Avari is now one of the chain hotels of the family which have their other establishments at Karachi and Swat. The Avari has an ideal location because in its vicinity is the famous Jinnah Gardens for walking and jogging, Alhamra Arts Centre with its most modern facilities for stage shows, Assembly Chambers, WAPDA House and the Government House where top bureaucracy and business people are busy working and needing the genuine services of really proper hotel and restaurant. The Avari Hotel has an exclusive club

Lawrence Montgomery Hall

which affords an oasis setting that is peaceful and serene. There is reportedly a measure of privacy and attentive guest service and a feeling of luxury. There is a health club, swimming pool and a flood-lit tennis court. The jogging track, a modern gymnasium, steam bath and massage parlour. Several meeting rooms are also available in the hotel which can accommodate for such functions and meetings from 15 to 1500 people. Secretarial facilities, personal computer, laser printer and national and international communication is also available. A choice of fine and all day dining is available at the Fort Grill, Kim's restaurant and Sichuan style Dynasty. Another option for food lovers is the magic of the past comes alive at Tollinton barbecue. This place offers downtown cuisine with special flavour. A best confectionery is also available in the hotel with take away facilities. Traditional musicians play every night in the lobby and restaurant. The philosophy of the hotel management appears to be creating a customised environment of information, assurance and comfort for hotel guests. There are 186 deluxe guest rooms, including 12 executive guests and 3 large deluxe suites, 6 Jacuzzi rooms and a no smoking wing.

HOLIDAY INN

Located on the Egerton Road, opposite hotel Falettis eastern wing and facing Awain-e-Iqbal. Hotel Holiday Inn is a recent addition to the hotel market of Lahore city. The accommodation at the Holiday Inn consists of 120 tastefully decorated guest rooms with 4 Deluxe and 4 Executive suites. The rooms have independent control temperature system and direct international dialling facilities. The hotel claims to fulfil every requirement of the travelling executives. Several Satellite channels and in-house movie system provides a good entertainment in each room. There are facilities of rooftop swimming pool relaxation in the recreational floor in the sauna, jacuzzi and steam bath. The Professional 'masseurs' offer a great massage, of course with Beauty Salon and Barber shop. For local souvenirs and general utilities one has to visit the Art and Craft shop in the main Lobby.

The Dining facilities are available in the Coffee shop known as Tania with 24 hours customer's service. Restaurant known as orchards serve buffet lunch and dinner both in Pakistani and continental cuisine. Barbecue dinner is served at the pool-side on the roof top. The Executive Board room has a seating capacity of 50 peoples for meeting and presentation. For large conferences, conventions and weddings, there is arrangement for more than 450 to 850 people in the Blossoms and Daffodil Halls. A fully equipped business centre caters to the needs of travelling businessmen and provide every supporting equipment for Conferences.

Again the most plus point of this hotel is its location in the city centre close to Railway and Bus Station and equally distant from airport like other five star hotels.

LAHORE GYMKHANA CLUB

Just opposite the Government House in the nicely laid Lawrence Gardens stand the "Lawrence and Montgomery Halls." These premises housed the Gymkhana Club, a prestigious and favourite hide out of men of diverse talents and fortunes. The building infact comprises of two parts. The Lawrence and the Montgomery Hall. The Lawrence hall fronts the Mall and the Montgomery faces the central avenue of the Gardens. The Lawrence Hall was built in 1861–1862 mainly from the contributions raised from Punjab by the well-to-do and European for a memorial to Sir John Lawrence (Late Lord Lawrence 1st. Lt. Governor of Province of Punjab). He subsequently became Viceroy and Governor-General of India. Montgomery Hall was built in 1866, again from the subscriptions raised by the native chiefs, Rajas and Zamindars in honour of Sir Robert Montgomery. Both the halls are joined by a covered corridor. The original vaulted roof of the Montgomery Hall was dismantled and replaced in 1875 with a splendid teak floor for singing and dancing. The roof was over-laid, galvanised and corrugated iron sheets with an ornamental carved woodencling beautifully painted and fitted with glass windows. The style of building is frigidly classical but dignified. The walls are throughout of all bricks laid in morter and lime plaster inside. The interior and exterior of the halls are polished and joined in imitation stones. The floors are boarded with Deodar Wood except those of corridor and attached rooms. The roofs are trussed with ornamental wooden ceiling underneath. Originally the place was used by the British officers who were without families in India. Various parties and get togethers of the bureaucrats were also held here. In the afternoon the "Sahibs" visited the gardens, strolled around, had a drink or played tennis or cards and would leave. Infact the original facilities provided here were a station library, tennis court and a Reading room for the visitors or members. Even public meetings were also held in Lawrence Hall in addition to quite a few theatrical performances. Both the buildings were maintained by the Lahore Municipal Corporation. The corridor was painted by students of Mayo School of Arts in late 1870s and till partition portraits of various English celebrities were displayed there.

The facilities of the halls, library and reading room etc. formally got the name of "Lahore and Mianmir Institute", or the club which was founded on 1st of May 1878, in the Lawrence and Montgomery Halls. It evolved as such due to activities at the premises by the top bureaucracy. The facilities especially the exclusiveness of the place turned it into a club where most of the regular and irregular visitors got them registered as 'Members'. The name of the Lahore and

Gymkhana Club

Mianmir Institute was changed to Lahore Gymkhana on 23rd January 1906. It continued to stay in those buildings till January. 1972.

The Lahore Gymkhana started as an exclusive meeting place for the British Officers. Its location out of the city in picturesque situation made it all the more exclusive for the 'members' for their activities and social life of Lahore. Barring a few exceptions it was a domain of the white man. It continued to cater to the successors of out-going British and local landed aristocracy till about 1968 when there was a move for shifting the club to another place. This was partly due to change in the political set-up, the visitors to the gardens and propaganda by press and those publicising acceleration of the pace of Islamization by way of discouraging the activities at the clubs. Consequently the Lahore Gymkhana planned to have its own premises, at its present location, in 1968, again the land of the Provincial Government on long lease.

With the passage of time except for the bureaucrats who are in minority and a large number of memberships is now gone to the business and professional class. Infact the membership has increased to thousands and predominant element is from the trading community and industrialists. In a way according to the recent reports the management mostly vest in the aforesaid community. For some time the civil servants had the chairmanship of Gymkhana Club but for the last couple of years the businessmen occupied the position.

The foundation stone of the new building on the Upper Mall was laid on the 15th March, 1968 by Nawab Muzaffar Ali Khan Qazalbash who was chairman of the then Lahore Gymkhana. It took about 4 years to complete the Complex and the building was occupied on 16th January, 1972. The building works were executed from the collections/funds raised by the Club members. The present Club has reasonable facilities for the members including dining halls, Card room, library, auditorium and bar room in addition to quite elaborate Kitchen facilities. The Club is run by various committees, its elections are annually held with a whole time Secretary, generally re-employed from the retired army personnel. The club has swimming pool, badminton, tennis court and Golf ground facilities. The families of the members can also avail of the facilities. The Culture Committee of Lahore Gymkhana so often holds musical programmes both for the young and the seniors. The classical and pop music is equally patronized by the management. While there is certain deterioration in the quality of service facilities at the club, it still remains one of the prestigious place of Lahore where annually hundreds of applications are received for membership and people have to wait for years for enrolment. The club has also residential accommodation facilities which have recently expanded.

Since partition many changes have taken place, in the dress rules and other procedures of membership. The future will see more changes and as 'we have seen the last of the 'Awami' age, we are bound to grow a much more structured and so-called formal elite the members feel. This will mean that the Lahore Gymkhana will have to enforce its rules with more severity if it is to remain an exclusive place for its members. Probably a time may come when the dress rules will be tightened and tightened, they must ensure a higher quality of common dress behaviour if at all it is necessary. The food quality will certainly have to be improved along with service and even the furniture, the crockery and the entire environment will need much more professional handling. But of greatest importance will be the manner in which the club staff handles its members. 'In this respect there has been a general reluctance to complain, minus the few who are viewed as 'senile nagging folk'. It is for this reason that there is a general perception that the management does not care. The patronising approach is taken and matters not discussed. They seem to forget the classic statement that 'the client is never wrong', but for the client the member needs a better deal, and in return the members must accept more discipline. This is an unavoidable path that Lahore Gymkhana is destined to follow.'

Whatever constitution of the club, its facilities and environment the building of the club has hardly any character of architecture. It is without any features of our heritage. It is infact a building which houses club without any regard for our history and art. As it is supposed to stay and continue as an institution for a longer time and cater to the requirement of the city elite it must have regards to our heritage and tradition. The very front of the building which is on very precious and valuable land hardly represents any feature of architecture either western or Islamic or what? The barrack and box like structure looks poor from the Mall and one gets an impression of a second rate structure with the exception of all the latest models of cars in parking, on its front. Even otherwise the furnishing, painting and interior decoration leaves much to be desired. Some times a serious look into the economics gives the impression of wastage of the funds of the members whereas an imposing monument should have been the permanent abode better than Lawrence Montgomery Hall, if not of the same standard. The only pleasing points are two pieces of sculpture done in marble which absorb the outsider who is bound to say "jis bhi fankar ka shahkar ho tum us ne sadion tuhmin socha ho ga"

THE PUNJAB CLUB

The Club was originally located in the building now occupied by the Administrative Staff College, opposite Hotel Pearl Continental. It is said that the club was divested of these premises after the 1957 Martial Law. Later after hectic efforts by members they got the premises (now occupied) in GOR-I, in sixties. Unlike Gymkhana the membership of this club is restricted and allowed only on the availability of a position or expiry of some members. In the recent years there were

Punjab Club Now Administrative Staff College

protests against this club on the eve of new year and Christmas celebrations. Some 'Islami Jamiat' students attacked the place and caused lot of damage.

The Punjab Club was established in 1904 and was exclusively used by British and Europeans. The Club was transferred to the Pakistanis during 1962. The club is most conveniently located in the midst of garden city of Lahore, with an exclusiveness and privacy in a residential area of the bureaucracy. The Punjab Club is a fully service & private club with membership of 600 only. The club has first class dining facility apart from residential accommodation, Library, Card Room, Conference Hall, Lounges, Squash, Tennis Court and Swimming Pool etc. All these facilities are open to the members of reciprocating clubs, on presentation of introductory card.

COSMOPOLITAN CLUB.

Another old club still existing and still operating in the Lawrence Gardens is the Cosmopolitan Club. It came into existence much after the Lahore Gymkhana. It has a mixed membership. It premises are not well maintained. The members do have small functions. It has the facility of tennis courts. For reasons best known to the management the premises, fittings and furniture are not worth a Club.Apparently its only plus point is that it is located in the Lawrence Gardens. The staff was shy of giving any details.

RAILWAY CLUB.

Located across the Allama Iqbal Road and going along the canal up stream about two miles from the Mall on the left side is the Railway Club in vast and shady grounds. Mostly Railway but quite a few other officials and businessmen are its members. Its grounds are generally liked for the golf. It is small place but very private and exclusive to the members.

EATING OUT.

With revolution in communication, transport and international travelling, western foods and eating varieties are being introduced in this city. There is a strong tendency, in modern educated youth and newly rich families, whether from business class or bureaucrats, to prefer and opt for on their own kitchens and eat out in restaurants the burgers, French Fries, Chicken Chips, fast food and miscellaneous items which are essentially western and taken with soft drinks like Coke, Pepsi and 7-Up etc. It has become choice number one of the College and University students. This class of youth likes to take the food as a fashion and don't mind eating on streets and roadside corners.

Of late, additionally a new trend has developed, of course, in the absence of very little entertainment opportunities, for the resourceful and rich, to have eating out usually with families and friends on week-ends. Routine parties, family functions, birthday celebrations, are generally organized in restaurants located in posh localities. The most popular and first choice of the well-to-do is to have an evening dinner in a Chinese Restaurant. For the last over 5 years quite a few Chinese Restaurants have come up. The first one named 'Shanghai' started on the Mall and later on in Gulberg, Fortress Stadium, Kashmir Road, Defence Housing Society, Cavalry Ground, Garden Town, Faisal Town, etc., etc. found quite a few establishments. Normally these Chinese Restaurants are run by some Chefs of Chinese features hailing from Hong Kong who found their way illegally into Pakistan from Calcutta and hardly any from Republic of China. The Chinese find local sponsors to invest. The Chinese food is made to the taste of locals by adding or changing a little quantity of spices. The most popular items of Chinese Restaurants are a variety of soups, different kinds of fried chicken, fried prawn, noodles and fried rice either with chicken or eggs etc. This business is so popular that on week ends especially it is difficult to get a table without prior reservation otherwise one has to wait outside. The most popular Chinese restaurants are Lung Fung, Yeefa, Taiwah, Sichuan in Gulberg and Tung Fung in Defence and Lahore Cantt and Dynasty in Avari and similar sections in Holiday Inn and Pearl Continental.

Further the latest fast food outlets which have been opened in Lahore and are talk of the town are the Kentucky Fried Chicken at Garden Town which continues to attract a large number of customers each evening with every one seeking to try out, the special recipe chicken, known all over the world. The same goes for Pizza Hut, which has joined the growing row of restaurants on M. M. Alam Road in Gulberg and the latest excitement has been created by the next expected arrival "McDonalds", which can easily lay a claim of being the best known burger giant around the globe.

However, the best and most popular fast food liked by Lahore continues to be served at Abbot Road and other areas around Regal, Mozang Chungi, Jail Road with 'Tikkas', 'Ram Roast', 'Kababs', Taka Tak Tin Chicken and Mutton Karahi, Chops etc., etc. from 11.00 a.m. in the morning to 2.00 p.m. in the night. In the walled city there is a fashion to buy curries and Kababs instead of cooking in the evening at home, but it is not true of all.It is an acknowledged fact that Lahore's restaurants and wayside food shops serve some of the best Pakistani dishes. These food items include typical Lahori specialities' which are really tasty and any-body's wish. I will mention for record some places which have come up in the localities outside the old city. Of course these are the places where well-to-do have the food.

People go out for expensive dishes in a pleasant atmosphere but all of this is not within the reach of an average person.

TABAQ RESTAURANT

For the standard known curries and barbecue items, the Tabaq Gulberg is known. This is one of the city's good restaurants. It serves not only Lahori dishes but also some Chinese and English food items. It presents excellent steam-roast-chicken and steam-roast-mutton-leg. These continue to be its specialities. The dishes worth mentioning at Tabaq include chicken, mutton, ginger mutton, chicken korma 'seekh Kababs' biryani, grilled prawns, mutton chops etc. There is choice of tandoori roti and 'roghni nan' both equally delicious.

SHEZAN ORIENTAL

The Shezan Oriental in Dayal Singh Mansion serves excellent Lahori dishes. Its specialities include chicken biryani, shami, tikka, kabab and chicken dehi. It is nice and neat place to go with family. Shezan outlet at Fortress Stadium also serves some Pakistani dishes like "karahi" 'seekh kabab' etc. but this place is more known for the Western dishes. Take away facilities are also available. Especially the Shezan Bakeries in the city arrange for this. Working lunches are known for the place.

KABANA

There are quite a few branches of Kabana in town, specialising in Lahori dishes. Best of them is located in the main Gulberg and known as 'Gulberg Kabana'. It serves excellent chicken ginger, karahi chicken (barcecue) & chicken Kababs. The other Kabanas are located at Liberty and near Sherpao Bridge in the Cantt. with a variety of specialities. There is a choice of Tandoori Roti or the Roghni Nans.

KABABISH

It is located on the Main Gulberg Boulevard and a known point for Barbecue particularly in summer for service in its lawns. One has a choice of curries of mutton, chicken ginger and Karahi Mutton Chops, grilled chicken barbecue and at some time, grilled fish on the skewer are its specialities. Kababish probably prepare the best roghni nans in Lahore.

Of the wayside food in Lahore. Khan Baba restaurant at Chauburji Chowk gives you delicious mutton curry. It used to be located in a katcha place but now it has shifted to multistoreyed restaurant. Many people have this dish every day especially in lunches.

Another restaurant, inside Main Market Gulberg, serves 'mutton joints curry', a speciality of its own type. The curry is spicy and juicy with meat very tender. Some typical Lahori families like the dish and take their guests for a change.

TAKA TIN

In addition to Restaurants there are countless number of wayside 'Taka Tin' stalls which serve you 'mutton', 'Gurda', 'Kapoora', 'Chops' and 'Taka Tin' which is cooked on a big open pan in your presence. Some butter and fresh 'masalas' comprising of ginger, green chillies, tomatoes, chopped onions and coriander are added to the Gurda Kapoora after slicing them into about ½ to ¼ inch pieces. After cooking this mixed stuff this curry type dish gets ready. It is indeed very tasty. Once you taste this fast food of Taka Tin you will never miss on your next visit to Lahore. Oven hot, Tandoori Roti and Dehi Chattani make it all the more delicious. The shops are spread all over, but the best are on the Abbot Road where you can choose ingredients of the dish to your requirements. It is not very expensive too.

MOVING TIKKA & KABAB STALLS

Bundo Khan's is another Chicken Tikka shop. It operates in the evening only and is the latest addition to the city. Its barbecue food and dishes are served at various points in the city. The known ones are (I) opposite High Court, (ii) Fortress Stadium; and (iii) Liberty Market. These restaurants open up in the evening and they have the stools made which are movable table-like which are placed on the road side wherever the customers like. Infact quite a few people prefer to take barbecue standing.

With the arrival of the fast transport, means of communication and international travelling the western food varieties are also being introduced in the city. Younger lot of modern educated and rich families especially from business and bureaucratic class prefer to have such varieties. These include burgers (chicken and beef) and the chicken chips consumed with soft drink like Coke and Pepsi. It is a fashion for the College and University students to have Burgers with Coke. In addition, of late, a new trend has developed, in the absence of real entertainment, by the resourceful and rich too have dinner out in the evenings. Usually the families go out on weekends. The people organise parties and family functions in Restaurants located in posh localities.

The Lahore city has over-grown and it would require a separate full volume to discuss the Hotels, Restaurants and other eating out places with their menues and specialities which is just out of the scope of this write up. I am, however, appending a list of few known hotels and restaurants of the city just for reference. These are:-

Lung Fung, Chinese Restaurant, Kashmir Road, Lahore.

National Hotel, Abbot Road, Lahore.

Hotel Sanaee, Abbot Road, Lahore.

Hotel United, Abbot Road, Lahore.

Tabaq Restaurant, Lakshmi Chowk, Abbot Road, Lahore.

Lasani Restaurant, Lakshmi Chowk,

Orient Hotel, Mcleod Road, Lahore.

New Hotel, Montgomery Road, Lahore.

Gillani Hotel, Montgomery Road, Lahore.

Lahore Hotel, Mcleod Road, Lahore.

Gulistan Hotel, Mcleod Road, Lahore.

Manora Hotel, Mcleod Road, Lahore.

Uganda Hotel, Mcleod Road, Lahore.

Shan Hotel, Mcleod Road, Lahore.

Hotel Plaza, Mcleod Road, Lahore.

Roballa Hotel, Mcleod Road, Lahore.

Jubilee Hotel, Mcleod Road, Lahore.

Zamindar Hotel, Mcleod Road, Lahore.

Victory Hotel, Mcleod Road, Lahore.

Grand Hotel, Mcleod Road, Lahore.

Parkway Hotel, Chowk Australia, Railway Station, Lahore.

Shabistan Hotel, Chowk Australia, Railway Station.

Al-Munawwar Hotel, Mcleod Road, Lahore.

Al-Asad Hotel, Mcleod Road, Lahore.

City Hotel, Chowk Australia, Railway Station, Lahore.

Ghausia Restaurant, Chowk Australia,.

Asia Hotel, Australia Chowk.

Chamber Hotel, Talab Mela Ram Road, Railway Station.

Kamran Hotel, Talab Mela Ram Road, Railway Station.

Ittehad Hotel, Talab Mela Ram Road, Railway Station.

Al-Imran Hotel, Railway Station.

Decent Hotel, Railway Station.

Shamshad Hotel, Railway Station.

Saiban Hotel, Railway Station, Lahore.

Karachi Hotel, Railway Station.

Pak Royal Hotel, Railway Station.

Kamran Hotel, Mela Ram Road, Railway Station.

Alhamd Hotel, Railway Station.

Hafiz Hotel, Railway Station.

Rex Hotel, Boharwala Chowk.

Shobra Hotel, Nicholson Road, Lahore.

Shah Taj Hotel, Nicholson Road, Lahore.

Al-Umer Hotel, Mcleod Road, Lahore.

Bundu Khan Restaurant, The Mall, Lahore.

Indus Hotel, The Mall, Lahore.

Rajena Hotel, The Mall, Lahore.

Saloos Restaurant, The Mall, Lahore.

Shezan Hotel, The Mall, Lahore.

Go-Go Hotel, The Mall, Lahore.

Bell Pearper, Fortress Stadium.

Shezan, Fortress Stadium.

Village Hotel, M. M. Alam Road, Lahore.

Bundoo Hotel, Fortress Stadium.

Hevely Hotel, M.M. Alam Road.

Kafazon Hotel, M. M. Alam Road.

Pak Tea House, The Mall, Lahore.

Pizza Hut, M. M. Alam Road.

Kababish, Main Boulevard, Gulberg,

Kung Fung, Main Boulevard, Gulberg.

Taiwah, Main Boulevard, Gulberg.

Yeefa Hotel, Main Boulevard, Gulberg, Lahore.

Shanghai Hotel, Main Boulevard, Gulberg.

Al-Syed Hotel, Railway Station.

Modern Hotel, Chowk Australia, Lahore.

Bolay Da Hotel, Railway Station.

Nau Lakha Hotel, Railway Station.

Station Hotel, Railway Station.

Metro Hotel, Railway Station.

Kabana, Main Boulevard, Gulberg.

K. F. C., Garden Town, Lahore.

Khan Baba Hotel, Chauburji Chowk.

Ma Sha Allah Restaurant, Ferozepur Road.

Ajmeri Restaurant, Ferozepur Road.

N. T. Restaurant, Ferozepur Road.

While mention has been made of hotels and places of eating out, there are some specialities of eatable items which are only made and are available in Lahore with a typical taste. The name of the proprietor, address and the item separately has been listed very briefly and is also given below:

Mochi Gate, Lal Khoo, Lahore.

Sain Seekh Kababwala Lal Khoo,
Inside Mochi Gate, Lahore.

Abdur Rahid Cholaywala,
Azam Cloth Market.

Hussain Kanjiwala, Dehli Gate.

Malik Yousaf Pan Shop, Chowk Rang Mahal.

Bhaya Cholaywala, Sonehri Masjid.

Hareesa House, Nisbat Road.

Shoka Gur ka Sharbatwala Circular
Road, Nawan Bazar.

Billa Bongwala, Circular Road
Near Pan Gali.

Shaikh Haleem, Pan Gali.

Mullan Kheerwala, New
Anarkali Corner.

Manna Taway Machliwala, Urdu Bazar Chowk.

Bha Cholaywala, Papar Mandi.

Baba Kulfiwala, Shahalmi,
Lal Masjid.

Haji Abdur Rashid Murgh Haleemwala,
Shahalmi.

Chota Chargha Farosh, Soha Bazar.

Chacha Saeed Bhathooraywala, Rang Mahal
Chowk.

Prince Chargha House, Inside Lohari.

Javed Machli Farosh, Rang Mahal Chowk.

Tabaq, Lakhshmi Chowk.

Lasani Baryani and Chargha,
Lakshmi Chowk.

Rahman Hani Goashatwala,
Lakshmi Chowk.

Cheema Pehlwan Dal Tikkiwala,
Lakshmi Chowk.

Nishat Takka Pak, Lakshmi Chowk.

Yasin Payeewala, Royal Park.

Yasin Halwa Puriwala, Royal Park.

Butt Karahee Goashat, Lakshmi Chowk.

Manna Cholaywala, Lakshmi Chowk.

Bara Pan Shop, Royal Park.

Amin Hotel Almashoor Kanjar Hotel,
Lakshmi Chowk.

Kashmiri Sabz Chayee (Komal Sanake)
Lakshmi Chowk.

Al-Shaikh Chatkhara House,
Inside Lohari.

Haji Sultan Nahariwala, Inside Lohari.

Lahore Nan Shop, Mcleod Road.

Kaka Gurda Kapoora House,
Mcleod Road.

Sheefa Gurdah Kapoora Karahee
Goasht, Mcleod Road.

Haji Allah Ditta Kabab Ferosh,
Landa Bazar.

Khalifa Kabab Farooh,
Kashmiri Bazar.

Jamil Bhaya Cholaywala, Dehli Gate.

Chacha Seed Falsay ke Sharbatwala, Rang Mahal Chowk.

Jaboo Fruit Chat, Dabi Bazar.

Bhaya Dehi Bhallaywala, Kaseera Bazar.

Idrees Chikar Cholaywala,
Chowk Rang Mahal.

Shahbaz Fruit Chatwala, Khaee Bazar, Near Dera Shaiba Pehlwan.

Fajja Sri Payeewala, Hira Mandi.

Fazal Haq Sri Paayeewala,
Main Bazar, Hira Mandi.

Kashmiri Dal Chawal,
Lakhshmi Chowk.

Ittefaq Dal Chawal,
Lakshmi Chowk.

Shahi Murgh Cholay,
Lakshmi Chowk.

Tooba Murgh Cholay,
Lakshmi Chowk.

Khalifa Nanwala, Masjid Wazir Khan Chowk.

Kaman Tikkianwala, Dehli Gate.

Kashmiri Dal Chawal, Old Anarkali.

Sindhi Baryani, Old Anarkali.

Kaka Gurda Kapoora, Old Anarkali.

Yousaf Faloodah & Machli Shop, Old Anarkali.

Nazir Faloodah Shop, Old Anarkali.

Abdur Rahman Hotel, Old Anarkali.

Nehmat Kadah, Lohari Gate.

Khan Baba Hotel, Chauburji.

Pak Tea HouseThe Mall, Lahore

16

FOREIGN
Cultural Centres In Lahore

As one observes the Lahoris are and have always been proud of their cultural heritage and a typical ambience of the city, its history, traditions, archaeology, palaces, mausoleums, mosques and gardens. The distinct classical features of the walled city, the narrow and winding lanes, the dress and costumes, food and cuisine, fine arts and crafts distinctly give the Lahoris an edge over others. Succeeding the Mughals and Sikhs, the British introduced their own building designs which can be termed as frigid classical style; though not very massive yet public-oriented in all respects. They have their own status. The suburbs, which have now become a part of the metropolitan city, have their own history and magic of outskirts. The traditional cultural traits inherited by the residents have trickled down and have been preserved although in a slightly modified form due to outside influences in addition to the technological advancements.

With the emergence of Pakistan as an Independent country, diplomatic and cultural relations had to be established with the comity of Nations. To foster relations some of the friendly countries set up their culture centres in main cities of Pakistan. Amongst those who established proper offices in Lahore were the United States of America, United Kingdom, France and Germany. The United States culture centre operates in its United States Information Centre with a full-fledged Director heading the Organisation. Similarly United Kingdom has its office in the name of British Council. The Government of Germany had its offices in the shape of Goethe Centre/German Culture Centre. The Government of France set up its Centre in the name of French Culture Centre (Alliance Franc'e)

These centres operate under bilateral agreements for propagation and promotion of their culture and projection of policies, finding common friends amongst the local citizens. Their activities are reportedly cultural, academic and artistic. It is understood that these cultural organizations spend quite a bit of money on the promotion and propagation of their activities through cultural programmes for the local people. Stating more specifically the profile of each organization is as under:

THE AMERICAN CENTRE LAHORE

The American Centre or United States Information Service started its office in Lahore, in Bank Square, in late 1949. It was then called United States Information and Education Service. Dr. George Candreva was the first head of United State Information Service, Lahore. Mr. Gibson was the first US Counsel General. Dr. Candreva with a small group of Pakistani assistants pioneered the USIS Lahore. The Centre comprised of Press Branch, an Education Section, and a Film unit with a few hundred books from US Army Libraries after World War II. Later on William A. Withus, the first Public Affairs Officer 1951-55 really built up USIS Lahore. With his wide contacts he also organized Pak – American Society in Lahore.

In October 1951 a proper library with 5000 books and 50 magazines was established on 54-The Mall. This was not only the first foreign Mission library opened in Lahore but also the first free-lending library with open bookshelves on entirely new novel concept in library service. There was no entry ticket, no membership fee nor any security required by any. One could visit the library browse through books, read magazines, consult a dictionary or an Encyclopaedia. Any body who could fill in a Membership form and get proper attestation could become a library card holder to borrow books. It soon became very popular with educationists.

The location of the library was a definite advantage on the Mall of 50s, which until 60s was much quieter, cleaner, and prettier place. The automobiles had not yet invaded and there was a grassy strip with flowerbeds along one side of the Mall, right from the Canal Bank to 'Gol Bagh' in the town. It was social and cultural hub of the town with many Cafes and Clubs where in the evening the elite of Lahore got together to sip tea, coffee or drinks. They would discuss art, literature, politics, take a stroll, browse through books in book stores and visit the USIS. The Lorangs and Nedous Hotel were the most prestigious hotels of Lahore and points for the intellectuals for tea and gossip. The library building on the Mall being next door to the office of Civil and Military Gazette. People coming to see Kipling's room would just also look into USIS Library.

Since Lahore was then major Centre of book publishing in Pakistan USIS was entrusted with the task of periodically selecting new local publications for shipment to the library of Congress. USIS continued to function on the Mall until the end of 1955. By that time a new multi-storeyed building constructed to USIS requirement had been completed in Bank Square. Thus the Library moved to the Bank Square in 1956. The Centre had new furniture, new collection of 12000 books, a separate room for magazines and an auditorium. The press publication exhibits and culture sections were also located in the same building. When it came to be known as USIS information Centre, the membership increased and there were number of regular programmes in the auditorium and US Centre became the hub of academic and cultural programmes. In 1956 the USIS Lahore provided all possible support to the three day international Islamic Colloquium which was sponsored by Princeton University. During the year 1956-68 the USIS set up a centre at Murree which operated there for three months from June to August. There was an exhibition gallery, which arranged film shows, music programmes, talks and lectures. In 1957 USIS Lahore launched a mobile Library service. There were two book mobile vans each stocked with 1200 books and 50 magazines. In 1958 the USIS Lahore initiated a book translation programme under which more than 50 books on history, literature, Economics foreign policy and education etc. were translated by Pakistani writers and scholars. The former Chief Minister Punjab Mr. Hanif Ramay translated Galbraith's Economic Development in Perspective, Famous Pakistani Painter A. R. Chughtai designed the book jacket of a book on Jacqueline Kennedy. Before the Asia foundation had opened their offices, the USIS carried a very active book on presentation programme. Thousands of books on various subjects were presented to Colleges, University and public libraries and other Government agencies.

CULTURAL PROGRAMMES

To this city of poets USIS Lahore arranged to bring, during the 60s, a number of contemporary American poets who recited their poetry and discussed their craft with local poets. In 60s the following three outstanding music events took place:

Black Singer Marina Anderson's moving performance in the Odeon Cinema Hall.The great Duke Ellinton thrilling young Jazz lovers of Lahore performed at the Open Air Theatre. Punjab Governor, Akhtar Hussain was the Chief Guest. A delightful performance by the Minneapolis Symphony Orchestra, led by famous conductor Andre Dorati was also held at the Open Air Theatre.

PARTICIPATION IN LOCAL EVENTS

The US Culture Centre had also been participating in important local and National events of literary and cultural interest. In 1963 USIS participated in the first International Book Exhibition organized by Booksellers and publishers in Punjab University Hall. It was inaugurated by President Muhammad Ayub Khan. A programme of dance and music was also arranged at the centre. Iqbal Day, Mirza Ghalib's centenary in 1969 and one thousandth anniversary of great poet and musician Ameer Khusrau along with performance by Iqbal Bano was also arranged.

Film shows have been a part of USIS activity since its very inception. It has its film library, which has thousand of films on variety of subject. The American Centre had a lot of work in connection with President Nixon's visit to Lahore in 1969. In January 1973 USIS Lahore moved into its present building on Shahrah-e-Fatima Jinnah. It provides a magnificent auditorium, executive gallery, proper canteen facilities, and a very fine library.

There is no doubt that USIS Library and Culture Centre has been providing a great facility to the students and scholars and mediamen. Being next door neighbour to Fatima Jinnah Medical College for Girls, American Centre provided 12000 volumes of collection on Medical books and journals which has proved a boon to the Faculty and college. The American Centre auditorium offers excellent facilities for cultural programming film shows, seminars, lectures and music performances by American artists. The four-day showing of "Roots" had attracted a capacity crowd of viewers all invited guests. With the collaboration of local theatre groups American plays such as Tennessee Williams' "Summer and Smoke" were staged in the auditorium. Shortly after USIS moved into the present building, auditorium facilities were offered to an outstanding Urdu novelist (Adamjee Award Winner). Jameela Hashmi, to launch her new book. Besides, being a well-known writer, she was also a well-connected person. Consequently, the function was attended by a full house of creative writers, Literary critics, journalists, radio and TV officials, and bureaucrat intellectuals, not only from Lahore, but also from Islamabad and other places. The function helped to introduce the (new) American centre to the intellectual community of Lahore.

Film shows, seminars, lectures, music performances by American artists, American plays, etc., etc. are a regular feature now. Of late the Centre also sponsored local plays, exhibitions, talks and lectures by local literary figures. The library due to its qualitative staff attracts its patrons from amongst Judges, Members of the Bar, Government officials, leading journalists, creative writers and intellectuals.

THE BRITISH COUNCIL

The British Council was established in 1934 and incorporated by Royal Charter in 1940. The Council is supposed to promote knowledge of Britain and English Language abroad, maintain cultural relations between UK and other countries. It administers programmes of education co-operation with developing countries. In 1976 it had offices in 78 countries overseas, Pakistan inclusive. The British Council's estimate yearly expenditure runs into millions of pounds and the major part is provided from the public exchequer. The Council's education work includes organizing training courses at home and overseas in supplying printed material etc. to the personnel. It undertakes recruitment for overseas educational appointments, and also arranges for British Specialists to go over-seas on advisory and lecture tours. It also provides information on the teaching of English as second or foreign language and all other aspects of English education. As an extension of works in education the British Council undertakes on full cost contractual basis, co-operative projects specifically designed to meet the particular education and man-power planning and development needs of Government and education establishments. It administers many programmes for visitors, scholars and students from overseas including British Technical Co-operation Programme student and youth exchanges. It provides administrative and welfare service for overseas students in Britain. The most important aspect of the Council assignment is promotion of the British performing visual arts abroad by supporting tours of theatre and ballet companies, orchestras and chamber groups and fine arts and documentary exhibitions from U. K.

The above being the Charter of British Council in general, it started its operation in Pakistan since 1947 with its Headquarters in the capital city of Karachi. It has a regional office in Lahore with a Library Project Management Unit and English Teaching centre.

The aim of the British Council is to enhance the relationship between Pakistan and Britain and to create partnerships through cultural, technical and educational co-operation, which contributes to Pakistan's social and economic development. The key areas of work of the British Council are:

- Promoting English as the language of international communication, and as a vehicle for development.
- Providing Britain's contribution to the global information society in Pakistan.
- Demonstrating the breadth and fertility of British culture.
- Promoting fundamental areas such as good government human rights and improving the position of women.
  Major components of the work are:
- Art Work: a showcase for the quality and vitality of British arts.
- Examinations: Access to the British examination resources in Pakistan.
- Teaching Centres: top quality English teaching at all levels.
- Education counselling service: detailed information for Pakistani students on all aspects of the British education scene, and support for British education exporters.
- Publishing promotion programme: major libraries and information centres in Lahore, Karachi, Islamabad and Peshawar and support to the book trade.

- Supporting development: project development in key development areas.

"The arts are excellent ambassadors for British. They demonstrate Britain's vitality, capacity for innovation and rich cultural resources. They are central to the British Council's role as Britain's role as British international network for education, culture and development. In our arts work, they help create international partnerships, refresh international perceptions of Britain and provide close support for Britain's political and trade relations with other countries. Above all, we celebrate the innovation, creativity and excellence of the arts in Britain today. A new programme of cultural co-operation aims to stimulate artistic development through contact with Britain. With sponsorship support they now have an ambitious and wide ranging arts programme, During 1997 the focus was on "From Thames to Indus Festival, their contribution to the celebrations to mark the 50th anniversary of the creation of Pakistan."

The British bring to Pakistan a variety of high quality and exciting arts events, exhibitions and performances supported by a team of specialists in Arts Group in London, they keep in touch with the best of the British Arts Scene. Committed to excellence and championing innovation, their aim is to refresh and update perceptions of Britain by introducing new work and new artists to international audiences. Through arts work their aim is to encourage partnerships with organizations both in UK and internationally. A successful arts project is always a collaborative venture and in Pakistan they worked with local government arts organizations and colleges to present British Arts and cultural activities.

British Council work represents the best of the British arts scene, including festivals and showcases, performance tours and exhibitions. In 1997 the Council brought the Royal Shakespeare Company to Pakistan for the first time, to perform, in Lahore. 'Traditions of Respect' a visual exhibition celebrating the close ties between Islam and Britain, toured Pakistan. A changed world, a contemporary sculpture exhibition was displayed in Lahore. High quality information resources and publications complement the activities they present.

The British Council supports development through academic link and exchange programmes with an increasing emphasis on in-country programmes. They have a highly professional and well-regarded project management capability in education and health, which has been recognised by the awarding of a number of major, contracts to them. Although the majority of the Council's project management work is funded under the British Government's aid programme, significant work is already undertaken for the World Bank and the Asian Development Bank.

FRENCH CULTURE CENTRE

The French Cultural Centre was established in Lahore in the year 1963. It is located near the Hockey Stadium in Gulberg, Lahore. The Organization works direct under the control of the French Embassy in Islamabad. The French Cultural Centre attends to the following two major activities:

1. The Language course (school level in French conducted by Pakistani Teachers)
2. Cultural activities at Lahore

The French Centre arranges alternately each month an exhibition of Paintings, Sculpture and Architecture etc. by Pakistani artists and the next month by any French Artist. During the Pakistan's Golden Jubilee celebrations the centre arranged musical shows at Alhamra Arts Council Cultural Complex on Ferozepur Road. There was also a jazz programme plus rock and roll dance. Still another programme of cultural troupe was organized at the Lahore Aitchison College. The French Cultural Centre has a big library, which has a rich collection of French and English language books in thousand. These are lent to the students and members of the Centre. Most of the books are on Art, Music, Literature and Museum etc. It is learnt that the centre arranges workshop with local educational institutions and collaborates with the sister organizations in France in this respect. The Centre has also arranged collaboration between the French Civil Service Academy and Pakistan Civil Service Academy along with National Institute of Public Administration for instructions in French Language. The Cultural centre is also running classes at University of the Punjab, the Kinnaird College and Aitchison College. The staff is provided and paid by the Centre.

GERMAN CULTURE CENTRE

This cultural centre again established under the bilateral cultural pact between Pakistan and Germany started its activities in the year 1961. Originally it provided facility for a German Reading Room in the locality of Nila Gumbad in the vicinity of Anarkali Lahore. Later on this was converted to Goethe Institute and was designated as Cultural Centre for the Federal Republic of Germany. A few years later it shifted to Fane Road Lahore where it built a Library, and reading room etc. In 1978 the Goethe Institute shifted to 5-H, Main Gulberg, Lahore. In 1978 the Goethe Institute again changed its premises to 92-EI G-XIII where it functioned till 31.3.1998. The Institute was closed down by the Central Administration of the Goethe Institute in Munich - Germany by their Government.

This organization was offering German Language Course and extending library facilities and a reading room. These consisted of material and literature on history, culture and art. The other main function of the Goethe Institute, which they propagate, was to promote culture. In this field the German Centre was holding and financing local groups under the banner of parallel theatre. These theatrical performances belonged to a particular Leftist school of thought which were exclusively funded by this organization. Their shows/ performances were held in the premises of Goethe Centre as also financed outside the Centre. The centre used to arrange exhibitions, Lectures, Seminars, Workshops, film shows etc. The main beneficiaries on account of theatre were the AJOKA Group. They as reported by the members felt shelterless and staged their play Bala King on the final closing date of the center. According to their version the Goethe Institute was engaged in dissemination of liberal thought and patronized this type of theatre. However, the local staff of the defunct Goethe Institute has purchased all the furniture, fixtures and library etc. and set up a Private German Centre in 237-A/3 Gulberg-III, Lahore. It is learnt that this private organization will continue to provide people information about tourism, trade and education etc. in Germany. They also plan to start their cultural activities in the manner the defunct Goethe Institute was carrying on.

Goethe Institute was offering German language courses and library facility with 5000 books on history, literature, culture and art.

The other main function of the Goethe Institute was to promote culture. In this field it was offering parallel theatre, exhibitions, lectures, seminars, workshops, film shows etc. The closure of the Goethe Institute was an end of a cultural era in Lahore. But after the closure of the Goethe Institute in Lahore the local staff of the Institute has opened an Institute with the name "Lahore German Centre" which will continue the German language classes and provide the people information about tourism, trade and education in Germany. It has also plans to start in near future the light cultural activities.

Following the closure of Goethe Institute in the city, some of the staff, as reported earlier, decided to open a centre of their own for the promotion of German languages and to provide employment to those who were left in the lurch.

A businessman who is an old student of Goethe Institute joined the venture and lent financial support. The Lahore German Centre thus came into being, and it was inaugurated by Mr. Waldemar Kroders, honorary consul of Germany.

Almost all Goethe teachers, including German nationals, will be teaching at the new centre, which is located near the 7-Up factory. Starting from May, they shall be offering basic German language courses. Weekend conversation class for those who have no time on normal working days will also be held .In addition to painting classes for children on Sundays, music classes and some light cultural activities are also on the agenda of managers. Information about trade and education in Germany will also be provided and the centre will be a centre for local German residents and German speaking Pakistanis.

The Goethe Institute was all along disseminating and promoting liberal thought. Various theatrical groups were promoted and financial support for production provided under different cultural titles. They used to allow even stage productions which were not generally enncouraged by the Government at their forums. Always supporting adaptations and portraying a typical school of thought were not usually welcome.

IRANIAN CULTURE CENTRE

The cultural, religious and literary relation of Iran and Pakistan need no comments. For centuries Persian has been official language of Lahore. A lot of our literary and historical material is recorded in that language. After Independence like other countries the brotherly Iranian Government also thought of opening a cultural centre at Lahore. The earlier exchanges took place when Dr. Saeed Nafeeci visited Lahore and founded a Majlis P-i-Pharcy Pakistan in 1956. With the efforts of Sufi Ghulam Mustafa Tabassam, a pharcy teacher and poet of Lahore, Khana-i-Farhang Iran came into existence. Sufi Ghulam Mustafa Tabassam was its first Director. The office was located on the Mall Road near Regal Chowk. Its Directors who later on came from Iran were Aqa Yousaf Rehbari, Aqa Ahmad Ali Panahee, Aqa Ahmad Ali Mahrpur, Aqa Fatehullah Mujani, Khanum Maryam Behnam, Aqa Rashid Farzanapur, Aqa Ali Ahmad Saji and Aqa Sadiq Ganji.

Prior to establishment of Iranian cultural centre a similar centre was working in Karachi. Iranian Culture Centre is managed by Iranian Culture Counsel and this office is attached with Ministry of Education who administratively and financially managed the institution. In 1979 the kingship in Iran changed into a Islamic Republic which was led by Imam Ayatollah Khamini from 1979–1982. The literary activities of the Centre remained slightly slow. These revived into full after 1982. The Iranian Culture Centre runs various courses on Persian language and literature. There is a big library and reading room. Various types of educational and literary magazines published from Iran are also available there. In addition to literary activities the Iranian Culture Centre holds many literary functions at different venues in the city .e.g. Alhamra, Hotels, College Halls etc., etc. The office of Iranian Culture Centre is now located in Gulberg. Recently they have also started teaching in Fine Arts and paintings.

THE HONORARY CONSULATES

In addition to regular Cultural Centres some of the countries have their nucleus offices here which are managed by the local Honorary Consuls, and local men of means of status. At a time when any cultural troupe or team visits Lahore for performances, they conduct them and also co-ordinate with local Art Council and other offices.

These Honorary Consulates are:-

Consulate of Austria
4-Lawrance Road, Lahore.
Consulate of Belgium
6-Egerton Road, Lahore.
Consulate of Brazil
LCCHS, Lahore Cantt.
Consulate of Denmark
27-Main Gulberg, Lahore.
Consulate of France
41- Zafar Ali Road, Lahore.
Consulate of Greece
71-A, Main Gulberg, Lahore.

Consulate of Italy
95-B, Gulberg-III, Lahore.
Consulate of Malaysia
86-D, Model Town, Lahore.
Consulate of Netherlands
Kashmir Egerton Road, Lahore
Consulate of Germany
60-Main Gulberg, Lahore.
Consulate of Norway
295/3, Sarwar Road, Lahore Cantt.
Consulate of Philippines
Gulberg Lahore.

17

LAHORI FOOD
And Cuisine

The history of human evolution has also helped the man to make food. Originally it may have started with the hunting and killing of animals by hurling rocks on them. The growth and evolution of human body, as the story goes, caused furtherence in this process. The food quest had helped to transform ape into man. The atmospheric changes forced the man to develop more rapidly and then more man than ape. Later, the man discovered the use of fire. Light, warmth within caves must have had a powerful effect on humanizing process. This was followed by the appearance of a pre-historic race on Homosapines the larger brand successor of Homosapiens known as Neanderthals. After the disappearance of Neanderthals, man a more advanced breed of men who, in a temporal mild climate, were able to develop refined tools. The bones and horns were used as hunting weapons, fishing hooks developed and so on. This was followed by climatic changes where the man, animal and vegetation all began to adapt themselves accordingly with more radical changes. Thus in this manner food played its part in the making of man. Now it was to make history, the pre-historic hunter was undoubtedly skilful. Killing of his prey may have a less problem to the hunter than those carrying it and conserving it. The pre-historic man, when within the range of sea coasts and rivers and lakes made considerable use of shell fish of all kinds, whether he killed by spear or traping. If men and boys went for hunting and fishing, the elders of the tribe were busy making tools. The women and girls set on their own for special food task of cooking the edible roots, green stuff not berries and small fauna, root vegetables were always important. Turnip, onion, large types of radish certainly date back to this pre-historic period. The womenfolk also collected small animals for purposes of food whenever it came in their way. There is evidence of wild man forced to take great variety of food of not only snails but river crabs and small turtles, pistachio nuts and such other material. They also learnt to trap partridges and migratory water fouls for hundreds of thousand of years. The human race ate its food raw. But some time between the first taming of fire and the appearance on the pre-historic scene of Neanderthal man cooking was discovered. This helped to make a number of formerly indigestible foods edible. It also increased the nutritive value of others since heat helps to break down fibres and release protein and carbohydrates, the introduction of cooking may well have been the decisive factor in leading man from primarily animal existence into one that was more fully human. Till date little is known about pre-historic cooking. Infact what happened in the kitchen between first culinary use of fire and evolution of pottery containers, tens of thousands of years later is almost entirely open to conjecture. Broasting–probably the first method used may have been discovered first. At some stage later the pre-historic cook discovered that meat done in the embers last less weight than it did when tossed on blazing fire. Cooking the roots in the embers was the next logical step. On a flat stone next of the fire, however turnips and onions could be baked. Pot cooking is certainly of considerable antiquity and it may have evolved during early tribal migrations over open terrain. The finding, the beginning of process of boiling is still a difficult question to be answered. But pot was first step and that followed evolutionary process.

The neolithic revolution i.e. the change from a primarily hunting fishing gathering existence to one in which man became a settled farmer and stock-breeder took place in different times in different parts of the world. However, none is sure where and when it really began. It was not the field of cultivated grain that brought villages into being but new and abundant fields of wild grain. The mellowing climates of near East resulted in conditions which favoured fast growing plants. The roasted grain and making of grain paste and solving the digestive problem led to an epoch making discovery in pre-historic time enabling man despite the limits of his technology to make a quantity of solid food out of tiny insubstantial seeds. It was portable food, too, which could be carried on a journey either ready-made or in the form of groats to which liquid would be added when required. The first unleavened bread may have been invented when man discovered that a piece of grain paste laid on the hot stone next to the fire developed an appetizingly crisp crust. The plain flour and water flat bread still survives in many parts of the world. Some time improved by addition of little fat or other ingredient to make it more delicious. The Mexican "tortilla" and scots "oatcake" the Indian "Chapati", the Chinese "Paping", Ethopian "Injera" are all direct decendants of neolithic bread, utilizing virtually the same balance of material. It is mainly the difference in the basic grain, maize, oats wheat or millet which makes the end products seem so dissimilar. Of course, this was subject to availability of grains, hunting fishing eatables and soil conditions with favourable climate. Slowly the knowledge about agriculture increased and similarly about the plants and animal domestication. Then followed immigration and population increased. Changes in quality of food cooking in a given climate, area and availability of supplies also progressed and improved. In the context of food history it certainly goes with Indus Valley

Civilization. The most important food crop raised in the early days was a small seeded foxtail millet and small amount of wheat. Rice was originally cultivated south of Yangtse, a wooded and marshy land of China.

DEVELOPMENT OF COOKERY

Cities are the index of civilization admired for their palaces, temples, art and aqueducts but as a rule for granaries. Yet, the whole magnificent structure of the world and first great civilization. Sumer and Egypt rested on those granaries and men who worked to fill them. This being the general scene in retrospect, in case of India it was another matter. Domesticated animals had already been common at the height of the Indus Valley Civilization though meat did not form the mainstay of the diet. With the collapse of Harrappa and Mohenjodaro and arrival of Aryan nomads, livestock and cattle in particular assumed great importance. Aryan food was mutton and beef, milk, curd and cooking medium was ghee. The Aryans seem to have introduced dependence on dairy products. Buddhism and Jainism however, brought a belief in the sanctity of all life and resultant advocacy for vegetarianism. Subject to change of economic conditions the diet of nobility responded to changes. The conditions of absorbing foreign food and foreign techniques of cooking were also conducive with sudden surges of innovation. The food of peasant, however, took an air of permanence. The Arabs under banner of Islam swept along Mediterranean coasts up to Persian Empire. The change from austre desert life to civilization and cosmopolitan luxury of Baghdad and subsequent innovation of cookery and food of green valleys thus trickled down to the sub-continent through Northern invading forces. Infact when Aryans arrived in India they also brought animals. The religious sanction here also gave birth to new food and changed dietry habits but with passage of time these adjusted. The Indian curry is a sauce designed to add relish to rice or the pliable wheaten chapatis equally accepted by the immigrants. Quite a large number of generalised recipes have earlier Indian cooking and are known for that period but describing true nature of each at the time is difficult. Variety in rice cooking, meat and beef dishes, poultry, drinks, syrups, liquors, grape-wines, honey and sugar were the few items which can be luxury ingredients of royal cookery. With the growth of towns, the market places, sale of merchandise, need for ware-houses, movement of people for sale and purchase at the given points caused the need for cooked food and thus came into being the cook-shops. The establishment of the Muslim rule in India in the sixteenth century had far reaching effects not only on Indian society but on Indian food. For about four centuries, followers of Islam had been drifting into northern India bringing with them their every day food and cooking methods. But at the court of the Mughals, a new haute cuisine was introduced into India. 'Mughal' style cooking was almost directly derived from that of Central Asia and Isphahan in Persia, a place which was a symbol of splendour to the sixteenth century Muslims as Versailles to the seventeenth-century Frenchmen.

Kababs, pilaf (or Pulao) dishes of rice with shredded meat, the technique of mixing fruits into fresh dishes, the use of almonds and milk, rose water, the garnishing of all kinds of food with fragile strips of tissue beaten out of pure gold and silver, all these were absorbed into the Indian cuisine. The Muslims were quite prepared to eat beef, but their cuisine was based on mutton and chicken, and non-vegetarian Hindus were therefore able to adopt it without hesitations. The region in which Muslim food became most common was in the north, the heartland of the Mughal rule. Even today, the cooking of the Punjab has almost as many links with the food of the near East as with that of traditional India. And what is Punjab, practically it means Lahore, the headquarters of the Mughals and their Government. One innovation which spread throughout the sub-continent was the Muslim addiction to sweetmeats, Just as Spain had learned of marzipan's of nougats from the Arabs, so India discovered the delights of sugar candy. Confections of all kinds, made from sugar alone, from sugar and almonds, from sugar and rice flour, from sugar and coconut, became immensely popular, as did sweet desserts such as Halwa. But although Hindu Indians ate candies with enthusiasm, it was Muslims who were most expert at their manufacture, Predominantly Muslim cities such as Dacca and Lucknow became, and have remained, the great sweetmeat centres of the sub-continent but these come after Lahore's "Barfi" which people take as present for their relatives & friends. In the anarchic early decades of the eighteenth century, the English, French, Portuguese, Dutch, and Danish travellers would all have found a number of their compatriots in India, settled comfortably in trading posts, living in semi-Indian style and eating semi-Indian food. They had already embarked on the development of Hindu-Muslim-European cuisine which has been passed off ever since in the West as 'Indian' Punjabi-Muslim food. Perhaps, they loaded their 'curries' with meat, poultry, and fish which entirely changed the character of the dish.

The above being brief of food and drink history in general, Lahoris absorbed the traditions and techniques of food, drink and cuisine from India, Central Asian States, Persia, Afghanistan, the Turkish and Greek invadors. The in-coming forces naturally caused change in cuisine and eating habits. These also under-went a change with over all human progress. The agricultural and industrial products also played their role in this direction. The barren and deserted lands developed into agriculture farms. The Jungles turned gardens, advancement of scientific knowledge and abundance of food products, coupled with institutionalization of family system and better education improved a great deal in effecting changes in finished cuisine products, but till late they were mostly dominated by local ingredients except that of meat. It was late in the 19th century that the western in-puts and stuffs entered the Lahore cuisine. Any way this was the evolution of grain becoming a staple food and millets and other wild grown groats contributed towards daily food. The wheat, rice, wine, liquors, birds, foul and poultry was the food for the rich. The poor and peasants subsisted on low quality stuff, i.e. grams, Moth, Millets etc. During the Sikh period the economic conditions were not very good and food and drink patterns continued deteriorating. No improvement could happen due to little attention towards productions in general, in the Province. However, the fact that across Sutlej, the British Government was working and the Sikh Regime had full diplomatic relations and movement of people both regular and irregular was there it might have brought changes and improvements in food preparation and Kitchen wares. During the Sikh period Lahore gave a very dirty look, streets full of garbage and litter. The population consisted of Muslims, Sikhs, Afghans, Kashmiri and some Persians. It was estimated around 50000 in 1830. Immediately on occupation in 1849 the British introduced the canal system and the Lower Bari Doab was fully operative in the late 1860s. Aggressive measures were taken to regulate the land and water management system. The Revenue system was also enforced which resulted in increase of agricultural produce and consequently the food and cuisine under-went change mainly due to abundant production and supplies. The British in their reports after some years of occupation made following observations on the food conditions of Lahore.

GRAIN AS STAPLE FOOD

The cultivating classes generally consume grain of the poorer kinds. Before the Bari Doab Canal brought water into the Majha, wheat was seldom eaten by the people except on the occasion of weddings, when it was purchased from the lowlands, and considered a great treat. It is now grown so much more largely that it will no doubt soon take its place as the staple food of the country; but even now barley, gram, moth, Indian corn, chural and chin't are more generally the food in use. The grain is ground, and kneaded with water and made into round cakes or chapatis. Rice is too expensive to be much used, and has to be carried from distances. Meat is also eaten, particularly the flesh of the goat or kid. Vegetables are also sought after; the saag of serson or leaves of the mustard plant is the most used. The people are very fond of curds, and butter-milk, and consider the want of the latter a great hardship and deprivation. Gur and Shakkar, the unrefined sugar, is also much used, particularly at weddings and merry meetings; it is an expensive item, for it is used not only with food, but also as a drink mixed with water or made into a sharbat. Salt is indispensable for every meal, and it is also largely given to cattle. Ghee, or refined butter, is much valued as a relish with chapatis or in cooking, and several kinds of dal are also in common use. The cultivator eats well, for his labour in the field whets his appetite; and being always in the open air, he requires food to sustain him. He seldom eats before 12 O' clock in the day, and will have another meal at night-fall.

As we know the Lahori cooking and cuisine developed in the Muslim courts of India and widely known as "Mughal" cuisine, is part of the stock national repertoire. It relies for its flavours on a blend of the more exotic herbs and spices such as saffron, cardamom, sesame and poppy seeds (the last too often roasted). The subtly bud-bursting quality of the resulting tastes and fragrances would be forfeited by the over-liberal use of chillies, consequently this food is perhaps the best choice for palates unaccustomed to very hot food.

MUGHAL COOKERY

Most menus offer a selection of meat and poultry served in a variety of spicy sauces. The word Mughlai (a la Mughal), often a misnomer, is frequently appended to the name of the dish to emphasize its aristocratic origins and indicate the school of cooking described above. Other words pertaining to cooking methods appear as part of the name given to dishes bhuna gosht (meat sautee in which the meat is fried with a variety of spices and comes in a paste rather than a sauce), 'machli ka salan' (fish curry) or 'bheja masala', (meat in spicy yoghurt gravy) may be suffixed with the word 'mughlai or zafrani' (with saffron) or indeed the name of a chef, establishment or region. 'Khara masala gosht' (whole spice meat), do-piaza' (two onion) chicken or mutton which requires onions to be added at two different stages of the cooking process and 'roghni gosht' (garnished meat) are just a few more popular dishes. These are variously garnished with fried onions, raisins, cashew-nuts, pistachios and slivers of almonds. Sliced tomatoes and boiled eggs, shredded lettuce, and raw or lightly cooked onions are also used to make presentation more attractive and colourful. As the restaurants become cheaper, the luxury elements in dishes are replaced with larger quantities of cheap ingredients such as tomatoes, onions, garlic, ginger, turmeric and chillies, making the food correspondingly hotter.

Another legacy from the Mughal era is the celebrated haleem claimed to be much loved by the Emperor Akbar. It contains succulent pieces of meat, cooked in seven grains including rice, wheat and various lentils ground to a sensuous, velvety texture. Its variant khichra, ground meat cooked with similar ingredients is a much "stodgier" concoction, equally if not more popular. Both are available from shops and stalls in disposable earthenware pots as are many other foods bought from street vendors and cheap stalls. Dalcha is a more mundane version consisting of meat and channe ki dal (yellow split-pea lentils) in a brown gravy, and may appear in many restaurants. Another perennial favourite dish is nahari which consists of large chunks of beef from the head and shoulder, with brain, tongue and marrow added to a highly seasoned gravy. Traditionally nahari was eaten at breakfast by workers to sustain them throughout the day. Ironically it is now a much sought-after delicacy and available only from selected restaurants on specific days but it is a speciality of the walled city. It is served with slivers of ginger, fried and raw onions, fresh chillies, chopped coriander and lime juice and eaten with nan.

Lahore's most famous contribution to the international gourmet scene is probably tandoori chicken, a chicken quarter steeped in marinade and barbecued in a tandoor (underground clay oven) from which it derives its name. Tikka Kababs made from cubes of chicken, mutton, fish or king prawns and sometimes beef, are a constant favourite and come in an enormous variety. Most tikkas and kababs are barbecued on skewers or baked in the tandoor oven unless the cooking method is specified as in karahi kabab (fried with onions and spices, in the work-like karahi). Seekh-Kababs are succulent sausage-shaped tubes of mince meat cooked in a tandoor or barbecued, after being moulded directly onto the skewer (seekh). Also commonly found and convenient to carry is the shami kabab, a meat rissole sometimes filled with a mixture of finely chopped onions, mint and coriander seasoned with lemon juice.

Nargisi koftas (meatballs) are coated in a spicy meat-paste and deep fried. Sometimes these are served in an onion sauce. Ghulvan kabab (dissolved kababs) and dam kabab (steamed kababs) are rarer and highly prized for the melt-in-the-mouth quality of their minced meat which is softened literally to a paste with the aid of natural tenderizers such as raw papaya or kachri (a species of melon). Traditionally kababs are eaten with naan, bread baked in a tandoor, or its variant kulcha sprinkled with sesame seeds. The paratha is also a popular alternative. Depending on the chef's recipe they can range from circles of airy, layered, puff pastry to a thicker, fried version of the ordinary chapati. Parathas also come stuffed with mince meat or vegetables. The versatile puri, a small, puffed circle of bread is enjoyed with meat, vegetables and lentils as well as desserts. Some places boast of special breads such as shirmal cooked with milk and eggs, which like nan, is one of the few yeast baked breads. Roghni bread is soft and slightly sweet and is also another favourite kabab accompaniment.

Biryani, rice cooked in rich meat sauce (or chicken, fish or prawns) possibly tops the national popularity polls and is reserved for special occasions due to its festive character. Like various sweetmeats and other celebration foods it is often decorated with finely beaten edible silver paper and partly dyed in attractive orange with saffron. Pulao is a lighter version of biryani and may contain meat, chicken or fish cooked in simple bouillon. Cloves, cardamoms, peppercorns and cinnamon are used to increase the aroma of rice dishes. Rose-water and kevra sprinkled over rice and other foods add further fragrance. The humdrum khichri, a mixture of rice and channe ki dal, is also favoured with aromatics. A masly version is eaten with a sauce of mint and natural yoghurt to cure diarhhoea. Traditionally most rice dishes are served with raita, yoghurt sauce seasoned with salt, pepper, ground fresh coriander and a sprinkling of chillies. Grated cucumber and mint flavoured raita is probably the most famous one worldwide. Elaborate recipes of raita may include fried vegetables, such as okra, aubergine or pumpkin and an infusion of fried mustard or cuminseed with turmeric.

Yoghurt is also a crucial ingredient of the pungent, strongly flavoured cuisine eaten at brunch or tea. The spicy chaat (literally "lick") dishes fall into this category and it is astonishing to see what can be achieved with boiled potatoes and chick-peas or gram flour. They are doused in yoghurt, chillies, and chaat-masala (a combination of roasted hot spices), sprinkled with fruit, chopped green chillies and onions, topped with hot red-chilly sauce, sweet and sour tamarind or green chutney made from mint or coriander in a base of lime juice and ground green chillies.

"Chutney" is the word for hot tangy dips made from ground ingredients and served in place of relishes and ketchup. Easy to eat finger foods perfect for filling gaps, include pakora, deep fried balls made from a batter of pale yellow gram flour, flavoured with spices and bhujia, batter-fried vegetables. These come with piquant chilli chutneys, spiced yoghurt or tamarind sauces. Kachuri, a crisp, round pastry filled with lentil paste is a delicious alternative. The authenticity of these tastes is an experience available only from the stalls of street-vendors and can rarely be replicated at home. Other cheap, convenient snacks from barrows include roasted peanuts (mungphali) and gram pulses (channa) available in slim paper cones. Kabuli channa is seasoned with salt, powdered with red-chillies and lime juice.

Devilled kidneys (gurda), liver (kaleji), brain (bheja) and sweetbreads (kapoora) are delicious flavours for those who enjoy offal. They are eaten with paratha or ordinary chapati. Alu-puri (spicy potatoes with puri) are also popular at breakfast which is often rounded off with suji ka halwa (semolina pudding) also eaten with puri. The rare and subtly delicious andey ka halwa is a taste not to be missed if the chance presents itself. Other desserts include shahi tukra (imperial pieces), a national version of bread pudding, coated in cream and slivers of pistachios and almonds and gajar ka halwa, a delicious dessert made from carrots and popular with wrestlers and body builders for the vitality and strength they claim to get from it.

Lahoris prefer meat to vegetables so the order of priority on social occasions is meat, poultry and seafood. Lentils and vegetables are regarded merely as accompaniments although some of these are delicacies in their own right.

The main meal for an average Lahori family probably consists of meat, poultry or fish cooked in gravy with a dish or two of vegetables or lentils, plain boiled rice and chapatis or its puffed variant roti, nan and the kulcha, the commonest of all Lahoris breads. Poorer households may forego meat in favour of more filling food such as potatoes.

The Lahoris dislike the sourness of tamarind, lime and raw mangoes, preferring the sustenance provided by energy giving meals of potatoes, meat and the freat regional favourite dal (lentils). When one of the many varieties of dal is infused with garlic, red-chillies, curry-leaves, cuminseed or onions fried in ghee (refnied butter) it is known as tarka (or baghar) and regarded as a great delicacy. Bread is perhaps the most vital part of the Lahori meals and in rural areas, is sometimes accompanied with little more than raw onion and a green chilli or two washed down with a pot of fresh milk or chach, a buttermilk variant of lassi. This may be followed with a lump of the fudge-like gur (a product of boiled sugar cane) which is used as a sweetener instead of refined sugar.

Lahoris eat sweets and confectioneries to celebrate happy occasions much as a bottle of champagne is popped in the west. Hence the demand of " mithai khilao" (distribute sweets) directed to people with reason to celebrate. A wide variety of milk based sweets is available from "sweet marts". The commonest of these are barfi (a fudge-like sweet which comes in coconut, pistachio and almond squares), pera (a similar, round sweet, harder and more crumbly in texture).

The ubiquitous paan (betel leaf) is worth a try. It is available from stalls on every street corner. A variety of fragrances and tastes are wrapped with chopped betel nut into the leaf and this is generally eaten after meals. Those addicted to it eat it at all times of day except directly before meals and spit out the red-stained liquid much like tobacco chewers.

All in all then exciting taste sensations await the more for the interested. While fast-food chains, food-stores and middle-to-expensive restaurants cater to more international tastes, the general status of food slightly differs in city. The Lahoris generally attribute their good health to the in-take of milk products in large quantities. This is in respect of the residents of the walled city who are least worried about the fat contents of butter, curd, milk and ghee etc. Be it evening meal or morning breakfast, lunch or supper; one would find that they are always up to eat something and hardly concerned with the hazards of consuming fattening foods. The vitamins, importance of minerals and proteins, the danger of high cholestrol and uric acid producing foods are apparently unthought of. The residents of city thrive on such food items i.e. milk, cream, ghee, meat, beef, poultry & even "sri-pai" unmindful of the risks of weight and negative effects on the physique and other distortion which these food ingredients may cost. Infact ghee was and is still regarded as a supreme source of energy. It is the modern scientific and medical education, better health care and health services that have now created awareness in the educated classes about heart problems, blood pressure and allied diseases which the fat rich foods bring. But the pattern of foods and cuisine continues in the traditional manner in the city. Infact there is a saying "jo kare gheu na kare ma na kare peau". Lahore and.Lahoris are known for their staple drink of Lassi which in summer is used both at the breakfast and the lunch. There are varieties of Lassi available in the market at the known points. It can be full cream Lassi and from curd and fat free variety from which the butter has been extracted. The other kind of Lassi is mixture of curd and milk which is mixed with 'Madhani' with appropriate quantity of sugar, salt and ice cubes. Still another variety of Lassi is which is mixture of curd and milk and 'paidas'. Generally the use of Lassi in the old city is that it is a part of the breakfast taken by all in summer months. During lunch time it is must but in winter months it is only in the morning breakfast that it is now taken by Lahoris. The Lassi is also used in the modern localities. Some of these localities are of the newly rich class of businessmen, Government servants and industrialists. The British introduced the use of tea which has replaced Lassi in most of the elite classes in the breakfast. It remains optional in the lunches but in summer months it is an essential component. Lassi is the only poorman's medicine to fight back the scorching heat. Since we are talking about the food drink and cuisine of Lahore we may also mention the availability points of Lassi shops and these are in Old Anarkali, Gowal Mandi, Lohari, Ravi Road, Chowk Rang Mahal, Delhi Gate and Sheranwala Gate are known for the quality and there are practically queues of those waiting for a glass.

Another bye-product of milk is milk mixed with Kasuri 'Falooda' and 'Tukhmlanga.' The two very known points of this delicacy of milk (which is sold added with a part of 'Rabri' is in the Old Anarkali where the business continues from 11.00 a.m. in the morning till 2.00 a.m. in the night and Mozang Adda, Gowal Mandi chowk shop, outside Bhati gate and Inside Lohari Gate. Still another preparation of the milk is "Pure Kasuri Falooda". This is a sort of spaghetti mixed with Tukhmlanga, sugar, syrup and Rabri (of milk), of course with ice. This is usually served in Chinese Bowls and available in Old Anarkali, Hira Mandi, Delhi Gate, Chowk Rang Mahal, Chuna Mandi and Ichhra. The other bye-products of milk are 'Barfi' and 'Khoya'. These are two specialities of Lahore. 'Barfi' is invariably made by every 'Halwai' (milk & curd alongwith Paidas made from Khoya). But the best Barfi is that of Lal Khoo inside Mochi Gate. The quality of this Barfi is known and it has taken a commercial shape and under its banner many shops are opening up in the new colonies around Lahore.

In the morning breakfast the Lahoris love to have 'Halwa Puri", 'Kachuri', 'pura' and 'Aaloo Chholey' a sort of spicy cooked curry with Achar (pickle). Immediately after partition and even till late in 70s the quality of 'Halwa Puri' and "Aaloo Chholey" used to be A-one. However, this has deteriorated. The cooked combination is not very delicious but still there are some points in Old Anarkali, inside Lohari Mandi, Shahalmi and Hira Mandi, where one could have a quality stuff compared with the ordinary places. Of course one has to wait for his turn for this stuff on the shop early in the morning.

There are special shops for Nahari in Chowk Gowal Mandi, Inside Lohari Gate, Chowk Chakla, Rang Mahal, Delhi Darvaza, Ichhra, Mozang, Qila Gujjar Singh where people leave their utensils in que for taking away Nahari (right from 4.00 a.m. in the morning). Nahari is a product of beef which is cooked all the night and is consumed with 'Nan' and 'Kulcha'. It is a sort of salty soup with some pieces of beef. Yet another item of breakfast which has gained popularity and importance for the last about two-three decades is the consumption of 'Sri Pai". Sometime back these were generally not cooked and considered to be a poorman's food. However of late somehow there is a feeling that it adds to energy and rejuvinates the sexual power. Two kinds of sri pai are cooked. Those of the sheep and goat and the other of the beef rendering animals. In case of beef "Bohng" is the most popular breakfast item in the city. The 'Pai' are burnt on the fire to lose and scrub the hair on the skin which are then scrapped with knife and after giving cuts Pai cooked. The spices used in this pais are cooking with appropriate quantity and a very thick greasy and gum like soup is considered to be the main quality of the Pai. People invite their friends inside the city to have this food specially in their dinner from the far off localities. The best known 'Pais' are those of 'Phajja' a shop in the Hira Mandi which is considered to be the sign of quality and spicy cooking. Not only that the people sit there and enjoy eating, they also use it as a take away food for their families. This food is now also sold in Ichhra, Misri Shah, Shad Bagh, Krishan Nagar, Lakshmi, Nisbet Road, Chowk Gowal Mandi, Rang Mahal and Taxali. This was the tradition for which the stuff used is known for its taste, variety and quality in and around city. Of course a countless number of petty shops have come up in other areas of the city where toasts, breads, biscuits, 'Rus' Buns, eggs, tea etc. are also sold as breakfast items. The latest addition to the breakfast items is that of mini mobile 'Paratha' preparation units. Some of the people take their stoves with iron pans and flour in the shape of paste and cook / prepare Paratha right sitting on the corners of chowks. The passers by, especially labour have their breakfast of Paratha with 'Saag' or butter as they like. Sometimes they also sell Paratha of maize flour with Saag. These Parathas are usually available in Bhati Chowk, near District Courts, around Data Darbar, outside Mochi Gate, Akbari Gate and Inside Sheranwala Gate.

We have already mentioned in the preceding paragraphs wheat bread only became available to the common man with better irrigation and agriculture in Punjab. Prior to that he subsisted on wildgrown grain and millets etc. With the access of this food to every citizen different forms of bread appeared. There were ordinary breads. There was Paratha prepared with Ghee. There was 'Nan' essentially cooked in earthen oven (a name imported from Persia and Afghanistan). The flour of the wheat prepared into paste was made to stay for some hours until it took the shape of initial stage of yeast. In the earthen oven with appropriate embers and coal heat these were laid, and cooked. There developed a variety of 'Nan' in which the basic material of the Nan slightly differed from ordinary wheat bread which is generally known as 'Maida'. The other kind of Nan was Nan with 'Qeema' in two loafs a layer of minced meat with spices, chillies, salt and other ingredients was cooked, and an appropriate quantity of ghee applied, immediately after it was taken out of the oven. This is generally eaten on lunch time and served on picnic parties, used as take away food, ordinarily it is consumed with dehi or curd. The other variety of Nan is that of 'Aaloo Wala' Nan. The potato paste mixed with spices is used inside the Nan and cooked in oven. Still another variety of Nan is the simply baked loaf which is ordinarily used on the food shops. Another shape of Nan generally eaten with breakfast or one may call poormans, loaf is called 'Kulcha'. On the front side 'Sesame' are applied. These are usually taken by low middle class in the morning as the simplest form of breakfast. Another most common routine food of the Lahoris is Nan Chholey. Chholey (Grams) are cooked in different ways. Ordinarily cooked without any meat. These are known as 'Chikar Chholey' and are usually consumed by working classes and low income groups as lunch and dinner. These have their own other varieties as well. The grams cooked in chicken are called 'Murgh Chholey' and there are certain places in the city which are known for the best variety known as 'Shahi Murgh Chholey'. The stall of 'Manna' on the Abbot Road is probably number one in the city. In addition Murgh Chholey inside Lohari Gate at chaskara, Anarkali, Alfalah, Lakshmi, and Nila Gumbad are the best places to go.

The most popular eating places which developed after partition and in early 60s were the 'Tikka Houses' where poultry and red meat is cooked on the spot and served straightaway. The first shop of this poultry food appeared in 1962 where one Ghulam Muhammad commonly known as 'Mama' opened a sort of barbecue shop in Mozang (Chowk Safanwala). He used to sell the chicken pieces, chicken 'Boty' and chicken cooked in Karahi at the spot. Needless to add that prior to this the roast chicken had arrived in the city and the biggest sale point specially for lunches was 'Nehmat Kadah Hotel' outside Lohari Gate. Infact the owner of Nehmat Kadah used to sell 'murgh chholey' outside Lohari Gate and his sons subsequently set up a hotel where with the arrival of broiler (in the poultry) it was sold comparatively on cheaper rates. The Tikka Karahi shop at Safanwala Chowk got so popular that one would have to wait to get the tikkas, chicken boty or chicken Karahi. While chicken tikka were roasted on the coal fire, chicken boty was cooked in ghee added with tomatoes, green chillies, onion, salt, some spices fresh way. Those going in for a change would go alongwith families to eat out their new variety of food. This business of chicken tikka became so popular that a big market developed on Jail Road just on the left side of Mozang Chungi. Similar food stalls appeared in the Lakshmi Chowk who added more varieties to the poultry food. Thus the poultry food business has expanded to a large extent and in almost all the newly built colonies there are sale points for preparation of the poultry food on order. A number of points in Gulberg, Defence Colony, Garden Town, Fortress Stadium in Cantt., Ichhra, Samanabad and Krishan Nagar, Iqbal Town, Muslim Town, are known for their products.

Lahoris are also fond of another food generally known as 'Haleem'. All the 'daals' are mixed and cooked with a certain quantity of beef or meat. Quite a number of spices are added to make it delicious. The dish is cooked the whole night and in the morning it is mixed and ground to the extent that it takes the shape of a thick paste. People usually eat this with 'Nan' and it is very popular in the old city. Quite a few persons are seen carrying their products on hand carriers with Nans and selling in the streets and bazars inside the city and in localities of Misri Shah, Qilla Gujjar Singh, Krishan Nagar, Sanat Nagar, Samanabad. This dish is also prepared on the occasions of alms giving days and also distributed as 'Bhandara' on the tombs of saints to the poor. People have now specially developed 'Chicken Haleem' dish which is served on parties which are organized in connection with Basant, Moharrram and Eid. With the arrival of conquers from Central Asia probably the roasting of meat and beef started. In its crude form it continued to be roasted from ember fire but later on cutting small pieces of the bigger pieces led to development of minced meat which finally turned into "Qeema." There were number of ways to prepare/cook dish, out of this meat and the most delicious and important which finally appeared was the 'kabab' also cooked on coals. For certain reasons this discontinued during the Sikh period but in Muslim majority or Muslim dominated areas beef or meat Kababs continued to be made. After the British period this again appeared on the scene and immediately before partition and afterwards this was a known delicacy of Lahori Food. It was an item speciality prepared, for the feasts and also a commercial item on festivals and a most handy and complete take away food item. The minced meat is mixed with added variety of Indian spices and then placed around iron rods and roasted on coal fire. The most tasty Kabab is made from beef although the rich prefer to go in for Kabab of chicken or meat. The kabab is served in friendly feasts. It has a particular relevance on drink parties. Recently with the poultry developing on commercial farming basis, chicken kababs are also prepared, served and sold in hotels, restaurants, way-side eating places. The best known sale points for this are the one Inside Mochi Gate "Khalifa Dey Kabab". There are also very known Kabab shops in Landa Bazar. The kabab shops go side by side with the chicken tikka and there are quite a few in Hira Mandi. Garhi Shahu Chowk, Lakshmi Chowk, Jail Road, Dharampura, Model Town Market and Mozang and Fortress Stadium are the most known places.

The next important dish is that of fish. The city being located on the river side, the Lahoris had privilege of fresh fish from the river. The most delicious fish used in Lahore was 'Khhaga' of Ravi which was daily caught and brought to the market fresh, sometimes even alive. The fish market is located outside Mori Gate. From here variety of fish is sold to the various city sale points, who sell it raw or in a cooked shape. The Lahori fish is broasted or fried in ghee or oil specially the 'Rahu' is known for its taste and crispness. People visiting Lahore like to have a taste of Lahori fish. It is so sold in the high class eating places. The traditional fried fish is available in Bhati at Bashir Dar ul Mahi, in Gowal Mandi at Sardar Dar ul Mahi. There are two shops in Mozang Chungi who also sell fried fish of quality. In addition to frying the fish another technique in preparing the fish is that of its cooking on a big iron pan and this is the delicacy of its own type but only now available at two points one in Sheranwala vicinity and the other on 'Annha Mor' near Shalamar on G.T. Road just opposite the fruit market. The fish is generally taken with Nan and radish sauce. Recently fish kabab in the name of fish finger have also appeared but with the promulgation of Indus Water Treaty with India the river has dried up and most of the fish in the market is either coming from Fish farms or from the sea of Karachi.

Afternoon food and drink scene is totally different from the "Lassi" and Halwa-Puri" of the mornings. In the afternoon around at 3-4 p.m the 'Halwais' would get ready with their other preparations which include hot and crisp Samosas, 'Bedana', 'Jalebi', 'Ras Goley' and 'Ras Malai etc. Some of the sweet shops also use variety of "Dal ka Halwa; Gajar-Halwa', 'Kheer' and Kashmiri Tea. Talk of Samosa and no Lahori can forget the special Samosa prepared by Butts, on the Mcleod Road, Khan's Samosa on the Regal, and Taj Cinema, Garhi Shahu. The Samosa snd 'Pakora' becomes a speciality during the Holy month of Ramzan and on every street corner there is a stall selling hot 'Samosa' and 'Pakora',

'Chholey'and 'Kachuries' etc. The Halwais of sweetmeat shops in the afternoon wear on a totally different appearance with glittering display of sweetmeats and silvers "Warqs" on most of the items to tempt the passers by. Among the popular sweets is "Barfi", 'Laddu' 'Bedana', 'Gulab Jaman', 'Maisoo','Balu Shahi', 'Amrati', 'Mooti Choor', 'Pateesa', 'Andrasy', etc. The halwais have a brisk business during festivals, fairs and on Eids. It has become traditional to take big packs of 'Balu Shahi' on weddings and especially the "Mangni" functions of the girls. The Halwais place sweets in flat pans (Thals) raising the racks to near the ceiling of the shop and present it colourful as far as possible.

In the summer months in addition to 'Lassi' a variety of soft drinks are also sold. The most popular being 'Sharbats' of different kinds and flavours such as "Rooh Afza", 'Sharbat Sheeren', 'Almonds, Pomegranate, "Falsa", "Shahtoot"and Sandal are common names one could mention of. 'Morrabas' of Apples, Mangoes, Carrots and 'Araks' diluted from herbs are also sold. The cold milk shops in Anarkali, Old Anarkali, Mozang, Ichhra, Outside Bhati Gate, Gowal Mandi and Krishan Nagar also make a lot of business. In the rainy season the people like 'Shakanjvi' or Niboo Pani; a number of cold drinks prepared on western formulas have also become popular. Lemonade, Rose Ginger filled in green bottles was a common drink in and around the city during pre-partition days. Now Coca Cola, 7-UP, Pepsi, Jolt Cola, R.C. Cola are the main brands which are sold and consumed in abundance. A number of other beverages and drinks have emerged in addition to the tinned drinks of various fruits which are imported. The Companies selling the drinks have their well organized distribution net-work and cover the entire city and localities. The more recent arrival is that of mineral water, generally consumed by elite class in place of ordinary water. It has appeared in the market only for the last couple of years. Originally it was imported from France but now it is manufactured here. Sugar cane juice "Ganne-ka-Ras" and milk shake machines, machines for fruit juices, are also seen frequently in the city. One can always find a glass of "Ganne-ka-Ras" with black pepper and salt during scorching heat and it is really refreshing and reinvigorating to have Orange and Pomegranate juice, mango milk shakes, which are also available at various other points in markets of the city. The known ones are the Liberty Market, Beadon Road, Multan Road near Chauburji, Old and New Anarkali, Ichhra, Barkat Market Garden Town, Faisal Town, and the main Market Gulberg. The tea is also a most commonly used drink although in pre-partition days it was available on rare places. It is now generally used in place of milk. It is infact fashion for the youngsters to drink tea in hotels and restaurants. Some time coffee is also liked but it is only in the selected places. Hawkers go round in the streets of mohallahs, lanes and alleys of Lahore where one can always buy delicious 'eats' or 'drinks' at one's doorsteps. There are always carriers with

"Chatwalas", selling 'Ghol Gapas', 'kanji' 'kulchey' 'Chholey and hawkers with sprouted yellow boiled rice with curried grams "papars" and variety of 'kulfis'. At home the variety of food is always to the ones rank, income and class. While in pre-partition days Hindus preferred vegetarian food, the post partition period has seen an over-whelming tendency to eat meat, beef and poultry. Most of the people mix vegetables with meat. "Makki ki Roti" and 'Surson Ka Saag' is a delicacy of the old and few who like this typical local meal of Punjabis. The "Paratha" and 'Makki Ki Roti' made in butter or ghee and consumed with "Saag" or spinach are enjoyed, but now rarely made in modern homes.

With the poultry emerging as an industry in the recent years it has become customary to serve roast chicken on marriage parties. Special 'barbecue' stations are set up during marriage parties where chicken 'tikka' chicken 'karahi' and chicken 'boti' are served hot. Chicken 'Pulao' is a must in the marriages.

FOOD HABITS

In the middle and low middle classes the food is taken as a tradition by the family members in the kitchen whereas those slightly above the middle income living in the recently developed localities have separate dining rooms; where they are served. A big change has occurred after 1947 where the newly rich class generally go in their big bungalows extending over kanals of land and have most modern facilities of kitchen, cuisine and parks on the premises. The eating habits of Lahoris are also under going a major change. The advancement of medical sciences, better health condition, health care facilities and awareness created by media is affecting the traditional food preparation and cuisine pattern in the old city and localities. A new class of educated generation coming out from English medium institutions like to have Burger, French Fries, fast food and consequently there is a mush room growth of such places who supply this requirement. A variety of burgers are sold in the modern localities.

The problem of fat adding food with high cholestrol and food of diabetic tendency i.e. blood pressure and similar other ailments has little effect on the common man to avoid fat rich food. Inspite of all this the residents of the old city have their traditional cuisine which they inherited with special preparations. Another important aspect of food and eats is that now the commoners also relish the fresh and seasonal fruit. The improved agriculture techniques, more yield and variety have multiplied supplies. The apple, orange, banana, pomegranate, melon, mangoes, dates, and lichis etc. are available in abundance which are generally on the dinning table with meals. There are flourishing fruit markets in Lahore; one on the Ferozepur Road, and other near Badami Bagh and the third in Allama Iqbal Town. One often finds countless Hawkers and Vendors on roads selling fruits. A slump in the economic growth in the recent year has, however, caused lowering of the purchase power of the public and the Government had to usher in 'Sunday Markets' where fruit, vegetable, meat, fish and other items of daily consumption are sold at comparatively cheaper rates. These Sunday Markets are organized at open spaces in almost all the areas and one finds a lot of customers who rush to purchase the rations for the week. The Lahoris love food. They do not believe in eating to live and one is always proud taking his guests to the old city for having items of their choicest food at the established points.

Another aspect causing change in eating habits and food is the erratic behaviour of the prices of food items during the last few years especially from 1992 onwards. It is changing the daily habits of fixed income lower formations, the daily wage earners and the lower middle white-collared classes. Instead of regular meals the workers are those to have quick one bite single item eats.

In this context Kababs, Samosas and Pakoras come to the help of such unprosperous people. Some fixed income employees admit, that there is no harm in eating a "Chopri roti" with pakoras. You won't look undignified or uncivilised if you take samosa with a plate of Chikar Chholey. Poor labourers have raw onion, boiled potato and oil-fried pakora as their daily diet especially food. So why would it look odd if a clerk's family would have these items as their staple diet, and the same is true for a white-collar employee or daily wage earner.

The demand for samosa and pakora increases during Ramzan. And that's quite normal. What's abnormal is the abrupt rise in their prices, hitting the low-income people of the city. As the time for 'Iftar' draws near, sections begin to swarm the sweetmeat shops lest they should miss the chance of getting the samosa and pakora on first come-first served basis. That is exactly the hour to fleece the consumers. So a single samosa which was priced at Rs.2/- before the holy month now fetches the seller at Rs.5/-. Similarly pakora prices have been raised by fifty per cent. Pakoras are sold as high as at Rs.64/- to Rs.80/- per Kg. Kachuries, too steal the "show". Previously sold at the rate of Rs.5/- per piece, it cannot be had at less than Rs.15/- now.

There are two types of people. Those who practice the age-old notion: eat to live under medical advice and otherwise, while the sinful other half religiously live to eat. This fits all Lahoris like a very smooth glove. As the business of food in Lahore never witnesses a dull moment, without a shadow of doubt, Lahore remains the mecca of cuisine in Punjab. For the last 30 years 'Chicken Karahi' has been and will continue to be the craze with all those who like to nurse their taste buds. The 'Karahi House' located on the far end of Jail Road linking Ferozepur Road at Mozang Chungi in Lahore is tipped as the standard eatery for this particular dish. Suitably tantalising Karahi is also found amid the blinding bulbs in Ghalib

Market and Punjab Tikka in Main Market, Gulberg and Liberty Market. The place is also famous for spicy 'Seekh Kababs' which certainly needs to be tasted on visit to this place in the evenings. Other known places for the same specialities are the many scattered points on Mcleod Road and Abbot Road. However, these shops are better known for the heavy Mutton Karahi rather than their chicken offerings. This area also makes for a very swift and savoury "takka-tak". This brings to Champ Shops, a heaven of 'brainly' delights located on Abbot Road. Surrounded by cinema houses and delightful 'Gurda Kapoora' and 'Champ' shops, the road offers an interesting scene after 9.00 pm, as people come out of the cinemas after the second show.

"Takka-tak" is basically of many organs of an animal meshed together, Champ (Mutton) and 'Gurdey Kapoorey' (Yep balls). The most popular combination is of chops and brain. Brain by itself is also secuptious, while 'Gurdey' are also very tasty. But the preparation after being mixed with green chillies, tomatoes, salt and butter taken in hot pans makes one forget every dish. There are places which are called 'Family restaurants' because they have rooms attached where you can have meal in relative privacy. Apart from family restaurants, the other alternatives are road-side arrangements, almost in the middle of the street where one can consume standing. These are little cheaper than the likes of 'Nishat Champs", a little more greasy and a lot more Lahori. A good place for a true Lahori food experience is "Kakka Gee Champ" on Mcleod Road, opposite Lahore Hotel. However, Bhaiya's Kababs are the best and most popular and are known for their softness and the 'imli chatney' that is served with them. And like everything else, there are lots of 'Bhaiya Kabab Wallas' around the city, but the original is right next to Afghan Tikka Corner. Bhaiya Seekh Kababs are so good that one can consume two dozen pieces at a time.

"Khoiay Walley Kabab" are the latest speciality developed in Dharampura. But are not much known because people don't know about them, probably because they are only available at Saddar Bazar, Dharampura. This place is pretty hard to find, especially if you have never been there. The food is sold on a side road, just around Habib Bank Building, Saddar Bazar Branch. "Mame Walley Kabab", the potato cutlets and shami kababs are found at 'Mammay ki Dokan' on Temple Road. If you are a standard seekh kabab buff, you should go to Mochi Gate. Die hard kabab fans do not think much of the likes of Bhaiya and his genre. They say that a seekh kabab should be a little crunchy, and one should be able to taste the onions in it. Sadly, making kababs is almost a lost art and there are many varieties available in various localities. Landa Bazar used to be another point where one had to wait for turn for the kababs. Model Town Market has also very good shops for Kababs. However, there happens to be a man in Mochi Gate who is famous for his kababs.

He has a small shop on the right side of the bazar. "Bundu Khan" is an experience that simply should not be missed. His 'Bihari Seekh Kababs' are the best. One can have them with Karachi style 'Paratha' which are most like 'puris' and the chicken shashlik is also a must. This is probably the best place when you are hungry and broken.

'Punjab Tikka' is by far the best place for grilled cuisine. Their chicken and mutton tikka is extremely delicious. Although Punjab Tikka is known for Tikkas, they also make pretty good karahi and 'takka-tak'. If you don't feel like going all the way to Abbot Road for 'Takka-tak', the Punjab Tikka is probably the next best alternative. It is a little expensive, because it is in the Main Market, Gulberg and so the rates are also slightly elitish. When it comes to mouth-watering "Haleem", you have to be a little patient. There is a man who sits right in front of Regal Cinema, on Regal Chowk who makes extremely delicious Haleem and chholey. But he does not have any place to sit and there are not any fresh 'Nans or Rotis'. And then there is this man who has a hand-cart in front of Government College called "Lucknavee Haleem". There is also a place opposite Mochi Gate "Lahori Haleem". These claim of being the best haleem sellers. Chicken haleem spots are on Montgomery Road and Abbot Road in addition to the walled city. Chholey usually go with haleem places. There is also a very famous 'Chholey Wala' in Neela Gumbad who has small shop opposite the main gate of Kind Edward Medical College. The other Chikar Chholey shop is just behind Ewing Hall where again one has to wait for his turn. Another speciality is 'Pathoray' which is like 'Puri' except that it is thicker because there are lentils in it and is served with 'Chholey'. There are tens of Pathora shops on Fane Road ideal for Pathora orgy. There is also hand-cart in front of Government College and one on Hall Road in front of Cathedral School gate.

Hareesa is Haleem made from wheat rather than lentils. The only place where you should have hareesa is Gowal Mandi, opposite Tufail 'Machhlee Wala'in Gowal Mandi and on Nisbet Road, opposite Moonlight School. The Nahari king in Lahore is "Delhi Kay Al-Mashoor Nahari Wallay" which is found in Lohari Gate. There is also a fake "Delhi Key Almashoor Nahari Wallay" on Circular Road. Hajis Nahari is thick and has an after taste similar to 'pai'. On the other hand, Delhi Wallay's Nahari is very spicy. Another known point for the Nahari is Waris Nahari Walla. They have two branches one in Paisa Akhbar and the other in Moon Market, Iqbal Town. Some die-hard waris fans say that it is almost as good as Delhi Wallay, but it is debatable.

The only thing that makes Halwa Puri good is Aaloo Chholey. If you don't have good Chholey, then out goes the fun. Royal Park Montgomery Road and Mcleod Road are very famous for Halwa Puri. There is also a place in Purani

Anarkali, opposite Yousaf 'Doodh Wallah' and Halwa Puri does not get much better than that. There is also another delectable Puri place in Main Ichhra and one on Muslim Town Mor which are delicious too. You can also get Halwa Puri from Liberty Market, Gulberg as there are a couple of food places opposite the Cinema behind all shops which offer Halwa Puri, Haleem, Chholey, Aaloo Keema, Lassi, Parathay and Makhan.

Pulao of Lahore is heard by Biryani and the most famous points are in Gowal Mandi, Mcleod Road and Old Anarkali. But the Lahoris have yet to develop a quality dish of this type. For all food varieties of Lahore one should forget the medical advice before trying out these specialities.

THE FOOD PALACE OF MCLEOD ROAD

I made a mention of some items of food available in Lakshmi Chowk but the Lakshmi Chowk is not a small place, at the end of Beadon Road, the triangular food places on Mcleod, Nisbet Road and Link Mcleod Nisbet Road, the Abbot Road, and both sides of Mcleod in the area offer an amazing food bazar with a variety of food items for a different taste both for the rich and poor i.e. from 'Dal Chawal' to roast, broast, 'Tikkas' cooked to order and ready from 10.00 am. in the morning to   4.00 pm. daily. A prominent landmark of Lahore, Lakshmi Chowk, is one of the liveliest places in the city, full of hustle and bustle almost round the clock. This chaotic ambience gives the place a distinction which is totally Pakistani. Honking wagons, smoke-emitting rickshaws with silencers missing, tongas, jostling crowds of mainly males, tempting eateries, shops of all kinds, film hoardings and posters everywhere, the Chowk generates an excitement so typical of Lahore and its people. With all the film activity going on at Lakshmi Chowk for the past so many decades, it is understandable that the area should also house a number of cinema houses, some of which are among the oldest in the city Rattan, Capital, Odeon. Two more cinemas in close proximity are the Ritz and Moonlight.

The very special flavour of Lakshmi makes one's mouth water. After sunset, the place comes alive with activities of the culinary kind when edibles flow out and are relished. Of course it is desi delights which the area specializes in. Your brand dishes may attract the young with their inexperienced plates but the true connoisseurs head for Lakshmi Chowk. As you pass by the eating joints you are seduced by aromatic smells from various stalls. Skinned chicken and mutton legs dangle from iron hooks and the waiters standing outside invite you to step in and pamper your plate with dal chawal, chicken and mutton, curried, fried and barbecued, spicy Tak Tak crispy chops or finger licking biryani. Bismillah Karahi, Mashallah Karahi tikka, Jahangir Murgh Pulao, Lasani, Tabaq, Shahi Champ Corner, Shahi Murgh Chholey, Tuba Restaurant are some of the popular eating

'Luxmi' Chowk

places. And then there is Ittefaq Dal-Chawal which according to its signboard, is the area's oldest shop, established decades ago. Sweet stuff including icecream abounds, but 'Butt Sweet House' specializes in all kinds of Mithai and its ice-cream comes in many flavours. And then there is Butt Bakers & Confectioners where you can purchase a wide variety of pastries, cakes, biscuits, etc. Mehran Snack Bar has creamy firni, flavoured milk and Kashmiri chae. When the cold winter sets in the aromatic Kashmiri tea is in great demand. Colourful, tumultuous and wild, Lakshmi Chowk really comes into its own on misty winter evenings of Lahore offering warmth, good cheer, fine food when colourfully dressed ladies and gents are coming and returning in tongas to this wonderful area after the film show.

I will be failing in describing the known set up of food if I do not mention about the Abdur Rahman Hotel in Old Anarkali. Also known as "Piplewala" Hotel. It is a hotel located in the most simple and shabby environments but selling the most tasty and cheap food in the market. Living in the college hostel if one was short of money (which was so often the case) and one wanted to save on account of mess changes one could have his full plate in four annas i.e. a plate of "Dal" and breads any number in late fiftees. In case of vegetable a plate would be charged four annas and meat vegetable 8-12 annas. The hotel used to sell 'Biryani', chicken quorma, fish, brain masala, 'Qeema mater'and 'Zarda' as sweet dish. The hotel still operates and at time it is difficult to find a seat. The same items of food are selling with the same demand but prices have gone up. A simple "Dal" and two breads cost Rs.10/- whereas vegetable price is for Rs.8, the chicken for Rs.25/- and Zarda (as sweet dish) cost Rs. 8. But surprisingly it is hardly the price of the same stuff in the same bazar on the next shop with high quality and taste.

The other special items of eatables are the "Chat", "Dehi-bhalla" and Ice cream. The best of 'Dehi-bhallas' are found in Chowk Rang Mahal, in front of Ainak Ghar in Shah Alami, Anarkali and Regal Chowk. There are some shops in Lakhshmi and Garhi Shahu. The best 'chat' known throughout is that of Bano Bazar – a ladies market where youngsters taste 'Chat' and also prone the young girls. On the Beadon Road recently two or three Ice cream Parlours have come up. In the evening one finds himself in traffic jams where the boys run around to get orders. The most popular Ice-cream is Chaman Ice Cream. Nearby there are five or six shops who sell the dry fruit of best quality on the Beadon Road.

For thousands of years, the search for food has helped to shape the development of society. It has dictated population growth and urban expansion, profoundly influenced economic, social, and political theory. It has widened the horizons of commerce, inspired wars of dominion, played no small role in the creation of empires, precipitated the discovery of new worlds. Food has had a part in religion, helping to define the separateness of one creed from another by means of dietary taboos. In science, where the prehistoric cook's discoveries about the effect of heat applied to raw materials laid the foundations on which much of early chemistry was based. In technology, where the water wheel first used in milling grain was to achieve immense industrial importance. In medicine, which was based largely on dietary principles until well into the eighteenth century. In war, where battles were postponed until the harvest had been gathered in and where well-fed armies usually defeated hungry ones. And even in relations between peoples, where for twelve thousand years there has been a steady undercurrent of antagonism between those whose diet consists mainly of grain and those who depend on animal foods. In the last analysis, of course, food is not only inseparable from the history of mankind but essential to it. Without food there would be no history, no mankind.

The truth of this, it might be thought, self-evident proposition is frequently forgotten in a world preoccupied with economic disasters and energy crisis, but if, in the decades to come, population growth and environmental pollution follow the catastrophic course forecast by a number of modern ecologists, acute food shortages could prove a harsh reminder of it.

What most peoples eat today is the product of thousands of years of dietary choice, the outcome, in effect, of an almost Darwinian process of natural selection. The foods which have survived in different regions of the world have been those best fitted not only to cultivation conditions but to the specific requirements of the inhabitants, requirements originally shaped as much by work and living conditions as by taste and preference. Men who lived in cold damp countries found that rich, fatty foods were not only comforting, but helped to build up a layer of flesh which acted as insulation against the weather. In less extreme climates, the field labourer used up considerable amount of energy on digging, ploughing, hoeing, and other agricultural tasks; his need was for calorie-rich starches and sugars to replace that energy. In tropical lands, perspiration, evaporating from the skin, helps to cool the body; strong spices encouraged perspiration and also stimulated a thirst for the liquids which were necessary to replace it. Discoveries such as these, the product of observation and experience, not of scientific analysis laid the foundations of many food traditions. During the course of history, however, such logic as there may have been in the origins of food habits has become almost impenetrably complexed. It has been distorted by shortages, by surpluses, by the introduction of new foods, and by number of external developments. Even the commonplace human desire to catch up with those next higher on the social scale, has helped to alter adequate diets for the worse. Only recently, too, it has been appreciated that food preferences are not necessarily the same as food prejudices, that taste and custom are sometimes related to forces which cannot be readily adjusted by social manipulation.

But however, confused, from the modern viewpoint, the logic of food customs may appear to be, history suggests that there has always been a conscious or subconscious attempt to direct food production towards what tradition shows to be the 'best' kind of diet for local circumstances, and Lahoris relish the choicest.

18

CRAFTS OF LAHORE

C rafts are as old as human history. Originally fulfilling utilitarian purposes, they are now a means of producing objects of intrinsic and aesthetic appeal. Among the earliest basic crafts are basketry, weaving and pottery. Nearly every craft can be traced back many hundreds of years. In early human society every individual, adult or child, was a craftsman who made the things needed for daily use. But as society grew more complex and functions more specialised a division of labour got formulated. A section of the society became expert in craftsmanship, to design and manufacture them while the rest of society merely continued to use the products.

So long as society remains vitally craft orientated depending for its supplies wholly on handicrafts, the creative stream is continuously stimulated and fed and the Master Craftsmen with a rich imagination and fine skill keep on creating new designs and objects. But when this pattern is broken by the invasion of the machine for manufacturing, the handicrafts sector is weakened, and craftsmen lose their stimulation. Production becomes imitative rather than creative. The same old forms and shapes continue to be made and no new inspiration seeks expression.

The advent of independence brought handicrafts into the national economic orbit again, breathing a new life into their withering limbs. This led to the launching of a purposeful development of the crafts to enable them to assume their rightful place in the economy and life of the country. Crafts, as creative hobbies are practised primarily in the home with a minimum of specialized equipment. Crafts as so defined have certain functions. In a world that is becoming increasingly mechanized and standardized, they give people the opportunity to work with their hands and to express their individuality. Crafts also are often used in occupational therapy; for example, a patient might be taught a craft to develop weakened muscles or to help in gaining use of an artificial limb. An emotionally disturbed person might be taught a craft that would serve as an outlet for feelings. Craftwork also provides the disabled with purposeful activity that diverts attention from their handicaps. Many hobbyists find themselves going into business. A craftsperson who perhaps has at first sold craft items only to friends or at local bazars may find that increased demand leads to a wider clientele and sales by mail order, at crafts fairs, or through a shop.

There is a fine line of distinction between crafts produced by amateur hobbyists for their personal satisfaction and crafts that in the hands of gifted artisans approach or can be considered art forms, generally made with a view toward the use and enjoyment of others. The difference between hobby-produced crafts and formal decorative art objects lies in the degree of innovation in form and technique and in the intention of the artisan.

Crafts can be grouped by technique or medium. These can, briefly speaking, be grouped under different heads like Paper Crafts, Textile and Fibre Crafts, Leather Craft, Pottery, wood working, stained glass, metal and Jewellery.

Elphinston in his History of India observes of the India manufactures, the most remarkable is that of cotton cloth, the beauty and delicacy of which was so long admired, and which in fineness of texture has never yet been approached in any other country. Their silk manufactures were also excellent, and were probably known to them, as well as the art of obtaining the material at a very early period. Gold and silver brocade was also favourite, and perhaps original, manufactures of India. The brilliancy and permanency of many of their dyes have not yet been equalled in Europe. Their taste for minute ornaments fitted them to excel in goldsmiths work. Their fame for jewels originated more in the bounty of nature than in their own skill; for their taste is so bad that they give a preference to yellow pearls, and table diamonds; and their setting is comparatively rude, though they often combine their jewellery into very gorgeous ornaments. Their way of working at all trades is very simple, and their tools few and portable. A smith brings his small anvil, and the peculiar sort of bellows which he uses, to the house where he is wanted. A carpenter, of course, does so with more ease, working on the floor, and securing any object with his toes as easily as with his hands.

The Gazetteer of Lahore 1883, describes that occupation of women in town is chiefly limited to cotton-spinning, wheat-grinding, grain-parching, and so forth, where they are not engaged in domestic duties. In villages women are exclusively engaged in domestic work, except among the Arains and Jats, where at certain seasons they help in light work in the fields, such as hoeing or picking cotton. Julaha women, too, work at the trade of their husbands, as do the wives of dhobis, kahars and telis, but not so extensively. A more detailed picture of the local industrial scene is given by Mr. Kipling, Principal, Lahore Industrial School of Arts who states:

It is surprising to those familiar with the actual state of the industrial arts in Lahore to see in catalogues of Indian art collections in Europe so many arts and beautiful objects ascribed to this city. Glass, enamels and arms elaborately wrought are among these. In some cases Lahore has evidently been written loosely for the Punjab at large; but in others a decayed if not extinct craft is indicated. It is about eighty years since any good enamel was wrought in the city, and the armourers to whom so many richly decorated weapons are attributed are represented now by two or three very old men. Gold embroidery naturally flourished where there was a court; and the kindred wire-drawing business with it. The superiority of the Lahore Kandlakash (silver ingot gilder), brought about by severe enactments and kept by the guild, is now a tradition merely, and there are only two or three workers in tilla or gold thread. Glass bangles are made by two or three workmen, but in no great quantity nor are the colours brilliant; while the most important glass work made is the kerosene lamp chimney, which is produced in large numbers for the railways and for domestic use. This is scarcely a manufacture in any true sense, for, excepting borax, no raw materials are used, broken glass being simply re-melted and blown. The stuff is full of air bubbles, and the only annealing it receives is that it is cooled by being put on the top of the furnace-a precaution which does not prevent the country chimneys from frequently flying into pieces when in use. The arts that have disappeared have been succeeded by trades of a more useful character, dependent rather on the increasing prosperity of the people than on the luxuries of a limited class. Among these may be mentioned the manufacture of vegetable oils by steam-driven machinery, laboratories for the production of sulphuric and nitric acid; soap and candle making; and letter-press printing of a superior kind. These are in the hands of natives and are flourishing. The leather trade is a distinctly improving one, and a large quantity of saddlery and shoes is annually turned out.

SILK AND OTHER FABRICS

In cotton fabrics, Khaddar, the coarse white cloth worn by agriculturists all over the Punjab for the sufficient reasons that its solid texture with the native nap unsinged renders it warm in winter, while it is not too hot for summer; and dun coloured khes are the only cloths made. It is contended by some workmen that the fine pashmina woven at Lahore is superior to that of Amritsar. Whether this is true or not there seems to be some reason for the belief that the trade has somewhat improved of late years. Chadars, dhussas, patkas and other articles are made. In attendance on the loom-embroiderers are always to be found Kashmiris, and there are many in Lahore. Besides fine good coarse woollen blankets (lois) are made. The greater part of this hand-weaving, both cotton and wool, is entirely unnoticed by Europeans, very few of whom venture into the city or tread the narrow alleys of such suburbs as Mozang. One slight indication of the extent of this domestic craft is afforded by the fact that the shuttle-maker's trade is a busy one. At every fair one or two stands will be found where weavers' shuttles are sold. A good shuttle lasts for many years, and is carefully handled and cherished. Perhaps it is fair to conclude that handloom weaving after all is scarcely so dead as might be expected from the large import of English piece goods.

In silk there is a relatively large and prosperous trade. The ordinary Lahore daryai is a stoutish, somewhat roughly woven and, considered as silk, lack-lustre fabric, narrow in width, and usually crude in colour. A thinner sort, similar to the silks used for linings, costs about 12 annas per yard; others are sold at a rupee and upwards. Gulbadans are striped fabrics, and were formerly woven much stouter than at present and in wider widths. Dhupchaon is the name given to shot silks, a changing effect of colour being given by a warp of one tint with a weft of another. Red and green are favourite colours for this combination. The greater part of these silks are for Zenana use, the narrow widths and the crude colours preventing their adoption by Europeans. Sufis of fabrics of mixed silk and cotton do not seem to be regularly made. The trade of silk and gold pyjama strings, ornaments, bed-cords, braids, tassels, etc., make a considerable show in the bazar, but it is probably of small commercial importance. The taste and ingenuity displayed in these small articles are worthy of remark.

FURNITURE AND METAL WORKS

This furniture trade is a profitable one, although little pain and intelligence is spent on it. Until the dealer is himself a craftsman there seems no hope of any improvement. The Mayo School of Art has had a decided influence on the carpentry as well as on other branches of manufacture, such as cotton prints, metal work, etc. This is partly due to objects actually made in the school, to designs and suggestions given to bazar craftsmen, and to its connection with exhibitions held at Paris, Melbourne, Lahore and Calcutta, for which it has acted as an agent. Its aim is to recur as much as possible to the best types of indigenous design, and to make more widely known the actual state and capabilities of the arts of the province. In some branches it has been of great use, and has both stimulated demand and increased production.

The copper bazar in the city presents the usual busy and noisy scene. The greater part of the wares sold are imported. Roughly hammered and perforated copper pandans from Lucknow, finely beaten plain copper degchis from Delhi, and brass wares from other places in the Punjab are to be seen. Antimony bottles and some other small articles are cast in Lahore, but there is not a large production of cast brass.

There are only two or three silversmiths who work with real skill in native methods, although there are many who sell and lend money on silver ornaments, and who indeed are rather mere sarafs than silversmiths. The upper classes are supplied with Delhi jewellery by a branch of a firm from that city. There is nothing very characteristic in the ornaments sold. The massive patterns for bangles etc formerly in favour, are going out of fashion, and a mere flimsy style is succeeding. The batua, a silver scent bottle, triangular in form with an open-work body, from which hang clusters of little bells, is one of the prettiest, if not quite the most characteristic ornament made in Lahore.

There are large numbers of 'mchr kands' or seal-engravers, and some of them work with great neatness. They never attempt glass engraving, for which their tools are perfectly suitable, and are content with a small but regular practice in signet rings and amulets.

POTTERY

There is not much to report under the head of pottery. An examination after rain of the great mounds of brick-burning refuse which are the only hills Lahore can boast of, shows that glazed and coloured pottery must at one time have been more common than it is now. Probably when the country was ruled from Kabul where glazed earthen vessels are habitually used for domestic purposes, this anti-Hindu custom was introduced. There are signs that it may again come into favour. Glazed earthen chillams and drinking bowls are now commonly sold, and there is a demand for the cheaper kinds of English earthenware. A certain quantity of Celadon-tinted Chinese unhandled teacups, imported via Amritsar and Peshawar, is annually sold for domestic use. Improvements in matters of this kind must be slow. There is good ground for the belief that the potter's art is an improving one; one of the most convincing proofs being the fact that the best potters are not kumhars by casts, but are either of Kashmir origin or members of superior Hindu castes.

Connected with domestic pottery, bricks, which are infact the material of nearly all the pottery of the great Indian plains, may be considered. Lahore has naturally been always a great brick-burning place, for there is not a stone to be found for many miles round. The old-fashioned native brick is scarcely thicker than an English "quarry," but it was often so well made and burnt as to resist the alkaline efflorescence which is the bane of all buildings raised on this salt soil. Of late years bricks of English size have been used, and the results in a technical sense are admirable. The Railway Station buildings are excellent as brick work, and more recent buildings show a similar quality of workmanship. The Municipality and private firms are now producing first-rate bricks in considerable quantities. The introduction in the plinth of new building of courses of glazed bricks to prevent the attacks of the destructive alkaline efflorescence has often been talked about, and it is surprising that the Public Works Department has not hitherto attempted any cure for a canker which seriously threatens the life of every building it raises. The practice of cutting and carving burnt brick, formerly common in some parts of England, is here carried to unusual perfection; and finials, mouldings, columns and bases, and the small tabernacles in door-jambs in which lamps are placed, are skilfully wrought. The work is often done with no other tool than a chopping instrument like a tesha or adze. The practice of constructing a latrine on the roofs of native houses, which it is desirable to enclose for the sake of privacy, while securing ventilation has led to the manufacture of open grill work in large pieces cut through the clay with oblique perforations in geometric or sometimes floral patterns. In an architectural sense nothing could be more decorative, but it is an element of native design unaccountably neglected by our modern architects.

The plasterer's business, considering the vast surfaces covered with this material, is in a backward and unsatisfactory state. Two or three years play havoc with their work. Both the materials and the workmen are at fault, and nothing like the fine, hard surface of some old work is now produced. In architectural wood-work the rebuilding of parts of the city consequent on the demolitions for the Water Works showed that much of the skill which is so evident on the carved fronts of the last century still survives. This is due in great part to the fact that the elementary training of each youth who learns the carpenters' trade, largely consists of practice in drawing and carving flowers and foliage in relief. The more utilitarian methods of the railway workshops and other establishments ignore this, and year by year we shall probably see a decline in this branch of art.

It has been found that the superior quality of Lahore-made soap is of unusual excellence, and it is used in large quantities for washing wool, etc. in the Egerton Woollen Mills at Dhariwal. The trade in tallow candles is new, and seems to be a thriving one. The candles are moulded, not dipped, and considering their cleanliness and freedom from smoke as compared with the oil shamadan or chiragh, it is no wonder they are coming into favour. The kerosene oil lamp, too, among the upper classes, is supplanting the oil lamp, and the demand for vegetable burning oils has already begun to decline.

PRINTING AND GLASS WORK

There is perhaps no one of the arts imported from England that has been accepted with more cordiality and aptitude than that of printing. Though capable of being treated so as almost to reach the dignity of a fine art, the business is in itself not very difficult to learn. There are several native printing-presses where excellent work is produced. These are all hand-driven. It is a curious fact that a large daily newspaper like the Pioneer finds hand labour cheaper and more trustworthy than the steam engine. Here similar conditions obtain, and it will probably be long before it is worth while to print by steam. Lithography though much used for the vernacular papers etc. is in a poor way. Chromo and chalk lithography have not been attempted; indeed the only pictures produced are rude illustrations in outline to the many cheap books of legends and poetry which are sold at fairs and gatherings as well as at small shops in the city. Book-binding has been learnt by men employed at the Railway, Jail, Government and Mission presses; but it seems to be invariably lacking in finish, and has not been taken up as might have been expected; for it is one of these businesses which must be done in some fashion, and one that would seem to be congenial to native taste. Some of the work produced under European supervision would rival that of English book-binders; but once withdrawn from control, and working on his own account, the native workman, either from carelessness, poverty or greed, scamps the work both in labour and material."

Syed Latif describing the arts & crafts of Lahore observes (p.260-63) that the old methods of manufacturing articles of daily use and household requirements are invariably followed. A brazier, or tinker, makes his utensils in the same fashion, and the same rude tools, as his forefathers used five hundred years ago. The blacksmith can not do without his leather bellows and prodigious hammers, or the goldsmith without his blow-pipe.

Glass bangles are made at Lahore; but the colour is not brilliant. The most important glass-work consists of Kerosene oil lamps and chimneys, which are supplanting the old oil shamadan of brass and the earthen chiragh, and for which there is an increasing demand, both for the railways and for domestic use.

A trade in tallow candles had sprung up and is flourishing, and a superior quality of soap, manufactured in the city, is used in large quantities for washing wool. The art of letter-press printing is improving, and so is that of bookbinding, though both are lacking in finish. The leather-work has decidedly been improved, as is evident from the large quantity of saddlery and shoes that are annually manufactured. The native shoes of Lahore are of superior make, and are profusely wrought in gold and silver thread or embroidery work.

Cotton-printing is done by means of raised blocks, cut in hard dark-coloured wood. Geometrical designs and decorative forms of men, animals, horses, the chase, etc., are stamped, in black chocolate and soft green, on pieces of cloth suited for decorating walls, or for carpetting. A peculiar mode of printing muslins is carried on at Lahore by stamping them in regular pattern in pale yellow of the "old gold" type, and the pieces thus decorated are used for ladies' dresses. Of the cotton fabrics, the city produces only Khaddar, or coarse white cloth, and dun coloured Kheses, but the trade in silk manufactures is relatively large and prosperous. The Daryai of Lahore is a lack-lustre silk fabric, of narrow width, and the Gulbadan, a thinner sort of striped fabric, of great width. Both were largely in use of male and female trousers in the time of the Sikhs, and all classes, from a Sardar to a common soldier, delighted in wearing them; but they are still in high favour with the Sardar class and the upper classes of the zenana. The Dhup Chaon of shot silk, with a lustre of two colors when exposed to light, is also largely used by the zenana.

The Patoli, or Ilakabandi, work of Lahore, though of little commercial importance, is noted for the taste and ingenuity displayed by the workers in making fancy articles of silk that are not loom-fabrics. Beautiful silk strings or girdles of drawers, with the long ends knotted off, and ending in ornamental tassels, ornamented and with gold thread and beads,etc., bed-cords, silk fringes, edgings, braids,etc., are made and largely used by the people for ornamental and decorative purposes. The Patolis fit peacock's feather and yak tails with handles secured by an embroidered knot, to serve as Chowris to keep off flies. They also make silk tassels, used for horse trappings; silk threads for necklaces and charms worn round the neck; head ornaments of gold and silver thread, for plaiting in the hair; loops and buttons for cloaks and coats, etc.

ENGRAVING AND KANDLA KASHI

Seal engraving is carried on with much neatness in the Dabbi Bazar; but the work is not as good as in Kashmir, or Delhi, where the art has reached perfection. There is nothing peculiar to be noted in connection with pottery, except glazed earthen chillams, drinking bowls and large earthen jars (matkas), which are both good and in large demand.

Lahore, like Delhi, is also known as a centre of gold wire drawing (Tarkashi), ingot-making and gilding (Kandla Kashi), and tinsel making, and the work turned out there is considered chaster than that done at Delhi, though very inferior to it in elegance.

Gold and silver leaf is made at Lahore, as in other large towns, by beating out the metal under sheets of jhilli, or gold-beaters skin. Sheets of bright brass foil or orsden and tin foil, in pieces about 8 inches broad and 2 feet long, are made and used for decorative purposes. Of cutlery work Lahore produces knives, scissors, tweezers, sword blades, daggers of embossed steel, etc.

The inlaying in gold, and occasionally silver, on steel or iron is called Koftagari, and Lahore produces fine specimens of such work, but it cannot be a rival of Kashmir in the art. The art is identical with the damascening of Syria, and, in the time of the Muhammadan Emperors and the Sikhs, was confined to decorations of armour and weapons of war. It is on the wane at Lahore, and the greater part of the Koftagari work is supplied by the Districts of Sialkot and Gujrat.

The enamelling, or Minakari work, of Lahore, is not so famous as that of Multan or Bahawalpur, but a sort of black enamel is done at Lahore.

The British on occupation immediately surveyed, explored, assessed and took measures to exploit the local industrial products. Various measures were adopted. For this the District Officers were given the assignment with special instructions. They also established Museums of industrial products, established industrial technical institutes and many schools of Industrial arts. Shoe making, carpentry, industrial and vacational schools were set up. The patronage increased and flourished with the economic development. On the emergence of Pakistan the local industries suffered a set back. The craftsmen moved. The settlement of new people took sometime before they could start the work and traditional craft production encouraged by the local craftsmen. But the situation of craft production has changed all over the world with the latest technological development. More and more machines have come to the help of workmen which have definitely affected the quality of product. In some cases the quality might have improved due to mechanical precision but at the same time the craftsmanship suffers.

With the technological advancement even among the developing countries where crafts are fast turning into mechanised cottage industries, Lahore remains one of the last citadels of a hand-wrought heritage. More than other Arts, handicrafts are the easiest and closest source of city's indentification –their passion for tradition, their patience with intricate techniques and their pride in beautiful products, even when rewards are low.

Lahore's early history is welded in metals moulded in ceramics and woven in textiles. The bronze caster of the famed dancing girls unveils a high level of artistic expression from Harrappan Valley civilization. The jewellery and ivory carvings reveal cosmopolitan influences. The Hindu craftsmen seem to have been wizards in weaving, carving in the round and metal-mouldings to this land rich in grains, gold and gods, Muslims then contributed entirely different aesthetics. Craft historians of the west have recorded a unique ferment in the Muslim world spilling over in phases into the sub-continent.

The Mughal period witnessed the place as the imperial capital and glittering nuclei of arts and crafts excelling in textiles and tiled ensembles. Graphically recorded renaissance in crafts begins with the Mughal rule who not only perfected many crafts but introduced new highly developed ones. The royal ateliers gave designs to the workshops which were supervised by technical experts from abroad. After the sunset of the Mughal empire, the British could not sustain an ardent patronage of crafts, which had found their last asylum in the wealth of the princely states during Sikh occupation of the city. Since Independence, craftsmen have at last found a stable market reinforced by immigrant Muslim artisans from India.

CARPETS AND JEWELLERY ETC

Lahore as one of the Mughal capitals, continues, to carry the notes and strokes of a wider culture, Carpets remain the chief devours of Pakistan's heritage. During Akbar's reign the establishment of workshops in Lahore is recorded, but some existed much earlier during the Sultanate period. This craft is a total transplant, proudly retaining its classical designs and hall-marks named after the celebrated production centres of Iran. Originally confined to court-rooms, carpet weaving today has proliferated into nearly all the suburbans localities and Lahore is the leading emporia drawing on the mass production of the hinterland, selecting the choicest for export.

Metal craft is a tradition encompassing centuries of hereditary expertise in casting, chasing, incising, repousse, cut-work, filigree and inlay. Jewellery, the most ravishing form of feminine capitalism, is a legacy from the fabled past. Gem-inlaid Kundan and jarao have always been the preference of the affluent, while solid gold ornaments are an investment of the middle class. Enamelled ornaments are in vogue again in Lahore and silver jewellery is fashionable now in the cities, but has long been the standby of the masses. Apart from folk motifs, almost any design in gold jewellery is copied in silver by city shops. Fine Kashmiri silverwork and parcel gilt decoration pieces of the highest quality are found in the city. Birdri-silver inlay on a black metal amalgam is an exquisite survival from the seventeenth century in all forms, decorative and functional, from aftaaba to paper knives and studs. Damascene, perhaps an arab import and later known as koftagari, is gold or silver wire in inlay on steel for arms, armour, astrolabes, mirror frames, jewelcaskets and pencases. Sialkot and Lahore were the famous centres of damasceners, who switched over from weaponry to cutlery in the nineteenth century.

Copper and brass are fashionable again, supplying domestic demands for lamps, coffee tables, flowerpots and door knockers. Apart from Persian and Turkish traditions, Ghandharan forms and motifs have recently added to the metal repertoire; chic combinations of these glowing metals are worked with wood, marble and ceramics. Lot of chiselled and engraved copper work with fine arabesques is found in the market. Lahore abounds in unequalled talent in cut-work and repousse.

What we have today is a continuation of past tradition in Lahore. Lahore produces costly and comely brocades, raw silks and a variety of floral and patterned silks under the generic name of banarsi. Silk and cotton looms are active for such special works. Kashmiri shawls of soft wool, from the underbelly of the Central Asian goat originate from the enlightened reign of Zain-ul-Abedin, who is supposed to have brought the skills and twill-tapestry technique to Kashmir from Samarkand in the fifteenth century. The loom-woven pieces called tilli shawls, are not collector's acquisitions. Sometimes as many as 1,500 bits were woven each with a separate design and stitched together so remarkably well that the naked eye could not detect the joins. Loom-woven pashmina is still embroidered. During the Mughal and Sikh period this was greatly patronised and presented as gift to State guests. It shall hold the market.

The ancient carver made good use of rich timber reserves, but the fine treliefs, chiselled on temples, did not survive climate and vandalism. The Muslims brought with them the exquisite genre, mashrabiya, a kind of geometric wood-joinery avidly adopted by the North Western Regions and re-christened pinjra. These pinjra lattices inspired a new trend throughout Mughal sphere of influence.

The tarkhans of Lahore are not mere carpenters but real artists, shaping furniture and daily utilities in forms old and new, with both classical and folk motifs in almost every wood from shisham to teak. Tea trolleys, teapots cigar boxes, egg-cups, salad bowls almost anything is wire-inlaid.

Dyeing is as old as the first civilization, but block printing too was exported to China a little before the Christian era and later to Egypt. The earliest samples extent, however, are from fifteenth century.. The centuries under the Mughals marked the glowing peak of printed and painted fabrics, a specialized genre of which qalamkari was initiated by the Persianised dynasty of Golkunda. The designs to this day seen all over India and Pakistan are of the same inspiration, cypresses, paisleys, carpet-cartouches, arches, niches, floral creepers and all the vernal variety romanticized by Persian literature. Block-printing, however, in folk tradition is almost universal. Tie-dyeing is one of the oldest skills on record in the city and one is wonderstuck with the quality of work.

The cotton bed and table covers alongwith wraps are mass-blocked in all the leading towns of the Punjab and especially Lahore outstands chappey-walas of Lahore, secretive masters of their trade in floor coverings, table-linen, curtains, canopy-liners and the latest sartorial trends are just specimens. The finest block printing is now being done on silk kaftans where the effect is enhanced by embroidered trimmings of gold and silver.

Lacquer-work is potenially a thriving industry in Pakistan. Once the wooden objects have been lathe turned and rounded, they are lac-layered in fast rotations and patterned by etching out one colour from beneath another. Lacquer-work is now used for furniture, swinging cots, beds and divans. The Kharadis of Lahore employ contrasting colours, like black and white. Mirror-frames, tea-trolleys, hat-hangers, caskets and standard lamps are made in striking colour combinations.

EMBROIDERY AND CHIKANKARI ETC

There are two distinct divisions of embroidery; metropolitan and folk. The former, previously a favourite with harems and the nobilitity, is only patronised by the rich today, Zardozi, Kaar-Chob, jali, salma-sitara, kalabatoon, baadla or kaamdani, gota-kinari, gijai and dori cover the entire range of stitchery. The finest masters of the crafts are now employed by the leading shops of Lahore which are back-looged with orders both local and foreign.

Chikankari an echo from the nawabs of Murshidabad, Dacca and Lucknow is made by Muslim immigrant embroiderers on transparent muslin shirts, saris and table cloths. It involves shadow-work, running-stitch (tepchi) for outlines, knotted stitches (murri and phanda and network). Though the multi-hued rilli, patchwork, one of the salvage crafts made from bits and pieces, is a speciality in its broader conception. It is applique and is displayed by tent makers of Lahore. Phulkari – rust home-spun cotton lozenges of rosettes worked in free hand from the reverse in darning stitch, mainly of white silken flose is a lost craft. Its diluted versions hang in bazars, but the classic Hazara bagh and kakri are only momentoes in a family chest and Anarkali in Lahore.

Leather craftsmen were regarded as lowly untouchables in Hindu society, until the advent of Islam in the sub-continent gave them new status. Marco Polo in the thirteenth century gives details of Moorish mats portraying birds and beasts in silver and gold threads. After seven centuries Lahore still exhibits mats of sambar leather with a central medallion, borders and corners appliqued with different leather or embroidered in multi-hued silk, silver or gold threads. Handsome leather saddlery, jackets, purses and shoes, embellished with colourful stitches, can be bought in the city. The horse and camel gear with its accessories, poches, pommels, belts and bags are embroidered. Gold-worked shoes and sandals, zari khussas and chaplis alongwith waistcoats are sold in Lahore. These were the condition of crafts in general in the city. Some items are specially made and marketed in Lahore with their typical quality. These may be summed up as under.

The richest and most elaborate items of jewellery seen in Lahore are those inherited from the Mughal period. These include gold chokers, bracelets and ear-rings enamelled and inlaid pieces are often incorporated into stranded necklaces of pearls, emeralds and rubies in the form of pendants and clasps. In addition to such items, essential part of the common South Asian heritage, are the more solid, rustic examples. Mostly made of solid silver, these consist of chokers, coarsely moulded collars and long necklaces and chains, often representing the total wealth of the wearer. These may occasionally be mixed with base metal and studded with semi-precious stones with a marked preference for blue and red. Bangles and rings are particularly popular in Lahore where gold is highly rated as are pearls and rubies. The damani (jewelled headband), tika (jewel worn in hair-parting suspending a pendant on the forehead) and jhumar (clustre of chains or jewelled strands funning out from the parting over the side of the head towards the face) continue to be popular bridal and dowry items.

Other items of gold and silver are available for the wealthy in the shape of platters, trays, serving vessels, chalices and pan-dans (containers for betel-leaf serving paraphernalia). Infact metalware is available in many grades of workmanship. The city boasts of a flourishing production of metal objects d'art, many modelled on famous medieval pieces, in the full range of chased, repousse and inlaid metal from furniture to vases, jugs and wall-hangings. The most popular metalware design is probably the intertwined flowering vine composed of rosettes and arabesques seen on a large number of objects in the Punjab. The crescent moon, the eight-point star and other Islamic symbols appear in fascinating contrast to the stock motifs of lion and elephant heads and fish recently augmented by the reintroduction of human forms from authentic Ghandhara art. Bidri, silver inlaid on metal amalgam, produces a dramatic silver-on-black effect which has commanded admiration since it apogee in the 17th century.

Muslim wood-workers emigrated at Partition from Kashmir and made their homes in Lahore. They are particularly remarkable for their inlay work with metal, buffalo-horn and ivory. The wood-workers of Chiniot are highly respected for their brass inlaid products, the latter particularly for their bold freehand designs, specifically those incorporating scrolls and the wood-marketed in Lahore.

Another widely practised craft is basketry. Mats, blinds, fans, slippers and caps are woven from the leaves of the date-palm, wild rushes, reeds and wheat-stalks. This continues to be the work of women who traditionally wove bread-baskets for keeping warm the bread they cook in large quantities. Other useful domestic paraphernalia included winnowing-fans and lattice-work baskets for storing and carrying. Decorated basketry bearing intricate geometric patterns woven from pre-dyed grass, reeds and leaves is commercially the most in demand. Basketry shopping bags are seen in use in most of the markets in Lahore. Basketry screens are often used to curtain off domestic and work areas.

The contribution of women to hand-crafted produce in Lahore is far greater than is generally recognised. Women of various regions and tribes produce exquisite embroidery and are capable of applying their skills to materials as diverse as floor coverings, leather sandals and handloom cotton garments. Infact the intricate and infinitely varied range of embroidered products found in Lahore is a strong feature of its cultural profile.

Like most domestic crafts, carpet-making is a family occupation, drawing in children whose help is invaluable in vital peripheral areas such as spinning, winding thread and working on the looms. Children, with their tiny fingers are extremely adept at lying the line knots required to create patterns and as a result are also popular in the artisan-controlled area of carpet-making. Here the master-weaver remains in control of the work, designing the piece and calling out instructions to the workers who knot and weave the pattern, sight unseen, to completion. Traditionally the master-weaver would call out an instruction to create a barely perceptible flaw in the design. This was meant to avert the evil eye attracted by a too-perfect piece. The chappay-walas of Lahore remain acknowledged master of their art.

Contemporary artisans favour the jewel-like beauty of the floral carpets conceived in Persia and developed in India during the Mughal period. Medallion carpets, bearing a vase-like central motif echoed in quarter-circles in each corner, also continue in popularity as do hunting or animal rugs.After agriculture and industry, handicrafts provide employment for a larger proportion of the working population, hence its preservation is as much commercial as a cultural imperative.

19

THE STATUS OF WOMEN

In inquiring into the manners and culture of a nation, knowledge of the conditions of women is necessary. This can be gathered from their status in society, laws of marriage, customs and incidental observations & general regulations. Some scholars argue that the discovery of thousands of stone figures of female goddesses dating from the Paleolithic period and on indication that early societies were originally goddess-worshiping, matrifocal civilization. Male dominance, however, was pre-eminent from the time of the earliest written historical records, probably as a result of men's discovery of their role in conception as well as the development of hunting and warfare as prestige activities. The belief that women were naturally weaker and inferior to men also was sanctioned by god-centered religions. In the Scepters, God placed Eve under Adam's authority, and certainly wives are to be obedient to their husbands. In Hinduism the reward of a virtuous woman is rebirth as a man. Therefore, in most traditional societies, women generally were at a disadvantage. Their education was limited to learning domestic skill, and they had no access to positions of power. Marriage was almost a necessity as a means of support or protection. Pressure was constant to produce many children. A married woman usually took her husband's status and lived with his family, with the little recourse in case of ill treatment or non-support. Under Roman law, husband and wife were one, with woman as the possession of the man. As such, a woman had no legal control over the person, her own land and money, or for her children. According to double standard of morality, respectable woman had to be chaste but not the men. In the Middle Ages, feudal law, in which landholding carried military obligations encouraged the subordination of women to men.

Some exceptions to women's dependence on men did exist. In ancient Babylonia and Egypt woman had property rights, and in medieval Europe they could join craft guilds. Some women had religious authority;for example, as Siberian shamans and Roman priestesses. Occasionally women had political authority, such as Egyptian and Byzantine queens heads of medieval nunneries, and

Iroquois women, who appointed men to clan and tribal councils. A few highly cultivated women flourished in ancient Rome, China, and Renaissance Europe.

Of deeper significance for women was the Industrial Revolution. The transformation of handicrafts, which women had always carried on at home without pay, into machine-powered mass production meant that lower-class women could become wage earners in factories. This was the beginning of their independence, although factory conditions were hazardous and their husbands legally controlled their pay, lower than men's. At the same time middle-and upper-class women were expected to stay at home as idle, decorative symbols of their husbands' economic success.

The middle of the 19th century partly in recognition of women's war contributions, they were paid as workers. The number of working women increased substantially after the two world wars, but they generally had low-paid, female-dominated occupations, such as school teaching and clerical work. Little opportunity existed in high-paid, male-dominated professions and major government posts. Advocates of birth control agitated for decades before women's right to family planning was recognized.

In the world the women's rights movement has made some progress. In more than 90 percent of the nations, women can vote and hold public offices. Aided by the United Nations Commission on the Status of Women (1946), women in many nations have gained legal rights and fuller access to education and the professions. However, the advent of industrialization in non-Western nations had destroyed some traditional economic arrangements that favoured women and has made underpaid factory labour the only work available to them, while the reappearance of fundamentalism has sometimes brought about the re- emergence of oppressive practices toward women. In 1975 the United Nations launched a Decade for Women program, and major conferences were held in 1975, 1980 and 1985. These international movements have not left the women of Lahore in isolation. The womenfolk of this historic city have accepted and adapted to the changes in historical retrospect through a corroboratory process, which paced up especially after 1947.

WOMEN IN ISLAM

As against the position of women discussed in preceding paragraph paging through the history, one finds only Islam as the religion, which has taken care of the rights of Muslim Women. These rights in respect of property inheritance, marriage, children and maintenance are laid down in Quran and Muslim Fiqah. In other societies it is by struggle whereas in Islam it has been provided and protected by religion. Women have not been made to attend prayers in mosques. According to

Islamic tradition the Prophet himself had said that it was better that they should pray at home. It is still in its regulation of woman's role in society that Islam is most strikingly different from Jewry or Christianity. Jewish and Christian women have throughout their history always in principle enjoyed more freedom than Muslim women. The most obvious symbol is the veil, still worn by women in Islamic countries. The Quran has, infact, more to say on the subject of women than on any other social group. This all along is more favourable to women than was the law in many Christian countries.

Technology also offered women other freedoms. A huge number of separate inventions and innovations, in all sides of life, have reduced drudgery and made work in the home easier. Some were as simple as the coming of piped water to the house which meant an end of long, often weary trips to a neighborhood pump or the arrival of gas for lighting and then cooking which reduced the dirt and trouble inseparable from oil-lamps and open ranges. Outside the house, better shops, carrying larger stocks of mass-produced goods, increased the choice open to housewives and, therefore, the ease with which they could meet their family needs. Imported foods (made available by steamships and railways, canning or processing) slowly made family catering different and easier than that once based as it still often is in many part of Asia or Africa on visits to the market twice a day. Cheaper soap and washing soda were the products of the nineteenth-century chemical industry, and even the first domestic machines, vacuum cleaners and washing machines for the rich, hand-turned mangles for the poor were in use by 1914. Historians too often overlook such humble innovations.

The last force already beginning to affect women's (and men's) lives before 1914, though not outside the most advanced countries (and even then, it was hardly ever talked about openly), was contraception, the conscious control by physical or chemical means of the number of children in the family. Societies in the past had relied upon infanticide or delay in marrying to achieve this. By 1914 the application of technology and spreading knowledge to family limitation had already begun to produce measurable effects in the more advanced countries. In the early years of this century it was a trend most noticeable among the better off; the more educated and the wealthy were the keenest to limit their family size by artificial means. Still, the mere notion that this possibility existed spread.

All the factors already at work to change women's life before 1914 operated more widely and more forcefully as the twentieth century unrolled, most evidently in the most developed countries. But two great wars had their transforming effects in every country, bringing about a questioning and rejection of much in traditional ways, and producing a forced draught of economic, military and even intellectual mobilization which thrust millions of women into new roles not always to their regret. It was in those countries, too, that there was felt most strongly the effect of developments in communication. It was not only the formal communication of feminist propaganda, which promoted women's independence. There was also the generation of new notions of the possible, new alternative models of behaviour by, first, the cinema and then television, which entered the home, itself. Above all, there was advertising, from which not only knowledge of new facts especially technological advances which pleaded the cases of women.

The preceding paragraphs indicate social status of women in general and the unison factors which were responsible for the change in their lives. In case of India the situation was slightly different where the women from the place of a domestic servant in the 18th century to a claimant of equal rights in the 20th century is no less then a social revolution. It will therefore be appropriate to briefly portray the situation in India in historical perspective.

A wife is to be entirely obedient and devoted to her husband, who is to keep her under legal restrictions, but to leave her at own disposal, in innocent and lawful recreations. When she has no husband, she is to be in a state of similar dependence on her male relations; but, on the other hand, the husband and all the male relations are strictly enjoined to honour the women: "where women are dishonoured, all religious acts become fruitless;" "where female relations are made miserable, the family very soon wholly perishes;" but " where a husband is contented with his wife, and she with her husband, in that house fortune will assuredly be permanent." The husband's indulgence to his wife is even regulated on points which seem singular in a code of laws; among these it is enjoined that she be "constantly supplied with ornaments, apparel, and food, at festivals and jubilees." Widows are also under the particular protection of the law. Their male relations are positively forbidden to interfere with their property. The King is declared the guardian of widows, and single women, and is directed to punish relations who encroach on their fortunes as thieves. This was so until the period of the Muslim Rule. Before and after conditions differed.

There was little difference in case of Brahamans, and they, as usual, are placed under austere and yet puerile restrictions. A man of that class must not eat with his wife, nor look at her eating, or yawning, or sitting carelessly, or when setting off her eyes with black powder, or on many other occasions. In all classes women were "employed in the collection and expenditure of wealth; in purification and female duty; in the preparation of daily food, and the superintendence of household utensils." "By confinement at home, even under affectionate and observant guardians, they are not secure; but those women are truly secure who are guarded by their own inclinations".

Generally the condition of women in pre-British India was not different. The dress of the women was nearly the same as that of men but both the pieces of cloth are much larger and longer, and they are of various bright colours as well as white. Both sexes wear many ornaments. but the necklaces were sometimes made of a particular berry that hardens into a rough but handsome dark brown bead, and sometimes of particular kinds of wood turned; and these were mixed alternately with beads of gold or coral. The neck and legs were bare; but on going out, embroidered slippers with long point curling up are put off, and are laid aside again on entering a room. Children are loaded with gold ornaments, which gives frequent temptation to child murder. Women, however, do not join in the society of men, and are not admitted to equality with them. In the lower orders, the wife, who cooks and serves the dinner, waits till the husband has finished before she begins. When persons of different sexes walk together, the woman always follows the man, even when there is no obstacle to their walking abreast. Striking a woman is not so disgraceful.

Domestic slaves are treated exactly like servants, except that they are more regarded as belonging to the family. But slavery is nowhere exempted from its curse. The female children kidnapped are often sold to keepers of brothels to be brought up for public prostitution, and in other cases are exposed to the passions of their masters and the jealous cruelty of their mistresses. Marriages are performed with many ceremonies, few of which are interesting: among them are joining the hands of the bride and bridegroom, and tying them together with a blade of sacred grass.

In retrospect the above depicts the conditions obtaining commonly in this part of the world to which culture obviously Lahore was a party. It was only with the arrival of Muslims that the changes occurred as ordained by their laws and the ruled also followed some convenient changes. Describing the status and general position of women in Lahore the compiler of Lahore Gazetteer remarks that the women of the agriculturists are used more as domestic servants than as companions of their lords and masters; their time from morning till night is fully occupied in sweeping out the house, grinding corn, milking the cows, churning butter, warming it to convert it into Ghee, cooking and carrying food to their relations, working in the fields, fetching water, making thread from the raw cotton for home consumption, sewing, picking cotton from the plants, collecting vegetables; and in the harvest time they often thrash the corn for daily consumption, manufacture fuel by drying cowdung in cakes, and carry flour to large villages, where they barter it for chillies, salt, etc., these and various other occupations employed their whole time, and it is a most rare thing to find a cultivator a bachelor ; for without such a helpmate, his work in the fields would be much retarded. The higher functions of the wife, however, are not unknown. In addition to the duties already detailed she generally keeps the household purse and endeavours in every way to prevent her lord from extravagance. She also has the management of family marriages; and if a clever woman, her husband, if only for his own comfort, has to keep her in good humour. Marriages are generally preceded by betrothals at a very early date during infancy. The arrangement is made between a barber and the mother of the girl. The marriage takes place somewhat later; amongst the Hindu Jats there are some peculiar customs in the ceremony; they put up four stakes and cover them over with a red cloth called bedi, inside which enclosure they place two reed seats covered over with a cloth for the bride and the bridegroom. The Brahamans then makes them go through a ceremony of worshipping the heavenly bodies, and he recites from the Shastar shlok or verse, which, being interpreted, is an assertion on the part of the brides's hand he puts it into the birdegroom's hand and makes him repeat a shlok giving his consent to the union; this is called hathlewa. A fire is then kindled, and they are both made to go round it; this is called lanwan; the fire is supposed to be a witness of the ceremony. The marriage is then complete. Thus it may be seen that marriages are no empty forms, but are looked upon as sacred ceremonies, and cannot be lightly set aside. There is one other form of marriage which requires to be noticed, which is known by the name chadar oalua, literally throwing a sheet over the two parties becoming man and wife; the ceremony is of a light and easy kind, and is generally performed when a brother-in-law marries his deceased brother's wife. In other cases the marriage of a Hindu widow is rare, and this custom leads to great immorality, and consequently Hindu widows bear but an indifferent character in the country side. The Sikhs and Gulab Dasis permit the marriage of widows. Divorce is seldom resorted to, except in the case of adultery; adultery is said to be most common amongst women who have had no children. Marriages are seldom effected without the payment of money, and daughters are popularly supposed to fetch from Rs.100 to Rs.500; but the market price varies according to supply and demand. Some money is given on betrothal, and generally a further sum when the marriage is consummated and the daughter handed over to her husband. Sometimes the father will get a piece of land for his daughter's hand, but this is rare, and only given when an object is to be gained, such as marrying into a higher class or clan than the bridegroom could ordinarily aspire to. "Rains" do not accept money for their daughters, and infact this avarice is not so common with Muhammadans as with Hindus. Marriages are effected between members of the same class or tribe (zat); for instance, most Jats will give and take each other's daughters, but the particular clan or "goth" to whom she belongs is excepted, as being within the prohibited affinity for a marriage to take place. The Dogars intermarry amongst themselves, and are the only tribe who follow this practice.

The expense attendant on marriages is very great. The whole of the poor, maimed, and leprous beggars of the countryside collect at a marriage, and have to be fed before they will depart. Friends not invited to a marriage take offence and cease to be friends. Priests, Brahamans, purohits and faqirs all claim their due; and until a man has collected a large sum of money in hand, he does not wisely undertake a marriage for himself or any member of his family.

With the passage of time western education, better economic conditions and more streamlined and strict administration of police and judiciary a definite change occurred in the life pattern of women of Lahore after the British occupation of the city. In the family set up of 1920s the women enjoyed an extraordinary position, unknown to their counterparts of today. They dominated the household scene, exercising undisputed authority over family affairs. What they lacked in education, they more than made up by their wisdom, intelligence and shrewdness in coping with all kinds of situation. They acted as the guardians of family, property, money and jewels and more often than not had been the final say in such matters. Rarely did the men dare to oppose them. Their world was full of activity, liveliness and labour. With the respect that they enjoyed the women occupied the center stage at almost all-family functions, which they organized with much skill and great enthusiasm. They were at their best when there was an occasion calling for a celebration such as a child's birth or a grown-up's wedding. An announcement of expectation of a child birth was an event for merry-making by female relations and women of the neighbourhood who would gather to congratulate the family. The guests offer sagans (gifts in cash) a custom based on the principle of reciprocity. Admission to Mosque or school was another joyous occasion calling for a celebration with distribution of sweets and singing of songs by the womenfolk.

MARRIAGE

The most important occasion in the life of a woman was the marriage of her son or daughter, which she would look forward to, and prepare herself for, right from the child's birth. Months before the wedding day, she would start consulting others about the arrangements to be made and the duties to be allocated to members of the family. Festivities would start with daily sessions of singing to the accompaniment of the dholki (drum) an activity, which the women enjoyed most four to five weeks before the wedding. The women attending the sessions would display their singing talent and repertoire of songs. The men are kept away from this exclusive women's affair where they were often the butt of their jokes and somewhat obscene songs are sung. This continues so and in a much elaborate shape in the well to do families. At the conclusion of a singing session 'patasas' (sugar candy) were offered to the participants, now the lady musician is paid and the family's ladies who participate are served food. As the wedding day drew nearer, these musical evenings would become more hilarious with the participation of female relations who would have by then arrived from distant towns. This was, however, part of the festivities and no one took offence at it. The climax was reached at the time of the departure of the bride when the women would recite heart-rendering songs as the near and dear ones bade her farewell with tears in their eyes. The most touching moment came when the bride took leave of her mother, which has been aptly described by a Punjabi poet thus: "Mavan te dhiyan milan lagiyan Chare kandhan ne chabare diyan haliyan"

The tearful send-off was usually in sharp contrast to the warm welcome that awaited the bride at the bridegroom's house. The womenfolk there would crowd around to have a glimpse of the shy bride who had not yet recovered from the shock of having been separated from a swooning mother, weeping elders and sobbing brothers and sisters. Elderly women would strive to divert her mind and amuse her by extolling the virtues of her husband. Women played an equally significant role on occasions calling for fortitude to bear the loss of a near and dear one and to extend sympathy to the bereaved. They shared one another's grief and took pains to console the bereaved. The period of mourning for the deceased lasts for over a month during which women would assemble every day to do 'siapa' (bewailing the loss), a custom widely prevalent in Lahore. Sometimes, a professional mourner would sit in front of them beating her breast with cries of `hai'hai'. Addressing them she would shout. "Oh mothers and sisters, he has left you hai-hai". "Oh God, why have you snatched the young one; you could have taken away any of us- hai hai." Close female relations of the deceased would repeat the chorus of lamentation, slap their thighs and beat their breasts with cries of `hai hai'. Oddly enough, some of the women sitting at the back would gossip while extracting kernels from melon seeds with their mochanas (tweezers). Sporting in black ghagris and grey chadars the women at this mourning assembly would meet and talk about everything under the sun, even discuss marriage proposals for their children and relations.

Though not quite an angel, the mother-in-law of (those days) in Lahore was much more accommodating towards her daughter-in-law than her counterpart of today. What upset her more than the inadequate dowry the daughter-in-law might have brought was her inability to bear a child. This often made her treat the daughter-in-law harshly. Desperate measures, prayers at temples and charms and amulets were employed. Quacks took advantage of the situation. Quacks, veds and pirs exploited the women in their own way. One Miroo Maulavi in Kashmiri Bazar was known and used to prescribe a talisman which when tied round the waist of a woman lying in bed was supposed to work wonders in securing pregnancy. There were, however, no cases of bride-burning on account of inadequate dowry as we learn in the News papers of these days.

While evil-minded mothers-in-law were few and far between, there were reportedly some women in Lahore who were reputed to possess the evil eye. Mothers hid their children from these ill-disposed women for a mere glance from them was believed to cause illness and even untimely death. To ward off the adverse effects of the evil eye, remedies were prescribed by Mullahs and Pandits. The former would write out certain charms on small pieces of paper which were to be soaked in water and eaten by the victim (the Tawiz). The Pandits would jot down a mantra on a paper, which was burnt, and its smoke blown towards the target of the evil eye. They also recommended burning a piece of red chilli after circling it around the victim's head. Another antidote recommended by elders was Chhaya Patar, which involved seeing your reflection in a bowl containing liquid ghee or oil and giving it away after adding a copper coin to professional mendicants who made their rounds of the city on Tuesdays and Saturdays.

Until the late twenties, spinning was a common pursuit of women of all ranks but, with the advent of cheap mill made cloth, the "Charkha" went out of vogue. The pastime, the women enjoyed most was shopping. As hawkers and vendors of fruits and vegetables and miscellaneous goods would come to their doorsteps, they had seldom to venture out into the market. Pedlars of textile materials, saris, shawls, etc., would attract groups of women and the bargaining that followed often turned out to be a noisy and lively affair. As the pedlars offered a limited variety of goods, the women were fond of visiting Tota (cutpiece) Bazar, the famous cloth market for womenfolk. This bazar, covered with awnings and tin roofs to keep out the sun, branched off from Wachhowali and extended right up to Gumti Bazar. On colourful display in the bazar were all kinds of textile materials. Crowds of women could be seen moving from shop to shop. Rarely visited by men, the bazar provided full freedom of movement to the women shoppers among whom were Muslim ladies who wore burqas but had their faces uncovered. It must be said to the credit of Lahoris that they showed respect to the women by being careful not to make any unseemly gesture or remark, leave alone any attempt to insult or molest them. The clan of eve-teasers had yet to make its appearance, which is the gift of partition to this sublime city. This hustle bustle of womenfolk in bazars of the walled city namely Rang Mahal, Sooha bazar, Kasera bazar, Gumti bazar etc. still continue the same way. Rather the streets and bazars have outlived, and the numbers of visitors outgrown with unexplinable rush for purchases but traditionally their does not appear to be any complaint against men who are shopkeepers. The shopkeepers had been giving humorous names to some of the materials on sale, such as "ankh ka nasha" (alluring glances), "teri-meri-marzi" (mutual consent) "dhoop-chhaon" (sun and shade). These names had instantly caught on with the women shoppers who freely used them while asking for the materials to be shown to them. The shopkeepers vied with one another in beckoning customers loudly in a sing-song voice to catch their attention. All day long, they would carry on one-sided conversation irrespective of whether anyone was interested or not. Tough customers, the women were not taken in by the sales talk of the shopkeepers. Sitting on the extended platforms of the shops, the women shoppers bargained hard to get full value for their money.

WOMEN AND FASHION

In fashion, the women of Lahore were far ahead of their counterparts in other regions of the country. The most popular dress among the pre-war (1914-18) generation comprised of a ghagri (skirt) extending up to the ankles, a blouse-cum-shirt with the sleeves reaching the elbow, and a bhochhan or dupatta (head-cover). The bhochhan, the most graceful part of the costume, was made from a large sheet of the choicest of materials edged with lace or embroidery. It was worn in such a manner that its one end partially covered the body while the other end was carelessly thrown over the shoulders. Social propriety demanded that women should move out in streets properly dressed. On ceremonial occasions, women sported ghagris made from velvet and silk materials heavily embroidered with gold thread. In summer, they would carry pakhis (wicker handfans) of different designs, some of which were edged with velvet ribbon or embroidered with silk thread. The custom of 'Ghund' or 'ghungat', that is, covering the face with a veil, survived until the thirties. Women covered their faces in the presence of even their husbands when elderly man and women of the households were around.

The post-war generation during the thirties replaced ghagri with 'shalwar' suits and saris. Young women took to the sari influenced by other regions of India. It came to be considered the most attractive form of dress. Heeled (English style ladies shoes) and sandals replaced slippers without heels and with pointed toes. Next to clothes, the thing most dear to women was jewellery which they regarded as their wealth and inheritance. There were ornaments for every part of the body, from head to toe. With the march of modernity, some of them faded out of fashion. These were gold chonk and phul shaped like domes and minarets for the head, gulluband (neck-strap) for the neck, nant (armlet), bankan (bracelets weighing up to 100 gm each), tadhagi (girdle) and lachhe (anklets). By the mid-thirties, ornaments became lighter in weight and more elegant. Responding to the dictates of fashion, Lahore goldsmiths came out with superb designs and new items of jewellery. The nath (gold ring) set with precious stones, worn on the left nostril, which had since olden times been considered an important piece of adornment and a symbol of a woman's marriage status, was replaced with a teeli (jewel-studded nose-pin) This is again in fashion now after a lapse of over fifty years.

As regards cosmetics, the older generation used "Watna" (kneaded flour mixed with ghee) to add lustre to their skin. The use of dentifrice served as a dual purpose of cleaning the teeth and colouring the lips. For beautifying the eyes, collyrium and kohl were applied. It was only in the mid-thirties that face powder; cream, nail polish and lipsticks came into vogue. Even then, their use was extremely limited. Infact, obvious lip colouring was unusual until the forties. Besides, the use of cosmetics was considered to be prerogative of married women and even they used them with discretion so that their make-up might not appear too audacious.

The budding generation of women of the thirties, influenced by the wave of social reforms, spread of education and exposure to modern ways, acquired a new life-style, which marked the beginning of a new era. Sporting fashionable 'saris' or 'shalwar' suits; they began moving out of their homes-something, which the older generation did not approve of. A Bombay movie, Miss 1933, starring Miss Gohar, set a new trend in dressing. Some women began to copy the heroine's ultra-modern clothes, wear sunglasses and carry umbrellas. The anti-tawaif campaign, which was then in full swing, also had its impact on the lifestyle of those days. It dissuaded many a young men from visiting the "kothas" for enjoying the company of courtesans, thus enhancing the status of women as wives.

Likewise, films like 'Saub hagya Sundri' starring Sulochna and Gun Sundri with Gauhar glorified the Indian woman in the role of a wife and condemned the tawaif as a destroyer of homes. In this changing social environment, even music, which had been preserving houses of ill fame, came to be patronised in respectable homes. Music schools sprang up in the city where girls were taught to sing and play the harmonium. Soon this came to be regarded as an additional qualification for marriageable girls.

Marriage was necessary even if it was not made in heaven and practically the only career for a woman. Anyway, harmonium makers had a flourishing business as, along, with the Singer sewing machine, this music instrument came to be included in the girl's dowry, in case of Hindus. The Muslims used to offer a copy of the Holy Quran.

The older generation, aghast at seeing young women crazy about latest fashions, was highly critical of their behaviour. They felt that these fashions had ruined them. Gold worth twenty-five rupees is converted into a fashionable ornament at an additional cost of thirty-five rupees and after four days it is again torn apart for reconversion. They wear shalwar-suits costing three hundred rupees and high-heeled shoes, which will drive us to bankruptcy within three days.

Watches and sunglasses are a rage and they are fast spoiling their eyesight. They take delight in exposing their bodies, so they have removed veils from their heads and move about bareheaded.

The elders adversely commented upon the educated girls in fashion with work and goggles. They felt that Study of English had spoiled the girls. They used to wear heeled shoes and stockings; they carry umbrellas in their hands. The girls do not know the art of cooking. They shirk doing any household work. While men of the older generation were shocked by the new ways of the modern girls, the younger ones fell for them. What hurt the male ego most was the fact that women had started working for living, something which only widows, driven by the force of circumstance, had done so far. Now educated girls have begun to join the ranks of school and college teachers.

Sex without marriage was virtually unknown in those days. An average woman was not expected to have any sexual desires; she would submit to her husband but only to please him. It was also said that illnesses, which afflicted unmarried girls, could be cured through marriage. Any indiscrimination in matters of sex was fraught with grave dangers for a woman. It could even lead to her expulsion from the community. This is not to say that there were no sex scandals. Among the poorer women who shared the drudgery of outdoor work with men were the dhoban (washer woman), the "churhi" (sweeper woman) and the bhadpunja (baker). The last mentioned was a most interesting character. She plied her trade in every mohallah. In summer, she would bake bread in the evenings in her tandoor (oven) when women would assemble with their kneaded flour and take their turn. By way of wages she would keep a portion of the flour. Every afternoon she lighted a fire in her open hearth put on it an open iron vessel and heated some sand in it. Children would bring small quantities of wheat, gram or maize and get them parched. This was the popular afternoon meal or snack. She would shake the long handle of the sieve, pour the hot sand back into the pot, and then hand over the parched corn to the customer. She kept her eyes constantly on the sieve but her tongue would be wagging all the time, doling out news about happenings in the neighbourhood which every one loved to hear.

That was the world of women in Lahore over half a century ago. How different from today! It was full of activity, fun and laughter, free from the stresses and strains of the present times.

WOMEN AND PAKISTAN MOVEMENT

From 1920 to 1947 the women of Lahore fought side by side with men in freedom struggle. To have a correct view of their status & sacrifices we have to briefly survey this period as the status of Women cannot be discussed in isolation as it is a part of the social phenomenon and over all economic and political position at a given time in a country. The position of women is therefore a part of the struggle of Muslim Nationalist Movement in the sub-continent and it continued to operate till the achievement of Independence. In the early stages it was the men who led and fought for the cause and rights of the women, unlike the position obtaining in Europe and America where women were fighting for their rights and cause. The fall of Muslim Empire, succession by British, deprivation of Muslim community, led leaders like Sir Syed Ahmad Khan to think about the causes of sufferings of Muslims for which they established the educational institutions for western education so that the Muslims could also share the Government through the British system of Education and Administration.

Sir Muhammad Shafi was the first person in Lahore who founded Anjaman-e-Khawateen-e-Islam in 1908. Prior to that there may be no hesitation in remarking that women were defined exclusively in terms of re-production as a commodity and not a community. Of course this had a host of repercussion, which were certainly detrimental to the status of the women. First of all the voice for educational rights of Muslim women was taken up in the Muhammadan Educational congress in 1784 where Sh. Atta Ullah of Aligarh pleaded their cause. From 1886 to 1917 a lot of mileage was covered politically by the nationalists and women never lacked behind. The women actively participated in the politics of the sub-continent during Khilafat Movement when in 1921 Bee Amman, mother of Maulana Muhammad Ali Johar addressed the annual meeting of the Muslim League in Lahore. In the later years when the idea of Pakistan took a definite shape, the Muslim women became more involved in the political movement for Pakistan and the Muslim League formed a women section. In 1940 the women also attended a public function at Lahore in a large number. They also led processions and the biggest demonstrations in Lahore was on the 23rd April, 1940 to protest against the arrest of Muslim leaders. As the political activities mounted the educated women from upper classes provided patronage. In 1941 Lady Abdul Qadir, Fatima Begum and miss launched Muslim Girl Students federation. On the 13th January, 1942 Lady Maratab Ali from Lahore declared that days had gone when the Punjab Muslim women were considered fit only for cooking food and minding children. In 1942 M. A. Jinnah addressed quite a few gatherings of the women. In 1943 the women of Lahore worked a lot, raised funds for the help of their brethren. Women National Guard was formed with Pyjama, white Kurta and green dupatta as their uniform. In 1946 elections were held. Two Muslim women viz. Begum Salma Tassadaq Hussain and Begum Shahnawaz stood as candidates. When the Muslim League inspite of its majority was not allowed to form Government, 500 Muslim women in Lahore led demonstration and protested. Begum Shahnawaz was arrested. Most of these activities were originated and concentrated in Lahore. Until emergence of Pakistan the struggle of women was to assist and help the men and politicians in the independence and not for individual community rights.

POST PARTITION PERIOD

The birth of Pakistan marked the end of an intense phase of struggle in the sub-continent. The massive migration brought in other problems and miseries to be attended by both men and women at Lahore. Over seven million crossed the border, homeless, to take refuge with countless problems, of families torn apart, women widowed, abducted, children lost, panic stricken and with no belongings and means to subsist. The most urgent task was their rehabilitation. The women arose to the occasion and volunteers worked day and night in administering First aid, attending to health care, food distribution, fighting epidemics and clothing etc., etc. A women Volunteer Service was also formed under the guidance of Begum Raana Liaqat Ali Khan, the wife of Prime Minister of Pakistan. Begum Raana Liaqat Ali Khan founded the All Pakistan Women Association (APWA) in 1949. APWA started working for the education of women, for community welfare, raising funds for schools, dispensaries and industrial homes. The most important contribution generally appreciated by the different women platform is that it convinced the Family Law commission for Family Law Ordinance which is considered to be an important step towards protection of women in marriage. They also moved for reservation of seats in National and Provincial Assemblies. The other organizations which later on had their operations in the city were the Business Women Club, Family Planning Association of Pakistan, Pakistan Children Welfare Council, Pakistan Nurses Federation, the House wives Association and the Girl Guides Association. The earliest post-independence names appearing in the Legislature of Pakistan are Begum Jahan Ara Shahnawaz and Begum Shaista Ikram Ullah. They were instrumental in making effective the Muslim Personal Law of Shariat which recognised the women right to inherit property etc. The passage of Muslim Family Law ordinance discouraged polygamy and required compulsory registration of all marriages under a Standard Marriage Contract (Nikah Nama). In 1972 Begum Nasim Jahan from Lahore alongwith Ashraf Abbasi were on the Committee to draft new constitution. The 1973 Constitution gave more rights to women. Article 25 of the Fundamental Rights gives all citizens equality before Law and provides for an additional safeguard for women by stipulating that there will be no discrimination on the basis of sex. Further Article 27 provides that there will be no discrimination on the basis of race, religion, caste or sex for appointment in services of Pakistan. Article 32 guarantees reservation of seats or Women in Local Bodies. Yet another important provision under Article 34 lays down that steps shall be taken to ensure participation of women in all spheres of national life. There are many more provisions in this behalf. Since 70, onwards there has been a lot of improvement in the social status of women. They have equal rights to contest elections at any level from Local Bodies to the National Assembly. All along these years quite a few women are found in Assemblies and in the cabinet both at the Federal and Provincial level. The women have equal opportunities in professional and non-professional educational institutions on the basis of merit, sex being no bar to their admission in medical and science institutions. A number of females are joining the Civil Services, and the Secretariat, Health and Education Department. They have their exclusive educational institutions and occupy the highest positions in the Government machinery. Above all Pakistan has had a Prime Minister, from the women, who has had two tenures (as Prime Minister) in the country. This should brush away any negative and discriminatory views of anybody, which they may have formed earlier in respect of women in Pakistan. It was general assumption that Islamic Jurisprudence did not favour the Muslim women and they were always treated discriminatory. This position and status of women in services, in politics offer a total changed scenario in Lahore where a century ago Muslim Women were confined to home, rearing the children and contributing no more towards social output. The world of women has totally changed now and they are playing their role in the developmental activities in educational, health publics and other allied fields.

The world of women has undergone a total change after Partition and migration of 1947. The institution of family as it was in existence prior to undivided India is no longer found. The migration totally up-set social fabric prior to 1947. It is very rare and in some conservative families that the elder/senior family members in the house enjoy some dominating position whereas it was taken as part of the book previously. The post partition family system is different and gradually deviating from the past traditions. The younger lot of women is mostly educated in the city and they do not want to give in to the old. On marriage they try and it is true in over 75 per cent of cases that the parents have to part with sons after they are married. The reason being that the newly wed bride wants independence where none should interfere in their routine living and privacy whether it is due to the impact of the modern education, economic conditions, education or changed traditions can be argued any way. The sharing of abodes by all the members with their parents is story of the past. To some extent, the position of holding the centre stage in the family functions, and celebrations, the elders are simply ignored and it is will of the youngsters that is followed. The migration has brought another change in the family life in which the education of the girls is now considered a priority whereas in pre-partition it was only the enlightened and well off who thought of this. Not only this most of the girls on acquiring their Intermediate or Graduation look for jobs in case of a middle and lower middle. The over all female population of the city has surpassed the male figures and with the prevalent economic constraints the educated girls try to find jobs as a compulsion. The taboo that Muslim Women observed Purdah and did not attend Colleges and Universities is a story of the past. People just get mad to get admission for their children into schools. The admission to professional institutions in the field of health, education, electronics, engineering, nursing etc., etc. is an uphill task. The modes and practices of marriage have undergone a change while in pre-partition days people used to arrange marriages within the families, the present situation differs. The family bond especially that of caste is just fading out. The parents want to see that their wards are safe and economically well off and go in for suitable matches. Another aspect besides caste is the integration of locals with those who shifted to city in 1947. The inter-marriages and consequent emergence of the new generation has changed the total scenario. The educated and well off classes avail of the services of the Newspapers and advertisements in dailies for finding out suitable matches after considering the placement of the boys or girls along with the qualifications. Another interesting informal arrangement, which has been institutionalised, is the Marriage Bureaus. There are hundreds of Marriage Bureaus now operating in the city, which find for you suitable match according to your status, financial position/educational qualifications and income level. Of course in the cases these marriages are finalized after negotiations of parties. But the bureaus operate on commercial basis and charge quite a bit of money. While pre-partition ceremonies were over-shadowed by Hindu customs, the present marriages have taken another turn. Once an informal understanding has taken place then the routine marriage ceremony starts with "Mangni" by parents of the boy going formally to the house of the girl where they take some clothes, jewellery etc. and in return the parents of the girl visit with gifts etc. It is either on that date or somewhere later that a date for final marriage or rukshati is fixed. While the poor and low income groups invite only a few and receive Barat in front of their house by closing the streets, now a days the well off arrange these, in the marriage halls or hotels. There are dozens of marriage halls in the city which are having good business. On weddings, sitting arrangements, food and other service facilities are provided against heavy charges. This business of marriage halls apart, the hotels are so busy in the city that one has to wait for a 4 or 5 Star Hotel upto 4/5 months for a reservation. The exaction of dowry from the parents of the girl and the choicest Menu on Barat have become so exorbitant that it had just gone out of the reach of the common man and the present Government had to intervene and bring an Enactment putting restrictions on food on the occasion of weddings. Now under the latest Law, parents on the both sides are bound to serve hot or cold, soft drinks and snacks if necessary. The violation has been declared punishable. The middle class feels greatly relieved.

Referring to the changed position of women in Lahore one may not miss the latest trend in this city especially in the modern families, about freedom of sex and love marriage. This happens in cases of well off, rich and highly educated. If the parents do not agree the boys and the girls go in for civil marriages through the courts. Another trend where the parents oppose such freedom is the indulgence of some of the NGOs generally supported by western countries. Such couples go to the judicial forums, and there are so often scandals in the Press. In the recent past Saima Arshad case is an instance in the Lahore High Court. The parents who believed in consent under the usual practice opposed where a Lecturer eloped his female student and secretly entered into Nikah. The case was heard in Lahore High Court and made headlines in the newspapers, finally being decided in favour of the boy and the marriage being declared legal. A similar type of case also took the shape of feud where the girl belongs to a conservative Pathan family and boy came from modern background. It is pertinent to mention that it has become a fashion for the boys and girls to wander in the public parks, hoteling or going to movies during the courtship period secretly. It is also learnt that some of the parents are in the know of such occurrences but they do allow. A great part is played in the life pattern of young women by the media. The newspapers, magazines, the radio, TV, VCR and Cinema have played havoc with traditions and values. The International newspapers, magazines openly discuss sex. Their economic independence, their right for votes, their claim for jobs with no education as to their responsibility towards society, family and the parents and above all their own future is at risk in these circumstances. The latest addition in worsening this situation is the onslaught by Dish Antenna on which free sex, permissiveness, living as friends, blue print films, stage performances and open discussions have led astray the younger generation. They try to keep and ape the models of media usually to their aggrandizement. Indian channels have brought in the most cursing effects where their secular society and new generation do not believe in any morals. This has caused deterioration and deprivation of our social and institutional framework of parenthood, children, elders and the youngsters. This has aggravated to such an extent that it has become a problem to see the smaller screen with the children.

The dress of women has also undergone big change from simple pieces of cloth to a well-designed dress. While the ordinary house wife wears Shalwar Qameez and Dupatta, the ladies of high status put on "Saris". In some families which are generally termed more advanced, the girls also put on jeans and trousers with haircut of different styles. On marriages special clothes are stitched like

Gararas, Langhas, blouses and specially embroidered dresses of brocade. Ordinarily the college and schoolgirls wear Shalwar Qameez and Dupatta. A sizable portion of the female population of city is working in education, health, TV, Newspapers, Radio, markets, Hotels, hospitals and many other professional or organizations including airlines, architectural Firms, and army. Many ladies are also seen chairing departments, heading institutions and holding executive jobs. From the status of domestic servant and slave to a sovereign, means a real revolution over a period of time in the status of the women in society.

20

HIRA MANDI
Another Institution

Prostitution is the oldest profession on earth. It may be fair to remark that it is as old as humanity. It exists today as it has existed always. No sermon and preaching have been able to stop it. What is prostitution: the performance of sexual acts solely for the purpose of material gain is generally deemed as prostitution. Persons prostitute themselves when they grant sexual favour to others in exchange for money, gifts or other payments and in so doing use their bodies as commodities. Legally the word 'prostitute' refers only to those who engage overtly in such sexual economic transactions usually for a particular amount of money. Prostitute may be of either sex but throughout history the majority have been women reflecting both the traditional socio-economic dependence of women and the tendency to exploit female sexuality. If prostitution is often characterised as the oldest profession, the concept of women as property, which property, prevailed in most cultures until the end of the 19th century, meant that the profit of the profession most often accrued to the men who controlled it. Men have traditionally characterised procurers and customers, but they are gradually and increasingly being also identified as prostitutes. They generally serve male customers and sometimes impersonate women. Prostitution in various forms has existed from the earliest times. It is dependent upon the economic, social, sexual and moral values of a given society. It has been secular or sometimes under guise of religion. Women have usually entered prostitution through coercion or under economic stress. In most societies prostitutes have had low social status and restricted future, because their sexual service was disapproved and considered degrading by money.

Prostitution was widespread in pre-industrial societies. The exchange of wives by their husbands was a practice among many primitive peoples. In the ancient Middle East and India, temples maintained large numbers of prostitutes. Sexual intercourse with them was believed to facilitate communion with the gods.

In ancient Greece prostitution flourished on all levels of society. Prostitutes of the lowest level worked in licensed brothels and were required to wear distinctive clothing as a sign of their location. Prostitutes of a higher level usually were skilled dancers and singers. Those of the highest level wielded power and influence.

In ancient Rome prostitution was common despite severe legal restrictions. Female slaves, captured abroad by Roman legions, were impressed into urban brothels or exploited by owners in the households they served. The Roman authorities attempted to limit the spread of slave prostitution and often resorted to harsh measures. Brothel inmates, called meretrices, were forced to register with the Government for life, to wear garish blonde wigs and other distinctive raiment, to forfeit all civil rights, and to pay a heavy tax. In the Middle Ages the Christian church, which valued chastity, to convert or rehabilitate individual prostitutes but refrained from campaigning against the institution itself. In so doing the church followed the teaching of St. Augustine, who held that the elimination of prostitution would breed even worse forms of immorality and perversion, because men would continue to seek sexual contact outside marriage. By the last Middle Ages, prostitution reached a high point in Western history. Licensed brothels flourished throughout Europe, yielding enormous revenues to Government officials and corrupt churchmen. In Asia where women were held in low esteem and no religious deterrent existed, prostitution was accepted as natural.

During the 16th century prostitution declined sharply in Europe, largely as the result of stern reprisals by Protestants and Roman Catholics. They condemned the immorality of brothels and their inmates, but they were also motivated by the perception of a connection between prostitution and an outbreak of syphilis, a previously unknown disease. Brothels in many cities were closed down by the authorities. Under a typical ordinance, enacted in Paris in 1635, prostitutes were flogged, shaved bald, and exiled for life without formal trial.

No restrictions, however, throughout known history have been able to stop it. In recorded history evidence is found for its spreading in Greece, in Roman Empire, the Middle East and in the East, in China and India. The assumption that prostitution is a disease is rebutted by an assumption that it is a panacea to save the society from larger epidemic. Who is a prostitute, what are causes of prostitution, where does the demand come from, who is responsible for it, individual or society or State are not the questions to be answered here. Neither we are discussing here the components of prostitution which sometimes are adopted as way of life suiting some and peculiar circumstances. Is it a moral question or social problem again are abstract terms and economic subject for Sociologists and religious scholars and preachers. My premise in this writing is that prostitution exists very much. It had partially legal cover to a certain extent. It may knock hard on the family system or save the institution to a large extent is not debatable here. I have simply to go in its background, functional character and to some extent about the community it serves, the methods and mode of its operation as it is an institution of Lahore.

We have discussed elsewhere that Lahore was the principal seat of Hindu State and thus centre of Hindu culture prior to arrival of Muslims. It will therefore be interesting to survey the prostitution as a part of Hindu history and tradition in terms of the provisions of their laws (i.e. Shastras and Vedas). Thereafter Buddhism only sanctified this profession both for the individual and the State. We will thereafter discuss the Muslims period where inspite of Quranic injunctions the Muslims indulged in the business and in cases left Hindus behind.

Some three hundred years before the birth of Christ a Brahaman called Kautilya or Vishnugupta wrote a treatise on the art of government, the Arthasastra. The Arthasastra consists of fifteen books in which every aspect of governing a kingdom is discussed. In the twenty-seventh chapter of the second book the duties of the Superintendent of Prostitutes are dealt with. We are thus provided with one of the earliest Indian accounts of how prostitutes behaved and how their lives were ordered.

The Superintendent of prostitutes shall employ (at the king's court) on a salary of 1,000 panas (per annum) a prostitute (ganika), whether born or not of a prostitute's family, and noted for her beauty, youth, and accomplishments.

With a view to add to the splendour of prostitutes holding the royal umbrella, golden pitcher, and fan, and attending upon the king seated on his royal litter, throne, or chariot, prostitutes shall be classified according to their beauty and splendid jewellery; likewise their salary shall be fixed by thousands. She who has lost her beauty shall be appointed as a nurse (matrka).

That several prostitutes were employed at court is implicit in the existence of the office of superintendent.

The existence of such provisions suggests that the status of court whores was considerable – they were not regarded merely as a group of pleasure. But they were there to be used for pleasure so that if a prostitute does not yield her person to anyone under the orders of the king, she shall receive, 1,000 lashes with a whip or pay a fine of 5,000 panas.

The most famous Indian erotic work, the Kama Sutra, dates from the first century after Christ. The author, Vatsyanyana, deals with all aspects of sexual love. Inevitably there is a section dealing with prostitution. Vatsyanyana tells us that he based it on a treatise written by one Dattaka for the women of Patna. We must remember that the prostitute or courtesan was an established part of Indian life. It would be immediately stigmatized as immoral and disgusting. With ourselves the prostitute is barely tolerated – with the India of (that) period she was an essential, and at times honoured, part of human society.

'By having intercourse with men courtesans obtain sexual pleasure, as well as their own maintenance. Ancient authors are of the opinion that the causes of a courtesan resorting to men are love, fear, money, pleasure, returning some act of enmity, curiousity, sorrow, constant intercourse, Dharma (duty), celebrity, compassion, the desire of having a friend, shame, the likeness of the man to some beloved person, the search after good fortune, the getting rid of the love of somebody else, the being of the same class as the man with respect to sexual union, living in the same place, constancy, poverty. But Vatsyanyana decides that desire of wealth, freedom, misfortune, and love are the only causes that effect the union of courtesans with men. The authorities agree that money is one of the major causes making a woman resort to prostitution. But in Indian society it would appear that many of the other reasons quoted above would have a bearing on the decision taken. A woman who became a prostitute did not turn her back on society, as is the case today, she could feel that she was serving society in an acceptable way.'

The section of the Kama Sutra concerning prostitutes ends with a classification of courtesans. This consists of bawds, female attendants, unchaste women, dancing girls, female artisans, women who have left their families, women living on their beauty, and regular courtesans. The fact that regular courtesans form a separate category shows that the majority of the others were not full-time professionals but were engaged in other forms of activity in addition to prostitution.

An other interpretation of Vatsyanyana's classification of prostitutes has been given by an Indian writer. The lowest type was the Kumbhadasi or common harlots. They were at the disposal of anyone who could afford their low price. All they had to offer was their bodies. A Paricharika, or attendant, was a daughter of a courtesan who went through a form of brothel marriage. Her marriage contract allowed her to act as a prostitute for a specified time but her husband was to be preferred over clients. A Kulata was a married woman who practised prostitution on the side. Similarly a Swairini was a married woman who took up the profession with the consent of her husband. A Nati was a dancer or actress who combined entertainment with selling her body. The artisan's wife, or Silpakarika, belonged to a low caste, the Sudras. Such women were often employed in higher caste families as domestic servants. Their presence offered opportunities for their seduction by the male members of the family. An affair of this kind meant not only money for the woman but the possibility that she might have a son with a high caste father.

We have seen from Kautilya and Vatsyanyana that prostitution was well-established from an early period in India. The great Indian epic of the Mahabharata gives various versions of the subject.

Whatever the origins of prostitution in India the popular classical literature of that country (India) not only contains frequent references to this type of sexual activity, but in some cases is devoted to instruction in the art, as well as to stories of courtesans. What emerges from the ancient law books is that each caste had a morality of its own – what was incumbent on a Brahaman did not necessarily apply to those of lower caste. Caste in other words dictated the sexual morality of the individual. For the women of the three highest castes prostitution was a unforgiveable crime. For those of the lower castes it was not only acceptable, but it might be their duty to act as prostitutes.

In the Laws of Manu (X, 47) it is stated that 'To sutas (belongs) the management of horses and chariots; to Ambashthas, the art of healing; to Vaidehakas, the service of women (that is prostitution); to Magadhas, trade.'

Yet another classification of courtesans is given in the sacred Tantras of mystic books. At the head of the profession were the Rajawesyas or royal whores who gave pleasure to kings. Next came a Nagari who dwelt in the city and drew her patrons from the well-to-do citizens. A Guptveysa was a clandestine prostitute who operated secretly because she wished to avoid bringing scandal on her family. Fourthly came the Devavesya or Devadasi, the strumpet of the gods. Lastly was the Brahmafesya or prostitute of the ghats or bathing places. She catered for pilgrims who came to the sacred rivers.

It was not only in armies that prostitutes found their place. Any expedition on the part of great men or princes had as its inevitable accompaniment the courtesans. To celebrate victories the courtesans must be there.

Hospitality also demanded that every want of a guest should be catered for. The more important the guest the greater honours given to him. 'To him came running up quite fifty pleasure-girls, splendidly light, fair-hipped, young and tender, sweet to gaze upon, wearing a thin red garment, decked with gleaming gold, well versed in speech and honeyed words, skilled in dance and song, speaking mid smiles, like the Apsarases in loveliness (heavenly beings), practised in the service of love, gifted with the knowledge of the heart's stirrings, in all things skilful. When he had eaten, they showed him in all its details the enchanting pleasure-wood by the women's abode, and playing, laughing, and singing gloriously, thus did the women, wise in their knowledge, wait on the youth of the noble nature. These glorious women offered him a heaven-like couch worthy of the gods, adorned with precious stones, spread with priceless rugs.

So far we have discussed prostitution as it functioned in an India dominated by Hinduism. With the advent of Buddhism there appears to have been little change. Inspite of the adverse public opinion and in spite of punishments, courtesans persisted into the Buddhist days, when they formed a far from negligible portion of the community, as is shown by the very ease with which they are used in smiles.

Buddhism created an opportunity for pious women to serve God as Almswomen or disciples devoted to religion. It also provided the courtesan with an avenue of escape from her profession. The literature is full of stories of courtesans who attain arahanship (holiness) through regeneration. One famous prostitute, Ambapali presented the Buddha with a mango grove which he accepted. She joined the order and eventually achieved arahanship. Some, however, tried to become respectable without invoking religion and failed.

Buddhism did not abrogate the traditional view of the prostitute which had evolved under Hinduism. She was not honoured but at the same time it was seen that she had to work out her destiny according to her birth. It was believed that you were reborn as a whore for some transgression in your previous life. But what Buddhism did offer as against Hinduism was an opportunity for such women to achieve a state of grace in this life by renunciation and regeneration. It is an important difference.

"The Muslim invaders of India who began to penetrate into the country before 1,000 A. D. brought with them the austere faith of the Prophet. The Quran, unlike the Hindu sacred books, turns its face resolutely against prostitution. 'If any of your women be guilty of whoredom, then bring four witnesses against them from among yourselves, and if they bear witness to the fact, shut them up within their houses till death releases them, or God makes some way for them'. (Sura, IV, 19.) In the very early period of Islam, adultery and fornication by women was punished by their being literally walled-up. This was modified for a maiden to banishment for a year and 100 stripes, and for a married woman to stoning."

"The status of prostitution according to the Quran is abysmally low. 'The whoremonger shall not marry other than a whore or an idolatress; and the whore shall not marry other than a whoremonger or an idolater. Such alliances are forbidden to the faithful'. (Sura XXIV, 3.) Their activities were to be severely punished. 'The whore and the whoremonger – scourge each of them with a hundred stripes; and let not compassion keep you from carrying out the sentence of God, if we believe in God and the last day: And let some of the faithful witness their chastisement'. (Sura XXIV, 2.) Prostitution was just not to be tolerated. 'And let those who cannot find a match (because of poverty) live in continence till

God of his bounty shall enrich them. Force not your female slaves into sin, in order that you may gain the casual fruitions of this world, if they wish to preserve their modesty'. (Sura XXIV, 32.) For those who had female slaves but who could not marry even this loophole was forbidden."

"It is interesting to speculate what led to this fanatical opposition to venal love. One possibility is that the religions which Muhammad (PBUH) had to overcome before Islam were the complete antithesis of the faith He created. They were compounded of fetichism, the worship of nature deities, and fertility rites. In the new faith there was to be no room for the free expression of the senses – man could indulge himself with four wives and his concubines, everything else was to wait for Paradise.

"Alas for the fine sentiments of the Quran. It was only a question of time before the puritanism of the conquerors from the North succumbed to the abounding sensuality of the Hindu. After six hundred years in India it can be remarked that: All Muhammadans are very fond of women, who are their principal relaxation and almost their only pleasure. The upper classes seemed to have concentrated on concubines rather than courtesans thus following the letter of the law."

The whole of India did not fall all at once under the dominion of the Muslim. Hindu and Muslim kingdoms remained side by side for centuries. In the fifteenth-century a Shah of Persia, Rokh, sent Abd-Er-Razzak as his ambassador to the king of Vijanagar, a Hindu state. Abd-Er-Razzak left an account of his journey in which he described the country and the people in great detail. What is extremely interesting from our point of view is the enthusiasm with which he, a Muslim depicts Hindu prostitution at that time.

"The organization of prostitution in Vijanagar appears to have been based on a far-sighted policy. The army was maintained and sexual pleasure provided for the people in great measure. A considerable amount of the soldiers' pay must have reached the prostitutes in return for their services. The delight with which the ambassador describes the scene in the bazar suggests that he was jealous that his own country could not supply similar spectacles. Despite his enthusiasm Abd-Er-Razzak managed to survive the sensual temptation of his embassy and return safely to Persia."

It has been our contention that prostitution in India was established from the most remote times, and that although the Muslim invaders arrived with a religion which condemned the strumpet as a thing of evil, they succumbed to the easy pleasures of the land they conquered – in some instances they went even further and that which had been a natural part of the social landscape was systematised. A ruler, such as Aurangzeb, remembering the words of the Prophet, might attempt to cast out the evil.

"In the reign of Shah Jahan dancers and public women enjoyed great liberty, and were found in great numbers in the cities. For a time at the beginning of his reign, Aurangzeb said nothing, but afterwards he ordered they must marry or clear out of the realm. This was the cause that the places and the great enclosures where they dwelt went to ruin little by little; for some of them married and others went away, or, at least concealed themselves. Such reforms did not last. A more truthful picture is presented by conditions under the great Mughal Emperor, Akbar the contemporary of Queen Elizabeth of England."

"The prostitutes of the realm (who had collected at the capital, and could scarcely be counted as large as was their number) had a separate quarter of the town assigned to them, which was called Shaitanpura, or Devilsville. A Daroghah (Superintendent) and a clerk were appointed for it, who registered the names of such as went as prostitutes, or wanted to take some of them to their houses. People might indulge in such connections, provided the toll collectors heard of it. But without it, no one was allowed to take dancing-girls to his house. If any well-known courtier wanted to have a virgin, they should first apply to His Majesty, and get his permission. Such arrangements were typical of those in many Indian cities under Muslim rule. The incontinent were gratified and the state prospered."

So far we have discussed what might be termed by prostitution. There was another, and very important aspect of prostitution in India – that which was associated with religion. The sexuality which informs so much of Hinduism here found dramatic expression.

The Deva-Dasi, or temple harlot, was a woman who was dedicated to the service of a god – married to the god and who served both man and god by prostituting herself, and by dancing. There is no mention of such women in Kautilya's Arthasatra. The rise of the caste and its euphemistic name seem both of them to date from about the 9th and 10th centuries A. D. during which much activity prevailed in South India in the building of temples and elaborating services held in them. Duties were to fan the idol with Tibetan ox-tails, to carry the sacred light called kumbarti, and to sing and dance before the god when he was carried in procession. In other words its origin seems to lie in India's mediaeval period.

"The association of temples dedicated to the sun and dancing girls is well-established. A Chinese traveller, Huien Tsang, in the seventh century A. D. remarks on the great number of Deva Dasis that thronged the temple of Surya at Multan. There was apparently, opposition from certain puritanical elements to the spread of the practice. This is recorded by an Arab commentator, Al-Beruni, early in the eleventh century. A tenth century inscription from Rajputana confirms the statement of Al-Beruni. It records the express instructions of a chieftain to his attendants that if the arrangements he had made about the services of dancing girls at different temples was interfered with by ascetics and Brahamans, they should at once be stopped."

Opposition was of no avail and the institution of the Deva Dasi became a prominent feature of religious and social life. There were many different ways by which a girl could be dedicated to this life of religious prostitution.

The Deva Dasi as an institution has persisted to our own day. In the Indian Law Reports at the turn of the century numerous cases are given which concern some aspects of temple prostitution. The majority of such cases have to do with the abduction of minors, dedication of a girl after puberty (which was forbidden) disputes between dancing girls and temple authorities, disputes concerning inheritance, adoption, and similar matters.

Whatever the criticism advanced and refuted the facts remained – there were two hundred thousand Deva Dasis in the state of Madras alone at a time (1927) when its total population was approximately five million. They even possessed their own union or association.

"There are temples in certain isolated places, too, where the most disgusting debauchery is the only service agreeable to the presiding deity. There, children are promised to women who, laying aside all shame, grant their favours to all persons indiscriminately. At such places a feast is celebrated every year in the month of January, at which both sexes, the scum of the country side, meet. Barren women, in the hope they will ease to be so, visit them after binding themselves by vow to grant their favours to a fixed number of libertines. Others, who have entirely lost all sense of decency, go their in order to testify their reverence for the deity of the place by prostituting themselves, openly and without shame, even at the very gates of the temple."

We are attempting in this chapter to trace the course of prostitution in India in historical times. In developing the theme of the temple harlot we have brought the story up to the present – to have done otherwise would have been to confuse the reader. From the evidence we have presented it is clear that India presents a unique phenomenon of a society which from a remote period evolved a system of prostitution, both lay and religious, that became an essential part of the fabric of living. That there were abuses cannot be denied, and the modern counterpart of ancient practices show degeneration from the classical past. Nevertheless the world of the great epics of Arthasastra, for the prostitutes under Buddhism, created a place for the prostitute in society which was unique. In the past of India the whore achieved dignity and status in a way which was rarely achieved in Europe, for the dark gods of generation had given her their blessing.

The above depicts the background and culture of Institution of prostitution in Hindu Society in general, in sub-continent and Lahore was no exception. These conditions prevailed until the Sikh period and Ranjit Singh was himself known patron of prostitutes.

The Hira Mandi, gem or diamond market must have appeared with the founding of the city. From historical evidence, there did exist a market in the time of Mughals. According to one account in the East men and women who earned their living horizontally often joined esteem. They were invited to weddings, feasts and public affairs particularly in India, the courtesans were associated with purity and respect. She was held to exert a potent charm against the evil eye. She the supreme mistress of the sacred science of copulatory, gymnastics became an envy of all. Prostitution was not forbidden because it swelled public revenue, kept officials and priests in prosperity, reduced fornication and adultery and because of its origin retained a consecrated aspect. In several countries it had been regularised under Government control.

Lahore until Partition, being economically dominated by Hindus had all dominant cultural traits of a Hindu Society. Rather it had a multiple characteristics, as historically the city had been a place often sought by the invaders from North. Some would loot and return, some would exploit the resources and wealth, some would use it as a temporary stop to reinforce their supplies, proceed ahead but indulgence of each armed force in sexual exploitation of the local women folk is a proven and established fact. One hardly needs to describe details of the treatment of young girls at the hands of occupying forces. They would not only capture the girls and have sex but the good looking were taken away by the forces while advancing from Lahore towards south or returning to the north. Each time a different force, a different race and a different commander would cause an intermixture and cross breeding of distinct nature. They included Greeks, Persians, Turks, Tatars and Afghans etc. This cross breeding and as a result of forced sex had genetic and racial effects. It also introduced changes in the attitude of men and women towards marriage and sex without marriage. This was in addition to the hindu religious sanctity whereby they used to spare the girls as "Deva Dasis" at the temples and regularised the free or paid sex at these temples or sanctuaries. Needless to state that the absorption or flexibility of Hinduism also played a vital role. Not only that, according to one version perversion in sexual habits and existing modes of prostitution, entered into the sub-continent through this process of consecutive entries of various armies which also induced male prostitution, fornication, lesbianism and many other perverted sexual behaviours.

The Hira Mandi of Lahore was in existence in the walled city during the Sikh period. The area was so named after a Sikh Sardar who had a haveli around. Immediately before annexation of Punjab by British it was also partly located in the Old Anarkali. The present locality of Dhobi Mandi in the Old Anarkali is said to be the exact Mohallah. When this area was converted into a camp of British forces (in 1846) and subsequently cantonment, the prostitutes were made to move. They settled inside Lohari Gate and partly in some adjoining quarters of new Anarkali. Their quarters, it is learnt extended upto Risala Bazar. Another version is that this area touched Akbari Gate and outside. Besides various other factors an important reason for increased prostitution in this city was that in addition to having been consecutively exploited by invading armed forces, its minimal status was that of a provincial headquarters. Sometime Emperors and rulers of India also made it their abode, at least all of them temporarily. Emperor Akbar made Lahore his capital for over 14 years. This would naturally attract visits of Governors, Commanders, Rajas and Maharajas including nobility who would need the womenfolk for their temporary stay in the city and thus it had become an establishment place and a fertile market of prostitutes. Sikhs who succeeded in Punjab on the fall of the Mughal empire also provided endless patronage to the prostitutes.

THE SIKH PERIOD

The Sardars and well off Sikhs extravagantly indulged in this. Maharaja Ranjit Singh alongwith other courtiers was very fond of prostitutes and was a regular visitor to their places in the city of Lahore, Kasur and Amritsar. The Maharaja used to witness their dances (mujras) in addition to other pleasures. Infact according to one report the best gift to the Maharaja was that of those young girls and beautiful women by other Sardars. Maharaja himself married the sister of Moran prostitute. Thus during Sikh period according to one estimate half of the city consisted of brothels. Infact it flourished and the city equally served the needs of the courtiers and visitors.

Mr. Jacquemont, a French scientist describes an interesting account in his journal about the condition of prostitution prevailing in Lahore and observes that "One knows that Orientals are debauched; but they have some shame about it. Ranjit's excesses are shameless. The fact that this grey beard has had and has a number of catamites is nothing shocking in this country; but, apart from this, he has always consorted publicly with the women of the bazar, whose patron and protector he is. At great festivals there are hundreds of them at Lahore and

Amritsar, whom he makes dress up as Amazons in the most ridiculous way, ride on horses, and follow him; on such occasions they form his bodyguard. He always has some of them in his camp, and they follow him everywhere riding upon elephants. One of his pastimes when he has nothing better to do is to watch their flirtations with the young men of his court.

In his youth he was passionately in love with one of these women. She had to be always near to him. The inhabitants of Lahore saw him a hundred times in those days sitting with her and that in broad daylight, surrounded by a large escort and talking and laughing with them all the time. The Sikhs have a horror of tobacco. A Mussalman would never smoke in the Punjab in front of a respectable Sikh. This woman who had such influence over the Rajah, smoked in his presence in his howdah and he even assisted her to light her hookah, probably the most outrageous exhibition he has made in Lahore."

Mr. Soltykoff in his travel account and stay at Lahore, when he had an interview with Maharaja Sher Singh on March 22, 1842, described about Lahore as under:-

"I speak of the streets only; when one looks up one sees the windows and balconies full of courtesans and dancing girls, brilliant with gold and precious stones, and making gestures of welcome. Other balconies are full of cocks and hens, filling the air with their cackling. The mixture of girls and birds is arresting, and, when I saw these young things shaking with laughter at my European dress, I forgot the dangers of the execution." Continuing about the party arranged by the King in honour of Mr. Clark and Mr. Soltykoff describing the dinner arrangement and drinks mentions about the girls who were also made available."

"Then the girls arrived, some thirty in all, pretty but small and delicate, in splendid costumes with their little noses so loaded with jewels and their foreheads and eyebrows so gilded that one could hardly distinguish their features. Their feet and hands, adorned with rings, and mirrors were very pretty though dark. The transparent veils that covered them were of gold, silver, or bright colours. Their short coats of velvet or other costly materials and their tight trousers of silk were very pleasing to the eyes. These charming girls approached the King one by one and gave him one or two rupees. The King, who was in conversation with the ambassador, turned to them with an air of coreless good humour. There is so much that is good natured and straight forward about him, that, although his figure is awkward, he is charming and one would say that, inspite of his nervous air he possesses plenty of pluck in danger. Sometimes he took the rupees mechanically, sometime he gently pushed aside the hand that offered them, sometime he added a handful of silver himself."

It seemed a curious household. The girls approached without any fear, most of them laughing, and looking about them. They sat down together on the ground between the tables. Suddenly, a plaintive melody was heard, and two of them began a slow dance, while the others sat, looking like butterflies. The king desired us to see the rest of his apartments, where his wives lived - on the third and fourth storeys. He, therefore, ordered them to conceal themselves in some corner or other; for, since the Muhammadans have invaded India, and introduced their customs here, the Hindus have also taken to concealing their women, and the pretty courtesans are the only ones to be seen."This truly depicts the state of prostitution during the Sikh period in the city and how common it was!

In the city, Hira Mandi had some spacious areas in terms of location as compared to the crooked and narrow streets where one has to rub shoulders while moving. There were indeed lovely and colourful evenings, the place is also euphemistically called the gem or diamond market which was generally assumed to be an institution of Lahore city, the 4th biggest in Indian sub-continent and smaller to none in Asia. It was an earmarked and known area as compared to small lanes in other cities and towns.

THE BUSINESS

Hira Mandi, at day time is quiet, dry and deserted but the evenings would appear dazzling and amazing. One can have glimpses of different styles of Punjabi living in the market, wherefrom middle class area onwards people of all communities lived in streets and behind the "Kothas" of courtesans. In the afternoon the population of the market i.e. girls after taking rest for the night performance used to loll about the houses and exchange notes about the men and visitors with comments. Sometime cursing the paramours and sometims praising kind exceptions. One could also sometimes see strayed ones in the bazar walking about desultorily in their slept in clothes, chewing pan, some smoking cigarettes and of course looking untidy. The musicians and accompaniments lurking around could be heard making cracks and loafing, were also visible. Slowly the girls would drift back to prepare for the evening which included a scrub, a bath, shaving the whole body, powdering, perfuming, combing, plaiting, selection and colourful choice of clothes of course facial treatment including eye-lid etc. All ready, the darkness deepening the evening, they would wait for instructions of the mistress (Naika) or another, who hoping against hope may accompany her for a treat of an evening assignment away from 'Kotha' outside Hira Mandi. Till partition the tradition was that after such an order the girls were taken out in "Purdah" to the destination lest they were seen and noticed. They had really hard life but in most of the cases the prostitutes were reported simple at heart and in the heart of hearts would pray for a love-affair which was rare but not unknown. Some say 'kanjries' used to make truly good wives, some thought that they would invariably return to the profession as the society would never accept them and treat decently. They were always looked down upon contemptuously. This was one category which was booked and taken out. Those who intended to stay for the night would so arrange and pay and enjoy at the Kotha. There was a category of those who would come for gaiety and one-go. They would enter the market, take a round and have a look of the stuff, settle the fee and after a short meeting would make room for others (in waiting) It was not always the case for all the women. Sometimes those in fading years would sit idle and wait for anyone and would be willing to accept without bargaining. Still another category was of those who would come for listening to the singers, have drinks and subject to their arrangements could either stay or leave the house late in the night.

SINGING

In the absence of any regular educational institution or Performing Arts Academy, Hira Mandi also served as a feeding area for the singers. It was the only place where musicians would impart regular instructions to newcomers and train them in solo or public performance. Still another category was of those visitors especially aged ones who would come to the place for mental relaxation. There is no doubt that the evening darkened, lights started coming up, and the girls would go up. The institution of Hira Mandi produced some of the best known singers from this place. The names of Noor Jahan, Zubaida Khanum, Zahida Parveen, Munawwar Sultana, Mukhtar Begum and Farida Khanum etc. can be mentioned in this context. Not only that, quite a few classical (male) singers also lived in this area including Ustad Barkat Ali Khan, "Bade Ghulam Ali Khan", "Chhote Ghulam Ali Khan" and so on. It would not be out of context to mention that the place was more visited by zamindars, important politicians and bureaucrats. Some of them did wed the prostitutes.

At a time it was an assertion that if someone wanted to learn about culture, manners, decencies and etiquettes, it was in the Hira Mandi, especially at the kothas of singers. This was true in case of courtesans hailing from Lucknow, Delhi, U.P. and the South of India, in general. They were graded to be the most cultured than Punjabis. Continuing the routine in Hira Mandi as balconies and take the appointed point / place. The rooms, houses and kothas were spread in Bazar Shaikhupurian, Kucha Chaitram Road, Neevan Chaitram Road, Tibbi Gali, Fort Road, Sabaz Pir Gali, Gujranwali Gali, Haideri Gali, Said Mitha, Hira Mandi Bazar, and Kucha Shahbaz,

There were various categories of houses. The select ones were occupied by singing girls, dancers' houses, places of the courtesans and finally the common prostitutes. There were of course different categories within each such group. The leading singing girls with attractive bodies and sexy features lived more luxuriously and enjoyed a measure of respectability and prestige. Their names usually carried the courteous suffixes of Begum or Bano and in case of non-Muslims "Bais". These singing girls were frequently invited and taken out to wedding parties and other family functions. They also used to sing for some of the Recording Companies and Radio Station. In case of films, sometimes they were booked as playback singers. To visit their places was quite respectable as a person of ordinary means could never afford to be with them and only well to do could go.

In their balconies the courtesans many beautifully (even in their prematurely tired youth), would sit in a strong light and look smilingly down at the men roaming in the line below. There were Kashmirans, Punjabans, grey-eyed Paharans, blue-eyed Pathanis who came from all over the North of the hills, dressed in different clothes with typical hairstyles. Men from below would look up, vacillating in their choice till someone would separate from the crowd and dive into the dark winding staircase, lit by a solitary light. As one entered into the glare of the reception room the girls left the balcony, she would come and sit near the man and they exchanged formal pleasantries, while the maid sat in a corner watching them ingratiatingly and shrewdly. The girls would size up what kind of a man he was and what to ask. It was routine with weak and old, young and fumbling, mean and demanding men, prudish and hypocritical men, an endless monotony of types that she knew by sight, but occasionally there came a simple man, undemanding, generous, with deep emotions, reaching uncertainly for a fulfillment somewhere but not daring to ask for it, not willing to talk about. Instinctively she would rise and tell the maid to close the shutters of the balcony, bolt the street door and go away. Sometimes the girl would bring him something to eat or drink, and indulge in other exciting gossip. Almost shyly she would hold his fingers and lead him to her room, both trying to forget herself and who the other was. The rough room existed behind the curtain, would disappear and get busy in the adjoining room if there was no separate place.The environment has changed and the prostitution is prohibited by law,.even the singing and dancing takes place after 10.00 pm. now a days

These courtesan girls are superstitious and insist on some kind of religious sanction. Most of them become Shia by faith so that by a simple invocation they could marry each man as they look him, and dissolve the bond afterwards. The Shia law, it is said permitted marriages of such temporary nature. In the houses of the 'nautch' girls there was much gaiety, music and drinking. But for these girls North Indian dancing might have perished as an art. They were a merry, wily lot who loved dancing and enjoyed their life; they danced and made love because the rythm in their limbs and their quivering bodies needed a relaxing fulfillment. There were some among them who became famous and kept exclusive establishments like the well known singing girls.

The houses of the common prostitutes were gay and busy, men coming and going all the time, and the girls exchanging ribald repartee with them. They were popularly known as the two and four Rupees women. Their bodies exhausted, their looks faded prematurely, they provided just a strayed satisfaction to lustful. When they failed to do even that they joined the ranks of "naikas" etc. except the few who were wise enough to become independent during their heyday.

It was patronised by the young and the old, the married and the unmarried, the rich and the famous, out for an evening's entertainment in the company of singing and dancing girls. For the young and the unmarried it was an adventure into the forbidden land. Old people frequented it more for mental relaxation than for any sensual stimulation. Married men, bored with their wives and domestic life, sought to experience new delights, more exacting both intellectual and sexual. For the rich, patronage of Hira Mandi was a status symbol, which enabled them to boast of being lord of the most beautiful of courtesans. On their part, the singing and dancing girls, were supposed to give their clients their money's worth. They were at their best when trying to please the affluent, while the ordinary customers had to be content with a routine performance. It was not always all song and dance. Greater delights were reserved for the few who could pay for.

DANCE

It would not be fair to take Hira Mandi only as a prostitute' street, which certainly it was not, even though some of its inmates carried on the world's oldest profession for a living. The courtesan's home was essentially a place of culture, particularly in Mughal times, when some of the singing and dancing girls found their way to the royal court. There they enchanted the nobility, with their accomplishments in the fine arts: music, poetry and dance. Witty conversationalists, they were engaged to teach etiquettes and gentle manners to young men of aristocratic families. The elders visited them to enjoy their enormous company.

With the advent of British rule and disappearance of the old nobility, much of the grandeur of Hira Mandi was lost. But, thanks to the patronage of the new moneyed class and the emerging landed gentry of Punjab, the pleasure houses of Hira Mandi continued to thrive. Troupes of singing and dancing girls were engaged to perform before Nawabs and rich landlords. Their presence on the occasion of a wedding was considered to be a status symbol and an auspicious sign and is so till date. The art of music had been confined to these families of Hira Mandi for generations. They had produced some of the most famous artists in the fields of dance and music.

Theatrical Companies during the twenties provided some opening for the courtesans of Hira Mandi but it was the advent of cinema in the thirties that came as a real breakthrough for them to display their talents. Later, many of them grew up to be leading stars. Broadcasting saw some others take to singing as radio artists. One of them was Umrao Zia who, with her naghma (song) "mera salam lay ja taqdeer kay jahan tak" overnight became a singing star around 1935.

Meanwhile, Hira Mandi continued to cast its spell on the Lahoris. In the evening, the place was transformed into one of gaiety and laughter. Soon after sunset, a row of tongas would line up outside Lohari Gate at the portals of Anarkali, where most of the restaurants and bars were located, to convey the travellers to their destinations. These four-seater shining Peshawari tongas, drawn by sturdy horses, would race towards Bhati Gate, proceeding to Hira Mandi via Ravi Road and Taxali Gate. Some of the merrymakers preferred to walk through the walled city. Passing through Lohari Gate they would go straight to Hira Mandi after crossing Chowk Chakla, Lohari Mandi and Said Mitha Bazar.

Walking through Hira Mandi, one could see the curtained windows behind which the singing and dancing girls entertained their clients. The strains of the sarangi and the beatings of the 'tabla' could be heard from outside. One visiting a Kotha was received downstairs at the entrance by the agent of the establishment and a flower-seller. He was expected to wear these stringed flowers around his wrists before proceeding upstairs. Amidst glittering lights, he took his seat on the carpeted floor covered with cool white sheets (chandnis) with bolsters to support himself. The singing girl would sit in the centre with a team of musicians behind them ready with their instruments to accompany the singer. An elderly woman, acting as impressario, positions herself in a corner holding a silver plate containing betel leaves, After a brief introduction by her, the visitor settles down for an enjoyable evening. On a signal from the matron, one of the singing girl goes around offering betel leaves to the patrons who are expected to make a token present of some money. The singing girls are dressed in shining silk shalwars or tight pyjamas and shirts embroidered with gold or silver threads with the upper parts of their bodies covered with a fine gauze veil. They wear gold pendants, necklaces, bracelets and anklets.

Soon the stage is set for the evening's entertainment by the musicians playing their instruments. The singer gets into her stride as she sings thumris, dadras and ghazals. She addresses each song to one or the other of the patrons who, enchanted by her sweet smiles and languishing glances, invites her to come closer to him. He rewards her with cash which she accepts gracefully and flings it towards the matron. She responds to the requests of the patrons in turn. The cries of 'wah wah', 'bahut khub', 'marhaba', 'mukarrar' from the patrons encourage her to repeat the couplets with gestures to emphasize the meaning of the words. The musicians in turn get into the spirit of the song animating the whole atmosphere. This establishes a rapport between the singer and the listener. At times, the patrons, in a hilarious mood, ask the singer to dance to the tune of the song. The sound of anklebells (ghunguru) in unison with music and the graceful movements of her supple body, hands and feet enthral the spectators. The repeated applause encourages her to display her seductive charms. Visiting a kotha was indeed an enjoyable experience.

An event celebrated with pomp and show in Hira Mandi was the deflowering of singing or dancing girls known as the nose-ring opening ceremony. The nose-ring, made of gold or silver, was traditionally recognised as a symbol of her virginity. Its removal signified her initiation into her new profession. The performance of the ceremony was considered an honour conferred on the wealthiest of the aspirants. The payment varied according to the charms of the girl. The ceremony was marked by festivities comparable to those of a wedding in which leading professional households of Hira Mandi and their numerous friends and patrons took part. There were lavish feasts lasting for two or three days where the choicest of dishes consisting of meat, kababs and aromatic pulaos were served. Beggars and the poor were fed generously to seek their blessings for the initiation ceremony. For the girl, it was a momentous occasion heralding her entry into the profession. This was followed by a series of briefing sessions where the elder profsessionals gave her advice and instructions on the secrets of success in her new career.

With the coming of cinema and the film industry taking roots in Lahore,as already mentioned, Hira Mandi emerged as a centre for recruiting budding stars; actresses, singers and dancers. Many of them rose to become leading figures in later years. Some others distinguished themselves in singing and acting and attained countrywide fame.

The post partition period saw the birth of a new class of patrons of Hira Mandi from among contractors, businessmen and merchants who were making money. These affluent pleasure seekers set a new trend and the Hira Mandi inmates spread out to other parts of the city to cater to their needs. This expanding clientele marked the beginning of the call-girl institution. These girls would visit hotels as well as private homes to entertain their customers. However, Hira Mandi

'Mujra'

continued to prosper. It was made even more lively by the affluent of the nearby towns, whose spending power could not be matched by the Lahoris or even by the landed aristocracy of Punjab who had until then dominated the social scene. Some landlords hailing from West Punjab, were Members of the Legislative Assembly; When in Lahore to attend its sessions, would bring a wave of gaiety to Hira Mandi. Driving to Lahore in their costly vehicles, they would wine and dine at the posh restaurants, Falettis, Standard, Park Luxury, Lords etc. on the Mall and then proceed straight to Hira Mandi for an evening of amusement. They would patronise its blossoming beauties most bountifully, dazzling the Lahoris with their extravagance.

With the passage of time, the practice of inviting singing and dancing girls to add glamour at weddings lost its popularity. There was, however, a revival of a sort during the forties when the rich began organising private mujra parties mainly for their male friends, sporting shimmering silks, shining jewels and gold pendants, the audience with her lilting ghazals and provocative gestures.

Encouraged by admirers and patrons, some of the Hira Mandi beauties even began visiting the race course and leading restaurants on the Mall, Metro in particular. The mushrooming film studios of Lahore were always on the lookout for young female artists. The budding directors, producers and financiers scouting for new talent found these places a happy meeting ground. Some of the girls were lucky enough to be picked up as actresses while some others ended up as mistresses of affluent pleasure-seekers.

I visited Hira Mandi in connection with this write-up, though one would otherwise long to visit once again to that memorable haunt of the young and the old where they went in search of joy, fun and amusement a resort of sorts. This was the Hira Mandi in its historical retrospect also commonly known as "TIBBI'. It is indeed an old institution of Lahore.. Glittering and gay it had an honest immorality about it. No one can raise his finger against it and neither ever-proposed restrictions. It was here for those who needed it and such needy came from all classes and the well-to-do from all over Punjab. It absorbed a great influx of the promiscuous lava and saved the normal tiers of society from big shakes and ensuing troubles of crime.

Hira Mandi scenario changed in its dimension to a great extent after partition. The cross section population shifted only non-muslim prostitutes, singers and dancers. Some converted and stayed on. The great migration brought more of poverty stricken inmates in the community. Those included shelterless and those who had been lost, abducted, defrauded in the name of marriage and further sold and resold. It also brought in those of dubious character economically deprived, fond of learning singing and music. Those perverts seeking variety of sex and finally those trapped by pimps and proprietors of the brothels.

The nature and status of the visitors also underwent a change. Now the 'Tamashbeen' was from amongst those who had grabbed the Hindu evacuee property, those who dealt with property, Mafia of Settlement Department and few spoiled from amongst the landed aristocracy. The place after short period of slump regained its glitter and was patronised and revived by the young and the old. However, the atmosphere and conditions of work totally changed after the year 1961 when the Government imposed restrictions in the name of suppression of prostitution laws. The creation of Pakistan, its ideology, Islam as religion of the State, preaching by fundamentalists, the economic development, diminishing landed gentry caused decay and depression in the glamour market. Those coming to Hira Mandi would plan their visits secretly as often with the change in the laws, police harrassed the so-called gentry and ordinary visitors. Of course 90% of the law clauses were waived with appropriate bribery to the police officials on duty. However, those who could not afford and handle the police were in trouble, challaned, arrested and the newspapers would publish their photographs and reports. This was really an embarrassment. Any police official would be ready to spend any amount for a short period posting in Tibbi Police Station. Sometimes those casual visitors for just a walk through were also arrested and had to pay to escape. This was of course an open licence for police officials to arrest visitors coming upstairs. The police would recover their booty both from the customers, pimps and prostitutes. This caused a slump in the market and the customers would find other ways to reach the courtesans. The common practice now was of the agents and pimps on various entry points such as Ravi Road, Fort Road, Ali Park site etc. who were always in search of the customers who intended to visit the place for a good time. Their attention was invited by pimps waiting in the shades and darkness by different cues and signs and if the customers (were interested) informed, the pimp would explain the number of the girls, their age, colour, features, domicile and induct into the room where the courtesans awaited. If someone wanted to stay he would pay and would have a go in the attached room often dirty, stinking and full of rubbish. In case he wanted to take out the girl for a night, bargain would be struck about the charges. The procurer would bring in a taxi or rickshaw for their next destination. If, however, the selection was not made by the customer he still had to pay a sum of Rs.50/- to Rs.100/- as "chehra krai". These pimps sometimes would still use another tactic in connivance with clever constable of police who would check the taxi and run away from the place of booking, ask for their identification and threaten them to arrest or pay reasonably to get rid of. Normally the first time visitor would go and most likely be trapped but the experienced would always slip away on the promise of returning. Still some of the prostitutes continue to occupy their places, engage one or two musicians and in the name of singing would indulge in sex business. There was still another category slightly different from the ones selling only flesh and that was mostly on the ground floor of Chait Ram Road, Bazar Shaikhupurian and Haideri Gali where some of the girls would start their rooms after 10.00 p.m., make their customers wait in the reception rooms and close their doors in the name of singing. This of course was in line with some provision of law. The customers subject to their payment and agreement could either stay or leave after some time. Yet another category of singers existed who would open their quarters on the fixed hours, sing for 'Mujra' etc. and generally do not indulge in sex except those who pay them on monthly basis and take care of the entire family and the dependents. Similarly there are categories of visitors i.e. those coming for one go and gaiety, those coming for 'mujra', those visiting their 'Rakhails' and still a category who just visit and roam about in the bazar to while away time. Of course, those taking out customers are in addition last but not the least is of very negligible minority of customers which are aged but well-off who visit the place for only 'mujra' and singing.

As already mentioned Hira Mandi remains closed during day time but the 'Naikas' and 'Malkins' have regular arrangements for their young girls for learning music and dance for which expert dance teachers are engaged. There are some old dance masters who have set up some sort of dance academies where, on charging lavish fees, they impart instructions to the young girls. This was the scene and the situation obtaining in the Hira Mandi until early 70s.

SUPPRESSION LAWS

The political conditions changed and more Islamization propagated and preached. This further caused the downfall of the institution. The populace of Hira Mandi thought of devising other modes to save themselves from the highhandedness of the police and law enforcing agencies. Infact the Suppression Law had a negative impact. The business of prostitution was taken by the cunning pimps and prostitutes to the new localities in the entire city in different colonies where they would hire a place and start their activities in a masked manner living like ordinary residents. They were at liberty to work both during the day and at night. Gradually the disease spread. The women-folk in the neighbourhood (some) finding easy money to meet their financial constraints would go for 2-3 hours at the place, get handsome amounts and continue the business in a hidden and concealed manner. These houses are spread over in all the vicinities. The dimensions of the prostitution have swelled to an extent that the proprietors and owners of the brothel houses or such 'Kothi Khanas' regularly pay the local police. A 'Tibbi Gali' has thus emerged in each locality due to the suppressive laws. The worst of this is that the Naikas or Malkins entice away the young girls of the Mohallahs and for attractive amounts of money induct them in this trade as part time business of making money. This category of girls leave their homes early morning for going to certain institutions and slip in-between to such dens where they make money. This disease has multiplied in the mohallahs and reached the educational institutions. The modern technology has greatly contributed towards the advancement of the cause of these mini prostitution cells. Their business has flourished and multiplied with the facility of celluloid telephone especially the mobile gadgets. The customers and clients, pimps and the prostitutes are all equipped with these handy machines, contact each other without creating any botheration in the neighbourhood and reach the appointed places, of their own. The latest situation is that the trained, seasoned and mature women recruit a variety of needy girls whom they supply in their own vehicles, on demand, both during the day and the night. Each den has sometimes dozens of girls on its waiting list. Another mode of this business, as has been regularised, by well-to-do have opened guest houses. They have long lists of call girls where people go and stay, they pay separately each for wine and women of their choice and enjoy a spree. One can remark on the variety that in the guest houses the girls themselves contact the counter and register their names, telephone and address for contact if someone wants to book her. It is further learnt that quite a few girls from the medical colleges, university and other colleges go there and make money. On a very reliable evidence this scribe was confirmed by a client that he booked a medical college student who explained that she did the business to meet her educational expenses and living in Lahore. These are the places from where people book the girls for holidays outside city and some even outside the country. There is no definite figure about the number of casual prostitutes operating outside the walled city in different localities. However, according to a survey at the moment there are over 1500 prostitutes of all categories residing in Hira Mandi which number has shrinked to a large extent. Most of the singers and performers of 'Mujra" live outside Hira Mandi and come only after 10.00 p.m. where they open their 'Daftar' dispose off their clients and leave late in the night. It was further surveyed that at least a population of over 500,000 is dependent on this in the shape of families of the prostitutes and those running their petty business of hotelling, markets and other general supplies in the area.

The merit of services of this old institution of Lahore apart from it would be unfair if one doesn't record its contribution towards the radio, television, film, and theatre as we know there is no performing arts academy in the entire country and in the absence thereof all the singers young and old have all along been provided by

Hira Mandi to both radio and the television. The hypocritic attitude of the people, hesitation of girls coming to television again provided a fertile ground for the producers to book the girls for their programmes from Hira Mandi. It is only for this reason that some so-called modern and advanced families have started sending their girls to television. The other major contribution towards public entertainment by Hira Mandi is their role in the cinema industry. Right from the beginning both the extras and good looking heroines(A to Z) were all from red light area whether these were the silent films, whether it was the side role and whether it was extras, all were taken from Hira Mandi. Their dances, singing and exposure with 'Tamashbeen' gave them an extra edge on the ordinary women to work in films. Infact, cinema which is slightly in depression these days is a polished market of singers and dancers who perform on the larger screen. This was all about Hira Mandi which inspite of all prohibitive measures have continued to prosper and serve those who need and patronise it.

MALE PROSTITUTES OR GIGOLOS

We have had a review of the prostitution in the city which was all about female prostitutes and prostitution dens. Interestingly of late, a new situation of male prostitution has emerged which has been beautifully summed up in a column of newspaper. It is only a latest development on social scene of the city. Since not much of evidence is available the said column is reproduced in original from the Daily News:

"Female prostitution and prostitution dens have always existed in the city, catering to all classes, from the elite to the lower middle-class. However, recent evidence suggests, a new phenomenon has hit the city. Now male prostitutes and gigolos (a professional male partner) have made their organised entry onto the local scene, operating through carefully concealed channels."

"The daily News revealed as many as five 'outlets' are currently engaged in this lucrative, new business and are operating in the posh localities of the city. The prostitutes operating from them have to undergo a month long 'extensive' course, designed to teach them the finer aspects of the trade, before they are dispatched to the client."

"My boss served for several years in Japan as a gigolo and male prostitute before starting this business here. There are others who are also in the business, but they lack class," said a young man who joined this business a few months back."

"He further revealed that when he joined this outlet, there were nine prostitutes but now they are seven, as two prostitutes had gone abroad after cultivating their rich clients who made their travel possible."

Tracing back the roots of the business, it is learnt that when prostitution dens shifted to posh localities and became 'kothi khanas' in the early 1990's, a sudden boom in the business was witnessed in the city. The massive earning and influence of 'kothi khanas' generated fierce competition, forcing the people running the businesses to undertake frequent 'study tours' to the Far East Asia, Dubai and Europe to introduce new ideas in their business.

Following the overseas exposure, the concept of male prostitution was introduced in Lahore. "I heard about this business, but when police raided a den recently, we came to know that she (the woman running the outfit) was also a supplier of male prostitutes," said a police officer, who asked not to be named. He further held the scale of this business is very small, and therefore it should not be reported, because this would create bad feeling.

It is learnt that these male prostitutes are welcomed to select female parties, to please the 'distinguished guests' and perform a striptease. "Recently at a party rich 'aunties' gave me heavy tips. I returned with Rs.23,000 beside my fee of several thousands," admitted a prostitute.

It was also learnt that most of the women who avail of this service are middle-aged with marital problems, while a very few women do it for the sake of fun. "I have gone to several women, rather I call them 'aunts'. They complained of their husbands who had no time for them. One lady told me that her husband is an alcoholic who is too busy with his golf and drinks and having affairs and hardly comes to her," said one model-cum-prostitute. He added, "for me this is safer and more discreet than having an affair myself."

It is reported that a new trend is also in fashion where 'hen' parties among the elite are arranged solely for the purpose of inviting gigolos and availing their services. Male prostitutes prefer these parties because within a short time they can earn large amounts, which is not possible in simple prostitution assignments. A former civil servant said that this is a new chapter, after wife-swapping, which was limited to the elite. He added that it seemed the immorality in society, till recently associated mainly with men, had also filtered down to the women.

Another prostitute claimed that with the organised and confidential networks of this service, elderly 'aunts' have no worries about hunting down a boy on their own. They simply have to pay Rs.5,000/- and pick a boy of their choice, usually between 21 to 24 years old.

He further said since these ladies are rich and resourceful, there is always a chance of getting a visa or a good job.

Such developments reflect how far we have degenerated on all fronts. Young boys now realise education and degrees stand little chance of providing them with a secure job. Some of them have resorted to earning easy money, like many college girls who entered the trade primarily for economic reasons.

A senior police officer claimed male prostitution had always existed, but it had just changed its face. "Everybody in the city knows that from Mall Road, Canal Road and Main Boulevard one can pick a male prostitute," he added.

The rising level of prostitution in the country, male or female, appears to be running parallel with the cry of the maulvis. So far it seems evil has outrun good, but if one analyses the sordid situation objectively, many elements, especially economic ones, appear to contribute to this unbridled surge of immorality"(The Daily 'News', April 15,1998). Before concluding this write-up it will be appropriate to list some of the singers who came from this area. They have big contribution in the field of music.

1	Zubaida Khanum	37	Sheedi Siranwali
2	Mala Begum	38	Malika Shahida
3	Naseem Begum	39	Bibi Eidoo
4	Farida Khanum	40	Api Rozi
5	Sayyan Chaudhry	41	Eidoo Gujratan
6	Samar Iqbal	42	Kalo Saranwali
7	Tasawwar Khanum	43	Eidoo Meedoo
8	Niggo	44	Kaloo
9	Roshan Ara Begum	45	Jaro Anewali
10	Musarrat Nazir	46	Zohra Bai Agraywali
11	Nazir Begum	47	Babi Adaa
12	Bilquees Khanum	48	Mumtaz Dengewali
13	Noor Jahan Begum	49	Shamshad
14	Zahida Parveen	50	Dafai
15	Shahida Parveen	51	Sardaran urf Dadi
16	Zahida Sultana	52	Azra Pathani
17	Tarannum Naz (Naz Laila)	53	Inayat Bai
18	Humaira	54	Aati Zori
19	Humaira Channa	55	Chheemo & Chajoo
20	Naheed Akhtar	56	Sheran Bai
21	Naheed	57	Eidan Gujratwali
22	Mehnaz	58	Shamshad Kausar
23	Arifa	59	Jia Wasian
24	Zamurrad Begum	60	Surraya Bijli
25	Shabana Chaudhry	61	Kajan Bai
26	Mumtaz Begum	62	Fehmida Sanponwali
27	Khurshid Begum	63	Khurshid Bai
28	Azra Jahan	64	Mizla Bai
29	Afshan Butt	65	Saba Bai

30	Nadia Jahan	66	Mumtaz Lakhanwali
31	Iqbal Bano	67	Mushtari Bai
32	Samina Iqbal	68	Kako Saranwali
33	Fareeha Pervaiz	69	Robeena Baro
34	Riffat Naz	70	Naseem Saranwali
35	Amrozia Begum	71	Alan Gujratwali
36	Sheedi Pondanwali		

The relative assessment that what boundaries in a given social set up this profession needs a very thorough study on which different people have different views. The fact remains that it has continued to grow in a variety of ways right from stone age through the space times.

The slow and painful rise of humanity from the promiscuity of the horde through slave-owning societies, serfdom, despotism and the age of enlightenment to modern forms of democracy is a circumstance that cannot be partially eliminated. The advanced industrial nations of the West are aiming at the realization of a set of ideals among which the life and personal development of the individual take the lead. Very real differences of opportunity and resources still prevail even among citizens of the same country. But on the whole they can be said to have been accorded, during the last few decades at any rate, equality in principle and impartial recognition of their claims to happiness and enjoyment.

Among the many who continue to misuse the new liberties and opportunities must be reckoned prostitutes and those who procure and maintain them, as well as the entire subsidiary host of caterers for sexual pleasure, from the last of the white slavers to the first specialists in improvised teenage parties. Throughout the long history of social progress prostitution clung like a vampire to the shoulders of every community and could not be shaken off. During the slave-owning centuries the male had tasted blood. For a prolonged period women as slaves and booty constituted a prize of war intelligible to the most barbarous Scythian without a great deal of proclamation. In a society almost wholly unproductive, with neither industry nor an agriculture capable of exporting its crops, with trade at an extremely low level, women and boys schooled to act as the slaves of appetite were commercially exploitable objects of special importance, since they were all that the backward regions of central and northern Europe could barter for the weapons and other manufactured articles supplied by oriental merchants.

The inordinate sensual excitation caused by the view of women as mere commodities again set Europe alight, as though from a spark, after the decline of the slave economy, when the Crusaders came in contact with the civilization of the East. The lady of the manor in her castle, courted as she was by poets, minstrels and her masculine guests, remained a prisoner. The walls of the bower were just as thick as those of any harem. The male also ruled and the female served in every other interior, from the baths to the women's quarters on an estate or in a town. Any woman, moreover, who might venture to claim a measure of personal freedom would be doomed. Death by drowning or burying alive would unquestionably be her fate.

In the ever-present shadow of such capital sentences women had no standing. They traded their persons and their affections unprotected but also unpursued by the law, eventually coming to be regarded as essential for the health of society. Otherwise, the Christian Church, for so long all-powerful, would have exterminated them all, one after the other, at the stake. Even the popes, however, who administered their own city and before whom emperors often knelt, took no measures against prostitution, which flourished in Rome more exuberantly than anywhere else in the world.

The conspicuous numbers, social success and impudence of prostitutes were first evident in the full radiance of the Renaissance, with its brilliant courts and festivities, only too popular with a dominant class living gaily on the proceeds of its conquests and the labours of its inherited serfs. The accident of legal immunity ensured asylum if some monarch had an attack of moral scruples. An austere Habsburger could always be exchanged for a particularly vivacious Valois. One could desert the court of a strict pope for such liberal seaports as Venice of Genoa. The oldest profession developed under dozens of rulers, in the course of centuries, an adaptability comparable only with that of those resourceful personages who financed the whole foreground splendour of more or less capable princess from a position in the background. With the help of a few eminently gifted prostitutes and their keepers like, for instance, Madame du Barry and her count, or some equally valuable team of adventurers on a grand scale, the already weakened resistance of the old-fashioned to these innovation was widely breached. Courtesans were ennobled, bastards usurped thrones, entire groups of morganatic offspring had to be provided for out of public funds and made their way into the corridors of power.

Since the Revolution (French), wrote Jean-Gabriel Mancini, 'there can no longer be any such thing as a history of prostitution, but only an account of the whole system of toleration in which prostitution is a mere item and for which not even a name has yet been found. The trade in question profits from the indulgence which has at last been granted to it and thus reveals one of the strangest associations which has ever come to light, between religion and sexuality. Freedom of thought and the now guaranteed impunity of attitudes which had formerly led to the take and eternal damnation found natural expression in the struggle against sexual taboos, which proved to be remarkably tenacious. Although modern intellectuals belong, at least theoretically, to an actually pluralistic society in which a man's religion and personal philosophy have at last been declared his own affair, the sexual customs and opportunities open to mankind today are contained in a social community still only slowly acquiring a homogeneous character and marked as clearly as ever by class distinctions. What seems normal to a peasant appears heathenish and primitive to many townsmen, while what is commonplace to the city-dweller strikes a provincial citizen as aberrant and perverse. National differences, moreover, go even deeper than the social.

The army of prostitutes and their adherents, better equipped than ever, had forgotten nothing and learnt much. With unparalleled agility it has occupied all the positions which the democratically constituted Welfare State has had to surrender. An unprecedented intensity of influence brought to bear on the masses and their permanent exposure to the glitter of allurements of every kind have not yet indeed rendered the code of morality invisible. But it is becoming more difficult to distinguish the more often the dazzling light alter. Nor, of course, should prostitutes and their adherents be regarded as the chief beneficiaries of the growing insecurity of society any more than their clients should be supposed of the most imperilled by it; no community has ever been ruined by this marginal feature of it. But all communities have tried to make scapegoats, for the future of those who are already in any case outlaws, burdening them with the responsibility for the society's own decline, senseless as it is to do so. The very ancient and deeply rooted dissatisfaction of the individual who has outgrown the horde and unexpectedly found himself living on a monogamous group, lends fuel to the fire to which prostitution in any age contributed little more than a slightly scented cloud of smoke.

Whatever the merits and demerits, the history of prostitution from ancient Greek sex markets and Dev-Dasis of Hindu temples to the sophisticated call girls and gigolos, is really interesting and colourful and the city of Lahore has not remained behind in anyway.

BIBLIOGRAPHY

The theme and subject of this book is so closely interwoven with the culture and history of the city that it has not been possible and practicable to cite form all the works, sources and material consulted. However the titles of all the studies to which reference is made or invairably quoted in the text and have been listed below. Items of international literature and reference works especially some historical accounts by well known authorities are not expressly mentioned. These consultations are gratefully acknowledged and include:-

1.   A Brief on The Arts Council, Annual Report 1963-64, Lahore,
2.   Aanant Soom, Batain Lahore Ki, Lahore 1997
3.   Addison C. G., The Knights Templars, London 1853
4.   Agarwal Chiranjiva Lal, Lahore Old and New, An Upto date Guide to its History, Buildings and Institutions, Lahore
5.   Ahmed Sohail, Jadeed Theatre, Lahore 1984
6.   Airi Em, Sexual Truths, Lahore 1944
7.   Allah Bakhsh Paintings Exhibition, at Alhamra (Pakistan Art Council), December 1952.
8.   Amjad Ali S., Anna Molka Ahmad, An Artist and Institution,Islamabad 1987
9.   Amjad Ali S., Painters of Pakistan, Islamabad 1995
10.   An Arts Center for Lahore, Building Project Report, Lahore 1965-66
11.   Anand Mulk Raj, Curries and other Indian Dishes, London
12.   Annual Reports, 1959-60 & 1960-61, Pakistan Arts Council, Lahore.
13.   Babree, Dr. Laeeq, Culture of Pakistan, Lahore 1997
14.   Bassermann Lujo, The Oldest Profession - A History of Prostitution, London 1967.
15.   Bezzant Bro. Reg. A Story of An Ancient Lodge London
16.   Bhavnani Enakshi, Decoration Designs and Craftsmanship of India, India 1968
17.   Bruce J. F., The History of University of the Punjab, Lahore 1933
18.   Brown Percy, History of Lahore Museum , Lahore.

19. Butt Khalid Said Dr., Ahmad Pervaiz (Fun Aur Shakhsiat), Idara Saqafat-e-Pakistan, Islamabad 1986
20. Chakldar H. C. Social Life in Ancient India Faisalabad 1987
21. Chisti Noor Ahmad, Tahkekat-I-Chisti, Lahore 1993
22. Chughtai M. Abdullah Dr., The Badshahi Masjid - History and Architecture, Lahore 1972
23. Chughtai M. Abdullah Dr., The Wazir Khan Mosque Lahore - History and Architecture, Lahore 1975
24. Contemporary Arts In Pakistan, Vol. IV: Number 3, Autumn 1963
25. Cunningham Joseph Davey, History of the Sikhs London 1849
26. Cunnigham Alexander, Ancient Geography of India, Calcutta, 1924.
27. Devi Tandra, Village Theatre the Foundations of the Indian National Theatre, 1937
28. Edwards Allen, The Jewel in the Lotus, A Historical Survey of the Sexual Culture in the East, London 1961
29. Elphinstone Mountstuart, History of India (Vol-II), London. 1841
30. Elphinstone Mountstuart, The History of India (Vol-I), London 1841
31. Exhibition of Chinese Art and Craft, Organised by the Pakistan Art Council
32. Exhibition of Thirty Portraits of The Quaid-I-Azam, By Anwar Jalal Shemza, December 25, 1954, Alhamra (Pakistan Arts Council)
33. Fifty Years of Visual Arts in Pakistan, Sang-e-Meel Publications, Lahore 1997
34. Garrett. H.L.O., History of Government College Lahore Lahore 1914
35. Garrett. H.L.O., Events at the Court of Ranjit Singh, Lahore 1935
36. Garrett. H.L.O., The Punjab - A Hundred Year Ago, Lahore 1997
37. Gazdar Mushtaq, Pakistani Cinema (1947-1997), Karachi 1997
38. Godley J. C., Record of the Aitchison College Lahore, Lahore 1901
39. Goulding H. R. Colonel, Old Lahore - Reminiscences of a Resident, Lahore 1924
40. Government of the Pakistan, Arts and Crafts of Pakistan, Karachi 1994
41. Government of the Punjab, Gazetteer of Lahore, Lahore 1989
42. Government of the Punjab, P & D Board, Punjab Development Review and Prospects, Lahore 1980
43. Halliday Tony, Insight Guides Pakistan, Singapore 1990
44. Hameed A., Lahore Ki Yadain, Lahore 1992
45. Hardy P., The Muslims of British India, London 1972
46. Hariharam M. Kuppuswamy Gowri, Royal Patronage of Indian Music, Delhi 1984
47. Henriques Dr. Fernando, Stews and Strumpets, London 1961

48. Hew Shirley, Cultures of the World Pakistan, Singapore 1953
49. Hoag D. John, Islamic Architecture, New York 1977
50. Hunter W.W., The Indian Mussalmans, 1968
51. Hussain Ed. I., Pakistan, Karachi 1997
52. Imperial Gazetteer of India, Provincial series Punjab (Vol-II), Calcutta 1908
53. Indian Film, Oxford University Press, New York 1980
54. Jacquemont V. & Soltykoff A., The Punjab A Hundred Years Ago Lahore 1935
55. Kamal Yousaf, Introduction to Lahore Division,Lahore 1996
56. Kashmiri Shorash, Us Bazar Mein, Lahore 1994
57. Khan Muhammad Walliullah, Lahore and its important Monuments, Karachi, 1964
58. Kipling J. L. & Thornton, History of Lahore, Lahore 1873
59. Krishna Rama Lajwanti, Punjabi Sufi Poets A.D. 1460-1900, London 1938
60. Lahore Art Circle, Group Exhibition at Alhamra, 1955
61. Lal, Kanyha, History of Lahore, Lahore 1987
62. Latif Khan Bahadur Syed Muhammad, History of the Punjab from the Remotest Antiquity to the Present Time, Lahore 1997
63. Latif Khan Bahadur Syed Muhammad, Lahore History and Architectural Remains Antiquities, Lahore 1892
64. Living in Lahore, By Committee for Living in Lahore, Lahore 1962
65. Malik Latif Muhammad, Auliay Lahore, Lahore 1994
66. Malik Saeed M., The Musical Heritage of Pakistan, Islamabad 1983
67. Mufty Naseera, Prostitution in Lahore, A Study Of Eight Professional Prostitutes In Lahore Corporation Areas (un- Published) Lahore, 1959
68. Mumtaz Khawar and Shaheed Farida, Women of Pakistan Two Steps Forward, One Step Back, Lahore 1987
69. Museum Bulletin, Vol.IV January-December, 1894.
70. Music Academy, Prospectus, The Pakistan Arts Council, Lahore 1964
71. Naheed Nargis, The Musical Heritage of Pakistan, Islamabad 1987
72. Narasimhan Shakuntala, Invitation to Indian Music,Delhi 1985
73. National Geographic, Vol. 177 No.5, Washington 1990
74. Nevile Pran, Lahore A Sentimental Journey,New Delhi- India 1993
75. Oliver G. D. D., The Golden Remains of the Early Masonic Writers, London
76. Open Air Theatre Complex, Lahore Arts Council, Lahore 1991
77. Pakistan Arts Council, Revised Rules & Regulations, 1967
78. Pakistan Arts Council, Revised Rules and Regulations, Lahore 1963.
79. Pakistan, Past & Present, Stacey International, London 1977

80. Pakistani Culture, National Book Foundation, Islamabad 1997

81. Quddus Syed Abdul, Punjab The Land of Beauty Love and Mysticism, Karachi 1992

82. Quraeshi Samina, Lahore the City within, Singapore, 1988

83. Rahmani Ishrat, Agha Hashar, Lahore 1954

84. Rahmani, Dr. Anjum, Lahore Museum Bulletin, Lahore 1994

85. Rehmat Maqbool, Pakistan Studies, Lahore 1997

86. Rhode Eric, A History of the Cinema, London 1976

87. Richmond Farley P., Darius L. Swann, Zarrilli B. Phillip,Indian Theatre Traditions of Performance, Delhi 1990

88. Rosenthal Ethel, The Story of Indian Music and its Instruments, London 1928

89. S. Safdar Exhibition of Paintings, at Alhamra on 12th January, 1955

90. Saeed Muhammad, Lahore A Memoir, Lahore 1989

91. Sahukar Mani, Indian Classical Music, Delhi 1986

92. Sarkar K.M., The Grand Trunk Road in the Punjab, Lahore 1926

93. Sethi R. R., The Mighty and Shrewd Maharaja Ranjit Singh's Relation With Other Powers, Delhi 1960

94. Sharb Zahoor ul Hassan Dr., Tazkara Auliay Pak-o-Hind, Lahore 1965

95. Shaw Isobel, An Illustrated Guide to Pakistan Hong Kong 1988

96. Shehab Rafiullah, 50 Years of Pakistan, Lahore 1990

97. Shehab Rafiullah, History of Pakistan, Lahore 1989

98. Sheila & Crowe, Gardens of Mughal India

99. Sherman Henry C., Foods: Their Values and Management, New York 1946

100. Sidhwa Rustam Sohrabji (Justice Retd), The Lahore High Court and Its Principal Bar (1866-1988), Lahore 1966

101. Sidhwa Rustam Sohrabji, District Grand Lodge of Pakistan, Lahore

102. Simon Robert Leopold, Spiritual Aspects of Indian Music, Delhi 1984

103. Singh Kashmira & Chand Tara Dr., Chughtai's Indian Paintings, New Delhi 1951

104. Soviet Union Handicrafts Exhibition at Alhamra 1956

105. The Star,Karachi supplement onLahore

106. Tannahill Reay, Food in History, Suffolk U.K. 1975

107. The Food of India, Authentic Recipes from the Spicy Subcontinent,

108. The Pakistan Arts Council Lahore, In Brief Lahore

109. The Partition of the Punjab 1947 (Vol-1-IV, Lahore 1993

110. Tufail Muhammad, Naqoosh Lahore No.II, Lahore 1962

111. Vista, Fine Arts,Deptt. University of the Punjab, Lahore 1961

112.   Wheeler Sir Montimer, Five Thousand Years of Pakistan, London, 1950

Punjab Government Archives

Book No.195 page 7 letter No.4, 1848
(Residency and Agency record.)

GENERAL DEPARTMENT PROCEEDINGS

1.   April, 3rd 1852 No.64
2.   March 30th 1864 No.22
3.   November, 20th 1852 NO.34-5
4.   July, 17th 1852 no. 30-32
5.   March, 22nd 1851 No.41
6.   November, 9th 1850 No. 31-2
7.   November, 1870, No. 4-A
8.   November 19th 1855 No. 36-37
9.   October 19th 1861 No.63-64
10.   July, 27th 1861 No. 62-64
11.   August, 31st 1861 No. 5A-5C

REVENUE DEPARTMENT PROCEEDINGS

12.   March, 24th 1855 No. 22-25
13.   September, 29th 1855 No. 53-55
14.   June, 12th 1852 No.38
15.   Proceeding dated 28th March No.597 No.31 – 1855
16.   General Department Punjab Archives
       Proceeding No.597 – 31 March General Department 1855
17.   Punjab Government Archives
       Punjab Government Gazette 1858 Page 310
18.   Proceeding No.60 – 61, 6th October General Deptt. 1860
19.   (Letter No. 1277 of 1860)
       Proceeding 22nd June 1861 No.20-21 General department
20.   Punjab Government Archives
21.   General report on the Lahore Central Museum March 1868
       Punjab Government Archives
       Proceeding No. 20 15th April 1867 No. 978
22.   General Department April, 1867. Punjab Government Archives
       Proceedings No.19 of 15th August 1867 Punjab Archives

23. Museum Bulletin, Vol. IV January December 1894
24. Rahmani Dr. Anjum Lahore Museum (Article)
25. Lahore Residency Record 1847 Vol. 71 Letter No.507/A
26. Proceedings 22nd April 1865 No.57-60 General Department.
27. Proceedings No.146-51 Home General Department 1917
28. Proceedings File 1918 No.78-79 B Home General Department.
29. Proceeding 1918 N/A file-B.
30. Proceedings 1910 File No.188 H. Genl. B.

NEWSPSAPERS

1. The Daily News Lahore (1997-98.)
2. The Daily Muslim Islamabad (1997)
3. The Daily NationLahore (1997-98)
4. The Daily Pakistan Times Lahore (1976)
5. The Daily Dawn Lahore (1998)
6.

REPORTS

Reports on Central Museum Lahore.

INDEX

Index

Index

Index

Index

Index